THE

Western World

AND

Japan

The *Western World* and *Japan*

A STUDY IN THE INTERACTION OF EUROPEAN AND ASIATIC CULTURES

BY

G. B. Sansom

Was bedeutet die Bewegung?

Bringt der Ost mir frohe Kunde?

WEST-ÖSTLICHER DIVAN

1950 ⸗ New York   Alfred A. Knopf

FIRST EDITION

THE WESTERN WORLD AND JAPAN *is published by Alfred A. Knopf, Inc., and is distributed in co-operation with the International Secretariat, Institute of Pacific Relations.*

PREFACE

THE CONTENTS of this book and its arrangement seem to call for some explanation. It deals with many persons and events of which the reader may well ask: "What are they doing in a history of Japan?"

I have to admit that they are there chiefly because I found them interesting and thought them significant. I had first intended to supplement a short cultural history of Japan that I wrote in 1931 by describing in some detail the effect upon Japanese social and political life of the Western influences to which she has been subjected in modern times; but the more I pondered this aspect of her history, the more I felt that it ought to be treated as part of a much greater sequence of events: to wit, the process by which the intrusive civilizations of the West have, since even before the Christian era, affected the life of Asiatic peoples, first only slightly and spasmodically and then with increasing power.

This was of course a difficult, not to say rash undertaking, but there was still a further reason for attempting it. When I reflected upon specific examples of what is called cultural influence, I found that I had only a vague idea of what it is and how it works. Of late a number of books have appeared which — though they testify to a commendable growth of interest in relationships between East and West — seem to me to be based upon assumptions that experience does not confirm, both as to the action of one civilization upon another and as to the very nature of intercourse between peoples. We do not yet know enough about these matters to allow of laying down rules or making predictions; and it therefore appeared to me that there might be some advantage in first examining the question on a large scale and then going on to a more detailed study of the particular case of Japan. It is with that purpose in mind that I have in the first part of this book touched in very general terms on the early history of relations between Europe and Asia and then, against the background so provided, tried to furnish particulars of the history of Japan that would show how she reacted to Western influence from the days of her first contact with Europeans down to the time of her entry into international life in the nineteenth century.

A survey of the enterprises of Europeans in Asia after the great voyages of discovery shows that during the sixteenth, seventeenth, and eighteenth centuries neither their colonizing and trading activities nor their missionary work brought about any significant change in the life of the peoples with whom they came into contact. The presence in Asiatic countries of small groups of European officials and traders made little impression upon indigenous cultures outside a very narrow circle. Even where, as in British India, Malaya, and the Dutch Indies, Asiatic peoples were for long periods under European government, the essential nature of their civilization was little modified by their foreign rulers, who saw no profit in tampering with native customs and were inspired by no reforming zeal. Indeed, far from Europe affecting Asia, it was Asiatic goods that changed and enriched European life, and Asiatic ideas that attracted some European minds.

As for the efforts of the Catholic Church to spread its gospel in Asia, remarkable as they were, they can for the most part be dismissed as failures, for (with the possible exception of the Philippine Islands) in all Eastern countries Christianity evoked among the inhabitants, especially in the governing class, more antagonism than interest. But because cultural differences between peoples are expressed most clearly in their religious beliefs and practices, I have felt obliged to treat of Christian evangelism in what may seem excessive detail.

It was not until well on in the nineteenth century that a great increase of trade, improved communications, and a rapid growth of machine industry began to exercise strong pressure on the life of Oriental countries. It was then that they began to feel the influence of Western civilization, which raised new problems by disturbing their economic systems and upsetting their social and political traditions. The greatest Asiatic cultures — those of India and China — resisted these European influences, if only passively, and, despite some superficial changes, preserved their own character. It was only Japan that after long hesitation voluntarily and of set purpose decided to meet Europe halfway and to remodel her national life upon Occidental lines. The case of Japan is therefore of peculiar interest for the student of cultural relations. For that reason I have in the second part of this book treated the history of Japan in the modern age by first giving an account of her civilization as it had developed in comparative seclusion, then tracing the gradual penetration of Western influences, and finally describing the steps by which she adopted some Western practices and rejected others. I have dealt at some length with economic problems of the seventeenth and eighteenth centuries because I think they are important to students specializing in Far Eastern history.

Similarly it may be thought that I have paid too much attention to details of political controversy in the first two or three decades (1868–95) of the Meiji era; but it seemed to me that there was a more than topical interest in showing how tradition fought against new doctrine and how, beneath a "modern" surface, many features of earlier Japanese political life survived without substantial change. At the same time, anxious not to neglect the more picturesque or less forbidding aspects of the national history, I have tried to give an outline of literary and artistic movements, and the part played in them by Occidental ideas. I wish I could have found space and time for a fuller picture of Japan in the eighteenth century, for it is a most interesting period, full of striking parallels and contrasts. Its sympathetic treatment by an Orientalist familiar with the contemporary cultural scene in Europe would prove a valuable document in the history of Taste.

It is a pity that the student of cultural relations cannot stop short at describing exchanges of ideas. It is a pleasant pursuit for him to trace the influence of the painters, poets, and philosophers of one country upon those of another. He is reluctant to leave that enticing garden, with all its seductive flowers and trees; but he is bound sooner or later to ask himself what this amiable vegetation has to do with the harsher realities of intercourse between nations. He then finds himself faced by a baffling question. He learns that the concept of an international society — developed after the age of discovery, as the divergent commercial interests of rising national states created new conflicts — is relatively modern; and he begins to wonder whether it is valid. He observes that even between contiguous states differences of language and habit prevent more than a modest cultural interchange, while there are political and economic barriers that make rather for isolation than for comity. As between distant states, it is difficult to see any link but commerce that can be said to bind them in one society, as individuals with common customs and common standards live together in an organized community with some approach to harmony. Such states maintain diplomatic relations, it is true, but these are concerned almost exclusively with economic matters, as anybody who has experience of diplomatic business will agree. Or if they are not economic, then they are concerned with actual or possible conflicts between members of this reputed society. It is difficult to see what its constituent states have in common except a desire to expand their trade and increase their strength.

Perhaps this is only an elaborate way of saying that communities are even more quarrelsome, competitive, and jealous than the individuals who compose them. But it is a point on which one ought to be clear before reaching conclusions as to the nature of cultural intercourse between nations or peoples, and its effect upon their political dealings with one another.

In this study the history of Japan is carried only as far as the outbreak of the war with China in 1894, because that is the end of a very definite phase, which in the following period gives place to new trends. To describe and analyse these would require the handling of a mass of material too complicated for inclusion in this volume. Yet perhaps it already contains enough to show that foreign cultural influences can produce unexpected political results.

To that extent it touches, if only at the very fringe, the question of the true nature of the relationship between nations. But this enigma cannot be settled by inquiry into past history alone, for in the last analysis it resolves itself into a disagreement between the cautious idealism of Grotius and the relentless logic of Hobbes, and thus becomes a matter of faith.

So we may hope, though we cannot prove, that *Leviathan* is only a bogy. But it is prudent in these troubled times (which seem to encourage what its author called "the frequency of insignificant speech") to bear in mind his bleak verdict on "the general inclination of mankind," that it is a "perpetuall and restless desire of Power after power, that ceaseth onely in Death."

Note on Transliteration

THE WRITING of Japanese in the Roman alphabet always presents a difficulty, and in this matter I do not regard consistency as a virtue. I have therefore felt free to write familiar words, especially names, without marking a long vowel if it seemed fussy or pedantic. Thus, *Goto* not *Gotō*, *Okubo* not *Ōkubo*. But where there seemed a possibility of confusion I have used diacritic marks; e.g., *Shōzan, Daté*. I have also at choice used English plurals such as *daimyos, shoguns*.

These methods will offend purists, but I am consoled by recollecting what somebody said of Robespierre: *"Cet homme est dangereux. Il est pur."*

Japanese names of persons are given with the family name first.

ACKNOWLEDGMENTS

I OWE special thanks to my friends and colleagues at Columbia University, in particular to Professor Tsunoda, a teacher full of wisdom and learning ungrudgingly and modestly imparted to his pupils, among whom I am happy to count myself; to Professor Carrington Goodrich, head of the department of Chinese and Japanese, who responds to requests for Sinological information with great amiability and promptitude; to Professor Hugh Borton, for useful advice on Tokugawa history, in which he is so well versed; to Professor and Mrs. John Orchard, for guidance in economic regions where they are at home and I am lost; to Mr. Howard Linton, librarian in charge of the East Asiatic collections, and his assistants, whose good nature and patience are remarkable even in this country where librarians press books into the hands of a borrower and do not look at him as if he were probably illiterate and possibly dishonest.

I am also indebted to the courteous officers of the Library of Congress, and especially to Dr. Hummel and his associates in the division of Orientalia, who know how to take the drudgery out of research and make it almost a pastime for the reader.

Professor Percy Corbett, of the department of Political Science at Yale University, was kind enough, out of his store of knowledge, to give me valuable suggestions as to the nature of international society.

In England I received generous help from Professor G. C. Allen, of the University of London, who took pains to elucidate for me several points in an analysis of the economic history of Japan; and from Mr. Basil Gray, of the department of Oriental Antiquities at the British Museum, who kindly assisted me in the choice of illustrations and in other matters.

From Professor Kurt Singer, of the University of Sydney, I received some fruitful suggestions out of his wide knowledge of economic history and his familiarity with Japanese institutions.

To my friend Major Charles Boxer, Camoens Professor of Portuguese at the University of London, I am especially beholden for copious information and advice relating to the history of the Portuguese and the Dutch in Asia; and I have drawn freely and unblushingly upon his published and unpublished works on those subjects.

Professor Duyvendaak, of the University of Leiden, generously allowed me to use the plate of the Auspicious Giraffe which adorns his learned and entertaining essay on the Ming voyages in *T'oung Pao*.

Finally I should like to say that I owe a great debt to Mr. Geoffrey Hudson, of All Souls College, Oxford, whose distinguished writings are the envy and inspiration of all students of Far Eastern history and politics. It was after first reading his *Europe and China* that I made bold to plan the present study, though it has since then taken a somewhat different form.

Having quoted so many high authorities, I must hasten to add that none of them is responsible for any error of fact or opinion which this book contains.

I am indebted to Theresa Garrett Eliot for her faithful drawings of Meiji celebrities, from old photographs that were too faded for distinct reproduction. These are included among the illustrations not only for their historical interest but also because I thought that they displayed a striking variety of facial types.

G. S.

C O N T E N T S

Contents

ILLUSTRATIONS

Illustrations

MAPS

PART ONE

Europe and Asia

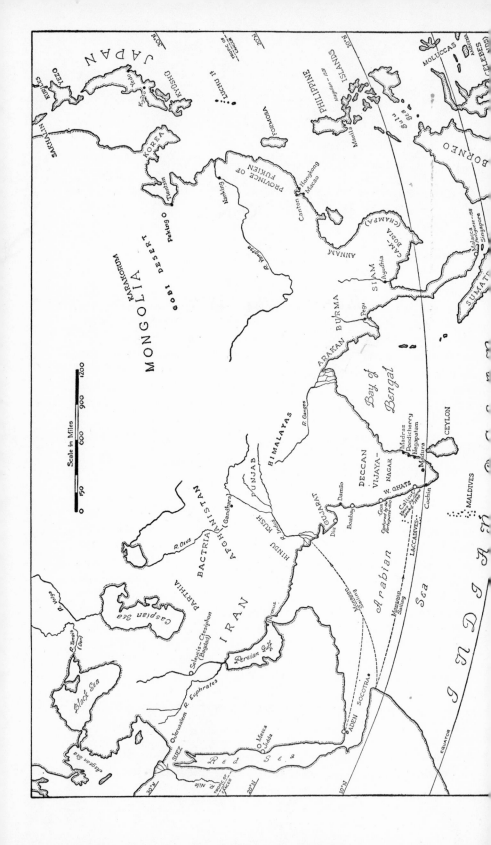

CHAPTER
I

INTRODUCTORY

1. Europe and Asia. The Frontier

THE modern history of Japan is in essence a record of the clash and fusion of two cultures, the development of an Asiatic civilization under the impact of Western habits of life and thought, the response of a crumbling feudal system based upon agriculture to the demands of industrial society. If we are to understand the nature of this process we must know, at least in a general way, the shape and the character of traditional Japanese institutions as they had evolved before they came under direct and continuous Western influence.

It would be sufficient for that limited purpose to furnish a summary account of the condition of Japan in the first half of the nineteenth century which would pay little attention to the course of events and opinions in the outside world. Because Japan until modern times has been remarkably isolated and self-contained, it happens that the nature of her traditional civilization is so distinct, so peculiarly *sui generis,* that it is relatively easy to describe in its own terms. But to treat it only in this way would be to lose sight of much of its interest and significance. The evolution of Japan, in the present as well as in the past, is part of a great sequence of events in the relations of Eastern and Western peoples. It is a particular and clear case of a general discord between European and Asiatic cultures which since antiquity has taken many forms but has not yet been resolved. Much of Japan's internal evolution and of her outlook upon the world at large becomes intelligible only if it is studied in the light of history on a scale so large as to appear at first sight excessive.

If Japanese civilization is unique, if it presents many variations that mark it off clearly from others, it does nevertheless in the basic elements of its growth conform to a general Asiatic pattern; and before considering its distinguishing features it is worth while to examine the major group of cultures to which it belongs. The first part of this study is therefore devoted to that purpose. It is designed to furnish a historical background against which the events that led to the emergence of modern Japan will appear in some relevance and proportion. More specifically, it seeks to trace the process by which European culture, having been subjected to Asiatic pressure in the first millenium of the Christian era, began to reassert itself and to spread eastwards, first slowly and cautiously and then with increasing vigour and determination, until at last its influence reached the eastern edge of the Asiatic continent and then touched the islands of Japan.

If we are to discuss the intercourse of Europe and Asia we ought to begin with some idea of the nature of Asiatic culture, having made the bold but necessary assumption that we understand the nature of our own. A captious reader might well argue that there is no such thing as a typical Asiatic culture and that therefore to speak of differences between the cultures of Europe and Asia is to treat of abstractions that do not correspond to realities. He might go further and say that even the name of Asia is only a label found useful by geographers. There would be substance in both of his objections. Certainly Asiatic civilizations differ greatly among themselves, while the geographical limits of Asia are not now, and have not been in the past, the same as its cultural frontiers. The influence or the power of Greece and Rome for long periods extended beyond the shores of the eastern Mediterranean. There were times when Asia Minor and Syria were at least as European as they were Asiatic in important aspects of their life. There were other times when peoples of admittedly Asiatic origin settled or controlled great stretches of territory within the borders of modern Europe. Mediæval travellers spoke of Asia as beginning at the river Don. Herodotus wrote of the river Don as the "terminus of Asia and Europe." William of Rubruck, describing his journey from Constantinople to Mongolia in 1253, says: "We came to the great river Tanais, which divides Europe from Asia as the river of Egypt divides Asia from Africa."

More recent geographers would say that the region loosely known to Europeans as the Near East has undefined boundaries both east and west. In both ancient and modern times a great part of it has been subject to Occidental influence and it includes all the classical lands that surround the eastern Mediterranean. Its farthest western boundary might be put at the eastern shore of the southern Adriatic. On the east there is no natural boundary before the "waist of Asia," the marsh, mountain, and desert territory that lies between the Caspian and Indian seas. The Near East up to this point has looked in varying measure to the Western centres of civilization, and access to it has been easier from Europe than from Asia, while "what lies beyond has always retained its own springs of development." [1]

The Semitic peoples, again, present a difficulty in classification. Geographically they certainly do not belong to Europe, but (as a recent writer on relationships between Europe and Asia observes) "the Moslems have something of the West about them." [2] It is difficult to classify them definitely as Asiatics, and the same can be said of the Jews.

So it is true that a strict line cannot be drawn between Europe and Asia even in a purely geographical sense, and the cultural boundary is equally undefined. But this need not prevent us from making a rough distinction on grounds of convenience, nor will anybody deny that the life of most Asiatic peoples differs in many essential features from the life of most European peoples. Perhaps the most obvious and important difference lies in their respective attitudes towards religion. This is an extremely difficult question, which cannot be treated fully here, though it will arise frequently in following chapters. But there is one field in which a distinction can be drawn in more simple terms than are needed for a study of things of the spirit, and that is the economic basis of life in these two great divisions of human society.

2. Asia and Europe. The Economies

THE typical Asiatic culture, as contrasted with the typical culture of European origin, is based upon an agrarian economy. It is of its nature a conservative culture, since it is supported by peasant masses engaged in simple agricultural pursuits, generally closely attached to the soil, living very near to the margin of subsistence and therefore concerned only with matters that bear directly on their livelihood. Their condition is not such as to allow, still less to encourage, an interest in problems of government. At most they may devote their thoughts to forms of corporate effort such as will simplify their task in the fields. They may in favourable conditions work out efficient arrangements of community life for that purpose. These, however, are rarely more than methods of local organization designed to maintain and develop, but not to reshape, the kind of society in which they live. The nature of that society is, for them, fixed in perpetuity, for they are not conscious of power to change it. They are inert, and centuries of tradition dispose them to accept the dominance of a small ruling class as part of the natural order, no less to be es-

[1] D. G. Hogarth: *The Nearer East* (1902).
[2] R. Guénon: *East and West* (1941).

caped than the burden of toil and hardship laid upon them by their calling.

So, throughout Asia until and indeed during modern times, in every culture (with the significant exception of the nomadic communities, whose life is pastoral and whose institutions are tribal ³) we find, irrespective of race or language or religion, a common pattern of peasant masses governed by a small class of warriors, priests, or officials subsisting upon the revenue from land. The form of government may vary. It may be monarchical or aristocratic, feudal or bureaucratic, even republican, but in essence it is always despotic. The whole aim of government is to ensure the maintenance of the agrarian economy and the rigid social structure that sustain the ruling class. This means that the rulers frown upon change and discourage initiative in the cultivator, whom they tend to keep in a condition of subservience; while the peasant, for his part, by the nature of his occupation is tenacious of his own habits and beliefs.

It may be objected that this description applies to European as well as to Asiatic cultures, and it is of course true that it represents a normal phase in the progress of all human societies once they have arrived at settled agricultural life. But the distinction between Asiatic and European cultures lies in the fact that, while the true Asiatic cultures have not yet emerged from that phase, the European cultures have all, in a greater or less degree, moved on to a new phase, where the simple agricultural economy is combined with or even displaced by a mercantile economy, which creates new functions and new classes, promotes the importance of the town and the town-dweller, diversifies the life of the community, and ends by changing its very nature.

Most European historians detect the first sign of this divergence from the ancient pattern in the city states of the Ægean Sea. For a number of reasons, all of which are not clear but which mostly have to do with geography and climate, this region developed new cultures differing somewhat among themselves, but all in striking contrast to the old. While, for instance, in China and India of the first millennium B.C. there were great stationary populations tilling vast areas of land, on those small islands and promontories washed by Mediterranean waters there lived peo-

³ The Arabs, though mainly tribal and pastoral, had developed in some regions an advanced urban life before the rise of Islam, and therefore cannot strictly speaking be put into the category of nomadic peoples. Yet they did not form a settled society comparable to the great agricultural societies of the rest of Asia, while their further developments took place outside their homeland and in collaboration with many alien elements. For purposes of classification they may perhaps be grouped with nomadic peoples, though they partook of both characters. They really are a class apart, nearer in many respects to the trading, colonizing Greeks than to the sedentary peoples of Asia.

ples who could scarcely subsist upon the produce of their own soil but were obliged, by circumstance and temperament, to traffic freely overseas. This maritime trade, as it grew, brought into being a new social class of merchants, shipbuilders, navigators, and other specialists upon whom the prosperity of their community largely depended. They were not numerous, but they were important. Maritime trade brought as much benefit as agriculture, so that the merchant rivalled the landlord in wealth and influence. There was now interposed between the traditional landlord ruler and the passive peasant serf an active middle class, with special interests of its own that inevitably gave it special political power.

From such origins there developed in the great age of Greece — during the fifth and the fourth centuries B.C. — a new type of society dominated by concepts of political and economic freedom, devoted to navigation, colonization, and trade and active in the study of mathematics, astronomy, geography, and kindred sciences. This, despite its fluctuating fortunes in subsequent history, is the forerunner of that element in European life which has produced its characteristic political and social features — democratic principles of government, individualist doctrines, and the spirit of scientific inquiry.

It may be argued that the great Asiatic communities also had considerable commerce within themselves and with one another; that their merchants also undertook extensive journeys by land and by sea; and therefore that the political importance of trade in the Hellenic world is not exceptional. But the significance of the merchant in the Ægean city states lay not so much in the length of his journeys or the volume of his trade as in his relative importance to a small community, in his status as a citizen.

The great Asiatic communities were in general self-supporting and self-contained. Trade within their own frontiers was of importance because of their size, and there was often an extensive traffic between the various parts of great countries like China, where for example the products of widely separated provinces would be exchanged by long overland or coastal journeys. But flourishing as this internal trade may have been, it was ancillary to the agriculture which provided the lifeblood of the state. It was an extension of the agrarian economy, not a rival to it. The trader, therefore, did not as a rule achieve in these communities any outstanding social or political importance. In most of them indeed he was despised and oppressed by the ruling class. The merchant and the artisan usually ranked below the farmer in the social scale. The town was more important than the country only in so far as it was the seat of government and the centre to which revenue flowed. Even in those countries or regions that, being favourably placed for overseas traffic, developed a considerable sea-borne foreign trade, the shipowner, the shipbuilder, and the specialists upon whom they depended attained only a local or subsidiary importance.

Here a useful illustration is provided by Chinese history. It shows a long and distinguished record of maritime commerce, particularly between ports in southern China and the Indian Ocean, going back possibly as far as the later Han and reaching its zenith under the early Ming emperors, who seem to have had some inkling of the importance of sea-power. But in general it is true to say that Chinese maritime enterprise stemmed from no national impulse and received no consistent benefit of national policy. Until the nineteenth century the diplomatic and military effort of China was directed almost entirely across her land frontiers. The great movements of Chinese expansion progressed mainly overland to the west, while her defensive movements looked towards her northern borders. She rarely faced seaward, because there was no circumstance obliging her to increase her naval strength or her sea-borne trade for truly national purposes. No serious or continuing danger threatened her from the sea, and her own domestic economy was so massive and self-sufficient that foreign commerce was little more than a means of obtaining luxuries or curiosities to satisfy the whims of courtiers and high officials.

What has been said of China in these respects is true also of India. Indian ships made long voyages in classical times, for from the earliest recorded history we know of traders sending freight westward across the Indian Ocean to Africa and eastward to China. Indeed, by the beginning of the Christian era Indian peoples had already begun a considerable enterprise of colonization, which later extended as far as Malaya and Cambodia. Nevertheless, "in all the earlier ages India looked inward, not outward." [4] In subsequent history also, time after time the expansive impulse fails, and Indian life turns in upon itself. It is not sensibly affected by influences from across the sea, and even alien conquerors pouring in across the land frontiers cannot change its essential nature though they may modify its outward forms.

This relative unimportance of foreign relations in the life of the great settled communities of Asia is but one expression of their self-sufficiency, for in general their history shows that, just as they have felt no great need of foreign merchandise, so they have been under no inner compulsion to seek wisdom or knowledge outside their own borders.

Seen in this aspect China and India appear as prime examples of the characteristic Asiatic culture upon which a great uniform peasant population confers an independence and stability in strong

[4] E. J. Rapson (ed.) : *Cambridge History of India,* I, 385.

contrast to the active, experimental temper of the cultures of the West. It is doubtless this contrast that has given rise to Western aphorisms about the "unchanging East"; for while it is true that Asia has seen great developments or mutations in religious and philosophic thought, great movements in art, great advances in knowledge, and great vicissitudes in the fortunes of peoples and nations, there has been throughout recorded history until very recent times but little change in the fundamental social and political habits prevailing in Asiatic countries. The life of the peasant, his attitude to his rulers, and their attitude to him remained in the early nineteenth century, and in some parts of Asia still remain today, what they were in the days of Confucius in China or the Buddha in India.

The European scene is livelier. Onward from the days of the Ægean city states it continues to manifest the restless energy that impelled Hellenic culture to expand, to reach out to other lands and peoples. There are dark and silent intervals, and sometimes the Hellenic spirit seems to be in danger of extinction; but it reasserts itself and continues to exert upon the Eastern as well as the Western world an influence that cannot be permanently resisted.

The intrusion of this disruptive, challenging element into the sequestered and conservative life of Asia must be a dominant theme in the modern history of any Asiatic state. The process has gone so far and so fast in Japan that her modern history is apt to be regarded as something surprising and exceptional. It is true that what marks off modern Japan from other Asiatic countries is the fact that she has gone farther and faster than them in the adoption of Occidental practices; but events in Japan in both ancient and modern times have followed in general a common Asiatic course. Her history, or for that matter the modern history of any single Asiatic state, to be fruitfully studied needs to be viewed in this wider perspective, for it is a particular case of a great general movement.

Such wider perspective should ideally include within its range the history of all Asiatic states in their relations with Europe, or at least the history of the Iranian and the Hindu and the Islamic worlds as well as of the great Chinese society, and it should touch on the seafaring and trading accomplishments of Arab peoples. Fortunately for both reader and writer the history of Japan presents on a sufficiently large scale most of the necessary elements of description; and our purpose will be served if we further examine in some detail the impact of Europe upon Asia mainly as it is exhibited in the foreign intercourse of India and China, though with occasional reference to other parts of Asia. But before passing on to particulars, it is useful to consider briefly whether it is possible to discover some general principles that in the past have governed the relationships of European and Asiatic cultures.

3. Asia and Europe. Mutual Influences

PERHAPS it is to push generalization too far to speak of a historical reluctance of Asiatic peoples to engage in close relations with Europe. Asia is too vast and diversified to allow of such a sweeping statement, as is clear if we recall the movements of her nomadic races from the earliest recorded times down to the Mongol invasions of the thirteenth century. But it can be said that, as a matter of historical fact, from antiquity until very recent times the settled Asiatic peoples as a whole have shown no stronger or enduring disposition to approach the European peoples either by way of trade or by military adventure.

However this lack of interest is to be explained, it is fair to say that the conservative nature of Asiatic cultures, from whatever causes it arose, is in contrast to the aggressive and often militant character of the efforts of Europeans to break into Asiatic seclusion. It is not necessary to argue that the strongest Asiatic cultures are or have ever been of their nature either lacking in aggressive qualities or impervious to foreign influence. But it is true that until modern times Asia has not looked towards Europe as Europe has looked towards Asia; and that Europe has been unable to maintain in Asia for long enough or on a sufficient scale the kind of contact or pressure by which one civilization can affect another.

The reasons are various. Sheer physical difficulties have played an important part. Great natural barriers are interposed between Europe and Asia. The Hindu Kush presents a formidable obstacle to those who would enter India overland from the north, and inhospitable country defends her against aggression from the west; while the central Asian mountains and deserts have always forbidden easy access to China by continental routes. But these factors of geography and climate which have prevented movement from Europe into Asia have at the same time influenced the nature and growth of Asiatic cultures. It is not only that they were for centuries physically secluded from European influences, but also that their own shape and quality were in great measure determined by an environment differing in important ways from that in which the main European cultures were born and grew to maturity.

It is therefore not unreasonable to say that Asiatic cultures are in general of a character that resists all but the most powerful and sustained influences of European origin. This is borne out by what we know of the efforts of the Western world to make and extend contacts with China, and further evidence is supplied by the failure of one wave of European influence after another to make any lasting impression upon the civilization of India. Even the most ambitious of the enterprises of antiquity directed by Europe against Asia, the invasion of India by Alexander the Great, failed of its purpose because the effort could not be maintained, and left but little trace upon the cultures that it disturbed. Whatever may have been his plans, it is admitted that he exerted no influence upon any part of India other than the country watered by the Indus, and it is most likely that the rest was not even known to him. Some historians indeed hold the view that the only influence that he exerted upon the Indus plain was to hasten the political unity of its diverse tribes and so to help the formation of the Maurya Empire. In other words, he consolidated rather than modified the culture of the region he invaded.

Such Hellenistic influences as persisted after Alexander's day were those exercised by Greeks living among Asiatic peoples under Seleucid or Bactrian rulers, whose kingdoms lay on the edge of India. It is true that, thanks to the survival of the Greek colonies he planted in central Asia, there persisted in Bactria and beyond the Hindu Kush for several centuries a strong Hellenistic tradition, which had some effect directly upon the native art of India and indirectly upon the art of China and even of Japan; but this, though providing an interesting episode in the history of painting and sculpture, was not more than a superficial and transient influence, which wrought no essential change in the nature of Indian or Chinese life.

It was only upon those Asiatic countries much nearer to European Greece — upon Asia Minor, Syria, and adjacent regions — that Hellenistic influence took some lasting hold; and even there that influence was later to be diluted or submerged by successive military or cultural invasions of Asiatic origin. Indeed, the historian who attempts to strike a balance in the account of cultural exchanges between the two continents is bound to conclude that at least until the modern industrial age Europe has owed a considerable cultural debt to Asia. The ancient and powerful civilizations of Iran and Babylonia, though they took some superficial imprints of Greek culture, were never radically influenced by its spirit. They stood firm in their own essential tradition, and it is even possible that they gave more than they took. The influence of Hellas never touched Chinese society, and though it reached beyond the fringes of northern India, it never sensibly affected the core of Indian life. Such traces as it left were swept away by Scythian or Parthian invaders, or they were overgrown by ripening indigenous cultures in Hindustan or central India. One authority goes so far as to say that, except for images of the Buddha, "the history of India would in all essentials have been precisely what it has been, had Greeks never existed."

This statement as to images of the Buddha, being taken from its context, needs some elucidation. It means that, while Greek influence had no effect upon Indian thought or doctrine, it did modify the Indian attitude towards the representation of deities in religious art. The early ritual of Hinduism did not include the worship of images. In early Buddhist art the person of the Buddha is not represented. But in those parts of India and adjacent countries where Hellenistic art flourished, men were accustomed to seeing the likeness of gods and kings on coins and in statuary. From this it was a short step, which the Indian religions took, to adopting the practice of portraying divinities in human shape both in painting and in sculpture. In the sculptures known as Gandharan the Buddha actually appears in a form like that of Apollo, or shows other plain traces of Greek or Roman influence. Apart from such transient elements in Indian art as we have just noticed, nothing alien of importance survives into a later age. The native institutions continue to preserve a secular stability. Only the military caste is restless and unsatisfied. One conqueror succeeds another, dynasties rise and fall, but the basic forms of social and intellectual life remain unaffected.

By contrast the pattern of European life presents an almost alarming appearance of instability. Europe seems to be the home of incessant movements, of *perepeteiai* or violent reversals of fortune, in human affairs. Unlike the Asiatic world its social order is constantly subject to change and crisis, and in its periods of greatest confusion it is particularly sensitive to foreign influences. In one such period it adopted the foreign religion that is Christianity, in another it submitted to the power of Byzantine culture, which had a strong Eastern flavour, and throughout the Christian era it has from time to time listened to voices from the Orient.

It was not until the nineteenth century that this trend was definitely reversed. Before that, although European influences continued to attack the strongholds of Asiatic tradition, they made little impression upon its defences. Despite the material power of European states, despite even their military conquests of Asiatic soil, the Asiatic peoples remained imperturbably confident in their own institutions.

Nothing could better illustrate their attitude than the often-quoted pronouncements of the great Emperors of China K'ang Hsi and Ch'ien Lung. The former, who reigned in the seventeenth century, was an urbane monarch who treated Jesuit missionaries at his court with consideration and took some interest in scientific and literary studies under their guidance. But he once observed, on perusing a papal bull, that if this was the way in which foreigners' minds worked, he could only say that they were small-minded people. Ch'ien Lung, who flourished in the eighteenth century, received with great courtesy an embassy from King George III of England that came to negotiate a commercial treaty. But he said to the Ambassador among other condescending things that although it was praiseworthy of the English to try to partake of the benefits of Chinese civilization, it would be quite impossible for them at such a great distance to acquire even the rudiments of civilized behaviour, while as for trade, he added, "China possesses all things in abundance, and we do not want your products."

This, it should be noticed, was in a century when Europe was approaching a political and social crisis and when (whatever Chinese sages may have thought of Europe) European philosophers were apt to admire and even to recommend for imitation the stability of Chinese institutions and the elegance of Chinese life. It was before the French Revolution had changed the political atmosphere of Europe and before the industrial revolution had released in the world forces that the ancient cultures of the East could not permanently withstand.

But from that time onward they could not remain indifferent; they must either submit to those forces or endeavour to turn them against those who had let them loose. This was the challenge that confronted all Asiatic countries in the nineteenth century. The Japanese were the first to take it up with vigour, and the way in which they met it is the substance of the history of modern Japan.

Notes on CHAPTER I

HELLENISTIC INFLUENCES UPON INDIAN ART. This is a controversial question. Some authorities rate the influence of Gandharan art very high, others doubt whether it was really the cause of the end of the aniconic period. The latter is the view of Ananda Coomaraswamy, stated in the *Encyclopædia Britannica* (1945) in his article on "Indian Art." The point is discussed in the *Cambridge History of India*, Vol. I, pp. 384 ff. and p. 648. Further discussion will be found in most works on early Indian art and notably in *Les Origines de l'art bouddhique* and other studies by Foucher. An article by H. Buchthal on "The Common Classical Sources of Buddhist and Christian Narrative Art" in the *Journal of the Royal Asiatic Society* (1943, parts 3 and 4) brings out most interesting parallels and gives useful references to literature on the subject.

K'ANG HSI'S OPINIONS ON EUROPEANS. Accounts are to be found in most works relating to the Rites controversy in China; for example, Latourette's *History of Christian Missions in China* and Rowbotham's *Missionary and Mandarin.* The exact words of the Emperor's Vermilion Endorsement on the Chinese version of the bull *Ex illa die* may be rendered as follows: "After reading this document all I can say is: How could the Occidentals, stupid men as they are, dispute the great teaching of China? Not one of them thoroughly understands Chinese writings, and when they speak, most of them are ludicrous. The bull, which I have now seen, resembles the superstitions of Buddhists and Taoists, but there is nothing so full of blunders as this."

Ch'ien Lung's pronouncements are given in English in *Annals and Memoirs of the Court of Peking,* by Backhouse and Bland; and a Chinese text is in the dynastic chronicle *Ta Ch'ing Shih-lu,* under Kaotsung, ch. 1435/11b.

CHAPTER

2

EARLY INTERCOURSE BETWEEN EUROPE AND ASIA

1. Trade and Navigation

IN studying the earliest recorded intercourse between Europe and Asia one is struck by a contrast between the strong interest in Asia displayed by European peoples and the indifference of settled Asiatic peoples to the affairs and customs of the inhabitants of distant regions. The Chinese, though inveterate chroniclers, have always affected to regard the outer world as barbaric. Their dynastic histories and even their great books of travel seem usually to state facts about foreign countries with a dry reserve. They are interested but not excited by the outside world.

As for India, it is remarkable that, despite a long history of relationships with peoples beyond her northwestern frontiers, commencing with a prehistoric affinity between Hindus and Persians and continuing down to close cultural contacts with Greeks and men of Greek descent, there is in Indian literature or tradition nothing about Europe or even western Asia to compare with the copious information about India furnished by early Greek and Latin authors.

Indeed, so little, it would seem, did the sages and scholars of India concern themselves with examining the nature of the visible world of matter, so immersed were they in speculation upon loftier themes, that the modern student must rely for much of his knowledge of ancient India upon the notices of Herodotus, Strabo, Pliny, and other classical historians and geographers who drew upon European sources of direct observation, such as Megasthenes and Ctesias. He can depend but little upon direct description in native Indian literature, since most of the information on political and social matters derived from that source is built up by inference out of religious and ethical writings or epic poems. These, while they are wanting in important historical details, testify to a rich and complex civilization evolving from its own original elements and

15

little subject to influence from outside. "Where such influence might be looked for with greatest certainty," says an authority, "namely in the effect of Greek domination, it is practically nil." [1]

Only the Yavanas or Yonas — the "Ionians," peoples of Greek descent — who appear in Indian records from the third century B.C. to the second century of our era, remain to show that Alexander and subsequent Greek invaders left any trace. "Political and social relations do not appear to be affected at all either by Hellenic or Persian influence. . . . The social theory remains practically the same, save that a place among degraded 'outcastes' is given to Yavanas as to other barbarians." It is significant that, of all the Greek or Greco-Indian princes who ruled either north or south of the Hindu Kush, only one is celebrated in the ancient literature of India. This is Menander, who figures in Buddhist legend not as a powerful monarch — which indeed he was — but as a philosopher who was overcome in debate and at length converted by an Indian sage. Similarly a later foreign ruler, Kanishka, appears in Indian chronicles not as a sovereign who made the Kushana Empire paramount in northern India but rather as a great patron of Buddhism, second only to Asoka.

From these and many similar indications, one must conclude that Indian culture, by the time that Greek influence was brought to bear upon it, was already so deeply rooted as to be no longer open to change. The position is clearly described by an authority on the Greek, Scythian, and Parthian invasions of India in the following words: "In Bactria the Greeks ruled supreme amid peoples of a lower culture. On the south of the mountain barrier, in the Kābul valley and in India, they were brought into contact with a civilization which was in many respects as advanced as their own and even more ancient — a civilization in which religious and social institutions had long ago been stereotyped and in which individual effort in literature and art was no longer free but bound by centuries of tradition." [2]

Turning to China, we see a picture of relationships between East and West that, although it presents some special features due to the remoter situation of China and the distinct character of its people, does in its essentials resemble that of the intercourse between Europe and India. There is fairly abundant material in Greek and Latin works as well as in Chinese records giving accounts of commercial and diplomatic exchanges between China and the West in classical times. Much of it is obscure, but there is sufficient evidence to show the general character of this intercourse and its extent.

[1] E. W. Hopkins, in *Cambridge History of India*, I, 225.
[2] E. J. Rapson, in *Cambridge History of India*, I, 545.

We need not concern ourselves with the earliest indications of Western knowledge of China, which are of uncertain value; but for the closing years of the second century B.C. there is good documentary proof of relations between China and the western parts of Asia in which people of European stock resided. This came about through Chinese initiative. It was the result, however, not of a desire for intercourse on a footing of equality but of a search for possible allies in China's struggle against the Huns (Hiung-nu) who were then threatening her northwestern borders.

This is a point of some significance, because the history of Asia tends to show that such changes as took place in the institutions and ideas of her settled peoples were usually the result not of internal evolution but of external pressure brought to bear by migration or invasion originating beyond their frontiers. Thus in the great movements and clashes of nomadic peoples which were disturbing Asia at this time, one of the migrating hordes, the Yue-chi, was driven by the pressure of its rivals to enter Bactria and Sogdiana and so to destroy the Greek kingdoms established there. The Greeks were forced to withdraw to the south of the Hindu Kush, thus enlarging for a season the Hellenistic influence planted in India by Alexander the Great.

Meanwhile, if we may believe the Chinese chronicles, the great Han Emperor Wu-ti, now master of all China and anxious to consolidate his power, sent an envoy to central Asia to look into the political and military situation there. The report of this inquirer, whose name was Chang Ch'ien, is summarized in a Chinese chronicle. It relates that in 128 B.C. Chang Ch'ien visited Ferghana, Bactria, and adjacent regions and took back also accounts of countries farther west, such as Parthia, Scythia, and Babylonia. The Emperor was impressed by what he heard, and decided to open up relations with both the tribesmen and the settled peoples. His plan appears to have been to win them over to his side by means of trade, for he began to send frequent missions to the countries described by Chang Ch'ien. These were on a large scale, and they carried with them gifts, which were most acceptable to the courts and camps they visited.

We have here the beginnings not only of regular diplomatic intercourse but also of commercial traffic between China and Europe, for very soon Chinese produce, at first reaching only as far as Ferghana, Bactria, and Parthia, found its way to Syria and then to Rome. The chief article of commerce was Chinese silk, and this fact points to a feature of the trade between China and the outside world which reappears throughout subsequent ages. It is characteristic of the historical traffic between Europe and Asia that its driving force is a European demand for Asiatic goods. This must hold true for so long as the Asiatic cultures remain self-supporting and self-contained because their needs are fulfilled within their own economies. Wu-ti embarked upon trade with the countries on his western borders not because he wished to supplement by imports deficiencies in the domestic production of China, but because, as a matter of national policy, he wished to impress the peoples of central and western Asia with his wealth and power. In return for his presents he was glad to receive rare and curious things that would minister to his luxury or his prestige. But whereas Europe was unable to offer to the Asiatic peoples in quantity any commodities that they urgently needed or desired, Asia was able to furnish articles of trade that were, or soon became, indispensable to the prosperous classes in the Roman Empire.

In examining lists of articles imported by China, not only in the earliest period of her foreign trade but also in much later days, it is rare to come across anything that can be regarded as essential or even important to her economy. This is true also of the traffic of Western countries with India and indeed of the traffic between the greater Asiatic communities themselves. The ancient and mediæval trade between India and China consisted largely in an exchange of precious metals, precious stones, or objects that were rare and curious but had little intrinsic value. Greek, Latin, and Chinese authors in their accounts of the Asiatic trade tell of such articles of sale or tribute (there is often no distinction between the two except in name) as ostriches' eggs and jugglers; dwarfs and musicians; horses that sweat blood; parrots, peacocks, and apes; incense, perfumes, and aphrodisiacs; ivory, rhinoceros horn, and tortoise-shell; and even "pretty girls for concubines." This kind of commerce, while it gave profits to traders and pleasures to those who enjoyed frivolities or luxuries, represented no important demand that must of necessity be satisfied. It was thus natural that foreign trade should not appear to most Asiatic rulers as something essential to the welfare of their countries, an activity that in their own political interest they must promote and expand.

The great Western empires on the other hand derived much of their power from the sustenance afforded by trade, both internal and external, and their policies were governed to a large extent by the needs of commercial expansion. A glance at the history of the Macedonian, Seleucid, and Ptolemaic empires and their succession states shows that, in peace and war, one of their chief concerns was to secure or protect trade routes by land and sea; and much of the warfare of the centuries between Alexander's campaigns and the Battle of Actium was a struggle not only for territory but also for commercial opportunity. The political and military history of that period gives a confused picture of rivalry between states or cities for mastery of the traffic in staple commodities. Pirates and robbers prey upon convoys and caravans, and states fight among themselves for the power to levy toll upon merchandise in transit or to divert trade to channels they control. Nations as well as individuals develop to a high point of efficiency the prototypes of those arts which are known in our day as smuggling, bootlegging, and highjacking, so that in the end only the boldest of merchants will take the risks of traffic with distant places, and only the wealthiest clients can afford his merchandise. It is no wonder that, in such circumstances, the Asiatic trade should have been little more than a trickle of goods in both directions, accompanied by no important cultural exchanges. The wonder is that, despite all hazards and discouragements, the trade did continue and on the whole increased in both quantity and scope.

Its most rapid increase took place during the first two centuries of the Roman Empire, when Roman rule extended over most of Europe and the Near East. Under the protection of Rome, merchants could now send and receive cargoes through the Mediterranean, the Red Sea, the Persian Gulf, and the Indian Ocean with a degree of security that they had not before enjoyed, while the land routes, though still in places hazardous, became increasingly safe for trade. Foreign commerce was encouraged not only by the elimination of brigandage and piracy, but also by the reduction of customs duties within the dominion of Rome and the disappearance or diminution of commissions, tolls, and other forms of blackmail that had hitherto been levied by middlemen or other parasitic groups along the trade routes.

These new conditions, together with a great increase in the wealth at the disposal of the leaders of Rome, created at the same time an insistent demand for foreign goods and a new possibility of its satisfaction. Roman ships sailed (from Red Sea ports) to India, first only by coasting but later, as the nature of the monsoons began to be understood, by running free before the wind from Aden to the mouth of the Indus.

A later development and one of great consequence in the history of trade and navigation took place in or about A.D. 50, when an open sea route from Aden to the southwestern shores of India was found by a shipmaster who steered with rudder and sail so set that the southwest monsoon blew from his starboard quarter and carried him from the Gulf of Aden to the Malabar coast. Thenceforward the trade between the Roman Empire and India increased rapidly in volume and variety. By the first half of the second century most of the west coast of the Indian peninsula was known to Roman traders (or rather Greeks in Roman service), and soon after that they began to find their way about the Bay of Bengal, eventually reaching Upper Burma, then Lower Burma, Malaya, Sumatra, passing on by the Malacca Straits to Cambodia and Tongking, whence they at last made direct contact with China.

A culminating-point in the early history of communication between Europe and the Far East is reached in A.D. 166, when we have it from Chinese sources that an ambassador came from Antun (Antoninus = Marcus Aurelius), the King of Ta Ts'in (Rome), with tribute, and this was the beginning of direct intercourse between the two empires.

It is evident that this and subsequent missions, which the Chinese in accordance with their practice chose to regard as embassies bringing tribute, were not in any sense official efforts to open diplomatic relations with China, but private ventures by enterprising merchants in search of new openings for trade. It cannot be said that official intercourse between the Far East and Europe developed because of these contacts. But Rome and Nanking did learn something about one another, and the commerce between them did grow in volume. It was, as we have seen, a commerce more important to Europe than to Asia.

Fairly precise accounts of the nature of the trade of the Roman Empire with Asia in the first three centuries of the Christian era are furnished by contemporary writers. Though they show that the goods imported from India and the Far East by the Roman Empire were mostly of the nature of luxuries, we have to remember that in a developing economy the luxury of today becomes the necessity of tomorrow. The most important single article of trade was Chinese silk, for which the demand grew and spread until its use, once condemned by Roman moralists as a shameless extravagance, became common among well-to-do people in western Asia and Europe.

Other commodities, at first rarities beyond the reach of all but the wealthiest, as trade channels were developed and organized and as peace under Roman rule raised the levels of consumption, became articles of everyday use in most Roman households. Notable among these were spices and aromatics from India, of which pepper was the commonest, though cinnamon, ginger, and cloves were in frequent use. We need not consider further the list of imports of this kind, beyond mentioning that it includes a great number of plant products used in cookery or medicine, mostly of Indian origin except for rhubarb, which came from China overland.

All these articles, it is interesting to note, played an important if not an essential part in the life of the urban population of the Roman Empire, and they have been since then in urgent demand by European peoples until our own day. In that sense it may be argued that China and India exerted an influence upon the social habits of the West at this early date. It is characteristic of the relationship between the two groups of cultures that no similar influence was brought to bear upon the life of the people of India or China by the European products they received in exchange. What went from Rome to Asia may fairly be described as luxuries or curiosities, things to suit the tastes of kings and courtiers rather than articles that might find their way into ordinary Indian or Chinese households and so bring a new element into common life. The chief European exports to China were glass, some textiles, amber, tortoise-shell, and coral, while there were a number of other products, such as precious stones, ivory, pearls, drugs, and perfumes, which were handled by Roman or Greek traders but were of African or Asiatic origin.

To India the Roman Empire sent coral, some linens, copper, tin (from the British Isles), glass, and some drugs, unguents, and perfumes. There is little else in the list, and it is established that India received much less in value than she exported. The urgency of demand was not equal on both sides because, as we have seen, the Asiatic economies were in general independent and conservative, whereas the European economies tended to expansion and diversity, largely no doubt because of their greater development of urban life and their greater spread of purchasing power.

It resulted from these differences that the balance of trade was against Europe. The West being unable to furnish to the Asiatic peoples in quantity any commodities that they urgently needed or desired, the Asiatic trade was for the most part an exchange of Asiatic products against European treasure. It involved a drain upon the wealth of the Roman Empire, which, it seems, could not be offset by any available means. The subject is a difficult one to discuss in the absence of exact data, but there is no doubt that as the Asiatic trade grew, the Empire as a whole was obliged to meet its deficit by exporting gold and silver. The loss of this capital may not have been a direct cause of the economic collapse that began to overtake Rome in the third century, though it was certainly one of the symptoms of decline. Possibly the fundamental economic weakness of the Empire was due to remoter causes, such as a failure to develop productive enterprises by which capital could be accumulated. If this were so, it would not be the first or the last time in history when a nation, having acquired great resources by war or good fortune, has failed to develop them and spent its substance without regard for the future. However that may be, the point of interest for the purpose of this inquiry is that, whether of necessity or by some fault of policy, the Western Empire was unable to redress the balance of its trade with Asia; and this was a condition that persisted until modern times, when at length the trading peoples of the West were able to create a demand for their products and to reverse the eastward flow of gold and silver.

It is clear that we have here an economic factor of overriding importance in considering the general nature of intercourse between Europe and Asia. The flow of commodities from Asia to Europe is a natural result of the difference in size between the two continents. The civilized part of Europe in the most flourishing period of the Western Roman Empire occupied a very narrow range of latitude — roughly speaking, from 35° N. to 55° N. Its range of natural products was accordingly restricted. It included very few of the crops that flourish in subtropical climates. It had in the Mediterranean area certain indigenous "southern" fruits such as the fig, but the lemon and the orange are of Asiatic origin.[3] It had no dates, sugar, cotton or rice, and none of the gums, spices and aromatics that are abundant in Africa and Asia. Though well supplied with coal, iron, copper, and tin, it was not rich in precious metals, particularly gold, and was deficient in most of the important precious stones. It was thus by contrast with Asia, though favoured by climate and geographical configuration, poor in the variety if not the quantity of its own material resources.

It follows that Europe, as its economy expanded, required from Asia an increasing number of commodities that the several Asiatic countries could find, if not within their own borders, at least in accessible regions of their own continent — a land mass which, with its adjacent islands, stretches from the Arctic Circle to south of the equator and presents the greatest possible diversity of soil and climate.

2. Politics and Religion

WHETHER Rome could by remedying her economic weakness have afforded to continue her lavish purchases from India and China is a matter we need not discuss, for by the third century both her economic and her political power began to decline. Barbarians ravished her territory, she suffered from internal disorder, and she could no longer protect the trade routes leading to India and beyond.

The Asiatic trade continued and at first probably saw no great falling off in volume, since Byzantine pomp and luxury surpassed that of Rome. But before long it was largely in other than Roman hands, because Abyssinians, Arabs, and Persians controlled the channels by which Asiatic merchandise reached the shores of the

---

[3] Europe owes many of its fruits and flowers to Asia Minor, while only the grape and the olive supplied exports that were appreciated outside Europe. They provided Anatolian and European Greece with two very important commodities for sale in Asia: wine and oil.

Mediterranean. It was on account of the importance to Byzantium of the silk trade that, as a means of escape from blackmail by middlemen straddling the lines of supply, the culture of silk was developed in the Roman Empire after eggs of the silk moth had been secretly brought to Europe, which was thus rendered independent of the import from China soon after A.D. 550.

By such developments Europe was cut off from the Indian Ocean and from regular communication with China by the land route; but trade from China and India by land and sea did not cease. It was too profitable to be abandoned, and what Rome was unable to afford, other customers were anxious to purchase. The roads remained open to those who had the courage to travel them.

The third century, which saw the decline of Roman power, began a period of strife and confusion in China, lasting from the collapse of the later Han dynasty until about A.D. 600, when China became united under the Sui and then the T'ang emperors. There is some evidence of visits to the T'ang court by European travellers, who were perhaps official envoys from Byzantium and not private traders. Such intercourse may well have been sought by Roman emperors or at least by the rulers of distant Roman provinces, since under the T'ang emperors the military power of China reached westward to Bokhara and Samarkand, while her political influence extended beyond the Oxus.

Certainly under the T'ang dynasty (A.D. 618–906) China began to learn more about Western countries than she had known before and to display more interest in them. A Zoroastrian temple was erected in Ch'ang-an, the capital, in 621; a Sassanian prince died there a little later as a refugee from Arab invaders of his home in Persia; the Nestorian teaching was commended; and we know from both writings and images that throughout the T'ang era Buddhist monks from India, envoys from central Asian kingdoms, nomads from Siberia and Mongolia, as well as men from Annam, Tonking, and Malaya, were not unfamiliar figures in the city, so that it is highly probable that visitors from different parts of the Roman Empire made their way to China in the seventh century. Chinese chronicles mention the arrival of embassies from the Eastern Roman Empire at intervals until the middle of the eighth century. These may have been composed of traders or Nestorian priests from Syria, but it is quite possible that a Roman emperor sent a mission or missions to the T'ang court because he had learned of the growing strength of China.

This was indeed one of China's great ages of expansion. The western borders of the Chinese Empire in the seventh century were close to the eastern extremity of the Roman Empire, so that a Chinese official stationed at Merv might have exchanged visits with a Roman governor of Armenia. Chinese vessels sailed into the Indian Ocean, and Chinese travellers passed by land routes into India. Notable among them was the Buddhist pilgrim Hsüan Tsang, who in a book called a *Record of Travel in Western Lands* described what he saw (A.D. 629) on his way to India across the western desert, through Kashgaria and Bactria and down into the Punjab.

The journeys of Hsüan Tsang and other pilgrims illustrate conveniently certain important features of the growth of Asiatic cultures in his period.[4] China, usually impermeable to alien influence, had accepted during the late Han period the doctrines of Buddhism, which first reached her by the route later followed by Hsüan Tsang in the opposite direction. This Indian religion prospered in China and — a curious phenomenon — served as a vehicle for Chinese culture transplanted into other lands, in this respect proving itself superior to Confucianism, which, so strong was its indigenous character, never flourished in foreign soil (except in the adjacent and tributary country of Korea and to a much less extent in Japan). Buddhism was carried by Chinese missionaries to Korea, to Japan, and to Annam, while Buddhism as it developed in Mongolia and Tibet, perhaps also in Burma and Siam, had a certain Chinese colouring. In China itself, though it never succeeded in displacing Confucian doctrine, it had a considerable influence on Chinese intellectual and artistic life and it persisted within China and Japan long after Buddhism in India had submitted to the older Hinduism which it had for a time challenged.

This fragment of history is mentioned here because it has some bearing on the question of the interaction of civilizations in Asia. It tends at first sight to show that, whereas Chinese culture offered resistance to European influences, it was open to Asiatic influences. But on closer examination it appears that, although Indian Buddhism had an important effect upon Chinese thought and left its mark upon art, literature, and popular beliefs, it was in the end conquered by traditional Chinese attitudes towards life and society, just as in Japan, where in early ages it proved a potent civilizing factor, it succumbed at last to the more deeply rooted indigenous beliefs. Neither in China nor Japan today is organized Bud-

---

[4] In the history of travel he takes a high place not only as a devout pilgrim but as an indomitable sightseer. There are two other great names: Fa-hsien, who in A.D. 399 went by a caravan route across the Tarim basin to India, collected copies of Buddhist sutras, and returned to China by way of Ceylon and the South China Sea; and I-tsing, who went from South China to India by sea *c.* 671 and returned, after a sojourn of over twenty years, with books for translation. During the seventh century many other Chinese pilgrims visited India. The names of at least fifty are on record, and there were doubtless many more. The knowledge they and their predecessors gained was passed on to Japan in the sixth, seventh, and eighth centuries.

dhism a living force, despite its past strength and the numbers of its nominal adherents. The same is true of other religions that have gained a hearing in China. Islam, so powerful in its influence in western Asia, never succeeded in competition with native Chinese systems, and though there is a considerable Moslem population in China, Islam has had to conform to Chinese notions of the place of religion in the state and can claim no favours.

The Chinese throughout their history have, with occasional lapses, displayed a peculiar tolerance in regard to foreign creeds. T'ang emperors permitted the propagation of Nestorian Christianity in the seventh century. Neither they nor their predecessors appear as a rule to have raised objection to the religious practices of foreigners residing within their dominions. Sometimes they went so far as to give them official encouragement and patronage, as when the T'ang court issued a pronouncement in favour of Nestorian doctrine; and Zoroastrianism and Manichæism, if not specially favoured, were at least admitted. This tolerant attitude expresses not a thirst of the Chinese for religious truth but rather a supreme confidence in the validity of their own institutions. They were always prepared to examine interesting doctrines that came to their notice, because they respected learning and were addicted to discussion of the principles of human behaviour.

It is for such reasons that they studied the Buddhist scriptures industriously and with respect, developing a considerable literature of commentary and exegesis and (since problems of organization appealed to them) paying attention to church discipline and sectarian differences as well as to doctrinal subtleties. Buddhism was too great a force, its metaphysical speculations were too attractive, to allow of its neglect by a people with strong intellectual tastes. Nevertheless, though it came nearest of all foreign influences to modifying Chinese life, it did not ultimately succeed in penetrating the inner shrine of Chinese culture. When it seemed to the rulers of China to be disturbing or threatening the civil power or undermining the established social order, they took prompt action. In A.D. 845 the authorities decreed the confiscation of Buddhist property, the destruction of monasteries, and the secularization of monks and nuns. This drastic rule was in practice relaxed and Buddhism survived in China, but it never regained its former strength. It had come into conflict with the cult of the governing class, the Confucianism which was the embodiment of traditional Chinese thought. Other foreign cults were proscribed at the same time lest they should, as the edict significantly put it, "contaminate the customs of China.[5]

---

[5] Manichæan missionaries provide a curious and exceptional instance of foreign influence upon Chinese culture. They began to visit China in the second half

Something of the same kind can be said of India. No foreign influence sensibly affected her ways of life and thought, unless it was exerted by military conquerors remaining long enough upon her soil to impose their will upon her peoples. On the contrary, in periods where there was some degree of national unity, it was Indian influence that spread outwards. The power of Buddhism we have already noticed, in its movement overland to China. It was also spread in countries east of India, by a migration of Indian population that began at a very early date but reached its height during the first five centuries of our era.

This expansion of India was part of a considerable movement of colonization, which established Indian political influence in the regions now known as Burma, Siam, Cochin China, and Cambodia, as well as in Malaya and the islands of Sumatra and Java. With political power and a flourishing commercial intercourse there went a strong cultural influence exercised principally through the medium of religion. Buddhism and Brahmanism were both carried eastward by this movement, and the rivalry between the two systems which took place in India was repeated in these settlements in Farther India and Indonesia.

Today the vestiges of this early Indian influence are plainly visible in the civilizations of both regions. Burma, Siam, and Cambodia are still Buddhist countries. Archæological evidence (such as the ruins at Angkor) throughout Farther India testifies to a once flourishing Hindu culture, which persisted for centuries. In Indonesia there is little that remains in the form of living religion, except in the small island of Bali, which has retained a strongly Hinduistic character. Elsewhere it was expelled by Islam, brought to the islands by Arab traders perhaps as early as 1100, but reaching its fullest influence in the fifteenth century. But even there, not very deep under an Islamic surface, lie considerable and lively vestiges of Indian customs, legends, and beliefs, to whose origins the monuments of Borobudur and Prambanan bear impressive witness.

It is clear that geographical proximity — and the monsoons — made it possible for India to influence both Farther India and China to an extent that was certainly not open to any non-Asiatic country, and it is hardly worth while to speculate what cultural in-

---

of the seventh century. They were made welcome because they were learned in astronomy; and when the Chinese calendar went wrong in the early part of the eighth, throwing sacrifices and other ceremonial observances out of order, they were called in to help in its revision. Planetary names in Sogdian were given to the days of the week, and the Chinese equivalent of Sunday was marked on the calendar in red ink with a phonetic symbol for Mithra. Consequently, though Manichæism was proscribed and persecuted, it retained some influence and survived in secret for several centuries. It is even said that some Manichæan texts were incorporated in the Taoist canon as late as 1019.

fluence might in other circumstances have been brought to bear by Europe upon Asia. All we have to go on is the fact that Hellenistic culture did not take a lasting hold upon India, that it made no impression whatever upon China, and that (until the spread of Islam, which is later than the period under discussion) the one great vehicle of cultural change in Asia, the only external influence that did in fact substantially affect ways of life and habits of thought in eastern Asiatic countries, was a religion evolved in Asia itself — the great, proliferating teaching of the Buddha.

Yet, as we have seen, this powerful system not only in course of time lost ground or was debased or even destroyed in nearly all the countries of its adoption, but also in the country of its origin gave way to the more ancient system, the Hinduism from which it had departed.[6] One is tempted to conclude that the main Asiatic cultures have a quality of conservatism which European cultures do not share.

This may seem too bold an assumption, ascribing to Asia a homogeneous character that it clearly does not possess. Asia presents more than one type of civilization, since it includes not only the great Chinese and Indian societies but also the Iranian and the Islamic worlds, while there is a fourth grouping, that of the central Asian peoples, who, though they have been distinguished in warfare rather than the arts of peace, have by their invasions and migrations carried cultural influences from one region of Asia to another and have thus played an important part in Asiatic history. It is obvious that we cannot expect to find one characteristic common to peoples so diverse in their history, their situation, and their habits; and in that sense one may dismiss as without basis in ancient or modern history such doctrines as the Pan-Asianism propounded by Japanese and other tendentious political writers.

Nevertheless there are certain respects in which Asiatic peoples, without being uniform among themselves, do differ in general from peoples of European origin, and the most important of these differences is in their attitude towards religion. It cannot be a mere accident of history that all the great religions of the world — Brahmanism, Buddhism, Judaism, Christianity, Islam, and (if they can be treated as religions) Taoism and Confucianism — have originated in Asia, and that of these only Christianity was received in Europe, where it flourished largely because it underwent essential changes at European hands, thereby losing much of

6 Buddhism vanished so completely from Indian life that traces of its practice are now scarcely visible, and we find modern books with such titles as *Discovery of Living Buddhism in Bengal* (Sastri, Calcutta, 1897). It is true that Moslem iconoclasm resulted in destruction of monasteries which were the home of Buddhism, whereas Hinduism was widely diffused and did not depend upon books and buildings; but it was not Islam that destroyed Buddhism in India.

its Asiatic character. Since Europe has never adopted without change an Asiatic faith and Asia has never accepted a European philosophy, it seems fair to conclude that, even if we cannot allege some common characteristic which can be called Asiatic, we may agree that "there is clearly a deep-seated difference between the religious feelings of the two continents."

These were the words of a great scholar, writing a generation ago. He did not seek the remote causes of this difference, but permitted himself the generalization that "Asiatics have not the same sentiment of independence and freedom as Europeans. Individuals are thought of as members of a family, state or religion, rather than as entities with a destiny and rights of their own. This leads to autocracy in politics, fatalism in religion and conservatism in both." [7]

Even had the main Asiatic societies been less conservative in habit than has been argued in the foregoing pages, the European influences brought to bear upon them until long after the period we have been considering were not as a rule great or continuous enough to affect their strong individualities. The growth of intercourse between European and Asiatic peoples, which depended upon the maintenance of stable conditions not only in the terminal countries concerned but also along the great stretches of land or sea between them, was impeded by the rise of new forces. All but a thin stream of communication between Europe and eastern Asia was cut off by barbarian invaders pressing upon Europe or by nomad powers plundering and threatening the roads through central Asia or by Arabs gaining command of the Indian Ocean. The dark age of Europe; the period of seclusion and civil strife in China from the closing years of the T'ang dynasty to the end of the Sung struggle against invaders from the north; and the similar period in which, after the collapse of the Gupta Empire, India was subject to repeated incursions first by Huns and subsequently, after a long interval of seclusion, by Mohammedan invaders — these three periods, while not closely coinciding, include a space of some five centuries during which the mutual knowledge of Europe and Asia was diminished almost to the point of hearsay founded upon the tales of a few adventurous travellers.

Notes on CHAPTER 2

MONSOON SAILING. The importance of the monsoons in Asiatic history can hardly be overestimated. The part played by monsoon sailing in spreading cultural influences is by no means confined to the commerce between Europe and Asia. The use of the regular alternation of winds

[7] Sir Charles Eliot, in *Encyclopædia Britannica* (1911), under "Asia, History."

in the whole monsoon area contributed to the spread of Buddhism and Hinduism, which was much accelerated from the beginning of the Christian era and reached Cambodia, Java, and Celebes at a very early date. This was something much more tremendous in scale and enduring in effect than the trading intercourse between the Roman Empire and Asiatic seaports.

The accounts usually given of the first use of the monsoon for deep-water sailing between Aden and the southwest coast of India are not very clear as to the actual method of steering. In Warmington's *Ancient Explorers* the voyage is described as follows: "About A.D. 50 a nameless merchant, bolder than the rest, by ordering his helmsman to pull constantly on his rudder and his sailors to make a shift of the yard, found an open-sea route from the gulf of Aden in an arc of a circle (bent northwards) to the south Indian coast, which he touched near the greatest of all Indian marts, the town of Muziris (modern Cranganore)."

The phrase "pull constantly on the rudder" puzzled me, and I asked Admiral of the Fleet Sir James Somerville, who is very familiar with the Indian Ocean and its beautiful sailing craft, if he would explain it. His vivid reply will, I am sure, be of great interest to students, and I reproduce it here with his permission, although he modestly denies that he is an authority upon such questions:

Since ships of the period could not sail to windward and would not have been able to stand up to the full force of the monsoon, the voyage of the merchant who in the reign of Tiberius sailed before the south-west monsoon to the mouth of the Indus could not have been made, I think, except during one of the short "light" periods of the south-west monsoon, i.e. before the June "burst" or after the end of August. This gives our Roman merchant half of March, all April and the beginning of May, during which time the winds would vary between S., S.W. and W., from light airs to nine knots. He would no doubt start from Socotra, where he could pick up reliable weather information, since both monsoons develop their greatest intensities here and the inhabitants would therefore have been weatherwise from earliest times.

A prudent merchant might have taken the advice of the Socotran weathermen and, starting on April Fool's Day, or the next day, would have set course N.E. by E., and if he made good four knots with a seven to eight knot Soldier's wind, would arrive at the mouth of the Indus ten days later. Alternatively he might have travelled safely in September, but this is doubtful, since the Autumn transition is followed by contrary winds, whereas the Spring transition is followed by increasing but favourable winds — a fact which must have been known to the Socotrans.

This man's achievement possibly proved to others that the late winter transition period, when the monsoon changed from N.E. to S.W., was succeeded by a "safe" period, during which steady and unboisterous weather would assist them to the coast of India.

The second merchant, therefore — the nameless one of about A.D. 50 — probably chose this period, but rather later, for his voyage. The course he made good (disregarding the great circle effect) being about E. by S., could not have been achieved during the north-east monsoon. It seems likely therefore that he too started from Socotra at the end of April and, anxious to make maximum progress with minimum leeway, kept the wind dead astern or as near thereto as he could until he was about half-way across the Arabian Sea. This point he may have reached at about the time of the year when the prevailing wind in that area tends to be westerly rather than south-westerly (viz. some time in May). With this gradual change of wind direction a series of small alterations to keep the wind astern would bring him in the arc of a circle (bent northward). On approaching the west coast of India the seasonal wind resolves itself into a strong north-westerly component. Again, if the wind astern assumption is correct, he would tell the helmsman to bear up and would trim his yard accordingly. He might then have left the Laccadive Islands to starboard and made a landfall in the vicinity of Cochin; or he might even have sailed through those islands. The crossing would probably have taken about fourteen days.

Another construction which might be applied to the words "pull constantly on his rudder" is that the merchant would make the crossing during October, when the wind is "variable and unsteady" but is likely not to exceed nine knots. The *constant* pulling on the rudder and shifting of the yard does suggest that these actions were more or less continuous in one direction; yet "constant" may also mean "frequent," and if we substitute one for the other we see an alert merchant, with his weather eye always open to take advantage of every shift of the wind.

ISLAM IN CHINA. Moslems and non-Moslems lived together in China without serious strife for nearly a thousand years. There was a rebellion in 1648, another in 1785 and frequent risings during the nineteenth century. But these occurred in distant provinces in the northwest and southwest, where there was a Moslem majority composed largely of non-Chinese. It is true that the Moslems in China are in many ways distinct from non-Moslem Chinese and tend to be segregated, not only by religion but also by physical characters and occupation, so that they are conscious of certain economic and social disabilities, out of which capital can be made by unfriendly neighbours. But it cannot be said that there is a Moslem problem in China as there is in India, for in general Chinese culture has acted as a unifying force tending to reduce the importance of ethnic and religious differences.

CHAPTER
3

CHRISTIAN ENDEAVOUR AND TRADING
ENTERPRISE

1. The Mongol Empire

IT was not until the light began to shine again in Europe, and Christendom summoned forth its latent vigour to attack the Moslem world, that the way was once more open to intercourse with central Asia and beyond. That astonishing outburst, compounded of religious zeal, princely ambition, military ardour, and economic enterprise, which formed the impulse behind the crusades, marked a new phase in Western civilization that included not only important political and social developments within Europe but also a new attitude towards Asia. By the thirteenth century the whole of Europe [1] and part of Asia Minor were Christian, and the crusades had produced alongside of militancy a strong missionary activity, which in its turn led to a knowledge of central and eastern Asia that amounted to a new discovery.

The intercourse now resumed between Europe and Asia contained a new and important element, for the motive force behind it was no longer only a desire for trade. The Christian world, stirred by visions of a universal church, sought to convert the peoples of eastern Asia and perhaps to enlist their aid in the destruction of the Islam which it could not defeat alone. This strong impulse inevitably gave a new character to missions that passed from west to east, since they stood no longer only for traffic between merchants but also for direct converse between nations through representative men.

The first approach was made by the Papacy not to China but to the great Khan of the Mongols. This was in 1245, at a time when the Mongol power extended to central Europe, to Armenia and Persia, and well into former Chinese dominions. China at that time was governed by the Sung dynasty, which under nomad pressure had withdrawn to the south, leaving the north to rulers of

---

[1] Except parts of Spain and Portugal still in Moslem hands.

31

nomad origin. It thus came about that when Europe was in a period of vigorous development, the true China was going through a phase of extreme isolation. Never, perhaps, had the two cultures, the expansive Latin and the self-contained Chinese, been in more characteristic and opposite moods. The Mongols, however, showed some disposition to respond to the overtures of the Catholic Church.

The first Christian envoy, John de Plano Carpini,[2] reached the camp of the Great Khan in Mongolia, where he found other foreign envoys and a number of European specialists in Mongol employment. Nothing much came of Carpini's visit, except that on his return in 1247 he was able to make a valuable report of what he had seen and heard. Though he furnished a useful account of the military organization and tactics of the Mongols, which was one of the purposes for which he was dispatched, the response of the Great Khan to the Pope's letter was rude and discouraging.

But subsequent missions, although they obtained no diplomatic concessions, were not ill received, and the Mongols at least gave the impression that they were determined in their enmity to Islam and well disposed towards the efforts of the crusaders to destroy the infidel. It even seemed possible that Mongol rulers (some of whom had Christian wives) might accept the Christian faith; and this was not an entirely baseless judgment, since the Mongols were growing aware of the shortcomings of their own nomadic culture. Proud of their military achievements and confident in their armed strength, they were none the less doubtful of their capacity to administer the sedentary peoples whom they had conquered. In the West they had more than once withdrawn from territory they had overrun, because after they had plundered, the effort of occupation did not seem worth while. It was rather in rich and highly organized states that they saw advantage in establishing themselves permanently, and they were wise enough to perceive that there they required the help of persons experienced in government. After they had entered Poland and Russia they were no doubt tempted to press on to the well-developed countries of western Europe. These, however, were far away, difficult of access, and equipped with considerable military capacity.

But near at hand, across the edges of the territory that they and their ancestors had roamed for centuries, lay a country at least as rich, extensive, and populous as any region elsewhere in the world

2 Carpini was sent by the Pope (Innocent IV) from the Council of Lyon in 1245. It is clear from his *Ystoria Mongalorum* that, as well as being a diplomatic and religious mission, his visit was intended as an expedition to gain information on the military organization and methods of the Mongols. The Church and European monarchs wanted to know what their enemy was like in his home and perhaps whether he could be used against the Mohammedans.

that they might have had thoughts of conquering. This was the great realm of China, which was already held in part by people akin to their own, and it was to this tempting prize that the effort of the Mongols was most consistently directed from the time when they were united under Jinghis Khan until his descendant Khubilai [3] established a Mongol dynasty as the first Yüan Emperor of China in 1279.

This choice, or perhaps it should be called a compulsion, by which the greater part of Mongol power was concentrated upon China, so reducing the pressure upon Europe, may be regarded as an important if not a decisive event in world history. Occidental historians dealing with the Mongol invasions are naturally most concerned with their effect upon Europe, but their effect upon Asia should not be overlooked. The Mongols threatened Europe, but they actually conquered and ruled China and great parts of central and western Asia. The Mongol Empire at its period of greatest extension reached from the shores of the Pacific to the Black Sea and the Persian Gulf, from Siberia to Annam, Burma, and the Himalayas. On all this vast area the Mongols imposed peace. Jinghis Khan and his successors established and maintained highways along which officials and traders could travel in comparative safety, if not without hardship. The Mongols themselves, when their thirst for fighting and plunder was satisfied, settled down to the encouragement of regular trade and to the orderly administration of their dominions. They had in their campaigns learned to appreciate the value of other civilizations and were wise enough to employ competent persons irrespective of nationality in posts of importance.

Such circumstances as these combined to produce a new phase of relations between Europe and eastern Asia. Earlier intercourse had been of a groping, indirect nature, whereas now it expressed a new attitude of political and religious expansion on the part of the Western world, matched by some disposition on the part of the East to respond to such advances. It is interesting to observe that it was not a settled Asiatic civilization which of its own motion so responded, but a nomadic culture which served as intermediary between China and Europe. This, indeed, was (as we have already noticed) the great service that the central Asian peoples rendered — something more important and enduring than their military conquests; for it seems that the migration of peoples hastens the transplantation of ideas and institutions and that when

---

[3] This of course is the Kubla Khan of Coleridge's poem, just as Xanadu approximates to Shandu. Khubilai is a more correct equivalent, and something like this was evidently intended by the Vatican secretaries when they addressed a letter from the Pope to his *Carissimo filio Quolibey Magno Chamo.*

transplanted they may sometimes flourish better than in their original soil.

Certainly it is doubtful whether China would of her own accord have borrowed directly from Europe, but she did in fact, when under Mongol rule, receive certain cultural influences from outside which reached her through Mongol intervention. The conquerors themselves, conscious no doubt that their own culture might succumb to the wider and deeper culture of the Chinese, feared the authority of the Confucian tradition and took care to employ in administrative posts (for which their own roving temperament disqualified them) a number of capable foreigners to counteract the forces of Confucian orthodoxy. Arabs, Persians, Greeks, Russians, and Italians worked for the Mongols as civil servants or diplomats, and at Mongol headquarters there were to be found specialists of almost all known nationalities — linguists, workers in arts and crafts, and, notably, men who could tell the Khan about affairs in other countries. Prominent among the latter were the Polo brothers, those bold Venetian merchants who, having set forth without other thought than profitable trade, found themselves in about 1264 in the Mongol capital at Cambaluc,[4] where they were welcomed at the court of Khubilai, questioned by him about Europe, and entrusted with a mission to the Pope.

The errand on which they were sent marked a change in the nature of relations between Europe and China, for what Khubilai requested was instruction in the Christian religion. This was a new departure, since it is impossible to imagine any monarch of pure Chinese descent stooping to ask a European barbarian to impart to the Chinese people a new faith. But the Mongols, having no religion of their own beyond a somewhat primitive Shamanism and a faith in oracles, were interested in the creeds of other people and anxious to adopt any principles that seemed likely to increase their capacity as rulers. They were not especially interested in Christianity, but very sensibly wanted to know what were the springs of behaviour in the peoples with whom they had to deal. They accordingly made a practice of summoning holy men before them to engage in debate on points of religion and morality. Jinghis Khan himself, in an interval between campaigns, had in 1219 sent for a Chinese Taoist priest, who made a long journey from Shantung to the Mongol camp by the banks of the Oxus and stayed there for some years. Sometimes great public debates were held between exponents of different creeds, and in course of time the Mongol rulers gained fairly clear ideas of their various natures.

4 More correctly Khan Baliq, the Khan's Headquarters — the modern Peking.

Their attitude was on the whole tolerant. It is well expressed in the language used by Mangu, the Great Khan, to William of Rubruck, a Franciscan friar who visited his camp in 1254, carrying letters from St. Louis of France. Mangu said: "We Mongols believe that there is only one God . . . but just as God has given different fingers to the hand so He has given different ways to men. To you He has given scriptures, but you Christians do not observe them. To us He has given diviners, and we do what they tell us and live in peace."

Despite this rather uncomfortable remark on the difference between Christian doctrine and Christian practice (which embodies a sentiment by no means rare in Oriental countries), Nestorian priests enjoyed the bounty of Mongol chiefs and their wives and daughters. Indeed exponents of many creeds followed the Khan — *sicut muscæ mel*, "like flies after honey," according to Rubruck — and each claimed success, not without some reason, for the Mongols, while not abandoning their own cult, patronized any religion that seemed to offer a cure for spiritual or bodily ills.

In due course Buddhism was accorded Imperial patronage, and Tibetan Lamaism was established with official support not only in Mongolia but in parts of China proper, including the capital city at Cambaluc (Peking). Islam, which had penetrated China in the eighth century, was not interfered with, possibly for fear of conflict with Moslem people in central Asia, and some prominent Mongols seem to have been converted.

In general it is clear that the Mongols as a people came under Western influence, part of which was European, while their empire extended into European territory. Their own nomadic culture was such that it could absorb influences from sedentary cultures only at the expense of its own character. It has therefore not survived except in so far as it has remained isolated in appropriate surroundings. But the Mongols undoubtedly served as agents for the transmission to China of certain Western ideas and the introduction into China of a number of Western products, so long as the Chinese were under their rule. Some foreign plants such as sorghum came to China during that time, together with the knowledge of some industrial processes such as sugar refining. These may be said to have had an influence upon Chinese life, just as the introduction of cotton from India at an earlier date led to its cultivation in the thirteenth century, and to the weaving of cotton cloth, so affecting Chinese dress. Perhaps more significant were innovations in the sphere of learning, such as methods of measuring and calculating in astronomy.

Most of these importations, however, were not of European origin, but stemmed rather from western Asia; and even if they added to Chinese knowledge or modified Chinese habits, it can scarcely be argued that they affected more than the surface of Chinese life. Iranian and other western Asiatic motifs can be detected in Chinese religious and secular arts of this era. In such ways no doubt Chinese culture was diversified or enriched, but there is little to show that its essence was changed in any important respect; while, if we limit our survey strictly to the effect of European ideas upon China, it is clear that they made much less impression than did Chinese ideas upon Europe.

The proselytizing effort of the Papacy following upon the report of Carpini resulted in a number of missions to China, of which the most notable was that of the Franciscan John de Monte Corvino, who travelled from Rome by way of Persia, taking ship at Ormuz for Quilon on the Malabar coast and, after a year's stay in India, proceeding by sea to China. He was the first of a noble procession of Catholic missionaries to establish himself in China. He translated the New Testament and the Psalter into "the language of the Tartars" (probably Mongol, but perhaps Chinese), and secured the favour of the Mongol Emperor. Writing to Rome at the age of fifty-eight, he said that he was already worn out with toil and tribulation, but he continued to labour until his death in Peking at the age of eighty-one, after more than thirty years' service in China. In point of courage and devotion he was one of the greater apostles in Christian history. Measured in terms of success his mission was not remarkable, but, like most of his distinguished successors in later periods in India, China, and Japan, his high character made an impression upon Oriental notables who were indifferent or even hostile to his doctrine. This is an aspect of missionary endeavour which, as we shall see, has played an important part in intercourse between Europe and Asia.

Monte Corvino and the Franciscans who came after him established Christian churches in both Peking and the port of Zayton in South China. The Mongol rulers treated them generously and gave them protection, so that they could make converts freely. Their flock numbered several thousand, though it is doubtful whether many Chinese became genuine Christians. Most of those baptized were foreigners — some Mongols but chiefly Alans, Armenians, Georgians, Ruthenians, and Hungarians, captives born in the Christian faith to whom the Nestorians had refused the sacraments. But what Monte Corvino had built up was swept away, leaving little trace, when the Mongols were at last driven out of China in 1368. The reaction against foreigners which accompanied this expulsion of a foreign dynasty was naturally severe, and explains in some measure the failure of Christianity to gain a foothold in the Far East at this time. But it is significant that Islam in China did not suffer a similar eclipse. Partly because it was an Asiatic religion and therefore more easily assimilable than a European system, but mostly no doubt because it was the native creed of a very numerous element in the population of China, introduced in the T'ang period from Turkestan and at intervals replenished by large and small migrations from central Asia, it was never in real danger of suppression. The Moslem communities in China today, which are thought to include some ten million people, have been politically assimilated without losing their cultural identity.[5]

Among the foreign religious communities in eastern Asia under the Mongols, the Nestorian Christians deserve special notice. Their history is perhaps interesting rather than important, but it offers a useful commentary on the several attitudes of European and Asiatic peoples towards theological disputes and it throws some light upon the general problem of cultural interchanges between Europe and Asia.

The Nestorian sect arose from one of those bitter doctrinal controversies which raged in the Christian church as soon as it began to develop political power upon its adoption as the state religion of the Roman Empire in the fourth century of our era. In the list of heresies — Arian, Sabellian, Pelagian, and others — that influenced the minds of both ecclesiasts and laymen in those days, none roused more violent passions than the beliefs of Nestorius, Patriarch of Constantinople, who held that Christ was two persons, one divine and one human. Quarrels over this subtle point of theology brought about (to use Gibbon's words) "a secret and incurable discord," which, besides leading to immediate cruel persecution, had remoter and more lasting consequences. At the fantastic Council of Ephesus — that "episcopal tumult" of A.D. 431 — Nestorius was condemned as a heretic, and his followers, who were numerous in Syria and Persia, presently founded the sect that is known by his name.

The already widening breach between the Eastern and Western branches of the Church now grew to the point of fission. The Church in eastern Syria broke off from the Church in Greek and Latin countries, and it was this easternmost extension of Christianity that, thanks to its separation and its geographical position, in course of time gained entrance for the Christian faith into India and China. The chief centre of the sect was Seleucis-Ctesiphon on the Tigris, where its distance gave it independence from the Greco-

---

[5] Though it is true that there have been revolts in frontier provinces where the population was mostly non-Chinese.

Roman world. Its position on the trade route to Bagdad and eastwards gave it an influence perhaps out of proportion to its real
strength. It displayed, moreover, especially in its early days, an
evangelizing zeal which was no doubt another aspect of the ardour
that informed its theological disputes, for certainly it would be
hard to match in the history of Buddhism or even Islam the fury
of sectarian discussions in the Christian church at that time.

Very soon earlier Christian communities in Persia joined the
Nestorian movement. In the sixth century if not before, there were
Nestorian bishops at Merv and Herat, and thenceforward Christianity was carried by the Nestorians along the overland routes
through central Asia to China, and by land or sea to northwestern
and southern India. Researches into the early spread of Christianity in central Asia and the Far East show that evangelization had
some success among people of Mongol race. There were Christians
among Turkic people on the Oxus as early as A.D. 200, and by A.D.
650 there were Nestorian bishoprics from central Persia to the Pacific. The date of the entry of Christianity into India is uncertain,
but there is some evidence that Christian communities in southern
India came from Persia in the fourth century to escape persecution. We know that by about A.D. 500 there were Nestorians in
Ceylon and Malabar, whose bishop was appointed from Persia;
and today there are in southern India some five hundred thousand
Christians of the Syrian rite, many of whom undoubtedly descend
in a doctrinal sense from those evangelized by Nestorian missionaries in the remote past.

Here, at first sight, we seem to have a convincing example of
the influence of European religious thought upon an Asiatic people; but we must pause before taking that view. Nestorian Christianity can scarcely be regarded as a European religion. The doctrines of the Roman Church, despite their origin in Asia, are to
be regarded as essentially European, not only because Palestine,
though geographically part of Asia, was within the Mediterranean
cultural sphere, but also because the elements of Christian belief
in Europe were compounded by European minds. Nestorian Christianity, however, in its eastward progress took on an increasingly
Asiatic character. Its rite was Syrian, and as it moved through central Asia towards India and China it became more and more distinct from the parent religion because it made concessions to the
customs and beliefs of Asiatic communities. It allowed marriage
to the clergy and the Nestorian Church in Malabar had already by
the middle of the seventh century adopted many Hindu customs
and rites and developed into a closed caste with no missionary activity. In T'ang China, where it arrived in the seventh century, it
suppressed mention of the doctrine of atonement and of the cru-

cifixion, which embodied ideas repugnant to many Oriental peoples, as Jesuit missionaries discovered in a later age.[6]

At that period it seems still to have preserved some of its early purity; but in course of time, losing touch with the mother Church and falling largely into the hands of tribesmen of Turkish origin (Uigurs), it suffered degradation. William of Rubruck described the Nestorians as ignorant, given to usury, drunkenness, and polygamy. He was no doubt intolerant of heresy, but in general probably correct in his estimate; and however true a pattern of Christianity was presented to the people of Asia in his day, it is clear enough that few Chinese were impressed by it.[7]

The Nestorian converts were almost all people of foreign race whose native religion was of a rudimentary kind. One cannot say that Christian doctrine, even in a form modified to suit Asiatic tastes, had any lasting influence upon the great Asiatic civilizations.

Some scholars have argued that the Nestorian priests in central Asia and in China consorted freely with Buddhist monks in the seventh and eighth centuries and that Chinese Buddhism borrowed something from Nestorianism. But there is no proof and little probability of this. The Chinese tolerated and even at times bestowed favours upon such foreign religions as Nestorianism, Manichæism, and Zoroastrianism, but this was due to their indifference or to their wish to keep on good terms with border peoples, not to any positive approval of their doctrines. There were, indeed, occasional proscriptions and even persecutions of foreign faiths, though these arose from political and not from religious reasons. Disputes on fine points of doctrine of the kind that convulsed the Byzantine Empire, had they arisen in China, would have scarcely stirred a ripple on the surface of the national life. The Chinese felt safe and satisfied in their own moral and religious climate. To them the outer world was barbaric, just as to

[6] William of Rubruck mentions that the Nestorians whom he encountered among the Mongols did not put the figure of Christ upon their crosses and seemed to be ashamed of his Passion.

A picturesque passage in Rubruck's letters, recording one of the religious discussions in which he took part, shows his own pessimistic estimate of the prospects of conversion:

"There was present there an old priest of the sect of the Uigurs, who say there is one God but nevertheless make idols. With him the Nestorians spoke at length, relating all things up to the time when Christ came to trial and explaining the Trinity to him and the Saracens by gestures (or parables? — *per similitudines*). They all listened without contradiction but none said: 'I believe. I wish to become a Christian.' Then the Nestorians and the Saracens sang together in a loud voice, but the Buddhists kept silent. And afterwards they all drank deeply."

[7] In a later day Newberry, the leader of the first English commercial expedition to reach India (1584), engaged two Nestorians as interpreters at Aleppo, because of their knowledge of India, but had to dismiss them because they "were so lewdly given."

the Greeks and later the Romans in their pride all that foreigners said was nothing more than uncivilized babble.

It thus appears that, despite the relatively favourable circumstances in which knowledge of European civilization was brought to the notice of the Chinese under the Mongols, it made little stir among them. Far otherwise was the effect upon Europe of the reports taken home by returning missionaries and merchants who had seen the marvels of China. Descriptions of its populous cities, its roads and bridges, its civic competence, its wealth, and the diversity of its products at first amazed the people of Italy, then aroused their interest and their cupidity, and soon set them planning to increase their commerce with its inhabitants. A new world was revealed to them. What they learned made a powerful impact upon their minds and stirred them to thought and action. This is something that certainly cannot be said of the effect upon the Chinese of their contemporary information about Europe. It may be that, had the Mongols remained longer in power, European influence exerted through them might have taken some root in China, but this is pure conjecture. The bare fact is that no such influence did take root, while knowledge and speculation about China exercised the European mind and prepared it for subsequent enterprises in the Far East.

Perhaps it is pertinent to add here, while casting cultural accounts between Asia and Europe, that although the Mongols exercised little influence upon European civilization beyond the stimulus afforded by their invasions, they did leave in eastern Europe a legacy of some importance. The Tartar and Mongol elements in the population of European Russia at the beginning of the twentieth century are stated to have numbered about three million. These derive of course from a variety of ethnic movements, but such Mongol invasions as those of Batu in 1241, when he conquered a great part of Russia and entered Bulgaria, Poland, and Hungary, must have left an enduring mark. Maternity homes in the poorer quarters of many eastern European cities report a considerable proportion of babies showing the birthmark known as the "Mongol spot," which is thought to testify to a strong admixture of Mongol blood. This same spot appears on most Japanese children at birth; but here, of course, it is evidence not of invasion but of the existence of a very early Mongol or Tungusic element in the ethnic constitution of the Japanese.

2. Asiatic and European Expansion

As the Mongol Empire disintegrated, the later members of the Yüan dynasty found themselves unable to cope with the strong tide of revolt flowing against them. They could no longer stay in power by force, and they began to defer to Chinese tradition. They even attempted to enlist Confucianism on their side, but it often happens that in matters of civilization the victor is subdued by the vanquished. *Capta . . . ferum victorem cepit.* The strength of Chinese culture reasserted itself, and those Mongols who were not expelled were absorbed. By 1368 the Yüan dynasty came to an end, and with it all early prospects of a change in the nature of Chinese society.

North and south were now united under the Ming emperors. whose general line of policy was to restore and protect the native culture and to erase all traces of Mongol influence. Apart from securing themselves against renewed Mongol aggression, they engaged in no important foreign military enterprises directed towards regaining lost territory, but concentrated upon internal reorganization. There was a pause in intercourse with the West along the central Asian trade routes, and China seemed to be entering upon a new phase of isolation. But by the opening of the fifteenth century there took place a remarkable revival and expansion of Chinese maritime enterprise under state control. Great fleets, carrying many thousands of sailors, soldiers, officials, and merchants, were sent to Java, Sumatra, Ceylon, India, Arabia, and the Persian Gulf in the period from 1405 to 1431. These expeditions ceased suddenly, and there is no satisfactory explanation of either their end or their beginning. They were no doubt intended to raise the prestige of the new dynasty in the southern seas and the Indian Ocean. In this they seem to have had some temporary success, for envoys from many of the countries visited appeared in Nanking or Peking — some, it is recorded, having been forcibly carried to China.

Indeed, it is worth observing here (because one of the purposes of this book is to trace the methods by which European peoples forced their often unwelcome attentions upon Asiatic countries) that Europe has not held a monopoly of aggression. China, in particular, has a long history of imperialism, commencing with the great expansive phase of the Han dynasty, which was after a pause repeated under the T'ang. It was again renewed, when she had released herself from the bondage of an even more far-flung Asiatic empire than her own — the Mongol dominion, which reached at its greatest extension from the Pacific to the Black Sea, the eastern Mediterranean, and the Persian Gulf. It may be argued in defence of Chinese expansion that the earliest campaigns of conquest were intended to defend the Middle Kingdom against barbarians threatening its frontiers. This was no doubt sound strategical doctrine, though it can be pressed too far; and it does not usually convince conquered peoples or, what is less important, the theoretical opponents of imperialism.

Similarly there are good reasons to justify the expansion of Indian empires in the past, particularly where it resulted in conferring the benefits of Indian culture upon backward countries. Its method was not always in keeping with the principle of *ahimsa* or non-violence, which is sometimes said to have been a controlling factor in Indian history. Apart from a long record of internal wars fought for the expansion of individual states within the Indian subcontinent, the colonizing activities of Indian peoples, which from the beginning of our era extended to Burma, Indo-China, Malaya, and Indonesia, were sometimes assisted by the force of arms. It must be admitted, however, that in general the expansion of India was peaceful and gradual. It was fostered less by the ambition of princes than by the slow permeation of Indian ideas and customs through the influence of Indian traders and the effort of Indian missionaries, neither of whom had any persistent military or even political support from India. Indeed, although Hinduism may have made some of its gains in Cambodia, Sumatra, Java, and elsewhere in the East thanks to strong colonizing pressure or even to local military conquests, Buddhism owed its position outside India to pure evangelism unstained by political motives, thereby contrasting favourably with Christianity, which from the fifteenth century onward did not in its progress eastwards disdain the support of the secular arm. Certainly by the time that the Portuguese had appeared in the Indian Ocean, Indian expansion had long lost whatever aggressive character it may have had in the past.

As for China, the overseas expeditions of the Ming emperors did not manifest a determined spirit of imperialism such as was displayed under previous dynasties. They were, however, by no means free from an aggressive character. Soldiers were landed in distant parts of Asia, where a good deal of fighting and destruction took place. They ranged as far as the Persian Gulf and the Somali coast, exacting submission and tribute from rulers great and small. They even carried off to China in 1410 a King of Ceylon who had offended them. Perhaps in the light of subsequent history the most interesting episode is the attack delivered upon the port of Calicut in southern India. Of this we have an account from an unexpected source — a priest of the Nestorian community in Malabar, who was given passage to Portugal by Cabral after that captain had bombarded the same port in 1500 in retaliation for the massacre of some of his men on shore. The priest's account says: "About 80 or 90 years ago the Cataio [that is, the Chinese] had a factory at Calicut, but because the king of that country committed outrages against them they rebelled and having gathered a very large armada they came to the city of Calicut, which they destroyed." We may therefore at least conclude that in point of priority the Portuguese must cede to the Chinese as aggressors in India. But it must be granted that the Chinese effort was not sustained.

It is clear moreover from the name of "jewel ships" given to the vessels in Chinese records that an important if not the principal purpose of their voyages was to acquire precious stones and other rare products of foreign countries. Ostriches, zebras, and giraffes are among the curiosities mentioned. The expeditions were led by palace eunuchs, and financed from the palace treasury. They may perhaps best be regarded as combining political and commercial objects, but it is noticeable that the trade in which they engaged was definitely a luxury trade. It did not arise from any popular demand for useful commodities and therefore cannot be compared in importance to the efforts that had already for a long time been made by European traders to secure Asiatic goods. The urgency with which for centuries Europe had sought the silks of China and the spices of the Indies finds no true parallel in the motives of vanity which led the Ming emperors to send abroad for exotic things. Whatever may have been their purpose, the great maritime voyages came to an end without having produced any important effect upon Chinese life and without having substantially increased Chinese strength. The fact that historians are not agreed on what they were meant to achieve is an indication that there was no clearly conceived policy behind them. The so-called tribute was obtained at high cost and, though the fleets of great junks may have impressed some petty kings of Indonesia, Chinese prestige in general did not for long stand high in eastern Asia.

China was really on the defensive from the time when the voyages ceased. The Japanese raided her coast incessantly, and pirates of all kinds, many of whom were Chinese, sacked and burned coastal cities so frequently that their inhabitants had to move inland. Tibet and Annam freed themselves from Chinese suzerainty, and even the now diminished Mongol power was able from time to time to strike at Chinese forces in the north. Chinese shipping was forbidden to leave Chinese waters, Chinese subjects could not go abroad, and the country entered upon an era of seclusion.

This was at a time when Europe was on the threshold of an age of maritime discovery and commercial expansion which was to alter the whole course of world history. It is difficult to say what were the prime motives of this activity. It was something new not in kind but in degree, since, as we have already seen, Europe had stretched a hand out towards Asia since very early times. One cannot help being struck by the persistence throughout European history of the demand for Asiatic commodities, first for silk and then for pepper and other spices.

The part played by pepper in the development of both overland and sea-borne trade with India and beyond is truly astonishing. It is comparable in its influence upon commercial effort to those materials like petroleum and rubber which in modern times have shaped the foreign policy of leading Occidental states. Rome bought off Alaric in 408 not only with gold but also with pepper; and the international rivalry of that and subsequent periods centres almost entirely upon the control of the trade in spices, of which pepper was the most important. In all accounts of the plans of the great European explorers, from the pioneers of the open sea route between Aden and Malabar (the indigenous home of *Piper nigrum*) down to Columbus, Vasco da Gama, and Magellan, a search for the spice countries figures as a leading motive.

Even after their discovery by the Portuguese the main effort of other European maritime peoples was directed to breaking the Portuguese monopoly by providing alternative routes into the Pacific Ocean. The brave but ill-fated attempts to force a northeast or a northwest passage, in which such navigators as Cabot, Frobisher, Willoughby, Chancellor, Gilbert, Cartier, and Hudson played a leading part, were chiefly designed to break through icy wastes into warm tropical waters. There is, indeed, a tragic irony in the fate of some of those seamen who, after years spent in struggling against the hazards of arctic exploration, ended their careers in southern seas while engaged in efforts to loosen the Portuguese hold on trade in the Indian Ocean and beyond the Strait of Malacca, which consisted largely in traffic in spices. Among them were John Davis, who was killed by Japanese pirates off Singapore in 1604, and William Baffin, another famous polar navigator, who was killed by a Portuguese shot during fighting in the Persian Gulf.

Yet it is clear that the urgency of demand for tropical products is not of itself enough to explain the great revival and increase of European activity in trade and navigation which, beginning with the rise of Venice, reached a peak in the epoch-making voyages of the end of the fifteenth century. The question is one of considerable interest, because until it is answered we cannot understand why the great eastern Asiatic states, despite their wealth and capacity, failed to pursue consistently a policy of maritime expansion and seem when they did on occasion embark upon such a policy to have lacked the will to sustain it. The Chinese, or rather their Mongol rulers, twice attempted to invade Japan, but were defeated. They had some success in attacks from the sea upon the coasts of southeast Asia, and even sent a fleet to attack Burma, but by the end of Khubilai's lifetime they had withdrawn from all these regions. Their failure may be ascribed to ignorance of the art of naval warfare, which obliged them to depend upon Chinese and Korean sailors, who were lukewarm assistants. But the cessation of the overseas expansion of Ming China more than a century later cannot be accounted for only by naval weakness, since the Chinese were by then at the height of their development in navigation and shipbuilding.

In view of the previous achievements of the Chinese in the conduct of great land and sea expeditions, it cannot be supposed that they lacked the capacity for such undertakings. One can only conclude that their political constitution and their social order did not, in the period following the Mongol conquest, afford the stimulus that sustained the contemporary European effort to expand. Similarly it may be supposed that the effort of Indian colonization, which once had carried Indian influence westward to Socotra and eastward to Sumatra and beyond, lost its motive power through the growth of political confusion in India itself.

But to say that internal conditions in China and India were not such as to promote an active interest in overseas trade and enterprise on a national scale is only to state historical facts. It does not explain them. It does not show why, in those great Asiatic countries, there was no impulse comparable to that which produced the commercial expansion of European states, where in the late Middle Ages and increasingly from the fourteenth century onwards the driving force came from their sovereigns and their governing classes. It was those leaders who, no doubt under the persuasion of ambitious explorers and energetic merchants, by their favour and interest gave a high place in the national policy to voyages of discovery and trade. It would be hard to match among the titles of Eastern monarchs such a style as that of Prince Henry of Portugal, who is known as the Navigator, or of King Manoel, who assumed the title of "Lord of the Conquest, Navigation, and Commerce of India, Ethiopia, Arabia, and Persia." Though Oriental monarchs often claimed something like universal rule, calling themselves by such proud titles as "Lord of the World" or "Lord of Life" or "Master of the Four Oceans" or "King of Kings, Companion of the Stars, and Brother of the Sun and Moon" or even "Eminent King of Kings, Ruler of the Beautiful Impregnable Metropolis of the World," it would not have occurred to the most vainglorious of them (with the exception perhaps of Moslem rulers, whose sacred book gave a high place to merchants) to speak of themselves as concerned in buying and selling. They would be alert to share in the profits of trade by the taxation or, if need be, the confiscation of swollen fortunes, but they did not as a rule regard the promotion of foreign commerce as a vital affair of state.

In order to seek an explanation for this difference in attitude between European and Asiatic states it is necessary to go far back in European history. The militant, expansionist phase of European history is not to be ascribed simply to some aggressive quality in the character or habit of European peoples. Indeed, Europe was for centuries before the period with which we are dealing constantly and perilously on the defensive. This is true enough even of Europe as a geographical expression, and if Europe is taken as standing for a continuing cultural unity, then it is beyond all doubt a just description of the condition of European civilization at least from the decline of the Roman Empire until the turn of the tide in the sixteenth century, when Europe began to exert force upon Asia. It has been well said that the history of Europe is the history of a civilization produced, preserved, and developed by the pressure of alien powers that threatened it almost from its birth.

Certainly the shape which that civilization took from the period of the Hunnish invasions was largely determined by the need to withstand the irruptions of peoples of Asiatic origin. It has often been pointed out that, in a geographical sense, Europe is a mere peninsula or promontory at the western extremity of the great land mass of Asia; and it was only by a long and arduous resistance that Europe could preserve its identity in the face of formidable attacks which, had they succeeded, would have made it also a political and cultural appendage of Asia. Freed from the menace of the Huns by the defeat and death of Attila in the fifth century, the Roman Empire had to face new trials, more severe and disruptive than the Germanic invasions. These last intruders had altered the political shape of Europe but had brought no fundamental change to European economic, social, and intellectual life. As Henri Pirenne observes, they did not destroy the Empire; they became part of it, though perhaps they lowered its tone, as when a palazzo becomes an apartment-house with some new and socially undesirable tenants.

But the Empire had to meet another threat in the sixth and early seventh centuries, when the conflict centred on the recovery of Christian provinces and partook of the nature of a crusade; and hardly had this danger been averted when with the rise of

Islam there appeared a new peril to Christendom. Now, as two religions with universal claims stood face to face in conflict, what
was in question was no longer only the defence of territory and
people against barbarian intruders, but the preservation of a system of life and thought that was European in body and spirit and
could not compromise with Asiatic blood or doctrine. The Christian civilization of Europe thus developed under constant assault,
and it is not surprising that it should have acquired a militant
character and in course of time have achieved a unity, however
precarious and imperfect, in opposition to the forces by which it
was threatened.

The struggle was long and hazardous. In the seventh century
the armies of Islam swept over the old Roman provinces of Asia
and Africa and in the eighth century they pressed on to southwestern Europe. They overran the Iberian Peninsula, where in
course of time they developed a civilization of their own which
exerted considerable influence upon the intellectual life of Europe
in the Middle Ages. To the north they were stopped from further
irruption by the Battle of Tours in 732, but their conquests elsewhere had the effect of confining Christian civilization to Europe
and cutting off the Western nations from access to trade with the
East. This confinement, this sense of pressure, naturally produced
a reaction, which finds its first full expression as a European movement in the crusades. Christendom feels hemmed in by the infidel, its frontiers shrink, and the fighting men of feudal Europe
are easily induced by the call of Papacy to take arms against the
Saracen.

The movement is not, of course, only religious in character. It
goes forward under a Christian banner, but it is in essence the
work of expanding political and economic forces. Despite the rivalries of Christian states, Europe began from the close of the
tenth century to oppose a growing political and economic unity to
the threatening power of Islam. It was the economic expansion of
Europe rather than its military effort that in the long run turned
the tide that had for centuries flowed from the east and had threatened many times to engulf European culture. It is true that the
power of Islam was but little diminished by the efforts of Christendom to crush it, and that Europe was threatened in the thirteenth
century by the Mongols and later by the Ottoman Turks; but
these dangers only served to give strength and coherent purpose to
the development of European life. The power that lay across the
trade routes to Asia and barred the way to any eastward movement of European states evoked a strong desire on the part of European peoples to break out of their confinement and to extend
the frontiers of the *respublica christiana*. No student of the his-

tory of late mediæval times can fail to be impressed by the great change that comes over the European outlook from the beginning of the fourteenth century. The dominant theme of European thought is shown by the number of works, influential at that time, which discuss methods of breaking the encirclement and expanding beyond the borders of the Mediterranean.

Among them are the *De recuperatione terræ sanctæ* of Dubois (1307), which advocates a general council of Europe, a blockade of Egypt by an international navy, and an alliance with the Moslems in Persia. The celebrated *Secreta fidelium crucis,* presented by its author, Sanuto, to the Pope in 1321, is a story of the crusades and represents the last lingering hope of reconquering Palestine, a land he describes in such a way as to show that Europeans were no longer familiar with its geography.[8] These, and other works bearing titles like *De modo Sarracenos exstirpandi,* while offering different suggestions for the defeat of the infidel, all for unity among European leaders and a European strategy against Islam. The growth of interest in the world beyond the Mediterranean is shown by such a work as the *Libro del Conoscimiento,* the Book of the Knowledge of All the Kingdoms, Lands, and Lordships that are in the World, which belongs to the middle of the fourteenth century. Even more significant is the *Libro di divisamente di pressi e misure* of 1348, which gives information for travellers in Asia. It is a kind of commercial geography for the use of merchants and contains useful facts that Pegolotti, its writer, had learned on his own journeys to central Asia, China, and India.

All these works, in their different ways, deal with European policy in terms of an offensive strategy of expansion. They are expressions of a sense of confinement and of an urgent need to repair the failures of the crusades, which had culminated in the loss of Acre in 1271. No single cause accounts for the new spirit which animated European life from that time onward, nor indeed are all the known and probable causes taken together sufficient to explain the strong and coherent purpose that seems to gather itself together during the fourteenth century and then to display an outburst of energy carrying Europe far beyond Asia in the many fields of material endeavour. There is some element that escapes analysis here, but the results are clear enough. Europe at the close of the Middle Ages entered upon a phase of constructive effort at a time when the great Asiatic communities were severally in phases of conservatism if not of decadence. Perhaps it can be argued that this constructive phase was a necessary sequel of the destruction of all but the germinating power of classical pagan culture by the

---

[8] He copied a good deal from Burchard's description of the Holy Land (*c.* 1283), whose maps he used. Burchard had visited Palestine, but Sanuto had not.

fall of Rome and the rise of the Christian church. It seems that the Asiatic civilizations, since they did not suffer a like experience, were under no compulsion to renew themselves. They did not need a Renaissance for their salvation and consequently were able to continue without startling change in their intellectual life, their political forms, or their social order until long after the nature of European civilization had undergone a thorough transformation. The assault upon their traditions was to develop later, at a time when they were by comparison with Europe as weak as pagan Europe once had been in the face of attacks by barbarian invaders and the challenge of a new creed.

It might be said, in more general terms, that it was the birth in Europe of a doctrine of perfectibility that impelled European states to extend their influence into Asia. As Europeans, under the influence of startling scientific discoveries, came to think that an increase in material benefits could be equated with an advance in human happiness, it was natural that they should look abroad for more wealth and knowledge, since these were the true ingredients of that continuous progress in which they were beginning to believe.

In Asiatic countries no such optimism prevailed as to human destiny. In the great religious and philosophical systems of India the life of mankind is not conceived of as having an end towards which it gradually moves, and certainly man is not seen as the master of his own fate, able to subdue natural forces or at least to turn them to his own ultimate benefit. The flux of existence is thought of not as a progress towards a desirable goal but as an infinite series, without beginning or end, of cycles of growth and decay. Nothing can be more uncongenial to the European mind than the teaching of Buddhist scriptures (which is not contradicted by Hinduistic beliefs) as to the lack of meaning or purpose in the material universe. Their descriptions of worlds that grow only to perish by flame or flood or stormy violence are such as to induce melancholy in all but the most sanguine and eupeptic Occidental.

When a cycle is ended by fire, at first a great world-destroying rain-cloud rises and a great downpour takes place in the hundred thousand myriad world systems. Men bring forth their seeds and sow them, but when the crops begin to grow, the rain is completely cut off. Water dries up, and it does not rain for many hundred years, many thousand years, many hundred thousand years. After a long time has passed since the end of the rains, burning suns manifest themselves, one after another. Their heat strikes down uninterruptedly and at length the hundred thousand myriad world systems are a mass of flame. Then after a long time the

49

rains begin again, and presently the sun and the moon and the constellations reappear, and the sequence of day and night, summer and winter, sowing and harvest is resumed. But lust and greed and craving also return, and in due time the æons of dissolution and quiescence and formation begin again in an eternal repetition of cycles. But there is no progress, no beginning and no end.

Such a view of the fruitlessness of man's endeavour doubtless explains in part why the confidence of European invaders was met by no determined opposition from the peoples of countries under strong Buddhist or Hinduistic influence. At the same time it is significant that as Buddhism moved towards the Far East its pessimism grew thinner, and (as we shall see) Far Eastern peoples, notably the Chinese and the Japanese, proved less acquiescent than Indians in their attitude towards Western intrusion.

Though the reader may wish at this point to reflect further upon the historical reasons why Europe was able from the fifteenth century onwards to exert a growing pressure upon Asia, it would be out of place to pursue such broad inquiries here. It is better to continue the study of the relations between the two continents by a survey of Portuguese maritime and commercial policy in Asiatic waters, and its execution. It throws some light upon the difference between European and Asiatic states in their attitude towards foreign relations and especially towards foreign trade. It is a picturesque story in itself, and it has a bearing upon later history because, the Portuguese being the first in the field, the problems that they encountered and the way in which they solved them did in a very large measure fix the pattern of subsequent European commercial enterprise and colonial expansion in Asia. The experiences of the Portuguese in the Arabian Sea influenced their policy as they moved farther east to Burma, to Indonesia, to China and Japan; and although the policy of later arrivals — principally the Dutch and the English — differed in important respects from that of the Portuguese, they were building upon foundations laid by Portugal. It is not excessive to say that the modern development of commercial and political relations between Europe and Asia, and in particular the history of European colonization in India and the Far East, cannot be thoroughly understood without knowledge of its earliest stages.

In considering these it is worth while to remember that when direct intercourse between Europe and Asia, interrupted by the power of Moslem states, was at length resumed in the closing years of the fifteenth century, it was by water and not by land that Europeans travelled to the East. The armed and mobile ship was less vulnerable than the slow caravan, since what is thought of as the "salt, estranging sea" presented fewer obstacles to traffic between peoples than the land that separated them. The land contains natural barriers more difficult to overcome than wind and waves, and it is peopled by inhabitants more hostile to strangers than are the monsters of the deep. Horace was surely wrong when he said that a prudent God had severed lands from one another by unfriendly waters — *oceano dissociabili;* for it was advances in navigation that not only made possible but also promoted the extension of European influence to distant parts of the world. The ships that Vasco da Gama sailed to India in 1498 were freighted with consequences to Asia more far-reaching than those carried by all the overland expeditions from Europe in preceding centuries.

Notes on CHAPTER 3

CHRISTIANITY AMONG THE MONGOLS. The best single source of information from missionary sources is *Sinica Franciscana* (4 vols. to date), published by the order at Florence. Vol. I contains the texts of the reports and letters of the Franciscan missionaries in eastern Asia, together with a valuable Latin commentary and notes.

MOSLEMS IN CHINA. See note to chapter ii as to Moslem revolts.

THE CHRISTIAN CHURCH IN SOUTHERN INDIA. Readers interested in the growth of the ancient Christian church may wish for further details of a community whose members profess to regard European Christians as "recent converts." The following particulars, derived chiefly from official sources, relate only to the two states of Travancore and Cochin in 1931.

Out of a total population of 6,301,000, the number recorded as Christians is 1,939,000. These may be classified in round numbers as follows:

Eastern (Syrian) Church	....	515,000
Roman Church		
Latin rite 470,000		
Syriac rite 632,500	....	1,102,500
Protestant churches	....	322,000
		1,939,500

Although the origin of the Eastern Church in Malabar can certainly be ascribed to Nestorian missionaries, its present-day members do not admit that their church ever accepted the Nestorian heresy. The sectarian divisions among the members of the Eastern Church are interesting and remarkable, when one remembers that they are almost without exception indigenous people. They are usually styled Syrian Christians because they use the Syriac rite and Syriac liturgies. When the Portuguese established themselves in India they naturally sought to bring the Indian Christian communities into the Roman Church.

In 1599 the Archbishop of Goa convened the Synod of Diamper (Uda-yampur), near Cochin, and induced mass conversions — a rather strik-ing if not complete parallel to the forced vote of the Council of Ephe-sus, A.D. 431.

The whole Malabar Church remained ostensibly Roman until 1653, when a revolt against the supremacy of the Pope took place. A great number of Syrian Christians renounced allegiance to Rome and formed a sect of Jacobite Syrians. In both cases, however, relationship with the Nestorian Church diminished, being kept alive only by a small number of Syro-Malabar Christians in Cochin, who still follow the Chaldean (Nestorian) rite and claim succession from the Patriarch of Babylon. The present subdivisions of the Eastern (Syrian) Church are:

Jacobite Syrians	363,700
Reformed Syrians	144,500
Chaldean Syrians	6,800
	515,000

The Jacobite Syrians are Monophysites who use the Antiochene rite in Syriac and (with some qualifications) acknowledge a Patriarch of Antioch in line from the first Patriarch installed by Jacob of Edessa (d. 557), who revived the Monophysite heresy. The Reformed Syrians result from a split in 1875 among the Jacobites and do not recognize the authority of Antioch, but have their own Metropolitan. They use a modified Antiochene rite but conduct it in the vernacular (Ma-layalam). The Roman Syrians — that is, originally those who in 1653 kept their allegiance to Rome — now include a number of Jacobite Syrians who seceded in 1930 and joined the Church of Rome, but retain the use of the Jacobite Antiochene liturgy.

The Roman Catholics of the Latin rite are persons, mostly of the "depressed" classes, who have been converted by Catholic missionaries from the West since the arrival of the Portuguese in India.

Both the Jacobite and the Roman Syrians are further divided into two or more social groups, which do not intermarry.

It will be seen that, although the total number of members of the ancient Christian church is small in relation to the total population of India, it has shown a notable power of survival and an astonishing variety of sects which does not represent any difference in doctrine. The number of Archbishops and Bishops in the two states of Cochin and Travancore is remarkable. There are twenty-two in all.

It is difficult to explain this persistence of an alien creed in a coun-try so imbued with religious sentiment, though of course the strength of that sentiment accounts for a strong interest in ritual subtleties. It is perhaps due to its deep historical roots in a region cut off by the Western Ghats from other parts of India, and by its coastal situation particularly open to influences from overseas. But, however it is to be explained, the growth of the Syro-Malabar Church is a singular episode in the history of religion; and it is worth noting that, far from losing influence, today its adherents can be found in other parts of India, sometimes occupying positions of importance in public and private life. The Syrian Christians have been fitted into the caste structure of Indian society and some are said tò rank with the Nairs, an exclusive land-owning community.

An account of recent conditions among the Syrian Christians in Travancore by the Right Reverend Stephen Neill appeared in the London *Spectator* of December 21, 1945.

The legend that the Church in India was founded by St. Thomas is not generally believed by historians, but the tradition has persisted for many centuries.

THE PORTUGUESE IN ASIA

1. Colonial Policy

WHAT is at first sight most difficult to understand in the early history of European colonization in Asia is the seeming ease with which small European states were able to impose their will upon highly civilized, rich, and populous Asiatic countries. Portugal at the end of the fifteenth century had a population probably not greater than one and one half million.[1] She was poor, although she had begun to increase her wealth by trading and by bringing gold from the Guinea coast. She certainly does not seem except in the light of after events to have possessed the elements of power that would enable her to challenge the Arabs, who had for centuries dominated trade in the Eastern seas, and to impose her will upon Asiatic peoples a hundred times more numerous than her own. She had, obviously, great courage, which had been tried and tempered in struggles against the Moors; great confidence, which had been nourished by successful voyages of discovery in the Atlantic Ocean; and great zeal for the destruction of heresy and the spread of the Christian faith. But with the physical assets that one would have thought essential for such a great enterprise she was but poorly equipped.

It is true that the seafaring peoples of the Mediterranean had by this time made considerable progress in the science of navigation and naval warfare. The maps and charts available in the fifteenth century to the sailors of southern and western Europe were much in advance of those of the thirteenth century, thanks to the evolution of astronomical and geographical studies. The possibility of extended voyages had brought about improvements in naval architecture and the arming of ships with cannon. But these advantages were not the monopoly of the Portuguese. It is usually

---

[1] Other estimates are higher, some as high as 2,500,000, but this seems unlikely. Spain at that time had 7,000,000, France 16,000,000, and England less than 5,000,000.

said that it was thanks to superior achievements in nautical and military science that they were able not only to make long voyages of discovery but also to overcome their more numerous but less capable enemies at sea. This is no doubt true in a general way, but it is not the whole truth. The task of the Portuguese, when they entered the Indian Ocean for the purpose of monopolizing the trade of the Indies with Europe, was twofold. They had to overcome the supremacy of the Arabs on the oceanic routes from Red Sea ports to the Malabar coast and thence through the Strait of Malacca to Java and the Moluccas. They had also to overcome substantial naval forces maintained by native rulers of countries on the western seaboard of India who did not resent or challenge the Arab supremacy, since it was peaceful and mercantile and involved no threat to Indian sovereignty.[2]

When the King of Portugal, after Vasco da Gama had in 1498 opened the sea road to India by way of the Cape of Good Hope, claimed the sole right of navigation and trade in Asiatic waters, he was bound to come into conflict with both Arab and Hindu. His captains were as a rule men of high courage, strong determination, and abundant self-confidence; but any convictions they may have felt as to an inherent superior capacity in Portuguese or other European seamen in matters of war and commerce were soon shaken. The first trial of strength came in 1500 when, following upon Vasco da Gama's voyage of reconnaissance,[3] Pedro Alvares Cabral was sent to India with a large fleet under instructions to conclude a trade agreement with the Zamorin of Calicut, the strongest ruler on the Malabar coast.

Cabral carried a very piously worded letter to the Zamorin from King Manoel, in which he explains some elements of Christian doctrine, points out that evidently God ordained the miraculous feats of navigation of the Portuguese not only for the purpose of "traffic and temporal profits . . . but also the spiritual of souls and their salvation, to which we are more bound." He refers to the legend that St. Thomas and St. Bartholomew had preached in India, says that he is sending, as well as captains, ships, and merchandise, religious persons (namely, Franciscan friars) to expound the Christian faith, refers to wicked sects (namely, Islam) that had hitherto prevented intercourse between Europeans and Indians, and invites the Zamorin to join in a profitable friendship with Portugal. The letter ends with a scarcely veiled threat: "And if it should happen that . . . we find in you the contrary of this

[2] At this time Hindu merchants were engaged chiefly in coastal traffic, leaving ocean voyages to the Arabs. But they did continue to trade direct with their own communities overseas, particularly in Farther India and Malacca.

[3] Vasco da Gama's ships brought back to Lisbon valuable cargoes, which repaid the cost of the voyage many times, and thus whetted the appetite of the King.

. . . our fixed purpose is to prosecute this affair and continue our navigation, trade, and intercourse in those lands which the Lord God wishes to be newly served by our hands."

This letter is cited here because it reveals very clearly the attitude of mind of the Portuguese of those days. They were no doubt sincere in the belief that their mission was to spread Christianity as well as to engage in profitable trade. Indeed, the Christian kings of Europe were under an obligation to the Church to convert the heathen in lands that they might conquer.[4] Dom Manoel himself was not only Lord of Conquest and Navigation, but also the Governor of the supreme pontifical Order of Christ, while the vigorous quality of his people no doubt owed much to the religious element in their long struggle to maintain their independence and to expel the infidels from the Iberian Peninsula.

But, however strong the impulse behind the Portuguese policy, it could not be executed without preponderant material strength. The Portuguese leaders could not hope to overcome great land forces in Asiatic countries, since they had not the means to transport and maintain abroad any considerable numbers of troops. Their policy must be to apply their limited strength to the weak points of their enemies. One of those weak points in India was the political disunity that prevailed, especially among the numerous small rajahs and chieftains on the Malabar coast. This region was both geographically and politically isolated from the rest of India. When the Portuguese reached India the powerful Hindu kingdom of Vijayanagar, almost the sole bulwark against Mohammedan invasion from the north, was able to exercise some influence upon political conditions in Malabar, and might presently have induced or imposed unity among the rulers of the many small states along the coast. But it was cut off from them by the Western Ghats, it was preoccupied with its own struggles against the sultans of the Deccan; and meanwhile the various Malabar rulers were concerned more with promoting their own several fortunes than with forming a confederation that might have protected them against aggressors.

Chief among these small principalities was the kingdom of Calicut, whose sovereign (styled the Zamorin) had by the end of the fifteenth century become the richest and strongest ruler in Malabar. Calicut was a considerable city, largely Hindu in population, but sheltering also a flourishing community of Arab traders who

---

4 This injunction is contained in several papal bulls. Henry the Navigator obtained a bull from Nicolas IV in 1454 granting to Portugal and the Order of Christ authority to trade and spiritual jurisdiction along the west coast of Africa and *usque ad Indos*. This was confirmed from time to time. The bull *Ineffabilis et summi* of 1497, while conferring upon Dom Manoel possession of lands conquered from the infidels, specifically enjoined him to establish the Christian faith therein.

had been settled there for some centuries. They did not interfere in politics, but they had a virtual monopoly of the foreign and some of the domestic trade of the state, to which they thus brought not only wealth but also a claim to the good will of the rulers of Cairo, Ormuz, and other Mohammedan dominions whence they came. The Zamorin, anxious to extend his authority, had built up his naval forces, and he had at his command not only experienced seamen of a race that had sailed the Indian Ocean for more than a millennium but also soldiers of the Nair caste, a warlike community that had a well-developed military organization of a somewhat Spartan character.

But at that time neither his men nor his guns were a match for those of the Portuguese, who were able to sink his ships and bombard his cities almost at will. The Nairs had a traditional method of fighting in which each side paid great attention to the convenience of the other and battles were conducted with a high regard for ceremony and decorum. They were obliged to abandon these amiable practices when they came up against Portuguese soldiers, who were better armed and more ruthless fighters than the Indians, and who reserved their punctilio for encounters among their own fidalgoes. The Indians had little artillery, and that not very serviceable, until they began to employ Italian and other advisers, who gradually improved their ordnance until, after about a dozen years, a Portuguese commander had to admit that "the people with whom we wage war are no longer the same . . . artillery, arms, and fortresses are according to our usage." This is a significant statement, because it shows that the wisest Portuguese, whatever may have been their first intentions, no longer contemplated the conquest of a large area of Indian soil. They perceived very soon that though they might take it they could not hold it. They were familiar enough with the fighting qualities of Mohammedan peoples to know that they could never maintain enough troops in India to secure themselves against land attacks by the Moslem rulers in the north, even supposing they could establish dominion over the small Hindu kingdoms in the south.

It was considerations such as these that shaped the colonial policy of the Portuguese in subsequent years. If they were to enforce the monopoly of navigation and commerce that they claimed in the Indian Ocean, they must establish not only trading stations but also bases for their warships. Further, they must capture or at least contain the bases of their rivals, the Egyptian and Arab sultans who had hitherto controlled the trade with India and beyond from their harbours on the Persian Gulf, the Red Sea, and the African littoral. This was not so easy a task as getting a foothold on the Malabar coast, where one rajah could be played off against another. Fortunately for the Portuguese, during their first decades in India the Mohammedan rulers of the Deccan were engaged in struggles among themselves or in attacks upon Hindu kingdoms, so that no combined military power was brought to bear upon the European intruders until they were well established. But the Indian Ocean trade was a matter of life and death to the Egyptian and Arab states, both large and small. It was something that they would vigorously defend, and they were not outclassed by the Portuguese in fighting spirit, in seamanship, and in the use of artillery. The success of the Portuguese in their Asiatic adventure depended therefore upon their ability to defeat their Moslem enemies at sea. This they managed to do, but only by a very narrow margin.

In reviewing the early history of European conquest and colonization in Asia, Occidental historians tend to ascribe its rapid progress to an unexplained superiority of Western culture, not only material but moral. A learned English writer on the history of Portugal, to explain how the Portuguese achieved their naval and military successes with so few ships and so few men, says: "The answer is to be found in the moral superiority of the white man, in the self-confidence and reckless valour of the conquistadores, in their armour, stouter vessels and better, though not so numerous artillery." [5] We may leave aside the question of moral superiority, which needs some further definition; but we may accept as substantially correct the view that the arms and equipment of the Portuguese were more advanced than those of the Asiatics whom they encountered. Yet in their early struggles with the "Moors" for the command of the sea, their victories were by no means decisive. In 1502 Vasco da Gama with a strong naval force, after burning a helpless ship carrying pilgrims from Mecca, destroyed a fleet of small vessels sent against him by the ruler of Calicut. The Mameluke Sultan of Egypt soon saw that he must take measures to protect his own interests and began to prepare a strong fleet. The Turks and Levantines and the Christian renegades whom they enlisted were good fighters, by no means unpractised in naval warfare or deficient in artillery. They defeated a squadron under L. de Almeida off the Indian coast in 1508. The designs of the Portuguese were in jeopardy and they had to make a supreme effort. Fortunately for them, in the following year they were able to inflict a defeat upon the Egyptian fleet and a number of Indian craft that came to its support, in a battle off Diu. This was a really decisive victory, which gave the Portuguese a command of the Indian Ocean and enabled them in due course to establish themselves in shore bases controlling the trade routes. The victors pro-

[5] Edgar Prestage: *The Portuguese Pioneers*, p. 302.

ceeded towards Cochin, celebrating their triumph by stopping off Mohammedan settlements along the coast and bombarding them with the limbs of prisoners of war whom they had carved up for that purpose. This grisly *feu de joie* was not merely a display of wanton cruelty. Like many other atrocities committed by the Portuguese in the Indies, it was part of a deliberate policy of frightfulness designed to make up by terror for deficiencies in their military strength.

Despite their successes, their troubles were not yet over, and indeed throughout the period of their ascendancy in Asia they were handicapped by a shortage of ships, men, and money, while their enemies, learning by experience, soon took to improved methods of warfare both on land and at sea. As related by European historians, the conquest of the Indies appears as a glorious epic, where Christian paladins lay low the infidel and the gentile — the Moor and the Hindu — in a succession of fights against fearful odds. It is indeed a heroic achievement, stained though it is by barbarities and greed. But seen from the Asiatic point of view it assumes another complexion. One Indian historian argues that the Portuguese never had any real power or empire in India, that they never got beyond acquiring a little local authority confined to small areas round the ports which they built along the coast, and that such successes as they achieved were due not so much to superior military prowess or political insight as to the disunity of India, which gave them a fortuitous advantage. He does not think highly of Vasco da Gama's feat of navigation, pointing out that it was an Arab pilot who took him from the African coast to Calicut; and in general he casts doubts on the claims of the Portuguese and other Europeans to primacy in maritime discovery, on the ground that the seafaring peoples of the East had developed oceanic navigation long before the days of Columbus and Magellan, and even before the Phœnicians and Greeks had learned to sail across the Mediterranean or out into the Atlantic.[6]

These arguments are perhaps not entirely convincing, but they deserve attention because they raise an important issue. They pose questions as to the relative merits of European and Asiatic civilizations in general. They suggest in particular some qualification of the common view that European advances in philosophy and natural science gave to European countries a moral and material advantage that found its clearest expression in a decisive military superiority.

[6] K. M. Panikkar: *Malabar and the Portuguese* (Bombay, 1929) , and *India and the Indian Ocean* (London, 1945) . Mookerjee's *History of Indian Shipping* (Bombay, 1912) , an erudite but not entirely convincing work, gives a very high estimate of Indian maritime development in antiquity.

Such assumptions hardly accord with all the historical facts in regard to the sixteenth century. When the West had to face a great danger from the sweeping invasions of the Ottoman Turks, the lords of Christendom failed to rise to concerted action and certainly they could not summon forth a degree of moral or material strength sufficient to subdue their common enemy. For years after the disaster of Nicopolis, until the great naval battle of Lepanto (1571), they were at a continuous disadvantage. Even after this victory, usually styled decisive, Turkish maritime power reasserted itself. Corsairs, if not organized fleets, continued until the seventeenth century to infest not only the Mediterranean but also Atlantic waters as far afield as the Bristol Channel. As late as 1645 a number of Cornish men and women were carried off by raiders who landed at Fowey from Turkish galleys. One of the Azores islands was twice raided by Barbary rovers in the second half of the seventeenth century, and the whole population abducted.

It is perhaps pertinent to mention here that Chinese ships also were in many respects not inferior to Portuguese. Fernão Peres de Andrade describes a war junk built by the Sultan of Damak beside which his own flagship "did not look like a ship at all" and on which his cannon balls made no impression. This was in 1513. The Portuguese suffered severe naval reverses at the hands of the Chinese in the first half of the sixteenth century, as for instance when Coutinho's fleet was defeated by them off Canton in 1523. There are also Japanese sixteenth-century accounts of great three- or four-deckers, built by the Chinese for use against Japanese pirates, which carried two thousand men.

Turkish successes, though admittedly due to the Ottoman Empire's ruthless and single-minded organization for war, could not have been achieved without proper technical competence in gunnery and manœuvre. It is hardly correct to account for the later collapse of Turkish power by regarding it as due to a growing moral or material superiority on the side of its European antagonists, except in the limited sense that the Ottoman Empire decayed through its own internal weakness. The efforts of European princes at Malta and Lepanto did, it is true, contribute to its fall, but good fortune was as important here as military capacity. It is probable also that the successes of the Portuguese in their struggle against Mohammedan power in the Indian Ocean were due not entirely to superior capacity but also to lucky political circumstances.[7] Support for this view can be found in the further narrative of Portuguese military and civil policy in India.

---

[7] One of the difficulties that hampered the naval efforts of the Moslems was the absence of timber in the Red Sea. To build ships for fighting in the Indian Ocean the Sultan was obliged to obtain timber from the Taurus forests in Alexandretta,

After the defeat of the Egyptian fleet off Diu in 1509, Affonso Albuquerque, who had assumed office as Governor of India (from Gujarat to Cape Comorin), perceived that the Portuguese were wasting their strength in attempts to hold points on the Malabar coast which involved them in constant intrigues and struggles between rival Indian principalities. They had, for example, some success in winning to their side the Rajah of Cochin, who became a vassal of the King of Portugal; but this drove the Zamorin of Calicut to plan a league of Malabar princes against the Portuguese and such Indian rulers as had taken their side. For years after Cochin received his golden crown from Portugal, there was constant strife between him and Calicut, in which the Portuguese were obliged to take a hand. The Zamorin, as well as calling upon the Sultan of Egypt for help, built up his own land and sea forces. Sometimes he would give the Portuguese a drubbing, sometimes he had to make peace with them; but for many years he was a thorn in their side. His people were not all mild Hindus. There were in the Malabar population the Nairs already mentioned and, in addition to Jews and Christians, a number of Mohammedans, including the fanatical Moplahs. Most of these were good fighters. The seafaring Arabs in particular were of great service to the rulers of Calicut, providing them with hereditary admirals. Fleets of small, speedy ships under their command, while avoiding pitched battles, continued to harass the Portuguese, intercepting their merchantmen and occasionally sinking an armed caravel, a galliot, or a frigate. It was not until the end of the sixteenth century that the power of these seamen was broken, and this was not accomplished by the Portuguese alone. The last of the Kunhali admirals (they were of Mappila or Moplah family) was attacked in his fortress by Calicut land forces in alliance with the Portuguese, because he had become swollen with pride and had gone so far as to cut off the tail of one of his sovereign's elephants.

Although conflict with the Malabar chieftains thus dragged on for nearly a century, it had already in 1510 become clear to Albuquerque, the wisest and greatest of Portuguese statesmen in India, that Portugal could succeed in her policy of dominating the trade routes only if she concentrated her strength in easily defensible places. He had learned a lesson, which some of his successors failed to understand, when Portuguese arms suffered a severe reverse at the hands of the Zamorin's land forces during an abortive Portuguese attack upon the city of Calicut. He decided that he

---

whence it was shipped to Alexandria and then taken up the Nile and sent to Suez shipyards overland. The slow vessels carrying the timber from Alexandretta were open to attack in the Mediterranean. Half the supply sent for building the fleet that was to meet the Portuguese was destroyed by the Knights of St. John from Rhodes in 1506.

must find a safer and more convenient base for naval operations, since what the Portuguese needed was a place that could be easily defended against land attacks while furnishing shelter and supplies for the warships that must protect the trade routes. This he found on the island of Goa, which was in the territory of a Moslem ruler, the Adil Shah. But it was also adjacent to the state of Vijayanagar, a Hindu kingdom still holding out in southern India against the Moslem power threatening from the Deccan.

This is a point of special interest, because it shows that even the new and limited policy of Albuquerque depended upon the good will of a native prince. Vijayanagar helped him because it needed a port through which to obtain supplies of arms and above all of Arab horses for its wars against the Moslems. After some reverses the Portuguese were able in 1510 to establish themselves in Goa, which thus at the end of a decade of indecisive fighting and diplomacy on the Malabar coast became the chief center and stronghold of Portugal in India, remaining in Portuguese hands through many vicissitudes until the present day.

Goa was the capital of the Portuguese Empire in Asia, the focal point of its trade, and the seat of the Patriarch of the Catholic Church in India. From here flowed the missionary effort of the Dominicans, the Franciscans, and the Jesuits; and here in 1583 a magnificent welcome was given to an embassy to Rome composed of noble youths representing feudatories of western Japan. Their mission had been arranged by the Jesuits, now well established in Japan, so that on their return they could tell their countrymen of the power and splendour of European countries and the commanding influence of the Catholic Church.[8]

More must be said about the ecclesiastical importance of Goa, but first some attention should be paid to its character as a Portuguese possession.

It may be regarded as the first of the European colonies in Asia in modern times, and one of its important features is that, like many later colonies, it was secured almost by accident and not as the result of a considered national policy. The Portuguese government, or more correctly perhaps the Portuguese kings, when they promoted exploration and maritime commerce, had not in their minds any plan of territorial expansion in Asia. They had a general intention of gaining trade monopolies in the Indian Ocean and beyond, and they knew that they might have to use force for

---

[8] By a strange coincidence I wrote this sentence just before breaking off to listen to a news broadcast on December 6, 1945, which reported that the Supreme Commander for the Allied Powers in Japan had ordered the Japanese government to withdraw its envoy to the Vatican.

that purpose. They at first supposed that, so far as concerned the Indian rulers, they might be able to achieve their ends by negotiation backed by a display of strength. This was in part due to their ignorance of actual conditions in India, which they completely misunderstood.[9] Indeed, despite the existence of a considerable European literature on India, including classical works, the reports of Franciscan and other missionaries in the thirteenth and fourteenth centuries, and travel-books of Mohammedan writers, Europe knew very little about India until the Portuguese had been there for some time. Even then the accounts of good observers were most incomplete and misleading because they failed to grasp the nature of Indian civilization. The earliest Portuguese invaders might be forgiven for such ludicrous mistakes as supposing that the Virgin Mary was worshipped in Hindu temples or attempting to convert Hindu rulers whose very kingship was a religious office; but it is remarkable that the Western world did not until the end of the eighteenth century become aware that India possessed an ancient literature and a philosophical tradition comparable in maturity and distinction to those of Greece and Rome.[10] Even this advance in knowledge was due not to an awakened enthusiasm for Indian lore but to the East India Company's recognition of the practical importance of Sanskrit studies as an aid to administration and judicial business.

But if the Portuguese misjudged the Hindu character, they knew a great deal about Islam and they were well aware of the struggle they would have with Mohammedan nations. In fact their policy, while it aimed at the acquisition of wealth by trade, at the same time sought to cripple the Mohammedan power not only by direct attack in the Indian Ocean but also by depriving Islam of its strength in the Mediterranean in so far as it was derived from the Oriental wealth that sustained the Mohammedan fleets and armies in Europe. Though it is true, as Vasco da Gama's men said on first landing in the Indies, that they came "in search of Christians and spices," this was only a local aspect of a national policy. The crusading zeal and the chivalrous sentiment which, though already outmoded in the rest of Europe, still inspired the Portuguese

9 One of the most interesting pieces of evidence on this point is the nature of the presents offered by da Gama to the King of Calicut. They were some striped cloth, hats, strings of coral beads, wash-basins, and jars of oil and honey. These were curious gifts to bring to the classical land of treasure, and the King's officers found them laughable. The King, when he received da Gama, had in his hand a golden spittoon, and by him a golden basin for his betel. He was wearing a crown set with pearls, and golden anklets set with rubies.

10 It is true that some of the Jesuits in India in the 17th century translated and refuted certain Hindu theological works, but their writings remained in manuscript and were not generally known.

nobility in the sixteenth century gave to Portuguese expansion in its early stages a romantic quality in contrast to the practical character of later imperialisms.

But the ultimate driving force behind the Portuguese and Spanish voyages of discovery in the fifteenth century was a desire to rid Europe of the threat of Mohammedan invasion. Spain and Portugal had ejected the Moors from the Iberian Peninsula, but the Ottoman Empire was a continual menace to all European states from the capture of Constantinople by the Turks in 1453. Until Vasco da Gama reached Calicut in 1498, the greater part of the world's oceanic carrying trade was in Mohammedan hands. The carrying trade of western Europe was almost insignificant in comparison, and even the most opulent of European mercantile states, Venice and Genoa, depended for their prosperity upon the overflow of commodities from India and the Far East that was spared to them by Bagdad, Damascus, Cairo, and Constantinople. It was as a part of the great struggle between Christian and Islamic powers that the Portuguese, with support from the Church, endeavoured to cut off and divert to themselves the stream of wealth that flowed from Asia to the Turkish Empire or its allies and without which the Turks would scarcely have been able to maintain their military pressure upon Europe.

Of course the Portuguese coveted the profits that the Moslems derived from the Eastern trade. But their motives were not entirely commercial. It has been said that one of their principal objects was to reduce the price of spices and that this is sufficient to account for their policy of breaking the Moslem monopoly. There is little evidence for this view, while there is plenty to indicate that the Portuguese, or at any rate their more far-sighted leaders, had in mind a grand strategy of encircling the Turks. Albuquerque even revived an old idea of diverting the flow of the Nile so as to ruin Egypt, while he saw the importance of taking and holding key places in the Red Sea and the Persian Gulf, from which, as Camoens said, "the Soldan drew a profit great and pleasing." [11] It thus appears that Portuguese expansion and colonization in Asia, the first manifestations in the modern age [12] of what is now called European imperialism, have their origin in an effort on the part of European states to thwart the imperialist ambitions of a people of Asiatic origin fighting under the banner of an Asiatic religion.

The menace continued through the sixteenth century, and was in some aspects intensified by the Asiatic campaigns of the Turks

[11] Referring in particular to Jiddah: *"Gida . . . De que tinha proveito grande e grato O Soldão que esse reino possuia."*

[12] The crusaders' colonies in Syria, etc., are on a different footing. They were an attempt to transplant feudal régimes, not national power.

under Selim (1515–20) and his son Suleiman the Magnificent. They inflicted defeat upon the Persians and by crushing the Mameluke sultans of Egypt they became paramount in Egypt, Syria, and the Hejaz. Their power, more unified than that of their Mohammedan predecessors in those regions, extended down the Red Sea and the Persian Gulf into the Indian Ocean. It was here that they came into conflict with the Portuguese, who, as well as establishing themselves in Goa, found it necessary to strike at the Mohammedan strength in Aden and Ormuz and to gain control of Diu, a harbour in the Mohammedan sultanate of Gujarat, which was important for the pilgrim ships and a centre of the trade in Arab horses.

This, in view of the scope of Portuguese designs, was a rather modest plan of territorial acquisition and it is important to note that it could not be fully accomplished. The Portuguese established a protectorate at Socotra, but they never could control Aden, they had trouble from time to time at Ormuz, and it was only after frequent reverses that they were able to establish themselves permanently in Diu by its capture in 1546. None of these places except Goa and Diu could be regarded as colonies in a strict sense.

The acquisition of the Portuguese colonial holding in India was so little the result of a considered policy that it was almost accidental in its nature, as were many of the colonial enterprises of the nations that followed the Portuguese. When Albuquerque took Goa, the court at Lisbon was surprised and suggested that he should return it to Abdul Khan, its ruler, because the King and his advisers had never contemplated direct Portuguese rule of any foreign territory. They had expected at most some kind of arrangement by which local sovereigns would grant trading privileges, with permission to erect a "factory" and a fortress for its protection. But as the Portuguese gained experience they learned that such arrangements were not sufficient. They found themselves involved in the unending disputes and intrigues of petty rajahs, and they could never feel secure. What they needed most of all was a base for their ships and a centre for the control of their various trading enterprises, in which they could keep a permanent garrison. It must be easily defensible against assault by land, and must afford shelter against storms or attack from the sea. For these purposes Goa was ideal. The men on the spot, with their knowledge of local conditions, could not be bound by policies laid down at home, which if carried out would have rendered their own task impossible. So Albuquerque and his council proceeded with their plan for the permanent occupation of Goa as a colony under direct Portuguese rule, just as three hundred years later Raffles took possession of Singapore in disregard of the policy of his home government, because he was convinced that the expansion of British trade in the Far East could not proceed without the acquisition of a strategic base.

So began and so continued the process of colonization in India, not as the result of any national plan of conquest, but as an inevitable corollary of a policy of obtaining trade by a monopoly of sea transport. As the Portuguese extended these activities towards the east, they found themselves obliged to acquire further bases. They captured and held Malacca in 1511, though they did not attempt to exercise direct rule over the natives of the region. Moving on to China, in circumstances that will be presently described, they established themselves in Macao, though here again they were unwelcome but tolerated guests rather than rulers. In extent the Portuguese Empire in Asia was small. It consisted of the few square miles comprising the island of Goa, the small port of Diu, the post at Malacca, and the lodging in Macao, and brought within full Portuguese sovereignty only a few thousand alien people. Portugal had also a somewhat loose hold upon considerable territory in Ceylon (from 1587 to 1658), and was in control of districts round Bassein until ejected by the Mahrattas in 1738. Her settlements at Muscat, Ormuz, Daman, Cochin, São Thomé, Amboina, Ternate, and Tidore were not, strictly speaking, colonies but fortified "factories" or trading posts enjoying by force or sufferance a kind of extraterritorial standing.

Though not impressive in area or population, the Portuguese Empire in Asia within a few decades of da Gama's first voyage to India represents a considerable achievement, which depended less upon superior power than upon strength and continuity of purpose. The Europeans went into Asia in a spirit of determination to succeed that was stronger than the will of the Asiatic peoples to resist. Europe in the sixteenth century could not boast of unity, for it was riddled with political and religious dissension, but on one point there was at least general agreement, and that was the need of expansion towards the east in order both to resist the pressure of the Ottoman Turks and to gain wealth from Asiatic trade. In this enterprise it was Portugal that took the lead, largely because, standing remote upon the western edge of Europe, she was not very directly concerned in contemporary European politics and could thus afford to devote all her national energies to the task of overseas expansion. Henry the Navigator and King Manoel gave the first place in national policy to equipping and supporting ships and men dispatched on voyages of exploration or adventure. There was no comparable singleness of purpose in the Asiatic countries against which these enterprises were directed; and even the Moslem power in the Indian Ocean, which stood to lose so much by Portuguese success, did not bring to the defence of its own interests the continuous and whole-hearted energy displayed by its European rival.

There seems to be no doubt that a policy of expansion cannot succeed unless it is executed with full and confident determination. These were the qualities that enabled three of the smallest and least powerful of European states in the sixteenth century to carry out undertakings that reason would say were beyond their strength. In the circumstances of the age, expansion was the law of their being, the condition of their independent survival. Though it may be condemned on moral grounds today, it was historically inevitable; and this historical character ought to be taken into account in forming judgments upon the past and future of colonial possessions.

A cynical view would pretend that the expansive, proselytizing movement of European civilization from the thirteenth century onwards was a mere cloak for mercantile cupidity. But it was much more than this, for it was an outpouring of strength acquired and knowledge accumulated in the long period since the fall of the Roman Empire. The record of the invasion of the Asiatic world by European intruders includes some regrettable chapters, but it cannot be said with certainty that it was in general harmful or retrograde. It was the expression, the inevitable expression, of a civilization on the march. It may have — indeed, it has — destroyed much that was gentle and beautiful, and those who have known at first hand the simple grace of some Asiatic cultures must grieve at the thought of their contamination. It may be that such cultures carried within themselves the germs of new life, but it is idle now to speculate as to what course they would have run had they not come under the influence of new forces from the Occident.

Those forces, it is useful to recall, first appeared in small seafaring communities in the Mediterranean, and it was the mediæval successors of those communities that led the way in the extension of European trade and the projection of European influence into the Indian and Pacific Oceans. It was the small maritime republics of Venice and Genoa, heirs to the tradition of the Greek city states, that explored unknown deserts and seas for the sake of trade, further developed the arts of shipbuilding and navigation, encouraged the spirit of scientific inquiry, and, thanks to their advances in invention, made that progress in naval warfare and also in methods of trade and finance which enabled them, and later the Portuguese and the Spaniards, the Dutch and the English, to gain ascendancy in all the oceans.

Seeing how notable have been the achievements of Asiatic peoples, remembering how the Asia of antiquity often surpassed Europe not only in the realm of abstract wisdom but also in the field of practical discovery, it might have been expected that, when later in their history Asiatic peoples were confronted with new ideas and inventions from the West, they would have displayed some active interest, some wonder whether here was not material that they might usefully incorporate in their own systems. It might, for instance, have been supposed that a people which had invented paper, printing, gunpowder, and the mariner's compass would have wished to apply to their own lives some of the scientific principles brought to their notice by Jesuit missionaries in the sixteenth century or by subsequent travellers. They were by no means behindhand in certain techniques, having for example made progress in the application of mathematics, in medicine, and in agricultural science. But for a millennium or more their economic and social conditions had been such as to inhibit the development of science beyond the empirical stage, and therefore the rulers of China showed little curiosity in matters of scientific speculation. True, they paid some attention to methods of astronomical calculation and map-making shown to them by the Jesuits, because calendars and land surveys played an important part in their system of government; and they were not unwilling to learn something about the manufacture of firearms, since this might be useful for the protection of their own order. But in general they looked with superb disdain upon other products of the European hand and brain, because they felt that their own institutions were near perfection and their own economy complete.

The position in India was not unlike that in China. Although in ancient times Indian ships had sailed distant seas and had carried Hindu colonists far from their native lands, later Hindu customs, particularly the caste system, were unfavourable to foreign travel. Brahman orthodoxy, for instance, required (and still nominally requires) a purification (*panipatya*) of every man who has crossed "the black water," which to the Greeks was the inviting wine-dark sea. For such reasons, and also because Indian sea power was overcome in the eleventh century by Indonesian sea fighters and subsequently by Arab corsairs, by the fifteenth century the seaborne trade of India both eastward and westward had long fallen from Indian hands into those of Moslem traders. These not only controlled the traffic routes to India but also were settled in communities on the coast of southern India, where they had a practical monopoly of the distribution of imported merchandise and the purchase of goods for export.

Internal political conditions in the Indian peninsula moreover were not favourable to the development of trade on a national scale, since the Moslem invaders in the north were interested in conquest rather than in trade, while in the south, especially in Malabar, where Moslem military or political power had not yet penetrated, petty Hindu rulers were at odds with one another and concerned more with gaining territory than with promoting commerce. Their need for foreign products was of no importance and they were content to leave buying and selling to strangers who were skilled in the business and even prepared to pay for the privilege. The tolerance of these rulers towards foreign trade and foreign religions, besides being a mark of their civilized condition, was a measure of their indifference to the matters that governed the thoughts and the actions of the foreigners. Long before the arrival of the Portuguese, peaceful communities of Arab traders had settled along the Malabar coast, where they conformed to the laws of the land and rendered useful services to its economy. In return they were treated with consideration by the native rulers, who did not interfere with their religious practices.

Nothing could have been in sharper contrast to this liberal attitude than the ruthless determination with which the European intruders, in particular the Portuguese, pursued as a national policy the active propagation of their own faith, the destruction of heresy, and, above all, the indiscriminate seizure of wealth. Certainly the record of the Portuguese in their early dealings with Asiatic peoples was deplorable, even by the modest standard then prevailing in Europe. But there does not appear to have been in the minds of their explorers any plan of conquest or annexation. Trade was their object, and when it became clear that they could not permanently control the trade routes unless they held protected bases, they were committed to the building of forts and the maintenance of garrisons on foreign soil. Thence it was only a short step to colonies.

This was of course not a new thing in history. It was only an extension of the process that reached back to the colonizing activities of the Phœnicians and the Greeks. They and their successors found by experience that any policy aimed at a monopoly of sea power and trade must lead to colonization and — if the necessary strength could be maintained — to empire. It is true that the Portuguese Empire of the sixteenth century was small in area. Depending upon sea power and unable to deploy large forces on land, the Portuguese could not occupy extensive territories but had to content themselves with seizing and holding strategic coastal points or small islands. There is in fact an inherent contradiction between the conditions that impel states to expand by colonization and the conditions necessary to sustain their effort of expansion. In both ancient and modern times it is the political units with little territory and small populations that make the strongest and most persistent efforts to supplement their poor resources by trade and colonies.

The small Greek cities by their trading voyages and settlements laid the foundations of Hellenic strength; Rome herself, type of the imperial city, was the core around which a great empire grew by the accretion of new parts; and in later days it was autonomous seaport towns such as Venice and Genoa that, adding to their scanty material resources by trading enterprise, achieved power out of all proportion to their own size. Even the greater states that inherited their commercial supremacy in the modern age — Portugal, Spain, Holland, and England — were of modest dimensions by comparison with states possessing great space and large populations. It is clear that their strength lay not in their size but in their character, and that a most important element in their character was a political and social structure which enabled them to devote their full energies to commercial enterprise.

If on the other hand we look at the history of states that are great in extent and population we find that they do not usually figure as important trading or colonizing powers. Their main energies are devoted to the development of their internal resources rather than to foreign trade. Expansion of their wealth and strength is achieved in that way or by the incorporation of adjacent territory. In a large measure their very size dictates the nature of their policies, since they are bound by the facts of their geography to have extended land frontiers, which occupy their attention and give importance to land forces rather than to naval strength, to roads and fortified towns rather than to ships and harbours. Even those whose seacoast is considerable have as a rule, until the development of modern sea transport, felt free from serious danger of sea-borne invasion. India is a case in point, and China as we have noticed was free to extend her empire overland, while she never felt vulnerable to attack from the sea. Indeed, her indifference to naval matters, arising from this sense of security, resulted in her failure to maintain supremacy over such weak countries as she did from time to time subdue by naval expeditions; and it gave Japan an opportunity to develop in safety for a thousand years.

It is doubtless this preoccupation with land, this neglect of the sea, that has made such great continental powers as India and China an easy prey for vigorous maritime states which, though vastly inferior in size and numbers, had the great advantage that they could bring their undivided national strength to bear upon points where the great land powers were weakest. The great land powers, moreover, tended to conservatism in political and social matters for reasons that we have already noticed, and their size was often an element adverse to national unity, as the history of both India and China amply testifies.

By contrast with the massive and often inert structure of the great land powers, the small maritime states show a vigorous continuity of purpose, which is a valuable source of strength and even, it may be said, an indispensable condition of their survival. When that purpose fails, as it did in Portugal, the capacity to exercise power at a distance vanishes, the momentum that sustains maritime enterprise and colonizing activity is lost. Conversely, whatever may be said on moral grounds — and there is much to say — against aggression and exploitation, there is no doubt that successful colonization is an expression of health and vigour in the colonizing people. There has grown up in recent years a habit of condemning colonial powers as exceptionally wicked and predatory. They are represented as backward and unrepentant, their vices in deep contrast to the shining virtues of those countries which have not found it necessary or possible to engage in overseas adventure. By a further step the Asiatic or African peoples whose countries have been entered by European intruders are made to appear as Arcadian innocents who have never stepped across a frontier or coveted a neighbour's goods or cracked an alien skull. But peoples who live across land frontiers are seen as savages who must be reformed or chastised or even exterminated.

Such views betray some blindness to historical perspective and a failure to understand the evolutionary steps by which Occidental cultures have been brought into contact and often, unhappily, into conflict with cultures of other regions of the globe. The critics of what is called colonialism, deceived by the fact that the most spectacular colonial undertakings have been carried out by the exercise of sea power, seem to consider that movements of expansion which do not take place across salt water have some special justification. By such reasoning the Portuguese seizure of Goa, the Dutch occupation of Java, the British hold upon India and Malaya, are particularly sinful, while British and American progress across the North American continent or the Russian spread eastward into Siberia appear almost as high enterprises of benevolence and enlightenment. But it cannot be that the Red River, the Colorado, and the Rio Grande, or the Athabasca or the Yenisei, contain cleansing elements that are absent from the salt seas. The truth is that the expansive urge of the capitalist society born in Europe after the Renaissance has expressed itself in many forms, of which direct colonization was the earliest and the power of modern finance and industry is the most recent. They are all of the same essence, and all industrial states are implicated, for good or evil, in the world-wide organism of trade, money, and inventions by which modern industrialized life is sustained. The nature of present-day relationships between East and West cannot be fully understood if they are regarded not as a stage in a continuing process but as something accidental that can be removed by strong gestures of disapproval.

After this digression, which will be found not altogether irrelevant to our main theme — because it places the eastward trend of European influence in its historical setting — we may return to the story of Portuguese colonization in Asia.

2. The Ecclesiastical Power

A SEQUEL TO the maritime discoveries of the fifteenth century not less important than commercial expansion was the growth of missionary endeavour beyond the frontiers of Europe. Not many years after the discovery of the Americas and the opening of the Cape route to India, Christian missionaries were making their way to almost every part of the now circumnavigated globe. They followed the explorers, the conquerors, and the traders, and though their rulers no doubt supported them for reasons of national policy, their labours were undertaken with a burning zeal and a selfless devotion that compel respect. Franciscans, Augustinians, Dominicans, and Jesuits carried the gospel westward to Brazil, Mexico, Central America, and Peru, eastward to Africa, India, and the Far East and the islands of the Pacific. This was evangelism on a scale for which there was no precedent in the history of religions, and it expressed a significant and characteristic European attitude.

It is true that in previous ages peoples professing one or other of the great Asiatic religions had made conscious efforts to spread their faith beyond their own borders. Buddhism in its early history had a strong evangelising quality, which was displayed in particular in the days of the great King Asoka. It was he who, after his conversion, expressed remorse for the bloodshed attending his military victories and announced that henceforth he would devote himself to conquest by means of the Dhamma — that is, by the Buddhist doctrine. He sent missionaries to parts of India beyond his own dominions and even, it seems, to the Hellenistic kingdoms in western Asia and Egypt. Thereafter Buddhism spread in the course of centuries to almost every part of Asia north and east of the Indian subcontinent and probably influenced the thought of foreign countries more than any other religion before or since. But in general the adoption of Buddhism outside India was the result not so much of deliberate missionary enterprise as of a gradual diffusion of Indian culture by peaceful travellers and immigrants. It was not, save perhaps in a few exceptional cases, imposed upon foreign peoples by invaders or recommended by powerful princes on political grounds. Its spread was due to the nature of its teaching and in later periods to the beauty of its art and the appeal of its ritual.

The spread of Islam, on the other hand, is to be ascribed principally to the extension of Mohammedan rule by conquest. It cannot be said to be the result of a deliberate policy of conversion, for although the Arab wars of conquest were described as holy wars, the Mohammedans were on the whole indifferent to the religious beliefs of the people whom they conquered. They gave to those who did not resist them by force of arms a choice between conversion and payment of the *jizya,* or poll-tax, with the result that Islam was adopted in many countries by native inhabitants whose own faith was not highly developed. But such conversions were not as a rule due to missionary ardour on the part of the Mohammedans. Their attitude towards subject peoples was based upon political rather than religious grounds.

The attitude of the Christian church in this matter of conversion was more positive from its very beginnings, since it was derived from the teaching of its founder. Christianity, by its emphasis upon the brotherhood of man, was bound to break loose from the narrow limits of Judaism and to assert itself as a universal religion, and the acts of the apostles are the first phase of a continuing missionary effort that spread first within the Roman Empire and then beyond its borders. The Franciscans who in the thirteenth century went into Tartary, the Dominicans who sought the Mongol leaders in Persia or accompanied Marco Polo to the court of Khubilai, and the members of the mendicant orders who followed the conquistadores to America and the East Indies — all these were in a true line of succession from Stephen, Philip, and Barnabas and the apostle who assayed to go into Bithynia.

The opportunity offered by the new empires of Spain and Portugal was eagerly seized by the Church, though her early efforts in India were ill-organized and unfruitful.

It cannot be said, however, that the Portuguese made any strong effort to impose their culture upon the peoples of India, except in so far as the Christian missionaries endeavoured to gain converts by methods varying from exhortation to force. The Portuguese administrators in general respected Indian customs (with the exception of *sati* [suttee], the immolation of widows, which they forbade) and interfered very little with Indian life. Albuquerque, though he set up in Goa itself a form of government modelled upon that of Lisbon, left it largely to Indian officials to administer judicial and financial affairs that directly concerned the native community. In rural districts under Portuguese control he was firm in maintaining old customs and charters, while the authorities in Lisbon frequently and in considerable detail admonished his less scrupulous successors to put an end to vexatious interference by Portuguese officials with local self-government. There is ample evidence in collections of Portuguese documents to show that the home government and the more enlightened viceroys were generally actuated by liberal motives and were concerned for the bodies as well as the souls of their Indian subjects. But, it must be admitted, the record of events shows that the greed and ignorance of Portuguese functionaries was beyond the control of their superiors, while the proceedings of the Holy Office were marked by an intolerance and severity that bore hard upon both Hindu and Moslem, convert and heathen.

By the end of the sixteenth century the quality of Portuguese leadership, both military and civil, had sadly deteriorated, partly no doubt because of a failure of purpose at home, where the union of the Portuguese and Spanish crowns in 1580 appears to have destroyed the fine temper of the instrument that had been forged by adventure and hardship in earlier years. But other and not less important causes contributed to this decay. Chief among these was the debilitating effect of tropical life upon the Portuguese in India. They were perhaps the best fitted of all Europeans to withstand the influence of hot climates, but what was more insidious was the ease and luxury they enjoyed. All contemporary observers, both Portuguese and foreign, agree in their accounts of the mode of existence of the Portuguese soldiery. Descriptions of Golden Goa, of its buildings, its wealth, and its peculiar manners, show that it was a splendid city, where the humblest Portuguese gunner's mate, in the long intervals between voyages on active service, could live in lazy comfort. The soldier who, when he left Portugal, might have been a poor impressed peasant or even a jail-bird, found himself in India receiving the attentions, both amorous and domestic, of one of the ladies of mixed parentage who abounded in the colony a generation after Albuquerque's heroes were married to the widows of Moslems whom they had killed in the course of their professional duties. But this kind of intimate relationship did not serve to spread the benefits of European culture in India. On the contrary, it produced in the long run a dissolute society that was foreign to both Indian and Portuguese life, but contained some of the worst features of both. India had much more effect upon Portugal than Portugal upon India. The passengers on the annual voyages from Lisbon to the East used to throw overboard their spoons when they rounded the Cape of Good Hope, to show that they would thereafter eat rice with their fingers — a gesture sym-

bolic of their intention to drop European standards of behavior
and to indulge in an agreeable Oriental laxity. No menial tasks
were performed by Portuguese of whatever rank, for slaves were
plentiful and cheap. There were of course many sober and industrious officials and some soldiers who took their military profession seriously; but on the whole the life of the European in Goa
was devoted to the pursuit of pleasure while accumulating as much
wealth as possible without scrupulous regard to honesty.

The profits of trade and office, as well as sustaining the
pomp and luxury of Goa, went to the enrichment of the home
country, and here again the influence of India upon Europe was
great, while the influence of Europe upon India was negligible.
The wealth that poured into Europe from the Indies, from Africa,
and from Brazil changed the nature of life in Portugal. It produced
a lavish and elegant social life in Lisbon, which became one of the
most brilliant of European capitals. It fostered rapid advances in
the arts and sciences. The sixteenth century was the golden age
of Portuguese literature, and it saw an intellectual revival inspired
by the new knowledge as well as the new wealth drawn from the
Indies. Camoens wrote the great Portuguese epic, the *Lusiads,*
which was based upon the adventures of the conquistadores in
Asia, in which he himself played some part. Palaces, monasteries,
churches, and cathedrals rose up in greater numbers than ever before, and their style was influenced by motifs of form and decoration drawn from India and Africa.

By contrast there is little to record of Indian borrowing from
Portugal. The current of Indian life ran too deep and strong in its
ancient channels to be disturbed by the influence of a few thousand
strangers living among the teeming populations of Asia. In Indian
history the changing fortunes of kings have passed almost un-
noticed over the heads of most of their subjects. The conqueror
comes, but institutions remain unchanged because they are the
very substance of indigenous life, which the new master, in his
own interest, refrains from disturbing. Even those great waves of
invasion which have from time to time in her history seemed to
overwhelm wide regions of Indian territory lost their strength as
time elapsed, and the invaders were merged into the Indian scene
unless they came and stayed in such great numbers and for so long
as to penetrate into essential areas of Indian life, such as its laws
or its religion or its organization for agriculture and trade. No
such influence could possibly be exercised by the Portuguese, since
they were not only few in numbers but also indifferent to all but
their own immediate concerns. During the period of their power
in India they could exercise direct political authority over only a
few native people, and those mostly of low caste. Their settlement

at Goa was populated chiefly by Kanarins, who were small traders, shopkeepers, artisans, farmers, or fishermen, by bannias from Cambay and Surat, and by Mohammedans from Gujarat and other coastal regions in India, as well as from Persia and Arabia. There were few persons of education or quality, since most Brahmans and better-class Mohammedans were irked by foreign rule and preferred to move to Calicut or other Indian towns where they could enjoy liberty and respect.

The life of these humbler inhabitants was too poor to be open to Portuguese influence, except in one respect. They were open to conversion to the Christian faith because it offered some improvement in their lot by giving them a certain protection and a claim to charity. No doubt Christian doctrine had some appeal to many of them apart from material benefits, but the record of Christian missions in most Asiatic countries, it can scarcely be denied, does show that their most conspicuous successes, at least in point of numbers, have been achieved among simple folk whose daily life was deficient in comfort and consolation. To say this is not to underestimate the zeal and self-sacrifice of Christian missionaries, but to note the extreme difficulty of the task they undertake; for a people's religion, notably in Asiatic countries, is often the embodiment of all their traditional ways of feeling, thinking, and living. To disturb these is to subject them to a sometimes unbearable strain, to tamper with the roots of their existence.

In reading the voluminous literature of Christian enterprise in Asiatic countries one cannot fail to be impressed by the recurring theme of failure, the tales of promising pupils drawing back on the brink of conversion for fear of named or unnamed consequences. We have already seen William of Rubruck among the Tartars and the Saracens sadly confessing that for all his eloquence nobody would say: "I want to become a Christian." Sometimes the incidents are such as to arouse almost a comic despair, as in the story told by Rubruck of a certain Saracen who "on the day of Pentecost came to us, and when we began expounding the faith and when he heard of the blessings of God to man . . . said he wished to be baptized. But while we were making ready to baptize him he suddenly jumped on to his horse, saying he had to go home to consult his wife. The next day he said he could not possibly venture to receive baptism, for then he could not drink Cosmos." This was *kumiss,* a fermented liquor that in Mongol life was regarded as essential to health, whereas the Christians living among the Mongols would not allow that a man could take intoxicants and remain in the faith.

This early example can be matched in the subsequent history of missions in India, in China, and, as we shall see, in Japan. The more highly developed a civilization, the less easily could it accommodate an alien principle without damage to its own nature. This was particularly true of India, where the native religion was not only of high antiquity but also so closely related to daily life as to furnish its substance as well as its form. For a Hindu of high caste the adoption of Christian tenets meant the abandonment of beliefs and practices that together constituted his very mode of existence in the community to which he belonged. An intending convert was faced with virtual expulsion from the society of which he was an important member even if he could bring himself to accept intellectually the doctrines put before him.

The Christian missionaries in India were confronted with this obstacle as soon as they perceived that their purpose of spreading the gospel in India could not be adequately served if they confined themselves to bringing within the fold the poor, the humble, and the oppressed. They must make an effort to convince Indians of education and rank that Christian doctrine was, if not superior to, at least not incompatible with the religious and social habits of Brahmans and other believers in Hinduism.

It was not until 1606 — after a hundred years of missionary effort — that the Jesuit father Roberto de Nobile, with the approval of the Society of Jesus, undertook a serious study of Hinduism in order to learn how it could best be criticized and confuted. Before that the Portuguese in India had gained some knowledge of the nature of Indian religious beliefs and had come to understand that many Indian social institutions had a basis in religious principles. They no longer supposed that Hinduism was something corrupt and barbarous, without theological or metaphysical foundations; but they saw only very dimly that its philosophy was far-reaching and profound. Father de Nobile devoted himself to arduous research into sacred texts at Madura, the chief seat of learning in southern India, where he was able by his ascetic habits and scholarly zeal to persuade a number of Brahmans to assist him. After some years of intense study and discussion he produced a work in Sanskrit that, it appears, presented a syncretic plan designed to reconcile on a high plane the Brahmanistic and Christian philosophies. This experiment failed, for though he persuaded some Brahmans to receive baptism, he found himself obliged, in order to gain general acceptance of his thesis, to give way on many subsidiary points of doctrine and ceremony. We need not here go into details, but those who like to disinter ecclesiastical controversies will find a rich deposit in such works as the *Storia do Mogor* of Nicolas Manucci. In his description of Mogul India this engaging Venetian shows what a pitch of acrimony had been reached a century after de Nobile's time by disputes between the Jesuits and other orders over what the latter called the "unholy compromise" with Hinduism. For our purpose it is sufficient to note the general nature of the issue, which was fought with a degree of invective, intrigue, and even persecution that must have given to cultivated Brahmans a strange idea of the practice of Christian virtues by their professional exponents in India.

In order to secure Hindu converts, the Jesuits in the light of their experience deemed it permissible to make many concessions to Indian customs. Other orders, in particular the Capuchins, charged them with a long list of offences, which included allowing the use of heathen charms or medallions (the *talī*) at weddings, performing marriage rites of girls of six or seven years of age, permitting superstitious ceremonies such as the symbolization of sex by the leaves of the pipal tree, and — most serious of all — recognition of the caste system by permitting the use of the ashes of burnt cow-dung for caste-marks and by discriminating among castes in administering the sacraments. The following extract from a Capuchin manifesto addressed to the Governor and Council of Pondicherry in 1707 will give some idea of the method as well as the matter of controversy between missionaries in this question of the Rites or, as it was called, the Accommodation:

You should not wonder, gentlemen, if the Malabari Christians, who had nothing about them of the heathen when under the guidance of their legitimate shepherd, have become more heathen than Christian after falling under the rule of thieves and robbers. You who are on the spot see every day the poor Christians smearing themselves over like masqueraders. Some cover their bodies with heathen marks, others cover their foreheads with cow's ashes. . . . The men wear jewels in their ears representing the attributes of false gods, the women hang *talīs* on their necks with a cross on one side and the head of an idol on the other. These ornaments are blessed by the reverend Jesuit fathers, and in their church they cause them to be put by the bridegroom upon the bride. One caste is separated from another in church, and the wretched pariahs receive the Most Holy Sacrament at the door, while other castes are admitted to the Holy Table.

Into the merits of this controversy we need not enter. It is adduced here only to show that when the Portuguese attempted to impose the religious elements of their culture upon a people whose institutions were more ancient and deeply rooted than their own, they laid bare a fundamental conflict between two civilizations. This experience was repeated in all the Far Eastern countries that they tried to convert, though it differed somewhat both in kind and in degree according to the nature of the resistance they encountered. Their successes and failures in India, Farther India, Indonesia, China, and Japan have each their peculiar character;

and a comparative study of the work of Christian missions in all those regions throws much light upon the nature of their respective civilizations. The reception of Christianity by the Japanese in particular shows some special features that contribute to an understanding of their later history in so far as it displays a readiness to consider imported doctrines.

While dealing with the subject of conversion it may be useful at this point to say a little about the development of Islam in India. It is obvious that the circumstances in which the Mohammedan faith was spread in India were very different from those in which Christianity was presented to the Indian peoples. In the first place, Islam was brought to their notice from a very early date by a series of invasions and conquests over the northwest land frontier, which put Moslems into close and often violent contact with Hindus over a long period. Even if we leave out of account early raids upon northern provinces by Arabs and other Moslem invaders, we may say that great parts of India were under strong and continuous Islamic influence onwards from about 1200, when the first Mohammedan dynasty was established.

Christianity first came to the knowledge of Hindus through the presence of Nestorians, perhaps as early as A.D. 400, but they cannot be said to have exerted any important religious influence, since they were confined to one locality and were refugees with no political power behind them. Subsequently, when Christianity was again introduced on the Malabar coast by the Portuguese, it was in conditions of temporal supremacy almost negligible in contrast with the extent and duration of Moslem rule in the rest of India. Therefore no valid comparison can be made between the two religions in point of success in gaining proselytes during the period with which we are now concerned. But there are some facts as to the attitude of the Mohammedan rulers towards the religion of their Hindu subjects which have a bearing upon the problem of conversion encountered by the Jesuits and other Christian evangelists.

The history of Mohammedan rule in India includes episodes of religious persecution ranging from forced conversion to massacre, but during the long period and over the great areas covered by Mohammedan conquest and occupation of Indian territory these were surprisingly rare and sprang rather from the fanaticism or the cruelty of individual sultans than from a consistent policy of making proselytes by force or by very severe discrimination. The Arab conquest of Sind, which took place at the time when the Prophet's successors were threatening Christendom in western Europe, had little effect upon the rest of India. It was accompanied by some massacres, as when the Moslem commander in 711 slaughtered all the Brahmans in a captured city who refused to accept Islam. But later even he, when the heat of battle had subsided, treated Hindus with tolerance so long as they did not resist him. For a century or so the Arab masters of Sind respected the authority of the caliphs, but gradually they became independent of Bagdad and concurrently relaxed the strict application of the Koranic law, so that, while endeavouring (not without some success) to propagate Islam by persuasion, they were wise enough, in view of their own small numbers, to leave the Hindus and their worship undisturbed.

The later dynasties of Mohammedan invaders of India, the so-called Ghaznevids and their successors, included certain rulers who figure in Indian history as intolerant bigots.[13] But, with these exceptions, in practice Hindus usually enjoyed under Mohammedan rule a great deal of religious freedom. The strict interpretation of the Koranic law requires an orthodox Moslem to exert himself in waging a holy war *(jihad)* against non-Moslem countries so as to bring their peoples within the realm of Islam. Early Islam allowed some moderation in the treatment of *ahl-i-Kitab,* "people of the Book" — that is, Jews and Christians, who followed a sacred scripture and were not idolaters. They were accordingly permitted, while suffering certain civil disabilities such as a poll-tax, to practice their own religion unobtrusively and to retain their own property.

Other infidels in conquered countries were in theory either killed or made slaves unless they accepted Islam. But this rigid doctrine was generally disregarded by Mohammedan rulers, partly because it was politically inexpedient in countries where Moslems were in a minority and depended upon the collaboration of their native subjects and partly because they themselves, by the lapse of time and their independence of the Caliphate, grew more moderate. Indeed, many of the sultans and emperors who reigned in India were themselves lukewarm believers, while some of them displayed a considerable interest in Indian religion and philosophy.[14]

13 Among them were Ala-ud-din, who introduced (1296–1316) discriminating laws against Hindus, which were cruelly administered; Firuz Tughluq (1351–88), who was at times tolerant and at times cruel; Sikandar Lodi (1489–1517), a bigot who destroyed Hindu temples; Jalal-ud-din (1414–32), a Hindu convert to Islam who persecuted and forcibly converted Hindus in Bengal and is thought to have been in part responsible, by his vigorous campaign of proselytization, for the present high proportion of Moslems in that province; Sikandar of Kashmir (1394–1416), known as the Iconoclast for his fury against idolaters, who was so ferocious in his zeal that under duress many apostatized in his kingdom, with the result that Hindus are in a minority in Kashmir today. Aurangzeb among the Mogul emperors was the most thoroughgoing and consistent in his policy of suppressing Hinduism and encouraging conversion to Islam by discriminatory laws.

14 Such as Zain-ul-Abidin (son of Sikandar the Iconoclast), who was a patron of learning and had Hindu works translated into Persian.

Akbar had dreams of a universal religion, and Ala-ud-din long be-fore him had some ideas of the same kind; neither regarded Islam as the quintessence of spiritual truth, and indeed Akbar was ready to abjure it in the interest of toleration. Moreover many Moham-medan rulers were in close relation with Hindu sovereigns through political or matrimonial alliances and some employed Hindus in high offices. Altogether it may be said that in general the sultans and emperors were remarkably tolerant of a faith that by strict Moslem standards was idolatrous and even obscene.

It might be supposed that, because Moslem dynasties enjoyed some degree of temporal power in India for almost a millennium, in the last half of which their supremacy was hardly contested north of the Deccan plateau, the progress of Islam would have been so great as to bring something near to an equality of numbers as between Hindu and Moslem. Conditions were in many respects favourable to conversion. Material benefits, such as lucrative em-ployment and security, might well dispose many classes of the Hindu population to change their faith, and Hindus of low caste or in particular those who were outcastes might find a strong in-centive in the improved social status that was open to them on con-version, since Islam knows no caste distinction. There were, more-over, wide regions of India where the religion of the people was only a rudimentary Hinduism or an indigenous animism with some Hinduistic tinge. Yet an examination of the facts shows that the success of Islam was much less than might be expected on a superficial view. The areas in which Moslems predominate are the sparsely populated North-west Frontier Province, Baluchistan, Sind, and the Punjab, all regions that geographically and histori-cally are close to lands where Islam was always strong. They are also in a majority in parts of Bengal, which contained a great num-ber of aboriginal people who were never fully Hinduized and who were persecuted by Jalal-ud-din in the early part of the fifteenth century; and in Delhi, which was the seat of the Mogul emperors.

Moslems comprised (in 1941) slightly less than one fourth of the total population of India. This is, of course, a high proportion, and the presence of so many adherents to a foreign religion is a fact of great importance in the history of religions as well as a po-litical phenomenon without close parallel. But, seen from the his-torical viewpoint, the success of Islam in India has been less than might have been expected in circumstances so favourable for its spread. Its strength in the northwestern provinces in the Punjab is due in some measure to immigration, in eastern Bengal to the fact that it was imposed upon backward people. These are parts of India in which the military and political supremacy of the Mohammedan invaders became overwhelming as they gradually moved eastward and established themselves from the Hindu Kush to the Ganges delta. But southward of this area the influence of Islam progressively diminishes. Today in British India the percentage of Moslems in the United Provinces is 15, in Bombay 9, in Madras 6,[15] in the Central Provinces 4, in Orissa 2. These figures tend to show that, despite its great advantages as the religion of long-established conquerors who were able to use every method of conversion from persuasion to force, Islam did not make a great impression upon Indian thought. It is true that the majority (probably nine tenths) of Moslems in India today are not the descendants of Moslem immigrants but of converted Hindus. Nevertheless, in terms of proportions, the success of Islam in India is not comparable to its success among the population of Persia, Egypt, and Indonesia.

The reasons are clear enough. Hinduism was a system of thought and behaviour at least as powerful and deeply rooted as the faith of the Moslems, and though there were under the Moguls some movements towards fusion, the two systems are fundamentally irreconcilable.

Islam has the remarkable power of creating a community of feeling between peoples of different racial or national origins. This is due not only to its simple and direct nature, but also to its attitude towards converts, who, in theory at least, are treated on an equal footing with all other Moslems and subjected to no discrimination on grounds of race or colour or social position. For this reason it proved attractive to many Indians; but as a theology it could not compete with Hinduism, which has a prodigious amplitude. It is for this reason that where efforts were made to reach a compromise between Islamic and Hinduistic ideas, it was usually the Hinduistic element that in time prevailed.

The history of these syncretic movements brings out an interesting aspect, sometimes overlooked, of the influence of one religion upon another. Attempts from outside to alter a system of thought[16] sometimes produce a reaction that strengthens rather than moderates that which it is proposed to change.

The two chief examples of compromise between Hinduism and Islam seem to bear this out. The first is the small sect founded by Kabir in the fifteenth century. He was a Moslem who believed in one God, of both Hindu and Moslem, and rejected caste and idola-

15 The Moslems in Madras province include a great number who are descendants of communities of Arab traders settled in seacoast towns since very early times, some even before the earliest invasions.

16 This is true also of other than religious traditions. Foreign artistic influences sometimes bring about an intensification of a national tradition, and, in modern times at least, foreign political doctrines tend to produce a traditionalist reaction in countries to which they are recommended.

try. But though his teaching excluded these two important features of Hinduism it retained the Indian idea of transmigration, and his successors seem to have reverted to pantheism and to have laid increasing emphasis on the traditional Indian sentiment that matter is unreal and illusory.[17] Following upon Kabir came a more important and far-reaching movement of amalgamation which was led by Nanak (1469–1538), the founder of the Sikh religion. He was a Hindu who was influenced by the teaching of Kabir and desired a means of reconciling Islam with Hinduism. He, like Kabir rejecting caste and idolatry, taught that there is but one God, and his concept of the nature of God is nearer to Mohammedan than to Indian thought. But he could not divest himself of the traditional Indian idea that the universe is uncreated and unreal except in the sense that it is an expansion of the Deity, and he held to the doctrine of reincarnation.

Under his successors the sacred book known as the Granth was composed, no doubt as an equivalent to the Koran, and Nanak's sect developed into a national community. Though its growth was influenced by the example of Mohammedanism in that it depended upon a sacred book and its leaders claimed both spiritual and temporal authority, its beliefs and practices were not such as to win the approval of devout Moslems or orthodox Brahmans, so that the Sikh community tended to acquire a separate social as well as religious indentity and in time developed a distinct political character. Its fifth Guru or leader, Arjun, displeased the Mogul Emperor Akbar, who approved of eclecticism in religion and even promulgated a new creed of his own but did not like the aggressive qualities of the Sikhs. In time the community became so hostile to the Mogul government that Arjun was put into prison, where he died; and thereafter the Sikhs became a militant society, making war upon Mohammedans.

This curious evolution of a sect designed by its founder to reconcile the two faiths seems to teach that experiments in composing religious differences are likely to be disappointing and even dangerous. At least it shows that Hinduism has great powers of resistance to change, for the Sikhs today, while antagonistic to Islam, do not hold any strictly religious beliefs that are objectionable to Hindus. The truth is that Hinduism is not so much a religion that has created Indian beliefs and customs as the expression in religious form of ancient and stubborn Indian sentiments. It is, as was pointed out by Sir Charles Eliot,[18] "not a religion which has moulded the national character, but the national character finding expression in religion." It is not to be wondered at, therefore, that

[17] Though this sentiment appears also in Islam among the Sufis.
[18] In his *Hinduism and Buddhism* (New York: Longmans, Green & Co.; 1921).

Christian evangelism in India should have made little headway with a task which, to be successful, must destroy much of the life that it endeavours to reform.

It should be understood that the cost of the ecclesiastical establishment in India was borne by the Portuguese crown. In recompense for political and commercial concessions granted to the King of Portugal by papal bulls, the crown undertook to further the interest of the Church in new-found lands. The whole undertaking of the Estado da India was thus conceived of as an extension of the personal domain of the sovereign rather than as a national enterprise. All expenditure was met and all income was received by the royal treasury. The King was under obligation to finance out of the profits that he received from his monopoly of trade the work of evangelization as well as the foundation and support of bishoprics, seminaries, churches, and clergy. This special feature of Portuguese colonial enterprise, known as the Padroado, naturally influenced the nature of the ecclesiastical organization in countries under Portuguese rule or control, and in the long run it hampered missionary effort in the East, since it prevented the Holy See from co-ordinating the work of the separate Catholic missions and gave rise to many unseemly rivalries both national and personal. It was not until 1622 that the organ known as the Propaganda (that is, the Sancta Congregatio de Propaganda Fide) was established in Rome for the purpose of superintending the propagation of the faith in foreign countries; and even then the claims of Portugal under the Padroado made it difficult for Rome to assert authority.

The Portuguese missionaries who first reached India were ill prepared for their task, being selected on no grounds other than their willingness to enter the field. In the days of the earlier governors and viceroys the churchmen had to submit to the requirements of the military commanders. A few Dominicans arrived in Goa in 1510, and Albuquerque more than once had to curb their intolerant zeal when he found them acting counter to his policy. But gradually the influence of the Church grew to a point where it could challenge and thwart the secular authority. The Franciscans established themselves in Goa in 1517, and from their headquarters there they visited other parts of India, Burma, Ceylon, and the Malay Archipelago. They were the dominant order in India for over twenty years, and their efforts were regarded by the Pope as so successful that in 1534 he made Goa a bishopric with spiritual jurisdiction over all Portuguese possessions between the Cape of Good Hope and China. It became an archbishopric in 1557. The first bishop was a Franciscan friar, who arrived in Goa in 1538. Soon after, in 1542, St. Francis Xavier came to Goa and founded the College of St. Paul, for the training of native missionaries. His ardour and energy contributed to the growth not only of the influence of the Jesuits in India but also to the general increase of arbitrary ecclesiastical power throughout the Portuguese Empire in Asia.

The Church had moreover the strong support of the King of Portugal, who instructed all his viceroys that they must encourage the spread of the Christian religion not only by direct missionary efforts but also by the grant of special privileges to converts. Taking advantage of this royal patronage, the religious orders committed many acts of intolerant bigotry, such as the destruction of all Hindu temples on the island of Goa in 1540 and the confiscation of temple funds subscribed by villagers.[19] Ecclesiastical courts tried and condemned heretics even before the Inquisition was set up in Goa (1560), and the civil power was obliged to carry out their sentences. In 1546 a Vicar-General invested with great powers by the King carried out such violent measures of persecution that he was poisoned, and the Bishop of Goa was accused of complicity in the crime. He was defended by Xavier against this charge, but the fact that it was made shows how disgraceful were the relations between the religious orders and the clergy, and how unruly were all the ecclesiastics in India at this time. Apart from their subversive behavior, which greatly hindered civil administration, their pecuniary claims were a serious drain upon the royal revenues, and it is probable that expenditure upon ecclesiastical establishments, combined with private breaches of the royal monopoly, was one of the factors that in the long run brought about the bankruptcy of Portuguese India. The King was warned of this danger as early as 1552 by an honest official,[20] who pointed out that such ardent and costly promotion of Christianity was having the effect of depopulating the country under Portuguese rule, because "there are some who want to force people to be Christians and who worry the Hindus so that people fly from the land."

When Xavier, sent by the Pope as nuncio and by the King as inspector of missions, arrived in India he reported that the moral and religious condition of the colonists was deplorable. Writing in 1545, he spoke bitterly of the corruption and greed of Portuguese officials and said that after his experience in India he never ceased to wonder at the number of new inflections that had been added to the conjugation of the verb "to rob." It was not long after this that Xavier, disgusted with conditions in Portuguese India, de-

---

[19] A curious form of persecution, which has its humorous aspect, was to compel Hindus resident in Goa to listen to sermons of one hour in length on alternate Sundays.

[20] This was Simão Botelho, a revenue officer, who in 1543 was denied absolution because he had attempted to reform the customs at Malacca without obtaining the approval of the Dominicans.

cided to spend no more time there but to strike out for China and Japan. Allowance must be made for the rigour of Xavier's standards of behaviour, but there can be no doubt that most of the clergy in Goa were lax and self-indulgent, if not positively corrupt. The city was crowded with priests. It had eighty churches and convents by about 1550, yet its religious activity scarcely extended beyond the narrow zones directly ruled by Portugal, and there was little missionary activity in Indian territory. It was due chiefly to the inspiration of Xavier that the Jesuits took the lead in missionary work, which carried them beyond India to the Far East, where in their struggle against great hardships and dangers they displayed an astonishing combination of patient self-sacrifice and intolerant zeal.

Note on CHAPTER 4

THE INQUISITION IN INDIA. It is interesting to note that the Inquisition was more vigorous in India than in the African and American colonies. It was not introduced into Africa until 1626, and its activity was small. In Brazil, though active intermittently, it was of no great importance.

In India, on the other hand, it was asked for by Xavier as early as 1546, though it was not inaugurated until 1560. The first auto-da-fé took place in 1563. There were 19 victims in 1575, 17 in 1578, and these numbers appear to have been usual. The charge usually brought against Hindus was that of practising magic.

The classic account of the Inquisition at Goa is that of Dellon, and Manucci's *Storia do Mogor* gives valuable detail. In Portuguese there is *A Inquisiçao de Goa,* by Antonio Baião (Coimbra, 1920). This is a selection of reports by the inquisitors to their superiors in Lisbon and of instructions from Lisbon, between 1569 and 1630. They contain much detail, including a good deal about sodomy, an offence that was vigorously attacked.

Maurice Collis: *The Land of the Great Image* (New York: Alfred A. Knopf; 1943) contains a summary of Dellon's experiences.

It need hardly be said that the special interest of the history of the Inquisition in Asia lies in its application of ecclesiastical law to native peoples with the support of the civil authority of Portugal. It was this kind of thing that stimulated both theologians and jurists in the sixteenth century to consider the legal bases of European relations with the native inhabitants of colonies and thus gave rise to the arguments of Grotius and others concerning a *jus naturale* or *jus gentium* of universal validity.

CHAPTER
5

THE CONFRONTATION OF EUROPE AND ASIA

1. India

THE SETTLEMENT of numerous Europeans upon Asiatic soil brought about the first true confrontation since classical times of European and Asiatic cultures. Though it was on the small scale already described and never reached the dimensions of later British settlement in Indian territory and intervention in Indian affairs, the contact between Portuguese and Indians was extremely close. It was not of sufficient scope, however, to make any impression upon Indian life, except perhaps as one of a number of disturbing influences, among which Mohammedan rule was far more important. The presence of the Portuguese in India was scarcely felt except by a few individuals in a few places. Its effect is to be found in a wider field, for what the Portuguese did was to make India aware of the existence of Europe, to alter the direction of Indian foreign trade, and, because Portuguese naval and military forces were used in conflicts between Indian rulers, to exercise some influence upon the rise and fall of Indian states. But all these things in combination did little to modify the domestic history of India, and it is probable that had the Portuguese abandoned their Indian empire at the end of the sixteenth century they would have left even less trace than did the Greeks, Scythians, and Parthians — perhaps some coins, some mutilated words in the language of the bazaars, some dwindling communities of mixed blood, and some fading traditions of foreign warriors and priests.

The contact of peoples, even on a much greater scale than that of the meeting between Indians and Portuguese, does not necessarily result in the transfer of ideas unless they are of transcendent power or are the property of a civilization manifestly superior to that which they confront. These were not the conditions in which the two peoples met, for each saw the other as backward in the arts of living and misguided in things of the spirit.

At least in the early days of their power in India there was little in the conduct of the Portuguese to show that they had any feeling of superiority on account of race or colour. They had full confidence in their military prowess, but they appear in their social intercourse to have mixed freely with Indians on terms of equality. Even with their Mohammedan rivals, though at first they displayed bitter enmity and though Christian knights professed in sanguinary metaphor that they could best do penance for their sins by washing their hands in infidel blood, they later established close personal relationships in many well-known cases. It was a matter of policy with Albuquerque to encourage mixed marriages between Portuguese soldiers and Indian women. He hoped thus to create, particularly in Goa, a settled population of fighters and skilled workmen who, while loyal to Portugal, would feel that India was their home. He found no difficulty in carrying out this plan, for the Portuguese men-at-arms, quite apart from the strong promptings of masculine instinct, had no prejudice against mixed blood. Indeed, Portuguese history had been such that her population contained a strong admixture of Semitic and African elements, so that there was no common feeling against miscegenation.[1]

Long contact with the Saracens had left in Portuguese minds an idealized picture of a *Moura encantada,* an enchanted Mooress, as the most desirable type of woman, "brown-skinned, black-eyed, enveloped in sexual mysticism." [2] It is not surprising, therefore, that Portuguese rule in Asia should have left some visible legacies, for there grew up in course of time, particularly at Goa and along the Malabar coast, a numerous population of mixed blood, part Portuguese, part Indian. Its members, at least nominally Christian, perpetuated their religion and some other features of Portuguese culture that can still be discerned in India and Ceylon and throughout the Far East. The Portuguese language, though in a corrupt form, became a kind of lingua franca, and Portuguese names are common in most seaports on the coasts of southern Asia. The influence of these mixed communities was reinforced by the evangelizing zeal of the Roman Church, while the native populations of territories under Portuguese control, irrespective of race or creed, naturally took some colour from their European masters, who were

---

[1] Freyre, in his *Brazil* (New York: Alfred A. Knopf; 1945), says: "Iberian culture rests upon an accommodation of diverse elements, Christians, Moors, Jews . . . and the general result was integration rather than segregation. . . . It is difficult to find a modern people with a more heterogeneous cultural pedigree. Ligurians, Celts, Gauls, Phœnicians, Carthaginians, Romans, Suevi, Goths, Jews, Moors, Germans, French, English, and a large number of Negroes and some East Indians *before* the colonization of Brazil."

[2] Gilberto Freyre: *Casa Grande & Senzala* (*The Masters and the Slaves*; New York: Alfred A. Knopf; 1946).

obliged to employ them in large numbers as clerks and artisans, since the Portuguese themselves were short of men.

2. Southeast Asia

THE PORTUGUESE reached Malacca as early as 1509, but the first visit, made by a squadron under Diogo Lopes, was unsuccessful. The Malays were hostile and the Portuguese reckless and overbearing, so that a large number of his men were seized and held in captivity. The importance of Malacca to the Portuguese was vital if they were to carry out their plans of trade monopoly. As Ormuz and Aden commanded the approaches to the Persian Gulf and the Red Sea, so Malacca commanded the gateway from the Indian ocean to the Pacific, and consequently the maritime trade routes from India to Java and the spicy Moluccas, China, and Japan. Malacca was moreover an emporium for the distribution of merchandise from those places to Siam and Indo-China. Full control of shipping along all these routes was impossible unless the Portuguese had a suitable base, and therefore Albuquerque, as soon as he had completed his arrangements at Goa, led an expedition to Malacca in 1511.

Malacca was inhabited or visited during the trading season by a mixed population of Malays and Javanese, together with traders from Gujarat, Malabar, the Coromandel coast, and China, as well as some silent hard-bitten men from Japanese ships. Most of the Indian traders were of the Moslem faith, as were also the local rulers, descendants of refugees who had been defeated in civil wars in Java early in the fifteenth century; but it seems that each community had its own leader and that all lived together in comparative harmony. The town was rich and the Mohammedan traders soon saw that the Portuguese threatened their fortunes. After some unsuccessful parleys in which Chinese traders gave assistance to Albuquerque he decided to attack. The defence was stubborn, and it was not until the tenth day of bombardment and desperate fighting that Albuquerque was able to establish himself on shore. A fortress was rapidly built. The town was thoroughly plundered. The rajah of the Javanese community, a Mohammedan, was treacherously killed, but his adherents were not subdued and, moving not far away, for many years they made the position of the Portuguese uncomfortable.

Albuquerque and his successors never tried seriously to conquer territory or to rule over native populations in Malaya or Indonesia. Their object was to control shipping and to monopolize the spice trade. Consequently, satisfied that they could hold Malacca as a naval base, they lost no time in sending expeditions to Siam, China, and the Moluccas. This last was of the greatest immediate importance, for a monopoly of the spice trade, besides bringing great pecuniary gain, would contribute to the grand political design of Portugal, which was to seize the source of income that maintained the prosperity of the trading cities of Syria and Egypt and thus to strike a blow at the finances of the Sultan of Turkey, who, as we have seen, depended in an important degree upon these trading profits for the maintenance of his naval power in the Mediterranean. We need not trace the complicated details of Portuguese fighting and intrigue in the archipelago, but some general account of their activities is of interest as throwing light upon their relations with the people of Indonesia.

The problem of stopping the transport of spices from Indonesia to the Red Sea and the Persian Gulf was not difficult for the Portuguese with their superior sea power. They had enough well-armed ships to make it hard for the Moslem traders to get their freight through the blockade. But there were other problems, since the Portuguese must make sure of securing the spices themselves from the centres of production. Here they were unfortunate, because most of the people living in the coastal regions of the islands were of the Mohammedan faith, though only recently converted; and to reconcile their two conflicting purposes of fighting Islam and obtaining spices was a task requiring political skill and tact, which the Portuguese, schooled in brusquer methods, did not as a rule possess. They found themselves therefore in some anomalous situations. On one occasion they allied themselves with the ruler of a kingdom in the interior of Java who was an enemy of Islam, and so found themselves supporting a devotee of Shiva, one of the divinities of Hinduism. At another time, in order to secure a monopoly of the clove trade, they entered into an alliance with the Sultan of Ternate (a small island off Halmahera in the Moluccas), who was so strongly given over to Islam that he would have no dealings with islanders of other faiths. They thus were tied to an enemy of Christianity, and the Jesuit missionaries, many of whom were not Portuguese and therefore not interested in Portuguese trade, protested violently to Goa and Lisbon.

It will be seen from these instances that the diffusion of Portuguese culture in Indonesia, in so far as it was represented by Catholic missionaries, had little success and poor prospects. The power of Islam at this period grew with remarkable speed, aided no doubt by the hostility of Moslem traders to the Portuguese, whose policy, if successful, would have deprived them of their wealth and their influence, both of which were considerable. Within some twenty years of the arrival of the Portuguese most of Java and large parts of Sumatra, Borneo, and the Moluccas had gone over to Islam, so that the Christian missionaries were obliged to direct their efforts to converting the pagan populations of regions that had not yet come under strong Moslem influence. It is for this reason that the principal Catholic missions were established on the island of Amboina, in the northern part of Halmahera, and on a few smaller islands.

It is not easy to explain fully the great proselytizing power of Islam, but there are certain clear reasons for its success in the countries of southeast Asia and for the failure of Christian missions to compete with it. Among these is the fact that the Moslem trading communities on the Malabar coast and their counterparts in Indonesia (who came mostly from Gujarat) were peaceful and well-behaved, they brought prosperity to the cities in which they resided, and so long as they were fairly treated by local rulers, they did not attempt to acquire political power. On the Indian coast, as we know from the testimony of travellers, the good behaviour of the Moslems rested upon the tolerant attitude of the Indian rulers, who allowed to each alien community the free use of its own customs and religion. The Persian traveller Abd-ur-razzak, who visited Calicut in 1442, said of that place: "Security and justice are so firmly established that merchants bring thither from maritime countries considerable cargoes, which they unload and unhesitatingly send to the markets and bazaars, without thinking of the necessity of checking the accounts or watching over the goods. . . . Every ship, whatever place it may come from or wheresoever it may be bound, when it puts into this port is treated like other vessels and has no trouble of any kind to put up with." It is not surprising that the people among whom these Moslems lived should have looked upon the Portuguese as barbarous and cruel by comparison, and should have thought little of a religion professed by men who flouted native customs and beliefs and whose object was to oust other traders by force and fraud.

In Malaya and Indonesia the Arab traders did not, it is true, encounter a civilization so high as that of southern India, and no doubt they had, at times, to take forcible measures to defend themselves against attack. But they were generally satisfied if they could establish a self-governing community of their own, and if they made converts, it was because the Malay rulers with whom they came into contact were pagans impressed by the superior culture of the Arabs and ready to share in the prosperity they could bring. Their Hinduism was perhaps wearing thin and did not offer the same resistance to Islam as did the more ancient and deeply rooted beliefs of the Brahmans in India, while Islam in these remote parts was not too exacting. It was thus not difficult for the Moslem communities in Malaya and Indonesia gradually to acquire personal and then political influence, and as their political influence grew, the half-civilized people within their orbit voluntarily adopted Islam. They might perhaps have adopted Christianity had the Portuguese been able to exercise a widespread and stable authority, just as most of the inhabitants of the Philippine Islands became Christians under the firm and continuous rule of Spain. But the Portuguese came too late, and the Arabs were Asiatic enough to know how to deal with Asiatic peoples and how to avoid the blunders of Europeans who had no consistent policy and vacillated between force and persuasion.

The Portuguese settlements in Malacca and the Moluccas were under constant threat, but despite their precarious situation they were able to extend their trading activities, gaining a large share in the export of pepper from Bantam, in western Java, of nutmeg from the Banda Islands, and of cloves from the Moluccas. These successes had results that were ultimately to the disadvantage of the Portuguese. The great abundance of Eastern produce that reached Lisbon through Portuguese channels had to be purchased there for distribution to European markets by merchants from Holland, England, and other trading countries because the Portuguese had no organization of their own for this purpose. They had destroyed the efficient arrangements that existed up to the close of the fifteenth century by expelling the Portuguese Jews by whose capable hands their commerce had been managed. The English and the Dutch, no longer able to visit the Lisbon market because of their war with Spain, were stimulated to open their own trade channels with India and the Far East.

By the closing years of the sixteenth century the fabric of empire of the Portuguese in Asia was showing signs of collapse. They had built it up by remarkable military valour and proud self-confidence, but they were wanting in the discipline and the consistent national purpose that were necessary if it was to be preserved. They left a name in the Far East for bravery, but the alien peoples with whom they dealt and whom they often maltreated did not regret their downfall, and even in many places hastened it by taking sides with their rivals when the Dutch and the English began to appear in Eastern seas to challenge the exclusive claims of the Portuguese and to follow their trading example without the complications of Christian evangelism. Even so, individual Portuguese traders held out for a long time against their competitors. Their "inter-port" carrying trade in Asiatic waters was efficiently organized by private enterprise and continued to prosper until the end of the eighteenth century.

We need not pay detailed attention to the doings of the Portuguese traders in Farther India, the countries now known as Burma, Siam, and Indo-China; but a brief outline of their activities will help to round off the picture of intercourse between Europeans and Asiatics in the sixteenth century.

The Portuguese royal trade monopoly did not in practice extend to those countries. Albuquerque on his return from Malacca had sent envoys to Siam and Burma as well as to continental Indian states and he received missions from their rulers in those countries, who were impressed by Portuguese power when they learned of the capture of Goa. But Burma and Siam were far off the strategic route between Malacca and Goa, and did not supply the spices and other commodities that were the main object of the eastward voyages.[3] The trading opportunities those countries offered to the Portuguese were provided chiefly by their sale or purchase at Malacca of commodities which Moslem ships could carry only at the risk of confiscation or destruction by Portuguese patrols. These opportunities were seized by a number of private traders and adventurers who made their way to the coastal regions of the Bay of Bengal, where they found good customers among the wealthy Moslems of Upper India, which in the second half of the fifteenth century was under the rule of Mogul emperors. These men were either fugitives or persons of enterprising character to whom the official restrictions of Goa were irksome. They settled at Hugli, where they formed a considerable colony engaged in trade, some of which was legitimate, though it included a good deal of piracy, kidnapping, and dealing in slaves. Moving eastward a great number of them took employment as mercenaries in the armies of the warring kings of Arakan, Burma, and Siam.

Thus in the wars of the Burmese with Arakanese to the west, Shans to the north, and Siamese to the east, Portuguese soldiers of fortune played an important part, fighting on any side that offered an attractive reward. It often happened that Portuguese fought against Portuguese in this endemic warfare, which by the end of the sixteenth century had brought great areas of Lower Burma to famine and desolation. The Portuguese *Decadas* relate, for instance, that a well-known captain, Diogo Soares de Mello, in 1548 led an attack on Ayuthia, the Siamese capital, which was successfully resisted by mercenaries under another Portuguese, Diogo Pereira. On another occasion de Mello was employed by a Burmese king to crush rebels in his own dominions who in their turn were assisted by Portuguese soldiers. Some of these adventurers, not con-

---

[3] The Portuguese did, however, in 1519 establish a trading post at Martaban and another in Tenasserim, which commanded a relatively safe route overland to Siam. Here they sold some European products (cloth and velvets), but the chief imports were pepper from Sumatra, camphor from Borneo, and porcelain from China.

tent with paid military service, attempted to hold cities for themselves, as when Felipe de Brito took and retained for several years the town of Syriam, then the chief port of Pegu. When he was finally expelled by the King of Burma in 1613, the remnants of his force were taken as prisoners and settled in village communities whose descendants numbered four thousand by 1800.

It might be supposed that such exploits did not serve to promote the good name of Portugal, but the condition of Farther India in those days was so chaotic, murder and robbery and piracy were so rife, that by contemporary standards in those parts Portuguese soldiers were probably as much respected as they were feared and their buccaneering exploits were not thought of as exceptionally wicked. This is a point that should be borne in mind when considering the behavior of early European adventurers in Asia. They were living in an age of violence and misrule, when cruelty was common and pity was rare. The annals of Farther India from the period with which we are now concerned until about 1800 are black with episodes of barbarism and treachery. The Arakanese and the Burmese needed no lessons in those kinds of behaviour from their European assistants, though they did depend upon the steadfast bravery and the superior military skill of their Portuguese mercenaries. Their own raiders, carrying off slaves by hundreds from Bengal, "would pierce the hands of their captives, pass a strip of cane through the hole and fling them under the deck strung together like hens." Their kings would conduct themselves like Thirithudhamma, the Defender of the Faith in Arakan, who plucked out the hearts of six thousand of his subjects to serve as ingredients of an elixir of life; or like Bayinnaung, a devout Buddhist King of Burma, who offered the Portuguese immense sums for the Buddha Tooth in Kandy, but who lost tens of thousands of soldiers in insensate campaigns which not only laid waste the territory of his enemies but also depopulated the richest areas of his own country and spread abroad starvation and disease.

Conditions in India itself were little better, although the Mogul emperors, until their power collapsed, were competent, when they so desired, to administer their dominions with some respect for justice and the well-being of their subjects. Nobody can read the history of their dynasty without feeling that all their acts were governed by an assumption that the people must subserve the ends of the ruler, and that the ends of the ruler were the subjection of other peoples, for, as Akbar said, "a monarch should be ever intent upon conquest; otherwise his neighbours rise in arms against him." To serve this purpose of never-ending conquest the Oriental monarchs did not scruple to sacrifice the lives and the property of their own subjects as well as of their enemies, and they stopped at no treachery or duplicity in their relations with their rivals. This was true not only of Moslems but also of Hindus. The condition of the peasantry in Vijayanagar and other Indian kingdoms was no better than in the Mogul Empire. In rare times of peace they were subjected to an execrable tyranny by the tax-collector, and in times of war their fields were ravaged and their young men conscripted. The coming of the Portuguese did not, therefore, except in particular local instances, impose any unfamiliar hardships or oppression upon the native peoples of Asia or reveal to them any new variations upon the theme of cruelty. They accepted the strangers as a new kind of master, mentally odd and physically distasteful because they were *feringhi* or foreigners, but neither worse nor better than the despots to whom they were accustomed.

It would be wrong to suppose that the rough European intruders broke into scenes of Arcadian simplicity and happiness when they showed themselves upon Asiatic shores. Many unhappy things can be laid at the door of European expansion, but its pioneers cannot generally be charged with making conditions worse than they found them under the despots with whom they sometimes fought and sometimes made alliances. In some respects they even made efforts, admittedly imperfect, to remedy evils they perceived. This is true of a few administrators and officials, and of a great number of missionaries who faced tasks of supreme difficulty complicated by their own bigotry and the powerful traditions that it was their business to challenge.

In Farther India they met with peculiarly unfavourable conditions. The teeming life of its quarrelsome kingdoms, in its varied environment of swamp, jungle, and mountain or in cities richly adorned with palace and pagoda, was, beneath a brightly coloured surface of royal luxury and religious splendour, often poor and backward. Their peoples were of many different origins, principally Mongoloid, and their culture was a mixture of various elements, for a foundation of pagan beliefs which they had brought with them as they migrated from north and west had been overlaid by successive influences of Hinduism, of Buddhism, and, though in a much less degree, of Islam. The debt of the civilization of Burma, Siam, and Cambodia to India is immense, and in examining the influence of European culture upon Asiatic peoples it may not be out of place here to pay some brief attention to the way in which the powerful example of Indian life had, long before the arrival of Europeans, shaped the religious and social institutions of a vast region extending from the Bay of Bengal to the South China sea.

It is difficult to imagine what would have been the condition of this region if it had not come under the influence of India, which was clearly a potent civilizing force. Not much is known about early contacts, either as to their date or as to their nature, but certainly from at latest the beginning of our era, and probably much sooner, bands of migrants, companies of traders, and no doubt some colonizing expeditions began moving west from India by sea as well as by land routes and reached as far as Cambodia. The landward movements from eastern Bengal were probably peaceful in character, for the mountainous country of Arakan is such as to protect Burma against conquest on that side and at the same time to preserve its peoples from the forcible imposition of Indian culture. It is therefore the more remarkable that a country so isolated should bear so deep an imprint not only of Indian religion but also of Indian customs, art, and architecture, as well as having adopted an Indian alphabet and incorporated in native lore a good deal of Indian legend. The other countries of Farther India — Siam and Cambodia — also submitted to the same influences, at some times direct from India, at others from Ceylon, at others by way of China and possibly of Java or Sumatra.

We need not stop to examine the different histories of the development of Buddhism and other aspects of Indian civilization in these several countries, for they are extremely complex and in many respects uncertain. For our purpose it is sufficient to know that in the sixteenth century they all were, as they remain, Buddhist countries. They follow the early form of Buddhism, the simple teaching of the Hinayana rather than the later and more complex doctrines and practices of the Mahayana, so that they preserve much of a religion which has vanished in the country of its origin and elsewhere is to be found only in Ceylon. At times, indeed, Burma contained great centres of Buddhist learning, and there was close intercourse with southern India and Ceylon, which tended to support the older type of Buddhism against Mahayanist influences from other parts of India. Something of the same kind is true of Siam, although here the earliest introduction of the Hinayana probably was from Burma. As for Cambodia, its religious history begins with a combination of Mahayanism and Brahmanism, in which the latter predominated, and continues from about the end of the fifteenth century with a gradual transition by which under Siamese influence the older faiths were replaced by Hinayana Buddhism, though certain vestiges of Brahmanism were retained, especially in the ritual of official ceremonies. Religion in the now defunct Kingdom of Champa followed a somewhat similar course, but did not reach a point where Hinayana ousted Mahayana, because the influence of Annamites to the north was stronger than that of the Cambodians to the west, and the Annamites drew their religion and the other elements of their civilization from China rather than from India.

It will be seen that, with the exception of Annam, the countries of Farther India display a fairly uniform religious pattern which testifies to the vitality of Buddhism beyond the land of its birth. But the influence of Hinduism is equally remarkable. In Burma, though Buddhism was supreme, Brahmans were employed at court to perform certain ceremonies and to cast horoscopes; in Siam there were many Brahmanic ceremonies, supervised by Brahmans attached to the court; and in Cambodia also court and other public ceremonies preserved a good deal of Brahmanic ritual. In all three countries religion was closely associated with the state, and the sovereign, if not the head of the Church, was intimately concerned with religious matters. The life of the people was strongly impregnated with religious influences, for their frequent festivals were in essence acts of worship, their scholars and artists were servants of the faith, and their landscape was dominated, as it is today, by holy edifices.

It is clear that such an ancient and widespread religious tradition presented almost insuperable obstacles to the small missionary effort that Europeans were able to put forth in these Buddhist lands where, as in India, religion was not a mere ornament or adjunct to daily existence but an element that gave it colour, shape, and substance. Even Islam, which in the Malay Archipelago was strong enough to displace or at least substantially to modify a long-established Indian culture, had little success in Farther India. These were small Moslem communities in coastal areas, no doubt formed by Arab traders. A number of the people of Champa were at one time converts to Mohammedanism, and their descendants, the Chams, in Cambodia today are still of that faith. But in general it is true to say that Islam made no headway against Buddhism in Farther India, and the only alien influence that competed successfully with Indian culture was that of China, which, thanks to propinquity, was imposed upon Annam, where customs, beliefs, and writing have a strong Chinese character, though even here some traces of Hinduism remain.

Apart from the inherent difficulties of the task of conversion among peoples so devoted to Buddhism, there was another obstacle to missionary effort in the countries of Farther India. The Portuguese communities, consisting chiefly of ruthless men whose trade was robbery and slaughter, did not favour the presence of missionaries, who, besides disapproving of their sinful lives, might encourage rival traders to come and disturb their monopolies. Consequently, although from the lonely Christian outposts in east-tern Bengal or from Goa or Malacca a few friars did visit Arakan, Burma, Siam, and Cambodia, and a few churches were established in those countries, the fruits of their labours were scanty. But, strange to say, there were other Christians in Burma and Siam than the natives of those countries, for the bodyguards of their kings sometimes included fighting men from western Japan who had before leaving home joined the flock of Xavier and his followers when they preached the gospel in the feudal baronies of Kyūshū from 1550 onwards.

So it happened that when the Augustinian Manrique was in Arakan in 1630 he was visited by a Japanese captain who asked for spiritual consolation and for the friar's help in obtaining the King's consent to the building of a church. This soldier showed himself a devout Catholic, and he and his companions busied themselves on behalf of the friar by bringing silken hangings and flowers to ornament the room in which he celebrated Mass. This incident is of interest in that it illustrates the ubiquity of Christian propaganda in Asia, its spread from India to the remotest country of the East, and shows at the same time that while the Portuguese were everywhere on the move, Japanese adventurers could also find their way to distant countries.

There is one other aspect of missionary endeavour in Asia that may be suitably mentioned here. The Christian evangelists found much difficulty in gaining a hearing for their doctrines in countries where a powerful religion was already established and where a priestly body was well entrenched. They were handicapped by their ignorance of native languages and traditions and by a natural fear of foreign influence. What usually impressed the people among whom they worked was not the message that they brought, but their own personal qualities. Both simple and learned could recognize at once a man of high character and good breeding, for as a rule Asiatics show great discernment in their estimate of Europeans, their judgment being unclouded by irrelevant matters like social standing and conventions of behaviour. So it frequently happened that both dignitary and peasant, though not grasping the points in a missionary's discourse, were impressed by his learning or his dignity or his kindliness. This may seem to be a small point in the history of international intercourse, but the record of missions in many Asiatic countries shows that the soundness of a doctrine is often less important than the character of its exponent.

3. China

ALTHOUGH Portuguese power in Asia began to decline in the latter half of the sixteenth century, the activities of Portuguese traders and missionaries continued on an important scale for another hundred years, and their individual achievements, while not sufficient to arrest the decay of the military and political power of their country, exercised a considerable influence upon events in the Far East. In India and the Malay Archipelago, Portugal was handicapped not only by her own weakness at home and abroad but also by the growing strength of Islam and the rise of powerful European competitors. In China and Japan she was first in the field, and since both of these were highly organized states able to present a firm front to invading influences, her soldiers and traders no less than her missionaries soon discovered that they could not in those Far Eastern countries use the forceful methods they had employed in the Indies. It took them some time to learn this lesson, but after salutary experiences they gave up what ideas they may have nourished of gaining a colonial foothold like Goa, Diu, or Malacca and confined themselves to striving for the privilege to trade and preach within Chinese or Japanese dominions.

By about 1550 most thoughtful Portuguese leaders must have realized that they had enough to do to maintain their position in India and the Malay Archipelago and could not afford to extend their military responsibilities. They had great difficulty in holding Diu, which was in constant danger of attack from the Mohammedan sultans of Gujarat, sometimes in combination with the Turks. In 1538 the Sultan of Turkey sent a strong force that might well have defeated the Portuguese, since it was equipped with powerful artillery and skilful gunners. The Portuguese were saved by what had saved them often before — a want of unity among their enemies; but they could no longer count upon a permanent military superiority. Diu was again under attack in 1546 and was saved only by an extreme effort, which necessitated bringing reinforcements from other garrisons in India. The soldiers who went out to India in those years were poor material, and the quality of Portuguese leadership had sadly fallen, whereas the ecclesiastical power had notably increased. These facts are perhaps sufficient to explain why the Portuguese in China and Japan behaved, on the whole, with more moderation and more respect for native people than they had displayed in the Indies.

This is not to say that they were blameless from the beginning. The first expedition to China was that of Fernão Peres d'Andrade, who reached Canton from Malacca in August 1517. He carried an envoy to the Emperor of China, Thome Pires, who for two years was unable to obtain permission to make the journey to Peking. Andrade was able to load a good cargo in Canton, and was most careful to keep on good terms with the Chinese authorities. But the next visitor, his brother Simão d'Andrade, who came in 1519, outraged Chinese feelings by his conduct. He bought kidnapped children as slaves, built a small fort on the island of Lintin, tried to prevent other ships from loading, and refused to leave port when ordered. There were brawls in the streets of Canton, and in 1521 another Portuguese captain had to fight his way out to sea from Lintin.

The result of this unfortunate prelude to commercial intercourse was an embargo placed by the Chinese upon Portuguese traders so severe that any vessel carrying a Portuguese was liable to confiscation on reaching a Chinese port. The court at Peking was apprised of these events, and all prospects of a successful mission for the unfortunate envoy, Thome Pires, vanished if they had ever existed. When he at length reached Peking in 1521, he was sent back to Canton to be imprisoned, and there he died in captivity.

Although the official attitude of the Chinese was uncompromising, trade was not in practice discontinued. Chinese merchants were glad to take goods brought from other parts of China in Portuguese-owned ships, and the Portuguese traders were able to make profitable voyages to the Fukien coast, where they anchored off shore and engaged in barter. It was one of these vessels which, blown off its course by a storm, reached the shores of Japan in 1542 and, in the persons of a few Portuguese castaways, brought Europeans into contact for the first time with natives of that country upon their own soil. While the trading and missionary activity that followed shortly upon this incident was concurrent with similar activity in China, the position in Japan is better understood if it is considered with some reference to contemporary conditions in China. It is therefore convenient to treat of these first, though it should be understood that the Portuguese met with a much more friendly reception in Japan than in China and made a degree of progress in matters of commerce as well as religion which they did not for some time achieve in their dealings with the Chinese.

China under the Ming emperors, after the expulsion of the Mongols, regained for a time some of her lost power and prestige, but after the brief expansive phase that saw the great maritime expeditions of Yung-lo she entered upon a period of regression. When the first Western traders appeared in the South China seas she was disunited at home and weak abroad. She was on the defen-

sive both culturally and politically. The process of recovery from
the domination of the Mongols had, perhaps inevitably, brought
about a reaction in favour of the past, which took the form of protecting traditional Chinese culture against change, by an emphasis
upon orthodoxy. In the political field the trend was in favour of
contraction rather than expansion, for on the landward side no
steps were taken to resist the rising tide of Mohammedan power
in western and central Asia, while on the seaward side her coasts
and her shipping were subject to piratical attacks by Japanese
raiders and even by her own countrymen out of control.

She was in fact from early in the sixteenth century following
a policy of seclusion in many respects similar to that which a century later was deliberately adopted by the Japanese, and for similar
reasons. Both countries felt that for the preservation of their own
institutions they must protect themselves against the intrusion of
disturbing foreign influences. The Chinese Empire was less efficiently governed by its central authority than was Japan in her
period of isolation, partly because of its great size and the remote-
ness of the court at Peking from the main centres of wealth and
population, which now were in the Yangtze valley and farther
south, the northern provinces having suffered from a century or
more of Mongol depredations. It resulted from these circumstances
that, at a time when European civilization was developing with
great speed and energy, Chinese civilization was at a low ebb of
vigour. These historical conditions should not be overlooked in
considering the nature of the relations between China and the
Western world from the sixteenth century onwards. At least one
may say with confidence that the results of European intrusion
would have been different in some essential features had it been
faced by China in one of her creative phases.

But general statements as to the strength or weakness of a civilization at a given period require many qualifications, and it would
not be proper to assume that the reception of the Portuguese by
the Chinese was a direct result of political and social conditions
in China. It was due rather to the Portuguese themselves, whose
behaviour was such as to cause offence and anxiety even to the
most tolerant of peoples. The Chinese were convinced of the
superiority of their own institutions, and they affected to regard
all foreign visitors as at best barbarians bringing tribute or respectfully enjoying the privilege of dwelling in the Middle Kingdom;
but it had for centuries been the Chinese practice to treat alien
residents decently and to make allowance for their misfortune in
not having been born members of the Chinese race. This is clear
from the position acquired by many religious minorities — Nestorians, Manichæans, Moslems — at different periods in Chinese

history and by the privileges accorded to communities of Arabs and other traders in Chinese seaports from very early times.

Something that the Chinese would not tolerate — indeed, something that they could scarcely comprehend — was that foreigners should knock at the door of China and claim admission not as a favour but as a right due to subjects of a foreign power. The Chinese view of the world had no place for a concept of sovereign states dealing with China on a footing of equality; and it must be remembered that even in Europe this was a new thing, since it was not until the collapse of the Eastern Roman Empire that the idea of a universal state gave place to the idea of a complex of national states, each claiming sovereign rights and all competing among themselves for power, territory, and trade on at least theoretically equal terms. The Chinese, in other words, did not understand the claims of foreign sovereigns to send ambassadors to their court, nor could they under their own political theory admit that foreigners could trade with them as of right. They would allow Chinese merchants to deal with foreigners or to engage in overseas trade, but, as we have seen, the government of China did not regard the fostering of foreign commerce as an important affair of state.

Consequently, when the Portuguese first came to China they were not positively forbidden to trade, though they were not granted any special privileges. It was the conduct of the Portuguese themselves that prevented for several years the resumption of authorized trading, and there is no reason to suppose that had they been moderate in their demands and sensible in their behaviour, they would not have gained a favourable position from the time of their first visit. Unfortunately for them, news of their buccaneering exploits and of their actions in Malacca (where China claimed a shadowy authority) reached the court at Peking at the time of Pires's visit and destroyed what prospects may have existed of a friendly agreement to permit trade and to accept, in some form consistent with Chinese pretensions, a diplomatic envoy from Portugal. It can scarcely be doubted that the suspicions aroused in Peking at this juncture injured the development of good relations with European powers for a long time to come, the more so since the Chinese, always a landward-looking people, were inclined to view with suspicion all strangers arriving off their shores, which were vulnerable and without defence. It is significant that Europeans were known to the Chinese as *yang-kwei*, or ocean devils, something new in their already abundant demonology; though it would be a mistake to think that only Portuguese misdeeds created such monsters in Chinese fancy, for their immediate successors — the Spanish, the Dutch, and the English — did not much improve upon the Lusitanian model.

For twenty years or so after their first arrival the Portuguese traders failed to obtain official licence to trade, and they were ejected from several ports where they had tried to establish themselves.[4] They did, however, manage to establish a precarious foothold on the small island of Shang-chüan, south of Canton, and because their well-armed ships were able to cope with the pirates who infested the South China seas they were useful to Chinese and other merchants and therefore were able to engage in the carrying trade despite official prohibitions of the central government. Before long (in 1557) they were allowed to occupy the harbour and town now known as Macao, which became their commercial base and the centre of European trading intercourse with China.

It is important to understand the nature of European trade in the Far East in this period. With few exceptions it did not consist in an exchange of European and Asiatic produce, because (as we have seen) there were no European commodities necessary to the Chinese economy in the degree that Asiatic produce was necessary to the economy of the West. The Chinese did, however, consume in quantity a number of the natural products of the countries of southeast Asia and India, as Albuquerque discovered on his visit to Malacca, where he found Chinese trading junks which had come to take on cargoes of goods brought for sale to that emporium from the Malabar coast, Siam, and Indonesia. It was the profits earned by the Portuguese as carriers and brokers that sustained their commerce with China, rather than the sale of the few European products for which they could find a market. Their commerce with Japan similarly depended to some extent upon the carriage of Chinese goods — for example, silk — from Macao to Japan, again because the Chinese and Japanese trading junks were not safe from pirates.

The uneasy relations of the foreign traders with the Chinese made it extremely difficult for missionaries to gain entry into China. The first missionary to seek admission was Francis Xavier, who had gone to Japan in 1549 and, as we shall see later, had been much encouraged by his reception there. He had gained the impression that since the Japanese derived their culture from Chinese sources they would be the more disposed to accept Christian doctrines if the Chinese would give them a lead. This was not very sound reasoning, but he was not a man to look for objections to his own theories, and on his way back to Goa in 1551 he began enthusiastically to plan a diplomatic mission to which he would

[4] They had for a time a settlement at Ningpo, which was destroyed by Chinese in 1545, the Portuguese staff being massacred. The Portuguese, for their part, occasionally laid waste villages on the coasts of Fukien and Chekiang, a practice in which they were only following the example of the Japanese.

be attached and which was to secure from the Emperor of China a treaty of friendship and the right to trade and preach the gospel in Chinese territory. This project was approved by the Viceroy, but could not be carried out because the Captain of Malacca would not allow an embassy to leave, probably because he thought, in view of recent news from China, that it had no chance of success. Xavier made his way with his companions to the island of Shang-chüan and tried to get over to the mainland, but the Portuguese traders would give him no help, fearing that an illicit landing of missionaries would only endanger their own very unstable position. Xavier stayed on, hoping somehow to find a passage, but he fell ill and died at the end of 1552.

It was some time before further attempts were made to establish a mission in China. There were Jesuits and others in Macao, and they made some efforts to convert Chinese, occasionally visiting Canton; but no permanent mission was established until 1583. It became clear to the superiors of the Jesuit order that it was not sufficient for ardent novices to come out from Europe to Goa, to spend two or three years there at St. Paul's College studying philosophy and theology, and then to step ashore in China to preach without adequate knowledge of the Chinese language or of Chinese thought. They might, by their sincerity and their charity, induce some poor peasant or fisherman to be baptized into the Catholic faith, but they could not hope to persuade an educated Chinese that the beliefs of his ancestors were mistaken. For that difficult task they would require, in addition to permission to live in China, a full linguistic competence and a considerable understanding of the nature of Chinese society.

It was only after some thirty years of ill-organized and abortive missionary effort that the Jesuits saw clearly that their evangelists must spend a lifetime in acquiring and using these indispensable qualifications. It was not until 1583 that the work began in earnest. By that time the Chinese antagonism to the Portuguese had somewhat lessened, perhaps because the captains and the traders had come to realize that their earlier policy of violence did not pay. Two specially selected and trained Italian fathers, Michael Ruggerius and Matteo Ricci, were allowed to reside in the capital city of Kwangtung province, and here as a matter of policy they set themselves to winning the friendship and respect of Chinese of the official class. Both were men of high attainments, and Ricci in particular was a good mathematician and astronomer. Their method of procedure was similar to that which was adopted by Father de Nobile in India at a somewhat later date. They endeavoured to recommend themselves to cultivated Chinese by means of their intellectual attainments and kept their religious motives in the background. It is interesting to note that whereas Nobile did not make his attempt to get on friendly terms with the Brahmans until 1606, Ricci was discussing European science with the mandarins a generation before that — a difference in time due perhaps to the fact that in China the Portuguese had no political influence, whereas in India they had a certain authority outside their own domain and could travel without much restriction. It is also significant that the missionaries who approached the major Asiatic cultures through science were usually not Portuguese, whose country was little affected by the Renaissance, but Italians, who came from its very fountain-head.

The Jesuits in China undoubtedly took a prudent course when, under the direction of their Visitor-General Valignano (also an Italian), they decided not to deliver a direct assault upon the Chinese intellectual tradition but to try to undermine it by showing that Europeans had advanced beyond the Chinese in certain branches of learning. There was some hope for such a strategy in a country administered by literati and singularly respectful of scholarship. They did not, it seems, allow their minds to be disturbed by a problem that has not been solved to this day, the question whether either precept or example can ever, even in most favourable circumstances, bring about radical changes in an indigenous civilization that has been formed by centuries of experience in its own environment. For their own sake they did well not to let their purpose be weakened by doubts in this matter, for Chinese society was as durable as it was ancient, and so closely knit that to deny one of its principles was to challenge the whole of its structure. They were, moreover, fortunate in that during the latter part of the Ming era there was among the Chinese themselves some disposition, if not to question their own institutions, at least to review the orthodox Confucian philosophy. The very fact that government was conducted on strongly orthodox lines seems to have evoked a certain spirit of criticism or at least a vague consciousness that all was not well in China's intellectual world.

4. Japan

THE PORTUGUESE castaways who reached Japan in 1542 carried arquebuses, which are said to have caused the greatest excitement to the Japanese, who met them in a friendly manner. Perhaps this incident, which is unlikely to be apocryphal, is symbolic of the nature of Japanese civilization at the opening of the sixteenth century and marks it off from the civilization of India and China, whose inhabitants when they first encountered the Portuguese are not reported to have displayed any particular interest in their weapons or to have regarded them as other than rough barbarians. The Japanese, for their part, welcomed the strangers, and it was not long before the first arrivals were followed by missionaries and traders who had little difficulty in establishing friendly relations with the people of the country and their rulers.

This contrast between Japan and other Asiatic countries in the treatment of foreigners requires some explanation. It may be stated as a fact that the Japanese were a friendly people, given to hospitality, disposed to good manners, extremely curious to learn new things; and this would go far to account for their attitude towards the newcomers from Europe. But something more is required, because we should like to know what in their past history and environment had given rise to these qualities. Though discussions of national character are apt to be inconclusive, some attempt may be made to discover what in the background of the Japanese had brought about their readiness to entertain strangers and consider unfamiliar doctrines.

Their early history gives an indication, for even before they formed a homogeneous nation they looked to the mainland of Asia for instruction in the arts of civilization. It was the bronze culture of China that enabled them to emerge from their neolithic phase in the first centuries of our era, and it was to China that they turned for the very foundations of an organized national life when they adopted the Chinese written language and studied Chinese methods of government. China was so mature when the Japanese were growing up that the prestige of her civilization was overwhelming. It was natural and indeed inevitable that they should welcome Chinese teachers who brought to them the treasures of learning and religion. These monks, doctors, and craftsmen crossed over in considerable numbers to Japan, where they were treated with great distinction — so much so that in a list of noble families compiled at the end of the seventh century over one third claim Chinese or Korean descent; and until the Japanese felt able to stand on their own feet, let us say in the tenth century, aliens might count upon receiving special privileges.

Since it was to China and indirectly to India that Japan owed all the enrichment for which her tribal life was groping, it is not surprising that in this early period of her history there was founded a tradition of respect for foreign wisdom. Though the Japanese from time to time in their later history reacted against the strong influence of China, their own civilization could not develop without frequent refreshment from its original source. Their earliest system of government was modelled upon that of China, their social philosophy incorporated with indigenous elements many

Chinese ideas, and it was to China that they owed their adoption of Buddhism, perhaps the most potent civilizing factor in their early national life.

It is easy to understand why Chinese influence should have dominated the intellectual growth of Japan, for China was an experienced adult when Japan first went to school, and there was no other civilized country within reach of Japan. What is exceptional in the case of Japan is the fact that Chinese culture was taken over not in submission to force or strong persuasion, but voluntarily and enthusiastically and on Japanese initiative. Until a native literature began to develop in the tenth century, Chinese studies were paramount in Japan. Scholars and statesmen tried to envelop themselves in a Chinese atmosphere. They would call themselves by Chinese names and, it is said, were happy if they could commune with a Chinese poet in their dreams. This, of course, is not a singular phenomenon, since it has had its counterpart in Europe, where some classical learning, including familiarity with Greek and Latin poets, has been necessary baggage for a man travelling towards eminence. Indeed, the comparison is close, for if Europeans studied the dead languages of Greece and Rome, so did the Japanese neglect contemporary Chinese and draw on models of long-defunct dynasties. But there was a difference, since the Japanese, even when their culture had acquired a strong and distinct national flavour, did not cut themselves off from living Chinese sources of inspiration. They continued for many centuries to look to China for new ideas in religion and philosophy, and until very recent times a quotation from a Chinese classic was felt to be a powerful support to any argument. By the time that the first Europeans arrived in Japan the cultural influence of China was waning, because of disturbed conditions in both countries; but it had been extremely strong, at least in art and letters, not many decades before, and as soon as Japan settled down to peace in the early seventeenth century, there was an important revival of Confucian studies and renewed intercourse with Chinese Buddhists.[5]

These fragments of history may help to explain why the Japanese, unlike the people of India and China, were disposed to take a friendly interest in strangers and anxious to learn what they had to tell. But there was another reason why, at the time when the Portuguese began to appear, the Japanese should have been especially open to foreign influences. Japan was then in the midst of civil war, which was breaking down old institutions, and such times of crisis usually favour a receptive mood. Some account of conditions in Japan at that period, known to Japanese historians

[5] Which resulted, for example, in the introduction of the Ōbaku sect as late as 1655.

as *Sengoku-jidai,* or the Age of the Country at War, will serve to furnish a background for description of the earliest intercourse between Japanese and Europeans.

For several centuries Japan had been accustomed to long periods of feudal warfare, in which contending factions struggled for supremacy. This endemic strife, though at times reaching a high pitch of intensity, had not been sufficiently widespread or destructive to prevent a considerable advance in the arts of civilization. Indeed, in the period before that with which we are concerned, though the central administration had lost most of its power to feudal chieftains, yet in the midst of confusion and turmoil there had taken place a very remarkable cultural phase, in which the arts flourished while government was neglected. These uneasy times encouraged a feverish activity, which expressed itself in a search for excitements and luxuries, so that commerce with China flourished and bold spirits, not content with legitimate trade, sailed out upon piratical voyages which carried them to the China coast and beyond. During the fifteenth century the Japanese were known and feared as corsairs along all the shores of eastern Asia, and adventurers were finding their way to the Malay Archipelago and Farther India. Thus when Europeans first entered the Pacific, the Japanese had already emerged from a seclusion which geography rather than temperament had imposed upon them, and by the time when the first Portuguese reached Japan they were in an expansive mood, not only willing but even anxious to extend their contact with the outside world and hungry for new commodities.

In the middle of the sixteenth century the protracted civil wars had eliminated all but a few powerful feudal groups from the struggle for supremacy. What must now follow was a final contest for mastery of the whole country, and it was at this critical point in Japan's history that the European traders and missionaries appeared upon the scene. The Emperor in Kyoto sat powerless upon his throne, his Shogun or Generalissimo could exercise no authority over the regional lords, and a feudal chieftain of obscure antecedents, Oda Nobunaga (1534–82), whose small fief lay in a good strategic position, was gradually building up his strength by skilful fighting and useful alliances. His enemies were still strong, for they included great feudal barons in northeastern and southwestern Japan who, singly or in combination, disposed of great military strength; while the leading Buddhist monasteries had both military and political influence.

Such a period of turmoil, when an old order was being challenged and new men were rising to power, was propitious for the European traders and missionaries. Here they could gain favour by giving their support to one side or another in the prevailing

quarrels, just as elsewhere in Asia they had been able to take advantage of disunity by siding with one faction against its rival. In
Japan they could not give direct military aid since their numbers
were small, but they were expert in the use of firearms and navigation, matters in which the Japanese were ignorant or backward.
They could also with their well-armed vessels carry cargoes safely
to and from Japan to the profit of Japanese merchants, and they
could introduce useful or attractive goods from Asia as well as
Europe.

These facts soon became evident to the feudal rulers, especially
to those in western Japan, where Portuguese ships first touched.
Trading vessels visited harbours in Kyushu once the Portuguese
along the China coast and in the Malay Archipelago heard of the
discovery of Japan by their compatriots, and by 1549 Francis Xavier with several companions landed at Kagoshima, the capital of
the lordship of Satsuma, one of the most powerful western provinces, where he was well received and given permission to preach.
We have noticed that the political situation in Japan at the time
of their arrival was favourable. The western feudatories, great and
small, feared for their own independence and saw that if they
could add to their wealth by foreign trade or if they could secure
from the Portuguese a little help in the way of weapons or shipping they would have an advantage over their rivals. The party in
central Japan which was striving for hegemony saw that a combination of the western feudatories would be hard to overcome,
especially if they could obtain help from or by means of the Portuguese. Consequently a number of barons made attractive offers
to the foreign traders, hoping to entice them to their own ports
and keep them away from their rivals; while, as we shall see, Nobunaga — though this was some years later — treated the Jesuits
with special consideration, having doubtless learned that the Portuguese captains paid deference to the missionaries.

So it came about that not only did the feudal leaders compete
for the services of foreign traders, but they also as part of this commercial policy gave special facilities to the Jesuit fathers, even in
some cases ordering the people in their domains to adopt the
Christian faith. This alacrity to receive and consider the offerings
of the West is in rather marked contrast to the attitude of India
and China towards alien importations. It is not difficult to see why
the Japanese in their remote and isolated situation should have
displayed an interest in the produce of distant climates, since they
had already traded with the southern regions, and the wealthy war
lords of the fifteenth century had spent freely upon luxuries from
China and beyond. But the enthusiasm with which the Christian
teaching of the Jesuits was received in some quarters requires fur-

ther study, for which, fortunately, ample material is to hand in the reports and letters of the missionaries to their colleagues in Goa and to the General of their order.

The progress of the early Christian missions to Japan is of interest not only in the history of evangelism. It is of great value as presenting a clear picture of the meeting of two cultures and seems to justify treatment in some detail in a separate chapter. Both the resemblances and the differences between what happened in Japan and what happened in other Asiatic countries are striking. But before concentrating our attention upon the Far East it is convenient at this point to look back and see what had been the effect upon European intellectual life of a century of European expansion. It was not much, but it was enough to set thoughtful men wondering about the future and asking themselves what would be their rights and duties in a growing world.

5. The International Society

THIS is by no means the place for an inquiry into the nature of international society, but it is germane to the theme of this study to pay some attention to the effect of European expansion in Asia upon sixteenth- and seventeenth-century thought about international life.

There is a certain irony in the fact that it was (in part at least) the search for Japan, the fabled Xipangu of Marco Polo, that impelled Columbus and other explorers to undertake their voyages of discovery and, by sowing the seeds of international rivalry in Eastern Asia, to raise in a new and urgent form the question of how to reconcile conflicting claims among the sovereign states of Europe. It was of course an old problem, but now it was presented on a larger scale than ever before.

In the Middle Ages the spectacle of a narrow European world of turbulent kingdoms continuously at war turned the minds of reasoning men to speculation on universal peace, and produced visions not of a regulated society of independent states but rather of an ideal empire, ruled in accordance with a supreme law by a benign and absolute monarch. This was the theme of Dante's *De monarchia,* which seems to have been inspired by thoughts of Imperial Rome as it might have been. But the idea of a society of nations bound to the observance of a universal law is of later growth. It appears in a rudimentary form after the discovery of the Americas and the Indies; and it is significant that among the first hints of a possible law of nations are suggestions made early in the sixteenth century by Catholic theologians who were brought to consider the rights and duties of temporal rulers by the behaviour of the conquistadores in the new-found lands. The Dominican Francisco de Vitoria, professor of theology at Salamanca, sat on committees dealing with Indian affairs and was moved to reflect upon international justice by reports of Spanish ill-treatment of natives of the Americas. This was in the first half of the sixteenth century. He propounded the view that Christian princes had no right to coerce or punish "barbarians," even with the authority of the Pope.

Other Spanish writers developed similar opinions, notably the Jesuit Francisco Suarez, who in 1612 wrote his *Treatise on the Laws,* in which he said: "Mankind, however divided into various peoples and kingdoms, has always a certain unity not only of species but also, as it were, political and moral, which is shown by the natural rule of love and compassion that extends to all, even to strangers of whatever nation. Consequently, though any single state, kingdom, or republic may seem to be a perfect society, complete and coherent in itself, nevertheless each one of these is in some way a member of the universal human society. None of these communities singly is so self-sufficient that it can dispense with the support of others, which it requires sometimes for its material advantage, sometimes out of moral necessity."

His meaning is sometimes obscured by the tricks of his pseudo-Ciceronian Latin and he is not explicit as to the vital part of his argument, which is the nature of "moral necessity." But he does conclude that some law is required to order the relations of states with one another. Neither he nor other theologians, however, ventured to postulate a world authority which should keep quarrelsome states at peace. Indeed, most of them balked at the idea of punitive or preventive war and took the view that it was permissible for a state to resort to arms only when attacked. They did not say how any nation or group outside the range of municipal law was to be stopped from wrong-doing or punished for misbehavior.

It was at this point that Grotius began to form his views on international law. He had been led to consider the works of Vitoria and his other precursors by cases of international discord that came to his notice as a lawyer. Retained by the United East India Company of Holland, he had to deal with suits arising from the capture of Portuguese prizes by Dutch ships in Asiatic waters, which involved questions about the rights of a chartered company and the freedom of the seas. He wrote his treatise on the law of booty (which included his chapters on *Mare Liberum*) about 1604, and by 1625 he had completed his *De jure belli ac pacis.* Here he laid it down that the international society existed as a legal community, and advocated a world-wide rule of law, to be enforced — he did not say how, though warfare figures prominently in his argument. His views were traversed later by Hobbes, who thought that nations should mind their own business and not go crusading, and said in effect that there was no such thing as the international society that Grotius imagined.

We must not enter into the disagreement between these two Titans. The point of interest for us here lies only in the circumstances that caused Grotius and his forerunners to give thought to a law of nations. It was the extension of conflict far beyond the borders of Europe — indeed, to all quarters of the known world — that brought home to the European mind the problems of relationship not only among European states but with the countries and peoples of Asia, Africa, and the Americas. It was thus that there developed the idea of a community of all states, governed by a law described as the law of nature or the law of peoples. While Grotius was in prison cogitating on such matters (1618–21), Spain was at war with the Netherlands, the rest of Europe was in arms, and in Asia and the Americas both the secular and the ecclesiastical representatives of European states were pursuing their rivalries with little or no regard for the native inhabitants of those regions. For long their jurists had argued that the highest duty of a Christian king was to convert the pagan, and for this purpose the use of force was necessary and legitimate. If it seemed that a foreign country would not voluntarily accept Christianity, then it was proper to make war upon it and take its territory, so that its people could be baptized and saved from idolatry. Even voluntary converts might be safer from temptation to backslide if they were under Christian government.

One of the most important departures that Grotius embodied in his treatise was an extension of the rule of law to benefit all peoples, without distinction of race or religion. He was brought to this view mainly by his knowledge of the way in which Dutch administrators in the East Indies disregarded the rights of native rulers. Similarly his thoughts on the freedom of the seas were stimulated by the monopolistic claims of Portugal to navigation and trade in the Pacific, as also by the doctrine of the closed sea proclaimed by Selden in his *Mare Clausum,* which suited England at that time but not the Netherlands. Ecclesiastical strife, indirectly involving the Protestant nations, revealed a fundamental antagonism between the Spanish and Portuguese missionaries in eastern Asia, for while the Spanish were moving westward to the Philippines, the Portuguese had established themselves in the Spice Islands, China, and Japan. It became necessary to decide their respective spheres of influence; and in default of a world authority the Holy See stepped in and bestowed upon the two temporal

ulers a Padroado covering half the globe for each, or with the
inion of the two crowns in 1580 all the globe for one.

This atrocious monopoly exasperated the English and the
Dutch and before many years, made the Indian Ocean and the
western Pacific the scene of European battles, fought between
armed men with ships and guns as well as between men of God
with bell, book, and candle, to say nothing of bull and brief,
pamphlet and sermon. In Japan and China the wrangles of the
Jesuits and the mendicant orders followed both national and re-
igious lines of cleavage; and because they could not bring force
o bear in those two powerful kingdoms as they had done elsewhere in Asia, they dabbled in domestic politics, thereby bringing
lamage to their own cause and injuring the trading interests of
others.

So it is not surprising that men with liberal, orderly minds like
Grotius, dismayed by the lawlessness that went along with trade
and the gospel in Asia and the Americas, should have turned their
minds to the problem of keeping order among ambitious kings
and insubordinate priests. And thus we have one more example to
how how, while Asiatic thought was little disturbed by Western
influence, events in Asia started new movements in the intellectual
ife of Europe.

Now we may return to the Far East, first looking at the results
of Christian missions in Japan and then observing the course of
he Asiatic trade and its effects upon Western economies.

Note on CHAPTER 5

The following works are useful for the study of the Portuguese in Asia
rom 1500 to 1650:

Boxer, C. R.: In addition to a number of papers in the Transactions of
the Japan Society, London, Major Boxer's studies of the missions
of Japanese to Rome promoted by the Jesuits are of great value,
as are his *Fidalgos in the Far East* and the forthcoming *Christian
Century in Japan*. In fact, all that he has written on these and
related subjects is indispensable.

Bernard, Henri, S.J.: All Father Bernard's books and his contributions
to *Monumenta Nipponica* are full of interesting material on
missionary activities in the Far East in the sixteenth and seventeenth centuries and related historical questions.

Cortesao, A.: *The Suma Oriental of Thome Pires*. Hakluyt Society,
1946. This deals with Portuguese affairs in China, 1512–15, and
with Pires's embassy.

Ferguson, D.: *Letters from Portuguese Captives in Canton*, (*1520–40*).
Most interesting and useful.

Gray, A.: *The Voyage of François Pyrard de Laval.* Hakluyt Society, Nos. 77, 78, and 80 of 1888–90. A mine of information.

Linschoten: *Itinerario.* Hakluyt Society, 1885–7. Gives a vivid account of Portuguese seafaring life and helps to explain the decline of Portuguese sea power.

Sanceau, Elaine: *Indies Adventure* (1936). A life of Albuquerque, which, though a popular work and somewhat romantic, is based on good Portuguese sources.

Whiteway, R.: *The Rise of Portuguese Power in India.* A classic. A little hard at times on the Portuguese administrators, it is still one of the best books on the subject and is extremely well written.

CHAPTER
6

CHRISTIANITY IN JAPAN, 1549–1614

T**HE BEST** single source for an account of the Jesuit propaganda in Japan in the second half of the sixteenth century is the *Historia do Japão* of Father Luis Frois, which covers the years 1549 to 1578. Frois was either an eyewitness of events that he describes or had knowledge of them from his colleagues in the mission field. His statements are therefore of exceptional interest and of patent veracity if one makes some slight allowance for his natural prejudices. His own career is something of an epitome of the life of the Jesuits who worked in the Far East. He was born in Lisbon in 1532, entered the Society of Jesus in 1548, and was almost at once sent to India. Arriving at Goa, he entered St. Paul's College, where his fellow students included half-castes, Negroes, Abyssinians, Mahrattas, Malabaris, Malays from Macassar and Amboina, and the first Chinese and Japanese students at the seminary. Among the latter was one Anjirō, baptized as Paul, whom Francis Xavier on his way back from the Moluccas to Goa in 1548 had found in Malacca, where (he said) he had come drawn by the father's fame as a holy man. Frois began the prescribed course of study at St. Paul's — two years of philosophy, two of theology, and one of Holy Scripture. During this period Xavier, who had sailed from Goa in June 1549, spent two years in Japan and returned to Goa in 1552, bringing with him a mission from a Japanese feudal baron, Ōtomo of Bungo. Xavier's reports on his visit to Japan were enthusiastic. "These," he said, "are the best people so far discovered, and it seems to me that among unbelievers no people can be found to excel them."

Frois was anxious to go to Japan, but he was first sent to Malacca in 1554, then returned to Goa for his ordination, and he worked as secretary to the Provincial, Father Melchior Nunes Barreto, where he was marked down as having good judgment and a gift for writing and speaking. Letters that Frois wrote from Malacca, Goa, and elsewhere bear out the judgment of his superiors, for they are vivid and full of interesting detail. He was sent to Japan in 1562 and stayed there until his death in 1597. His literary gift his long experience and his acquaintance with leading figures in Japan make his account a very valuable document. It is drawn upon freely in the following pages.

Francis Xavier was well aware of the dangers and difficulties of the voyage to Japan, but his determination to bring light to the heathen was such that, in a letter to the Provincial of Portugal written in 1549, he said that he did not fear shipwreck or pirates or any other perils, but only the anger of God if he should not be diligent in His service. These words express clearly the spirit in which the Jesuit mission to Japan was undertaken. This was no trading expedition including a few monks to give it an air of sanctity, but a purely religious undertaking arising out of Xavier's conviction that it was a sacred duty to combat the ignorance of unbelievers. He had said, in the letter just cited, that he was determined as soon as he reached Japan to go straight to the King of that country and to discover from what was written in their books what its people believed. Thereafter he would write to the Jesuit colleges at Coimbra and Rome and to all the universities reminding them that they must not be guilty of piling up knowledge for themselves while not troubling about the ignorance of the heathen.

This is an interesting statement of the policy of the Jesuits, who realized that to change the beliefs of a people it was not enough to preach to the poor and the unlearned, but that their leaders must be gained over; and for that purpose it was necessary to study the nature of their traditional beliefs. The Jesuit fathers in Japan followed this direction, with the result that in course of time, despite the great obstacles of strange customs and an extremely difficult language, they gained the friendship and respect of many Japanese of all classes and reached a remarkably good understanding of the nature of Japanese life. Their reports and letters give a picture of the civilization of Japan and of its contemporary history that is probably without equal for accuracy among sixteenth-century European accounts of foreign countries.

Their early steps in evangelism, it must be said, were somewhat faltering. Xavier and seven companions (including Anjirō and two other Japanese) left Malacca as passengers in a Chinese pirate vessel and reached Kagoshima in August 1549. Without delay Xavier visited the "King," or more correctly the Daimyo or feudal lord of Satsuma — Shimazu Takahisa, a very powerful ruler — by whom he was received in a friendly manner. He learned that the sovereign of all the sixty-six provinces of Japan lived in Miyako [1] — though he was not aware that in fact the Emperor exercised no secular authority — and begged for a ship to take him there. Takahisa promised this, but said that owing to the state of war then prevailing the voyage must be postponed.

[1] The capital, now called Kyoto.

While waiting for the opportunity, which Takahisa never meant to provide, the fathers set about their task of conversion. They were handicapped by their almost complete ignorance of the Japanese language, and it is difficult to understand how they were able to make converts; but they appear somehow to have persuaded a few people to accept baptism, probably with the help of Anjiro, the interpreter. They also set about translating into Japanese a statement of the elements of Christian belief — the creation, the coming of the Son of God into the world, the commandments, and the last judgment. This must have been a very hard task, even if they had sufficient linguistic competence, and one cannot help wondering what the simple Japanese made of these new ideas, for there is nothing more difficult to convey in a foreign language than an unfamiliar principle. Nevertheless, some progress was made, for if we are to believe Frois one hundred and fifty persons were baptized during the ten months spent in Satsuma by the company. Further Xavier contrived, evidently by the strength and charm and simplicity of his character, to get on good terms with some of the monks of an important Buddhist monastery in the vicinity. He appears to have made friends with an amiable and learned abbot of the Zen sect named Ninjitsu, of whom two instructive anecdotes are told. Both reveal the sceptical attitude of dignitaries of the Buddhist church at this time.

Ninjitsu one day took Xavier to the meditation hall of his monastery, where the monks were engaged in their usual exercise of Zazen, which consists of kneeling motionless in concentrated thought upon one object for the purpose of clearing the mind of all extraneous matters and thus approaching an intuitive grasp of truth. Xavier asked what these men were doing, and Ninjitsu replied: "Some are counting up how much they took from the faithful last month; some are considering where they can get better clothing and treatment for themselves; others are thinking of their recreations and pastimes. In short, none of them is thinking of anything that has any sense whatever."

The Jesuits learned in course of time that leaders of the Zen sect were likely to be formidable opponents, since they were as a rule men of strong character who, while well grounded in philosophy, rejected all conventional forms of religion and held that the truth could not be learned from books or sermons, but only by looking into one's own being. Frois describes them as believing that there was nothing beyond birth and death, no other life, no punishment for the wicked, no reward for the good, nor any creator who rules the universe. They were clearly most unpromising material for conversion, but Xavier seems to have sensed their importance and he took pains to argue with Ninjitsu. On one occasion he asked the abbot, who was advanced in years, which time of life seemed to him better, youth or old age. Ninjitsu replied: "Youth," explaining that this was the time when a man's body was free from illness and he could do what he wished unhindered. Xavier retorted: "Suppose you saw a ship that has left one harbour and must perforce at length reach another, when would you say the passengers should most rejoice? When they are on the open sea, threatened by wind and wave, or when they are in sight of their haven and begin to cross the bar?" Ninjitsu said: "Father, I understand you well. I know that the aspect of the harbour is pleasant and joyful to those who are bound thither. But it is not yet clear to me, and I have not yet decided, which is the best harbour, and so I do not know how or where I must land."

Xavier continued on friendly terms with the Zen monks and pressed Ninjitsu to accept baptism, but he refused, because (as Frois sadly relates) he would not give up the dignities he held and the respect he enjoyed and the wealth he possessed, "preferring to land lost and miserable in hell." Here, as elsewhere in Asia, the Jesuits found that for most men to adopt an alien faith was to abandon their own culture, because a culture is composed of many elements, and when one is destroyed, the whole structure disintegrates.

The missionaries, however, did not lose heart. Their confidence was indeed superb. Their zeal and especially the intemperate language of Xavier in his condemnation of Japanese customs aroused anger among the monks, and though a few conversions are recorded among humble folk, they made little progress in Satsuma. After a stay of ten months Xavier, finding that the Daimyo would not help him to get to Miyako, went to the port of Hirado, in a neighbouring fief some hundred miles distant, where a Portuguese ship from China had arrived. He went back to Satsuma for a brief visit, withdrew the mission, and returned to Hirado. The ruler of this territory, Matsuura Takanobu, treated him well, seemingly because he had been pleased by the visit of the ship; and Xavier, leaving Father Cosme de Torres behind, set out on foot for Yamaguchi, hoping there to find a passage to Miyako.

Yamaguchi was at this time the seat of a very powerful feudal lord (Ōuchi Yoshitaka) the head of the Ōuchi family. He kept a kingly state and his kingdom was prosperous. Xavier asked for permission to appear before this prince and to preach the gospel in his dominion. This was granted, it being generally supposed that, since the fathers came from India, they were bringing to Japan the teaching of some new sect of Buddhism. Xavier had an audience with Ōuchi, at whose request he told the interpreter to read in Japanese a document, already prepared, which gave the elements of Christian doctrine. This included a discourse upon error and sin. When the reader came to a passage on sodomy, describing those guilty of this offence as filthier than swine and lower than dogs, the Daimyo changed colour and dismissed them, no doubt because he, in common with many military men and monks in that part of Japan, was given to such habits. The interpreter thought that they might have their heads cut off, but they left safely and Xavier, without waiting for permission, began to preach in the streets of Yamaguchi. His knowledge of the Japanese language was poor, and he was obliged to depend upon his interpreter, who again read from a prepared document, while the Father stood by, praying for the success of his sermon. The discourse did not spare the feelings of the audience, for it pointed out three great sins of the Japanese: idolatry, sodomy, and infanticide or abortion. Many gathered in the streets, some to listen, some to revile, and some out of mere curiosity. One nobleman for his own amusement invited them to his house, where, having heard about the creation and the fall of Lucifer, he expressed his scorn of such myths. To this Xavier retorted that unless he abandoned his pride and wept for his sins he also would be stricken by God with the torments of hell.

Shortly before Christmas of 1550 Xavier decided at all costs to make his way to Miyako, where he was determined to see the Emperor of Japan. After a long and painful journey, mostly on foot through snow and storm, he reached the capital, but to no avail, for the place was in an uproar and the Shogun had left the city, while the Emperor was living in obscure retirement in an old palace. He therefore decided to return to Yamaguchi, concluding that there were better prospects in the fief of Ōuchi, who seemed at that time to be the most powerful lord in Japan. He obtained an audience and took with him some valuable presents, including a clock, a matchlock, some brocades, fine crystal glasses, a mirror, and spectacles, together with letters from the Bishop of Goa and the Governor. These seem to have pleased Ōuchi, who was impressed by Xavier's appearance in rich ecclesiastical robes. There were some monks present who started a theological discussion with the father. They belonged to the Shingon sect, which is devoted to the worship of Dainichi (the Buddha Vairocana) and has a strong esoteric character, regarding the whole universe as a manifestation of this Buddha. They professed to discern a close resemblance between the attributes of the God of the Christians, as described by Xavier, and their own conception of the nature of Dainichi. They said that though the language and the dress were different, the content of the doctrine was the same as their own, and they appeared (according to the Jesuit narrator) to be delighted by this foreign testimony to the truth of their beliefs.

It seems that Xavier himself gained the impression that Dainichi and God were identical, and according to one account in some of his preaching he exhorted the Japanese to worship Dainichi. But upon reflection he began to have doubts, and a few days after the discussion just recorded he approached the monks again and questioned them on the mystery of the Holy Trinity, asking whether they believed that the second Person of the Trinity had become a man and had died on the cross to save mankind. The Shingon monks were accustomed to mysteries, but these things were so strange to them that they seemed like fables or dreams, and some laughed at what the father said. Xavier then saw how the Devil had founded this accursed sect, and ordered Brother Fernando, the interpreter, to proclaim to the people in the streets that they should not worship Dainichi, but should hold the Shingon, and indeed all other sects in Japan, as inventions of Satan. He thus not surprisingly incurred the ill will of the monks, but he continued his preaching and made some converts, mostly among people in poor or modest circumstances. One of these was a blind lute-player and story-teller, baptized as Lourenço by Xavier in 1551, who was the first Japanese to be taken into the Jesuit order. He became a brother and catechist in 1563 and is recorded to have made thousands of converts in different parts of Japan during his long years of service.

While Xavier was in Bungo, the Jesuits had more trouble with the monks of Yamaguchi. One of their antagonists was a member of the militant Hokke or Lotus sect, whom they were satisfied they overcame by asking such questions as why the Buddha was born eight thousand times and by calling attention to the dissolute life of Hokke votaries. More difficult adversaries in debate were educated gentlemen who were familiar with Zen teaching and were able to put searching questions which, the Jesuits said, could not have been answered without divine assistance. Mission work was soon interrupted by alarms of war, and the fathers took refuge in the house of a friendly Japanese, meeting on their way some armed men who said: "Let us kill these men from India, for it is they who have caused our misfortunes. They have offended the Buddhas, who have now let loose this war." They escaped this danger, but were obliged to lie hidden until the fighting ended.

It was at this time that Brother João Fernandez set forth for the information of Xavier a list of questions that were frequently put by those Japanese who, for whatever reason, wished to discover the nature of Christian doctrine. Some of the more striking points may be recorded here, since they are of interest as revealing the trend of Japanese thought on religious matters. The idea of a soul was strange to them. They asked what was its shape and colour.

They asked: What is God, and where is He? Has He a body and is He visible to man? The Jesuits replied that, since all material things consisted of elements and since God had created the elements, He could not have a body composed of those elements, for if He had a body so composed, then He could not be the Creator. Then they asked: Can the soul of a good man see God when it leaves the body? Told that the truly good man saw God at once after his corporeal death, they asked why God should not be visible to a good man during life and argued that if souls were without bodies, then they must be gods, free from both birth and death. These questions reveal a great difference between the Japanese and the Christian conception of godhead, which has been at the root of much misunderstanding. The translation of the word "God" has caused many difficulties in Japan, where it has been most inadequately represented by the word *kami,* which means little more than "a superior being." In China too there was acute controversy as to the proper Chinese equivalent of *Deus,* an argument in which the Emperor K'ang Hsi took part when Pope Clement XI ventured to give a ruling on the point. Such are the semantic obstacles to a fusion of cultures.[2]

The Jesuits' letters from Japan frequently state that the Devil was busy in that country, aiding and abetting the enemies of Christianity. He inspired the monks in their attacks upon the missionaries and gave evil counsel to rulers who oppressed converts. The Japanese found it hard to understand why an all-powerful deity should have created an evil spirit who turned men's hearts to evildoing. They were familiar with the demons of their own mythology, but these were subsidiary spirits, grotesque and mischievous, yet yielding to spells and other suitable precautions. What puzzled them was that a merciful God who had created man for eternal life should have given to Satan such powers to prevent its enjoyment. Indeed, they could not understand why, if God intended us for bliss, He made the way so hard. They did not like to think of damned souls from hell coming to earth as evil spirits, as — so they were told — Satan does. Their own dead parents' spirits would come back once a year at the time of the Bon festival, but for refreshment and conversation, not to bewilder and tempt the living.

These and many other doubts the fathers did their best to re-

---

[2] There was a further difficulty in Japan. The Jesuits used the word *Deus* for want of a Japanese equivalent. But as spoken by the Japanese this became *Deusu,* very close in sound to *Daiuso,* which means a "great lie." This similarity was seized upon for purposes of vilification.

In Christian literature in the Japanese language, especially when written in Latin characters, the difficulty was met by the use of Latin or Portuguese words, such as *anima, martyrio, fides, perseguiçao, consciencia, graça, anjo* or *angelus, beato,* etc. It will be seen that most of these express ideas unfamiliar to the Japanese.

solve. Their house was crowded from morning to night with questioners, and if their arguments did not convince those whose daily life was governed by beliefs of different origin, at least they impressed their hearers by their kindness, their patience, and a certain proud humility.

The first phase of missionary endeavour in Japan may be said to have ended with the departure of St. Francis Xavier for India (1551). It was largely exploratory, for although converts were made and useful relationships established with Japanese of some standing, the fathers still had much to learn by experience as well as study. They did not yet fully understand either the political condition of Japan or the nature of Buddhism or the strength of certain indigenous beliefs and customs; so that they at times fell into the error of needlessly offending Japanese sentiment.

Perhaps their most serious lapse in judgment was their failure to make allowance for that strong feeling for the family which has always characterized Japanese life and which finds its full expression in what is, somewhat misleadingly, called the practice of ancestor-worship. It is not worship in the strictest sense, but rather the performance of simple household rites intended to console and comfort the spirits of departed relatives and so to preserve the continuity of family tradition. One of the chief objections raised by the Japanese to the doctrine preached by the Jesuits was, as Xavier himself wrote, that it had not been revealed to Japan in the past and that therefore their ancestors were unjustly condemned to hell. In reply to this complaint the missionaries argued that all men know in their hearts that killing and robbing and bearing false witness and other breaches of the commandments are wrong, and that therefore the heathen know the commandments without being taught. St. Francis stated that this solution of their difficulties aided many to become Christians, but it does not seem to dispose of the question in a convincing fashion.

It is evident that we have here one of the situations that must arise when a foreign idea comes into conflict with a deeply rooted custom. Theologians or philosophers may concede points in debate without much harm to themselves as individuals, but as members of an organized society they can hardly admit that one of its most important rules of behaviour is completely mistaken. For those who are neither philosophers nor theologians the shock of losing a cherished belief is likely to upset the balance of their lives and to disturb the social order of which they are a part. The early missionaries in Asia, thinking only in terms of religion and not realizing that religion in most countries is an expression of national temperament, found themselves confronted in Japan, as well as in India and China, by the difficult problem of reconciling their own principles with other people's practices. It is a problem that is most acute in the field of missionary endeavour, but it is of course also likely to arise where a new system of behaviour, whether political, economic, or social, is urged by one group of men upon another.

Some of the disagreements between Europeans and the Japanese can be ascribed to pure ignorance. The Jesuits, impressed by what they saw of corruption and laziness in the monastic life in Japan, were inclined to blame the Buddhist religion for the faults of its less worthy practitioners. Themselves ascetics of strong conviction and abundant vitality, they abhorred the easy-going scepticism and the self-indulgent habits of the Buddhist monks; and from this it was but a short step to condemning Buddhist doctrine as if it encouraged such misdemeanours. Some very strong language was used by the Jesuits about the religion of the Noble Eightfold Path. Xavier described the Buddhas Shaka (Sakya Muni) and Amida (Amitabha) as "those two demons." Valignano, the Visitor-General who was in Japan thirty years later and made some inquiries into the history of Buddhism, described Shaka as "a sagacious philosopher who, pretending to lead a holy and penitent life, commenced to preach the divine cult of Amida." Bartoli, writing about 1650 on the basis of Jesuit materials, said that in Buddhism the Devil had created a mockery of Christianity in Japan, transforming its sacraments into superstitious rites and its ceremonies into a sacrilegious cult. Such statements are neither good history nor good sense. They may perhaps be excused on the grounds that the origin and development of Buddhism are obscure and that Buddhism in Japan was in many respects degenerate when the Jesuits first reached that country. But they display an intolerance that must have deeply offended devout believers as well as antagonizing the leaders of a powerful institution.

In November 1551 Xavier embarked from Goa at the port of Funai in Bungo in a Portuguese ship. The presence of this vessel and the respect paid to the father by the Portuguese captain and his crew impressed the ruler of the province, who received him courteously and asked him to take with him an envoy bearing letters to the Viceroy of the Indies in which he expressed a wish to make a treaty of friendship. He was anxious to attract Portuguese ships to his territory and not too well disposed towards the Buddhist monks, who were unruly and addicted to political intrigue. He thus was helpful to the missionaries, who said of him that there was no heathen king in all Japan who favoured them so much. Xavier, therefore, on reaching Goa with the Japanese envoy was able to show good evidence of the success of his efforts. He had written from Malacca to Ignatius Loyola, pressing him to send more fathers to Japan, where there were too few reapers for the rich harvest that might be gathered. He spoke highly of the character of the Japanese, saying: "these people are my delight"; and he asserted that if only they knew how ready the Japanese were to receive the gospel, many learned doctors would leave their books, many priests their benefices, to exchange a sad and tiresome life for one full of true and sweet joys.

It is hard to judge how many genuine conversions were made in this early period. The style of the Jesuits' letters is at times so cloying, so sweet with joy, and so moist with tears that one is at a loss to know what allowance to make for the fervent belief of these lonely men. But, apart from numbers, the results achieved in the first two years were considerable. Most of their converts were made among poor and simple peasants. Their charitable works, said one of them, could attract only the humble and the wretched, and for a long time their religion would be considered as that of the ulcerous and miserable. The people of western Japan were in general backward and unenlightened as compared with those in the metropolitan region, and their existence was very hard. They lived in troubled times, in frequent danger of death or disaster, so that they were thirsty for such consolations as were offered to them by the new faith. Its observances gave them a scope for activity and an outlet for their emotions that was not furnished by the Buddhism of the day. Indeed, there are indications that many of them obtained an almost hysterical enjoyment from their acts of worship and penitence, as when at a Good Friday celebration in 1557 the converts engaged in such merciless flagellation that though the priest ordered them to stop they would not cease until he had rung his bell several times.

A further and important reason why the Jesuits had their greatest successes in western Japan is the fact, already mentioned, that the feudal rulers in those parts knew the importance of maritime trade and were ready to allow and sometimes even to encourage the spread of Christianity because they hoped it would bring ships to their harbours. Two examples are sufficient to illustrate this point. The feudal lord of Hirado had closed the church and driven away the fathers, but he changed his mind and readmitted them when the captain of a Portuguese vessel refused to enter port on hearing of this action. The lord of Bungo (Ōtomo Sōrin) wrote to the Jesuits in China in 1567 a letter in which he said: "My desire to win a victory over the lord of Yamaguchi is due to my wish to help the Bateren [the Jesuit fathers] to return there and to give them more protection than before." He then went on to say that, to ensure this victory, he needed a quantity of saltpetre, for which he would pay handsomely.

In the second phase of their activity in Japan the Jesuits, while not neglecting the fertile ground they had begun to cultivate in western Japan, turned their attention to the central provinces, in which lay the ancient capital, the seat of such central government as then existed. This region was the most advanced in civilization and it contained the most important religious establishments, such as the great monasteries of Hiyeizan, the headquarters of the Tendai sect, which looked down upon Miyako from a near-by mountain top. It was here, the missionaries realized, that their greatest effort must be made, for they knew that if they were to spread their faith widely they must have the temporal power on their side. "I was at pains to see the King," said one of them in 1556, "because in Japan everything depends upon the rulers." The Jesuits were handicapped by lack of men and funds. They depended largely upon the help of native catechists and interpreters and the irregular charity of a few Portuguese and Japanese sympathizers. In 1561 Father Cosme de Torres wrote to the Provincial saying: "We are only six and we preach in eight provinces. For the love of our Lord send us six or at least four of our Company, for not only in these parts but elsewhere the door is open for the gospel. Wherever we go we shall make converts. But provide us with fathers and brothers." By 1570 their number had been increased by twelve,[3] and they were able to extend the range of their work.

The first visit to Miyako after the failure of Xavier was made by Father Vilela in 1559. With the help of a Japanese who had been converted in Bungo and now lived near the capital and through the intervention of a friendly abbot he managed to gain an audience with the Shogun, who treated him courteously and after some delay authorized him to establish himself in Miyako. He was able to interest a number of men of rank and education in his doctrine and by 1564 could announce that, in spite of the prevailing disorder and the antagonism of the monks of Hiyeizan, five hundred converts had been made and a number of churches built in the capital and its vicinity. Early in 1565 he was joined by two helpers, Frois (the writer of the *Historia do Japão*) and Almeida, a rich Portuguese merchant who had joined the order in Japan.

By a combination of hard work and good fortune the position of the Jesuits gradually improved. They gained the friendship and support of several influential persons, not all of whom were converts. Among them were Miyoshi Chōkei, who was the Shogun's chief minister; Wada Koremasa, one of Nobunaga's best captains; and Naito Yukiyasu, lord of the fief of Kameyama in the province of Tamba, who was close to the Shogun Yoshiaki. Other Japanese

[3] Others had been sent, but were lost at sea. The voyage was still extremely hazardous. Every year ten or more lost their lives on the voyage out from Portugal.

noblemen and gentlemen, together with some ecclesiastics, showed a sympathetic interest in the Christian religion and were at times useful to the missionaries.

But their greatest support came from Nobunaga himself, who by 1568 had overcome his principal rivals and was the most powerful man in Japan. In the civil wars that had ended in his victory several of the most powerful Buddhist sects had taken side with his enemies, using their political influence against him, and even in some cases taking the field, for such monasteries as those of Hiyeizan were in strong defensive positions and sheltered large numbers of armed monks and mercenaries. Consequently Nobunaga hated all Buddhists, with the exception of some members of the Zen sect; and as soon as he had established his position in central Japan he took steps to break their power before proceeding upon a campaign to subdue the western barons. He destroyed all the monasteries and other buildings on Hiyeizan, slaughtering most of their inmates. He was particularly anxious to uproot the Ikko or Single-Minded sect, which consisted of powerful fraternities organized on military lines, and he destroyed them wherever he could, though he never entirely mastered them, for they held out against him for years in the fortified monastery at Osaka known as the Ishiyama Hongwanji, the temple of the "Original Vow" that Amida made to save mankind.

Nobunaga's hostility towards Buddhism gave valuable support and encouragement to the Christian community in Japan, which had suffered so much from the enmity of the monks. It was no doubt not the only reason for the friendly attitude he displayed. He was certainly impressed by the character of the missionaries; he liked to talk to them about foreign countries and probably thought that they might in some way be useful to him. Whatever his motive, he protected the Jesuits and their flocks against powerful antagonists. He treated the fathers who were established in the capital with great kindness and good humour, insisted upon showing them round the new palaces and fortresses he was building, and even on occasion served them himself at meals.[4] He also took an interest in their seminary for young gentlemen, for which he had given a piece of land. News of his friendly attitude soon spread in the city and beyond, so that the path of the missionaries was made easier. It became almost fashionable in some quarters to be baptized and to carry a rosary, and many who had hesitated to take the last steps to conversion now came forward when they saw that

---

[4] On one occasion Nobunaga carried in a tray of food from an adjoining room and handed it to a father, who took it in both hands and, as Japanese etiquette required, raised it to the level of his forehead. Whereupon Nobunaga said: "Don't spill the soup."

Christianity had such high protection. The new faith began to make rapid progress both in the home provinces and in the western baronies where it had first been introduced.

The number of Christians in Japan was estimated at 30,000 by Father Vilela in a letter written at the beginning of 1571. Most of these were in western Japan, the greatest number for any one province being 5,000 in Bungo, where the ruler himself was well disposed to the Christians. In the capital there were not more than 1,500 in 1577. Only a few years later Father Organtino, writing to the General of the Jesuits, reports that in six months he and his colleagues had baptized over 7,000 new converts. He was so hopeful that he said that in ten years the whole of Japan would be Christian if there were sufficient missionaries. Frois, writing in the same year, says that while in the first seventeen or eighteen years (that is, from 1550 to 1568, when Nobunaga became supreme in the home provinces) they made only 1,500 Christians, now they baptized many more than that number in a few months. In 1579 Father Cespedes, writing from Miyako, says that the number of converts in the previous two years in his district alone was about 10,000 and the total was over 15,000.

At that date the number of Christians in all Japan was put at 130,000. This was the position after thirty years of missionary endeavour, and seeing that the number of fathers and brothers was in the first decade or so never more than a dozen, it must be said that the results were remarkable. Even by 1579 there were only fifty-four members of the company of Jesus in Japan, of whom not more than twenty were fathers, the rest being brothers and scholars in the seminaries and Japanese catechists and novices. The situation in 1582, just before the death of Nobunaga, was examined by the Visitor-General Valignano. His conclusion then was that the number of Christians was 150,000, who were served by two hundred churches large and small and two seminaries. In the "kingdoms" of Bungo, Arima, and Tosa the rulers themselves as well as most of their subjects were Christians. Of the total of 150,000 the greater part were in western Japan, but the community of 10,000 Christians in the capital and the near-by provinces was of a significance out of proportion to its numbers since it included, as we have seen, many influential persons of high rank, both military and civil.

When Nobunaga was succeeded as the military ruler of Japan by his leading general, Hideyoshi, the prospects of the mission seemed very bright. Among Hideyoshi's trusted counsellors were several Christians of high rank, notably Konishi Ryusa; his son, baptized Augustin, who had been brought up by the Jesuits; and Takayama Nagafusa (Ukondono), a chivalrous captain who was of great help to the Church in times of danger. In 1583 through their good offices Father Organtino, the leader of the mission in Miyako, was received with a Japanese brother in most friendly fashion by Hideyoshi. He conversed with them at length and granted them a plot of land for a church in Osaka, where he planned to make a new capital. In 1586 he entertained in his now completed palace Father Coelho (the new Vice-Provincial of western Japan) and a large number of missionaries, catechists, and seminarists. According to Frois, who acted as interpreter, he praised the work of the Jesuits and discoursed at length upon his own projects, which included the conquest of Korea and China, where (he said) he meant to establish the Christian faith. The missionaries should help him by supplying good ships. The new ruler was as hostile to the Buddhists as had been Nobunaga, and destroyed several great monasteries with much bloodshed. It seemed to the Christians that their idolatrous enemy was doomed. Hideyoshi entrusted Christian generals with important tasks in his campaigns, and some of their troops carried banners emblazoned with a cross. When in the summer of 1587 he was on his expedition to subdue the daimyos of Kyushu he invited Father Coelho, the Vice-Provincial, to visit him at his headquarters, and at the end of the campaign he set aside a plot of land for a church in Hakata. He later went aboard a small but well-armed Portuguese vessel to see the father, where he showed himself extremely affable and interested.

Out of this clear sky there came on July 25 a thunderbolt. Hideyoshi issued an edict in which he condemned the missionaries and their teaching and ordered them to leave Japan within twenty days, but decreed that trade with the Indies could continue. The missionaries were at a loss to understand this startling change of mind. Their opinions differed, and in fact the reason for Hideyoshi's sudden decision has never been fully explained. Some suggested that he was angered when he learned that the Christian settlement in Nagasaki was protected by pieces of artillery that the Portuguese had brought ashore. Others that he had been impressed by the well-armed Portuguese vessel which had brought Father Coelho to Hakata and that he had marked with displeasure the close relationship between the churchmen and the military. No doubt such ideas passed through his mind, but it is probable that he was less moved by particular reasons than by a more general feeling of alarm at the growth of Christian influence among important rulers and generals. Like any new ruler not entirely sure of his position, he feared a movement that by attacking national traditions might produce a division of opinion and weaken the loyalties upon which he depended. There is no reason to doubt the reasons Hideyoshi himself gave for his policy. He said quite clearly that he had no objection to the Christian religion. He thought that the missionaries were good people and their doctrine was good; but they were foreigners and were preaching against the gods of Japan.

He had no religious feeling himself, but he well knew that the indigenous cult of Japan, the worship of the *Kami,* the spirits of departed rulers and heroes, was the very foundation of the social order. It supported the whole pyramid of loyalties at whose summit he stood. From his standpoint as a despotic ruler he was undoubtedly right to regard Christian propaganda as subversive, for no system can survive unchanged once the assumptions upon which it is based are undermined. However high their purpose, what the Jesuits were doing, in Japan as well as in India and China, was to challenge a national tradition and through it the existing political structure. This last is an animal that always defends itself when attacked, and consequently Hideyoshi's reaction, however deplorable, was to be expected and does not seem to need any fuller explanation.

What is surprising is the mildness with which his edict was enforced. When the Jesuits protested that there were no ships to take them away he gave them six months' grace and subsequently he took no action when he found that they remained in Japan and unobtrusively carried on their mission. They made no public appearances, but celebrated Mass in private houses, and in the district surrounding Miyako they travelled at night in closed palanquins. They hoped that by behaving with great discretion they might persuade Hideyoshi to withdraw or relax his proscription. Some of their converts apostatized, but for the most part the missionaries, far from needing to fortify the spirit of the native Christians, felt obliged to discourage many who were ready (in the words of Organtino) "to hasten to martyrdom as if to a festival." All the Jesuit observers are agreed in describing the Japanese as a people whose traditional manners and customs so predisposed them to a disregard for life that it was necessary for the missionaries to preach to them vigorously against suicide. The Jesuit letters refer frequently to their devotion to the cross, their love of Christ crucified, and their cruel flagellations, which made the blood flow. "It was difficult to moderate their spirit of love and penitence." A striking phenomenon of this period is the growth of Japanese Christian literature on martyrdom. It includes exaltation of martyrs, discussions of the purpose of martyrdom, and letters written during the persecutions exhorting the faithful to be steadfast. A Japanese authority considers these writings to be admirable in style and comparable to the best Buddhist literature of the preceding period.

This curious sidelight upon the Japanese character may be left to psychologists to explain, but it has a historical interest in that it seems very clearly to mark off the Japanese as different from other Asiatic pepoles in their attitude towards the crucifixion. To most people in other parts of eastern Asia, if one may judge from the records of Christian endeavour, the doctrine of atonement was repugnant. They were shocked by the idea of a divine person undergoing torture and death and disliked a symbolism that had to do with blood. This was particularly true of Buddhist countries, and it is somewhat surprising to find a masochistic strain in Japan, where the religious ascetic usually mortified the flesh only by living frugally in a mountain hut or by practising such minor austerities as bathing in very cold water. But it is an undoubted fact that the Japanese people throughout their history have been remarkably ready in peace as in war to suffer as well as to inflict death; and this may account both for the ferocity with which Japanese Christians were persecuted and for the fortitude with which they went to martyrdom.

But severe persecution did not follow the first edict of Hideyoshi until after a lapse of ten years. Organtino with several priests and brothers was allowed to reside in Miyako on condition that he performed no baptisms and opened no churches. In secret a number of catechumens came to him and he baptized several notables. In the southwestern provinces similar conditons obtained, particularly in Nagasaki, where the Governor permitted private gatherings and where the Jesuit printing press was busy putting out devotional works. The missionaries held their regular assembly in 1592 and, reporting that the persecution would soon come to an end, asked the General of their order to send more workers to Japan. According to their records the number of conversions in the south during the five years from 1587 to 1592 reached 52,000, and they predicted that the number of Christians could soon be carried to several hundred thousand. Faith, said Organtino, might be tried by persecution, but like the seed that falls upon good soil it would bear fruit in the midst of suffering. In an interesting passage in one of his letters he says: "Our consolation is to think that in Japan we are sharing the trials and tribulations of our holy martyrs in England." By this curious comparison he unconsciously testified to the fact that behind the persecutions in both countries was a strong political motive. The Jesuits in Elizabethan England and in Japan were feared as agents of a temporal power that threatened national security by fomenting dissension within the realm.

An unfortunate but probably inevitable combination of circumstances served to increase the suspicions of Hideyoshi and to induce him to enforce his edict more vigorously. It is quite likely that the Jesuits, who were experienced and circumspect, were right in believing that had the field been left to them they would, despite the edict, have been able to continue their work and in the long run convert a very large proportion of the Japanese people. But an unseemly rivalry on the part of other orders, notably the Franciscans, destroyed these prospects. In disregard of the understanding that evangelization in Japan should be reserved to the Jesuits — an understanding confirmed by the papal brief *Ex pastoralis officio* of January 28, 1585 — Spanish Franciscans from the Philippines began from 1593 to make their way to Japan. Displaying great apostolic fervour but little political sense, they openly flouted the edict, building churches, preaching, baptizing in the capital itself, under the nose of Hideyoshi. Even so, that despot held his hand, partly no doubt because he was preoccupied with more urgent matters, but also because he was interested in commerce with the Philippines and even professed to regard those islands as belonging to him. He was in negotiation for a commercial arrangement with the Spanish Governor at Manila, who used Franciscans as his emissaries. Hideyoshi received them courteously enough, but evidently he was keeping a careful watch.

Late in the year 1596 a Spanish galleon was driven ashore in eastern Japan and salvaged by the Japanese ruler of the district, who claimed its cargo. The Spanish pilot angrily boasted of the power of his own sovereign and hinted, it seems, that traders and priests were the advance guard of expeditions to conquer distant countries.[5] When this news reached Hideyoshi he was quick to act. He arrested certain Japanese catechists of the Franciscans, had lists of converts in the capital prepared, and sentenced to death twenty-six Christians, including six Spanish Franciscans and the catechists just mentioned. These were all crucified at Nagasaki in February 1597. To the protests of the Governor of the Philippines he replied that the Spaniards had no more right to introduce their religion into Japan than had the Japanese to preach the worship of their own gods in the Philippines. Moreover, these Franciscans had been sent to prepare the conquest of Japan, just as they had prepared that of the Philippine Islands, where the Spaniards had dispossessed the native rulers.

Thenceforward the Japanese Christians in most parts of Japan were liable to persecution at the hands of their rulers. Some were killed, many were exiled. Churches and seminaries were burned, missionaries for a time had either to go into hiding or to go about their business with the greatest circumspection. Hideyoshi himself after the edict of 1597 did not legislate further against Chris-

---

[5] The truth of this story has been questioned, but there is no doubt that some such language was used, either by Spanish officers or by Franciscans from Manila.

tians. He was busy with preparations for a second expedition to Korea, the first (in 1592–3) having failed. He was already suffering from an illness that proved mortal in September 1598, and was succeeded in power by his colleague Tokugawa Ieyasu after a struggle against recalcitrant barons, which was brought to an end by his decisive victory in the battle of Sekigahara in 1600.

It was not until 1615, however, that he completely subdued all opposition, so that for some years after 1598, though there were severe local persecutions, in general the work of evangelization was not seriously disturbed by Ieyasu himself.[6] He had more urgent matters to deal with and he was a cautious ruler who knew how to bide his time. He was much interested in foreign trade and therefore disposed to keep on good terms with both Spanish and Portuguese at least until he could develop his own merchant marine. He even approached the Spanish government of the Philippines, through a Franciscan intermediary, offering to open harbours in eastern Japan to Spanish ships, proposing reciprocal freedom of commerce, and asking for naval architects. He also gave it to be understood that he would not enforce the anti-Christian edicts. The missionaries made good use of the respite afforded to them. Valignano, writing in 1603, said that by 1600 all the residences and most of the churches had been rebuilt and great numbers of new converts had been made. He put the total number of Christians at 300,000, the population of all Japan being at that time probably about 25,000,000.

It is not easy to understand why Christian doctrine should have appealed to Japanese minds so much more strongly than to those of other advanced Asiatic peoples, but there is perhaps a clue in the resemblance between the ecstatic states of mind reached by Japanese Christians and those enjoyed by devotees of the Pure Land and Lotus sects, which are both distinctly Japanese versions of Buddhism. On the Pure Land sect there are some enlightening

---

[6] The recorded martyrdoms, after the crucifixions at Nagasaki in February 1597, are as follows:

1600	1	
1603	6	
1605	102	(A vassal of the Daimyo of Yamaguchi with all his family and retainers. All decapitated by order of the Daimyo.)
1607	2	
1608	1	
1609	7	
1610	8	
1612	5	

No foreigners were executed in this period. The figures do not, of course, include Japanese Christians who were stripped of their property and banished. Of these there were several thousand.

From the year 1613 the number of executions increased as the persecution gained in ferocity owing to a change in the attitude of Ieyasu.

passages in the writings (*o fumi*) of Rennyo Shōnin. Speaking of the effect of their faith upon the minds of believers, he says, in a well-known stanza: "Formerly happiness was wrapped in the sleeve, but tonight it is even too great for the whole body," by which he means that after repeating the invocation to Amida the congregation is filled with an overflowing bliss, whereas before their lives had never known more than a pocketful of rejoicing. The hymns composed by Rennyo and his general teaching dwell upon present happiness as contrasted with the pleasure of paradise to come. One such hymn says:

> Since we have heard the Saviour's vow
> We are no common sinful men.
> For though our bodies still are stained
> Our hearts are filled with heavenly joy.[7]

The conviction of future birth in paradise leads to bliss in the present life, and thus faith and joy are so closely related as to be one.

It seems that the Pure Land teaching satisfied some emotional need of the times, which were full of hardship and danger, especially for those in the lower ranks of society, whose lives were wretched. It is perhaps significant that in those parts of Japan where the Jōdo sect was most firmly established, there were few converts to Christianity, presumably because believers in Pure Land Buddhism found it a satisfying faith. Similar arguments would apply to the Lotus sect, whose members were given to apocalyptic visions, trances, and states of high excitement induced by beating drums and chanting litanies. There can be no doubt of the attraction of "revivalist" gatherings for simple people, denied all but the most elementary pleasures. It may be added that the Christian gospel furnishes some analogy for the Jōdo doctrine of salvation by calling upon the holy name. Thus in Romans x, 9: "If thou shalt confess with thy mouth the Lord Jesus and shalt believe in thine heart that God hath raised him from the dead, thou shalt be saved"; and in Romans x, 13: "Whosoever shall call upon the name of the Lord shall be saved."

There is also in Romans iii an interesting analogy to the distinction made in Pure Land Buddhism between salvation by works (*Jiriki*) and salvation by faith (*Tariki*).

---

[7] This is a very free translation, but the sense is preserved. Students of Japanese may be interested in the text of the verse first quoted, which is in very simple language:

> *Tanoshisa wa*
> *Mukashi wa sode ni*
> *Tsutsumikeri*
> *Koyoi wa mi ni mo*
> *Amarinuru ka na*

THE ASIATIC TRADE

1. The European Background

ONE of the remarkable aspects of the Portuguese claim to a monopoly of maritime trade in Asia is the deference paid to Portuguese pretensions by European nations. Neither the Dutch nor the English were at the beginning of the sixteenth century strong enough to challenge the authority of the Pope in giving to the crowns of Spain and Portugal the exclusive rights of navigation to newly discovered lands. The French, though they sent a ship to Sumatra as early as 1529 and made voyages of exploration along the Atlantic coasts of North America, did not for some time make any persistent effort to rival the Portuguese in the Eastern trade. The Netherlands, France, and England, recognizing for political reasons the position assumed by the Spanish and the Portuguese, respected the papal bulls and the doctrine of *mare clausum,* and accordingly their seamen felt obliged to seek an alternative way to China, Japan, and the Spice Islands. Their efforts were thus for a great part of the sixteenth century confined to valiant but abortive striving to open a northeast or a northwest passage, because their sovereigns would not take the risk of embroilment with Spain or Portugal.

The evolution of maritime trade was in fact governed to an important degree by the political development of Europe, for the Portuguese and Spanish were by no means alone in feeling a strong urge for expansion. All the vigorous European peoples were seeking for means to expand their wealth and power as the pattern of national states began to form at the expense of the waning political authority of the Catholic Church. It was by this struggle to increase national resources that the foundation of modern imperialism was laid. It cannot be regarded merely as an expression of European pugnacity and greed, for though it was not wanting in those incidental aspects, it was an inevitable outcome of the development of European political and economic life in the centuries leading up to the Renaissance. As feudalism meant economic regression, so the break-up of feudalism was bound to call for economic expansion. The smaller national states of Europe were obliged, in defence of their freedom and independence — in defence even of their very existence — to strive for additions to their strength, either in goods or in territory, if they were to resist their more powerful rivals. This is clear enough if only from the examples of England and the Netherlands, since it was these small countries that, by throwing off the authority of the Catholic Church and by resisting the domination of Spain and the Holy Roman Empire, were able to take the lead in the development of free institutions. These ends they could never have achieved without the strength they drew from the expansion of their maritime trade; and therefore in considering the rights and wrongs of colonial rule we should not fail to take into account its full historical context. We may deplore an effect, but in assessing blame or praise we should recognize its cause.

These general observations may be fittingly expanded by examining the position of the countries that, though lagging behind at the time of the Portuguese and Spanish discoveries, ultimately created the greatest colonial empires in Asia. In the sixteenth century both England and the Netherlands were poor and weak. The Low Countries indeed were in the first half of the century part of the empire of Charles V, who handed them over to Philip of Spain in 1555, so that, while the separate provinces kept their ancient rights, a national state did not exist. But the doctrines of the Reformation had spread over all the provinces before the accession of Philip, and after Alva's reign of terror hostility to Spain grew powerful enough to allow the counties of Holland and Zeeland to maintain some degree of independence and to wage war on Spanish sea-borne commerce. It was not until 1581, however, that the northern provinces disowned Spanish sovereignty and formed an independent union (finally recognized by Spain in 1609), which was able in time to attain great prosperity, whereas the southern provinces remained in decline because of their association with the decadence of Spain. The northern provinces were able to free themselves largely because of the strategic advantage given to them by their coastal position, and it may be said that the later maritime achievements of the Dutch were nourished by their struggle for freedom against Spain. In that struggle they received aid from England, whose developing hostility towards Philip gave them some respite while he was preparing the great Armada.

If England was, unlike the Netherlands, free and independent in the sixteenth century, she was none the less weak and poor. Her margin of safety was very small, and her overseas expansion was not undertaken in a spirit of romantic adventure. The picturesque and stirring episodes in which the great Elizabethan seamen figure, their astonishing successes in buccaneering, and their brilliant naval exploits tend to conceal the truth that their country was engaged in a desperate struggle for life, which required sober planning and bold execution.

In the early part of the sixteenth century, while Spain and Portugal were strong and were beginning to add to their wealth by overseas trade or, to be more exact, by confiscation of the wealth of America and the Indies, England was only beginning to recover from the Wars of the Roses, which had ended in 1497, the year of Vasco da Gama's voyage to Calicut. Henry VII, by a cautious foreign policy devoted largely to securing advantageous commercial treaties, began to improve his country's trading position, and he also encouraged maritime exploration. British seamen in search of fishing grounds — for the cod and the herring played a great part in the economy of western Europe — had already sailed well out into the Atlantic before Columbus, and after Cabot's voyage under royal charter which ended in the discovery of Nova Scotia in 1497, Henry encouraged exploration of the North American coastline.

But England was still needy, and time was wanted for the development of her navy and her merchant fleet and the organization of her foreign trade, both of which depended upon capital that was slow to accumulate. Caution was still required before national policy could be openly directed to rivalry with Spain and Portugal and it was not until Elizabeth's reign was well advanced that the English felt strong enough to challenge those maritime powers openly. Meanwhile ventures in navigation and trade were left for the most part to private enterprise. There were plenty of bold spirits in England and elsewhere attracted by the prospects opening out in the rapidly expanding world, for while fortune gave the early successes to Portugal and Spain, the whole of western Europe was alive with a passion for discovery. This was not a mere movement to gain trade, though the desire for commercial profit was of course a strong incentive.

Though the age of discovery was opened by the great voyages of Columbus and Vasco da Gama, it depended upon much more than national enterprise, for its exploits were made possible by the totality of European intellectual achievement — by advances in geography, astronomy, and navigation and other sciences, to which Genoese and Venetians, French and Germans, Flemish and English had all made some contribution. But if the movement of expansion was cosmopolitan in its origins, it was decidedly national in its development; and while it may be regretted it cannot be denied that European rivalries gave a special character to the intercourse of European and Asiatic peoples from the end of the six-teenth century onwards.

The march of European influence towards the East can be fully understood only if it is seen as an extension of conflicts between European states at home. Once Portuguese supremacy was challenged, it was not possible for the Dutch and the English to expand their trade in Asia by peaceful rivalry, for the Portuguese were bound to defend their monopoly by arms, and the other maritime nations of Europe, being intermittently at war with one another, carried on a foreign commerce that was an inseparable part of their naval struggle. This aspect of the Asiatic trade is familiar to students of European history and need not be treated in detail here, though it must be referred to from time to time. But the attitude of Asiatic peoples towards the efforts of Europeans to open trade relations on a great scale is less well understood and requires some general explanation. This may be prefaced by a brief summary which will refresh the reader's memory of the main events in the competition for Far Eastern trade that took place in the seventeenth century.

After 1580, when Portugal was united to Spain, the Lisbon market came under the control of Madrid, and free access was denied to the Dutch and the English. The effect of Spanish policy was to raise the price of pepper and spices and thus to stimulate other trading nations to go direct to sources of supply. The Dutch were first in the field. They expelled the Portuguese from Bantam in 1596 and traded on their own account, forming the Netherlands East India Company in 1602 and thenceforward establishing factories on the Malabar coast, at Amboina and other strategic points. They took Malacca in 1641, controlled Ceylon by 1658, and dominated the spice trade by 1660, thus cutting deeply into the Portuguese monopoly. They did not succeed, however, in gaining a footing in China, where the Portuguese, after inauspicious beginnings, were firmly settled in Macao. Seeking for alternatives to direct trade with China, the Dutch built up an ingenious system whereby they purchased Chinese goods in Japan, Bantam, Calicut, Surat, and later Formosa, whither the produce of China was brought in Chinese junks. Their trading position was not achieved without clashes with their Portuguese and English rivals, but they were generally successful because they disposed of superior naval forces and had behind them the strong support of their home government.

The English East India Company, founded in 1698, was preceded by a company of "Governors and Merchants of London trading into the East Indies," which was formed at the end of 1600 under patent from Elizabeth. Its trade was less successful than that of the Dutch, its exports for the nineteen years from 1601 to 1620 amounting to £840,000, or about £44,000 per annum. Of this total £292,000 represented the value of woollens, metals, and other English products, while the remaining £548,000 was silver bullion and coin.

The disproportion between goods and cash was a great handicap to English trade. This was an age of monopolies, begun by the Portuguese and continued by the Dutch. Both were anxious to keep out a third party and used all possible means to check the growth of the English company and also the activities of interlopers such as Weddell's expedition to China in 1636–7. When Weddell reached Macao the Portuguese did all they could to thwart him; and when he arrived off Canton the Chinese officials were unfriendly. After some abortive negotiations, when Weddell landed some men by force, his ships were attacked by Chinese war vessels. He was in the end allowed to load some cargo after a face-saving declaration, but the desire of the Chinese was evidently to get rid of the intruders in the hope that they would not come again. This was at a time when the Ming government was declining. The high provincial officials did not want trouble; the lower officials wanted not trade but bribes and plunder.

Thus the English ventures in China were unsuccessful. They tried elsewhere, in Formosa, Japan, Siam, and Tongking, but results were very poor. Friction with the Dutch was unending and English settlements in the East Indian archipelago could not be profitably maintained in the face of Dutch obstruction, which often took violent forms. The English effort in the Far East therefore tended to diminish, and greater attention was paid to the development of trade with Red Sea ports, the Persian Gulf, and notably with India, where the foundations were laid of a commercial empire that was to prove vastly more profitable and to have greater political consequence in both Asia and Europe than the Dutch monopoly of the spice trade.

2. The Adverse Balance

THE TRADE relationships between Europe and Asia were until recent times of a somewhat one-sided character, the Europeans showing a firm resolve to sell and the Asiatics a reluctance to buy. The Roman Empire was, if historians are to be believed, drained of gold because the peoples of India and China had little need of European produce, and a similar obstacle to trade was encountered by the Portuguese not long after their arrival in India. Although trading communities in both India and China were anxious to make commercial profits and were skilled and experienced practitioners, governments in those countries did not look upon foreign trade as something to be encouraged and protected as a matter of state policy, but were inclined to leave merchants to themselves as a class of people to be taxed and tolerated but not especially favoured. Consequently the Portuguese, unable to furnish to India or China or the countries of southeast Asia enough useful commodities in exchange for the silks and spices that were indispensable to Europe, found themselves obliged to seek means of acquiring gold and silver with which to purchase them. This they did by acting as brokers and shippers, and by the beginning of the seventeenth century they had established themselves in both the Indian Ocean and the Pacific as the chief carriers of goods between Asiatic countries. Their earnings from this traffic allowed them to purchase and convey to Europe in home-trading ships such Eastern goods as they required.

It may be asked why the several Asiatic countries did not themselves engage in this carrying trade, and the answer is that they did, but that Portuguese ships were faster and better armed than their own craft and could therefore make longer and safer voyages in waters infested by pirates. Consequently, by establishing themselves in protected trading stations at a number of key points in the Indian Ocean and in Indonesia and by obtaining trading privileges in China and Japan, they were able to build up an organization that extended, with many ramifications, between Sofala and Nagasaki. So firmly planted were they by 1600 that, although they soon afterwards lost the spice trade and much of their direct trade with Europe to the Dutch and the English, they continued to dominate the interport trade of Asia, which was the real basis of their commercial supremacy. They carried cotton piece goods from Gujarat and Coromandel ports; silk and silk fabrics from China; silver bullion from Japan; gold and ivory from east Africa. These they disposed of in other parts of Asia. It is noteworthy that of these commodities it was the gold and silver that were absorbed by India and China respectively. This is clear evidence that those great countries stood in no need of European products, wanting only luxuries and treasure. The political difficulties encountered by European nations seeking trade agreements with Eastern potentates are to be explained largely by the indifference of the rulers of the self-sufficient countries to the manufactures of Europe.

We have already noticed how the Emperor of China told King George III that China possessed all things in abundance and wanted no foreign goods. In this Ch'ien Lung was only professing sentiments that had guided Chinese sovereigns in the past, for even at the time of their greatest maritime expansion the Chinese gov-

THE BIBLE IN MING CHINA

A page from a small book published in China in 1605, containing simple versions of three Bible stories prepared by Father Ricci, the Jesuit scholar who laboured in China from 1582 to 1610.

By the side of each character is a rendering of its sound in Roman letters, in the hand of Father Ricci. This is the earliest attempt at a systematic "romanization" of Chinese. In Japan the Jesuits had produced devotional works in "romanized" Japanese a decade or more before 1605, their system being already well established when they printed their Doctrina Christiana *in 1592.*

(Reproduced from Westernized Art and Roman Script in the Ming Period, *by Ch'ên Yüan, Peking, 1927.)*

rnment had been only mildly interested in foreign trade. In our lay, when it seems like a law of nature that all countries should mutually buy, sell, and chaffer, this attitude appears as a kind of prelapsarian innocence and is a little hard for modern man (whether European or Asiatic) to comprehend. But it was part of a view of the world not uncommon in Asia, and therefore deserves a little study, especially as the process by which it was broken down is by far the most important of all influences exerted by Europe upon Asia. It was not fortified trading stations or even the seizure of territory that forced Asiatic people to buy European exports. These were steps on the way, but what at length overcame their resistance was the provision of cheap manufactured goods.

Perhaps the best example of Asiatic indifference to foreign trade is furnished by the nature of the great Ming voyages of the early fifteenth century. They are of especial interest because they may be looked upon as a historical prelude to the troubles encountered by the Portuguese after their first visit and the subsequent experience of the English, which led to the "Opium War."

3. The Auspicious Giraffes

DISTINGUISHED Sinologists have written fascinating studies of the Ming voyages, which provide historians with much ground for speculation. These remarkable and enigmatic expeditions have already been referred to [1] in connection with the arrival of the Portuguese in China, but it is useful to bring out some further points bearing upon the reversal of Chinese foreign policy by which they were followed. They commenced in 1405 and continued until 1433. Nobody knows why they began or why they ended. They appear to have been planned by a eunuch of the Imperial court, one Cheng-ho, who commanded the first of a series of seven voyages, which were made by scores of ships, carrying thousands of soldiers, sailors, officials, and merchants. They visited the harbours of the Southern Sea, the Bay of Bengal, and the Indian Ocean, sailing on as far as the Persian Gulf, the Red Sea, and the east African coast. Immense and costly undertakings, they seem to have been designed not to increase trade but to satisfy the luxurious tastes and the curiosity of the court, while ministering to the ambition of the eunuchs. The civilian authorities and the literati disliked them and went so far as to hide or destroy the records that Cheng-ho must have submitted. This action may have been inspired by jealousy of the eunuchs, but there is nothing to show that the Emperor, who must have been formally apprised of the ex-

---

[1] See Chapter iii, pp. 42, 43.

peditions, viewed them with any enthusiasm. His successor stopped them on the day of his mounting the throne.

It is to be presumed that the missing records said something about trade, but it is certainly not mentioned in Cheng-ho's memorials to the Emperor. These dwell upon the size of the fleets; the transforming power of the Emperor's virtue, which caused many kings to submit to him and send tribute; the punishment of those who did not pay respect to China; and most of all the wonderful presents brought back from foreign parts. He has a great deal to say about a kindly goddess named the Celestial Spouse; about the god of the South Seas, who was promoted to an earldom for his services in arranging good weather; and about certain Auspicious Giraffes which were brought from Africa for the Emperor. The Board of Rites wished to present an address of congratulation on these creatures, but this the Emperor declined, saying that if the ministers exerted themselves for the welfare of the world, auspicious animals could be dispensed with. But it does not appear that the expeditions had acquired much useful knowledge of the world, and the Auspicious Giraffes may be regarded as symbolizing the official Chinese attitude towards foreign countries.

These immense undertakings brought back to China some ambassadors who professed submission to the Son of Heaven and some tribute, doubtless requited by handsome Chinese gifts. There was little else to show for this great and costly effort, beyond a few exotic birds and animals. After the last voyage China withdrew once more into seclusion. Her people were forbidden to leave the country or to communicate with foreigners, and Chinese ships could no longer make ocean voyages. This attitude towards the outside world was maintained for more than three hundred years and influenced the course of Far Eastern history in important ways.

At first sight the Ming policy in regard to foreign trade looks as if it were a policy of closing the country similar to that adopted by Japan in 1640. But there is an important difference between the Chinese and Japanese attitudes. China simply did not recognize the existence of independent foreign states and therefore the question of opening or closing the country to them did not arise as a legal problem. There were edicts preventing ships and men from leaving China, but these did not constitute an exclusion policy. The instructions or legacy of the first Ming Emperor said that "not an inch of plank" should go down to the sea, and this, strictly interpreted, meant that there should be no coasting trade as well as no ocean trade. But it was usually taken as referring to voyages which would carry coasting vessels into areas of piracy. In principle the Ming government prohibited Chinese from emigrating to or trading with foreign countries. Infractions were common, however,

GANDHARAN SCULPTURE

This Buddhist image shows drapery of the Roman type.
(Reproduced by permission of the British Museum)

THE AUSPICIOUS GIRAFFE

(By kind permission of
Professor J. J. L. Duyvendak)

and there were frequent orders against "private commerce with barbarians," while large numbers of Chinese went overseas and stayed there, forming considerable colonies in Java, Sumatra, Malacca, Luzon, and Siam.

The purpose of these bans upon foreign trade and travel is not entirely clear. They doubtless formed part of a general policy of seclusion that began when the Ming, having rid China of a foreign dynasty, settled down to resume their native way of life and to shelter it from foreign influences. This would explain the first Ming Emperor's ruling (1404) that the "people should not go down to the sea in ships"; and although these strict rules were from time to time modified or disregarded, for a long period it remained the official view that foreign trade and foreign relations in general were unnecessary and dangerous.

Apart from this general theory, there were specific reasons for discouraging commerce with foreign countries. The shores of China were constantly raided by Japanese pirates during the fourteenth and fifteenth centuries and also by sea robbers from Chinese coastal areas, who were quite as numerous as the Japanese. In fact the crews of many Japanese pirate vessels were composed largely of Chinese. It was to check their own subjects as well as the Japanese that the Ming government restricted the movements of Chinese shipping and tried to keep disorderly sailors from joining pirate bands. But despite these restrictions there was never any prohibition against the visits of foreign vessels bearing customary "tribute," which was in fact foreign merchandise. Special offices known as Merchant Shipping Controls were open at ports in Fukien and Kwangtung to deal with them. The rule or principle was that China did not exclude ships sent by countries that were impressed by the virtue of the celestial court. It was only when the Portuguese towards the end of the Ming dynasty behaved badly that other countries (in southeast Asia) suffered from injunctions aimed at the Portuguese; and when at last the Portuguese did gain a foothold, they were able to drive a profitable trade because, owing to the disabilities imposed upon Chinese subjects, Portuguese merchants at Macao were able to monopolize the purchase of Chinese silk and other goods for export. The Ming policy was carried on for a time by the Manchus, but the ban on foreign trade was lifted from 1684 until 1717, when trade with the South Seas was forbidden.

It will be seen that the Chinese policy was not one of deliberate and determined exclusion like that of the Japanese. The Chinese theory was that if foreigners came respectfully and peacefully to China and asked for goods, they were allowed to trade, because the Imperial grace extended over the four seas; but this was a privilege that could be withdrawn at once if there was any bad behaviour. The Japanese prohibition was absolute, except for the licensed trade at Nagasaki, and foreign vessels venturing to other Japanese ports were liable to destruction and their crews to death. Thus, although the Japanese attitude to foreigners was less contemptuous than that of the Chinese, the trade policy of the Tokugawa period (1640–1858) was in practice less liberal. But European traders never fully understood the reasoning behind Chinese policy, always thinking in terms of the right to trade while the Chinese regarded it as a gracious concession. It was not until after the collapse of the Manchus that China could treat foreign countries on a basis of equality, by abandoning the idea that China ruled the world. Accordingly the relationships between China and foreign countries seeking trade opportunities were constantly bedevilled by misunderstandings, which culminated in the Anglo-Chinese war of 1840. Even that bitter experience did not really change the Chinese point of view. They agreed to the terms of the Treaty of Nanking only in order to keep the foreigners quiet and did not abandon their historical position. The Japanese, on the other hand, saw clearly the implications of opening their country to trade, and when they took that step they knew that it involved a refashioning of their institutions.

A confusing feature of Chinese policy towards foreign trade is the difference between principle and practice. It is worth some mention here because it helps to explain several seeming anomalies and illuminates in a rather striking manner the contrast between Chinese and Japanese standards of the enforcement of law. The Ming edicts that forbade Chinese men and ships to leave their shores were often disobeyed and officials on the Fukien coast were always ready to wink at illicit trade. Even when relations between China and Japan were severed as a result of Japanese piracy and the Korean campaigns of Hideyoshi (1592–8) the Chinese trading colony in Kyushu continued its pursuit of legitimate trade and smuggling. Early in the seventeenth century one I-quan, the leader of that colony, had a fleet of a thousand junks and was "master of the seas from the Yangtze to the Pearl River." In 1628 he was used by the Ming government against pirates, being put in command of the Imperial fleet. When the Japanese exclusion edicts came, Chinese trade was permitted in Nagasaki and nearly one hundred junks entered in 1639, though the Ming edicts had not been rescinded.

Many more instances could be cited of the Ming failure to enforce its policy. It was due no doubt in the first place to the weakness of the central government and the great extent of its territory, but a certain partiality for compromise seems to have had something to do with it also. The Japanese for their part were less accommodating. The Ashikaga shoguns were not able to control all their feudal lords and in the fifteenth century they had allowed trade with China under somewhat humiliating conditions, going so far as to accept the Chinese calendar, which is an act of submission. But once the Tokugawa family had established a central government, they carried out their exclusion policy with ruthless thoroughness. No Japanese official would dare to tolerate infractions of the law.

Seen in their historical setting all these difficulties were inevitable sequels of the adverse balance that had characterized the trade of Europe with Asia since the days of the Roman Empire. Asia did not need foreign goods, and Europe did not wish to spend gold in the purchase of Asiatic produce which was so important to her. The Portuguese, as we have seen, used their earnings as carriers for the purchase of Indian and Chinese goods; the Dutch and the English followed their example, but did not succeed in capturing the interport trade from them. The history of English commercial enterprise in the Far East shows a continuous but abortive effort to find a "vent" for English woollens; and it was a failure to establish markets for English manufacturers that led in the long run to the sale of opium for the purpose of redressing the adverse balance of which Roman writers had complained. They had in the first century decried the waste of Roman treasure upon gossamer fabrics for shameless Roman women; and early in the seventeenth century English pamphleteers deplored the export of bullion for the purchase of fine Indian muslins and calicoes, things "light as cobwebs, light commodities for light women." They described the ladies who wore these flimsy stuffs as "Calico-Picts, who would have shocked their naked woad-stained ancestors."

4. Eastern Trade and Western Life

It will be clear that the trading enterprises of Europeans in Asia, profitable as they were to merchants of both continents, were the cause of disturbances in European as well as Asiatic life, and it is worth while to look further at the nature of the Asiatic trade from this point of view. One is apt to think of European intrusion as producing disturbances in Asiatic life and to forget that from their adventures European countries experienced effects which were not all beneficial.

When one considers the various forms of intercourse between nations, it appears that trade relations, which are usually thought of as nothing but the exchange of things, are in fact those which exercise the greatest influence, especially as between countries separated by long distances. Attempts to impose ideas by means of religious missions or books or other means of persuasion seem to have less effect than the objects of trade, which are silent but convincing. What we have seen so far of the history of evangelism in Asia does not encourage a belief that religious or philosophical ideas are easily transplanted. The influence of ideas is at any rate slow to operate and almost invariably evokes a resistance that is not met with by — let us take for example — guns, tobacco, potatoes, watches, and clocks in Asia or silks, gums, and spices in Europe. These are accepted at first without qualm and often with alacrity, and it is only after a lapse of time that their true influence becomes apparent, for better or for worse.

One of the evils laid at the door of European trade expansion is the harm it has done, especially to the inhabitants of colonial territories, by disturbing or even destroying their customary economic life. The introduction of new commodities displaces native products and throws people out of employment; or a demand for native products for export induces the cultivator to grow them at the expense of articles needed for consumption at home; or the colonist for his own purposes interferes with an old custom of land tenure or a method of trading, thus throwing the native economy out of balance. Such charges have been levelled at British and Dutch administration in the Indies, and they are not easy to rebut. But it is sometimes forgotten that the development of foreign and particularly of colonial trade often disturbed the economy of the colonizing country, and this is a feature of the intercourse between Europe and Asia that should not be overlooked. We talk of the influence of one country upon another, of one culture upon another, but we are inclined to forget that these are not simple one-sided processes. Where there is action there is reaction, and in the measure that one country influences another its own life is often subjected to change. The very existence of relationships close enough to affect one party is almost invariably the cause of change in the other. The whole history of intercourse between Europe and Asia bears out the truth of this proposition. It is particularly well illustrated by the record of the East India trade, which may therefore be appropriately discussed here.

The commercial successes of the Portuguese in India brought prosperity to Portugal in their earliest phases and enriched the cultural life of her cities. But it can also be argued that the digestion of the wealth of the Indies caused serious pains to the body politic of their country. It strained her agrarian economy and proved too much for her trading machinery to handle, with the result that the Dutch and the English ultimately profited and Portugal suffered.

An even more striking example of what might be called reverse influence is provided by the history of the English East India trade in the seventeenth and eighteenth centuries. It produced a crisis or at least a disturbance that had important consequences in the economic life of the British Isles. This was at a time when England had only recently developed as a national state in which economic policy was deliberately pursued with a view to strengthening the country against powerful European rivals and possible aggressors. The formation of the Board of Trade and Plantations in 1672 shows how important it was in the minds of contemporary statesmen that trade and industry should be regulated in the interests of the country as a whole. This high and persistent regard for manufacture and commerce is in marked contrast to the indifference displayed by the rulers of most Asiatic countries.

In seventeenth-century England not only did the state begin to take an energetic part in protecting trade, but trade was a constant topic of public discussion. It was the East India trade that provoked the most violent controversies. The root of the argument, from which grew a tree with many branches, was the old fear of the drain of gold. When the English pamphleteers professed to be shocked by the transparency of Indian fabrics their care for the modesty of English females was a disguise, not less transparent than muslin, for the objections of those who on general grounds deplored sending gold and silver abroad or on particular grounds were anxious to protect domestic industries.

The controversy was long-drawn-out. The East India Company was attacked in the early years of the seventeenth century on the ground that most of its trade with India involved paying out specie, so denuding England of its wealth, just as in the nineteenth century Indian patriots were to resent the so-called Drain — the transfer of gold from their country to England. In the battle of the pamphlets and broadsides the East India Company found writers to defend its practices and make out a good case for its contribution to the general wealth of the realm. But there was a strong feeling against the company which argument could not abate. Private traders and the general public resented its monopoly, while the beautiful Indian cottons, becoming first fashionable and then popular, upset the domestic manufacture of both woollens and silks. As early as 1695 Parliament was urged to prohibit the use of Indian fabrics, and in the debates "cheap foreign labour" was assailed. The Indians were said to work for a penny a day to destroy Christians, and the French were charged with underselling the English by living on a low diet and wearing linen breeches and wooden shoes. The war between cotton and wool was bitter and protracted. In 1677 Parliament had forbidden the use of other than woollen apparel in the winter months and later decreed that every corpse should be buried in a woollen shroud. By 1690 the English factors in India were deluged with orders for cotton goods, and the strange Hobson-Jobson names of different types of cloth had become familiar among drapers. There were, besides the muslins, dimities, taffetas, and other terms that have been naturalized in English speech, such designations as allebanies, charconnays, hunhums, malmulls, sallampores, betellees, colloway-poos, seersuckers, saderuncheras, salpecadoes, and a hundred similar outlandish versions of Asiatic words. This great variety of weave, colour, and pattern shows how fashion was influenced by the East Indian trade and how everyday English life was changed by the use of cheap, light, gay, and — most important — washable garments and draperies.

Nor was it only the clothing of the English people that was affected, for presently the pamphleteers who fought the case of the English weavers were reinforced by those pleading for other trades. The Fan-makers, the Joyners, and the Japaners began to protest against the importation of fans, cabinets, and lacquered goods from India, China, and Japan. That the processes which these artificers used were for the most part of Asiatic origin testifies to the further influence of Asiatic crafts upon European ideas of decoration and furnishing. Indeed, the English tradesmen were obliged to use in their defence such arguments as those of the Japaners, who declared that "the curious and ingenious art and mystery of Japaning has been so much improved of late years and is withal so beneficial to the nation" as to deserve support at home. This, it may be observed in passing, was at a time when the Japanese had made astonishing advances in the art and mystery of *makiye,* the superb decorated lacquer in which Kōrin excelled.

So, but for the Asiatic trade, the picture of social life under Queen Anne would have been vastly different. At a time when Japanese textiles and Chinese ceramic wares had reached a pinnacle of brilliant fancy, there would have been in Europe no figured silks and muslins, no screens and cabinets, no delicate porcelain, no tea, and therefore no sprightly talk in elegant drawing-rooms. These direct and material influences have been amply explored by many writers, who have also dealt with the effect of Chinese theories upon political thinking in Europe, especially among the encyclopædists and physiocrats. But the impact of Asiatic goods upon English economic development has attracted little attention outside of academic circles and therefore deserves some mention here, as showing that things have sometimes a more powerful influence than ideas. The Asiatic trade not only changed our mode of dress and introduced new æsthetic principles, but also altered in the long run the constitution of English commerce and even the trend of English economic thought. It was the controversy over calicoes that presented in an acute form to people and Parliament the choice between protection and free trade and ultimately — after a protectionist phase — led to the adoption of those doctrines of free enterprise and laissez-faire which dominated English theory and practice for many generations.

The free-trade view was first presented, though imperfectly, by two pamphleteers, Josiah Child in 1690 and Charles Davenant in 1696. The latter, writing to defend the East India Company against proposals to prohibit the import of Indian cottons and silks, argued in favour of the territorial division of labour. He proclaimed that there was "no trade so advantageous, especially to an island, as that of buying goods in one country to sell them to another." The arguments of his adversaries were powerful, however, for they could point to visible depression and unemployment in domestic industries. The weavers of wool and silk made violent demonstrations and the government was alarmed, but the East India Company had strong support in Parliament and it was not until 1700 that a bill was passed prohibiting the home consumption of silks and dyed or printed calicoes of Asiatic origin.

These measures did not suffice to kill the calico trade. Consumption increased because the bill allowed the import of plain cloths to be printed in England, and also of muslins, while there was a good deal of contraband. A long struggle ensued, in which the free-trade cause was fought vigorously. The arguments for the company were put cogently in an anonymous pamphlet of 1701, entitled *Advantages of the East India Trade to England Considered*. This work is regarded by economic historians as a well-reasoned protest against mercantilism, the most acute analysis of the problem of free trade and protection before *The Wealth of Nations*. But neither reasoned argument nor scurrilous pamphleteering nor the pressure of vested interests could prevail against the case of the weavers. The woollen industry was, with some justification from history, regarded as the foundation of English prosperity, and the government was always disposed to protect it. Moreover, the agitation of the weavers and their allies took a violent form, which influenced the views of an administration nervous of Jacobite plots. In what were called "calico-chases" women were molested, sometimes stripped, and in other ways roughly handled by mobs of weavers. Parliament was flooded with petitions, and at length in 1720 an act was passed forbidding under severe penalty the use of all printed, dyed, or stained calicoes.

Thus England, as a result of the Indian trade, was forced into the adoption of a decided protectionist policy. At this time calico was similarly prohibited in France and all other European countries with the exception of Holland, where the Dutch saw clearly that to them at any rate foreign trade was more important than domestic industry. But cotton, whatever governments might do or say, was a material that could serve more purposes of use and beauty than the respectable wool, while because it was forbidden most women were determined to wear it. The prohibition did not succeed. Smuggling and other devices, licit and illicit, somehow furnished a supply of muslins, chintzes, and prints. Traders and manufacturers turned their thoughts to ways of producing cotton goods at home, and by the end of the eighteenth century ingenious minds had made it possible to spin and weave cotton in England as such low cost that the Indian trade in calico and chintz began to dwindle. Before long the Indian weavers of cotton were in a situation like that of the English weavers of wool. They in their turn were suffering from the competition of imported articles. Asia was beginning to take goods, not gold, from Europe.

Such were the entirely unpredictable results that flowed from the visit of Vasco da Gama in 1497 to the port that gave its name to Calico. India, which had supplied the world with cotton fabrics since remote antiquity, in the nineteenth century was buying her calico from Lancashire, and the English, prospering by much commerce, had turned from protection to free trade.

The foregoing fragment of economic history has taken us a long way from our theme, but it is not without bearing on the general question of cultural influences and, moreover, the trade in cotton textiles continued until most recent times to be one of the most important features of both political and economic relations between European and Asiatic countries.

We may now turn to the effects of the Asiatic trade upon Far Eastern countries as it was conducted by the Dutch and the English, the chief features of Portuguese commercial enterprise having already been described in outline. The English traders, as we have noticed, had little success in China or Japan or the Spice Islands during the seventeenth century. It was the Dutch who dominated the scene. They were kept at arm's length by the Chinese, and such effect as their brief presence in India may have had was expunged by the subsequent English supremacy. The record of their influence upon the peoples of Indonesia belongs rather to the history of colonization and is too long and intricate for treatment here, though it may be said that in many respects it is similar to that of British influence in India. But there is a special interest in the Dutch position in Japan, where without exercising much direct influence themselves they served as a channel through which, during the centuries of seclusion, the Japanese obtained their knowledge of the world at large. It was in the light of that knowledge that Japan prepared herself for the resumption of intercourse in the nineteenth.

There is not much more to say about the influence of European traders upon Asiatic life in the seventeenth century. Such as it was, it was exercised mainly by the introduction of new commodities rather than by the communication of ideas, though we shall see that the Dutch language became the most important medium for Japanese students of Western science, and that the occasional visits of learned Europeans to the Dutch factory provided rare opportunities of viva-voce explanations to supplement knowledge slowly acquired from books. The Dutch were careful to avoid all religious discussion, for it was because they were not Catholics that they were allowed to remain in Japan after the Portuguese were expelled. Consequently the history of Christian evangelization in Japan came to an end in 1639, and thenceforward the most important field of Catholic endeavour was in China.

CHAPTER
8

CHRISTIANITY IN CHINA, 1582–1742

1. The Jesuits in Peking

We left the record of Christian evangelism in China at the point where after some thirty years of unsuccessful effort by Jesuit missionaries the Visitor-General had decided that no progress could be made until members of his society had gained the confidence of the official class. This decision was followed by the dispatch of Fathers Ruggerius and Ricci, both men of considerable attainments, who took up residence in the provincial capital of Kwangtung in December 1582 and set themselves the task of impressing educated Chinese by their scientific knowledge. They applied themselves to the study of Chinese culture and for the time being they refrained from the discussion or even the mention of religious topics.

The further history of the Jesuit mission to China is one of the most interesting and illuminating examples of a deliberate and organized plan to exert cultural influence on a grand scale, for what the Jesuits were attempting to do was to introduce into an ancient, powerful, and highly developed civilization modes of thought and standards of morality which, if they were adopted, would change its very essence.

The story of their effort and its ultimate failure is too long, too rich in complicated incident and difficult controversy, to be told here, and we must confine ourselves to the briefest summary designed to bring out only some of its more significant features. It is important in the first place to understand that the Jesuit policy of conversion was opposed to that of the other missionary orders. The Dominicans and the Franciscans, who had gained their experience in Mexico and the Philippines, believed in the *tabula rasa*. They argued that no compromise must be made with the tradition or the prejudices of the people to be converted. The missionaries must beg their way through the country and preach to the masses, their aim being to destroy the existing order from below. This, according to the Jesuit view, might be well enough in poor and backward regions, but it could not succeed in highly developed states. The difference between the two principles is succinctly expressed by Father Bernard, S.J., who says that the policy of the *tabula rasa* *"ne tient guère compte du présupposé culturel chez les peuples à évangeliser,"* while by contrast the Jesuit policy requires *"la méthode de la préparation providentielle, qui étudie préalablement les populations afin de s'y adapter."*

Ricci and his companions therefore made no attempt to convert the populace, but devoted all their energies to learning the nature of Chinese social and intellectual life. While demonstrating their own learning to educated Chinese with whom they came into contact they sought an intellectual basis for harmonizing Christian teaching with Confucianism. In this they had no small success, though only after twenty years of labour, darkened by ill treatment and neglect and brightened only by the help of a few friendly officials. At length Ricci actually found himself in Peking, where by the Emperor's favour (which had in the first place been secured by interesting gifts) he was allowed to remain. Ricci was an impressive figure, who gained the respect of several members of the governing class by his assiduous study of the Chinese classics, his evident appreciation of Chinese culture, and his superior knowledge of mathematics and astronomy. He had the great advantage of not being associated in the minds of Chinese officials with any particular foreign authority. He did not rely upon the support of the Portuguese crown, had no connection with foreign traders, and was moreover allowed considerable discretion by his own superiors in the Society of Jesus. Had it not been for this independence he would have found it impossible to carry out his mission, which depended for its success on some degree of official approval. No illicit propaganda would have been possible, since no European could reside in China without official permission. The only hope of making progress lay in proceeding along lines that were not inconsistent with Confucian orthodoxy. Once again we see that the character and attainments of the teacher are as important as the doctrine. The Chinese literati, who despised soldiers and traders, could not withhold admiration from a scholar who, in the scientific field, possessed knowledge in which they were lacking.

When at last Ricci ventured to discuss religious matters he argued that Christian tenets were supported by the moral principles of Confucianism, and his best-known work of Christian apologetics (*T'ien-chu Shih-i*, or *The Teaching of the Lord of Heaven*) cites appropriate passages from the Chinese classics. He was on slightly dangerous ground here, because he was neglecting reinterpretations of Confucian philosophy, which dominated much of contemporary Chinese thought; but he had the advantage of appearing friendly to Confucianism and hostile to Buddhism and other beliefs not approved by the official class. He was on the side of the school of thought that permeated the government and thus was able to maintain fairly close relations with influential men. He was wise enough to see that this position, though favourable, would not of itself protect him against conservative opposition, and he took every opportunity of showing how useful his special knowledge could be to the court, especially in regard to astronomy. In China, as in Japan, the calendar played a most important part in government, since it regulated ceremonies that in their origin had to do with agricultural seasons and also with certain astrological concepts as to the exercise of sovereign power. So intimately was it connected with the fortunes of the state that acceptance of the Chinese calendar was regarded as a necessary act of submission by a tributary kingdom. Accordingly Ricci arranged for the dispatch to Peking of a skilled astronomer, Father de Ursis, who arrived in 1606. Ricci himself died in 1610, worn out by his vast labours, but within a year de Ursis had reformed the Chinese calendar, and the Jesuit mathematicians had become quasi-official advisers to the court, displacing the Moslem experts who had been proved wrong. This was a step of the greatest value to the Jesuits' cause, for in a land of bureaucrats they had gained a footing in the bureaucracy. They had their ups and downs, but they remained official astronomers until well into the nineteenth century, and such success as they achieved in their task of evangelization could not have been gained without the benefit of this position.

The subsequent history of the Jesuit mission to China, in its purely evangelical aspects, is one of gradual and guarded concession to Confucianism. Ricci on his death-bed is said to have told his colleagues that he left them "facing an open door," and this was true. Had his successors been able to continue his policy the Christian church in China might have been well established within another generation. But they were not all prepared to pass through the door he had opened. Even during his lifetime his colleague Longobardi, who was to succeed him, had nourished doubts as to the wisdom of the "accommodation," and after his death more than one of the missionaries had argued that the Chinese philosophers upon whom he had relied had no knowledge of the true God. The Jesuit confraternity, however, preserved a certain solidarity, which was due in part to their habit of discipline and in part to their anxiety lest the Dominicans and the Franciscans, by entering the field and using their uncompromising methods, should ruin the position the Jesuit pioneers had so painfully acquired.

The chief points in dispute turned on the nature of Confucianism. Were its ritual observances civil or religious? Could a Christian properly take part in ceremonies of ancestor-worship or of reverence to Confucius? Was the word *T'ien* a proper translation of the word "God"? And in general were traditional Chinese beliefs consistent with Christian faith? The Jesuits could not agree among themselves, and under pressure from other orders these questions were referred to the Holy See, where in 1645 Pope Innocent X gave a decision *parte inaudita* that was unfavourable to the Jesuit position. This was followed by a decree of Pope Alexander VII in 1656 which appeared favourable but was qualified by a further decree in 1669 in a contrary sense. The situation became extremely confused and the Rites controversy dragged on for many years, turning into an unseemly wrangle in which European theological and even political quarrels obscured the original issue of evangelical procedure in the Far East. The climax was not reached until 1742, when a papal bull finally ruled against the Jesuit compromise.

During this long interval the Church continued to make progress in China under Jesuit leadership, though it was subject to occasional reverses and even to persecution, as well as suffering setbacks from the activities of Franciscans and Dominicans in parts of China (notably Fukien and Chekiang) to which they had obtained access. The success of the Jesuits was maintained largely by their usefulness to the government.

They not only gave advice on astronomy but were often consulted on matters of foreign and even of domestic policy. They were fortunate in their choice of successors to Ricci, for Father Adam Schall and Father Ferdinand Verbiest were both remarkable men who, apart from their scientific knowledge, were able, thanks to their strong characters, to obtain great influence at court. Some of the Jesuit leaders in Japan had succeeded in gaining the confidence of such powerful dictators as Nobunaga and Hideyoshi, but they never reached the point of intimacy with the ruling sovereign that was achieved by their colleagues in Peking. Schall (1591–1666) was in Peking during the last years of the Ming dynasty and there, as well as being appointed director of the Bureau of Astronomy, he was called upon in 1636 to make cannon to be used against the Manchus. When the Manchus displaced the Ming, the first Manchu Emperor, then a youth, conceived a strong liking and respect for him and bestowed upon him many honours. Probably no European has ever played so influential a part at a great Asiatic court. The Emperor's favours to Schall were valuable to the mission, for a church was built upon land that he granted, and after Christianity had been commended in an official rescript of

1692 the number of converts grew by thousands. When the young Emperor died in 1661 Schall was appointed tutor to his successor, the Emperor known as K'ang Hsi, then a minor. But court intrigues against him ended in his arrest on an absurd charge of treason. After cruel imprisonment he was condemned to death, but the sentence was not carried out and he died of illness in 1666, a few months after his release. He was succeeded by Verbiest, who had reached Peking in 1660 and had shared his sufferings.

After Schall's trial Verbiest and his colleagues were kept in Peking for scientific work, but were denied freedom of movement until 1671, when the young Emperor K'ang Hsi began to take an interest in them and in the foreign learning they possessed. Verbiest was very favourably treated and was for some years in daily attendance at the palace as tutor or adviser. He, like Schall, was director of the Bureau of Astronomy, with Mandarin rank, and he also made cannon for the Imperial forces, as well as giving general advice on mechanical matters. K'ang Hsi used to take Verbiest with him on his hunting expeditions — great month-long battues in the northern camping-grounds of his nomadic ancestors. These strenuous exercises and the strain of his duties at court wore out the elderly missionary, who died in 1688. He was given a state funeral and the Emperor bestowed posthumous honours upon him.

This was near the end of the great days of the Jesuits in China. K'ang Hsi continued, however, to favour the missionaries in Peking, and in 1692 he was persuaded by a friendly nobleman at court to approve an edict tolerating the Christian religion. He even took a personal interest in the appointment of missionaries, deciding which should stay in the capital and which should go to the provinces, and he gave the fathers land for houses and a church, with a sum of money towards the cost of building. There are no satisfactory statistics of the number of converts, but it is said that there were 150,000 Christians in the Chinese Empire in 1650 and that this number was doubled by 1700. Perhaps more important than numbers was the fact that a few Chinese in high places had gone over to the Christian faith in Ricci's time and had been of service to the cause.

But after the first decade of the eighteenth century the tide had begun to turn and the development of the Rites controversy hastened the decline of Christian influence in China. The Emperor did not withdraw his favour from the leading missionaries in Peking, whose merits he appreciated; but he grew weary of theological bickering among the missionaries of different orders and he took offence at the attitude of a papal legate who was sent out to China in 1705 to inquire into the question of the Rites and to explain the attitude of the Holy See. It is a long and unedifying story, which need not be told here but can be studied in the vast polemical literature to which it gave rise. For our purpose it is enough to notice that the Jesuits maintained in substance that Confucianism was not a religion. It was an ethical doctrine, laying down principles entirely consistent with Christianity. The rites of veneration offered to ancestors and to the memory of Confucius were not acts of worship contrary to Christian duty but civil observances. K'ang Hsi himself, when the Jesuits in Peking had put these points to him in a petition, had categorically said that they were right. "To honour Heaven, to serve the prince and parents, to revere one's ancestors, to honour one's master and superiors is the universal doctrine of the Empire. In all this petition there is not one word to be changed." But the opponents of the Jesuits would not allow that a Christian could appeal to a heathen monarch for a ruling on matters under examination at the Holy See.

The controversy grew more widespread and bitter. In March 1715 the bull *Ex illa die* in unequivocal language forbade every item of the "accommodation" that the Jesuits regarded as both proper and essential. K'ang Hsi seems to have taken some interest in the dialectical and diplomatic aspects of the question and condescended to listen to the arguments of a second papal legate, Mezzabarba, the Patriarch of Alexandria, who was sent out by Rome in a last attempt to compose the quarrel. But the Emperor finally lost patience, said that Europeans were ignorant and contemptible people not fit to discuss the Great Doctrine of China, and declared angrily that they should not be allowed to preach their own religion. He dismissed Mezzabarba, whom he had treated correctly and even with distinction. He sent handsome presents to the Pope and asked in return for news of Europe and the latest books on mathematics.

This was a significant gesture, which may be taken as symbolic of his true feelings towards Christianity. He had no real interest in the Jesuits' religion, as is clear from the terms of the edict of 1692, which refers specifically to their services as astronomers, makers of ordnance, and diplomatic advisers. It was their useful knowledge that accounted for his tolerance. They could stay and propagate their faith so long as it was not antagonistic to the doctrines upon which Chinese society was based. The Jesuits in Peking were fully aware of this and they managed for some time to evade full compliance with the decree *Ex illa die*. Meanwhile, though anti-Christian edicts were issued from time to time and there was some persecution in the provinces, they remained established in the capital and were not interfered with. It is a curious fact that, despite the ban upon Christianity, the central government made no attempt to wipe it out, as the Japanese had done after 1637. It seems that the authorities did not regard it as a menace, feeling that the number of converts was almost negligible. Nor were they disturbed, as Ieyasu had been, by fear of armed risings fomented by missionaries in concert with the secular power of European countries.

The strength of the Jesuits in China was in part due to their care to dissociate themselves from any national authority. In Japan their order had been less discreet, for they had taken advantage of current disunity to play one faction off against another. They had directed Portuguese trading ships away from the harbours of feudal barons hostile to Christian teaching, and in fiefs where they were admitted they had offended Japanese sentiment by inciting their converts to attack Buddhists and to destroy Buddhist property. They had taken sides in feudal struggles and it is not surprising that they should have been mistrusted by the central government of Japan as soon as it was established.

By contrast the position in China was much more favourable to Christianity. China was a unified state and her great provincial officers were not competing for foreign trade as were the Japanese feudatories. Therefore the Christian missions in China did not come under suspicion of exerting commercial pressure for political ends, or of interfering in domestic politics and imperilling the reigning dynasty. Consequently the Chinese authorities did not feel called upon to enforce the anti-Christian edicts to the limit. But persecutions continued intermittently and in time they took their toll. In 1742 a last decree (*Ex quo singulari*) had settled the Rites controversy by deciding all remaining points of doubt against the Jesuits and thus preventing any form of accommodation with Chinese practices. In 1773 the Society of Jesus was dissolved and its work was carried on by the Lazarists. The number of Christians in the Empire was now declining. It was estimated at only 160,000 by the Jesuits at the end of the eighteenth century, as compared with the 300,000 at its beginning. These figures are doubtful, but they can be taken as evidence that official action and hostile feeling among the literati were gradually doing the work that a single edict had accomplished in Japan.

A survey of the history of Christian missions in China must give the impression that a great and indeed a noble effort produced a very small result. At any time from the end of the sixteenth century there were thousands of converts to the Catholic faith. By the beginning of the eighteenth century they may have reached as high as the figure of 300,000 named above; but it is improbable that more than a small proportion of these were so firm in their faith as to lead lives that involved a break with Chinese social and intellectual tradition. There were many heroic believers, especially among Chinese priests and catechists, who laboured faithfully in spite of persecution. But in relation to the total population, which was of the order of 100,000,000 in 1700, the number of professing Christians was extremely small. No doubt by their own lives they influenced non-Christian friends and neighbours, but the most sympathetic student is forced to admit that by the beginning of the nineteenth century Christianity had made almost no impression upon China. It had brought about no significant change in the moral and religious habits of the people, no modification of their social or political life. It has been argued that Christianity helped to swell a certain intellectual current which in the seventeenth and eighteenth centuries produced a small group of heterodox thinkers who challenged the classical tradition and so set in motion forces working for ultimate revolutionary change. This is a claim that it would be most difficult to substantiate. Even if some indirect influence upon Chinese political life can be traced to the cumulative effect of missionary labours in spreading Western learning, it was of no great consequence. The tide of Chinese life found its own channels. In the words of Dr. Latourette, a careful and impartial observer whose *Christian Missions in China* is an authoritative work, "had missionaries after 1835 gradually ceased coming to China . . . the Church would probably have passed out of existence within a few years, leaving behind it no permanent trace."

Such were the exiguous results, after more than two hundred years, of a highly organized and skilfully conducted propaganda, for which it would be hard to find a parallel in modern history. It illustrates very clearly the difficulties that attend any deliberate attempt to exert cultural influence upon a civilized community. Perhaps its most startling result was one which neither Europeans nor Chinese had intended or even contemplated, and that was the great effect of Jesuit descriptions of Chinese culture upon European thought in the seventeenth and eighteenth centuries. The effect was not lasting. It was made possible in the first place by social and intellectual changes that were then taking place in European countries and made them responsive to foreign influence. When those changes were accomplished there was no further need to cite Chinese practice, or rather, one should say, convenient versions of Chinese practice, in support of new philosophies. What is really remarkable about these Chinese influences is that they have left hardly any trace in European thought but a lasting imprint upon æsthetic sentiment. It seems that if social and political habits shrink from an alien touch, at least the arts may be dialects of some universal language.

2. Christian Doctrine and Chinese Tradition

THE RITES controversy is of such historical interest and the biographies of the great Jesuits are so fascinating that together they give the impression that the fortunes of Christianity in China were determined by a struggle between European missionaries and Chinese officials. This is true as a summary of events, since the general sentiment of the Chinese people was in harmony with the doctrines of their leaders. In China the official doctrine was not something imposed upon the untaught masses by scholars, but (like Hinduism in India and Shinto in Japan) it was the literary expression of indigenous views about life and society held by the whole people. It is possible therefore that, but for the Rites controversy, the Catholic Church would have continued to enjoy a tolerance such as had been accorded to it by K'ang Hsi. This would not have been alien to Chinese tradition, since not only Buddhism in its various forms but other foreign creeds also had in the past been given considerable freedom, as witness the record of Nestorianism, Manichæism, and Islam.

But even supposing that the Jesuits could have composed their differences with the governing class and kept clear of political troubles, it is by no means certain that they would have succeeded in spreading Christian influence very widely among the people. There were points of Christian doctrine which, however tactfully handled, were incompatible with the traditional way of life in China. Most important among these is the attitude of the Church towards the worship of the dead. This was always a difficulty, for quite apart from the so-to-speak theoretical problems of the nature of these acts of worship, the earliest missionaries often found it difficult to persuade even their most devout converts to abandon the practice. It formed part of the "family system" that is at the core of Chinese social life, and whatever concessions may be made by Catholic or Protestant missionaries, it remains true that the essence of Christian doctrine is against any ritual, and still more any belief, which assumes that the dead need the ministrations of the living. To define the acts of veneration performed before the ancestral tablets as civil observances with no religious character is to evade the issue. They are an integral part of the Chinese view of life, and it is life as a whole that religion professes to govern.

It should be added, if we may leap forward from the seventeenth century to the twentieth, that at least until a very few years ago, despite most sweeping changes in the nature of Chinese political and social life, the great majority of Chinese families continued to perform the usual rites before the ancestral tablets, even "modern" young men and women who profess rationalistic or agnostic opinion often taking an active or a passive part. Chinese Christians themselves have not earnestly fought against ancestor-worship and many of them say that "it does no harm" so long as it is understood that it does not replace the true worship of God. This again is an evasion, which can only be interpreted to mean that Chinese Christianity is not Western Christianity. Indeed, a modern Chinese Christian has suggested that such compromises will create "a Confucianized indigenous Christianity." What this means is obscure. It may be an excellent and desirable goal, but if it is reached it will prove an interesting example of a reversed cultural influence, the new religion being adapted to the convert, not the convert to the religion. This would not be a new thing, since early Christianity itself was adapted to conform to certain Hellenistic modes of thought, and many other examples might be cited to show that strong cultures rarely incorporate foreign elements without changing them.

There is another important aspect of traditional Chinese life which offers resistance to Christian teaching. The traditional Chinese view of the family, besides stressing its continuity, attaches importance to filial piety and considers that children are born to nourish their parents. This is certainly contrary to the Christian view, which in general puts the authority of the Church above that of the family and regards the parent as one who must "lay up for the children." It may be argued that traditional family life is breaking down in China and that this obstacle will disappear. No doubt this is true in some respects. The breakdown, however, is part of a general relaxation of old standards, which is to be ascribed to the influence of "rationalistic" thought and not of Western religion. It is in fact part of a process of change connected with the growth of an industrial society to which the old family life can scarcely be adjusted. The machine has brought with it the idea of progress, and this is the real, the overwhelming Occidental influence, by the side of which that of the Church appears to be almost negligible.

Yet it is a testimony to the power of survival of ancient beliefs in modern conditions that since the Rites controversy the question of ancestor-worship has remained until today a live issue for the Christian church in China. In 1890 in a *Plea for Toleration* addressed to a conference of Protestant missionaries at Shanghai the following statement was made: "If I were called upon to name the most serious impediment to the conversion of the Chinese I should without hesitation point to the worship of ancestors. Gathering to itself all that is deemed most sacred in family or state, it rises before us like a mountain barrier." There have been great changes in

Chinese life since that date, but in December 1938 the Sacred Congregation in Rome found it necessary to decree that attendance at public ceremonies in honour of Confucius was licit and that a likeness of Confucius might be placed in Catholic schools, to which the students might bow. Further, "inclinations of the head and other signs of civil respect" in the presence of the dead or before their images or tablets are to be regarded as "licit and proper." Of this decree the Catholic Archbishop of Nanking, a leading Chinese ecclesiast, said in 1946: "The Church stood free of its shackles. It was no longer the cultural invader of China." But at the same time he deplored the meagre results of centuries of missionary labour, saying that not one per cent of China's population was Catholic, and "even this is not an influential one per cent."

It should be added here that Protestant missions in China do not approve of an accommodation in respect of ancestor-worship and will not accept converts who adhere to traditional practices that are to be regarded as acts of worship.

3. Comparisons

It is convenient at this point to make some comparisons between the problems of the Church in China and those experienced in India and other Eastern countries. There is not much to add to what has already been said as to the methods employed by Father Nobile and his successors in an effort to compromise with Hindu thought. Their problem was not identical with that of the Jesuits in China, since most Indians have a strong tendency to religious tolerance, being intensely concerned with spiritual matters. If not inclined to welcome truth wherever it may be found, they are at least more eclectic than dogmatic. Accordingly the Jesuits in India did not have to overcome the indifference, the somewhat pragmatic materialism, that they met in China. Nor did the question of obtaining official sanction arise for them, since the Portuguese (and later the French) missions in India had the support of their own secular powers.

On the other hand they met with a resistance from Indian social life which was, if one may judge by results, stronger than the resistance of the family system in China. There are certain features of Hindu belief and practice which are, or were at that time, ineradicable and yet are in direct conflict with Christian principles. Chief among these was caste, an institution that, whatever its origins, is closely bound up with religious doctrines (especially the doctrine of karma) and has throughout Indian history stubbornly withstood attempts to destroy it from within as well as from without India. Buddhism itself failed to make any impression upon it and successive Indian reformers until recent times have challenged it in vain. The Jesuits were therefore obliged to go to extremes that make the "accommodation" in respect of ancestor-worship most plausible by comparison. Under the Madura mission (which worked outside Portuguese jurisdiction) not only was caste recognized, it was actually adopted in the organization of the Church. A missionary who worked among the lower castes would prostrate himself before a colleague who, posing as a Brahman, worked among Brahmans; and would even go to the length of covering his mouth to prevent his breath from polluting a superior. These methods, combined with the ascetic character of the missionaries, had some success, and the number of converts is said to have reached 150,000 by the end of the seventeenth century. Leaving aside judgments on the legitimacy of such compromises, which the Holy See at length forbade, one may doubt whether evangelization of this kind could have continued indefinitely, since it was based upon disguise.

It is true however that, after the Portuguese were displaced by the Dutch, Protestant missionaries arriving in 1706 tolerated caste distinctions among their converts, who were numerous in southern India. Yet these concessions and immense efforts by Catholic and Protestant workers produced hardly any result among the high-caste Hindus, and by 1850 the total number of Christians in India probably did not exceed 200,000, if the members of the ancient Syrian Church are excluded. The later history of Christian missions in India is beyond the scope of this study, being the special case of a vast region of Asia governed by a Christian country; but we may note in passing that, with all the advantages conferred by political supremacy and control of education, the combined missions in 1931 could point to a total of less than six million Christians, which is 1.8 per cent of the total population. It is interesting to observe that the membership of the Christian community in China, according to statistics of 1936, was little over 1 per cent of the estimated total population.

In one sense both these figures represent a remarkable achievement, and it has to be remembered that in Asiatic countries where political and social change is gathering speed the influence of Christian communities is in some ways out of proportion to their numerical strength. But important as the increase has been, it does not justify a belief that either India or China will eventually become a Christian country, or that the Christian church will acquire a powerful, still less a dominant position. In India, as in China, the demands of industrial society, the growth of national feeling, and the interest of youth in political and economic rather than religious questions are all factors which, while they tend to break down earlier obstacles to Christian influence, put new barriers in its path, since they are on balance adverse to the adoption of an alien doctrine. In India, in intellectual circles not particularly subject to modern influences though fully aware of them, there is too great a pride and confidence in the all-embracing character of Hindu thought to allow of the acceptance of a dogmatic religion, whatever its origin. Indeed, far from Western religious thought influencing the main current of Indian life, there are signs in contemporary Europe of an interest in Indian philosophies among intellectuals baffled and discouraged by the glaring contrast between scientific progress and spiritual decay.

However one looks at the cultural relations of Asiatic and Occidental countries, one cannot but be impressed by the fact that it is only upon peoples whose aboriginal civilization was backward that Western religious thought has left a permanent mark. The greatest successes of Christian missions in Asia, if success is to be measured by numbers, were achieved in the Philippine Islands. They are the only Christian state in the Far East and the islands were evangelized at a time when they had only an elementary cultural life and no political cohesion. For the most part their tribes were untouched by Hinduism, of which only slight and ancient traces are discernible, and they came under Spanish influence before the power of Islam had spread beyond the Sulu Archipelago.

PART TWO

Japan and the Western World
1600–1894

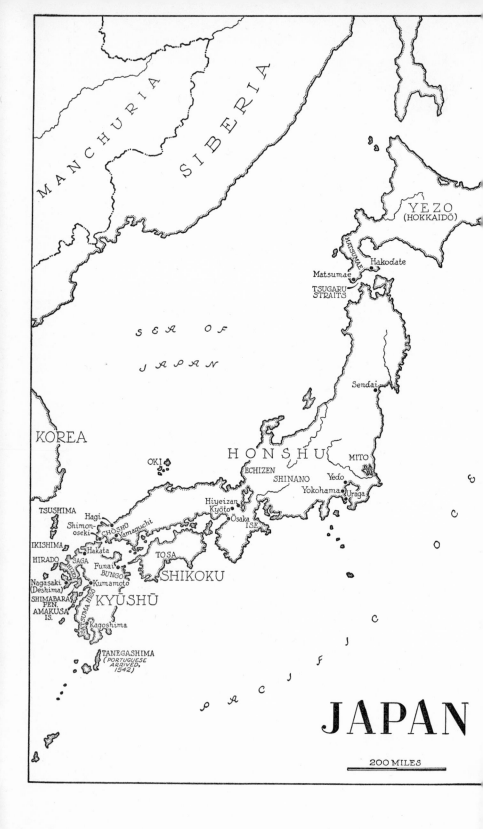

MANCHURIA

SIBERIA

YEZO
(HOKKAIDŌ)

MATSUMAE

Hakodate

Matsumae

TSUGARU
STRAITS

SEA   OF

JAPAN

Sendai

KOREA

HONSHU

MITO

OKI

ECHIZEN

SHINANO

Yedo

Yokohama

Uraga

TSUSHIMA

Hagi

Hiyeizan
Kyōto

Shimon-
oseki

CHŌSHŪ

Yamaguchi

Ōsaka

ISE

IKISHIMA

Hakata

HIRADO

SAGA

TOSA

Funai

SHIKOKU

BUNGO

Nagasaki
(Deshima)

Kumamoto

SHIMABARA
PEN.

HIGO

AMAKUSA
IS.

KYŪSHŪ

SATSUMA

Kagoshima

TANEGASHIMA
(PORTUGUESE
ARRIVED,
1542)

PACIFIC

JAPAN

200 MILES

CHAPTER
9

THE TOKUGAWA RÉGIME

1. The Closing of the Country

THE MAIN purpose of this and the following chapters is to describe, in the light of the first part of this study, how Japan in modern times has reacted to Western influences, particularly since her entry into international society in 1854. It was then that she began to feel the full impact of European civilization, for her experience of Western intrusion in the sixteenth century was only transitory and, far from modifying her institutions, it caused her to shrink from foreign contacts. It might therefore be sufficient to give some short account of Japan as it was in the decades just before Commodore Perry's visit in 1853 and then to go on to a study of the effects of Western intercourse upon the indigenous civilization. But the opening of Japan was not only the beginning of a new phase; it was also the end of an old one. It is not easy to describe changes unless we know the nature of the thing that is changed, and if we are to understand what Japan was like in the first half of the nineteenth century we ought to know something of the events and traditions that had shaped her society as it then was. It will therefore be useful, before treating of modern Japan, to give an outline of earlier history designed to explain the institutions that had grown to maturity before she emerged from seclusion.

Geography has played a leading part in Japanese history. The Japanese archipelago lies off the mainland of Asia just as the British Isles lie off the edge of the European continent, and this insular position has given a special character to the life of both countries, for, thanks to intervening waters, each was able at will to keep out of the main stream of continental life and so to protect its own individuality. Each in its early history received invaders or immigrants from the mainland and was subjected to the influence of more advanced cultures, but both invaders and immigrants were in the long run amalgamated in a distinctive culture that, though it included many borrowed elements, kept a strong native essence. Thus it came about that, as the people of the British Isles though belonging to Europe were not characteristically European, so the Japanese though belonging to Asia were unlike any other Asiatic people. The English were frequently at war with their nearest neighbours across the Channel, just as the Japanese often raided Korea across the Strait of Tsushima. The English owed much of their early civilization to the Christian religion, brought to them by missionaries from overseas, just as the tribal life of Japan was transformed and enriched by Buddhism from Korea and China.

Here and in several other respects the analogy is very close; but it is not complete. England at its nearest point is only some twenty miles from the mainland of Europe, while Japan is separated from the southern tip of Korea by over a hundred miles of rough water. Japan was therefore protected from armed invasion by her distance from continental seats of power and throughout her recorded history until modern times she could not be seriously threatened so long as no great maritime state arose in eastern Asia. The Chinese, usually preoccupied with their land frontiers, never persisted in a policy of expansion across water. It is true that China twice attempted an invasion of Japan, in 1274 and 1281, but this was under the rule of a Mongol emperor who was ignorant of maritime warfare, and both expeditions failed for want of naval competence. Even under the Ming dynasty, when the Chinese sent great fleets southward and into the Indian Ocean, they did not threaten Japan.

As to cultural influences, these the Japanese could accept or reject as they pleased, and though their civilization owes a great debt to China, they contracted it willingly and under no kind of pressure. By contrast the British Isles have from the earliest times been peculiarly exposed not only to armed invasion but also to successive waves of foreign cultural influence, beginning before the Roman occupation. Further, the English people, though their insular situation was a shield against aggression, were always compelled to keep a watchful eye upon the politics of Europe in order to guard their independence. The proximity of rival states provided them with a beneficial stimulus, which the Japanese did not enjoy since they had no close and dangerous neighbour, and this may account for a certain sluggishness in the development of Japan as a nation. On the other hand the British Isles may perhaps have been at some disadvantage as compared with Japan, in so far as the English, Irish, Scottish, and Welsh elements in their population have never reached the state of ethnic fusion which the peoples of the Japanese archipelago had achieved by the end of their neolithic period. But this is a doubtful point, for variety is lively and useful.

It will be seen that the civilization of Japan was formed in comparative seclusion, and this has given it a very special character. Its many foreign elements were borrowed in such circumstances that they could not overcome a stubborn indigenous character, and even until modern times Japanese life has preserved much of its earliest native quality. No nation has been more ready to consider new teaching, and yet none has been more tenacious of its own tradition. These circumstances have given rise to an impression, which a cursory study of history seems to confirm, that the geographical isolation of Japan has fostered a habit of seclusion, an aversion to foreign intercourse. But there is little to justify this opinion. From earliest times relationships with China and Korea, sometimes peaceful, sometimes warlike, were continuous despite an occasional diplomatic rupture, and from the end of the feudal wars in the twelfth century, when internal peace was established, there was a steady increase and extension of Japanese maritime enterprise. Recent researches have established that Japanese ships (from the Luchu Islands) visited Java, Sumatra, Siam, and Malacca in the fifteenth and probably in the late fourteenth century. From that time onwards Japanese vessels in legitimate or piratical trade sailed freely in Far Eastern waters and Japanese merchants or soldiers of fortune were to be found in most Far Eastern cities. It was during the early phases of a great movement of Japanese expansion that the first Europeans arrived in Japan; and the welcome accorded to Portuguese missionaries and traders, so friendly in contrast to their treatment in China and some other Asiatic countries, is to be explained by the enthusiasm for overseas adventure and trade which then prevailed among the feudal leaders of Japan.

Had the Portuguese and other Europeans not arrived upon the scene in the sixteenth century, it is quite probable that the Japanese within a few decades would have established themselves in Formosa, the Philippines, and parts of Indonesia, thus forming the nucleus of a colonial empire in the Pacific. But such designs, which were certainly harboured by Japanese rulers, had to be abandoned when it was thought that Western guns and ships might be turned against Japan by the foreigners. It was no failure of the expansive impulse, but only a reluctant recognition of weakness that caused Japan to withdraw into almost complete seclusion in 1640. The hazard that brought Western influence into the Pacific before Japan had achieved a stable central government thus gave the maritime countries a free hand in the Far East and so fixed for centuries the pattern of colonial enterprise in that region. During those centuries the rulers of Japan abandoned all dreams of empire, and only by exception did a few unorthodox thinkers turn

their minds to a day when Japan might renew her broken intercourse with foreign countries. The energies of the governing class
were devoted entirely to the consolidation of their power and to
devising instruments by which to preserve it. Theirs was a policy
of almost complete isolation.

The institutions of Japan under the régime that was firmly established by Ieyasu in 1615 need only a general explanation here.
The Tokugawa family had succeeded, after a series of victorious
campaigns, in reducing to submission the powerful feudal lords
who had opposed them. They thus acquired supreme authority in
the land, all other feudal rulers — the daimyo, as they were called
— being their vassals. Those who had fought on the Tokugawa
side were rewarded with fiefs commensurate with their services,
while the former enemies — known as Tozama or Outside Lords
— in return for their submission were confirmed in their holdings
but were not allowed authority beyond their own territories, and
in principle could not hold office in the administrative organs set
up by the Shogun for the government of the country as a whole.
Each daimyo was left in control of the people and property in his
domain, which was in theory not subject to interference by the
central government so long as the supreme authority was not endangered. All daimyo were obliged to swear allegiance to each
successive Shogun and were then confirmed in their fiefs, but they
could be deprived of all or part of their holdings at the will of the
Shogun should he deem them guilty of insubordinate conduct or
treasonable intentions. These powers were freely exercised by the
first three Tokugawa rulers, whose commands were so far-reaching
that Japan in their day already exhibited some of the features of
a centralized nation state.

The whole of Tokugawa policy was designed to guard against
revolt and thus to ensure the permanence of Tokugawa rule. The
geographical distribution of fiefs was made with an eye to strategy,
hereditary vassals being assigned lands at points that threatened
the line of advance of any Outside Lord who might plan an uprising. All daimyo were compelled to spend part of the year in Yedo,
the Shogun's capital, and to leave their families behind as hostages when they returned to their provinces. These and many
other devices were used to prevent the vassals from plotting mischief, and they did in fact secure for Japan unbroken peace over
more than two hundred years. But the Shogunate was never fully
at ease with respect to the Outside Lords, who for their part never
became reconciled to Tokugawa dominance. Out of easy reach
in the north and west of Japan lay powerful and warlike fiefs
which had, it is true, been brought to submission but which might
alone or in combination with other Outside Lords, or even with

disaffected hereditary vassals, rise against the Shogun and plunge the country once more into civil war. Such a prospect the Tokugawa could not face, for they had brought peace to the country by a combination of arms and diplomacy which they could not be sure of repeating.

This fear of domestic uprising has an important bearing upon the policy of seclusion, a policy that was not contemplated in the early years of the seventeenth century but was formed and executed precipitately after 1637. The sudden decision then taken to exclude aliens and to prohibit Japanese from going abroad was closely connected with the presence in Japan of foreign missionaries and traders. Its history is therefore most pertinent to the study of Western influences in Asia and calls for some detailed consideration here.

It will be remembered that, in describing the progress of Christian missions in Japan after the arrival of Francis Xavier in 1549, we stopped at the year 1600, when despite great persecutions the number of converts had risen to 300,000 and promised further increase. At this time Ieyasu had come into power but had not subdued the last of his adversaries. He was much interested in foreign trade, cherishing notions of expanding Japan's merchant fleet and perhaps of making some conquests in the southern seas. He was disposed to be friendly with both Portuguese and Spanish; he even proposed to open harbours in eastern Japan to foreign ships and showed no signs of any intention to diminish, still less to cut off, the foreign intercourse of Japan. He made it known that he would not enforce the anti-Christian edicts, and the work of evangelization went on without interruption, while foreign trade flourished.

But the truce was not to last for long. Though the number of converts steadily increased, there were isolated persecutions in different parts of Japan and hostility towards Christianity grew in high quarters, until after a series of perfunctory orders by Ieyasu, which may be regarded as warnings rather than as definite prohibitions, an edict banning the Christian faith was issued in 1614 and enforced with great severity in some regions, but still mildly elsewhere. By now it was evident that, sooner or later, the partial relaxation would come to an end.

When Ieyasu died in 1616, to be succeeded by the second Shogun, Hidetada, the Tokugawa family were supreme in Japan and determined to permit no activity that might develop into a threat to their primacy in the state. By this time not only the Portuguese and the Spaniards but also the Dutch and the English were competing for trade privileges in Japan, quarrelling with one another and prompt to reveal to the Shogun's officers real or imaginary designs of their rivals upon the safety of the Japanese realm. The news that came to Hidetada of the doings of foreigners in other parts of Asia was certainly of a kind to arouse misgivings in his mind, since he knew that they were all striving to increase their holdings of territory in the Pacific and would stop short at little to obtain new commercial footholds. In 1617 the persecution was continued with increased fury, and thousands of Japanese were banished or went to the stake, while the Jesuits, the Franciscans, and the other orders sank their differences in a common fortitude which led many to torture and death. The number of executions between 1613 and 1626 according to missionary sources was about 750, and in addition to these thousands suffered and died through imprisonment or exile and destitution.

Towards 1622 the Shogun discovered evidence that led him to suspect the complicity of the Catholic Church in alleged Spanish plots to invade Japan. Shortly thereafter he re-enacted the anti-Christian edicts and ordered the deportation of all Spaniards, both priests and laymen, while decreeing that no Japanese Christian should leave the country. During this later and more violent phase of repression unspeakable tortures were used in efforts to secure apostasy and whole families including infants in arms were mercilessly destroyed. Nevertheless the Jesuit documents report a continued enrolment of new converts and an almost joyful acceptance of death by believers of all classes. Their testimony to the bravery of the Japanese Christians is confirmed by a contemporary observer, the English captain Richard Cocks, who was strongly prejudiced against the "papisticall" missionaries. He described the government of Japan as "the greatest and most puissant tyranny that the world has ever known" and, writing of the Shogun's enmity towards Christians, said: "I saw 55 of them martyrized at one time at Miyako. Among them were little children of five or six years, burned alive in the arms of their mothers, who cried 'Jesus, receive their souls.' There are many in prison who hourly await death, for very few return to their idolatry."

By 1625 the persecution had reached its peak, and Christianity had been either eradicated or driven underground in most parts of Japan, though martyrdoms continued until as late as 1660. In remote districts, particularly on small islands where official scrutiny was imperfect, it was still practised in stealth and a few missionaries remained to carry out their task in hiding. The culminating tragedy took place in 1638 when a peasant uprising, in which Christians took a leading part, was ruthlessly suppressed by the government with great slaughter. Of about 37,000 peasants with their families and a number of disaffected samurai, who made a last stand on a headland of the Shimabara peninsula, only one hundred are said to have escaped alive. Even after this attempts were made by missionaries to smuggle themselves into Japan, but so far as is known they were all sooner or later discovered and executed or died in captivity.

The total number of martyrdoms recognized by the Church recorded for the period 1597–1660 is 3,125. This includes only those who were executed or died under torture and leaves out of account those who were stripped of their property, imprisoned, or banished. Many of these died of ill treatment or destitution. The Japanese statesman Arai Hakuseki put the number of Christians who had perished by 1650 at between 200,000 and 300,000. This though no doubt exaggerated may give us some indication of the number of Christians in Japan at its highest. There are no exact data, but only estimates. It is possible that by 1614 the number of Christians was of the order of 500,000, and in view of the drastic enforcement of the edicts after that year it is unlikely that it showed any increase in the next two or three decades. The Jesuits calculate the total number of adult baptisms between 1550 and 1614 at 652,900. Adding the estimated number of children baptized in Christian families they arrive at a total of 750,000. To these they add the converts made by Franciscans and others, bringing the number of Christians in Japan to nearly 1,000,000 about 1614. This computation seems to leave out of account the number of deaths in the whole period from 1550 to 1614, which must have been very large since the majority of converts were presumably adults and many were of advanced age. The average expectation of life in this period was very low; and since the Jesuits report a figure of 300,000 souls in their charge in 1597, against a total of 500,000 adult baptisms since 1550, it is probably not excessive to deduct from the estimate of 1,000,000 at least one half on account of death and backsliding, and thus to put the total number of Christians in Japan in 1614 at not more than 500,000. Persecution, as we have seen, was intense between 1597 and 1614, and although a surprising number of conversions was made during this period, there were many apostasies from fear and deaths from hardship as well as an outflow of Christians who took refuge overseas and formed Christian communities in the Philippines, Cambodia, Siam, and Burma. This movement of emigration continued until the exclusion edict of 1637.

All these calculations are, of course, based upon Jesuit estimates of the numbers of converts at given dates. If those estimates are over-optimistic, then the totals must be reduced.

If Arai Hakuseki was right in saying that as many as 200,000 perished for their faith before 1650 we may (allowing for apostasies) assume that there were left in Japan perhaps as many as 100,000 who practised it in concealment. We know that, even after two hundred years of seclusion, when Japan reopened her doors and the anti-Christian edicts were rescinded, a number of Christians declared themselves, particularly in remote corners of southwestern Japan, where their ancestors had continued to worship secretly.

Two aspects of the Christian propaganda in Japan deserve some further comment. The first is the attitude of the missionaries towards the Japanese people and the second is the attitude of the Japanese ruling class towards the missionaries. Both are of interest, since they throw some light upon the nature of Japanese civilization in the sixteenth and early seventeenth centuries.

Through all the copious Jesuit literature on Japan runs a strong current of affection and admiration for the Japanese people. The missionaries are impressed, almost against their will, by the power of Japanese rulers and by the good behaviour of their subjects. They praise their strong sense of duty and obligation, their courage, their anxiety to learn, their family affection, their skill in arts and crafts. Nowhere is there to be detected in the Jesuit letters any feeling of racial or cultural superiority. On the contrary, such good observers as Organtino and Valignano insisted, when writing to their colleagues in Europe, that only the best missionaries were good enough for Japan. "It must be understood," said Organtino in 1577, "that these people are in no sense barbarous. Excluding the advantage of religion, we ourselves in comparison with them are most barbarous *(siamo barbarissimi)*. I learn something every day from the Japanese and I am sure that in the whole universe there is no people so well gifted by Nature."

Much of the work of the missions was entrusted to Japanese helpers, who displayed a remarkable zeal for the conversion of their fellow countrymen. The number of European missionaries was never great, and they could not have achieved the results that rewarded their labours without the assistance of a large body of devoted and capable Japanese helpers.[1] One cannot wonder at the affection that the missionaries felt for the people of Japan, since nowhere else in Asia were Christian propagandists able to gain such a ready hearing for the gospel from all classes, and nowhere were they more kindly treated. Yet nowhere were they more savagely repressed. This paradox is to be explained by the dual character of Japanese society, which combined a strong sense of social ethics with a great ruthlesness in the enforcement of law.

Turning now to the attitude of the Japanese towards Europeans, it must be allowed that both they and the Chinese recog-

---

[1] In 1614, just before the dispersion, the Jesuit Province in Japan had 121 members, of whom 62 were priests (including 7 Japanese) and 59 were brothers, almost all Japanese; while there were 245 Japanese seminarists and catechists.

AN UTAMARO BEAUTY

Her slender limbs can scarcely support her frail body.
Contrast to illustration, page 215.

ANOTHER SLENDER BEAUTY

From a print by Bunchō (circa *1770*)
in the collection of the late Louis V. Ledoux
(Reproduced by kind permission of Jean Ledoux)

nized that the strangers had some knowledge in which they were lacking. But there was a difference in their outlook, for the Japanese felt themselves in no sense inferior to Europeans while the Chinese professed to feel themselves in every sense superior. The former attitude is obviously the better foundation for fruitful and friendly intercourse. Nobunaga, Hideyoshi, and Ieyasu perceived very quickly that they had something to learn from the Portuguese, while unlike the contemporary rulers of China they offered no resistance to foreign ideas as such but took the initiative in seeking new knowledge.

A factor contributing to the remarkable success of Christian propaganda in Japan was the absence of a concerted effort by the Buddhist clergy to refute it. This may not be due to tolerance, but at least it shows that, in spite of sporadic attacks upon missionaries and occasional destruction of church property, religious animosity of itself was not strong enough to bring about a really dangerous campaign against Christianity throughout Japan. So far as can be judged from surviving documents the first important refutation of Christian teaching was published in 1620 by an apostate Japanese, who until 1606 had been the principal *irmão* or brother in the church at Miyako. He prefaced his book by a statement that opposition to Christianity had so far failed because Japanese Buddhists and Confucianists had not troubled to find out what its principles were. There were other and later refutations, in which learned Buddhists set out to expose the falsity of Christian tenets and stated the arguments for pantheism against monotheism. But though some of these treatises display a great theological fury their strongest objection against Christianity was that to deny the national deities was to imperil the state. A similar line was taken by Confucianists, though some of them, being opposed to all religion, attacked both Buddhism and Christianity at the same time.

Several motives combined to create in ruling circles a deep suspicion and hatred of Christianity, but no doubt its chief cause was an unfounded fear of the political power of the Catholic Church, which might, it was supposed, be exercised in Japan with the secular aid of Catholic states — to wit, of Spain and Portugal. Dread of foreign intervention was so firmly fixed in the minds of the Tokugawa rulers that as late as 1673, when the East Indiaman *Return* came to Japan requesting permission to trade, the authorities, at first disposed to allow it, sent the vessel away when they learned that the English King had married a Portuguese princess. This at least was milder treatment than that given to the Portuguese mission that had visited Japan in 1647 for a similar purpose and only narrowly escaped the punishment decreed in the edict of 1640, threatening with death the crew of any Portuguese ship that should enter a Japanese harbour. Probably the Japanese here acted upon hints from the Dutch in Nagasaki, who did nothing to remove suspicions of Christianity from the minds of the Japanese officials. But their apprehensions needed no support from the Dutch, for they were so extreme as to be scarcely rational. The basis of their fears is well revealed in the oaths that apostates were obliged to swear after 1616. In denying the Christian faith each apostate had to repeat reasons for his disbelief in a prescribed formula, which ran: "The fathers, by threats of excommunication and hell fire can do what they like with the people, *and all this is their stratagem to take the countries of others.*" The remainder of the formula is an involuntary tribute to the power of the Christian faith, for the converts, having abjured their religion (generally under duress), were by a curious logic made to swear by the very powers that they had just denied: "By the Father, the Son, and the Holy Ghost, Santa Maria and all the angels . . . if I break this oath may I lose the grace of God forever and fall into the wretched state of Judas Iscariot." By an even further departure from logic all this was followed by an oath to Buddhist and Shinto deities.

There is thus very little to show that true theological ardour was an important element in bringing about the suppression of Christianity in Japan. The refutations just cited were all composed long after the first anti-Christian edicts and put political considerations in the first place. In this respect the reception of Christianity in Japan is not without interesting analogies in other times and other countries.

It is a far cry to Iran in the first centuries of our era, but the experiences of early Christian communities in that country are almost identical with those of the Jesuits and their converts in Japan more than a thousand years later. In the Sassanid period the native Zoroastrian clergy were intolerant, but only on political grounds. Zoroastrianism was not a propagandist religion and was not concerned to convert believers in Judaism or Christianity. The Sassanid rulers, though they disliked the Jews, did not fear them; but they resisted Christian influence almost entirely upon political grounds. Of several religious minorities in Iran it was the Christians who were most frequently in trouble because of their aggressive methods. At the beginning of the Sassanid dynasty a Christian mission was well established at Edessa, and in their wars with Rome the Iranians took many Christians prisoners whom they settled as colonists in Iran. It was not until the Christians, under ambitious bishops, began to show signs of consolidation and to display a fanatical zeal against heretics that they became objectionable. Even then the Sassanid rulers felt no great anxiety so long as Rome remained pagan. But after Constantine the Great the Christians came to be regarded as outposts of Roman influence, and persecutions began in A.D. 339 under Shahpur II, mostly in the provinces next to Roman Asia. These persecutions continued at intervals for two hundred years, but there were long periods when the Christians were left alone, especially when there was peace between Byzantium and Iran. At times the Iranian rulers even favoured Nestorians, because they were split from the mother church and were therefore to be regarded as representing a reaction of Asia against Europe, or at least a hostility to Hellenistic culture.

It will be seen that here was no consistent antagonism to a foreign creed, but a variable attitude based upon political grounds. If Nestorian Christianity survived for so long in Asia it was because it had no strong political power behind it; and the successes and failures of the Roman Catholic Church in India, China, and Japan have been closely related to the degree of political support that in the estimate of those countries was enjoyed by the missionaries. It is reasons such as these that best explain the apparent vacillations and inconsistencies of the Japanese ruling class in their treatment of Christian propaganda during the period we have been considering.

The action taken by Japan against Christianity cannot be considered separately from the exclusion policy to which it was a prelude. We have seen that the anti-Christian edict of 1616 was inspired in part at least by fear of Spanish intervention in the domestic affairs of Japan. The edict was re-enacted in 1624 because the Shogun had further grounds for suspecting Spain, or at any rate the Spanish in the Philippines, of aggressive designs; and this new edict was accompanied not only by the expulsion of all Spaniards but also by the stoppage of overseas travel by Japanese. The door was gradually being closed to both ingress and egress. The Shimabara rising that began in 1637 evidently caused further misgivings to the Shogunate, for it was followed in 1638 by the expulsion of all Portuguese, whether priests or traders. At the same time the prohibition of foreign travel was strengthened by imposing the death penalty on any Japanese who should attempt to leave the country or, having left it, should return. This embargo was extended to foreign trade by a law that forbade the building of any ship of more than 2,500 bushels' capacity and consequently prevented ocean voyages. Thus Japan deliberately cut herself off from intercourse with other nations rather than face the dangers it involved. In the history of relations between Europe and Asia this was the most decided rejection ever given by an Asiatic people to an approach by the Western world. It was a flat negative, to be supported by force where necessary, as is clear from the execution of Portuguese envoys from Macao who came to Japan in 1640 hoping to persuade the Japanese to change their minds.

From 1641 the only Europeans allowed in Japan were a few Dutch merchants who were confined to a small island (named Deshima) at the head of Nagasaki Bay and allowed to trade under very strict conditions. They and some Chinese traders, also under close surveillance, formed the only channel of communication with foreign countries.

Many different reasons have been suggested for the sudden and drastic exclusionist policy of the Tokugawa shoguns, which was in such striking contrast to the expansive temper of the Japanese only a few decades before. It is at first sight hard to understand why the Asiatic people who gave Europeans the most friendly welcome should have also given them the most violent dismissal. But, granted certain simple assumptions, it does not seem difficult to explain. It was clearly not due to a peculiar distaste for foreign intercourse, since that was resumed with remarkable alacrity once the country was reopened at a later date. It is true that, since the civilization of Japan was self-contained and her economy self-supporting, there was no compelling reason for cultural or commercial exchanges; and conservative sentiment, in Japan as in other countries, was naturally opposed to foreign influences, because to most people what is foreign is also disturbing. But the intense distrust which drove the Tokugawa shoguns to close their doors arose from no ordinary conservatism. They were moved by fear, and fear not of the contamination of national customs (such as had inspired the exclusion policy of the Ming Chinese) but rather of domestic uprising against themselves.

By 1615 Ieyasu, the first Tokugawa Shogun, had after long struggle imposed the authority of his family upon all his feudal rivals. But neither he nor his successors felt entirely secure for several decades, and it was a cardinal feature of their policy to take every possible precaution against rebellion by one or more of the still powerful western feudatories. The legislation of the Tokugawas shows a constant preoccupation with this danger, which was by no means imaginary. The Mōri family in 1600 ruled thirteen of the sixty-six provinces, the Shimadzu family were strong in Kyushu, while there were other feudal houses that also chafed under Tokugawa rule. Any of these singly or in combination could have seized a favourable opportunity to revolt, as indeed in the long run they did in 1867 when the Shogunate was overthrown largely by an alliance of the clans of Satsuma (Shimadzu) and Chōshū (Mōri) with other anti-Tokugawa forces. It is significant that this alliance enjoyed the moral and material support of Western powers.

In 1637 the Tokugawa government had good reason to fear that one or other of these great families might conspire with foreigners — Spanish, Portuguese, or Dutch — trade with them for firearms, get their help in procuring artillery and ships, and even call upon them for military or naval support. The leaders of the ruling house, firmly established as it was, did not feel strong enough to face this risk; and they took steps to remove it by closing the country to foreign influence, so far as that was possible.

It is interesting, though perhaps not very fruitful, to speculate upon what turn events might have taken if this exclusionist policy had not been followed. Japan would no doubt have suffered from further civil war, and it is just possible that after an interval she herself would have followed the European example and, with a rapid development of shipbuilding and the manufacture of ordnance, taken a part in the struggle between trading powers that began to develop in the Pacific after 1600. But all we can say for certain is that she would not have enjoyed the two centuries and more of undisturbed peace that followed upon the exclusion edicts. Perhaps this blessing was not too dearly bought by cutting off intercourse with foreigners who were just beginning to taste the varied fruits of the Renaissance and the Reformation.

Ieyasu died before the outbreak of the Thirty Years' War in Europe, and it is doubtful whether his successors heard much about it. But it might have afforded them some grim satisfaction if they had known that this devastating struggle turned on the principle of *cujus regio ejus religio,* for they had taken care that organized religion should have no power in the state, and proceeded to govern their country in accordance with Confucian teachings interpreted to their own taste.

It is important to remember that the principles of Tokugawa rule were entirely secular, because some foreign accounts of the modern political development of Japan tend to fall into the error of ascribing its peculiar features to the influence of a long-standing "Shinto" tradition. There was, it is true, a so-called Revival of Shinto just after the Restoration of 1868, but (as will be seen later) the fact that it was attempted is itself a demonstration that the Tokugawa rulers had no place for Shinto political concepts in their system; and the fact that it failed shows that Shinto as an organized cult had become obsolete and at that juncture responded to no strong national sentiment. The so-called State Shinto which was developed for political ends from the turn of the nineteenth century is an invention resembling and indeed anticipating the National Socialist perversions of Teutonic mythology. "Shinto," indeed, is a term that should be used with great caution, since it can be applied to an animistic cult, to a theocratic myth, to a simple folklore that expresses indigenous Japanese sentiment about life and society, and to an organized system of ritual with a certain political content.

2. The Tokugawa Government

THE GENERAL strategic dispositions taken by the Shogunate to forestall feudal uprising have been described in outline and we may now turn to examine its administrative methods, though only for the limited purpose of making clear the nature of the institutions that were to be destroyed during the Restoration period in the second half of the nineteenth century.

The first and most important point to establish is the relationship of the Shogunate to the throne. The Shogunate, as its Japanese name, *Bakufu,* implies, was essentially a military dictatorship, for the word means the headquarters of a military command. The shoguns conceived of themselves as exercising in times of peace powers first delegated to them by the throne in time of civil war. By custom and with the throne's consent — a consent that it dared not withhold — these powers were assumed by each successive Shogun and thus perpetuated.

One of the first steps taken by the Bakufu when all the feudatories had submitted was to draw up regulations governing the position of the Emperor. He was given fairly adequate revenues, but no administrative function of any kind was left to him. Powerful Bakufu officers and a suitable garrison were assigned to the capital (at Kyoto, or Miyako as it was called at that time) in order to supervise the Emperor and to acquaint him with the Shogun's policy. His prerogative was entirely formal. He made appointments at the direction of the Shogun, including the appointment of the Shogun himself, and he carried out ceremonial observances, mostly of a religious character. At no time did the shoguns ever attempt to claim the throne. The fiction of the ultimate authority of the Emperor was always scrupulously observed, and the military dictators submitted advice or requests to him in the humble language of a loyal subject addressing his sovereign. But they took care to underline any proposal that might prove unpalatable by a suitable display of armed force. To prevent the court from plotting with powerful daimyo the Bakufu forbade any vassal to approach the Emperor except through the Shogun's representative in Kyoto. This state of affairs was generally accepted and regarded as normal under the Tokugawa régime, though it was challenged by a small group of loyalists from the beginning of the eighteenth century in a literary revival that brought to light the history of the Imperial house and later developed into an active monarchist movement culminating in the Restoration of 1868.

Thus established as the supreme power in the land, the Bakufu embarked upon a new experiment in government. Not confining themselves to the functions of raising revenue and keeping order, they undertook to regulate the morals of the people and to prescribe their behaviour in the minutest detail. It is doubtful whether previous history records a more ambitious attempt on the part of a state to interfere with the private life of every individual and so to control the thoughts as well as the actions of a whole nation. These are matters that in most countries have been left to the Church, but in both China and Japan the secular authority has traditionally regarded it as its duty to promote ethical teaching, so that in both countries political and moral philosophy are combined in one doctrine.

The Bakufu depended for its existence on the support of a military caste, and most of its legislation was designed to promote discipline and obedience among its supporters. Careful steps were taken to develop an administrative and social hierarchy ruled by a rigid code of behaviour. This was embodied in a series of documents that legislated in great detail for the duties and conduct of each grade in the military class, from the daimyo down to the lowest rank of samurai — that being the general appellation, meaning "one who serves," of all persons under military obligation to a feudal master.

Some excerpts from these documents will perhaps give a better idea of feudal standards of behaviour than an elaborate digest of their contents. Thus we may take as illustrating a puritan strain in Japanese feudal morality the first of what is known as *The Hundred Articles* or the *Legacy of Ieyasu*. It reads: *Avoid things that you like and turn your attention to unpleasant duties.* This stern view of life is repeated in a statement attributed to Ieyasu which, among other bleak pronouncements, says: *Human life is like going on a long journey carrying a heavy load. You will not be disappointed if you think that hardship is the common lot. When desires arise in your heart think back to times when you suffered distress.* The code is severe and rigid. It dwells not upon the pursuit of happiness but upon the unquestioning performance of duties. Loyalty and obedience are its watchwords, and it allows no freedom of thought. In a society so governed every man has his appointed place; in principle none can leave the station in which he was born. It is a minutely regulated hierarchical structure, designed to continue unchanged from generation to generation, and in it there is implicit no idea of progress. This indeed is the characteristic feature of all Tokugawa legislation. It is intensely conservative, to such a point that the Edict of a Hundred Articles, which has just been quoted, lays it down that a law that has been in force for fifty years may not be amended although it prove faulty. The laws that the first Tokugawa shoguns enacted were regarded as fundamental and were reaffirmed by each of their successors in a solemn ceremony of investiture attended by all vassals, who swore to obey them. It is this determination to preserve the system over which they presided that accounts for the decision of the Tokugawa house to close the country to foreign intercourse, and it explains much that is difficult to understand in the domestic history of the subsequent period of seclusion.

We need not study this system in detail. It will be sufficient for our purpose to notice some general features that will help to make clear how Japan was governed when the Western nations in the early nineteenth century resumed their efforts to force the opening of the country to foreign intercourse. The Tokugawa shoguns, as we have seen, exercised sovereign powers delegated to them by the Emperor, and since the Emperor was an absolute monarch in theory, the Shogun was an absolute ruler in practice. For the first time in her history Japan was governed by a central authority that extended over the whole country; but whereas in Europe of the seventeenth century the feudal system was giving place to national government under a crown, in Japan the crown lost its power to a supreme feudal overlord. It has been said that this Japanese system was in fact a form of centralized national government, no longer feudal in character, and this is no doubt true of a later period, when certain economic changes had impaired its structure. But in the early phases of the Tokugawa dominance the political relationship of the several daimyo to the Shogun was of a feudal character, their local autonomy depending upon vassalage and their armed forces being, in theory at least, at the disposal of the Shogun in return for the grant or confirmation of their fiefs.

The central government under the Shogun had a dual function. It administered directly the Tokugawa family's own domains and it kept careful watch on the domains of the vassals. It interfered very little in the territories of the Outside Lords and exercised only a general surveillance over the hereditary allies; but there was a general tendency in all fiefs to adopt principles of administration similar to those of the Tokugawa, while the code of behaviour that regulated the conduct of the military class was substantially the same throughout the country.

The machinery of government was simple. Matters of high policy were decided by the Shogun, since he was both the Emperor's delegate and the head of the ruling feudal house, though after the first three shoguns a large share of the administration passed into the hands of a Council of Elders, who directed a not very numerous body of subordinate officials. Often, when the Shogun was weak or indolent, real power was exercised by a senior official or even by a palace favourite, but on the whole continuity and tolerable efficiency were preserved because the practice of delegation is characteristic of Japanese political life, and indeed of social life also. Just as the affairs of the family are regulated nominally by the head of the house, but in effect by a family council, so the functions of government are frequently exercised not by the ruler in person but by a group standing behind him, which gradually acquires permanent, even hereditary status, and then in course of time loses its *de facto* authority to anonymous deputies or subordinates. Consequently the student of Japanese history is often at a loss to discover where real power resides. There are of course parallels for this descent of authority down the stairs of rank, but in Japan the system of delegation has been carried to extreme lengths.

In the early days of foreign intercourse it proved very baffling to the representatives of foreign powers in their efforts to obtain undertakings from responsible Japanese quarters. Yet the system does not appear remarkable to Japanese eyes, and it has certain advantages. It has at times counteracted the hierarchical trend of Japanese life by affording scope to persons of low standing but high capacity; and one of the most striking features of modern Japanese history is the part played in the Restoration by talented young samurai of very modest rank. There is something ironical in the fact that the Bakufu, which was based upon the strictest of class divisions, should have been destroyed by small officers who had learned their business by deputizing for their seniors.

As to the political philosophy of the rulers of Japan in the Tokugawa age, we have already noticed that once the Buddhist church had been reduced to obedience and the Christian faith suppressed, they proceeded to govern the people in accordance with Confucian principles.

Japan's long history of feudal warfare had naturally brought to high esteem the martial virtues and had fostered the growth of a class of fighting men which prided itself upon courage, disregard for life, and contempt for material wealth. These, at least, were the ideals of this privileged caste and though we may be sure that conduct often fell short of principle, there can be no doubt that most samuari endeavoured in their fashion to be faithful to the code they professed. It was encouraged by their feudal superiors as a strong bulwark for the protection of the existing order. But in times of peace a warlike spirit may be troublesome to rulers unless it is tempered by some sense of civic duty, so that the Bakufu saw the need of turning the minds of the military class to peaceful pursuits. The Law of the Military Houses (*Buke Sho-Hatto*), which was promulgated by Ieyasu in 1615, lays it down that they must devote themselves equally to arms and to polite learning. This optimistic injunction illustrates the problem that faced the rulers of Japan when the country settled down to years of unbroken peace. There was no important call to arms after the feudal levies of Iemitsu, the third Shogun, had put down the Shimabara rebellion of 1637. Thenceforward the question was how to maintain discipline and fighting spirit among men who enjoyed abundant leisure, for most samurai had little but ceremonial duty to perform and they were supported in idleness from the revenues of the Bakufu or their respective feudal lords. These conditions made it necessary to impose strict rules of conduct upon them and to punish breaches with great severity. Justice under the Tokugawa was ruthless, as all seventeenth-century travellers to Japan observed.

The guiding principles of Tokugawa administration were laid down in a system of social ethics adopted as official doctrines by the first shoguns. It was derived from a version of Confucian teaching into whose complicated history we need not enter. It is enough to note that its chief tenets were concerned with loyalty. The vassal owes loyalty to his overlord, the samurai to his master and these obligations transcend all others, even the bonds of duty and affection between parents and children, husband and wife, teacher and pupil. This was a code which, though it might be practised alongside of Buddhism, was in essence antireligious, and during the Tokugawa period Confucian professors exercised a greater influence among the educated classes than did the Buddhist clergy. Many samurai, however, continued to profess the creed of one sect or another, and all members of the lower classes were compelled to register as parishioners of a local Buddhist church, though this was only a means of keeping a watch on their movements and was part of civil, not religious policy. Ieyasu treated all Buddhist sects with a large impartiality and seems to have belonged to several himself, a habit that was followed by most of his successors.

But their tolerance stopped short at sectarian quarrels, for they all set order above faith and were quick to punish a turbulent sect, whatever its beliefs. Thus an abbot of the Nichiren sect named Nichikyo, who had been so severely beaten by some Amidists in a quarrel that he could not take part in a theological debate, was declared the loser by default, whereupon he said that the Shogun was the greatest robber in Japan, an ignoramus who did not know the simplest principles of government. For this he had his ears and nose cut off, because the Bakufu did not care what the monks believed but would not tolerate civil disobedience.

Though the authorities approved of Buddhism and gave it a certain official patronage, it cannot be regarded as the state religion of Tokugawa Japan. In that respect one may say that its place was taken by the orthodox Confucian teaching. It resulted from these conditions that there developed among the ruling class, from the highest officers of the Shogun down to the lowest samurai, strict if narrow principles of conduct that were generally observed and were reflected in the standards followed by the rest of the people. Enforced as they were by severe penalties, they inculcated in the whole nation habits of discipline and obedience, which eased the task of government and enabled Japan to pass through two hundred years of unbroken peace with but little disturbance of the social order. Consequently when in the nineteenth century the course of world events made it necessary for Japan to enter the modern world and change many of her ancient habits, the most sweeping transformations were accomplished with relative ease, because the mass of the people was schooled in respect for authority and the privileged classes included a great number of men blessed with courage, trained in public affairs, and moved by a high sense of duty. The feudal oligarchs may not have discovered the secret of good government, but firm government was something they thoroughly understood.

The foregoing outline may have given the impression that throughout the Tokugawa age conditions remained substantially unaltered, and it is true that they kept their basic character for a very long time. But beneath a look of permanence there can be detected a continuous process of change in the nature of Japanese institutions. It cannot be said that they collapsed, for they displayed a remarkable durability; but peaceful conditions and the cessation of foreign intercourse faced the country with problems that obliged its rulers to accept and even to encourage modifications in the policy laid down by the founders of the centralized feudal state. The first three Shoguns (Ieyasu, Hidetada, and Iemitsu, who between them ruled from 1603 to 1651) were animated by a military spirit that found expression in their principles of government. This was natural enough, since in their day the memory of civil war was still fresh, and martial ideas were still in favour. But under the fourth Shogun the character of the régime began to undergo a change.

In the first fifty years of the Bakufu the return to peace and settled life, with the growth of cities and the improvement of transport, had favoured the use of money. The government was well provided with funds, for Ieyasu had accumulated great treasure and his currency was sound. Foreign trade was increasing until about 1610 and did not seriously diminish until the seclusion began, while the mining of gold and silver was fairly lucrative. These and similar circumstances brought a time of free spending and thriving business, which diverted men's minds from military matters and produced a certain relaxation of feudal discipline. Civil accomplishments began to rival warlike prowess. Ieyasu himself, as we have seen, had laid it down that members of the military houses should devote themselves equally to arms and learning, and he had given some encouragement to classical Chinese studies by installing a Confucian scholar as the official philosopher at his court. But it is only a rare paragon who can maintain a nice balance between outdoor exercises and learned pursuits. By the time of Tsunayoshi, the fifth Shogun (1680–1709), the military arts were being neglected and interest in Chinese literature had become a fashionable craze. The Shogun himself took the lead by endowing an academy for the sons of feudal dignitaries, whose examination papers he set. He even took advantage of his position to expound the classics to his vassals in lectures of increasing frequency, which they were obliged to attend.

This lapse from rigid martial standards was accompanied by some relaxation of the severity of the Bakufu towards the Imperial court and by easier relationships between Yedo and the feudatories, who were now allowed some discretion in matters of succession and marriages — favours that by reducing tension between the Bakufu and the fiefs made life more agreeable for provincial samurai and tended to diminish the number of discontented *rōnin*.[2] Though this moderation of policy is ascribed to the Shogun, it was not, of course, his directive that created the new mood. It was a natural reaction against the energetic and uncompromising authors of a planned society, those capable and restless people whose designs for the improvement of mankind usually end in making the objects of their solicitude more eager than ever to break the rules. By the end of the seventeenth century Japanese life in cities and towns had entered upon a new phase, a spring-like flowering of the native culture revealing qualities that had for long been denied expression.

3. The Cultural Scene

PEACE in Japan could not fail to stimulate learning and the arts, since even in times of war the æsthetic impulse had not failed. Indeed, many great captains, famous for bloody exploits, had been

---

2 The rōnin were samurai who either voluntarily or through the accidents of war had become masterless men, owing allegiance to no feudal superior.

not only patrons but also connoisseurs of literature, painting, ceramics, and such recondite pastimes as the tea ceremony and the lyric mimes called Nō. Official encouragement of the studious life produced before long a society in which intellectual and artistic pursuits took a high place; and the growth of Osaka and Yedo as populous centres of trade and government led to the formation of a prosperous and lively bourgeoisie also devoted to the arts, great playgoers, avid readers of romances, and good judges of painting and poetry. The stern rule of the Tokugawa, despite their frequent sumptuary edicts and their exhortations to frugality, did not succeed in keeping metropolitan life from cultivating elegance and luxury, while many castle towns became centres of provincial enlightenment. The fixed pattern of feudal administration was liberal enough to allow a measure of freedom in spheres remote from politics, so that during the eighteenth century Japan developed a society based upon law and privilege, governed by harsh principle, but nevertheless achieving in practice great urbanity and style. It was closed to outside influences and therefore could not be refreshed by the winds of new doctrine then blowing about the Western world; but probably no contemporary European community was more civilized and polished.

Consequently, when in the nineteenth century the policy of seclusion was gradually relaxed as Western peoples began to range the Pacific in search of new openings for trade, they were confronted in Japan not by a backward culture submitting easily to their influence, but by a highly organized civilization, which, though it was in a disturbed phase, was nevertheless supported by strong traditions and firm government, and by a vigorous nation filled with pride. This was something new in their experience of Eastern countries, for neither in India nor in southeast Asia nor even in China had they met with a people so united, so self-reliant, and yet so ready to learn.

It may be interesting in this context to examine the impressions of Japan recorded by Europeans from the earliest days of intercourse. Here are some of the most vivid, set forth in chronological order:

St. Francis Xavier, *c.* 1550:
 "These people are the delight of my heart."
Father Frois, *c.* 1560:
 "As gifted a nation as any in Europe."
Ortelius, in *Japoniæ insularum descriptio,* 1595:
 "Mortalitatis incommoda, famem, sitim, æstum, algorem, vigilias laboresque admirabili patientia tolerant. Acuta, sagax et bene a natura informata gens est judicio, docilitate, memoria."
Sir Edward Michelborne, *c.* 1605:

"The Japons not being suffered to land in any port in the Indies with weapons, being accounted a people so desperate and daring that they were feared in all places where they came."

Will Adams, the English pilot-major, 1611:

"The people of this island of Japan are good by nature, courteous above measure, and valiant in war. Their justice is severely executed without any partiality upon transgressors of the law. They are governed in great civility. I mean there is not a land better governed in the world by civil police."

The same, 1613:

"In this land there is no strange news to certify you of, the whole being in peace, the people very subject to their governors and superiors."

Don Roderigo de Vivero y Velasco, Governor of the Philippines, *c.* 1612:

"The streets and open places of Yedo are so very handsome, clean and well kept that it might be imagined no person walked in them. . . . In the one hundred leagues from Zurunga to Meaco a village occurs every quarter of a league. On whichever side a traveller turns his eye he perceives a concourse of people as in the most populous cities of Europe. . . . The Japanese are very industrious and expert. They are clever at invention and imitation. Their municipal government is excellent, the internal police is admirably regulated. . . . Pride, arrogance, and a resolution which is almost carried to ferocity are the distinctive traits of Japanese of all classes."

Englebert Kaempfer, 1692:

"United and peaceable, taught to give due worship to the gods, due obedience to the Laws, due submission to their superiors, due love and regard to their neighbours."

Anon. *Manners and Customs of the Japanese* (a compilation), London, 1841:

"Law and established custom, unvarying, known to all and pressing on all alike are the despots of Japan. Scarcely an action of life is exempt from their rigid, inflexible and irksome control; but he who complies with their dictates has no arbitrary power, no capricious tyranny to apprehend."

The captain of H.M.S. *Samarang*, 1845:

"The gentlemen of Japan were most polite and courteous, conducting themselves with refined and polished urbanity."

It will be seen that these observers agree that Japan was efficiently and firmly governed, and they praise the civic virtues of the Japanese people. They were for the most part not well enough acquainted with the Japanese language or familiar with Eastern philosophy to appreciate the literary and artistic life of circles of which they could have but little direct knowledge. But had they been able to understand it they would have agreed that it was not wanting in distinction. It is true that the greatest periods in Japanese art and letters had passed by before the end of the civil wars in the sixteenth century; but the seventeenth and eighteenth saw a modest renaissance that deserves some notice, because it contributed to the formation of that culture which in the nineteenth met the impact of Western civilization.

When the country had settled down to peaceful life in 1615, the growth of cities like Yedo and Osaka brought about certain changes in the constitution of the people. The great numbers of feudal officers and troops in residence in those places and the constant going and coming of daimyo between their provinces and the capital swelled the urban population and, by creating a need for the services of tradesmen and artisans, formed a large class of *chōnin* or townspeople. In former times under feudal rule there had been a strict division of society into four classes: soldiers, farmers, artisans, and traders. This division persisted throughout the Tokugawa era, though it tended to break down towards the end. In the seventeenth and early eighteenth centuries it was still maintained in principle, and to pass from one class to another was difficult and unusual. The trader came lowest in the social scale because in an agrarian economy the farmer is the pillar of the state. But in a large and thriving city such as Yedo the tradesman and the skilled craftsman gained a special importance by reason of their use to the community and their great numbers, so that in course of time they developed into a prosperous bourgeoisie. This was a new phenomenon in the social life of Japan, which later exerted a strong influence upon the country's economic development as the growth of a substantial mercantile class opened a breach in the rigid social structure of feudalism. The political and economic aspects of the rise of the chōnin need not detain us here, though it is worth while to note in passing that the descendants of the wealthy shopkeepers of Yedo and Osaka played an important, indeed an indispensable part in the movement which ended by overthrowing the Shogunate in 1868, because it could scarcely have succeeded without their financial backing. But what concerns us now is the contribution of this class to Japanese culture in the seventeenth century and after. Its history is remarkable in many ways, since it arose from small beginnings, was handicapped by inferior social standing, and had to strive against a virtual monopoly of learning and authority enjoyed by the military caste, the Buddhist clergy, and a few court nobles.

The Tokugawa oligarchs for some generations conducted their administration almost as if it were the enforcement of martial law, and they legislated very thoroughly on points affecting the conduct of each separate class, distinguishing in their standards between samurai and commoner. Strict rules were applied to the townspeople, who as time went on became extravagant in their habits, thus calling forth a stream of official rebukes. They were told to lead frugal, industrious lives, and not to wear fine clothes or give expensive feasts. But this endeavour to regulate the citizen's behaviour by edict, which was in accordance with ancient tradition, was not successful, though the government never learned by experience and thus repeated its fruitless policy time after time. The merchants and craftsmen had money in their pockets and were determined to spend it. The money they earned came from the purses of their social superiors, to whom their services were indispensable. It was the daimyo on duty in Yedo, their wives, and their retinues, or the Shogun's own officers, who converted their rice revenues into cash, to the great profit of brokers and dealers, and spent it on lavish entertainment or the purchase of fine dress and furnishings. It may be asked why the Bakufu did not frown upon this high-class extravagance, and the answer is that it was part of Tokugawa policy to encourage the daimyo to spend their fortunes on pleasures rather than on military preparations. Thus the old stern morality of the military aristocrats was being eroded by peace and leisure.

Such circumstances contributed to the growth of a new middle-class community, confined principally to the greater cities, enjoying comfortable incomes and devoted to amusement. By 1700 or thereabouts the citizens of Osaka and Yedo had developed a characteristic culture of their own, which showed a marked divergence from the severe and sometimes cramping standards of the classical Japanese tradition. Their taste was for the theatre, for romantic or comic novels, for salacious or witty lampoons, and for gay, coloured paintings and prints. It was vulgar in the eyes of the orthodox, but it was fresh, spontaneous, and by no means lacking in discernment. It brought into being schools of artists, authors, actors, playwrights, and master craftsmen who figure prominently in Japanese æsthetic history. Their work came to be prized outside of bourgeois circles and in time attracted into the artistic and literary coteries of the chōnin a number of men of samurai origin who were dissatisfied with what feudal life had to offer.

Like most nice arrangements, the class system that the Tokugawa attempted to fix did not remain unmodified. Apart from the rise of an influential bourgeoisie a new and disturbing element appeared in the peaceful Tokugawa society. This was the class of masterless samurai or rōnin which grew to important dimensions after the civil wars. It was not a new feature in Japanese life, for the end of fighting had often thrown out of employment a number of soldiers who found it hard to adjust themselves to peaceful conditions and were inclined to take up a roving and sometimes an unruly or criminal life. But when Ieyasu, having disposed of his enemies, proceeded to a redistribution of fiefs throughout the country, he created for himself and his successors a serious problem on a much larger scale. He abolished or reduced a great number of fiefs, some of which were incorporated in his own domains and some transferred to his favourite vassals. When these changes of ownership took place new incumbents did not as a rule wish to take into their services samurai bound to them by no previous tie, and accordingly within fifty years after the Battle of Sehigahara some 400,000 samurai are said to have become rōnin.[3] To these should be added a number of men who for various private reasons gave up their allegiances and led an independent life. Among them, it is interesting to note, were a number of Christian converts who fled from their homes when persecution became severe. Some went overseas to the Philippines, Macao, and Farther India, where they engaged in trade or took service with foreign rulers as mercenaries, but most remained in Japan, together with most of those samurai who, having been engaged in maritime trade licensed by the government, lost their occupation when the country was closed.

Thus from early in the Tokugawa period the population included a considerable number of men ill adjusted to the social order of the times. Some crossed the line and entered another class, becoming farmers or tradesmen or engaging in scholastic, literary, or artistic pursuits. But there was a large residue of unsettled men of no fixed occupation, always ready for excitement and tending to engage in subversive movements. They were rightly regarded by the Bakufu as a dangerous element, especially after the Shimabara rebellion of 1637–8 and again in 1651, when a conspiracy against the government came to light and implicated a great number of rōnin. As many as 100,000 of these desperate men who fought against Ieyasu are said to have been slaughtered during and after the siege of Osaka in 1615, and ruthless measures of repression were taken after the incidents of 1637 and 1651. But even when this generation had been destroyed or had passed away the rōnin as a class did not disappear. They were quiescent through most of the eighteenth century, though their ranks were from time to time refilled by economic depression, and by the end of the Tokugawa period they had regained importance as a menace to the existing order. It was men of this type who in the troubles leading up to the Restoration and in the years of political strife to follow were to play a part that was always active, generally vio-

---

[3] This does not, of course, mean a total of 400,000 at the end of the period, but shows that the ranks of the rōnin were added to each year after 1600 by from 5,000 to 10,000 men, the cumulative total being reduced by alternative employment or death.

lent, and sometimes useful. They displayed every character from a quixotic knight-errantry to a vulgar rowdiness, and Japanese political life for several generations thereafter bore the marks of their influence. It should be added that the rōnin who joined the anti-Tokugawa movement from about 1858 were not all vagrants and deserters. Many purposely divested themselves of their obligations to feudal superiors so that they could with a clear conscience support the Imperial cause.

The presence of a samurai element in the new bourgeoisie probably tended to raise its cultural level, for some of the rōnin were men of parts. The history of popular literature and art in the middle and late Tokugawa period shows that some of its most prominent figures were men of samurai origin. The celebrated playwright Chikamatsu, who flourished late in the seventeenth century, was a rōnin and so was Bakin, the great novelist, while many popular artists came from samurai families and began as pupils of "official" painters.

Tempting as it is, this is not the place for a full study of the intellectual and artistic life of the seventeenth and eighteenth centuries, which has unfortunately been neglected by Western students, who have so far paid attention mainly to political and economic matters in that era and have made few or no attempts to paint a comprehensive picture of the singularly interesting society of Yedo and Osaka in its more human and less statistical aspects. But it is necessary to have some knowledge of this society if one is to understand the culture which was later to come under strong foreign influence.

Its chief feature is perhaps its development of popular arts. Classical schools of painting, which had grown up in Kyoto, continued in Yedo, when the Shogun Tsunayoshi (1680–1709) invited painters from the Kano studios to his capital, because their work had a certain Chinese flavour and its sentiment was in harmony with the Confucian spirit cultivated in official quarters. But what most distinguishes the new art from the old is a profusion of genre paintings which portray faithfully and for the most part with only a faint idealistic tinge the common contemporary life in its many-coloured aspects. This is the heyday of a realistic art which takes for its themes the streets, the theatres, the tea-houses, and the easy-going ladies or the fashionable actors who frequent them. It does not belong to any of the early schools, but is a new thing, though compounded partly of older elements. Its patrons are the tradesmen and it satisfies a demand that gay city life has created. It forms, as it develops, an exacting taste among clients in bourgeois circles, so that presently the townspeople become severe critics and the one time aristocratic monopoly of culture is broken. The pictures of the passing scene, beginning with the work of such painters as Hishigawa Moronobu, are the forerunners of the colour print so familiar to the West, a form of art that apart from its artistic value testifies in a most convincing way to the spread of æsthetic interest among the rising urban class. The names of the great print artists were known to every citizen and their merits earnestly debated. They are the portrayers of the Ukiyo or Floating World. It is a term of which the origin is disputed, some deriving it from the Buddhist *ukiyo,* which means this world of sorrow. But there can be little doubt that, as referring to the work of Yedo painters, it connoted the world of transient pleasures. The Ukiyo-e is a picture of that world.

Much the same can be said of literature and the theatre. The romances and the stage performances that appealed to the military class did not satisfy the robust and sensuous taste of the townspeople and accordingly there developed in Osaka and Yedo a new kind of novel and a popular theatre, less refined but more actual and lively than their predecessors. These new demands called forth a new class of writer who depicted for popular entertainment the contemporary scene and thus extended the interest of the citizens in books and plays, their feeling for costume and their appreciation of acting. At the same time a rising standard of living promoted excellence in the applied arts, and by the end of the seventeenth century — in the very bright and showy period known as Genroku — it may be said that a distinct and advanced new culture had been formed, a culture which for lively æsthetic quality would compare favourably with anything that contemporary Europe had to show. As seen by the social historian, perhaps the most interesting feature of this new culture of the townspeople is the fact that it belonged to no particular class. It was born and nourished, it is true, in a society of commoners, but it cannot be called plebeian, for the creative artists and the master craftsmen who made it formed an élite in which all were merged without respect to social origins. This élite, like the society it served, had no pedigree. Its themes were those of the present and its past was only yesterday.

The spectacular work of the artists and writers of these popular schools has caused foreign and some Japanese writers, in reaction against their former neglect, to exaggerate their importance in the artistic and even the social history of Japan. They have given the impression that the new bourgeois culture replaced or overwhelmed an earlier cultural life in which the townspeople took no part. But in fact the bourgeois culture was very limited in its scope, and its superb artistic quality was confined within a very narrow range. The townspeople, for all their growing prosperity, were still subject to the disabilities of their class and not free from oppression at the hands of their feudal masters. It was in the world of entertainment, the world of make-believe, that they found escape from social restraints, and their free emotional life was led largely in resorts of fugitive pleasure — to wit, the brothel and the theatre. It was a life dominated by the influence of women, and it is not to be wondered at that it nourished in both art and letters an almost morbid preoccupation with the sensual. This is less apparent in the early Ukiyo-e painters than in their eighteenth-century successors, but from its beginnings the popular art of the cities was the expression — the charming, the delicate, and the accomplished expression — of only a narrow segment of contemporary life. There is a natural temptation to stress the Floating World school, in life as well as in art, because of its special sensitiveness and its distinctive repertory, but this should not lead us into neglect of more sober but still quite important movements in old-established schools. Something more must be said on this subject when we come to consider Yedo in the eighteenth century, but it is as well to emphasize here that old ways of life did not vanish with the growth of cities. The fine arts as practised and enjoyed in the upper circles of Tokugawa society did not display that preference for the actual and that instinct for the contemporaneous which were the marks of the bourgeois *fin de siècle* culture. But it would be mistaken to think of them as entirely traditional and closed to new influences.

Alongside of this cultural growth there took place also some changes in the nature of the more conservative parts of feudal society. Polite accomplishments had been encouraged among the samurai by their opportunities for leisure and by the official promotion of study as a means of turning the minds of malcontents away from real or imagined political grievances. No doubt a majority of these military men were little disposed to sit over their books, but on the whole it can be said that learning spread and flourished. The line of scholars was not broken, and the Yedo period is distinguished for the number of philosophers that it produced and the heat that their controversies engendered. Some students began to question the official philosophy, and in course of time the uniformity of feudal opinion was broken by heterodox schools, which challenged the assumptions at the base of feudal society and thus began an intellectual movement that was to bring it to ruin in the nineteenth century. It cannot be said, however, that in the seventeenth and eighteenth centuries the feudal system showed clear signs of impending collapse, though these may now be visible in retrospect to the historian. Yet a crack in its seemingly massive structure is revealed by one significant feature of the scholarship of the Tokugawa era. This is the attention paid to economic problems by its leading political philosophers. As early as 1712 we find Arai Hakuseki, the official Confucian scholar at the Shogun's court, whose natural interest was in rites and ceremonies, immersed in questions of currency and writing on monetary theory. He was followed by other distinguished Confucian scholars, such as Ogyū Sorai and Miura Baien, who wrestled with

KUMAZAWA BANZAN (1618–91)

A celebrated Confucian scholar
and political economist

problems that still vex economists, and propounded theories on value, prices, and other matters remote from the sphere of conventional scholarship.

It need hardly be said that this interest in questions of finance, production, and trade arose from practical necessity. The closed economy of Japan was disturbed by one crisis after another as population increased, as the use of money altered the distribution of wealth, and as the farmer's interests clashed with those of the merchant. The rise of the urban class whose culture we have been discussing was a challenge not only to the social structure of the feudal state but also to its economic foundation. Once the land-revenue economy, that essential support of feudal privilege, was disturbed by a growing mercantile, money-using class, the end was almost in sight, though it might be delayed for a space by the weight of tradition and the use of autocratic measures.

Perhaps it should be added here that when the leading Japanese Confucianists turned their attention to economic matters they were not departing from precedent, for these were often uppermost in the minds of Chinese philosophers. The advice that the Sages so copiously offered to distracted monarchs frequently had to do with land tenure, the growing and storing of grain, and the relations between producer and consumer. But they regarded such questions as a branch of moral philosophy and not as a dismal science. This was also the attitude of most of the Japanese scholars who were troubled by anomalies arising from the use of money. Their view was not unlike that of philosophers in mediæval Europe, for the Church thought of economic questions in ethical terms. It might prove an interesting exercise for a historian to trace the resemblances between the opinions of classical Far Eastern writers and the mediæval idea that production and profit were forms of evil unless their end was the general good.

Note on CHAPTER 9

ASTRONOMY AND MATHEMATICS IN JAPAN. Whether more valuable scientific knowledge was obtained from Dutch than from Jesuit and other missionary sources is not a question of much importance; but it is of passing interest to note that the Jesuits in China did not use the Copernican system until towards the end of the seventeenth century, whereas the greatest advances made by Japanese astronomers followed upon knowledge of the Copernican system, which they obtained through the Dutch.

Perhaps the most significant feature of astronomical studies in eighteenth-century Japan is not the zeal of the students but the ease with which the Copernican system found acceptance. In Japan, as in China, it met with no opposition on religious grounds, since Far Eastern beliefs were neither anthropocentric nor geocentric and were consequently not thought to be endangered by a theory that made the earth a satellite and diminished the importance of man.

For further details see an interesting paper by B. Szczesniak, in the *Journal of the Royal Asiatic Society,* parts one and two of the volume for 1944. The same writer deals with astronomical and mathematical studies in China in later parts of the same volume.

CHAPTER
10

EIGHTEENTH–CENTURY JAPAN

1. Domestic Politics

THE PERIOD called Genroku may be looked upon as the zenith of Tokugawa prosperity, and perhaps even the justification of feudal rule, for here was peace and plenty and a great flourishing of the arts — a happy society as human societies go. Thereafter Japanese history for a century or so may be read as a chronicle of the failure of a great experiment intended to maintain peace and well-being by conducting the affairs of the state in accordance with a fixed doctrine and preserving it from contamination by all new influences, whether arising from within or without its borders.

But when the Shogun Yoshimune succeeded to power in 1716, both internal and external circumstances had set in motion a process that by slow degrees was to wear down resistance to change. This new ruler saw that the samurai, or at least the samurai upon whom the Bakufu depended, had declined in vigour though they might have increased in knowledge; and he seems to have reached the conclusion that government on the advice of philosopher-statesmen and the substitution of learning for military discipline had gone on too long. There can be little doubt that a Japanese reading of a Sung version of an ancient Chinese philosophy was a most unsuitable instrument for governing a great country, as indeed was any doctrine pretending to have found the secret of guiding the mysterious, erratic behaviour of men. One Chinese sage had said that governing a great country was like cooking small fish, and if this means that attention must be paid to detail, then the Tokugawa rulers would have done well to follow his advice by neglecting theory and devoting themselves to practical matters.

If ever there was a need for straightforward empiric solutions of political problems it was in the days of the shoguns whose desire was to preserve their system intact. Something of this kind may have been in the mind of Yoshimune when he surveyed the feudal scene on his accession. He knew by experience the state of affairs in the clans, for he had been lord of a small fief before his appointment; and he decided that Confucianism was not enough. Some practical steps must be taken to revive the waning military spirit and to stop the decay of feudal institutions. Accordingly he endeavoured to restore the discipline of the days of Ieyasu by encouraging great hunting parties, which were in reality military exercises, and by other measures such as the issue of orders to all members of the military class directing them to cut down expenditure and lead simple lives. This kind of government by rescript was naturally not very effective and there is a plaintive note in some of the orders, which say: "In all things frugality must be observed, as we have laid it down already time after time." Little attention was paid to these sumptuary rules by either samurai or simple commoner, and perhaps the Shogun did not expect much of them.

He also struggled to make positive improvements by reforming a debased currency, encouraging agriculture, reclaiming waste land, and generally stimulating production, with some temporary benefit. But neither he nor his advisers grasped the fundamental weakness of the system over which he presided, for they did not realize or would not admit that once the merchant class had gained effective influence, the main principles of feudal rule were no longer valid. Perhaps the feudal rulers were groping for the right solution, since before long they began to engage in trade themselves. They had some success in government enterprises, either regulating or monopolizing the sale of such products as oil, iron, brass, coal, and sulphur. They also continuously endeavoured, though with no success, to control the price of rice and other commodities. But the object of such undertakings was not to improve the national economy. They were designed to increase the Tokugawa revenues while checking the power of the merchants. Similar policies were adopted by a number of daimyo, who made profits by the sale of local products.

This was a great change from the days when feudal authority was enthroned upon a pile of rice built up by industrious peasants, but the growth of a money economy only gradually encroached upon the privilege of the military class. The process was inevitable and relentless, but it took a hundred years from the days of Yoshimune to reach its culmination. Its interest at this point lies in the fact that a habit of state intervention in trade, developed in the eighteenth century, was carried over into the nineteenth, when it affected the economic policy of Japan as she began to develop into a modern industrial state.

Some knowledge of economic conditions in the Tokugawa era is necessary for a full understanding of its history and in particular of the events that led to the breakdown of the policy of seclusion. A short discussion of the main economic problems will be found in the next chapter, and here it is only necessary to say that from Yoshimune's day onwards the authorities were constantly harassed by the conflict between rural and urban interests, by questions of food production and prices. Their policy was never consistent or successful and their repeated failures made for social instability and discontent.

Much of the serious literature of the period is concerned with the agrarian problem in its various aspects, and even in more fugitive pieces one comes across frequent references to unpredictable changes in the price of rice. The scholars of the day can scarcely be blamed for failing to understand the weakness of their system. They were part of it, unable to see it from outside, and the very isolation upon which it depended deprived them of opportunity to compare their experience with that of other countries. The only example or precedent upon which they could draw was furnished by classical Chinese writings on political economy, and these were the produce of an environment not unlike their own in so far as it was dominated by ideas natural to a land-revenue society. In such circumstances it is most creditable that Japan in the Tokugawa age should have brought forth a line of scholars who, though by training they were exponents of Chinese moral philosophy, should have arrived independently at theoretical concepts that, in the opinion of competent students, are very close to those deduced by Western economists from a much greater wealth of material.

2. Foreign Influences

ONE of the dangers most feared by the Bakufu in its early days was the influence of foreign ideas which (as the Chinese also said on occasion) "might contaminate the customs of the country." Though the exclusion edicts do not appear to have been reinforced by a general prohibition of the import of foreign books, this was scarcely necessary since none but a few official interpreters could read a European language, and in any case the Bakufu could always legislate *ad hoc* as the occasion required. Thus the ban upon Christianity had been accompanied by a rigorous censorship designed to exclude not only all direct Christian teaching but all literature that might be suspected of promoting the spread of Christian knowledge. There was a possibility that Chinese books, which were at that time freely admitted, might contain matter infringing this rule, and consequently in 1630 an edict sought to close a gap in the proscription by forbidding "books intended to propagate

Christianity" and specifying certain works by Father Ricci and other Jesuit missionaries that had been published in the Chinese language in China.

This interdict was applied in an absurdly matter-of-fact way, the authorities confiscating any book that contained the slightest indirect reference to Christianity, even if it were only a single word like "Catholic" or "Western" or "Europe." But it seems that it was not consistently enforced, for there is good evidence that a considerable number of Chinese books reached Japan during the latter half of the seventeenth century. The arrival of cases of Chinese books from Cambodia is reported in 1663, and when Chinese loyalists escaping from the Manchus took refuge in Japan in 1683 and 1684 they carried with them choice items from their libraries which appear to have passed through the Nagasaki customs without trouble. Perhaps because of this the 1630 edict was renewed in 1685, and ten years later we hear of the Nagasaki censors' doubts as to a Chinese work that described the sights of Peking in twenty-eight volumes. It contained a reference to the tomb of Father Ricci and gave some account of that great man's life. The censors asked Yedo for instructions, saying that the guide-book did not teach Christianity but only praised the virtuous life of an Occidental person. But the higher authorities ordered the book to be destroyed, and the junk that brought it was quarantined, so that the crew could buy no food ashore.

These curious instances are quoted in order to show to what lengths the Tokugawa administration carried their detestation and their fear of Christian influence. They show at the same time that, despite the edicts, there was still a certain interest in foreign ideas in intellectual circles. Part of this was mere curiosity, but there is no doubt that there was some genuine thirst for Western knowledge, chiefly in scientific matters and notably in astronomy and surgery. Earnest Japanese scholars did not like being deprived of information that might further their studies and objected to censorship on general grounds. It is clear that despite the strict official policy they did from time to time manage to get hold of forbidden books, though (like certain works in Chinese on mathematical subjects by Ricci) these were usually confined to a very select group and circulated secretly in manuscript.

As the fear of Christianity diminished with the lapse of time the reasons for the ban on Western literature seemed even less valid than before and certain scholars began to protest openly against it. Ogyū Sorai, a celebrated Confucian scholar who was no liberal but a believer in absolute rule, nevertheless raised objections, saying: "Owing to these prohibitions nobody knows what Christianity teaches. But the officials should not leave us in ignorance on this subject, since we ought to know whether it is good or bad. . . . Buddhists, Shintoists, and Confucianists should be in a position to prove that it is erroneous or harmful, but they cannot do this unless they are allowed to see the books." Arai Hakuseki, the official Confucian scholar at the Shogun's court, was no friend of Christianity, but after having interrogated an unfortunate missionary who had smuggled himself into Japan, he decided that it was not dangerous. He was not against precautions, but he neatly summarized the objections to an indiscriminate censorship by observing: "There is danger in hunting wolves with tigers."

It will be seen that, severe as was the official attitude, there were means by which information about the outside world could reach Japan. Chinese sources were important because there was a regular approved trade between Japan and China, carried in Chinese vessels whose crews were not averse to smuggling and no doubt adept in bribery. The merchants in the Dutch factory at Nagasaki were scrupulously isolated from contacts with other than officials and interpreters, but some of these latter were professionally interested in foreign learning and thus provided a channel of communication that could be used by scholars in search of Western knowledge, though only illicitly and at great risk. Thus a trickle of intercourse always continued, though not even the boldest smuggler of scraps of information would dare to show an interest in any matter that might, by some stretch of official imagination, be connected with Christianity. Here the vigilance of the authorities was never relaxed. Anti-Christian edicts were constantly issued and reissued throughout the seventeenth and eighteenth centuries, and they continued in force until after the Restoration of 1868.

We have already touched on the reasons for the anti-Christian edicts and seen what were the circumstances that prompted their issue in the early part of the seventeenth century. But it is not easy to understand the persistence of an almost hysterical dread of Christian propaganda long after the missionaries had been ejected and all visible traces of the foreign creed removed. This enduring anxiety was betrayed not only by reiteration of the edicts, but also by repeated hunts for Christians in remote places, which are recorded as late as 1790, 1841, and 1856, to say nothing of a last search in 1868. In the period with which we are now dealing — it carries us to the end of Yoshimune's shogunate in 1744 — all persons suspected of a connection with Christianity were still obliged to prove their innocence by trampling upon a sacred picture, the *fumie*, a wooden or metal plaque bearing a figure of Jesus or the Virgin. By that time, however, well-informed Japanese no longer supposed that there was any likelihood of an invasion planned by Spanish or Portuguese priests. None of the anti-Christian edicts was withdrawn and precautions were not discontinued, but the attitude of the authorities had become less immoderate.

This change was part of a general liberal trend in the policy of Yoshimune, who in spite of his promotion of the military arts was well disposed towards scholarship. He did not confine his patronage to the orthodox Confucian philosophy and he became persuaded that Japan had something useful to learn from the West. In 1720 he relaxed the interdicts upon Western learning by permitting the importation of foreign books so long as they did not propagate Christian teaching. This meant that scientific works written by the Jesuits in China could now be brought to Japan. His reasons are not quite clear, though it is evident that he was acting in accord with a growing desire among Japanese scholars to extend their studies beyond the range of native learning. A clue to his motives is afforded by an episode that occurred when doubts arose as to the accuracy of the Japanese calendar — a serious matter in Eastern countries where government depended upon a kind of national horoscope. It was known that there existed in Nagasaki a copy of an astronomical encyclopædia compiled for the use of the Peking court by Father Adam Schall, and orders were given to dispatch it to Yedo. It is evident that the usefulness of this foreign book was one of the causes of the edict of 1720.

It may be asked why, after nearly a century of intercourse with the Portuguese, the Japanese had acquired so little Western scientific knowledge that they should now have to depend upon information from China. This is not easy to account for, but it is a fact that, if we exclude the effects of astronomical science as it was made known in the Far East by Jesuits working under the Portuguese *padroado*, Portuguese influence upon Japan, considering its duration, was remarkably small apart from the effect of Christianity, which was of great importance while it lasted but left little positive trace upon Japanese life beyond the deep-rooted mistrust it aroused. The Japanese learned from the Portuguese something of cartography, navigation, medicine, and the use of firearms, and the Portuguese may be given some credit for the system of "romanization" by which Japanese words could be written in the Western alphabet. But specific survivals of Portuguese influence are rare and perhaps one may say that the most important effect of the century of Portuguese intercourse was to make the Japanese aware of the world beyond eastern Asia, of the possibilities of extended ocean trade and at the same time of the strength of Western navies.

The really important, positive, and measurable Western influences on Japan, those which by promoting the study of mathematics and astronomy led to further interest in Western science and so prepared the way for profound changes in Japanese life, are strangely enough not visible until after the exclusion edicts; and they began to come in through the Chinese channels just described. This is to be explained partly by the chronology of the development of Western science, in which Portugal was relatively backward; and partly by the change of policy expressed in Yoshimune's decree. Thenceforward, principally through the medium of the Dutch trading station in Nagasaki, Japanese scholars were able to pursue their Western studies in comparative but by no means complete freedom, though they were of course handicapped by the difficulty of learning foreign languages, obtaining foreign books, and profiting by personal contact with Western men of learning.

The story of this small band of students, sedulously striving in the face of many obstacles to acquire the elements of unfamiliar science, is a fascinating one, which can be told here only in the broadest outline. Its historical interest is considerable, for it reveals a glaring contrast between the indifference of the Chinese towards foreign learning and the eager interest displayed in Japan, at first by a few obscure students and later by an increasing number of men of all classes. In China under the Manchu dynasty a band of distinguished Jesuit scholars, who enjoyed the patronage of the Emperors K'ang Hsi and Ch'ien Lung, could place at the disposal of Chinese intellectuals a great fund of learning in the Western sciences, but those gifts were disdained by most of the complacent Chinese bureaucrats, and the influence of Western knowledge upon Chinese life was hardly perceptible until the closing years of the nineteenth century. In Japan, on the other hand, where Europe was represented only by a few merchants and ships' captains confined to narrow quarters in a seaport town, it was the Japanese themselves who came forward to inquire into the nature of Western learning.

The first step was the study of the Dutch language, which gradually displaced Portuguese as Dutch and English rivalry diminished Portuguese power throughout the Far East. The Portuguese language, however, continued in use in Japan throughout the seventeenth century, and it was not until the early eighteenth century that Dutch became the accepted medium of communication between Europeans and Japanese. It therefore seems as if the introduction of Western learning was delayed by the supremacy of Portuguese as a lingua franca in the Far East. Doubtless other causes contributed, among them being a general mistrust of Europeans, which diminished only as the events that brought about a policy of seclusion receded into the past. In some branches of knowledge, particularly astronomy and mathematics, the ability of

Japanese scholars to read Chinese versions of the work of Jesuit scientists was a specific cause of delay in turning to original European sources.

Yoshimune's edict of 1720, though it applied to Chinese books and was inspired mainly by an interest in the calendar, was an expression of his general attitude towards foreign learning. When the head of the Dutch factory at Deshima made his annual journey to Yedo and was received in audience at the Shogun's court, Yoshimune used to show some curiosity about foreign books and pictures, and the members of the Dutch party (especially the physicians) during their stay in Yedo were always questioned at length by Japanese scholars thirsting for information on scientific matters. The official atmosphere was therefore more favourable to Western studies than at any time since the exclusion edicts.

There can be no doubt that the long era of peace had promoted among Japanese scholars a spirit of free inquiry, which began to raise doubts concerning some of the assumptions upon which Japanese life was based and to encourage the exploration of new fields of learning. By about 1700 a few of the official interpreters at Nagasaki had acquired not only a fair mastery of Dutch but also some general information as to the nature of Western civilization, which (it should be remembered) had undergone great changes since the days of the Portuguese. Scraps of knowledge concerning the history, arts, and sciences of European countries which they picked up and imparted to others began to arouse the curiosity of certain Japanese scholars and to induce them to take up the study of the Dutch language.

These were the founders of the group of Rangakusha or Dutch Scholars, who, at first in competition with the official interpreters and then in collaboration, pursued not only linguistic inquiries but also research into European "physic and natural history." The difficulties that they met and surmounted are recorded by one of them, Sugita Gempaku, in a work called *Rangaku Kotohajime,* or *The Beginnings of Dutch Studies.* He tells in vivid detail of their struggles to obtain and translate Dutch books, the dissection (in 1771) of a criminal's body, which they performed while following the plates in a Dutch work on anatomy, and their subsequent laborious translation of its text, word by word at the rate of ten lines a day. The translation was published in 1774, and though it contained little not already known to Japanese students, it was the first European work to be printed and published by Japanese in Japan, and therefore a landmark in Western studies. Another significant work was *Rangaku Kaitei,* or *First Steps in Dutch,* written in 1783 by Ōtsuki Gentaku, who may be regarded as the father of Dutch scholarship. It is an elementary work, yet it was widely welcomed among Japanese students, for there was no other; and this shows how painfully slow had been the progress of Western language studies, apart from those of the interpreters, until that date. These later developments took place after Yoshimune's death, but they laid a good foundation, and by the end of the eighteenth century Japan had made considerable advances in scientific knowledge, standard European works on astronomy, mathematics, medicine, and botany having been translated and published or circulated among specialists.

In tracing cultural influences one should not, of course, dwell exclusively upon literary channels. The contribution of individuals through personal contacts is often more effective than the cold printed word. It should therefore be noted here that, although these early cultural influences reached Japan mainly through the medium of books, much credit is due to certain European scholars who visited Japan and gave precious help during this period. Among them may be mentioned Thunberg, a Dutch botanist who was in Japan in 1775–6, and Isaac Titsingh, a very gifted Dutch scholar and official, who was head of the Dutch factory at intervals from 1779 to 1785, when he made good friends among Japanese in high places.

3. Native Learning

THIS growing knowledge of Western science, which was supplemented by increasingly detailed information on political and social conditions in Europe, naturally began to exert some influence upon Japanese intellectual life, and from that point of view the history of "Rangaku" is of peculiar interest to foreign students. But it should not be allowed to obscure the significance of truly indigenous cultural developments in the eighteenth century, for these were at least as important as Western influence in determining the future of Japanese institutions. A history of the later Tokugawa period would be incomplete without some account of the activities of native or naturalized schools of thought, since by their various challenges of orthodoxy they opened the minds of the Japanese to new ideas and so made them responsive to change.

We have seen that the Bakufu endorsed and encouraged the Confucian philosophy of Chu Hsi, which may be crudely described as teaching that knowledge of the nature of being is necessary for determining the moral law. It was a corollary of this dogma that wise men should instruct the people how to behave, and therefore that good government depended upon the wisdom of the ruler and the obedience of the subject. This doctrine provided a convenient support for autocracy and was naturally prized by all feudal authorities.

But already in the sixteenth century other schools had arisen which were in varying degrees critical of the official doctrine and sometimes hostile to it. We need not attempt to follow the controversies which ensued, beyond observing that one of the important points in dispute was the nature of the moral law. The out-and-out opponents of the official doctrine followed the lead of an idealist Chinese philosopher, Wang Yang-ming (1472–1529) or, in Japanese, Ō Yōmei, who held that self-knowledge was the highest kind of learning and that a man could discover the principles of right behaviour by looking into his own nature without wasting time on speculations about the laws of the universe. This rational empiricism commended itself to the best sort of samurai, because it relied upon intuition and self-control, precisely those qualities which were the essence of the Zen Buddhism that had appealed to military men from the early feudal age. Scholars of an independent habit of mind were inclined to favour Wang Yang-ming and, by implication at least, to disagree with the orthodox teaching. Some of them, who did not trouble to conceal their views, were rebuked or punished by the Bakufu, though it must be allowed that, so long as a philosopher committed no subversive act, the penalties for heterodoxy were not usually severe.

The first Japanese students of the Ō Yōmei school were Nakae Tōju, who died in 1648, and Kumazawa Banzan, who died in 1691 in comfortable banishment, which he had earned by criticizing the established order in a course of lectures to court nobles, an audience always ready to listen to unfavourable comments on their feudal masters. These and other variations of dissent continued to be propounded by a number of scholars and sages whose interesting characters enliven the intellectual chronicle of the eighteenth century. Their contribution to the culture of the times was, if not so picturesque, at least as significant of coming change as the engaging frivolities of the citizens of Yedo and Osaka.

One remarkable and admirable figure may be taken as an example. This was Ogyū Sorai (1666–1728), already mentioned, one of the leaders of a philosophical sect that described itself as the Ancient school because it refused to admit the modern reinterpretations of Chinese doctrine and went back to Confucius and Mencius. But on their way back to antiquity they had picked up some startling baggage. Sorai in particular was an original thinker, who had the courage to say that his own countrymen were poor philosophers and had misunderstood the teaching of the Chinese sages. This is a very interesting view, which is borne out by a superficial study of Japanese intellectual history and might well be confirmed by a deeper investigation. Be that as it may, Sorai was contemptuous of all efforts to reinterpret Confucius, whether Japanese or Chinese, and he did not hesitate to say so, thereby stirring up much hostility. In a search for first principles, which was itself unorthodox, he took a firm stand on the question that had since high antiquity divided the Chinese sages. Most of them thought that man was virtuous by nature and that good government would keep him straight. A powerful minority regarded him as incurably bad, and Sorai took this melancholy but tenable view. He believed and taught that in order to govern a state it was necessary for exceptional superior men (whom he did not precisely define) to invent a code of morality for the people to follow, and he thus cut the ground from under the feet of the philosophers who argued for a natural law and the innate goodness of mankind. Putting it bluntly, he said that morality was nothing more than a necessary device for governing a people. This position should be honestly accepted and not dressed up in a pretentious disguise of benevolence and altruism.

Though the Ancient school had many adherents, it does not appear that Sorai's views had any substantial effect upon his contemporaries. They are cited here not for their intrinsic value but as an example of the growth of a critical spirit and the spread of heterodox opinion in the eighteenth century. Sorai, though his cynical arguments were not at all palatable to the authorities, came down on the side of absolutism and therefore did not fall into disfavour. Even outspoken opponents of orthodox principles were treated with leniency in Yoshimune's day. It was not until the closing years of the century that the Bakufu, at the instance of official professors, forbade the exposition in any official college or school of doctrines other than those of Chu Hsi; and this line was followed by most of the feudal princes in their own domains, so that few unorthodox teachers and their pupils could find official employment.

The history of the two and a half centuries of Tokugawa rule presents an interesting picture of alternation between severity and laxity, a phenomenon that in itself may be taken as revealing the inherent contradictions in an insulated military society cultivating the insubordinate arts of peace. We have seen that on his accession in a period of gay insouciance the Shogun Yoshimune strove to restore order, frugality, and a serious outlook upon life. But his promotion of earnest study as a means of checking frivolous behaviour brought results that he did not contemplate, inasmuch as he unwittingly encouraged speculations which were in the long run to supplant the official dogma. Nevertheless he had some success in improving administration, in making legislative reforms, and even in stemming the tide of luxury. He probably represented the feudal administrator at his paternal best. He was succeeded, however, by two Shoguns who were incompetent. Power fell into the hands of avaricious and dishonest counsellors, and the laxity against which he had contended returned in double measure especially during the régime of one Tanuma, an able but peculiarly corrupt official who was a virtual dictator for some thirty years until shortly after Ieharu's death in 1786.

This was a period of bad government and of a decline in the moral standards of the ruling class. Contemporary accounts of social life in Yedo give a picture of extravagant banquets, drunkenness, gambling, and other dissipation which would make it appear that the culture of the country was at an extremely low ebb. On Tanuma's death the place of chief adviser was taken by an experienced administrator, Matsudaira Sadanobu, who became regent during the minority of Ienari, from 1786 to 1793. He tried to purify the government, to reduce expenditure, and to increase production. He put out a vast amount of sumptuary legislation, taking as his model the Shogun Yoshimune, who himself had based his policy of plain living upon the frugal maxims of Ieyasu. It is hardly necessary to say that these efforts to make men good by statute had no more than a temporary success. When Ienari came of age Sadanobu resigned and life in high circles and among the affluent townspeople became as unrestrained and as lavish as before. Nor was Sadanobu the last statesman to attempt to cure current evils by proclaiming that they must cease, for within fifty years of his retirement we find Midzuno, the Shogun's chief adviser, pouring out a stream of laws to regulate conduct in the minutest particulars.

It will be evident from this dull recital of failure that the rulers of Japan were attempting to check a process which was far beyond their control. The rising tide of luxury, the continuing lapse from orthodoxy in manners and morals, the increasing power of money, even the recurrent economic disasters that plagued the country and baffled the government — all these were, had they but known, symptoms of some radical weakness in Japanese society. It was a society struggling to expand and evolve, but confined within narrow limits by the national policy of isolation. It could not do other than turn in upon itself and expend its energies in ways that seemed wrong and dangerous to conservative statesmen. Seen in this light the periods of extravagance that they deplored appear as natural features in a process of emancipation. Even the corrupt Tanuma régime has its positive aspects, whereas the earnest and well-intentioned policies of Sadanobu and Midzuno were in essence reactionary or, at best, negative in character.

If this reading of Tokugawa history is correct, it will be seen rom the following outline of cultural development between the leath of Yoshimune (1751) and the opening of Japan in 1854 that llmost every event of importance forms part of a process of decay n the institutions of the mature feudalism of the Tokugawa sho-;uns. The period known as Genroku (1688–1704), which has)een briefly dealt with in a previous chapter, may be taken as the lividing line. After that the feudal society begins slowly to disin-egrate.

4. Subversive Trends

Ihe Dutch studies which had made progress under Yoshimune's 'ule continued without interruption in the times of his successors. Γhe corrupt Tanuma was indifferent to learning and took no in-erest in either Eastern or Western studies, but the administration, ιlways in need of funds, showed an interest in foreign trade and here is some evidence that Tanuma (or his son) was disposed to 'elax the navigation laws and allow freer intercourse with foreign :ountries. It is known that a proposal to build ships fit for ocean 'oyages was considered in 1769. Isaac Titsingh, already mentioned ιs in Japan at intervals between 1779 and 1785, noted that a ιumber of important Japanese of his acquaintance displayed a ;reat interest in Western culture at that time.

These stirrings of a desire to renew intercourse with other na-ions came to nothing, for under the conservative rule of Matsu-laira Sadanobu, which began in 1786, the orthodox Confucian tudies were restored to supremacy and in 1790 all but the official chool was declared by edict to be heretical. Other teaching was ιot forbidden, however, and the result of the edict was to stimu-ate critical studies in private academies or in the domains of eudal lords who could afford to disregard the wishes of the 3akufu. We need not follow this trend in detail, but it is worth ιoting that an interest in the Ōyomei school of political philos->phy, leading to inquiries into the principle of loyalty, naturally aised questions as to the legitimacy of the Shogun's position, since t was important that the object of loyal sentiments should be de-nonstrably worthy of them. Since it is sometimes supposed that he official doctrine could be read as warranting the Shogun's usur->ation of the Imperial prerogative, it may be as well to explain that his is not a correct view. Strict adherence to the nominalism which vas a feature of the orthodox Chu-hsi philosophy would lead to ιn examination of the correspondence between names and things n the political field, thereby bringing to light a discrepancy be-:ween the real and the nominal powers of the Shogun.

Doubts that assailed Confucianists were shared by scholars who devoted themselves not to Chinese but to native classical studies. They in their historical researches soon discovered the true sequence of events which had transferred the prerogative of the throne to feudal dictators, and thus sowed the seeds of a revival movement designed to restore the ancient religion of Japan and therefore to return to supreme power the imperial house, which

MOTOORI NORINAGA (1730–1801)

A celebrated scholar, who contributed to a Shinto revival and to the Restoration

traced its ancestry to the national gods. This was in effect to describe the Shogun as a usurper.

A revival of interest in classical Japanese studies began as far back as about 1680, when a Buddhist monk named Keichū, encouraged by one of the Tokugawa princes, engaged in researches into the earliest Japanese poetical anthologies. He was followed by a scholar named Kada Adzumamaro (1669–1736), who further advanced the cause of Japanese as opposed to Chinese learning. It was a natural sequel of their researches that a study of the native religion as it was before it came under Chinese or Buddhist influence should lead to further historical inquiries of a more political nature and foster sentiments of reverence for the Imperial house.

Three scholars in particular contributed to the development of this loyalist school of thought: Mabuchi (1697–1769), Motoori (1730–1801), and Hirata (1776–1843). It will be seen that they flourished at a time when Confucianist influence was dominant in official circles, and they undoubtedly represent an anti-Confucianist reaction, which not unnaturally took on an anti-Chinese complexion and acquired a potential anti-foreign and nationalistic character. It is true to say that Mabuchi and, in particular, Motoori inspired both the loyalty to the throne and the anti-foreign sentiment which in the years before the Restoration were expressed in the cry of "Revere the Emperor and Expel the Barbarian." [1] Too much weight, however, should not be given to the work of these individuals, which should perhaps be regarded as a symptom rather than as a cause of discontent. In the days when the great National Scholars were preaching a return to the ideals of antiquity it was not difficult to evoke nostalgia for an imagined past in which there were no military despots, no disturbing foreign creeds, no dreadful occasions of sorrow, but only a happy life of a people basking in the affection of a divine and virtuous sovereign. Even such earnest rulers as Yoshimune and Sadanobu had been unable to cope with the disasters that came crowding upon Japan in the second half of the eighteenth century. It had seen one catastrophe after another — floods, storms, great earthquakes, accompanied by famine and pestilence. The population is said to have decreased by more than one million between 1780 and 1792, and the survivors of those great trials found themselves at the turn of the century in conditions of economic and social disorder that might well throw doubts upon the competence and then the legitimacy of the Shogun's government.

The growth of such sentiments was very pleasing to the minds of the court nobles in Kyoto, and during Sadanobu's regency some bad blunders in the treatment of the Imperial house had given them special cause for grumbling. Consequently they listened eagerly to lectures by scholars who set out to prove that the Bakufu was a treasonable institution; and when in 1791 certain of them (Nakayama and Ogimachi) were punished by Sadanobu for a stand they took upon a matter of the Emperor's powers, even the townspeople of Yedo showed their sympathy and they were made the heroes of popular romances of the day. The novelist Bakin relates in his *Kyokutei Zakki* that a novel entitled *The Story of Nakayama* was so popular that the lending libraries of Yedo ordered several new editions. It represented Nakayama as rebuking

[1] It is a curious fact, which would probably have interested Vico, that the researches of the Kokugakusha or National Scholars were based upon philological inquiry. They carefully analysed the language of the earliest chronicles and drew therefrom conclusions as to the true nature of Japanese culture and the proper constitution of the Japanese state.

Sadanobu in very strong terms, and no doubt the citizens of Yedo much enjoyed any hit at the Bakufu.

It was not only the national scholars who began to doubt the legitimacy of the Shogunate. Even some Confucianists, while not going so far as to suggest that the shoguns were usurpers, began to emphasize the fact that their powers were delegated to them by the Emperor and ought to be used in the interests not of the Tokugawa family but of the nation at large. They were still a long way from the logical conclusion that the powers should be returned to the Emperor and thought at most that there should be a closer collaboration between the Bakufu and the court in matters of policy, executive authority being retained by the military class. This point of view had been reached by men like Kumazawa Banzan (1619–91) a century before. Banzan in particular arrived at his conclusions by a philosophical road, since he was an unorthodox Confucianist who believed in benevolent government for the benefit of the people and therefore regarded the Tokugawas as unfitted to rule on behalf of the Emperor. In this he was right, since the object of feudal rule was certainly not the welfare of the masses but the maintenance of oligarchy.

Sufficient has been said to show that towards the close of the eighteenth century the juridical position of the Bakufu was being slowly undermined by intellectual movements, while its practical administrative authority was being weakened by its failure to cope with pressing economic problems. But in addition to these domestic troubles it was faced by dangers from the outer world, against which the exclusion edicts could no longer give full protection. Some historians treating of the opening of Japan that took place at the instance of Commodore Perry in 1854 are inclined to ascribe it almost entirely to American pressure; but the influence of Russia was of great importance and should not be overlooked.

While the western European powers, following Portuguese example, were expanding eastwards by way of the Indian Ocean and the Strait of Malacca in the seventeenth century, a great overland movement was being made by indomitable Russian explorers and traders. It is sometimes forgotten that Russian sailors had reached the Sea of Okhotsk as early as 1639, and that a base was established at Okhotsk in 1649. For a long time after that only the overland route was used, but knowledge of Kamchatka appears as early as 1672 and it was explored in 1700 by Atlasov, who reported to Moscow on the Kuriles and their proximity to Japan. The Kuriles were visited in 1713–14 and an attempt to find Japan led to a landing on Sakhalin. Shortly after this there was some talk in Moscow and St. Petersburg of opening trade relations with Japan, but the project does not appear to have had strong official support and it was not until 1732 that Bering, then endeavouring to fix the geography of the Siberian coast and its relation to the American mainland, was instructed to send a ship to find a route to Japan. Outfitting difficulties delayed this voyage until 1738, and in 1739 on a second attempt a Russian vessel commanded by a Dane, Spanberg, appears to have put in at points on the east coast of the main island of Japan. Japanese records state that it was sighted off Shimoda, the harbour at which Perry arrived in 1853.

No results of importance followed this visit and for twenty years or so no direct approach by Russia to Japan is recorded, although further information was gradually collected by Russians from Ainu and Japanese settlers in the Kuriles. In 1771 an adventurer named Benyowsky, a Polish exile in Kamchatka, escaped in a government vessel that he had captured and sailed for Madagascar, where he founded a colony in 1773. On the way his ship was driven to the coast of Japan and (in 1771) he landed at two points, where he was well treated and left letters of thanks to the Japanese authorities, in which (out of his hatred for Russia) he suggested that the Russian government had designs upon Japan. There is little evidence to support this charge and it does not appear that the Bakufu was particularly disturbed.

In 1777–9 Russians in the Kuriles encountered Japanese from the fief of Matsumae, which controlled the northern island of Yezo. They proposed opening trade with Japan, but were told that it was against Japanese law, except that they could if they wished go to Nagasaki. European political events, such as the Russo-Turkish war, prevented further Russian approaches to Japan for some time, and it is clear that behind these attempts to enter into trade relations there was no positive policy, but only a somewhat indifferent support given to the projects of officials and merchants in Siberia.

An expedition commanded by Lieutenant Laxman was sent by the Governor of Siberia to Japan in 1792. Laxman wintered at Nemuro and went to Hakodate and thence by land to Matsumae, under a heavy escort of armed Japanese guards. Negotiations and feasting took place, but Laxman was told that, since Japanese law allowed no dealings with foreigners, he and his crew were liable to arrest and imprisonment. They would be allowed to depart because of their ignorance, but they must not visit Japan again except at Nagasaki, where trade might be permitted.

By this time certain far-sighted Japanese had already taken alarm, thinking that their country was in danger of Russian aggression. The Bakufu had not so far displayed any great anxiety. Such indifference was perhaps to be expected during the administration of Tanuma, but when in 1792 a patriotic scholar named Rin Shihei published a work called *Kaikoku Heidan* (an *Essay on the Military*

Problems of a Maritime State) calling attention to the weakness of Japan's coastal defences, he was punished by Sadanobu for his pains. Though there was much in Rin's arguments, he suffered penalties because he had published criticism of the Bakufu and also because he had confided his views to certain court nobles who were known to be hostile to the Shogun's government. This interesting episode shows that the Bakufu was growing sensitive to criticism, which was beginning to arise from more than one quarter. To the attacks of scholars upon the official Confucian doctrine and the new historical criticism of the Shinto loyalists there were now added the revelations of men like Rin, who did not deal in theory but pointed out specific faults in the Tokugawa administration, dwelling especially upon the dangers of a policy that forbade the building of large vessels useful for national defence.

Sadanobu, though he treated Rin unjustly, was impressed by his arguments, which were given point by the arrival of Laxman's ship in Japanese waters and the knowledge that there was a Russian settlement on the island of Yurup, uncomfortably close to Yezo. Sadanobu therefore ordered an inspection of Japan's northern boundaries and instructed all feudatories whose domains bordered on the sea to look to their coastal defences and to keep on the alert. Thus the eighteenth century ended for the Bakufu on a note of anxiety over the intentions of foreign powers, and in the early part of the nineteenth century they were to have further reasons for alarm. These must be set forth presently, but first it will be useful to attempt, against the background already described, some impression of the Japanese cultural scene as it unfolds during the eighteenth century.

5. Yedo Life

Wᴇ have already seen that by the end of the seventeenth century the growth of town life and the increasing power of money had favoured the development of a lively urban culture. It is a culture perhaps best symbolized by the bold design and strong colour of the fashionable costume of the day. It is not an accident that the mood of this society should be so well expressed by its æsthetic bent, for it is characteristic of Japanese civilization that in its expanding phases the decorative arts are vital and flourishing. Some account of painting and literature in the eighteenth century may therefore serve to throw light on the social scene as it developed after the gay, extravagant Genroku era.

It is sometimes supposed that the growth of popular arts was accompanied by a decline in those which had been practised or

A ROBUST BEAUTY

Early wood-block ukiyo-e *print; by Kaigetsudo Norishige* (c. *1714*)

patronized by members of the ruling caste. It may be true that the classical schools of painting produced few artists of distinction, and that popular taste, which was shared by many members of the military class, was satisfied by the new school of Ukiyo-e artists, who departed in many ways from old conventions. But the Ukiyo-e school did not spring fully armed from the soil of Osaka and Yedo. It had a good pedigree, for its earliest phase shows traces of the heroic quality of Momoyama screens and panels, and such artists as Hishigawa Moronobu (d. *c.* 1694), Nishigawa Sukenobu (1671–1751), and Miyagawa Chōshun (1682–1752) even in their painting of seductive women retain a classic dignity and use a strict technique that shows their training in one or other of the great traditional schools. The light and sensuous touch of the later Ukiyo-e is just apparent, but the grand manner is still there. It is a long way from the attractive and almost corpulent females of Kwaigetsudo to the drooping beauties of Utamaro who, though denizens of the fleshly world, can scarcely support the weight of their frail bodies. The later Ukiyo-e develops along its own lines and diverges into untrodden paths of sentiment and fantasy; but it is from conventional beginnings that it arises.

The older schools of painting, for their part, continued to flourish, for they belonged to a society that was ripe for change but had not yet lost its vigour. The Kano school, though tending often to stiffness, produced some good painting and maintained an all-round perfection of technical skill, occasionally reaching a high standard of accomplishment, as in the work of Kano Naonobu. But there was also some departure from the strict Kano style, a tendency to use its conventional brushwork but to apply it to genre paintings treated in a realistic fashion. This can best be seen in the work of Morikage (a Kyoto artist) and Hanabusa Itchō (1653–1724), both Kano men by training but unconventional and humorous in manner. These artists, who were both pupils of Tanyu and were expelled from the Kano school for nonconformity, represent a movement away from old canons, but they remain within the classical tradition. Following them, in the middle of the eighteenth century, comes the Maruyama school, eclectic and experimental. It shows the influence of a new, critical temper that developed with a growing interest in Occidental life. Its founder was Maruyama Okyo (1732–95), trained in a Kano studio but interested in Occidental technique. His successors developed in Kyoto a new style, the Shijō, in which European influence can be detected. Thus in the arts, it is fair to say, change was not confined to bourgeois circles, but made itself felt in more conservative quarters.

Yedo literature on its own merits is deserving of little comment. It has its interest as a social phenomenon and is at rare moments not wanting in a certain sophisticated fluency and even in a debilitated grace, but with few (though important) exceptions it is fundamentally vulgar, a literature of bad taste and exiguous content. The writing of the Floating World is strikingly inferior to its painting, for the Ukiyo-e with all its limitations contains some of the true essence of Japanese art. It is, as has been observed by Professor Yashiro,[2] an admirable record of the emotional life of the Japanese people, so eminently their *art intime* that "it lays bare those charming weaknesses which one does not readily disclose to others." This can scarcely be said of what is called *chōnin bungaku,* or the literature of the townspeople; but some of its features should be briefly noted if only because, as we shall see, late Yedo writing was so poor and thin that it succumbed almost without a struggle to European influence in the early Meiji period.

Perhaps the most characteristic form of Yedo literature is the *Ukiyo-sōshi,* a comprehensive name for novels and sketches dealing with the life of the city almost exclusively in its sensual aspects. These works are sometimes called *kōshoku-bon,* which is nearly enough translated as "sex books," though perhaps "love stories" would be a kinder rendering. The originator or the leading exponent of this school of writing was Saikaku, who flourished from about 1660 to 1693 and published a number of books under such titles as *Kōshoku Ichidai Otoko* (*A Man's Love Life*) and *Kōshoku Gonin Onna* (*Five Amorous Women*), which deal freely with the amorous proclivities of both sexes. In works of this class close attention is paid to descriptions of leading courtesans, their charms, their characters, and their professional manners. But it must be said on Saikaku's behalf that these unpromising themes are explored with an acute insight and an extensive knowledge of human frailty, so that they are still most readable as realistic psychological studies, fluent in style, original in treatment, but distinguished by wayward fancy rather than creative imagination.

The most commanding literary figure of the age is Chikamatsu (1653–1724), an extremely prolific dramatist who wrote both historical plays and what were called *sewamono,* pieces about modern life. Leaving aside their literary merits the point of interest in the works of Chikamatsu is the contrast between the two groups. Both are concerned with the conflict between duty and sentiment. But in the historical plays, where the theme is the loyalty of the samurai class, duty comes first, whereas in the "modern" plays there is a more sympathetic view of the claims of the affections. The drama-

2 In his *Nihon Bijutsu no Tokushitsu* (*Characteristics of Japanese Art*), a valuable work published in 1943, which ought to be translated for the benefit of art historians.

tist here treats not of ideals of chivalry but of the common lot of thwarted lovers, jealous wives, and disappointed parents whose tragedy lies in the triumph of passion over rectitude. Such plays clearly break new ground, because they are the product of a new kind of society, which is struggling against older standards of morality.

Apart from such delineators of daily life as Saikaku and Chika-

CHIKAMATSU MONZAEMON (1653–1724)

Japan's most famous playwright and a leading
figure in the literary world of the Genroku period

matsu, who may with suitable reservations be called "realists," there was a school of writers of sensational fiction led by Kyōden (1761–1816) and Bakin (1767–1848), who might be described as "romantic" or "idealistic." The label is of little importance, for the particular interest of work of this school is in its didactic flavour. It deals largely with the exploits of members of the military class, who perform prodigies of skill and valour, conforming in every particular to the samurai code as it had developed under Confucian influence. In Bakin's work, which draws freely upon Chinese and Japanese legend and displays much erudition, the characters are nearly all superhuman in their achievements. It is a branch of later Yedo literature which may be taken as an effort to reassert the ideals of the military caste, so strong is its contrast to the novels and sketches that explore the dark places of current urban life. Of these latter perhaps the most typical and the least praiseworthy are the *share-bon,* or "witty books," naughty works that deal mainly with life in the pleasure quarters and served in their time as a kind of Rake's Guide. Their nature can be judged by the title of one of the most celebrated, *Keisei-kai Shijūhachite,* which might be rendered *Forty-eight Ways of Commerce with Harlots.* It was written by the versatile Kyōden, who could in more respectable moods turn his hand to moral tales, and was also able to illustrate his own books in Ukiyo-e style.

These vulgar and salacious pieces are redeemed by no literary merits discernible to the foreign reader, but they are of special interest as revealing the important part played by the gay quarters in Yedo life. Denied informal social intercourse by the strict division of classes and the subordination of women, the citizens were driven to frequent these homes of entertainment to satisfy their gregarious as well as their amorous instincts. The sons of well-to-do tradespeople were not their only clients, for it is said that more than half the visitors to the best-known establishments were samurai of all ranks, not excluding the highest.

It is of course easy to overstress the importance of the haunts of the dissolute in the life of the great cities, for the conduct of virtuous citizens goes unrecorded. What interested the writers of the period was the surface of things. One should be careful in using the terms of European literary criticism, but it is not far out to say that the literature of the townspeople was dominated by realism. In this respect it evidently accorded with the mood of the times, which was in the cities one of satisfaction with the existing order. The townspeople were in general prosperous, their standard of living was high, and they could afford to look down on the needy samurai even if they had to make some show of deference. These were not times of doubt and difficulty, when men try to penetrate beneath the surface of things. The citizens lived in the present and were interested only in the day-to-day life of the town, for that is really what is meant by *"ukiyo."*

It is for this reason that Yedo literature is wanting in imagination and insight, though it is quick to note the oddities of the passing scene. Like the "ukiyo" paintings it shows a singular virtuosity in seizing and portraying the decorative, the entertaining, the comic, and sometimes the indecent aspects of the contemporary world as it was presented to the populace in their daily avocations. It should be added that, despite their plebeian origin, the townspeople developed a sense of style in living. It is significant that the qualities usually ascribed to the hero of a Yedo novel are *sui,* which is *chic,* and *tsū,* which is something like the *savoir faire* of a man about town, an expert knowledge of how to behave in all contingencies. In modern European literature its equivalent, though on a lower social level, might be the familiarity of the Baron de Charlus with all epicurean details from the qualities of pears to the etiquette of *maisons de passe*. Even in the great picaresque novel of low life, the *Hizakurige*, it is the shifts and stratagems by which its disreputable heroes extricate themselves from preposterous situations that make them true types of the sharp-witted, irrepressible vulgar order.

It is not easy to give a picture of life in more respectable circles, for it is not chronicled in any literary masterpiece and has to be pieced together from diaries and letters. Some hints may be found in the correspondence of certain literary figures and we may look at an interesting letter from Bakin, the leading Japanese novelist, in which he describes to a friend a monster entertainment given by him at the instance of his publishers. It takes us out of the eighteenth century into the early nineteenth, but it illustrates well enough the nature of the intellectual society as it had grown in previous years, and it is quoted here to show in particular how the expansion of urban life had served to break down social barriers.

Great preparations were made for this party. As presents to the guests three thousand fans and two hundred and fifty silk squares were got ready, and Bakin was asked to write his name on each, with a suitable eulogy of the painting, which had been done by a pupil of Hōitsu. He turned some of this work over to a friendly artist, but it required great skill and care, for in Bakin's circle taste was exacting, and so it took a long time and the banquet had to be postponed. Etiquette demanded that the host should pay calls on his principal guests, in order to invite them in person. For several days he was carried round in a palanquin, visiting prominent literary men. Less important persons received calls from his son-in-law and his grandson, who were accompanied by a number of employees from artists' studios and bookshops. These had to be entertained on the way and cost him no small sums in food and drink.

At last the day of the party arrived. It took place in a great restaurant called Manpachi-Rō in Yanagibashi. The arrangements were lavish. Members of Bakin's family and numerous friends received the guests in ceremonial dress, from early morning. There were a reception desk and a cloakroom for the deposit of swords and sandals; attendants handed out tickets for food and drink. By midday the place was thronged. All the upstairs apartments and the downstairs rooms were filled, and guests overflowed into the verandas. Geisha were employed to pour out wine, though Bakin did not much like this, thinking it not respectable, and only agreed reluctantly. "Anyhow," he says, "I scarcely saw these girls and much less did I talk to them." The account continues as follows: "On this day there were over eight hundred guests, including both the elegant and the vulgar. Then, in addition to the promoters and helpers there were more than two hundred who had not been invited. Meals were served for 1,284 persons. Three barrels of saké proved too little and we had to get more in a hurry. Some people in the confusion contrived to get three or even four meal-tickets, wrapping up the food and taking it home. I cannot describe to you

TAKIZAWA BAKIN (1767–1848)

The celebrated Yedo novelist

in a short note like this the strange vagaries of human conduct. . . . Anyhow, it was agreed that there had not been so successful a party for twenty years." The crush was immense. One of Bakin's friends who was helping to entertain the guests had a rush of blood to the head, because he was "drunk with people."

Among the distinguished literary men, artists, and others who attended were Confucian scholars; academic painters, carefully distinguished from the Ukiyo-e artists and including Tani Bunitsu (who represented his aged grandfather Bunchō), Watanabe Kwazan, Nanrei, and Settan; three renowned calligraphers; leading colour-print men including Kunisada and pupils, Eisen, Kuniyoshi, Hiroshige, Hokkei, and Hokusai; comic prose writers and poets including Tanehiko and Shunsui; and distinguished officials and scholars as well as a number of publishers, booksellers, paper-merchants, and wood-block makers. Glamour was added to the occasion by the presence of important military personages from the Shogun's court.

This glimpse of a literary and artistic coterie may have served to give some idea of the quality of late Yedo culture in its less solemn aspects. It is strange that this carefree society should have matured in an era when the nation as a whole was in the grip of calamity, for the wealth that was drawn into the cities to sustain it came from a countryside frequently ravaged by disaster and oppressed by bad government. But the slow economic decline was not apparent to the busy merchants and shopkeepers, who throve at the expense of overburdened agriculture. It was only by a few scholars and officials that the agrarian problem was understood, and that imperfectly. Yet what caused the impoverishment of farmers was at the same time relentlessly undermining the political edifice. This continued for a while, an imposing and even menacing fabric, but with the opening of the nineteenth century its prestige, carried along by inertia after its real authority had diminished, began to be challenged on all sides.

Note on CHAPTER 10

JAPANESE MISSIONS TO ROME. At first sight the missions sent to Europe by important feudatories seem to indicate an early interest in Western knowledge. But the first mission (of 1588–91) was arranged by Valignano with the definite object of showing the strength of Catholic countries, and the envoys were youths of no experience, likely to be impressed by magnificence rather than learning.

As for the second mission, sent by the lord of Sendai, Date Masamune, which was abroad from 1615 to 1620, it was arranged by the Jesuit father Sotelho, who wished to gain favour for his order in northern Japan, where Date was very powerful. Date, for his part, was anxious to trade with Mexico. A Japanese historian has said of this mission that the Jesuits wished to use trade for the kingdom of heaven and the Japanese wished to use the kingdom of heaven for trade. This is perhaps too simple a formula, but certainly Date does not appear to have had any serious interest in Western science. The point that has not been cleared up is the attitude of Ieyasu towards this mission. It is hard to believe that Date acted without his knowledge and, one would suppose, his approval. Ieyasu was at this time much interested in foreign trade, as we know from Adams and Cox as well as from other sources.

C H A P T E R

I I

THE END OF SECLUSION

1. The Economic Situation

WESTERN historians in their studies of the great political changes that ushered in the Meiji era are sometimes tempted to give too much weight to the pressure of external events. It is true that the arrival of foreign vessels in Japanese waters and the menace of Western expansion in Asia were proximate causes of the reshaping of Japanese institutions in the middle of the nineteenth century; but the continuity of Japanese domestic history is very impressive. Seen in its perspective, the unification of Japan under a constitutional monarch between 1868 and 1890 is a natural sequel of the last phase of the inadequately centralized government of the Tokugawa, and the development of that phase can be traced backwards step by step to the origins of Japanese feudalism in mediæval times. There was no sudden break with the past in 1868, but only a gathering of speed. To overestimate the part played by Western influence is to misunderstand modern Japanese history and in consequence to form an unbalanced if not a mistaken view of the relations between East and West.

It is true that Asiatic life was affected in the nineteenth century by the impact of the industrial revolution, which had been felt long before in the West. But some at least of the causes that produced the industrial revolution had been operating, though imperceptibly, in parts of Asia and particularly in Japan long before the ships of the foreigners came to Japanese shores demanding trade in the early 1800's. From the day when Ieyasu set up his administration in Yedo, Japan was destined to a struggle between agriculture and industry, between barter and money, between food and population, between feudal autocracy and the power of capital — in short, the protracted birth pangs of a modern national state. The long seclusion of Japan was only a delaying factor, which masked for a time the nature of the change her society was undergoing. Nothing reveals more clearly the slow and seemingly inevitable decline from the massive stability of the early Bakufu than the record of agrarian disturbances in the Tokugawa period. Peasant uprisings, common enough before Tokugawa days, grew more frequent and violent as time went on, and by the early part of the nineteenth century they may be said to have become endemic. The causes of these troubles were numerous and complex, but they may be summarized by saying that, since the peasant was the only regular taxpayer in the country and since he was obliged to contribute a high proportion of his rice crop for the maintenance of his feudal masters, he was exposed to hardship at all times. It was he who had to bear the brunt of the financial difficulties of the Bakufu, for almost every burden that was imposed upon the military and commercial classes was transferred by them to his shoulders, either by an increase in direct taxation or by currency manipulations from which he was the first to suffer. When his crop was good he did not profit in proportion to the yield, for he had to turn in more bushels than in an average year; and when it was bad he had little left for his own subsistence. His position grew worse as the use of money increased, for he then must suffer from violent fluctuations in the price of his grain, and a bountiful harvest often caused him as much distress as a poor one, because he must market his surplus at a sacrifice.

Though he was not in theory the owner of the land that he cultivated, his tenure was secure, largely because the territorial rulers were as a matter of policy opposed to the sale or mortgage of farm land. They wished to protect the peasant economy, by which their class was supported, against transfers of rights in land to any other class. It was for those reasons that in the early Tokugawa period laws were enacted that forbade the alienation of land under cultivation. But those laws were made difficult of enforcement by the rise of a merchant class with surplus funds for investment, and by the insolvency of many farmers arising from natural calamities or the contraction of money debts to usurers. It was not difficult to find ways of evading restrictions on the transfer of rights that for the purposes of the transferee were as valuable as ownership, and sometimes even more valuable since the cultivator could not contract out of his obligation to pay tax. In consequence there began to develop a new class of landlord, composed of city merchants or rural moneylenders gradually breaking into the monopoly of land revenue, which was the economic foundation of the feudal state. That foundation was attacked by other forces, or perhaps one should say by the same force in another guise, for almost all the evils that overtook the feudal economy can be regarded as aspects of the problem of population.

This problem seems to have caused anxiety to the Tokugawa

authorities from early in the eighteenth century, the first census having been taken in 1721. The methods employed were imperfect, but on the evidence available good authorities have formed the opinion that in the first half of the Tokugawa period population increased fairly rapidly, while through the second half it remained almost stationary at from twenty-nine to thirty million. It would seem that the peace and prosperity that followed the civil wars brought the population to a point where it began to press upon the limits of subsistence in 1735 or thereabouts. From that time onward the growing cities drew many workers from the land and thus created shortages of farm labour. Serious famines, aggravated if not caused by the consequent decline in production, are recorded in 1733 and from 1783 to 1787. Epidemics further reduced the population, which according to credible figures fell by over one million between 1780 and 1790. Yet this great decline did not solve the problem of food supply. Starvation and disease bore hardest upon the peasants, and the impoverishment of rural areas drove many more to abandon their holdings and seek work in towns. A recovery that took place between 1790 and 1830 was wiped out by another famine in 1834, after which the total population was rather less than it had been a hundred years before.

The causes of trouble were dimly perceived by the rulers, who from time to time legislated to prevent peasants from leaving the land and endeavoured to force migrants to return from the cities to the fields they had deserted. At times serious attempts were made to improve farming conditions and to induce the farmers to grow subsidiary crops, such as sweet potatoes. In Yoshimune's time a great deal of waste land had been brought under cultivation and there was a rice surplus for some years. But it was followed by local or general shortages, which baffled the administration, who had no sooner dealt with a famine than they were obliged to reverse their policy and deal with a too copious harvest.[1] The position was

---

[1] The extreme contradictions in Yoshimune's policy may be quoted as a useful illustration of the difficulties which faced the Bakufu in regard to food, prices, and currency.

In 1718 he reformed the debased gold and silver currency by increasing its content and reducing the amount of issue, thus bringing prices down very suddenly. Rice, which had reached a peak of 230 *momme* of silver in 1715 fell to 130 in 1717 and reached as low as 33 in the following year, when a bumper rice harvest coincided with a deflationary currency policy. For some years after this the price fluctuated between 30 and 100. Attempts at regulation had little success. Between 1730 and 1733 an effort to raise prices was made by various measures aimed at reducing the amount of rice on the market and controlling the rice exchanges. But again with little success. In the summer of 1732 insect pests destroyed the crop in western and central Japan and the price of rice rose to near 150. Now the Bakufu was constrained to promote an increase in supplies by devices aimed at controlling the market and preventing "cornering." These also were ineffective. A rich harvest in 1734 obliged the government to reverse its policy once more and attempt to raise prices again. In 1735 a law was enacted specifically forbidding fluctuations in market

well described by Dazai Shundai, an economic writer of the day, in his *Keizai Roku* (*Treatise on Political Economy*). Treating of the position in 1730 he said: "The price fell to two fifths of what it had been in the days when rice was precious. People looked on it like dirt. In samurai households after setting aside what they needed for food they tried to sell the rest of their allowance, but could not get enough money to meet even their most necessary daily expenses. If they sold enough for that purpose, then there was not enough left to eat, and their distress was extreme. Peasants were in the same case as samurai. In good years they have plenty of grain, but when they come to sell it the price is not enough to pay for carrying it away, so that they make no profit from what they do not eat themselves." And of course, he might have added, in bad years they have to go short of food.

It is clear from the recurrent failures of the Bakufu that the price of rice could not be regulated by official controls, and there can be no doubt that the dependence of Japan upon a single staple crop was a flaw in her economy. Even had there been a sufficient supply of auxiliary foodstuffs to moderate the effect of bad harvests it is doubtful whether administrative measures could have stabilized prices so long as rice was the measure of value in one segment of an economy that was as a whole governed by money and credit. It is a difficult question, which does not seem to have been exhaustively treated by Japanese historians, and the exact bearing of the economic troubles of the eighteenth and early nineteenth centuries upon the decline of the Bakufu and its ultimate collapse is not easy to determine. The reader whose interest lies in the purely cultural field may complain that economic discourse is dreary and irrelevant, and he has my sympathy. But the condition of Japan when she came under Western cultural influence determined the way in which she reacted to it. The economic legacy of the Shogunate shaped the development of political and social institutions in the early Meiji period. The grievances of samurai and farmers, the financial difficulties of the new government, the capital resources of the merchants, were elements that decided the course of the Restoration movement and many of its sequels; while agrarian problems that harassed the Bakufu continue in other forms to trouble the makers of policy in the present day.

Writers on Tokugawa economic history are inclined to use such generic terms as "the internal crisis of feudalism." This, though a convenient label, does not disclose the nature of the crisis nor is

---

quotations. All these efforts to deal with the market having failed, they then, in 1736, tried reducing the value of the coinage, also without obtaining the desired result. Between 1710 and 1735 the price fluctuated wildly between a maximum of 230 and a minimum of 30, but generally tended to fall.

it usually shown that it could not have been dealt with in a feudal setting by competent administration had other circumstances been favourable. It does not explain why the prosperity of the seventeenth century was followed by a period of economic confusion despite peaceful conditions and a general advance in both agricultural and industrial output. Is it not possible to account for this phenomenon without reference to the political system under which it occurred? There are some reasons for doubting whether it was an inevitable result of feudalism and even for believing that Japan, by the late eighteenth century if not sooner, was no longer a feudal state except in some formal aspects, but was in most essential particulars a centralized national state whose economy had lost most of the features that distinguish feudal régimes.

The following speculations on this point are put forward not with any dogmatic intent but only in order to suggest a line of thought in regard to the political and economic decline of the Shogunate which, it would seem, has not been fully explored.

A characteristic feature of the Japanese economy from early times until the Restoration was its dependence upon a single staple food crop. Where such an economy is closed, as Japan's economy was closed at first by geography and later by edict, fluctuations in supply are bound to occur from natural causes, and the effects of scarcity and abundance cannot be mitigated by imports and exports. These conditions cannot be ascribed to the political system under which they occur unless it can be shown that by its nature it prevents diversification of the economy or the growth of foreign trade. But there is nothing to show that Tokugawa rulers were opposed to diversification, and indeed efforts were made from time to time to encourage the cultivation of alternative crops and the growth of domestic industries. It is true that it was the Tokugawa Shogunate that severely restricted foreign trade, but that was after Japan had become a centralized state, whereas in the previous era, which was much more feudal in character, foreign trade was most actively encouraged. It is therefore difficult to believe that basic economic conditions in Japan resulted from its feudal constitution. Moreover, it should be remembered that until the eighteenth century was well advanced few if any countries, whether in Europe or Asia and whether feudal or not, could rely upon food imports to sustain an increasing population. They were obliged to improve their agricultural methods or to increase their cultivated area; and this was done by the Japanese, as is clear from the fact that the area under cultivation was doubled between 1600 and 1730, so that a steady increase in population could be supported.

But this increase was checked from about 1730, and population remained stationary for a century or more. The usual and no doubt correct explanation of this difference between population trends as between early and late Tokugawa is that, the internal resources of Japan being limited, the production of food could not keep pace with a further growth of population and, in the absence of other forms of relief, Malthusian adjustments took place in the shape of famine, disease, and other calamities. But it can scarcely be maintained that feudal institutions were responsible for these unhappy circumstances. It may be argued that the Japanese failed to discover or apply suitable methods of increasing the supply of food, but here again there is not much evidence that the political system was to blame. On the contrary there is much to show that the rulers of Japan fully understood the importance of agriculture and took what steps seemed possible to promote it, as their own interests obviously dictated.

Japanese history since the earliest times shows a constant concern with problems of agriculture. The early chronicles contain frequent references to matters of irrigation, the selection of seeds, the opening-up of new land, and the diversification of crops. As early as the seventh century we find notices of official efforts to encourage alternative or subsidiary crops such as wheat, barley, millet, buckwheat, beans, and peas, but both growers and consumers stubbornly kept to rice, despite constant famines. Coming to the modern age we find in the Tokugawa period a considerable improvement in agricultural techniques, encouraged by the Bakufu and enlightened daimyo; and there is in the eighteenth century an important body of literature dealing with methods of increasing and diversifying food production. It does not seem that agricultural policy as such was at fault, but rather that agrarian distress was local and partial and arose from oppressive methods of tax-collecting and from a breakdown of the traditional system of land tenure. In their general attitude towards agriculture the rulers may have made mistakes, but these were due to ordinary human fallibility and not to some hypothetical defect in feudal reasoning. Such mistakes were made in most European countries long after the disappearance of mediæval feudalism. Thus (for example) Malthusian checks prevented any significant growth of the English population until the agricultural improvements of the eighteenth century made it possible for more food to be grown; and perhaps it is pertinent to notice here that Japan managed at that time to support a population approaching thirty million on a farming area not much greater than that of European countries which supported only five or ten millions.

On seeking for reasons why in the latter half of the Tokugawa period the Japanese did not succeed in carrying out effective agrarian reforms it appears that what delayed improvements was not the persistence by inertia of old forms of tenure and consequently of old methods, but rather a deliberate policy of peasant protection adopted by the ruling autocracy. Here we have an analogy to the *Bauernschutz* of Frederick the Great, except that the purpose of German rulers was to obtain recruits for the army while that of the Japanese was to preserve the rural society from the intrusion of merchants and moneylenders. In neither case can the phenomenon be justly attributed to a feudal outlook, though it may perhaps be said that in Japan it arose from the resistance of feudal rulers to the penetration of money, which had already transformed the economic structure of the country. The truth is that late Tokugawa Japan can be described as a feudal state only if the word "feudal" is employed in a very loose way and without any mediæval connotations. It bore a close resemblance to the less highly centralized states of Europe in the eighteenth and early nineteenth centuries and was undergoing a process of change similar to that through which most European countries had passed or were passing in the same period. These developments were not a part of feudalism, though they might be, and frequently were, outgrowths of a particular feudal institution. In European countries as in Japan feudal survivals can be detected until well on into the nineteenth century, but their presence is consistent with a general disappearance of the essential features of a feudal state and its replacement by a "modern" centralized national state. Thus although copyhold and *métayage* are not "modern" forms of tenure, being rooted in a mediæval land system, they are not feudal; and similarly though in Japan the alienation of land to members of the non-military classes took place under a régime that had not lost all its feudal character, it was — like the leasing during the fifteenth century of demesne land in England by manorial lords to persons outside the feudal hierarchy — a breach in the system of feudal tenures and the beginning of "modern" farming tenures.

It may be objected that the slow progress of agrarian reform in Japan, as compared with the more advanced European countries, was due to a stubborn feudal conservatism, and it is true that the Tokugawa policy was based on a determination to prevent change. But conservatism was not peculiar to Japan. It existed in Europe until it was broken into by the struggle between nations which took the form of political rivalry and competition in colonial and commercial enterprise. Because of her geographical isolation Japan did not come under this powerful influence until late in the Tokugawa period, but when she did, as European powers began to press her, the process of change became extremely rapid. It can hardly be doubted that this speed was possible because her feudal institutions had withered and her condition resembled that of European countries in the days just before the industrial revolution. Once the process of change began, it was subject to no retarding influences such as the universalist tradition of the Empire and the Catholic Church.

One feature of the Tokugawa administration closely related to its breakdown was its deplorable fiscal policy, which depended almost entirely upon oppressive taxation, borrowing, and currency debasement. (See chapter x.) A simple explanation of the collapse of the Shogunate would ascribe it to the cumulative effect of generations of incompetent public finance, and this for general historical purposes is probably an adequate statement, since it gathers together in one formula the complicated causes I have tried to isolate. In so far as the collapse was directly due to fiscal misdeeds it may be said to have arisen from the, let us say, semi-feudal condition of Tokugawa Japan, where the central government, though responsible for many costly items of national expenditure, derived its revenues principally from Tokugawa domains and was able to supplement them only by contributions from vassals, which were voluntary at least in name and could not be levied as of right. But even so, since European states in the seventeenth century were also harassed by budgetary troubles, it is doubtful whether Tokugawa financial difficulties were exclusively feudal in their origins. It seems much more likely that they arose from the policy of isolation, which prevented Japan from embarking on mercantile expansion and thus replenishing the national exchequer as England and Holland had done. Had Tokugawa Japan thrown open her doors at any time between 1640 and 1853 she might have solved the problem of national finance and thereby eased the general economic situation. But the result of renewed foreign intercourse might have been the civil war that the Tokugawa rulers dreaded, or an expansionist, colonizing foreign policy that would have brought her into conflict with Western powers.

The foregoing arguments are perhaps not conclusive, but at least they warn the inquirer against reading political and economic conditions in late Tokugawa days solely in terms of feudalism. We need not labour this theme, but there is one further point of doubt that needs some attention. Most treatises on the agrarian situation in Japan at that period dwell upon the wretched and impoverished condition of the peasantry. For this the evidence of contemporary documents is so strong that it cannot be questioned. Yet there are some grounds for believing that the farmer's position in general was not actually deteriorating in the first half of the nineteenth century. Certainly a great number of peasants, especially those in marginal areas, suffered great hardship in times of short crops, and nobody can contend that the lot of the poorest workers on the land was a happy one. But descriptions of the countryside by foreign travellers, the records of festivals and pilgrimages, and in particular the specimens of peasant clothing, ornaments, and utensils which have been preserved testify to a comfortable life and in many instances to a rising standard of living. It can hardly be supposed that the edicts aimed at the "luxurious living" of farmers were entirely without reason. The ruling class no doubt had very modest ideas of what was luxury for a peasant, but there is plenty of evidence to show that some members of the farming community in fertile districts were much better off than poor samurai.

It is not always when economic conditions are deteriorating that complaints against the prevailing political system are loudest. What causes unrest and dissatisfaction is often the failure of a given class to maintain an increase in its standard of living, and this is a condition likely to arise where prices or incomes fluctuate wildly. Most people will accustom themselves to poor conditions so long as they are stable and will even acquiesce in a slow deterioration; but when there is a sudden drop in their money income or its purchasing power, even if it is temporary, they will struggle to maintain their standard and complain of the existing social order. This is not to say that rural life under the Tokugawa was uniformly easy, for that would be to fly in the face of facts. But it does give some ground for supposing that, in a purely statistical sense and without reference to individual cases, agrarian conditions were improving rather than deteriorating in the late Tokugawa period. Many poor peasants lost their holdings, but farming techniques improved and enterprising farmers could make good incomes. Even the poor peasants in many cases fell into distress not because they were oppressed but because they tried to maintain a higher standard of living than their fathers had done, and so fell into debt.

If this reasoning is correct, the discontent of the farmers is to be explained not by a general economic deterioration due to feudal misrule but rather by the fact that the benefits of a rising national income were unequally shared. The point is perhaps of no great importance, but it is worth taking into account when considering the causes to which the decline of the Shogunate is usually ascribed. Whether its crisis — if we are to use that word, which seems ill-suited to a long-drawn-out process — was due to administrative blunders or to radical economic weakness, it is true that criticism of the Bakufu was strengthened, if it was not produced, by growing dissatisfaction with economic conditions, though the line of attack was often political or even purely dynastic.

Among the important and effective critics, in addition to the National Scholars and the Confucianists already mentioned, were certain thinkers of a new sort, whose interests were scientific rather than literary. Perhaps the most influential and certainly one of the most interesting among them was Honda Toshiaki (1774–1821). He was an extremely gifted man, a samurai born in Kaga, on the west coast, in a Tozama fief remote from Yedo influences. There he developed an interest in sea voyages and learned about conditions in Yezo. He studied mathematics and astronomy and opened a school in 1797. He worked at the Dutch language and went to sea in command of a small coasting vessel on a voyage to the northern parts of Japan. He wrote a number of works on shipping, conditions in Western countries, and the conservation of natural resources; and he addressed himself to matters of national policy in his *Keisei Hisaku* (*A Secret Plan of Government*), which proposed state control of industry, commerce, and shipping together with the expansion of national strength by means of colonization. He was much concerned by the difficulty of adjusting population and food supply and was perhaps the first Japanese thinker to see clearly that the closed economy of Japan, a country with only modest natural resources, was incapable of supporting the standard of living to which the people had become accustomed unless foreign trade was increased. He therefore did not hesitate to argue for a merchant marine capable of overseas traffic, and specifically proposed trade with Russia.

He may be regarded as one of a growing class of intellectuals who were dissatisfied with traditional Asiatic life, and it is interesting to note that he, like the National Scholars, was opposed to Confucianism. He was even inclined to think that Christianity might be useful. He said that the most important things needed by Japan were gun powder, metals, ships, and colonies. It will be seen that his views were such as would be abhorrent to the Bakufu, especially those which concerned Christianity, a hatred of which was a canon of Tokugawa doctrine on international affairs. His opinions were much in advance of the times and most of his books remained unpublished during his lifetime.

One revealing aspect of his sentiments was his attitude towards Western painting, which he preferred to Chinese or Japanese styles. In this he shared the view of another interesting character, a man called Shiba Kōkan (1737–1818), who like Honda felt that his native culture was exhausted and stale. He was a restless man, constantly changing his occupation, always seeking for something new. Having had some instruction in painting as a youth, he earned a modest livelihood for a time by turning out competent but spiritless pictures in different styles, including that of the print artist Harunobu, whose name he disingenuously borrowed. But he was really not interested in Asiatic art and he wrote an essay on Western painting in which he argues that it is most useful and very superior to Chinese and Japanese painting, because it portrays light and shade, the shapes of solids, and their perspective. It is most valuable, he remarks, for illustrating in books things that cannot be explained in words. Far Eastern painting, on the other hand, is just something to amuse people at drinking parties.

His views are interesting because they show him as a man in revolt against contemporary Japanese life. He was impressed by the material and scientific aspects of Western culture, and what he really liked was natural philosophy and the exact description of things. In European painting what pleased him most was its representational side, which he called *shashin*, or "copying truth," using the Japanese word that now stands for "photography." How far he had left behind the traditional Japanese or Chinese view can be judged from an essay by an early nineteenth-century painter named Kuwayama Gyokusho. This artist says contemptuously of certain realistic Chinese paintings that they might be mistaken for the work of barbarians, by which he means Europeans. Painting that is a correct representation of things, he says, is work for artisans, not artists. A true artist wishes to show not the exact appearance of an object, but the spirit that informs it. "No artist," he observes, "would try to make faithful copies of objects he saw, if only because he would be afraid that his work might be mistaken for that of a common craftsman or a mere artisan."

Men like Shiba Kōkan were scarcely important or influential in their day, but they are significant figures, useful to historians in that they were typical of a growing class who were restless and dissatisfied and therefore in favour of change. It would be convenient if one could ascribe their discontent to one single cause, to economic instability or to maladministration or even to some obscure law which decrees that cultures must change or perish. But such explanations are of little use and it is better to keep to particulars. What is clear and so far as it goes instructive is the fact that each class early in nineteenth-century Japan had reason for complaint — samurai, farmer, artisan, and merchant, court noble and feudal lord. Let us take them class by class in the hope that some common feature will reveal itself.

2. Discontented People

THE SAMURAI had one very patent grievance, and that was lack of money. The finances of the Bakufu and of many feudal lords were in a parlous state, which led them to reduce the allowances of their retainers on one pretence or another. Often the stipend of a samurai in the late Tokugawa period was cut by as much as one half,

while his financial embarrassment was increased by sharp falls in
the money value of rice. It should be remembered also that the
majority of samurai were poorly paid men-at-arms with families
and dependants to support, so that an allowance of twenty *koku*,[2]
which might be reduced to ten, was beggarly. There was little in
the life of the average samurai to keep him from brooding on his
misfortunes. His military duties were very light and he suffered
from too little occupation as well as too little money. Complaints
of a decline in the character of the military class are common in
documents of the end of the eighteenth century. One of them
says: "Seven or eight out of ten bannermen and retainers are ef-
feminate. They are mean-spirited and behave like shopkeepers.
Those who profess a taste for military arts do it for the sake of
worldly success and to get appointments. . . . If on taking a test
they are lucky enough to hit a two-foot target and to dismount
safely after bestriding a horse as tame as a cat, they are promoted
for their exploits and after that they put their accomplishments on
the shelf." This was written by Sugita Gempaku, a scholar of Dutch
who naturally disliked military pretensions, and some allowance
ought to be made for his prejudices.

But there seems to be no doubt that a great number of plain samurai in cities and castle towns were leading useless and sometimes
dissolute lives, while those in higher ranks were frequently corrupt. A lampoon entitled *Efficacious Medicine* says: "Promotion
Pills. A large packet 100 *ryō*, medium size 50 *ryō*, small size 10
ryō." This was in the day of the notorious Mizuno Tadaakira, a
minister who died in 1835 after some thirty years of corrupt official life. We may well suppose that the base example set in high
places contributed to a decline in standards of conduct among the
samurai. But its ultimate reason is something more general and
fundamental. It is the contradiction inherent in the existence of
a numerous privileged military class throughout two hundred
years of peace. This was tantamount to a standing army of 500,000
men, since in addition to the samurai there was a considerable
number of servants or other dependants who, nominally at least,
were under obligation to follow their masters to war. The exact
number of samurai at the beginning of the nineteenth century is
not known, but when after the Restoration the population was re-

2 It will give some idea of the purchasing power of this income to explain that
1 *koku* is the average annual consumption per head. Thus, after deducting 5 *koku*
for food in a household of five persons, a samurai on 20 *koku* would have some 15
koku to convert into cash. At 100 *momme* of silver per *koku* this would give him,
for rent, clothes, and all other expenditure, 1,500 *momme* (or about $200 a year in
1868) provided that he received his full allowance, that he was fairly treated by
the broker, and that the coinage in which he was paid was not debased.

classified, the number of persons who registered as *shizoku* — that is, as former samurai — was 420,000.[3]

It was to be expected that many samurai would be dissatisfied with the condition in which they found themselves. Some became rōnin, some crossed over into the commoner class so as to make an independent living by commercial pursuits, others raised funds by adopting sons or daughters from the families of prosperous traders or farmers, thus conferring upon them the status of samurai, and others supplemented their income by teaching. But the majority fell into an indigent state, which naturally brewed discontent. The Bakufu were aware of these conditions, and made grants to relieve distress or issued orders allowing samurai to repudiate debts to traders or to reduce their interest payments; but such measures did not radically improve the situation of the samurai in general.

A small but active and intelligent minority began to see that only some sweeping change would better their position, and it was by these that the seeds of an anti-Bakufu movement were sown. It did not necessarily appear to them as an anti-feudal movement, though that is what it eventually became, and it resulted in the disappearance of the samurai as a class. Those among them who had some experience of official duties in their clans or who had been entrusted with financial dealings with the merchants and brokers or who had superintended the commercial enterprises that some daimyo undertook in order to increase their revenues were able when the change came to step into suitable employment. But most members of the military class were unfitted for a competitive life in which a sharp sword was no argument. The very idea of competition was strange to them, and when Western economic writings were first translated into Japanese it was necessary to make a new word for it. It was a combination of the separate words for "race" and "fight," and Fukuzawa, the translator, relates how shocked his colleagues were by such harsh terminology.

Turning now to the class of farmers, whose unfortunate condition has already been discussed, we find a very active expression of their discontent in the agrarian risings that became endemic from the close of the eighteenth century. Japan has a long history of peasant revolts, in which sometimes political, sometimes religious motives appear to be uppermost. But in almost every case economic grievances were a compelling reason for resort to violence. Riots on a large scale were not uncommon throughout the mediæval feudal period, especially during phases of disorder pro-

[3] This number is that of heads of families. The total number of persons registered as of *shizoku* status in 1872 was 1,282,000; and this had increased by 1900 to 2,168,000.

duced by civil wars; but they were generally local in character and cannot be said to have sprung from a universal agrarian discontent. In the early part of the Tokugawa period peace and a rising standard of living brought some measure of order and contentment into the life of the countryside, and there were comparatively few disturbances during the seventeenth century.

But from about 1700, following upon a series of natural calamities which produced famine and general distress, the number of uprisings began to increase. There were riots, in some of which several thousand peasants took part, in different provinces and at different times throughout the eighteenth century, and for the next hundred years or more — that is, until the Restoration of 1868 — their frequency was nearly twice as great. The size of these demonstrations was as remarkable as their frequency. Thus, in 1739 as many as 84,000 peasants in one province, objecting to an onerous tax upon rice, challenged the samurai of their feudal lord and forced him to give way to their demands. In 1764 the provinces adjacent to Yedo were much disturbed by emergency levies imposed on them to meet special expenditure of the Bakufu, and when officials arrived to make requisitions a body of 70,000 peasants revolted and began to march on Yedo, their numbers being increased by reinforcements collected on the way until they amounted to 200,000. From 1783 onwards there was a great increase in the number of uprisings for a decade or more, this being due to the severe famines and plagues which began in that year and presently affected almost the whole of Japan.

After it had recovered from these disasters (which, as we have noted, reduced the population by more than one million in a few years) the country remained relatively tranquil for a brief space of time, thanks in part to the reforming activity of Matsudaira Sadanobu. But the conditions that had produced riots in the past were not abolished, and from 1811 onwards there were many fresh outbreaks, usually violent and often on a large scale. We need not follow these in detail, for it is sufficient to say that thenceforward hardly a year passed without some serious manifestation of agrarian unrest, and it is significant that risings increased in frequency as the collapse of the Shogunate drew nearer, for this was a clear indication that the central authority of the Bakufu was diminishing. Two very significant risings were directed not against the lord of a fief but against the Bakufu itself. One of these, in 1840, was caused by a Bakufu order transferring the Daimyo of Shōnai to another fief. The peasants objected to this because he had been a benevolent ruler. They made repeated demonstrations and direct appeals to Yedo, and in the end the transfer was revoked. A large-scale demonstration against a resurvey of land conducted by corrupt

Bakufu officials in Ōme in 1842 resulted in the flight of the officials and the triumph of the peasants, though many of them suffered torture and death. Both of these affairs testify to the decline of the Shogun's power to exercise control in the provinces; and it is interesting to note that both arose indirectly out of Mizuno Tadakuni's efforts to improve the Bakufu finances by controlling more rice land and so increasing its revenue.

Outbreaks were especially numerous and serious for some years after 1833, when Japan was again visited by natural calamities, starvation spread to the cities, and lawlessness was rife throughout the country. Though relief was afforded from time to time by good harvests such conditions continued with little substantial change until the Restoration; and indeed the reforms of early Meiji, far from bringing risings to an end, produced further disturbances, which differed very little in character from those of the Tokugawa period.

It is evident that such determined revolts, spread over so long a period and involving so many people in so many places, were not fortuitous episodes but were blind attempts to remedy some deep-seated malady in the prevailing social order. It is not easy to single out one general cause for a discontent so grave that in the hope of alleviation great numbers of simple country people would brave death, torture, and cruel imprisonment — for that was the common fate of hundreds of those who took part in even the most successful insurrections. But it is safe to say that a feature common to all these revolts was a feeling of desperation induced by oppressive taxation. A glance at the petitions presented by the peasants to the authorities shows that almost without exception they included prayers for the reduction of special levies in money or in kind or in labour, or for fairer methods of assessment or for the dismissal of unjust officials. Often the complaints were directed not against the rulers themselves but against villagers whom they employed as their agents, or against landlords who were not members of the governing class.

It is a striking fact that nearly all the abuses that provided the motive force for these insurrectionary movements can be traced back to one overriding cause. That was the gross failure of the public finance of the Tokugawa administration and, in a secondary degree, of most of the daimyo. The fiscal difficulties of the Bakufu have already been touched upon and we need not revert to that theme, for what is of interest here is not the causes of agrarian discontent but its effects. It would be difficult to sustain the view that the peasant risings directly contributed to the downfall of the Bakufu. They were not revolutionary in intent, for (so far as can be judged from contemporary accounts) the leaders were not inspired by any organized hostility to the existing form of government but only by objections to specific injustices that were not connected in their minds with fundamental weaknesses of the society in which they lived. Indeed, it is a marked feature of the whole sequence of revolts of peasants in the Tokugawa period that these unhappy men accepted without question the right of the feudal nobility and gentry to govern their lives. They did not challenge the harsh law, but resisted excesses in its application, and in this they differed somewhat from the rural insurgents of the fifteenth century, who in several instances fought to secure rather than to suppress feudal privilege and in a few instances succeeded in setting up autonomous communities. But even these comparatively successful uprisings, which took place in times of anarchy, can hardly be looked upon as concerted revolutionary movements; and still less can the agrarian revolts of the Tokugawa period be treated as political in character. The main difference between them lies in the fact that the insurrections of the Middle Ages belong to a period when there was no clear distinction between soldier and farmer, while under Tokugawa rule, the peasants having been disarmed by Hideyoshi in his famous Sword Hunt, there was a rigid separation in both function and social status between the professional military class and the cultivators. This had become habitual and accepted as the Tokugawa régime was consolidated, and consequently it is difficult to accept the view of some Japanese historians, who argue that the peasant uprisings of the late eighteenth and early nineteenth centuries were the first stage of a social revolution designed to overthrow the Bakufu. To apply to the study of Far Eastern history the terms of a conventional analysis which may, or may not, be valid for European history can easily lead to error and confusion.

It is true, of course, that in so far as the peasant risings added to the mounting embarrassments of the Bakufu they must be considered as one of the causes of its collapse, but this is not to say that they formed part of a direct revolutionary movement. The position is well stated by Dr. Hugh Borton in his valuable study *Peasant Uprisings in Japan,* where he points out that they were "a continual protest against the economic distress in which the peasants found themselves," and that most of them were disconnected, "having little concern for the overthrow of feudalism as such, but caring more for a rectification of those minor injustices which were inherent in the feudalistic society of the times."

It may be objected that this is too fine a distinction, but it has nevertheless an important bearing upon the nature of the Restoration movement and of the subsequent reshaping of Japanese institutions, for both of these were the work of reformers who were

A FOREIGN BEAUTY

Oil painting ascribed to Hiraga Gennai, 1732–1779.
Primarily interested in natural history and applied science,
he merely dabbled in literature and the arts.

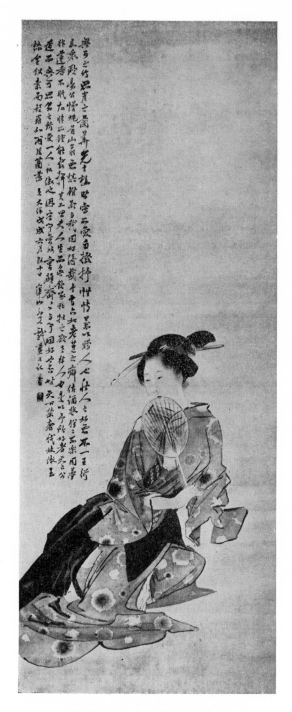

PORTRAIT OF HIS MISTRESS

By Watanabe Kwazan, 1793–1841

as conservative in some respects as they were progressive in others, and whose motives show no trace of a desire to improve agrarian conditions in a thoroughgoing manner. Indeed, some of their early reforms were accomplished at the expense of the rural population, as can be seen from the fact that agrarian disturbances increased rather than diminished in the first decade after the Restoration. Had there existed in Japan at the close of the Tokugawa period any organized and coherent sentiment among the peasants it is probable that the course of Japan's political development from that point onwards would have been accompanied by a violence and disruption that it in fact escaped. This was thanks to the submissive character of the mass of the Japanese people, which derived from the long tradition of firm, not to say ruthless, government established by the Tokugawa and their vassals.

That through centuries of subordination a sense of inferiority persisted among the peasants and was still strong in the early years of Meiji is shown in a striking passage in the autobiography of Fukuzawa Yukichi, one of the strongest advocates of Western learning at that time. He was a man who held strong equalitarian views, but he confesses in this work that he sometimes found it difficult not to address farmers in commanding tones habitual to a samurai. Unless he deliberately softened his manner he was treated by them in a most deferential, not to say cringing way. On one occasion, he relates, he met a peasant on horseback, who hastily dismounted as soon as he saw that he was about to meet a social superior. "I caught hold of his bridle," says Fukuzawa, "and said: 'What do you mean by this?' The farmer bowed as if in great fear and began to apologize. 'No, no,' I said, 'don't be a fool. . . . This is your horse, get back on it and ride on.' The poor fellow was afraid to mount before me. 'Now get back on your horse,' I repeated. 'If you don't, I'll beat you.'"

As for the traders and artisans, their grievances as a social class were not exceptional, though many town-dwellers suffered from poverty and at times from severe shortages of food. The power of the more prosperous tradespeople, particularly of the merchant bankers, was rising as the fortunes of the samurai declined. Their chief cause of discontent was their inferior social status, and the richest of them suffered from vexatious interference by the Bakufu in their financial and commercial dealings.

One important example of this interference was the action of the Bakufu in destroying mercantile and industrial guilds, and a brief account of official policy in this respect will serve to explain the attitude of the merchant class towards the administration of the Shogun's officers and of the several daimyo. The Bakufu was in constant financial difficulties from the beginning of the eighteenth century, and although drastic economies were made from time to time, the general condition of public finance was one of recurrent deficits, which had to be met by emergency measures since the organization of the country did not allow of the raising of national loans. These emergency measures usually took the form of levies upon the merchants, who lived principally in cities that formed part of the Tokugawa domain. There was in fact no other important source of increased revenue open to the Shogun's government, since agriculture was already overtaxed and the trickle of foreign trade passing through Nagasaki provided very little in the way of customs dues. The daimyo were occasionally called upon to help with contributions, which were described as gifts, but this was a practice that could not be often repeated.

Consequently it was the merchants who in the first place bore the burden of meeting budget deficits. They were invited by the government to lend large sums, which were frequently not repaid, for the feudal authorities had a long-standing habit of proclaiming Acts of Grace which were total or partial repudiations of debt contracted by members of the military class. It is said that one half of the *fudasashi* (the brokers who advanced money to vassals and retainers on the security of their rice stipends) were bankrupted by an act of this kind in 1843. These cancellations of debt were not all directly connected with the Bakufu's direct obligations, but were means of pacifying the hereditary followers upon whose loyalty the Shogun depended and whose allowances the Bakufu could not pay in full. In 1760 the Bakufu "borrowed" from members of the great trading guilds as much as 1,781,000 *ryō*, a sum of the same order of magnitude as the total ordinary expenditure of the government for one year.

Even shifts and devices of this nature were as a rule not sufficient to balance the budget of the Bakufu, and it resorted at frequent intervals to coinage debasement, a practice that began late in the eighteenth century and by early in the nineteenth had reached such a point that an item called *demé,* or profit from recoinage, appears almost every year under the heading of revenue, in amounts equal to from one fourth to one half of total expenditure. It need hardly be said that this kind of fiscal arrangement, while tiding over each annual crisis, had in the long run the effect of increasing the financial difficulties of the Shogunate. At the same time it worsened general economic conditions throughout the country, causing the wildest fluctuations of prices. Driven by the results of its own policy to attempt stabilization, the Bakufu legislated against guilds and other quasi-monopolistic organs in commerce and industry, thus arousing the antagonism of the strongest elements in the mercantile class. Such a policy might

have been justified in so far as the guilds acted in restraint of trade
— which to some extent they did — but the government, itself not
fiscally pure, could put nothing useful in the place of the system it
destroyed, and its measures merely resulted in the breakdown of
a well-organized if costly system of credit. Action of this kind naturally intensified the strain between military and commercial elements in Japanese society. The attitude of the trading class was
expressed with rueful humour by a contemporary wit who said
that while the townspeople were at one time rudely cut down by
samurai swords, nowadays they were politely ruined by samurai
borrowings.[4]

Nevertheless, so long as the authority of the Bakufu persisted,
the merchants and the moneylenders were obliged to submit to the
exactions of the ruling caste, who were their best, in fact their only
important clients. Consequently the townsmen did not as a rule
show open hostility to the feudal régime, though when the time
came they were ready enough to join in its destruction. Meanwhile
by pitting their knowledge and their wits against the military they
continued as a class to make handsome profits, accumulating capital, which no doubt soothed their feeling of social inferiority and
in due course proved an indispensable weapon in the destruction
of the government that had despoiled them.

The financial condition of the daimyo was not unlike that of
the Shogun. Most of them were heavily indebted to great merchant
bankers and resorted to expedients similar to those of the Bakufu
in the hope of making ends meet. They issued coins and paper
money (thus infringing the prerogative of the Bakufu) on very
doubtful security and set up commercial and industrial monopolies within their own domains. All such measures were attended by
a gradual disintegration of the established society, since they attacked the economic basis upon which it rested.

It will be seen that each of the main classes in this society had
good reason for desiring change. It was a society dependent upon
mutual obligations that could no longer be fulfilled, and upon a
division of classes that could not be maintained. It is easy to see
why, in the early part of the nineteenth century, the authority of
the Bakufu began to fail rapidly as the system over which it presided lost the last remnants of its feudal character. Its growing embarrassments were to be intensified by circumstances over which
it had no control. In the era called Tempo (1830–43) famine was
chronic and agrarian risings were frequent and violent. Rioting
spread to the great towns, where short supplies and bad management had caused starvation among the poorer citizens. In Osaka

---

[4] *"Nikui yatsu tote kiritaosare, amai yatsu tote karitaosare. . . ."* The play upon
words cannot be translated.

in 1837 their condition was desperate and their hatred of the rich was expressed in attacks upon the houses of the great rice merchants.

Such rice riots, known as *uchikowashi,* or "smashings," had been common enough since the early eighteenth century, but the one that took place in 1837 had a peculiar significance, in that it was led by samurai, who set an example which was followed in other parts of the country. Its moving spirit was Ōshio Heihachiro, a police official serving under the Shogun's magistrate in Osaka. He was angered by the failure of the authorities to cope with the problem of feeding the city and gathered together a small band whom he incited by saying: "First we must kill all the officials who have made the poor suffer, and then we must go on to slaughter all the rich men of Osaka and their minions who live in luxury." The rioters were not numerous. Apart from Ōshio and a dozen or so other determined samurai and rōnin, they consisted of a few hundred peasants and townsmen who were carried along by the ringleaders but were presently dispersed by troops from the garrison. What was remarkable about this rising was the incompetence of the officials and soldiers. They had had ample notice of the plot and yet they allowed the rioters a free hand for several hours, during which a great part of the city was burned down. The garrison commander had no plan, the chief magistrates at the head of the troops fell off their horses, and some of the soldiers ran away when they were confronted by the miserable rabble. These were representatives of a military and civil power which traditionally had never brooked the whisper of a challenge to its authority, so that it may well be imagined to what a low ebb the prestige of the Bakufu had fallen.

The need for reform was not unperceived by sensible men in high places, but it was not until 1841 that Mizuno Tadakuni, the Shogun's chief minister, attempted to restore feudal discipline. His method was that which had been used by Yoshimune in 1716 and Sadanobu in 1789, for he introduced a great number of sumptuary rules in astonishing detail. He had even less success than his distinguished models, possibly because the evils that he attempted to cure were more deep-seated than they had been a century before. There is no need to recite his failures in detail, but it is interesting to note that he interfered in the life of the townspeople, censoring and suppressing novels, segregating actors, forbidding the employment of women in barbers' shops and archery grounds, and in other ways diminishing the *menus plaisirs* of the citizens. While discouraging comic entertainments he arranged for improving lectures upon religion, ethics, and military science.

Apart from this fantastical legislation he attempted major economic reforms. It was he who abolished the guilds and came down heavily upon the rich merchants with levies, displaying an animosity that seems to have clouded the judgment of the ruling class. He also planned an increase in revenue by certain reclamation projects (which were never finished) and by obliging daimyo and hatamoto [5] who had domains near Yedo and Osaka to exchange them for less productive land at a distance. This was a policy not calculated to nourish loyal feelings among the vassals. His currency policy was also deplorable, for he relied upon recoinage almost entirely, deriving from it in 1841 a profit (*demé*) of 1,555,000 *ryō*, the highest amount ever reached and greater than the total of all other items of revenue. That a reformer should have felt constrained to use such financial methods is plain evidence that the Shogun's government was as bankrupt of policy as it was of money.

It is clear that by 1840 the Bakufu was already going downhill. The only thing that might have saved it was a resolute and consistent policy; but even Mizuno's poor efforts were not sustained. He resigned in 1843 for want of support among his colleagues, having done little but arouse all-round hostility; and when the citizens of Yedo heard of his retirement they assembled outside his mansion and threw missiles at the sentry box. One thing he attempted was a reform of the training of the Shogun's troops, and he paid special attention to gunnery. This involved the study of Dutch works on military science and on the manufacture and use of ordnance, thus encouraging a number of enterprising men who favoured the opening of Japan to intercourse with the West. It is humiliating to reflect that in Japanese minds Western culture stood for a knowledge of advanced methods of slaughter, but it cannot be denied that guns spoke with a convincing voice to a people with a long military history.

While the military-minded were thus looking to the Western world for science, the Western world was beginning to take an interest in Japan and seeking to break into her seclusion.

3. Occidental Intruders

WE have already seen how towards 1800 Russian approaches to Japanese shores had caused some anxiety to the Bakufu and induced it to strengthen coastal defences. By that time other menacing visitors had begun to show themselves. Owing to European rivalries the Far Eastern trade of Holland began to decline from about 1780 and the Dutch East India Company could not continue

---

[5] Hakamoto or Bannermen were direct vassals of the Tokugawa, but not territorial rulers as were the daimyo.

its regular voyages to Japan, although the trading station at Nagasaki remained in operation, but on a diminished scale. For want of Dutch vessels arrangements were made to bring cargo from Batavia in foreign ships, the first of these being the *Eliza,* flying the American flag, in 1797. This practice continued for some years and meanwhile ships of other countries began to appear in Japanese waters. These included an English and a Russian man-of-war. The former was sent away from a northern harbour after a short parley, but the latter entered the harbour of Nagasaki in October 1804, carrying a duly accredited envoy from Russia.

This was the *Nadiezhda,* commanded by Captain Krusenstern, who was making a voyage round the world, mainly for the purpose of developing trade with India and southeast Asia and supplying Russia's Far Eastern possessions by sea rather than by land. The mission of Rezanov, the envoy whom he carried, was subsidiary. Krusenstern stayed for six months while Rezanov endeavoured to open negotiations with Yedo. But he could get no satisfaction whatever, the Bakufu maintaining its stand that since Japan had no need of foreign goods, to permit trade relations would merely deprive her of useful commodities and risk the entry of foreign religious doctrine. Rezanov, who appears to have used angry and threatening language, at last gave up his plans, realizing that he would get no backing from the Russian government; but he left a bad impression upon the Japanese. This was presently made worse by the action of two of his subordinates, Chvostov and Davidov, who in 1806 raided points on Sakhalin and the Kuriles, attacked Japanese trading posts, and "took possession" of the country in the name of the Tsar.[6] Such events caused perturbation among the Japanese authorities, and their subsequent conduct shows that they definitely feared Russian aggression, although there was at that time no firm intention on the part of the Russian government to force Japan to open trade relations.

In 1807 Captain Golovnin, a Russian naval officer commanding the warship *Diana,* set out on a voyage of exploration in the Pacific. In 1811 he received orders from the Admiralty to investigate the southern Kuriles and landed at Kunashir in the summer of that year. He and some of his ship's company were captured by a Japanese armed force and imprisoned. They were held in captivity until 1813, when the *Diana* was allowed to enter Hakodate and take them away. During his long imprisonment (most interestingly described in his *Narrative of a Captivity in Japan*) Golovnin, after some cruel treatment, gained the esteem and affection of his cap-

---

6 It is interesting to note that Hirata, the great Shinto scholar, wrote in 1807 a work called *Chishima Shiranami,* or the *White Waves of the Kuriles,* intended as a guide to restraining barbarians and a manual of coastal defence.

tors and when he left they were reduced to tears. Their behaviour illustrates in a small way the nature of the subsequent attitude of the Japanese towards Russians, which shows a curious mixture of fear and a feeling that perhaps after all they would make good friends.

After Golovnin's release a few fruitless attempts were made to approach the Japanese in the Kuriles, but these were soon abandoned. It was not until 1849 that under Nesselrode as Foreign Minister, Count Muraviev, who stood for an active policy in eastern Siberia, decided that it would be to the advantage of Russia to make friends with Japan in order to check British and American influence in eastern Asia. In 1852 the Tsar, Nicholas II, agreed to send an expedition to Japan, and an embassy headed by Putiatin reached Nagasaki in August 1853, to find that Commodore Perry had already arrived in Uraga.

These details of Russian approaches to Japan are given here because American and English historians sometimes overlook the important part played by Russia in bringing about the opening of Japan by revealing to the Japanese their own weakness. The gradual movement of Russian influence towards eastern Asia has a history much longer than that of the American movement westward across the Pacific, for, as we have seen, Russians were in Kamchatka by the end of the seventeenth century and began to take an interest in Japan not long after that.

Bearing these facts in mind, we may return to the attempts of other countries to open relations with Japan, but first it may be useful to consider the attitude of the Bakufu towards foreign intercourse. The frequent arrival of foreign vessels in the closing years of the eighteenth century had caused the Japanese government to re-examine its policy in the light of new conditions. The strict legal position was that ships might enter Nagasaki for purposes of trade provided that their presence was not inconsistent with the anti-Christian edicts; and during their stay in harbour they must be disarmed. This did not necessarily mean that trade would be permitted, for the Japanese naturally were free to buy and sell or not as they chose. In fact, the Bakufu did not desire an increase of trade beyond what was carried on through the Dutch and the Chinese. They considered, or at least they argued, that it was to the national disadvantage to export Japanese products in exchange for articles of luxury, and they feared moreover that to extend trading rights to nations other than the Dutch and Chinese would lead to embarrassing political relations and then to a breakdown of the fundamental policy of isolation. Occasional displays of force by Russian vessels and the stiff attitude of Rezanov in 1805 caused them in 1806 to issue a new edict, directed especially at the Russians, in which local authorities were commanded to drive all foreign ships away from ports other than Nagasaki. This order was not always easy to comply with, since there were times and places where the defence forces were weak and the strict rule could not be applied, as in the case of Chvostov and Davidov.

In 1808 an English frigate, H.M.S. *Phaeton*, sailed into Nagasaki in search of Dutch prize and threatened to bombard the shipping in the harbour if food was not supplied. The Governor gave orders that the *Phaeton* should be attacked and burned, but nothing was done. The intruder, having obtained food and fuel, sailed out again. This incident, following shortly upon the Russian attacks of 1806, made a strong and disagreeable impression. It caused the Bakufu to take disciplinary steps against the officers at Nagasaki (who had shown a poor spirit), to strengthen coastal defences, and — with some prompting from the Dutch — to conclude that both England and Russia had designs upon Japan. Yet so irresolute were the Shogun's counsellors that within a few years they had relaxed their precautions and had to submit to a number of incursions by ships in search of water and fuel, which the local forces could not cope with.

At last, while the authorities at Yedo were considering what to do next, news came of acts of violence by the crew of an English vessel on an island off the Satsuma coast, and this stimulated the Bakufu to issue a new edict. It is known as the *Ni-nen-naku*, or "No Second Thought" Expulsion Order. It enjoined all local authorities to destroy any foreign ship that should come close in shore and to arrest or kill any members of its crew who might land. There was to be no hesitation, no discussion. This was in 1825. Several years later, in 1837, a small vessel, the *Morrison*, chartered by some American missionaries, brought to Uraga a number of Japanese castaways for repatriation. The officials who boarded her, seeing that she was unarmed, had her fired upon the following day. She withdrew and entered Kagoshima Bay, where she met with similar treatment.

But this action gave rise to some criticism within Japan, as well as making a bad impression among foreigners to whom it became known; and as the Japanese government began to learn more of the strength of foreign navies and heard details of the defeat of China in the so-called Opium War, they thought it wise to moderate the policy laid down in their Don't-think-twice edict of 1825. In 1842 local authorities were instructed to deal more leniently with foreign ships, supplying them with food and fuel and "advising" them to go away. Thus an English naval survey ship, H.M.S. *Samarang*, which entered Nagasaki in 1845, was treated with great courtesy, though difficulties were made about landing.

A French warship arriving in 1846 was not so amiably received, but that was because the French commander was known to have come from the Luchu Islands, where he had endeavoured to make a treaty with the King and had landed a missionary. This was alarming to the Bakufu, for the Luchuans were really under the control of the Daimyo of Satsuma, who was known to be in favour of foreign intercourse. After discussions in Yedo, Satsuma was told that he might use his own discretion, and it is possible that, but for the fear of Christianity, he would have made some kind of pact with the French. Actually he confined himself to arranging a certain import trade in arms and machinery by way of the Luchus, and thus made a breach in the seclusion policy.

It will be seen that the Bakufu was showing signs of vacillation, and it is worth while to digress here in order to consider what were the forces within Japan that were working against the principle laid down in 1639, when foreign intercourse ceased. We have seen that the pursuit of Dutch studies had already in the eighteenth century created a body of scholars who, primarily because of their interest in science, were anxious to see the opening of the country. This tendency had been strengthened as with the lapse of time more knowledge was acquired and more was needed, until at length it became clear that the Bakufu was too weak to withstand accumulating foreign pressure. By 1830 the students of Western science had begun to acquire such influence that the Confucian scholars intrigued against them and for a short time "Dutch" studies languished. But a number of courageous men continued their criticism of the authorities, and though some of them paid with their lives they succeeded in convincing a few members of the administration and some of the daimyo that Japan could no longer stand still.

Some account of the leading figures in this movement to break down the exclusion policy will serve better than a description of its growth in general terms and it has the advantage of throwing a little light upon conditions in Japan, especially among the samurai, in the period under discussion. But first it should be mentioned that in the history of European influences upon Japanese thought much depended upon the personal relationships of Japanese students with Western scholars who were attached to the Dutch factory at Nagasaki. It is of course impossible to assess precisely their contribution to Japanese learning, but many Japanese historians (though there are notable exceptions) are inclined to write in terms of trends, books, and documents and to neglect the importance of individuals. An interesting inquiry might be made into the share of foreign teachers in the transmission of cultural influences to Japan, for it would undoubtedly reveal that throughout Japanese history Korean, Chinese, Portuguese, Dutch, and other foreigners of learning or experience have given life to studies that might have been dry and infertile without their help. Certainly Japanese scholars under the Tokugawa owed a great debt to men like Kämpfer, the German scholar who was in Japan from September 1690 to November 1692; Thunberg, the botanist; Titsingh, a man of all-round accomplishment; and notably Siebold, the German scientist who from 1823 to 1830 was in close touch with Japanese students and scholars, giving them precious aid and counsel. Siebold indeed was on such friendly terms with his pupils that they broke the law by giving him forbidden information, and some suffered death on that account. He himself was expelled from Japan, to the great grief of his disciples.

The other side of the picture — and what most interests us here — is the persistence, in face of difficulty and often of danger, of a strong interest in Western knowledge throughout the period of seclusion. It ebbed and flowed in accordance with the official attitude, but it never entirely subsided. By the end of the eighteenth century it had spread from a small band of specialists to a great number of men in all ranks of society and in all parts of the country, and it had increased its range to include most aspects of European art and science. At the turn of the century students were influenced not only by a desire for knowledge for its own sake, but by a sense of urgency which they felt as the visits of foreign ships became more frequent and more menacing.

4. Forerunners of the Restoration Movement

WHEN in 1808 the saucy *Phaeton* sailed into Nagasaki harbour her complement can have had little idea of the commotion they were causing on shore. The commander of this crack frigate had come all the way from the Indian Ocean in search of fugitive Dutch vessels and doubtless his mind was only on his professional duties. He certainly had no scruples about entering neutral territorial waters on a warlike mission. But the appearance of this armed ship and its calm disregard of Japanese feelings brought home at once to the local and presently to the central authorities the weakness of the defensive measures they had taken in a rather half-hearted way since the Russian descents upon the Kuriles at the end of the eighteenth century.

At the time of the visit of the *Phaeton* a boy named Takashima was in his eleventh year, and there is no doubt that he and his family were much impressed by it. His father was a municipal officer of good standing. His family had since Portuguese days been established in Nagasaki and had a hereditary claim to municipal office as well as being recognized experts in gunnery. Young Takashima succeeded his father in these posts at the age of seventeen and before long was entrusted with important duties in the supervision of the defences of the harbour. He applied himself assiduously to the study of military science and soon reached the conclusion that the forts and guns installed around Nagasaki were quite

TAKASHIMA SHŪHAN (1798–1866)

A specialist in gunnery and coastal defence

inadequate for protection against foreign warships. He pointed out that the Bakufu orders to drive foreign vessels away were meaningless, since there was not sufficient artillery for their execution. Finding that his memorials had no effect, he devoted his energies and his private fortune to a study of Western military science and to the purchase from Holland of modern weapons, which included field guns, mortars, and muskets of recent design. In this enterprise he was assisted by members of the Dutch trading station at Deshima and by captains of Dutch vessels. From them he obtained a number of books, which he and his pupils translated, and by about 1840 he had made such progress that he was able to train in Western style two companies of infantry and a battery of artillery and had gained a considerable knowledge of the technical processes in the manufacture of ordnance. These efforts may be taken as the first serious adoption of modern Western military methods and the first concrete sign that feudal methods of fighting were obsolete.

These activities took place at a time when the outbreak of the Anglo-Chinese war of 1840 had made a deep impression throughout the Far East, but particularly in Japan. The naval strength that had enabled an English squadron to destroy Chinese warships without loss to itself came as a great surprise to most Japanese, though not to students like Takashima. News that reached Japan of the engagement and its sequels much exaggerated the number and strength of the English ships. Extraordinary rumours were circulated, and repeated by serious scholars, such as a report that the English navy was composed of 25,860 vessels, many with forty or fifty guns, and its total force of officers and men amounted to one million.[7] A scholar named Mineta, as late as 1849, when more exact information might have been expected, published a book called *Kaigwai Shinwa,* or *New Tales from Overseas,* which was an account of the war from Chinese sources. This work contains an illustration depicting the English fleet assembled below London Bridge for the expedition to China. There is a great forest of masts extending to the horizon, and immense crowds throng the embankment, while sightseers in gondolas are visible in the foreground. It is interesting to reflect that at this time probably not one Englishman in a thousand knew or cared about the China war, and in general the Japanese seem to have had very mistaken notions as to the British attitude towards Japan, for there is no indication in the history of the period that British merchants had any great interest in the Japan market or that British statesmen had any designs upon Japan's independence.

Similarly the Japanese seem to have overestimated the degree of interest that the Russian government took in the Far East. They did not know, for instance, that Rezanov's mission did not grow out of a deliberate official policy, but resulted rather from his connection with a company interested in the fur trade, which (he thought) depended for its success on the ability to obtain provisions and other stores in Japan. Rezanov was much more interested in the west coast of America than in Japan. In fact, it is not far out to say that much of the anxiety displayed by the party that was urging military preparation on the Bakufu was inspired by fears of imperialistic policies on the part of England and Russia that did not then exist.

---

[7] It should not be supposed that the Bakufu were ignorant of the facts. They were pretty well informed by the Dutch, and there is on record a questionnaire which the Nagasaki officials presented to the Dutch in Deshima, with replies in some detail concerning the strength of English squadrons in China and their positions, the reasons for China's defeat in 1840–2, and related matters. (Boxer: *Jan Compagnie in Japan.* The Hague, 1936.)

The anxiety, however, was genuine. Takashima, with other patriots of the day, concluded that the success of the English was due entirely to their superior weapons. In a memorial to the Governor of Nagasaki he argued strongly for military reform, saying that in fact Japan was no more capable of resistance than was China, and Chinese defensive measures had been "like children's play." Japan must at once adopt Western practice in artillery and infantry training. His proposals were transmitted to the Bakufu, where they met with strong opposition. In the light of Japan's martial history it might have been expected that, whatever objections were raised to Occidental ideas in general, improved methods of warfare would arouse the interest of a military autocracy. But the Bakufu had lost much of its early military complexion, and conservative, Confucian sentiment was powerful.

Takashima's memorial fell into the hands of an official named Torii Yozo, nicknamed the Demon, a sinister character who was a son of the official Confucian scholar Hayashi Jussai and hated foreigners and foreign learning. He held an important post as one of the chief magistrates of Yedo, with both judicial and police power. He objected to Takashima's views and recommended that they should not be adopted. His arguments were curious. He said that Western countries were unreliable, very different from civilized nations who understood manners and morals. They were always thinking of profit and relied entirely upon force. Such people were not at all to be trusted, not at all like the people of China and Japan, who depended for victory upon intelligence. He therefore deplored the activities of the Rangakusha, the students of Dutch learning, who were always running after some new thing; and he warned the Bakufu against the idea that some cannon bought from foreigners and manipulated by a few locally recruited soldiers of no standing would serve to protect the shores of Japan.

These old-fashioned views were not shared by all Torii's colleagues and superiors, among whom Takashima found some supporters. One of them was an important Bakufu official named Egawa Tarozaemon, who arranged for him to be summoned to Yedo. In June 1841 he gave a demonstration of modern infantry drill and gunnery exercises on a parade ground near the capital. He seems to have been obsessed with the importance of drills and parades. He had brought from Nagasaki a company of 125 men, dressed in a newly designed uniform, and before a distinguished company he put them through their repertory with muskets, mortars, and quick-firing guns, using Dutch words of command. This last feature was regarded as most unpatriotic and the official Master of Ordnance of the Bakufu was extremely upset. The drill, he said, was ridiculous. The men raising and manipulating their weapons all at the same time and with the same motions looked as if they were playing some children's game. And as for using Dutch words of command in what was called the Takashima style, it was most improper and should be stopped at once. These frivolous objections were not upheld. The Bakufu even rewarded Takashima and ordered him to give instruction in the new methods to responsible Bakufu officers, but not to anyone else. This proviso

EGAWA TAROZAEMON (1800–55)

A Tokugawa official, student of Dutch, surveying,
and military science

is interesting, since it shows that despite the national peril the Shogunate was afraid that if the feudatories obtained superior weapons and learned how to use them, they might be turned against the government itself. The restriction was soon withdrawn, however, and Takashima's knowledge was spread throughout the country, in particular by Egawa, who opened a school for that purpose. Among Egawa's pupils was one Sakuma Shōzan, a man who was to play a leading part in the introduction of Western scientific knowledge into Japan.

The successes of Takashima and other scholars infuriated the reactionary party, of which Torii was a leader. He sent an agent to Nagasaki to work up charges of treason, peculation, and espionage against Takashima, who was arrested and finally brought to Yedo for trial and imprisonment. Fortunately, but not until Takashima had languished in jail for some years, Torii fell out of favour and Takashima's punishment was reduced to a mild kind of house arrest. This was in 1846, and he was obliged to keep quiet until 1853, when, owing to the urgency of questions of coastal defence created by Perry's visit, he was pardoned and released, receiving an appointment as maker of ordnance for the Bakufu.

Takashima's experiences have been related here in some detail because they illustrate clearly the strength of conservative feeling in Japan at that time. It should be added that it was not only his addiction to foreign learning which displeased the reactionary party, for he was a strong advocate of opening the country on the ground that foreign trade was necessary for the support of Japan's economy and in order to prevent her culture from stagnating. Contemporary with him, but younger by some thirteen years, was another earnest and influential advocate of Western learning, who also suffered for his views. This was the aforesaid Sakuma Shōzan, a man who reached the same conclusions as Takashima, but by a different route. A comparison of their careers brings out in an interesting way not only the conflict between conservative and advanced schools of thought as to the future of Japan, but also the variety of reasons that were adduced for the opening of Japan when the problem became acute as foreign pressure increased.

Sakuma was born in 1811, his father being a samurai of the Matsushiro fief in the mountainous province of Shinano. His feudal lord, named Sanada, happened to have close family connections with collaterals of the Tokugawa and was therefore well thought of in Yedo. This circumstance was of advantage to Sakuma in later life, because it gave him a means of access to high officers of the Bakufu and afforded him some protection against his enemies. As a young man, singled out by Sanada for his talents, he went to Yedo for study and attached himself to older men who were interested in Western science. He devoted himself in particular to military problems and gradually became impressed by the advances made in gunnery and tactics by the leading Western powers. In this he was not exceptional, for it is characteristic of the early stages of Western studies in Japan during the Tokugawa period that it was the companion sciences of inflicting wounds and healing them that attracted the attention of ambitious young samurai. Those who did not study the manufacture and use of lethal weapons devoted themselves to medicine and surgery. These and astronomy were the features of Western culture that appealed to their minds, and it was only incidentally that they acquired some knowledge of other aspects of European culture.

Sakuma was much impressed by Takashima's demonstration of gunnery exercises in 1841. He studied for some time under Egawa,

Takashima's colleague and friend, and then, taking an independent line, he began to inquire into the question of national safety. Sanada had in 1842 been put in charge of coastal defences by the Bakufu, so that Sakuma had ample opportunity for examining such preparations as had been made. He wrote and spoke copiously on problems of national defence and put in a memorial of eight points which throws an interesting light on the views of men of his type. It reads in summary as follows:

1. Fortifications must be erected at all strategic points on the coast and equipped with adequate artillery.
2. The export of copper through the Dutch must be suspended and the metal used for casting thousands of guns for distribution to all points.
3. Large merchant ships must be built, so as to prevent the loss of rice through the wreck of the small coastal vessels which were all that the exclusion edicts allowed.
4. Maritime trade must be supervised by capable officials.
5. Warships of foreign style must be constructed and a force of trained naval officers built up.
6. Schools must be established throughout the country and a modern education provided, so that "even the most stupid men and women may understand loyalty, piety, and chastity."
7. Rewards and punishment must be made clear, and government must be conducted benevolently but firmly, so as to strengthen the popular mind.
8. There must be established a system of selecting and employing men of ability in official posts.

This document received no attention from the authorities and is of no historical importance, but reading between the lines one can find in it a useful picture of contemporary conditions. It shows that men of Sakuma's type were aware not only of the military and economic weaknesses of their country but also of defects in its social constitution. Sakuma felt that the ignorance of the people was one of these, and he favoured widespread education, taking the characteristic Far Eastern line that good government must be based on the moral instruction of the masses. But more significant than these commonplace proposals are the last two items in his list. They express a critical attitude towards the government which was shared by most of the intellectuals of his day. People of his kind resented its arbitrary character, but most of all they chafed under a system of preferment that denied opportunity to young men of modest origins. There can be no doubt that, among all the causes of the anti-Tokugawa, loyalist movement which ended in the fall of the Bakufu, the ambition of young samurai was the most powerful. Agrarian discontent, economic distress, financial blunders — all these would not have sufficed to bring about change without the fructifying zeal of a small number of vigorous persons anxious to exercise their talents and to rise in the world. That Western culture made a strong impression upon their minds is undoubted, but it is important to remember, in studying the growth of Western influences, that most of the young men in question were in the first place attracted to Dutch studies because they afforded opportunities of advancement that were not open to them so long as they confined themselves to the routine duties of a junior military officer.

At the time when he compiled his Eight Points, Sakuma, it will be noticed, was inclined to take an isolationist view. He saw that there was something wrong in the exclusion policy, but he was still of opinion that Western people were barbarians, "incapable of understanding virtue and righteousness," and therefore unfit to enter into relations of equality with Japan. In particular he feared the English, whom he suspected of treacherous designs against his own country. His views on that nation had been coloured not only by reports on their behaviour in China but also by warnings from Dutch informants. "Once they have finished off the business in China," he wrote, "they will send warships to Nagasaki, Satsuma, and Yedo. They are a people who are swayed only by a desire for profit, and they are not likely to go to the expense of sending a large expedition against us all the way from England. But they already have a considerable force just across the water from us, and all they have to do is to take advantage of the recent incident in Uraga [referring to the visit of the *Morrison* in 1837] and, making a warlike demonstration, to insist upon opening trade. If this were refused they would pester us until they gained their point at little expense and would stop at nothing. There is therefore no advantage in attempting to deal with them in accordance with the laws of courtesy."

If this pessimistic diagnosis were correct, what was the remedy? Here Sakuma's wisdom seems to have deserted him, for all that he could suggest was that it would be shameful to agree unconditionally to a demand for trade. Japan must hold firm and quickly strengthen her defences in accordance with his Eight Points. She was already losing much of her wealth in exports through the Dutch, and to give way to the English, besides being fraught with moral dangers, would only make her material condition worse.

He did not say what was to happen if those predatory Western countries should descend upon Japan before she was ready; and the truth is that his Confucian training and his reverence for the Imperial dynasty combined to make the idea of commerce with barbarians extremely repugnant to his patriotic feelings. He was, in other words, taking a reactionary view that later, in the pre-Restoration struggle, was to be expressed in the cry of "Revere the Emperor and Expel the Barbarian." The fact that so able a man should not have perceived the contradictions in his own views shows the strength of conservative sentiment in what for his day were advanced intellectual circles. But he was an indefatigable student, and his subsequent career shows that he was not afraid to change his mind. It is worth relating in outline, because his own conversion to a doctrine of qualified internationalism represents in miniature the intellectual history of the movement that culminated in the opening of Japan a generation later. So powerful were the forces working against seclusion that the experiences of individuals may seem to be of little significance, but Western influences had to work upon individual Eastern minds before they could affect Eastern cultures, and there is thus a real historical interest in tracing that process in typical cases. Sakuma's career is from this point of view especially instructive.

Alarming information as to the naval strength of Western powers reached the Bakufu not only from scholars such as Takashima and Sakuma but from many other sources, and — as we have noted — moved them to moderate the expulsion order of 1825 so as to allow local authorities to supply foreign ships with food and fuel. In 1842 officials were told that they must act in accordance with humane principles and not be unreasonably disturbed by the close approach of strange vessels to the shores of Japan. But on no account were foreigners to be allowed to land and all ships were to be instructed to leave after receiving supplies. Soon after this (in 1844) a Dutch warship entered Nagasaki bringing an envoy with a letter addressed to the Shogun by the King of Holland. This interesting document contained a friendly warning to the effect that the development of modern science and the growth of international trade were trends that Japan would find it impossible to resist, and she should therefore make up her mind to open the country. In a polite reply the Shogun's high officers said that the ancestral law of Japan prevented them from acting upon his well-intentioned counsel. They overlooked the fact that the ancestral law, if there was one, did not go back farther than 1639 or thereabouts; but the Bakufu was at this time in an obscurantist mood, the Confucianist clique that had brought about Takashima's downfall being still powerful. The position of the Dutch scholars was extremely uncomfortable. The Confucianists endeavoured to suppress the study of Dutch writings altogether, and they might have succeeded had there not been a strong feeling in high quarters in favour of Dutch medical science. It resulted that for some time students who wished to pursue their inquiries into Western learning took the precaution of enrolling themselves in the schools of teachers of medicine and surgery, because it was dangerous for those who resided in Bakufu domains to display an interest in other branches of Western science.

It was in such unfavourable circumstances as these that Sakuma, after putting in his memorandum on coastal defence, pro-

SAKUMA SHŌZAN (1811–64)

ceeded to make a more thorough study of the Dutch language, so that he might read books on military science and other branches of learning. On familiar terms with most of the leading students of the period, he plunged enthusiastically into grammars and dictionaries, and it was not long before he could read Dutch with some ease. In 1846 Sanada resigned from office and returned to his fief, taking Sakuma with him. There Sakuma continued his researches and put his knowledge to practical use by experimenting in making glass and refining chemicals in accordance with instructions that he found in a Dutch encyclopædia. By 1848 he had succeeded in casting three field guns, one three-pounder, and two small quick-firing pieces. At the same time he was rapidly increasing his general knowledge of Western science and endeavouring to promote Dutch studies by publishing a revised edition of a Dutch-Japanese dictionary, the so-called *Halma,* which was an incomplete translation into Japanese of François Halma's Dutch-French dictionary, begun before 1796. But this the Yedo authorities, in their hostility to foreign learning, refused to allow.

Meanwhile, as Sakuma pursued his inquiries he became more and more impressed by the wide range of Western learning and the importance of scientific knowledge. He no longer thought that China had been conquered by sheer weight of metal, but said in a memorial to Sanada in 1849: "How is it that Western countries have been able by devotion to learning to increase their national strength to such a point that even the country of Confucius has fallen victim to their assault? It is because foreign learning is rational and Chinese learning is not." There is much more in this vein, but his argument may be abridged by saying that he comes down heavily on the side of world-wide scientific knowledge, praises Western people for their assiduous study of the real nature of the universe, and condemns those who, sunk in ancient prejudice, despise foreigners as barbarians. He has come a long way from the young man who described the English as ignorant and savage, was opposed to foreign trade, and wished to keep the sacred soil of Japan free from the contamination of foreign footsteps. He now sees the need for avoiding conflict and is all for extending the range of his country's intercourse.

His mind was always on guns and forts, but his preoccupation with these matters brought him to an admiration almost amounting to fear of the scientific attainments of the West and led him, as we have seen, to an international view. He was a voluminous writer — the standard collection contains some 2,500 pages — but his intellectual growth is neatly summarized in a few lines that he wrote in 1854, and the circumstances in which he composed them give additional point to what he said. He was at the time in prison for conniving at an offence against the exclusion laws. He said:

> When I was twenty I knew that men were linked together
> in one province
> When I was thirty I knew that they were linked together
> in one nation
> When I was forty I knew that they were linked together
> in one world of five continents.

This shows his progress from the narrow loyalty of the fief to the sentiment of national unity and thence to a feeling of membership in an international society. But it must not be inferred that he had acquired a pacific, cosmopolitan philosophy. Far from that, he retained a fiery patriotism, and all he meant was that Japan could not remain secluded but must take her place in the world and hold it. This involved learning about other countries, associating with them, understanding them, and — most important of all — using their knowledge. All his views led to the conclusion that Japan must increase her armed strength, and it is significant that among the men whom he influenced were Yamagata and Inouye, respectively the founders of the modern Japanese army and navy.

His phrase "Western science and Eastern morals" summarizes his attitude towards the problems of the day. Though he was a reformer, the conservative instinct was strong in him. He thought it possible to reach a compromise between modern life and ancient tradition. To the end he still hoped for a reconciliation between the Shogunate and the throne, standing for the principle of amalgamation known as *"Kōbu Gattai,"* according to which the military houses could collaborate in government with the civil aristocracy. Despite his modern studies he was still under the influence of his Confucian training, which is visible in all his writings. His views on all matters are to be found in his collected works expressed through the medium of Chinese verse, and even his matter-of-fact travel diaries often drop into a poetical prose, as when he notes the imperfections of coastal defences near Yedo and says: "At this sight I lifted my eyes to heaven and wept. Long my bosom heaved and long my tears o'erflowed."

Among the young men who gathered round Sakuma was an ardent patriot named Yoshida Torajiro, who was anxious to go abroad to gain knowledge he could put to his country's service. In 1854 he, with another adherent of Sakuma, attempted to board one of Perry's vessels, was discovered, and was imprisoned for a breach of the edict that forbade Japanese subjects to leave their country under pain of death. The police found on his person a farewell poem from Sakuma, who was thereupon taken into custody. He does not come out of this incident very well, for he denied that he had encouraged Yoshida. He was imprisoned, however, but released in 1862 only to be murdered after less than two years of freedom by some anti-foreign fanatics.

Sakuma Shōzan, though a remarkable man, was of a self-righteous character, with a rather vain and pompous side. A more attractive though in a worldly sense less successful member of the company of samurai who in adverse conditions strove against the exclusion policy was Watanabe Noboru, better known by his pseudonym Kwazan. Talented and versatile, poet, painter, scholar, and patriot, he took a leading part in stimulating interest in Western learning and in forming a body of opinion that, after his death, brought about the results he had desired. His was a restless life with a tragic ending, which has been fittingly recorded in the form of a romantic novel by a modern Japanese author.

At a critical stage in his career his fortunes were entangled with those of another member of the group, a certain Takano Nagahide (or Chōei, as he was often called); and it is difficult to describe the one without reference to the other. Takano, who lived from 1804 to 1850, was probably the most accomplished Dutch scholar of his day in Japan. The list of Dutch books he read and Japanese works he wrote is impressive. He published treatises on a great variety of matters, including botany, medicine, mineralogy, geography, history, and military tactics. Naturally he could not have a profound knowledge of all these subjects, and indeed the very names of some European sciences were new to the Japanese when he wrote. The wide range of his interests shows on the one hand how imperfect was the picture of the outside world as his contemporaries saw it, and on the other hand how thirsty they were for even the smallest draughts of new knowledge. We find him and his colleagues noting with excitement the most elementary facts, and sometimes misunderstanding them in a ludicrous way. But they all displayed an admirable determination to learn, and little by little their vision grew fuller and clearer, until by the time of Perry's visit they had become familiar with the leading facts about Occidental life and had mastered the rudiments of many branches of foreign learning.

Takano was born in a family of physicians living in a rustic environment. At the age of sixteen he began the study of Western medicine, which involved learning the Dutch language. Quite penniless, he had to support himself by the practice of massage, earning a few coppers each night at the end of a long day's study. After many vicissitudes he at last obtained a post in the home of a daimyo (Matsuura of Hirado, where once the Dutch and English had trading posts) by whom he was employed in translating Dutch books, most of which dealt with natural science. He began to learn something of chemistry, physiology, and similar subjects. What he learned sharpened his appetite and by 1828, in his twenty-fourth year, he had made some reputation and could look forward to a life of useful study. His prospects were good. He hoped, as he said, to put his own thoughts on a sure foundation, to accomplish something of benefit to his country, and to be a credit to his parents — characteristic ambitions of an earnest young man of his generation. But this smooth course was not to be followed by him, for late in that year, when the Dutch [8] scholar Siebold had been found to possess forbidden information, the Bakufu arrested a large number of teachers and students who had been in contact with him, and

---

[8] He was in fact a German, but prudently posed as Dutch. Takano, among others, judged from his speech that he was not Dutch.

showed signs of suppressing Western studies. Takano thought that he was in danger and fled to Kumamoto in Kyushu, where he would be free from attention. When the Siebold affair had blown over he cautiously made his way to Yedo. He told his family that he had made up his mind to sever his connection with the clan to which he belonged and to devote himself to the service of the whole country, not of a single fief. He also, though reluctantly, resigned from family duties and declared that he could not return home to marry the young woman to whom he was affianced. This was in Japanese eyes a serious step to take, and he tried to make amends by legally adopting her as his daughter and then marrying her to a man who would first enter the Takano family, so becoming its head in place of Takano himself. This was a curious but not uncommon practice, designed to secure continuity by adoption and thus to ensure the perpetuation of ancestor-worship.

Takano, though distressed by his failure to carry out his family obligations, was determined to pursue his studies until he could practice medicine, and this was impossible if he lived in a remote country place. He settled in Yedo, where he soon became well known and respected among the Dutch scholars and made friends with a large number of men interested like himself in foreign learning and extremely critical of the Bakufu.

One of these was Watanabe Kwazan, who though not an advanced student of Dutch was much interested in national affairs and anxious to learn about foreign countries. With some companions of like views he formed and presided over a society that he called "The Old Men's Club," not because of the great age of its members but to show that they were prepared to learn from scholars who were their juniors, whether in rank or in years. They met to study geography and history and military science and to discuss ways of improving the condition of Japan by the use of Western knowledge. Kwazan was of higher rank than Takano and through his connections was able to assist him and some of his colleagues and to bring into their circle useful friends.

Among these were some Bakufu officials, and at a meeting of the club in 1838 one of them disclosed the government's intention to enforce the expulsion edict against a foreign ship that was expected to arrive shortly. It was (they supposed) the *Morrison*, bringing Japanese castaways back to their country; and when Takano and his friends heard this piece of news they were much disturbed. They thought it wrong to use violence against a foreign vessel coming on a humane mission and feared that such action would have unfortunate sequels for Japan. Takano decided to write a pamphlet against the exclusion policy, pointing out its dangers and the advantage of admitting foreigners to trade. It was a strange document, purporting to relate a dream, and was of course in substance a strong criticism of the Bakufu. It was full of errors and misunderstandings. Takano supposed that the authorities had mistaken the name of a well-known English missionary in China, Dr. Robert Morrison, for the name of a ship, and did not know that the ship *Morrison* had already come and gone, after being fired upon, in the year 1837, and that the Bakufu were discussing the possibility of a further visit. Such confusion shows how little the general public knew of what was going on, how they were kept in ignorance by a policy of secrecy which was characteristic of the Tokugawa regime.[9] However, the general intention of the pamphlet was very clear, and it was widely read.

It was a grave offence to publish any criticism of official policy, and the magistrate Torii (the "Demon," who has been mentioned above as the persecutor of the gunnery expert Takashima) recommended the arrest of Takano and his associates. No immediate steps were taken, however, and the Old Men continued to talk and write against the government. Torii meanwhile was spreading his net and by the summer of 1838 he reported to the Council of State a conspiracy in which, he alleged, a number of daimyo and samurai were implicated. He brought false charges against them, saying that they were in communication with the barbarians and planned to colonize some uninhabited islands off the coast of Japan, which could be used as a base of operations against the government. The chief Minister of State, Mizuno Tadakuni, hesitated to take open action, because the plot, if it existed, implicated some important persons in the powerful fiefs of Satsuma and Mito and some Bakufu officers who could count on protection in high quarters. There was a very thin substance to Torii's charges, since Kwazan and his friends had talked of transferring peasants to an island that could be developed as a means of relieving distress in poor farming areas on the mainland; and it was true that all or most of the people accused had been in communication with members of the Old Men's club. This in itself was a sign that dissatisfaction with the Bakufu was spreading in the clans, and showed that the Dutch Scholars were gaining influential support. But Mizuno knew that if he proceeded against persons of high rank some disconcerting scandals might be uncovered, and it was therefore decided to arrest only Kwazan, Takano, and a few minor figures.

Kwazan was summoned before a magistrate on June 24, 1839. He was able to warn Takano, who at once went into hiding. Kwazan was imprisoned that night and all his books and papers were confiscated. Takano was urged by his friends to escape from Yedo,

---

[9] It was not until a year after the *Morrison's* arrival that the Bakufu learned from the Dutch the name of the ship and the purpose of its visit.

but he refused, saying that since his pamphlet was the cause of all the trouble, he could not honorably remain free while Kwazan was in danger. "If I should conceal myself only for a short time, still I should be a man of darkness forever," he is reported to have said; and he gave himself up after settling his private affairs as best he could, being protected meanwhile by his friends.

From this point the histories of the two men followed different courses, though both came to the same end, taking their own lives in despair. Takano was condemned to life imprisonment after a perfunctory trial in which he conducted himself with courage. Accused of misleading the public by writing about things he did not understand, he was asked how he could describe in his pamphlets the condition of foreign countries that he had not seen. He had in fact given a very dreamlike account of the English and some remarkable views on the political influence of Dr. Morrison, which would have astounded that distinguished scholar, who, however, had died some years before the pamphlet was written. But Takano boldly replied: "We do not know that anybody has gone up to the heavens, but we have astronomers. We do not know that anybody has gone down into the earth, but we have geologists. . . . There is an inner eye with which such things can be seen." He was angrily silenced, and on Febrary 1, 1840 he was condemned. We may here leave the story of Takano's life, noting only that he escaped after a fire in the prison in 1844; led a wandering life for several years, never staying long in one place and living on fees for translating books on military science, paid to him by friendly daimyos; was traced by spies in 1846; evaded pursuit; travelled in disguise, translating and teaching when it appeared safe, always impelled by patriotic zeal to spread new knowledge; and at last reached Yedo, where (betrayed by a former fellow prisoner) he was come upon at night by police officers and, having killed one of them, calmly committed harakiri. This was late in the year 1850, only three years before the arrival of Perry's ships, which could not, as the Bakufu well knew, be treated like the *Morrison*.

Against this dark background let us now look at the career of Kwazan, not as a student of affairs and a political offender, but rather as a man displaying the most attractive aspects of the culture of his class in the late winter of feudal society. He was the son of a samurai of good standing in the small Tawara fief, which was situated on the seaboard of Mikawa, Ieyasu's home province. Like many daimiates it was in financial difficulties, and these were severely felt by samurai of all but the highest rank, whose stipends were reduced and often even unpaid. Kwazan's family was therefore poor, and as a youth he was obliged to support it by painting fans and lampshades for sale, alongside of his studies in Chinese.

He took lessons from Tani Buncho and other masters, displaying great versatility, and before long had gained a good reputation as an artist. During his turns of duty in Yedo he frequented the society of painters and writers (we have already seen him at a party given by the novelist Bakin), and among all those who knew him he was well liked for his lively and generous spirit and well thought of for his strong sense of duty. His services as an official of the Tawara clan were valuable, and he was picked out for promotion to the rank of counsellor, thereby arousing some jealousy among his colleagues. In this capacity he devoted himself to questions of coastal defence and to the improvement of economic conditions in the Tawara domain, which had suffered from the disastrous famine of 1833. His records of journeys of inspection and his notes on taxation, agriculture, peasant unrest, and agrarian problems in general show that he was a capable and popular official who, in difficult times, gained that kind of experience in administration which made it possible a generation later for comparatively junior samurai to take over the administration of the country without any serious breach of continuity. It was men of his type who were both the authors and the leaders of the revolutionary movement of the 1860's.

His entry into the company of students of Western science was of value to them, since he had a practical experience of affairs in which most of them were lacking, and so he easily gained their respect as well as their affection. When he was arrested all his friends, not least his fellow painters, rallied to his support at considerable risk to themselves. They managed to correspond with him while he was in jail awaiting trial and sent him small gifts to lessen the rigours of imprisonment, which were to be dreaded in those days. He was ill and wretched — his health never recovered from the effects of more than six months' incarceration — but he did not lose courage. In the letters he was able to smuggle out he dwells not on his own misfortunes but on the grief and trouble he is causing to others. There is at times a note of humour also, as when he relates that he is on good terms with his fellow inmates, who respectfully call him Master, and even the prison officials like to talk to him about art and pester him with their conversation. "In fact," he says, "I am not badly off here, only about as uncomfortable as I should be undergoing treatment at a medicinal hot spring." During those months he hoped for a mild sentence, but he was prepared for capital punishment and was even informed that this would be his fate. He had contrived to obtain paper and brushes and made a number of sketches of prison life. Among these is one that shows himself, in manacles, seated between two jailers, who have announced that he is to receive the death sentence. He has been perhaps overpraised as a painter, but his quick impressions show a great virtuosity, and none more than this unusual example. It may be noted here that his sketches for portraits are very telling, and show some Western influence.

A number of letters, diaries, and notes have been preserved which show that great efforts were made to secure his acquittal. They give an interesting picture of a grim aspect of life in those days of intrigue and suspicion, false witness and jealousy, underground negotiations, cruelty and fear. It is a picture in which all members of the military caste do not shine as virtuous figures. But it is relieved by the loyal conduct of his former associates. It also shows how widespread was discontent not only among samurai but in other ranks of society, for the ramifications of the anti-seclusion movement extended in all directions. In the list of suspects there appear the names of priests, artisans, and tradesmen as well as scholars. The Bakufu was on the alert to suppress its critics. There is a revealing passage in a letter in which one of Kwazan's friends discusses with another the draft of an appeal for clemency. It runs as follows: "Do not speak of him too favourably or give the impression that you are intimate with him. That would go against him, for what the authorities most fear in these days is a man of promise who is one of a party."

Kwazan was fortunate in his friends and, no doubt thanks to their endeavours, his penalty was reduced to life imprisonment. Because he was a trusted retainer of a feudatory of some consequence he was handed over to officials of his own clan for perpetual domiciliary confinement. This was in February 1840. Weak and ill from prison life, he was carried in a small locked palanquin over the Hakone Pass on a bitter winter's day, suffering agony from cramp and fainting on the way. But on arrival in Tawara he was well enough treated and lived in a small house under guard, studying and painting and carrying on a clandestine correspondence with his former associates, but on literary and artistic matters rather than political. He remained thus for a few months, but he had enemies in his own clan, and they spread a false report that the Bakufu was about to bring further charges against him. This came to his ears, as they had intended, and he felt that he might cause difficulties for his feudal lord. He decided to commit suicide and ended his life in November 1841. He left a number of touching letters, explaining his motives and condemning himself as a failure who had brought shame upon his clan and misery upon his family. His farewell letter to his younger brother is very brief. It begs him to take care of their aged mother, apologizes for his own conduct, and ends: "I will write no more, for this kind of letter is only a source of tears." Writing to his son, he tells him in two lines to carry out his filial duty to his grandmother and to his unhappy mother, and signs: "Your disloyal and unfilial father, Noboru."

It is sometimes said that the samurai code of behaviour was narrow and class-bound, essentially selfish. There is some truth in this charge, for it was a code that was developed to sustain a society dominated by a military caste and depending upon the ruthless maintenance of privilege. But it must be admitted that, as practised by men like Kwazan, it encouraged an admirable rectitude. His life shows also that it was consistent with warmth of feeling, breadth of interest, and devotion to the public good.

In reviewing the careers of men like him one is struck by their sense of dedication. Their writings, like their actions, all express deep feelings of loyalty and filial piety, the two virtues most esteemed in the society in which they lived, and it is noteworthy that the real tragedy of their careers arises from a conflict between two ideals that are often irreconcilable. They were exceptional people and though they failed to fulfil their immediate purposes their example had great influence upon the next generation, and they are still regarded as important figures in the history of their country.

They were followed by other ardent reformers who, though they played no great role in the politics of the Restoration period, inspired many of its leaders. Some knowledge of their lives helps to an understanding of their times — the twenty years before 1868.

Yokoi Shōnan, like his contemporary Sakuma, was assassinated for his views, which were regarded among reactionary samurai as unduly favourable to foreigners. Shōnan was a samurai born in Kumamoto in 1809, and starting like most of his kind as a student of Chinese philosophy, he displayed prodigious talent in his youth. He was in Yedo from 1839 and became well known among other Confucian scholars, forming a special friendship with certain members of the Mito clan, whose Daimyo, though head of one of the main branches of the Tokugawa family, carried on a tradition of scholarship hostile to the Bakufu and favourable to the Imperial house. Shōnan in the course of his studies had reached the conclusion that the official Chu Hsi philosophy "had form but not substance" and was therefore impractical. His mind turned to a kind of realism which under his leadership became popular among the more advanced or open-minded samurai. That several fiefs competed for his services can be taken as a sign of the current dissatisfaction. Mito leaders invited him to put his wisdom at their disposal, but he declined such offers and returned to his own province, where he set up a school, to which students flocked. His view was that the modern samurai were taken up, besotted almost, with art and letters, to the neglect of political and social studies which the times demanded; and the aim of his teaching was described as the encouragement of real, practical learning. His group, known as the Practical Party, aroused opposition especially among physicians of the old school of medicine, who discovered that Shōnan, having been cured of a complaint by a doctor of the Dutch school, was in favour of Western science.

From about 1849 he travelled throughout the country, observing conditions and expounding his views. He became more and more persuaded of the need for reforms as he began to take an interest in gunnery, navigation, and other branches of Western science. When Perry's arrival split opinion in Japan, Shōnan firmly expressed the view that the question of opening the country should not be decided in panic and anger, but on grounds of principle, which must be considered without prejudice. This sounds almost obvious, but the fact that he had to say it is a measure of the violence of controversy that Perry's visit had aroused. Shōnan considered that the country as a whole disliked the exclusion policy and that it should be reviewed irrespective of the demands of the foreign powers.

In 1857 he had been invited by Matsudaira Shungaku, lord of Echizen, to visit his fief as an adviser. Shōnan agreed to this and on his arrival was treated with great respect by officials of the clan. Shungaku had been ordered to retire because he had displeased the Bakufu, but in the last days of the Shogunate he played, under Shōnan's influence, an important part as a mediator, being by then strongly in favour of foreign intercourse and at the same time, because of family connections, sympathetic with the house of Tokugawa and anxious to protect its dignity. By the end of 1857, when negotiations with the American envoy had gone a long way, the question at issue was no longer the simple acceptance of further engagements but the extent to which impending changes in Japan's foreign relations would necessitate a reform of domestic institutions. Shōnan himself had by now become convinced that full international intercourse was necessary and a great expansion of foreign trade. He already saw that a drastic reform of the current system of government was necessary. When in 1858 he decided to accept Shungaku's offer of employment in Echizen, his friends had asked him how he reconciled this with the classic rule of undivided loyalty, the principle that a samurai could not serve two masters. He had replied: "The times are such that we must not be fettered by such old maxims," thereby knocking out one of the pillars of feudal ethics. In Echizen he worked out with like-minded people various plans for domestic reform. He showed one of his drafts to Okubo Ichio, a trusted Bakufu retainer who held relatively advanced views and saw the need for change. One article in the draft proposed that the periodical attendance of daimyo in Yedo should be abolished, and their families should be sent home. This was too much for Okubo, who said with truth that it would break down the system upon which the Tokugawa depended. Shōnan retorted: "Well, if the daimyo withdrew from Yedo without notifying the Bakufu, what could be done to prevent them?" and Okubo was obliged to reply: "Nothing!"

This incident — it occurred in 1862 — shows how much the authority of the Bakufu had declined. It had lost its power of decision and did not know where to look for advice. It even turned to such men as Shōnan himself, who was offered employment but declined. His mind was now on the future, and he began to take an interest in naval problems, proposing to send his son to America for training as a naval officer. This was in 1866, when he had of course become a convinced and open advocate of full intercourse with the West. He was now a target of suspicion and hatred among the anti-foreign party and was killed by assassins early in 1869, but not before he had received a high appointment under the Meiji government. He was in close touch with Yuri Kimimasa and Fukuoka Kotei, two men who drafted some of the fundamental documents of the Meiji era, and it is clear that his influence upon them was considerable. His name appears with those of Okubo, Kido, Saigo, and other Restoration leaders in the first list of counsellors issued by the Meiji government in 1868.

The development of his political thought provides an interesting study. As a young man he held very strong anti-foreign views and wrote some fiery poems about the disgrace of dealing with Western barbarians. But his "practical" reasoning brought him to the view that it was "in accordance with the laws of heaven and earth" to open the country. In a later phase he developed ideas of universal peace and the brotherhood of man, propounding a kind of One World doctrine. Looking back at the condition of Japan at that time, it is at first sight difficult to understand how Shōnan and many other patriotic scholars who had some idea of the nature of Western civilization could have seriously entertained the view that their own country could one day attain to world leadership. But it is clear that they saw nothing irrational in such ambitions, and it must be remembered that one of the central features of Chinese political doctrine was a belief that China was the centre of the world, the Middle Kingdom from which irradiated a gracious benevolence to the four quarters. This in substance was what the celebrated Commissioner Lin wrote in 1839 in a letter to Queen Victoria, saying: "Our Divine House reckons as its family all within the Four Seas, and our great Emperor with Divine Grace offers shelter to all distant lands." Such remarkable pretensions did not appear excessive to Japanese scholars brought up on Chinese history; and it must be admitted that other countries have often made similar claims to universal benevolence. Shōnan's idea is uncomfortably like the later proposals of Germany to spread her *Kultur* throughout the world, and — though he did not know it at the time — the Western nations that in the 1850's were pestering Japan to open her doors justified their action on the ground that they were bringing to that fortunate country noble principles and a better life. This was a prosy version of Ch'ien Lung's offer of the shelter of his divine grace.

Certainly Shōnan appears to have believed sincerely in the expansion of Japan by moral rather than by material force, though he thought that a big navy was necessary. But the celebrated journalist and popular (but very tendentious) historian Tokutomi Soho describes him as in essence an imperialist. Tokutomi himself (of the same clan as Shōnan, whom he much admired) was in his early days an ardent liberal and a supporter of the Christian movement. He later became a convinced nationalist and his writings took on a tinge of xenophobia. In one of his works written in 1916 with the object of stimulating the patriotism of Japanese youth he gives a list of the early advocates of foreign intercourse and says that they were all good imperialists. He cites Rin Shihei, Honda Toshiaki, Sato Shingen, and Yokoi Shōnan as favouring policies of expansion without limit. Thus, whatever may have been Shōnan's true feelings, they were later interpreted as supporting a national policy of expansion.

It may be that this was to do an injustice to Shōnan, but there can be little doubt that most leaders of the anti-Bakufu, Westernization movement before 1853 took the line that Japan must reform and unify her domestic government, engage in foreign trade and develop her armed strength with the ultimate object of expansion in Asia. Sato Shingen (a competent administrator and no mere visionary), who was in touch with Shōnan, wrote in 1823 a book called *Kondō Hisaku* (*A Secret Plan of Absorption*), proposing domestic reforms that, he argued, were essential before Japan could undertake the conquest of China and the rest of the world. A generation later came Yoshida Shōin, whose career merits some notice in this connection.

Yoshida Torajiro, or Shōin as he is usually called, is a puzzling character. A cursory reading of his biography gives the impression that he was foolish, fanatical, and ineffective. He was full of high ideals, grand visions, and ambitious projects, yet he failed in almost all his undertakings large and small, for want, one would say, of common sense. It is not easy for a foreign student to understand why he so strongly influenced the minds of his contemporaries and was so extravagantly praised by later generations. It is clear that there is something in his life which appeals to the emotions of his compatriots, and it calls for study on that account.

He was born in 1830 near the castle town of Hagi in Chōshū, son of a samurai of low rank, and was adopted as a child into a family named Yoshida, which carried on professionally the teaching of Yamaga Sokō, a distinguished Confucianist and professor of military science in the seventeenth century. Shōin turned out to be a small and skinny youth, very precocious and fond of study. It was characteristic of the simple and frugal life of most of the western clansmen — in contrast to the soft habits of the town-dwelling Tokugawa retainers — that his adoptive father, at the end of his daily official duties, would dig in his own small piece of land; and there are many pictures of young Shōin standing in a rice-field with a hoe in one hand and a book in the other. So strong was the hereditary principle in feudal society that when the elder Yoshida died Shōin at the age of six succeeded him as head of the Yamaga school of military science in the clan. This was, of course, only a nominal post, but by the age of eleven he was lecturing before his feudal lord on the Chinese military classic of Sun-tzŭ.

It is not surprising that he should have developed into a prematurely solemn young man, and no doubt this early training accounts for much that seems unnatural and even priggish in his character. From his early boyhood he began to hear tales of the doings of Western powers in Oriental countries, the advance of England from India to China, the threatening visits of Russian and American ships. These stimulated his patriotic feelings and led him to think almost exclusively of political matters. Reform of this or that was always in his mind. He wrote long memorials and delivered long lectures, he travelled about inspecting coastal defences in the Choshu territory — this was when he was about twenty years old — and he studied assiduously the while. He paid a visit to Nagasaki, where he learned a little Dutch and colloquial Chinese, observing the foreigners and their ways with grave attention. Passing on to Kumamoto, he listened there to much political talk and heard of the realistic views of Yokoi Shōnan. He was more impressed by the opinions of a party of loyalists who enlarged on the theme of reverence for the Emperor and its corollary, hatred of the Tokugawa. All over Japan earnest young soldiers and scholars were excitedly talking, talking, revolving in their minds this scheme and that for bettering the times, seeking for some golden rule that would resolve their doubts and dissatisfactions.

The doctrine of loyalty to the throne, the apotheosis of the Emperor, seemed to offer a solution for many of their difficulties, but

SKETCH BY WATANABE KWAZAN

*Made in prison, it shows himself, manacled, being informed
that he is to be sentenced to death.*

THE OPIUM WAR

The British Fleet assembles below London Bridge for the voyage to China.
A Japanese conception from New Tales of Foreign Lands (Kaigai Shinwa) *by Mineta (18*

they all felt deficient in knowledge and sought from one teacher after another a key to questions that troubled them. Something was wrong with their country, they did not know what. Perhaps it was that its culture had come to a standstill? It could not be that humanity was at fault, for there must be some principle, if only they could discover it, by preaching which they could set the world to rights. They were bewildered young men, they knew so little of that world, their lives were so cramped and confined. It is not to be wondered at that they should often have started upon wild missions or welcomed fantastic theories as if they were golden rules.

In 1851 Shōin went to Yedo with his feudal lord, to carry his studies further. There he met Sakuma Shōzan, under whom he worked for a time. But he wanted to travel and agreed with some friends to start for the northern provinces on a certain day — it was the anniversary of the suicide of the Forty-seven Rōnin. Because his passport did not come in time, he set off without it, thereby disobeying the rules of his clan. This meant that he must lose his samurai rank and the income that went with it, but he seems to have found pleasure in the thought that he was thus committed to a larger loyalty. He was now at the service of the whole country. So the small, scrawny, untidy figure of Yoshida, not very clean in his person, wearing a sword too large for him, was to be seen striding off on his way to the north. He called at Mito, where the scholars had for centuries been studying Japanese history, teaching that the Shogun was a fraud and the Emperor was a divine sovereign of a country with a divine mission. One day, so thought some of Yoshida's friends, Japan must spread to the continent of Asia and, perhaps making a defensive alliance with Russia, go on to capture lands in India and in South America, and even in Europe. He went about in the northern provinces and returned to Yedo impressed by the value of travel, conscious that he knew only a narrow world.

During all this time he was learning his own ignorance, but his mind was full of lofty designs. He went back to his province in 1852, where he was formally deprived of his rank, and then returned to Yedo in 1853 to resume his work under Sakuma Shōzan and to meet a number of young men interested in foreign studies. This was the year of the first visit of the American squadron under Commodore Perry and he soon conceived the idea of going abroad, encouraged by Sakuma. With characteristic enthusiasm he started off for Nagasaki, where there was a Russian warship; and with characteristic misjudgment he tarried too long on the way and found that the Russians had left. He had met Yokoi Shōnan in Kumamoto and been impressed by his views. He was a great one for listening to views, though sometimes loud-mouthed in contradiction, and he listened so much that he did not get back to Yedo until the end of 1853.

Long and frequent discussions with Sakuma strengthened his decision to smuggle himself aboard one of Perry's ships, which returned to Shimoda early in 1854. He and a friend, one Kaneko Shigesuke, made for the coast and hung about for days trying to find the ships and to make contact with an American. Yoshida carried in his bosom as well as a farewell poem from Sakuma a supply of paper and brushes for use in taking notes when he should reach foreign parts. He had made no other preparations, for his plans were of the vaguest and they always failed. Towards the end of April, after several disappointments, the two men at last managed during the middle watch to steal a fisherman's boat and row out towards the steam frigate *Mississippi*. They bungled this, breaking an oar-lock and drifting about helplessly, but they at length contrived to reach the ship blistered and exhausted, though they nearly fell into the sea as they jumped to the gangplank. The ship's officers sympathized with them in their plight, but could do nothing to help them, since the Commodore could not connive at a breach of Japanese law, and it seemed moreover possible that this was a ruse to test the good faith of the Americans. They were therefore put ashore in a ship's boat while it was still dark.

The full story of their attempt is told in *The Japan Expedition*, by J. W. Spalding, who with a comrade had that morning been stealthily approached by Yoshida and Kaneko on the beach near Shimoda. With great precaution they had pressed on him a letter in Chinese addressed to the High Officer of the American ships. A day or two later officers on shore leave saw a small cage in which two Japanese were confined. These were Yoshida and Kaneko. They had been arrested on the day following their adventure and were being held for transport to Yedo. [10]

After some months in jail awaiting a final verdict Yoshida was handed over to his own clan for punishment and carried back to his province, where at the end of a year's close confinement he was released and put under simple house arrest, his unfortunate companion having meanwhile died in prison. He then opened a small village school where among his pupils were Ito, Yamagata, and other young Chōshū men of about his own age, who were to figure prominently in the Restoration period. He taught here for over two years, and the lessons were on politics. He discussed the prob-

[10] Spalding's book is a useful corrective to the solemnities of the official narrative of Perry's expedition. He had a lively style and was addicted to poetical extracts. Describing the impression made upon the Japanese by the guns of the squadron, he refers to howitzers as "the mortal engines whose rude throats Jove's dread clamors counterfeit," and after those cacophonous lines he says that a blockade in the bay of Yedo would "stop the throat of the Japanese empire."

lems of the day, the treatment of foreigners, how to deal with the Shogun, how to serve the Emperor, how to protect the country.

There can be no doubt that this seemingly hopeless, helpless, ineffectual man was a most inspired teacher, of a selfless and inflaming zeal. Traces of his influence appear in political history after his death. His death was very near. In 1858 he and some of his pupils developed a raging hostility to the Bakufu and plotted the assassination of an official called Manabe, who had been sent to Kyoto to persuade the court to agree to a treaty with the United States. Like all his plans, this miscarried. He had no control over his own impulses, and once the idea came into his head he burned to escape from Chōshū and kill Manabe with his own hands, because he thought that by striking at the Bakufu he could bring about the restoration of the Emperor. He was persuaded to wait, but he could not check his own wild talk and he wrote indiscreet letters that caused the clan authorities to put him back under arrest. The Shogun's men had got wind of his conspiracy from his enemies in his own clan, and his fellow conspirators had been reckless. He was sent to Yedo for trial soon afterwards. This was the time of what was called the Great Persecution of Ansei, when the Bakufu was taking the harshest measures against its adversaries. In Yedo he was thrown into the Temma-cho jail, then crammed with loyalists awaiting judgment; and after three months he was beheaded on October 27, 1859. Kido and Ito, two Chōshū samurai who were within less than ten years to become leaders of the government, took his corpse from the execution ground and buried it in a near-by temple. That they should have undertaken this pious duty shows in what great respect he was held by his contemporaries.

To reach a just estimate of his character would require as well as sympathetic insight a careful study of his environment and many details of contemporary history. His life is briefly recorded here because, in spite of all his weaknesses and his perpetual failures, he must be regarded as an important figure, expressing the revolutionary spirit of his era. He wrote well and fluently, both prose and verse, as was the habit of his kind, although he was no calligrapher, being too impatient for an art that needs calm and poise. His literary remains are considerable. They contain besides some touching passages many alert and pointed observations and much elevated sentiment. In the last two days in jail awaiting execution he scribbled in prose and verse what he called *Ryūkonroku,* or the *Record of an Uneasy Spirit,* the tale of his unsatisfied wishes and his uncompleted plans. The prison diaries of those days are vivid pieces of historical evidence, and Yoshida's is among the most pathetic. He knew that he was a failure and he expressed

a kind of proud repentance, but the best thing that he said justified all his errors, for he declared: "I would rather be wrong in
giving than wrong in receiving. I would rather be wrong in dying
than wrong in living."

Perhaps the most ironic thing in a life full of ironies is the text
of his death sentence, which sets forth the following reasons for his
conviction:

Item: He tried to go to America.

Item: He advised the government on coastal defence while in jail.

Item: He opposed hereditary succession to office and favoured the selection of able men by popular vote.

Item: He planned to give his opinion regarding foreigners to the Bakufu.

Item: He did such things while in domiciliary confinement, thus showing great disrespect for high officials.

It is pleasant to recall that his story appealed to Robert Louis
Stevenson, who tells it in his *Familiar Studies of Men and Books.*
His piece is a somewhat garbled version of the facts of Yoshida's
life, but he seizes upon its essence.

CHAPTER

12

THE LAST PHASE OF THE SHOGUNATE

1. External Pressure

So far we have considered principally the visits of Russian and English ships to the shores of Japan, since they began earlier than those of American ships and continued at long intervals throughout the period of seclusion. But the visits of American ships deserve separate treatment, because it was in the long run American pressure that brought about the opening of Japan. [1]

Though Russian and British ships frequently entered Japanese harbours with requests for trade they had no success. Neither the Russian nor the British government appears to have had any firm policy as to opening trade relations, and the rebuffs of the Japanese authorities were accepted without protest. The only determined attempt of the English to force their way into commerce was that of Raffles, who in an endeavour to break the Dutch monopoly sent two vessels in 1813 and one in 1814, but did not succeed in his object and could obtain no government support for a further approach. From that time onwards with very few exceptions such English visits as took place were made by naval vessels engaged in surveying-operations, and these had no political or commercial purpose. Something of the same kind can be said of the Russian visits. Though rather more persistent they do not appear to have had a strong government drive behind them.

Both countries were interested in the Far East, but during the first half of the nineteenth century both were usually preoccupied with European problems and from the end of the Napoleonic wars the English effort in commercial expansion was concentrated upon the East Indian and the China trade. There is very little sign of a strong interest on the part of English merchants in the possibilities of a valuable trade with Japan, and even the China trade was re-

[1] The first recorded visit of an American ship was made by the *Eliza* in 1797, under charter of the Dutch, but flying American colours. Two arrivals in 1790 and 1791 are reported by the Japanese, but those ships appear to have taken refuge from storms.

garded by the British government (though not by the Canton merchants) as subsidiary or complementary to the East Indian trade. Indeed, just prior to the opening of Japan it was thought by many English business men that Japan, being a poor country, would have little to sell and therefore could not afford to buy English manufactures. It is significant in this connection that the agreement concluded by Great Britain with Japan in October 1854 by Admiral Stirling does not mention trade. The Russian agreement does, however, provide for trade at the open ports.

These are at this late date perhaps unimportant points, but they are of some interest in the light of the fears of Russian and English aggression entertained by the Japanese before 1853. As it turned out it was the American government and American traders that forced the issue. Their attitude was much more determined than that of other Western countries, for it so happened that they were developing a strong general interest in eastern Asia and had moreover a specific grievance against Japan. From before 1800 Americans had traded in the North Pacific and particularly after 1812 American ships had begun to play a leading part in the whaling industry. Whalers in the Sea of Okhotsk were from time to time driven by storms on to the shores of Yezo or the Kuriles, and the treatment of shipwrecked crews by the Japanese was a source of constant friction, as was also the treatment of American ships endeavouring to repatriate Japanese sailors whom they had picked up at sea. Public attention was drawn to these matters, and proposals were put before Congress that missions should be sent to arrange commercial intercourse with Japan and Korea. In 1835 the United States government had taken some preliminary steps by designating a diplomatic agent, Edmund Roberts, to make inquiries about opening communications with Japan. Roberts died in 1836 and was buried in the English cemetery at Canton, so that nothing came of this move; but in 1845 Commodore James Biddle, acting under instructions from Washington, took two warships into Yedo Bay and in the name of his government proposed the opening of trade relations. To this the Bakufu returned a flat refusal, and Biddle retired. The American government did not lose patience, but remained determined to persuade the Japanese government to agree to such arrangements as would ensure the good treatment of shipwrecked seamen, provide a badly needed port of call where American ships could obtain fuel and other supplies, and permit of an agreed trade.

The Japanese government knew very well what was coming; and it may be pointed out here that the warnings of such patriots as Takashima, Sakuma, and others, though useful as goads to action, conveyed no new information to the high officials in Yedo. In fact in 1852 they expected a visit from the then Commodore of the American squadron in Chinese waters, who had been instructed in 1851 to proceed to Japan with a letter from President Fillmore. When, therefore, on July 8, 1853, Commodore Perry (he having been appointed instead of the officer first designated) appeared with four men-of-war in the harbour of Uraga, his visit came as no surprise. Even the approximate date of his arrival was known to the Japanese authorities, for on his way to Japan he had first called at the Luchu Islands, whence news was speedily passed on to Yedo.

The story of Commodore Perry's negotiations is too familiar to need repetition here. All that need be said is that, after some preliminary obstruction by minor officials, he succeeded in inducing the representatives of the Bakufu to accept for transmission to the Shogun a letter from the President, his own credentials, and a letter from himself in which he made it clear that, although his country had friendly intentions, it would insist upon carrying out its policy of securing good treatment for distressed American seamen, and some facilities for navigation and trade. There was no open threat, but only a statement that he would return with a larger force next spring, when he hoped to receive a favourable reply. There can be no doubt that he was prepared to use force if necessary and that the Japanese authorities were left under no illusion on this point. In that sense the policy of the United States government differed little, if at all, from that which other Occidental countries had adopted in their dealings with Oriental countries reluctant to enter into relationships with them. Japan was brought to agreement by a demonstration of power. In an age when this was orthodox practice, Perry was as determined to achieve his object as would have been the representative of one of the countries that had perhaps less respect for national sovereignty.

It is clear from the voluminous records of his expedition that he and his government, though their aim was naturally the promotion of American interests, were convinced that they were acting in a most enlightened and benevolent way. Like most Western people at that date, they were thoroughly confident, not to say complacent, as to the rightness of their views and the perfection of their culture. Whether the Japanese liked it or not, the West proposed to confer upon them the benefits of Western civilization. It was good for them. Perry therefore would have felt no misgivings on moral grounds if he had been obliged to use force. The private records of the expedition are sprinkled with such phrases as the "nobler principles," the "better life" of a "higher civilization," which were to be put at Japan's disposal; and in the less lofty language of the official correspondence similar ideas are implicit.

But Perry was exceedingly anxious not to resort to strong measures if he could attain his object in other ways, and great praise is due to him for the combination of dignity, firmness, and skill which he displayed in his dealings with a very difficult people, masters of evasion and procrastination. His position was even stronger than he at first thought,[2] for every responsible Japanese official knew in his heart that Japan was powerless. Those concerned with the defences of Yedo in particular were aware not only of the uselessness of their forts and guns, but also of the danger to the city of an interruption of its food supplies. These were brought to the bay of Yedo in barges, which the American guns could easily have destroyed, so starving the city.

When Perry returned to Japan in February 1854 with a more powerful squadron, he had no great difficulty in completing his negotiations within a few weeks, and on March 31, 1854 a treaty was concluded that opened two ports (Shimoda and Hakodate) to American vessels and gave certain limited concessions in respect of trade, while it provided for American consular representation in Japan. Thus the period of seclusion, which had lasted for more than two hundred years, was brought to an end. The American treaty was followed by similar agreements between Japan and Great Britain (October 1854), Russia (February 1855), Holland (November 1855).

The details of the negotiations and the treaties do not concern us here, but some aspects of the meetings between the members of the American mission and Japanese officers may be singled out for attention, as bearing upon the condition of Japan at the time and upon the attitude of the people towards foreigners.

Once the bargaining was over and the Japanese negotiators saw that they could temporize no longer, the formality of intercourse gave way to a certain cheerful intimacy. In their strolls about the countryside the American officers noted a generally friendly disposition on the part of the people, which officials often endeavoured to check. More striking, perhaps, was the insatiable curiosity that most of their Japanese interlocutors displayed. They asked endless questions, examined the clothing and equipment of the Americans with the closest interest. There was much peering and prying and taking notes and making sketches. Everything interested them, and when it was permitted they visited the American ships in droves. Most of such visitors were mere sightseers, but at times, by night and in secret, a young samurai would row out and implore to be taken on board so that he could get to America and learn about the world. The law was against this, and the American

---

[2] But his officers soon perceived the great number of coasting junks and realized that a blockade would be very effective.

officers were obliged to refuse them. At times these adventurers were tracked down by the police and paid the penalty of death. One of them was that Yoshida Torajiro who has already been described and whose capture led to the imprisonment of Sakuma Shōzan as an accomplice. A genuine desire to learn was present, as well as mere curiosity; and much had been learned already, as the American officers soon discovered. Their general impression was that the Japanese were far better informed than they had supposed, and knew very well what kind of information they lacked.

One of the most interesting episodes of the expedition was the formal exchange of gifts that took place shortly before the signing of the treaty. There were displayed on the one hand such Japanese products as silken stuffs, gold lacquer, and porcelain, on the other such distinctive embodiments of the Western way of life as rifles, pistols, and swords; a miniature locomotive, with tender, passenger car, and rails; a set of telegraph apparatus, some books, among which were Webster's *Dictionary* and Audubon's *Birds of America;* and various strong liquors, including cherry cordials, champagne, maraschino, and one hundred gallons of whisky. The Americans were disappointed by the Japanese gifts, which they thought were meagre, and they noted the absence of rich and precious things which their ideas of Oriental magnificence had led them to expect. It might be supposed that the Japanese, with their high æsthetic tradition, would have thought poorly of the plain and practical objects offered by the Americans. But far from showing such feelings, they displayed great interest and excitement at the sight of the mechanical devices and the death-dealing instruments spread out before them. The working of the locomotive and the telegraph gave immense pleasure, and many of those present showed a good knowledge of the way in which various machines should be set up and manipulated. But most popular of all were the revolvers. Everybody wanted one of these delightful implements. And as for the liquors, the Japanese visitors to the American ships had already shown, sometimes all too clearly, their enjoyment of stimulating drinks. Indeed, one of the memories of the Americans from their last visit was a picture of the negotiator Kagawa, as his boat rowed away from the *Susquehanna,* knocking the neck off a bottle of wine and drinking a farewell toast. Even the most reserved of his colleagues had not failed to show that they needed no lessons in conviviality, once their business on board was done and they were offered refreshment. In the alcoholic world, there was a complete meeting of minds as between East and West.

The exchange of gifts was followed by agreeable entertainments, and here also the confrontation of cultures offers matter of interest to the student. To amuse their foreign guests the Japanese provided an exhibition of wrestling of the kind known as *sumō*, contests between very large and corpulent but extremely athletic men, which are conducted in a somewhat hieratic fashion. The Americans, though they could not but admire the strength of the wrestlers, found this performance disgustingly brutal. This was a very odd sentiment to come from fellow citizens of the Benicia Boy and other heroes of the prize ring.[3] But characteristically they turned to the locomotive, which demonstrated their national faith in the triumph of machines over muscle, and it must be said that the Japanese were not behind them in appreciating the value of steam engines and electrical apparatus. They swarmed round the track, climbed on to the little coaches, and thoroughly enjoyed the fun of riding at twenty miles an hour.

That evening the leading Japanese officials and interpreters were invited to dine on board the flagship. They ate and drank copiously and exchanged many toasts until they adjourned for a minstrel entertainment. It was a most hilarious occasion. The Japanese guests can scarcely have appreciated the finer points in the exchanges of wit between Mr. Bones and his colleagues; but though this exhibition of Western culture was something quite beyond their own æsthetic experience, they laughed heartily at the costumes and antics of the performers, and even the chief delegate, Hayashi Daigaku no Kami, the Lord Rector of the University and the Chief Confucian Adviser to the Shogun, a very grave statesman, was seen to share in the fun, though without any loss of impressive dignity.

So it appeared that most cordial relations had been established, and after one of the tipsy Japanese delegates had embraced the Commodore and announced that Japanese and Americans had the same kind of feelings, the signature of the treaty seemed assured. And so it was, for on March 31, 1854 the main purpose of Perry's mission was accomplished. He could well congratulate himself on his success in carrying out a most difficult task without the violence and bloodshed that might easily have occurred.

Apart from a few unfortunate minor incidents his men had behaved well and, to judge from the records, his officers were fine representatives of their profession. Before they left they began to see much to admire in Japanese life, even though they felt that, by their standards, there was also much to deplore.

But while the Commodore's negotiations had proceeded in an atmosphere of comparative calm and even at times of cordiality, the country as a whole was in a state of confusion and doubt, even

---

[3] Readers unfamiliar with that branch of literature called Fistiana may like to know that the Benicia Boy was John Heenan, who fought an epic battle with Tom Sayers in England in 1860.

of panic, of which the American officers could at best have had only a glimmering. When they landed they sometimes received ugly looks from armed men on guard duty, but in general they could move about freely and safely and found the ordinary Japanese citizen friendly and interested. It could not be said that there was any conspicuous anti-foreign sentiment. There was, however, such insatiable curiosity that it looked as if the nation at large appreciated the merits of Occidental civilization so far as they could understand it and might soon throw open their country with enthusiasm.

Yet if that was their view, they were mistaken.

2. Internal Politics

Even had Perry and his officers been given by a reliable Japanese informant an outline of political conditions in Japan in 1854, it is very doubtful whether they would have understood it. But it is quite certain that the situation as it developed in the following decade would have been far too mysterious for their comprehension. The domestic politics of this period were described by more than one contemporary writer in works with such titles as *Yumemonogatari,* or the *Story of a Dream.* That, though not so intended, was a fitting description of the plots and counterplots, the quarrels and arguments, the confusion between names and things, the misunderstandings and bewilderments which characterize this uneasy epoch. It is full of episodes that seem not to belong to waking life, but have the plausible inconsequence, the unearthly logic, of events in a dream. From the highest sources issue proclamations that do not say what they mean or mean what they say. The throne rebukes great officers for doing what it has already approved, or enjoins them not to do what it knows they have already done. Weighty memorials are submitted to the government by powerful nobles who on the basis of information that they have not understood recommend measures that are incompatible one with another. A fantastic ethos prevails throughout the land. Patriots assassinate other patriots for views they have never held or professed, and statesmen declare intentions that everybody knows to be contrary to their real purpose. Feuds become alliances, friendships become hatreds, and the whole nation is in a state of uncertainty and doubt. Yet from this welter of contradictions a solution presently emerges, nobody can say exactly how or why. Things and ideas cease their demented gyrations and fall into their appointed place. The dream is over, and the country is united under one leadership.

So far no Western writer has given us a full account of the process by which innumerable and often irrational conflicts of opinion and interest were resolved and the country at length turned from fear and hatred of foreigners to an excessive admiration. Abundant materials are now at hand, crowded with picturesque detail.[4] It would be an exacting task to arrange them in a lucid and convincing narrative, but it would throw light on many obscure places in the history of Japanese thought and it would prove a fascinating story of the behaviour of man as a political animal. But for our modest purposes here it is enough to select only a few of those events which bear upon the attitude of different divisions of Japanese society towards the opening of intercourse with the West.

When Perry arrived in 1853 the Bakufu was at a loss. It endeavoured to ascertain the opinion not of the samurai but of the court nobles and the feudal aristocracy. The very fact that it did so shows how confused the situation had become, for in the days of its strength and pride the Yedo government would never have dreamed of consulting its lieges and followers. It would have taken its decision boldly and called upon both the hereditary vassals and the Outside Lords to carry out its orders; and it would subsequently have notified the court of its treatment of a question of foreign relations, which was well within the sphere of the powers delegated to the Shogun by the throne. But, well knowing that the country was not strong enough to resist, the Bakufu had already reached the conclusion that the foreigners could not be immediately driven away and that some agreement must be made with them. The feudal nobles, when consulted, could not give any useful advice. Most of them were in favour of expelling the barbarians, and some supported their view by the curious argument that as the Shogun's title was Queller of Barbarians he should act in accordance with it, irrespective of other considerations. The best-informed of the daimyos knew very well that the Shogun had no ships and no guns to speak of, and some of them were already strengthening their own fiefs with artillery and introducing Western learning among their clansmen. But they rejoiced at an opportunity of embarrassing the Bakufu and were not much troubled by logic, so that they were not ashamed of offering advice that could not be taken.

Consequently, in this time of national crisis most anomalous situations continually arose. The view of the feudal nobles was

---

[4] No period in Japanese history is so richly documented. There are easily accessible great collections of official archives, correspondence, diaries, and biographies, while modern Japanese historians have written voluminously on the events of the years from 1853 to 1868. There are whole volumes that recite only the happenings of short periods of ten or twenty days and contain the accounts of eyewitnesses of much that is described.

adopted by the court and accepted by the Bakufu, which publicly announced the Emperor's wish to have the foreigners driven away and added some vague sentiments that recommended at the same time both boldness and caution. The government then proceeded to negotiate the treaty of 1854 with Perry, and the later agreements with other Western countries, as if it had received no instructions whatever. Copies of these treaties were handed to the Emperor by the Shogun's deputy in Kyoto, with a quite untruthful explanation to the effect that the negotiators had made no concessions of importance; and in February 1855 His Majesty gave them his approval and thanked the Shogun for his services.

This, one might suppose, should have settled the matter. The foreigners would be admitted and gradually intercourse would be extended or, alternatively, Japan would strengthen her defences, train men, build ships, purchase guns, and ultimately drive the foreigners away once more. Superficially, at least, that was a feasible policy and many patriots favoured it. But the policy actually adopted was one of drift. The first treaties gave only very limited rights to foreign commerce, but little advantage was taken of these for some years, while such trading vessels as did arrive met with annoying obstructions. The officials of the Bakufu had gained a breathing spell, which they felt they had best use in regaining some of their lost prestige, hoping meanwhile that the foreigners would not come back with new demands. True, there was one uncomfortable clause in the 1854 treaty, providing that the United States might appoint agents to reside at an open port if either government deemed such an arrangement necessary; but the Bakufu, resting on the Japanese text, considered that this meant "if the Japanese government thought necessary," and therefore shirked the issue.

The intention of both the American treaty and the Russian treaty was perfectly clear, however, and the English agreement also contained a reference to the appointment of consuls. Not all the officials of the Bakufu shut their eyes to the real situation, for the most powerful member of the Council of State, Ii Kamon no Kami (Naosuke) was an extremely capable and determined statesman who was persuaded that the policy of seclusion could not be maintained. He was not enthusiastic for change, but he saw that Japan could stand up against foreign countries only if she were strong herself, and he advised the court accordingly. His definite view naturally ranged on the other side all the enemies of the Tokugawa family and he therefore seems to have judged it expedient not to try to convince the anti-foreign party, but to concentrate upon strengthening the position of the Shogun. This would, in any event, have been his natural desire, since his family had been loyal supporters of the Tokugawa family since the days of Ieyasu. Accordingly the problem of Japan's relations with Western countries became entangled with and indeed subordinated to a number of irrelevant issues in domestic politics. The domestic situation was one of almost incredible complexity, and it was this which gave to the events of the next few years that inconsequent and irrational aspect already alluded to.

When Perry was in the Luchu Islands preparing for his second visit to Japan in 1854, he received a letter from the Governor-General of the Netherlands Indies informing him at the request of the Japanese authorities that the Shogun had died and transmitting their request that he should not come back to Japan while the situation was so confused. It was indeed confused for the reason that, the new Shogun being childless, the nomination of his successor had become a question of the first importance, which split the court and the feudal nobility into factions and engendered even more strife than the treaties.

The truth is that at this juncture antagonism to the Bakufu had in certain quarters grown to such a pitch that on any question, irrespective of its merits, powerful interests would range themselves on the side opposed to the government. The selection of an heir to the Shogun provided most welcome opportunities for controversy and intrigue, and many surprising alliances were made on each front. Among the most remarkable was the alignment of one of the great Tokugawa princes against the government of his own family. The lords of Mito were of one of the three senior Tokugawa houses, but by an old tradition they were barred from succession to the Shogunate, though there was nothing against the adoption of one of their sons into another house with a view to ultimate succession. By one of those strange contradictions in which Japanese dynastic history is so rich, the Mito branch of the Tokugawa had from the seventeenth century developed an attitude of independence, if not of hostility, towards the ruling Tokugawa house. Tokugawa Mitsukuni, who was lord of Mito from 1661 to 1700 had encouraged a school of historians whose researches tended to discredit the Shogunate and to give support to the Imperial family; and Nariaki, his descendant in the nineteenth century, was of the same vintage. He was very friendly to the court and had married a lady of the blood royal. His activities were so patently adverse to the Bakufu that he had been forced to abdicate in 1844, though he continued to exercise great influence in retirement. His conduct was characteristic of this era of anomalies, for while he joined loudly in attacks on the Bakufu for its failure to quell barbarians, he encouraged foreign learning in his fief — inviting such scholars as Yokoi Shōnan — and was so anxious to promote gunnery that he took the bells of Buddhist monasteries and turned them into cannon.[5] It was this action that persuaded the Bakufu to retire him, because they did not like great feudatories to increase their military strength. Yet while Nariaki was working against the Shogunate and on behalf of the court, he was also canvassing support for the candidacy of his own son Keiki, who had been adopted into another branch of the Tokugawa family and could therefore aspire to become Shogun. Thus Ii was on all grounds opposed to this troublesome lord, and the struggle between the two was likely to determine the more vital issue of foreign policy.

The forces arrayed against the leader of the Shogun's Council of State were considerable. There was a powerful party at court which favoured Mito, and some of the strongest feudal nobles were also on his side. This combination included most disparate elements, for there was no uniformity in their views on any subject except the suitability of Keiki as heir to the Shogun's office. They all criticized the Bakufu on one ground or another, but few made any useful suggestions as to how the foreigners should be dealt with. Ii, for his part, was in a fairly strong position. He was in office, he was responsible for national defense, could give orders to all Bakufu officials, and controlled the shaky finances of the country; while the Shogun could legally punish any daimyo for insubordination, and even confiscate his fief. He thus managed to hold his own, and by 1858 the succession dispute was settled by the appointment of his nominee.

But before that he had other difficulties to overcome, and the most troublesome of these was presented by the arrival in August 1856 of an American warship carrying a gentleman named Townsend Harris. This unassuming, upright, and sensible official might have been the Devil himself from the consternation he caused. The Japanese authorities implored him to go away, urging that there was no need for his services. No difficulties had arisen, and if he stayed, other foreign consuls would come and cause much trouble. But Harris stayed, though he must often have regretted it in moments of despondency. His purpose was to extend the scope of the treaty of 1854 and he carried a letter from the President that he intended to present to the Shogun in person. For some months, as one may tell from his diary (a little-known but fascinating book, which gives a vivid account of his struggles against a bureaucracy skilled in all the arts of temporizing), he encountered the most baffling obstruction and made little progress because he was unable to use the veiled threat of force that Perry

---

[5] The Mito rulers were traditionally anti-Buddhist. Mitsukuni had destroyed Buddhist temples in his fief and replaced them by Shinto shrines. This was part of his loyalist policy.

with his warships had found so useful. Ii was still engaged in his struggle with Mito and other insubordinate clans, and therefore was unable to concede immediately what Harris requested; but his position was gradually improving, and by June 1857 he was strong enough to carry out his intentions and to agree to the proposals of Harris.

A convention was signed opening Nagasaki to American ships, giving rights of residence at two other ports, settling some details of currency exchange, and providing for the trial and punishment of American offenders by American consuls in accordance with American laws. In practice this was only a modest enlargement of the 1854 treaty, but it was an important step, and it was to be followed by an unprecedented event on December 7, 1857 when Harris was received in audience in Yedo by the Shogun. At the time of Perry's visit the Bakufu would not have dared to go so far. It is probable that had they done so and frankly faced the ensuing domestic storm, they could have carried the country with them. But they were not bold or wise enough to stand firm, nor were they yet convinced that the foreigners could not be kept at bay by illusory concessions.

By 1857, however, a change had taken place in the situation, both at home and abroad, which calls for a brief examination. Under Ii's guidance, the Shogunate had somewhat reasserted its authority and Ii had, if only momentarily, got the upper hand of the lord of Mito. Meanwhile Harris, a very patient man, after several months of frustration, in March 1857 upon hearing from his government, had warned the Japanese authorities that the United States would not tolerate further evasion. This intimation had been conveniently underlined by recent events in China, to which he did not fail to allude. Early in 1857 the interpreters in Nagasaki had reported that, because the Chinese government had failed to carry out treaty obligations, a British squadron had attacked and burned Canton, with assistance from the French and Americans.[6] They ventured to warn the authorities that "in this country also, if great care is not taken, war may result from some trivial incident." This alarmed the procrastinating and shifty Bakufu officers, and the warning was made more impressive by a message from Curtius, the superintendent of the Dutch post at Nagasaki (now the Dutch Commissioner in Japan), who in respectful but unambiguous terms pointed to the example of China and warned

---

6 It was not true that American forces had shared in the attack on Canton in 1856. The American squadron had remained neutral; but, the Chinese having fired upon a small craft carrying an American official and flying the American flag, ships of the squadron had in retaliation bombarded and destroyed forts commanding the approaches to Canton. It was doubtless this incident that had come to the knowledge of the Japanese authorities.

the Bakufu against the evasive and dilatory behaviour of the officials with whom Harris had to negotiate. What they thought were triumphs of diplomacy were petty tricks calculated to goad the Americans and the British into violent action. This lecture had an immediate effect, for in March 1857 the senior Commissioner for Foreign Affairs (Hotta Masatoshi, who had recently been appointed to that post) addressed a note to the officials concerned, both in Yedo and at the ports, in which he repeated what Curtius had said, in much the same language. He told them that they must change their attitude at once. There must, he said in effect, be no more red tape and sealing wax, no more discussions and delays over trifling points of detail. They must show a genuinely friendly spirit in their dealings with foreigners.

All this correspondence — and there is much more in the same vein — shows that the civil service of the Bakufu was paralysed by addiction to details of procedure and concerned more with form than with substance. It could have given points to any Office of Circumlocution in the West. This was inherent in its character, because the penalties of error were so severe that none but the boldest official dared make decisions on his own judgment.

But there were other reasons why the officials who had direct dealings with foreigners should resort to shabby tricks. They were reflecting the general attitude of the Bakufu, which was so harassed by domestic difficulties that it tried from day to day to put off the solution of its problems in foreign affairs, desperately grasping at any opportunity to postpone decisions. It was struggling for its own life against powerful opposition, and to grant any favour to a barbarian was to give a weapon to its enemies at home. Thus it is known that the officials whom Harris encountered on his arrival at Shimoda in 1856 had been given orders to prevent any intimacy between Japanese and foreigners; and there is good reason to believe that, although the pressure of events obliged the Bakufu to take the lead in opening Japan to foreign intercourse, opinion in the inner circles of the government was more hostile to Westerners than that of some of the allegedly xenophobic daimyos. It was natural that the Tokugawa government should be loath to cultivate relations with foreign countries in the nineteenth century as in the seventeenth, since such a departure could not but bring changes into the constitution of the Japanese state which would at best diminish the authority of the Tokugawa family and at worst destroy it. The point is not one that can be definitely settled, but it is at any rate certain that the Bakufu entered into negotiations with Western countries decidedly *à contre-cœur,* and would have taken a much firmer line had it not been as short of money as it was of true political wisdom. The history of its tergiversation becomes more intelligible if the emptiness of its treasury is taken into account. It was chiefly because it was insolvent that it gave way to Perry's pressure in 1853, though this fact was not known to the country at large, and still less to Perry himself, who naturally took full credit for his own diplomatic skill. It was

KATSU AWA (1823–1900)

A Tokugawa retainer (hatamoto) who became
Navy Minister in the first Meiji government.
He arranged the surrender of Yedo castle
to the forces of the crown.

its subsequent dilatory action that caused its downfall, for a dictatorship depends upon its power of firm and prompt decision.[7]

When Harris first settled in Shimoda and (living disconso-

[7] Katsu Awa, a Tokugawa adherent who later played a leading part in the Restoration movement because he saw that the Bakufu was incompetent, writing of this period said: "From the day of Perry's arrival for more than ten years our country was in a state of indescribable confusion. The government was weak and irresolute, without fixed policy or power of decision." A later Japanese historian says of the same period: "The Bakufu had capable men, who knew what should be done. But it lacked the courage, the skill, and the sincerity to do it."

Many Japanese historians think that if the Bakufu had displayed more resolution, it could have carried through its policy of opening the country without great difficulty. One cannot resist the temptation to observe that, if this is true, Japan has been unfortunate in her military dictators. They were weak when they should have been strong in 1854, and aggressive when they should have been temperate in 1941.

lately on a diet of tough chicken, rice, and promises) began negotiations there with the delegates of the government, he met
nothing but obstruction. His official notes were left unanswered
because (he was told) "it is not customary to reply to the letters of
foreigners" — a statement that nearly a century later would have
been regarded as not entirely obsolete by diplomatic and consular
officers residing in Japan. He was surrounded by spies who tried
to trap him into indiscreet statements. So fantastic were the ideas of
the local officials that in response to an inquiry from Yedo as to
the alarming number of prostitutes who had been brought to
Shimoda, they replied that it was hoped that those ladies by their
charms would soften the hearts of foreign visitors and so make
them less determined to exact political concessions from Japan.
Both foreign and Japanese accounts agree in describing the
Bakufu functionaries as almost unbelievably addicted to petty
statagem and irrelevant detail.

The country was not lacking, however, in sensible statesmen
and officials who could read the signs of the times. Some of them
saw the foolishness of exasperating Harris (and other foreigners
also, for in 1855 the Dutch were negotiating at Nagasaki, in 1856
Captain Possiet was there ratifying the Russian treaty, and a visit
from the Governor of Hongkong was expected). In September
1856 a memorial was addressed to the Shogun's councillors by a
group of men who represented the most advanced view among
high Bakufu officials, and it is significant that their functions were
concerned with coastal defence and public finance. They urged the
government to bring about a change in the official attitude towards
foreigners. In the old days, they said, their country was strong
enough to do what it pleased in the matter of trade relations with
China and Holland, and could afford to treat their subjects like
slaves. This habit of mind had become ingrained in their countrymen, but they must realize that conditions change and they must
change with them. The memorial then complains of negotiators
who "make difficulties about the smallest trifles and neglect what
really matters." They argued for instance that no difficulties
should be raised about the treatment of foreign officials, or the
supply of beef, or the regulation of houses of ill fame — questions
that had taken up most of the time of the authorities at Shimoda —
but that broad-minded concessions should be made. Their general
intention was sound, but it was characteristic of the tortuous official
reasoning of those days that in recommending the supply of beef
(which according to Buddhist and Shinto belief was defiling)
they argued that it was essentially not different from supplying
pills to invalids. By an equally curious logic they suggested that
the Bakufu should proceed with a policy of concessions to foreign-

ers, but keep it secret from the public so as to prevent a decline in national morale. It did not occur to them that the morale of the Bakufu might decline also.

This fragment of evidence discloses the fundamental weakness of the policy of the Shogun's government. It was trying at the same time to keep the foreigners quiet and to give the country the impression that it was being very firm and would soon drive them away. It was this dishonesty that in the long run encouraged anti-foreign sentiment not only among those enemies of the government who were genuinely opposed to Western influence but among the general public, who were led to believe that it was the sentiment by which the Shogunate was inspired. These habits of double-dealing introduced complications into the domestic political history of the next few years which make it extremely difficult to understand. But it is worth some attention if only for its interest as study of the morbid anatomy of cultural intercourse.

Ii Kamon no Kami, now the most powerful of the Shogun's ministers, having made up his mind that it was in Japan's best interests to negotiate comprehensive treaties with foreign powers, agreed to negotiations that Harris proposed immediately after his audience with the Shogun in December 1857. The American treaty was to provide for full diplomatic and consular privileges; the opening of more ports to foreign trade by agreed dates; private import and export transactions, subject to an agreed tariff; and freedom of religion and extraterritorial jurisdiction. It was evident that it must bring an end to the policy of seclusion, since it would be impossible to prevent Japanese subjects from travelling or sending ships abroad, and thus the country would be exposed to strong foreign influence.

Naturally such a prospect stirred hostile feelings in the bosom of all conservatives, and it gave an excellent excuse for open or underground movements against the Bakufu to all those parties and individuals who resented Tokugawa supremacy. The Bakufu was of course well aware of these dangers and, having once decided that the treaty must be signed, embarked upon a series of intricate manœuvres designed to obtain the approval of the throne. The court refused to sanction the proposed agreement, although high officers were sent to Yedo to explain the circumstances and to allay the anxiety of the Emperor. But meanwhile the Shogun's ministers learned that British and French envoys were on their way to Japan to conclude new treaties, and Harris took advantage of this situation to warn the Bakufu that it would be prudent to sign the American treaty first, lest worse befall.

On July 29 the treaty was signed on board an American warship in Yedo Bay, and it was followed in the next few months by treaties with Great Britain, Holland, Russia, and France. Either specifically or by virtue of a most-favoured-nation clause, these and all subsequent treaties in the series provided for consular jurisdiction and for a fixed customs tariff at very low rates. These provisions, and the fact that none of the treaties was of specified duration, were to cause great heartburning in Japan a few years later and to lead to an outburst of anti-foreign sentiment that imprinted a special character upon the future relations of Japan with foreign countries. It can even be argued, though not proved, that they started Japanese policy, both domestic and foreign, upon a course that it would otherwise not have taken. It is at any rate quite certain that a desire to secure revision of the treaties determined, more than any other single factor, the character of political life in Japan for several decades.

The sense of weakness and frustration betrayed in the attitude of government and people throughout the period of the negotiation of the treaties is closely paralleled by the angry, humiliated feeling that was commonly expressed only a few years after the Restoration, when the Western powers could not be induced to listen to Japan's plea that those treaties were unjust. It will be seen from later chapters that it was in part a sense of inferiority that impelled the Japanese people to take enthusiastically to foreign ways, and it was this same zeal, soured and curdled by disappointment, that produced the strong anti-foreign reaction which followed. It is significant that the national watchwords in these two periods were "Expel the Barbarians" before the Restoration and "Revise the Treaties" in the first half of Meiji. Both were anti-foreign in character, and both were deliberately used for political ends because they were known to appeal to a common national emotion.

Katsu Awa, the statesman whose views on the incompetence of the Bakufu have just been cited, foresaw this development. He wrote after the Restoration that the Japanese people after hundreds of years of seclusion had no real understanding of the outside world. Yet this was necessary if they were to change their form of government and the nature of their life. He feared for the future, and the future confirmed his fears.[8] It is principally by reason of its bearing upon the nature of subsequent relationships between Japan and the West that it has been thought useful to

[8] Katsu's words were as follows: "From the arrival of Perry for more than a decade the country was in a state of disturbance and uncertainty. Today, after years of indescribably difficult negotiations, we have at last agreed to foreign intercourse and trade. But in those ten years the whole nature of our government has changed and the face of the country is to be altered. But shall we succeed? After three hundred years of seclusion our people, in all classes, have no knowledge of the outside world. It is impossible to measure or to estimate the great difficulties which await us."

describe in what may seem unnecessary detail the controversy that arose out of the signature of the 1858 treaties. It illustrates only too well the truth that foreign cultural influences, however beneficent in intention, may evoke an unforeseen and disagreeable response.

To return now to the situation in Kyoto, where the Shogun's officers had tried in vain to persuade the court to agree in advance to the signature of new treaties. Hotta, the Bakufu's Minister for Foreign Affairs, had found in the capital a widespread anti-foreign feeling and much hostility to the Bakufu, fomented by the retired lord of Mito and shared by a number of powerful daimyos. The Shogun was faced therefore not only with the disagreeable problem of dealing with foreign envoys but also with growing opposition among his own countrymen. The throne had consulted the feudal nobles and had found opinion divided as to the proper treatment of the foreigners' demands, though on the whole it was in favour of opening the country. But by this time the main issue had been lost sight of, and the court's decision was based upon reasons of domestic politics. The Emperor and the nobles around him appear to have been genuinely alarmed at the prospect of foreigners living and trading near the capital and not far from the sacred shrines of Isé; and there was a strong party at court that hated the military in general and the Tokugawa in particular.

Hotta returned to Yedo in June 1858. By that time Ii Kamon no Kami had been made Tairo, an appointment equivalent to that of regent, and was therefore the most powerful of the great officers of state. He was determined to assert his authority, and that of the Bakufu, by striking at his enemies and by carrying through his plan of making his own nominee the heir to the Shogunate against the wishes of Mito. He concluded the American treaty of July 29, 1858, as we have seen. In August the young prince of his choice was proclaimed heir, and actually succeeded to the Shogunate a few days later, when his predecessor died.

This combination of distasteful events enraged the opposition in Kyoto. Feudal lords and their retainers flocked to the city and added to the clamour against the treaty. They were breaking the rule of the Shogunate by attending at court, and the Shogun forbade the entry of members of independent clans into the capital, but the uproar continued. Mito and other daimyos wrote angry memorials and accused the Bakufu of disloyalty to the Emperor. The Regent struck back at once and imposed house-arrest on Mito and his heir, while forcing other influential daimyos to abdicate. He even went so far as to snub the court when he was ordered to proceed to Yedo to explain his conduct, and instead of obeying the Imperial command (which he knew had been pro-cured by his enemies) he sent an envoy named Manabe to press for the Imperial sanction to the treaties. The story of Manabe's mission is extremely interesting, because it reveals the nature of the court intrigues of the day and illumines the extraordinary cross-currents of opinion concerning foreign relations. Manabe reached Kyoto in October, and shortly after his arrival a number of nobles were — by prearrangement — arrested for plotting against the Shogun.

It will give some idea of the opposition that Manabe had to encounter if we quote from one of the numerous memorials and decrees which flew about the country at this time. Perhaps the best presentation of arguments used by the anti-foreign party is to be found in the memorial that Mito (Nariaki) addressed to the Regent on July 16, 1858. He said that it was absurd of the Bakufu to plead that they could not drive the foreigners away until the country had increased its military strength by the profits of foreign trade. Military preparations should come first and commerce later. If the foreigners attacked Japan they could not penetrate far into the country, as they had no maps. But if trade were permitted they would soon learn all about the geography and internal conditions of Japan, and that would be dangerous. If new treaties were made and foreign learning and religion introduced, the people would do as they liked, all discipline would vanish, and the country would be demoralized. He thought that if ports were opened for the American barbarians, then other barbarians would say that they could not live in the same places and would ask for more ports to be opened. If you comply with one request, he said, they will make others, and there will be no end to it.

This represents the extreme view of the party in favour of Jō-i, or Expelling the Barbarians. Mito was a self-indulgent, tempestuous man, who by most accounts does not deserve the reputation for wisdom that he somehow acquired, but it is unlikely that he really believed all he said. Since he was the most influential of Ii's antagonists, however, the sentiments he proclaimed were adopted by many nobles and samurai, some because they had a genuine fear of foreign contacts, others because they welcomed any support for their intrigues against the Shogunate.

That the anti-foreign movement was to a great extent dictated by hostility to the Bakufu is clear from the opinions offered by the leading members of the feudal nobility when they were consulted after Harris had been received by the Shogun at the end of 1857. Their attitude was much more enlightened than that which they had displayed at the time of Perry's visit. Not all of them replied to the questions put to them, but few were positively against foreign intercourse. Some had entirely changed their views and come out strongly in favour of new treaties. Only Mito was violently antagonistic, and he suggested that the negotiators should commit suicide and Harris ought to be decapitated. Echizen, advised by men like Yokoi Shōnan and Hashimoto Sanai, was in favour of full commercial and diplomatic relations, and other daimyos thought that a greater or less degree of intercourse must be accepted, even if only experimentally.

The court when informed of these views issued a decree in which a decisive line was avoided. It said that the Imperial Mind was distressed by these difficult questions and would not be at ease unless the matter was treated by the government with due consideration. The only express wish of the throne was that the foreigners should be kept as far away as possible and not allowed in provinces near the capital. The national honour must be preserved and the safety of the people assured.

Manabe remained for some months in the capital (from October to early April) and succeeded in inducing the court to agree for the present not to forbid the conclusion of new treaties. The arguments he used were remarkable. He said that the Yedo government was at heart opposed to extending relations with foreigners, but was helpless because it had no funds and no armaments. Its real intention was to complete the country's defences and then at a suitable moment to expel the barbarians. He even made the startling suggestion that if Japan so arranged matters that the foreigners could make no profit out of their trade they, being greedy people, would leave of their own accord.

This was at a time when a great many important Bakufu officials were already persuaded of the importance of foreign trade, and when the Council of State had before it memorials from its advisers presenting the case for future commercial relations and discussing the probable nature and volume of imports and exports.[9] It is clear that the Bakufu promised to expel the foreigners within a few years, and it is even said that an approximate date was set, about five years ahead. Consequently the Emperor, while maintaining his objection to relations with foreigners, gave an ambiguous and qualified consent to the treaties, which was sufficient for the immediate purposes of the Bakufu. It was embodied in a decree of February 1859, which was not made public.

[9] Among such documents is a well-reasoned essay by Tsutsui Masanori. In 1856 the senior State Councillor, Hotta Masayoshi, had been instructed to report on the pros and cons of foreign trade and had ordered all officials concerned to examine the question. Among the reports that he received was this reply from Tsutsui, which said that in his opinion good results would follow from the opening of trade and not the disorder that its opponents predicted. He said that it was wrong to suppose that trade would dwindle away for lack of products to exchange. The needs of both parties to buy and sell would inevitably increase production in Japan and at the same time diversify it. He was opposed to state interference and in favour of leaving trade to private enterprise.

The treaties (which had been signed in July and August 1858) came into force in July 1859 and foreign diplomatic envoys at once took up residence in Yedo, while the port of Yokohama was opened to foreign trade and residence. Like most of the edicts and memorials of the period, the Delphic utterance of the Emperor did not settle any of the current disputes. It merely gave the Bakufu a semblance of authority for their action. It did not abandon any principle and a majority of the ruling classes of the country remained fixed in their anti-foreign views.

Ii now turned to crushing the influence of Mito, who was still the head and front of the anti-foreign party, and he made a bid for harmony with the court by arranging a marriage between the Shogun and a younger sister of the Emperor. He was taking the first steps in a policy that had been for some time in the minds of adherents of the Tokugawa who, seeing a current of opinion setting against the Shogunate, hoped to restore its prestige and save a substantial part of its administrative authority by promoting a movement for what was called Kōbu-gattai, or the amalgamation of civil and military. In essence this was an attempt of feudalism to avert an anti-feudal tendency, which grew as the sentiment of reverence for the Imperial house was revived. It was not by any means confined to the Bakufu, for the notion of amalgamation was entertained by several of the leading feudatories as well as by a number of court nobles who, while anxious to reduce the power of the Tokugawa family, were so accustomed to military dominance that they did not see further than a state of affairs in which military and civil nobility would share in the government on approximately equal terms. There were some who thought of a system in which the Emperor would assume administrative authority and delegate it only in part to the Shogun or to a council of feudal and court nobles over whom the Shogun would preside.

It was this latter view that started a number of people thinking about national councils or assemblies and thus did something to prepare the public mind for the idea of parliamentary institutions a decade or more before the Restoration. Thus, although there was hostility to the Bakufu in many quarters, it did not necessarily bespeak an intention to abolish feudal rule entirely. Even such a powerful clan as that of Satsuma, a hereditary enemy of the Tokugawa, was until shortly before the Restoration in favour of a degree of amalgamation which would leave great powers to the military houses. The daimyos of Satsuma (the Shimadzu family) had for centuries had close connections through intermarriage both with the court nobility and with the Tokugawa family, and as late as 1856 Shimadzu (Nariakira) succeeded in arranging a match between his daughter and the Shogun. Thus simply stated, it appears as a political alliance of a common type, and so it was. But it was achieved only after the most roundabout negotiations and intrigues. These cannot be related here, but it is worth while to mention some of their more startling features, if only to illustrate the remarkable complexity of social life in Japan of that day. They also serve to show why, at a time when Japan was in a most critical situation by reason of the demands of Townsend Harris, the energies of her leading statesmen were taken up by dynastic problems which were in their view of the first importance.

Shimadzu's daughter, a girl of eighteen, was not really his daughter but the daughter of a collateral, and she was already affianced. But her engagement was cancelled, and she was adopted by Shimadzu. As there were objections on the score of rank to a match between the Shogun and a girl who was not even a descendant in the direct line of the lords of Satsuma, it was deemed necessary for her to acquire some additional quality, and this was done by having her adopted as a daughter by Prince Konoe, head of a family of court nobles closely related to the Imperial house and patrons of the Shimadzu since 1100. There were still many difficulties to overcome — objections by other daimyos (notably Mito, who wanted his own son to be Shogun), the outstretched hands of officials and court ladies who had to be persuaded by handsome gifts, and opposition from several other quarters on political or personal grounds. The negotiations lasted for three years, and a great many people took hand in them, in Satsuma, Kyoto, and Yedo.

The objects of the marriage were various. In the first place it was designed to strengthen Shimadzu's own position should he find himself opposed to Bakufu officials on matters of policy. It was also connected with the vexed problem of the succession to the Shogunate, upon which feudal society was split. But essentially it may be regarded as part of an effort to bring about the amalgamation of military and civil power, which has been alluded to above. Despite differences of view on matters of national policy, many of the great feudatories felt that if that amalgamation was to be successful, the leading military houses must present a united front to the court. It was for this reason that such prominent men as the lord of Echizen assisted Shimadzu in his negotiations with the Shogunate.

Conversely, of course, the court would ultimately profit by disunity among the feudal nobles; and this is in fact what happened, for the Kōbu-gattai movement failed. It turned out that the Shogunate had already lost its last chance when it referred the question of Perry's treaty to the Emperor, asked the advice of its vassals, and relaxed the fundamental rule of "alternate attendance" by daimyos at the Shogun's court in Yedo.

With the signature of the treaties and the arrival of foreign envoys the scene changes. The Shogunate is openly committed to one policy, the court to another, and opinion throughout the country is bitter and divided. A clash is inevitable, because evasion and concealment are no longer possible. The foreigners are there on Japanese soil, the ships in the harbours, and it is no use pretending that they have not come to stay.

3. The Dying Struggles

AFTER the treaties came into force the officers of the Shogun's government continued in their habit of making a promise and then avoiding its performance. They deliberately obstructed the foreign trade they had agreed to encourage and — though not deliberately — they failed to afford protection to the foreign officials and merchants whom they had admitted. They had, of course, got themselves into this absurd position by their ambiguous attitude, by allowing the country to believe that they really were against barbarians. It must be admitted that they had some very difficult people to deal with. The foreign merchants, thinking above all of profit, seized with alacrity upon a clause in the treaties that provided for the exchange of foreign gold and silver coin weight for weight against Japanese coin, for in Japan gold could be bought with silver at a rate that yielded an easy profit of about one hundred per cent. Gold was therefore rapidly exported and this combined with other circumstances drove up the cost of commodities and gave rise to complaints directed against the government and against greedy foreigners.

Feeling began to run high, and within a few weeks of the opening of the port of Yokohama there was an outbreak of murderous assaults. The victims were usually foreign merchants or their servants, and precautions taken in good faith by the government failed to bring these attacks to an end. The clans were in uproar, and though the clansmen might be restrained by their leaders there was no way of controlling the masterless samurai, the rōnin, who were sworn to kill foreigners whenever they could find an opportunity. These men were numerous and, as always, their numbers increased as conditions grew confused. They embarrassed their friends as well as their enemies by their irresponsible violence, and they naturally evoked in the government a ruthless spirit, which left some traces in later times.

The cry of *Sonnō Jōi*, "Revere the Emperor and Expel the Barbarians," resounded through the country, and those who might have suppressed the mounting agitation in fact encouraged it, because both of these watchwords increased the difficulties of the Bakufu.

Early in 1860 a Japanese mission had gone to Washington to ratify the American treaty.[10] While the representatives of the Shogun's government were abroad, the situation of the Bakufu was rapidly worsening. In order to maintain its prestige, the Regent, Ii Kamon no Kami, had taken very drastic measures against his enemies at court. Some of the minor conspirators had been brought to Yedo, where they were tried and punished by death or imprisonment. Persons of more consequence were deprived of title or office or placed under domiciliary arrest. Among these latter was the retired lord of Mito, Nariaki, who was disgraced, while Hitotsubashi, his candidate for succession to the Shogun, was confined to his house. These steps aroused bitter feeling in the Mito fief, and on March 24, 1860 a small band of clansmen assassinated the Regent as he was about to enter the castle at Yedo. They thus succeeded in removing a determined enemy, but they did no service to their clan, for its samurai were by no means unanimous. Many still supported the Shogun against the Imperial party, and internal dissension in his own fief thus prevented Mito from playing any significant role in national politics.

But the position of the Bakufu did not improve. As the chief supporter of the throne and the most powerful antagonist of the Shogun, Mito was succeeded by the leader (though not the titular daimyo) of the Satsuma clan, Shimadzu Saburo. The court, incited and assisted by Satsuma, pressed hard on the Bakufu after Ii's death. They insisted upon postponement of the opening of Yedo, Osaka, and Hyogo to foreign trade and residence, thus obliging the Bakufu to appeal to the treaty powers for consent to some delay. The diplomatists in Yedo were not unwilling to recommend this move to their governments since they understood the situation of the Bakufu and were, moreover, ready on personal grounds to leave Yedo for a time.

Attacks upon foreigners had grown more frequent and serious. The secretary of the United States Legation had been murdered in Yedo, and in protest the representatives of England, France, and the Netherlands had withdrawn to Yokohama, though the American Minister courageously decided to stay. The three representatives returned in March 1861 under guarantee of their safety from

---

[10] Despite the only qualified approval of the court, the treaty — which was already in force — was ratified in Washington on the part of Japan in the name of the Shogun.

he Bakufu, but some months later the British Legation was at-
acked by Mito clansmen in accordance with plans made a year
)efore. Other acts of violence directed mainly against foreigners
ollowed this in 1862 and 1863, and it is supposed that they were
lue to something more than negligence among Bakufu officials
responsible for the protection of the legations. It is known that the
ourt particularly resented the residence of foreign representatives
n Yedo. Soon after Ii's assassination his friends were dismissed
rom office and replaced by men more acceptable to the anti-
oreign party, who may well have wished to improve relations with
Kyoto by a deliberate failure to protect the legations. Such conduct
vould have been in keeping with the general ambiguity of the
ictions of the Bakufu after the death of Ii, for its relations with the
:ourt became more and more inconsistent with its professions to
he foreign powers.

Perhaps the most striking among many remarkable anomalies
vas the conduct of the Bakufu in agreeing with the court to fix a
late for the expulsion of foreigners at a time when its envoys, on
i second mission abroad, had just asked the treaty powers to agree
o deferring the opening of further ports on the ground of "opposi-
.ion offered by a party in Japan which was hostile to all intercourse
with foreigners." The powers' consent was given on the understanding that all other treaty obligations would be carried out and
10 obstacle put in the way of trade and intercourse. This was in
June 1862 (in London) and it was in the summer of the same
/ear that, in response to a command from the court, the Shogun
igreed to journey to Kyoto to consult with the nobles there as to
he future government of Japan and the time and method of expelling barbarians.

At the same time the Yedo government gave way to the court
on other important questions. It appointed Prince Hitotsubashi
Keiki to be guardian of the young Shogun who had been his suc-
:essful rival; it agreed to the selection of the Prince of Echizen as
President of the Council of State. Its effort to improve relations
with the court by a marriage between the Shogun and a sister of
the Emperor was made to look like an act of submission by an
)rder to the bride that she must use her title of Imperial Princess
ind not the customary designation of a Shogun's consort. Thus the
Shogun's government, by surrendering on one point after another,
was on the way to losing all but the outward forms of its authority.

The Shogun left for Kyoto in March 1863, and this in itself was
a further blow to his prestige, for none of his predecessors for over
two centuries had deigned to set foot in the capital, where their
deputies were accustomed to give orders, not to receive them.
Shortly after his arrival, at a council of nobles, it was decided that

the first step in closing the country should be taken on July 24 1863. On that day the foreign representatives in Yedo were no tified in writing that instructions had been received from the Shogun in Kyoto for the expulsion of all foreigners and the closing of the ports. This notice was accompanied by oral assurances that the Bakufu would do nothing. To these approaches the foreign envoys merely replied that foreign interests would be protected by the powers themselves. The implicit threat alarmed the Shogun- ate, though it can scarcely have surprised them. Meanwhile the Shogun — who had been detained in Kyoto against his will on the pretence that the Emperor must concert with him measures for expelling the foreigners — managed to extricate himself and re- turned to Yedo in July. He then addressed a memorial to the Em- peror, in which he said that the time was not ripe for expelling foreigners and action must be postponed. The court, which had received reports confirming what the Shogun said, reluctantly agreed. The Jō-i or Expulsion Party were of course enraged, and the foreign community was thought to be in such danger that British and French troops were brought to Yokohama for its pro- tection in 1863.

Certain other warlike moves by foreign powers had brought home to the court the fact that it would be impossible to drive the foreigners away by force. An Englishman had been killed by samurai in the retinue of Shimadzu when that old-fashioned noble- man was on his way back after escorting the Imperial messenger who had carried to Yedo the order to the Shogun to appear in Kyoto and discuss the expulsion measures. The British govern- ment, unable to obtain satisfaction from the Bakufu, had ordered the bombardment of Kagoshima (in Satsuma) in August 1862. The Bakufu was now fearful of similar action if the powers should be aroused by the notice it had just given of the plan to close the country. It hastily paid out of its own funds the indemnity de- manded of Satsuma and sent word to the court that in present con- ditions there was no possibility of executing the Imperial com- mands and expelling the foreigners. Prince Keiki, the Regent, sent a similar message and offered his resignation, which was not ac- cepted. The confusion at Yedo is revealed by his statement that on the Shogun's council there were no two councillors in agree- ment as to the expulsion of foreigners. The court was at last per- suaded to leave the date for the expulsion to the decision of the Shogun.

It might be supposed that at this juncture a decision one way or another would have been taken by the court or the Shogunate. But this is to assume that the announcements made on either side represented firm views or resolute intentions. Nothing could be further from the facts. The court, it is true, had scored some great successes over the Shogunate; but neither in the court nor in the inner councils of the Bakufu nor in the most anti-foreign clans was there any real unanimity. Each had its factions, its extremists and its moderates; and the edicts or proclamations that issued from those sources represented not fixed decisions upon policy, but only the views of persons or groups momentarily in the ascendant. To borrow a simile from a Japanese historian, opinion in Japan at this time was like a great whirlpool formed by a confusion of many smaller whirlpools.

Thus it would be wrong to accuse the Bakufu of sheer wanton duplicity, since circumstances changed so rapidly that they could not be faithfully described, and it was generally understood among the actors, if not the spectators, of the tragicomedy now being enacted that no statement was to be taken at its face value. The Shogunate, seeing that it was impossible to maintain its erstwhile supremacy, was struggling for its existence and endeavouring to conciliate both the court and the great feudatories in the hope of bringing about that amalgamation of civil and military power, the Kōbu Gattai, which has already been alluded to. Its repeated surrenders to the court have been noticed, and now, as it twisted and turned and faced both ways in its efforts to placate the foreign envoys while not antagonizing the anti-foreign party, it felt obliged to make more concessions to the clans. In October 1862 the Shogunate took a step that perhaps more than any other single act hastened its collapse. It so modified and relaxed the rule exacting periodical attendance by the daimyos at the Shogun's court that it virtually abdicated authority over its vassals. They were no longer obliged to leave their families in Yedo as hostages, their visits could be shorter and less frequent, and they were encouraged to give their opinions on affairs of state. The result was a scurry from Yedo of most of the daimyos and their households, and the sojourn of many members of the feudal nobility and gentry in Kyoto, where they engaged in activities usually unfavourable to the Shogunate.

Not that the relaxation of rules was needed to encourage the most powerful of the western clans to come out openly against the Bakufu. Satsuma and Chōshū, though they may have at one time thought it possible to amalgamate with the Tokugawa house on something like equal terms, were now prepared to act independently.[11] The history of the ensuing decade is concerned mainly with the activities of these two great clans; and as we shall see, the

11 Among the proposals put to the Shogunate by the mission that Shimadzu escorted to Yedo in 1862 was, besides the appointment of Keiki, the foundation of a council to advise the Shogun, which was to include five great daimyos.

government of the early years of Meiji was dominated by samurai who had gained political experience in the domestic affairs of Chōshū and Satsuma and the intricate triangular bargaining between the court, the Shogunate, and the leading feudatories. It was, by a paradox characteristic of the times, the anti-foreign activities of Satsuma and Chōshū that brought to birth a new government dedicated to the fullest extension of foreign intercourse. The clans that had uttered the loudest cries of "Expel the Barbarians" were those which led the way in spreading Western ideas throughout Japan. It is not surprising that Japan gained the reputation in the West of being a topsy-turvy land.

For a fuller understanding of the events that preceded the downfall of the Shogunate, it is necessary to return to the date fixed for the expulsion of foreigners — June 24, 1863. On that day the Chōshū clan had thought it proper to commence hostilities by firing upon an American vessel anchored in the Straits of Shimonoseki, on which Chōshū territory bordered. A French vessel was attacked on July 8, a Dutch warship on July 11. An American warship retaliated on July 16, firing at the batteries and sinking a small ship. French forces landed on July 20 and destroyed the batteries, putting their defenders to flight. At this point, in an endeavour to induce the unruly clan to desist, a message was carried to Chōshū by two young men who pointed out the folly of embroiling the whole country in war with several powers at once. One of these was Ito Hirobumi, a Chōshū samurai who had just returned, impressed by the power of Western states, from a clandestine visit to England and was within twenty years to become the leading statesman of Japan. The Daimyo of Chōshū would not listen to his advice, and the straits remained closed for more than a year, until in September 1864 a joint expedition of ships from the American, British, French, and Dutch navies attacked Shimonoseki and removed the guns. Chōshū thereupon gave way and agreed to pay an indemnity, the money finally being found by the Shogun's government.

This incident, like the attack on Kagoshima in 1863, though it doubtless inflamed anti-foreign feeling in many clansmen, resulted in the establishment of friendly relations between the foreigners and the leaders of the delinquent clan. Both Satsuma and Chōshū had received a valuable lesson, and though the action of the treaty powers has been described as unwarrantable there can be little doubt that it served a good purpose by showing the futility of the expulsion policy and by preventing the bloodshed and humiliation that would have followed an attempt to carry out the instructions of the court.

The court had already begun to hesitate when Chōshū fired

PERRY'S SHIPS AND THE EMBLEMS OF THE COASTAL DEFENCE FORCES

Part of a sketch by a Japanese artist,

from a manuscript book in the collection of the late Edwin Neville

SUMO WRESTLING

The ceremonial entry of champions. Illustrating the entertainment offered to Perry's offi by the Japanese treaty negotiators in 1854

upon the foreign ships in July 1863. When the Shogun upon his return to Yedo had told the court that he could not carry out its orders, the court had replied in a very haughty way, and reproached him for travelling in a steamer, a most undignified and barbarous method of transport. But the upshot of the communication was that the Emperor was getting alarmed and had lost confidence in his advisers. With strong approval from the Bakufu, some of these were dismissed and the Chōshū men, who had established themselves as guardians of the Emperor's person, were directed to leave Kyoto. They went off, carrying with them seven of their chief allies among the court nobles. One of these was the Prince Sanjō, who — not surprisingly, for this was an era of sudden changes of opinion — within five years became a leader of the new, pro-foreign government of Japan.

By now on all sides there were signs that the attitude towards foreign intercourse was changing, not among the majority of the samurai or the numerous irreconcilable rōnin, but in more instructed and responsible quarters. The Echizen fief, where, as we have noticed, foreign studies had made good progress, announced in decided terms that both the court and the Shogunate were mistaken in objecting to friendly intercourse with foreign states, and its leaders could therefore no longer associate themselves with Bakufu policy. Even the Bakufu took courage to inform the representatives of the treaty powers in November 1863 that the notification of June 24 no longer held good. It was not intended to expel foreigners. True to form, however, it stated in a public announcement that the Shogun was negotiating with the foreigners for the closing of the ports, and the clansmen must not resort to violence.

The Chōshū clansmen, however, remained insubordinate. The Shogun went to Kyoto early in 1864 and there he made still further concessions to the court, where friends of the Chōshū leaders were still intriguing in their favour. It was agreed that in future all feudatories, upon their succession, should receive investiture from the Emperor. This took from the Shogun almost the last shred of his feudal privilege; and when it was further agreed that certain feudal dignitaries (including leaders from Satsuma, Tosa, Echizen, and Aidzu) should be the advisers of the Shogun "because they had the confidence of the Emperor," then for most purposes it was the manipulator who had become the puppet.

The Bakufu had now little left to preserve but its dignity; and it was its remnants of stubborn pride that hastened its downfall. The Chōshū clan was divided into two factions, the peaceful and the warlike. The former, it is interesting to note, was known as the Party of the Vulgar View, which shows that its opinion was fairly widespread if not respectable. The latter having gained control, their men in Kyoto revolted in August 1864, professing themselves anxious to rescue the Emperor from evil advisers. The Emperor did not wish to be rescued, and the Shogun, whose function it was to suppress rebels, crushed the rising by the end of 1864, with the assistance of samurai placed at his disposal by Satsuma and other clans. At this time Satsuma and Chōshū were at odds, and Shimadzu Saburo, the Satsuma leader, was a better statesman than any of the Chōshū men. He knew how to control the refractory rōnin, restraining or encouraging them to suit his own plans; and he seems still to have had in mind the possibility of a compromise between the civil and the military powers. In the now very unstable position of affairs he could tip the balance as he wished, and from this moment the attitude of Satsuma was to be the most important factor in determining the domestic policy of Japan, which in turn would shape its foreign relations.

It was at this crucial point that the harassed Bakufu made an error of judgment which proved fatal. After their defeat the Chōshū leaders submitted, and the matter might well have been left there. Satisfactory terms were arranged on the suggestion of Saigo Takamori, an influential Satsuma samurai, and by the beginning of 1865 a settlement was in sight. But in the Bakufu rash counsels prevailed, and after much discussion and manœuvre it was decided to crush the Chōshū clan entirely. The conditions laid down were so harsh that Chōshū determined to fight to a finish. Satsuma no longer took the side of the Bakufu, and some prominent Satsuma men, among whom were Kido, Ito, and Inouye, were approached by the war party in Chōshū for help. Satsuma went so far as to purchase war materials from an English firm in Nagasaki and to present them to Chōshū. The Shogun led his troops in person to Osaka. Meanwhile on the side of the Bakufu there was much argument to and fro, much denunciation of rebels and warlike preparation. The clans that the Shogun summoned to assist him were slow to respond, and it was not until July 1866, more than twelve months after he had procured the Imperial mandate to "chastise the rebels," that Tokugawa forces marched west. They were everywhere unsuccessful, being driven back to their base in ignominious fashion. Thus the country was presented with the spectacle of the defeat of the Shogun's armies by a single clan. No doubt the Chōshū men were impudent and deserved a lesson, but the Shogun's advisers had made an error that no dictator can afford. They had made a threat they could not carry out. The Shogun himself died in Osaka on August 17, 1866, and hostilities were suspended under the pretence of mourning. Hitotsubashi Keiki succeeded the defunct Shogun, and the Bakufu, still struggling to maintain its prestige, continued its efforts to disgrace and diminish Chōshū, but met with firm opposition from Satsuma.

The hollowness of all Tokugawa pretensions had been exposed, and the most powerful clans were now arrayed against them. The idea of amalgamation — Kōbu-gattai — was no longer entertained, and Satsuma began to work for the destruction of the Shogunate. Its natural ally in this enterprise was Chōshū, and the two clans were soon reconciled by the efforts of Saigo Takamori and Okubo Toshimichi, who had no difficulty in persuading Chōshū to join them, since that clan had been uniformly hostile to the Bakufu from the beginning. A secret understanding had been reached already in 1866, and this soon became an alliance. During the preparations for the second expedition against Chōshū, a combined fleet of American, British, Dutch, and French warships with diplomatic representatives on board had anchored in Osaka Bay, to press for the opening of the court of Hyogo and the Imperial approval of the commercial treaties.

The foreign powers had for long suspected that there was dual authority in Japan, but did not understand the relations between the court and the Shogunate, which it must be admitted were not easy to define. But they had come to see that the centre of power was gradually moving to Kyoto, and they had decided to deal now with the throne, hoping to make an impression by a show of force. Their demand was unpalatable to the Emperor, but the Bakufu seized this opportunity to represent to the court the danger of a refusal and the court reluctantly agreed to ratify the treaties of 1858. The court refused to give way as to the opening of Hyogo, which was fixed for January 1, 1868, but the Bakufu, with its usual reserve, refrained from telling the foreign representatives of this condition. The Emperor at least had the dubious satisfaction of learning that the foreign powers were aware of his growing authority. It should be explained that he reached his decision on the advice of a majority of the leading clans, whose representatives he had summoned on November 21, 1865. Opinion was rapidly swinging in favour of foreign intercourse.

The question of foreign intercourse was thus solved, at least in principle. But the pressing question now was the disposal of the Shogunate. The times were very ripe for change. The Emperor Komei had died on February 3, 1867 and was succeeded at once by the youthful sovereign known to history as the Meiji Emperor.

Shimadzu Saburo, on the advice of Saigo, Okubo, and others, agreed to the formation of an alliance with Chōshū, which was to be joined by Echizen, Tosa, Uwajima. This was early in 1867, and in May of that year Saigo, escorting Shimadzu, led troops into

Kyoto and was shortly followed by the rulers of Echizen (Shungaku), Tosa (Yamanouchi), Uwajima (Daté), and others, who commenced activities at court and pressed upon Keiki, who was then residing in the capital at the Nijo Palace, reforms that in effect meant the surrender of power by him to the court and to his greater vassals. It is interesting to note at this point that the lord of Tosa, still nourishing a sentiment of loyalty to the Tokugawa because his ancestors had been Ieyasu's men, pleaded illness and did not join in the conversations with the Shogun. But one of his clansmen, named Itagaki Taisuke, was strongly in favour of Saigo's plan to restore the Emperor to his former power. Chōshū agreed, and other clans that had sympathized with Chōshū in its struggle against the Bakufu joined in the movement. They arranged to bring troops to Kyoto "for the protection of the Imperial city," and they approached certain court nobles who had hitherto been in favour of the amalgamation of powers but were now persuaded that the Bakufu must be overcome. Among these were Iwakura Tomomi, and Sanjo Sanetomi (already noticed as one of the Seven Fugitive Nobles). Both of these, with the clansmen named above, were to play leading parts in the Restoration, which was then approaching.

The new Shogun found himself pressed on all sides, the western clans urging him to resign, his own faithful vassals and the more uncompromising officials of the Bakufu pressing him to stand up for his rights. His position was by now untenable, and on November 8, 1867 he announced his resignation. In a dignified manifesto he blamed himself for faulty actions, saying that "if authority is restored to the Emperor, and matters of high policy are decided by His Majesty after national deliberations, then by unity in thought and effort the country can hold its own with all nations of the world." If he had stopped at this it might have been said that nothing in the life of the Shogunate became it more than its ending. The Shogun awaited further orders from the court, which had requested him to remain in office until a council of the leading feudal lords could meet in Kyoto and decide upon the next step. It seemed as if, even at this last moment, some high office might be reserved for the Tokugawa leader.[12] But the reform party, flushed with pride and success, easily induced the court on January 3, 1868 to abolish the Shogunate and the nominal regency with which the Shoguns had usually been invested. A provisional government was formed, in which no adherent of the

---

[12] Certain daimyo, including Echizen and Owari, who had historical links with the Tokugawa, did in fact propose an arrangement by which the Shogun should offer part of his revenues to the court and take his place in the new government on the same footing as great feudatories like Satsuma and Chōshū.

Tokugawa was included and the key posts were allotted to the five clans of Satsuma, Tosa, Aki, Owari, and Echizen; and as a last bitter insult Chōshū was pardoned and a Chōshū force appeared in the capital. The Shogun contented himself with a formal protest, but he was overruled by his supporters, who with the faulty judgment that characterized the actions of the Bakufu in its decline urged him to take arms against the court. He did so, was defeated, and returned to Yedo. There followed a brief civil war and, except for a stand made by a few Tokugawa adherents who held out for some months, the whole country submitted to the Emperor's rule without delay.

The Meiji era began on January 25, 1868. The name of Yedo was changed to Tokyo (Eastern Capital) in September 1868, and in that city the Emperor's residence and the seat of government were established in March 1869. There was confusion for a while. The new government no longer encouraged or tolerated antiforeign activities, but the sentiment of hatred did not at once subside. The mass of the people were ready to show signs of friendship towards foreigners, but there was a residue of irreconcilable rōnin and other agitators who displayed great hostility. Violent attacks both upon foreigners and upon Japanese associated with the new, pro-Western régime were frequent in the first few years of Meiji. In March 1868 the crew of a French picket-boat were murdered by Tosa samurai, and shortly afterwards some desperadoes attacked the British Minister as he was riding to an audience with the Emperor. In all such cases the new government was prompt to punish the offenders. Among Japanese victims was Yokoi Shōnan, who was murdered on February 15, 1869. The Official Gazette of the time contains several entries concerning this incident, from which it is evident that the new government were much perturbed by these affairs and made up their minds to use strong measures against unruly rōnin. Much of the ruthlessness displayed by the authorities in the ensuing decade can be traced to their determination, formed at this time, to suppress subversive activities without hesitation. They had not abandoned the feudal outlook in matters of discipline.

It is as well to recollect, before going on to a study of Meiji politics, that power was now in the hands of men who had been brought up as soldiers and were schooled to drastic action. Okubo and Saigo belonged to the Satsuma clan, the most stubborn fighters in Japan. Goto of Tosa was an experienced swordsman; Kido, Ito, and Inouye of Chōshū had risked their lives more than once in the troubles between their clan and the Bakufu, and most of their colleagues had gone through similar experiences. The character of these men, and the events in which they had participated, had much to do in shaping the political history of the Meiji period, which is hereafter described. It is a period that bears a very clear imprint of the character of individuals, whereas by contrast the policy of the ensuing decades appears anonymous and undirected. Most foreign observers who were acquainted with the great figures of the Meiji period are agreed in thinking that there was a great fall in the quality of statesmanship after they had departed from the stage.

One more observation may be suitably made here. The Meiji government was rich in talent but poor in money. The public finance of Japan, maladministered by the Shogunate for more than a century, was almost entirely ruined by expenditure on national defence, indemnities, and civil war after about 1800, and when the new government came into power in 1868 its coffers were nearly empty. This is one of the leading facts in the history of the early years of Meiji. Next in importance is the fact that by the beginning of the nineteenth century it was being said that hardly any daimyo had a fortune of more than 300,000 *ryō*, while many merchants and landowners counted their money by millions. The wealthy classes had to be used and conciliated by the new government unless its leaders were prepared for an economic as well as a political revolution; and this is not, or was not then, the way of revolutionaries who have accomplished one difficult reform.

As seen by foreign students the history of the years between Perry's arrival and the Restoration of 1868 is concerned chiefly with the struggles of the Western powers to induce Japan to emerge from seclusion. It is partly for that reason that a foreign writer can hardly avoid stressing the deceitful stratagems of the Japanese government and the general atmosphere of xenophobia that pervaded the country in those days. But examined from a different viewpoint, these aspects are of incidental rather than primary importance. The true interest of the events related emerges when they are studied as evidence of the way in which a society can decay and renew itself without changing its essence. The arrival of foreigners demanding admission brought to light and even resolved certain conflicts latent in Japanese political life, and in that respect Western influence was clear and decisive. But it was limited in its effect, and in the following pages an attempt will be made to show how in other fields it was circumscribed by the strength of ancient habits. No final conclusion can be reached, since it is early yet to say what are the lasting results of international intercourse. A century is a short time in the growth of a national culture, and all we can do is to inspect the passing scene, trying to draw from it some modest and tentative inferences.

Note on CHAPTER 12

COMMODORE PERRY'S EXPEDITION. An interesting account is given in Arthur Walworth's *Black Ships off Japan* (New York: Alfred A. Knopf; 1946). It contains some particulars of earlier American attempts to open trade relations.

The fullest account of relationships between Japanese and Americans before the expedition is to be found in a well-documented study in English by Shunzo Sakamaki, entitled "Japan and the United States, 1790–1853," which is Vol. XVIII (second series) of the *Transactions of the Asiatic Society of Japan* (Tokyo, 1939).

CHAPTER 13

EARLY MEIJI: THE POLITICAL SCENE

1. Prefatory

IT is not the purpose of this study to present the history of early Meiji in terms of strict political or economic analysis. It is of course possible to trace, as a number of modern historians have done, some tolerably close analogies between the development of capitalism in western European countries and the process by which the social and political order in Japan was transformed as the mercantile class developed and commercial capital was replaced first by industrial and then by finance capital. But the early stages of Japanese political development, at least from the Restoration to the Sino-Japanese war of 1894, present so many peculiar features that it is difficult to reconcile them with any rigid theory, deterministic or other. It may, for instance, be said that the demands of a rising mercantile class — a bourgeoisie, to use the popular label — resulted in the liquidation — another piece of jargon — of feudalism and in the kind of political change that had accompanied the industrial revolution in Europe. But in fact the capitalism of the early years of Meiji was feeble and in some respects rudimentary, and it can be argued that the early Meiji government, far from succumbing to capitalist pressure, created a régime that was in essence more feudal in character than the Shogunate in its decline. Certainly this was a view held by many of the opponents of that government, who frequently complained that it was a second and more resolute Bakufu.

The driving force at the Restoration and in political life for the best part of a generation thereafter was provided by leaders who had been brought up in a feudal, or at any rate a feudalistic, atmosphere. They were for the most part dissatisfied and ambitious samurai, and their outlook was coloured by their antecedents. It was these men, and not the bourgeoisie, who laid the foundations of a capitalist structure and at the same time developed a political system that bore little resemblance to those which came into force in the advanced industrial countries of western Europe under the influence of a powerful moneyed class. Consequently it would be misleading to treat the history of the first twenty years of Meiji as a simple case of the repetition in Asia of a process that had taken place in Europe. The fact that the Japanese exercised a choice between European models and did not follow any one of them exclusively tends to show that neither their political nor their economic development conformed to a theoretical pattern such as is postulated by some modern historians. Indeed, the chief interest of the study of Japanese history in its early "modern" period lies in its divergence from what is regarded as normal in the conversion of an agrarian into an industrial society.

In the following pages, therefore, no attempt is made to describe events in their relation to some preconceived notion of historical necessity. They are arranged in a loose fashion that will probably be painful to scientific students; but it may have the advantage, rather rare in these ideological days, of permitting the reader to select what interests him and to draw his own conclusions. The limited object of this chapter is to furnish a background for the subsequent discussion of social and other changes that took place in the period reviewed. It might have been more logical to attempt a description of the changing aspects of Japanese society and then to follow with an account of the political events it experienced. But because Japanese social and intellectual life in those years was dominated by political issues that dictated its chief forms of expression it seems best to pay attention first to political matters. What follows therefore does not pretend to be a detailed study of political history, but aims at giving only such information as will help in understanding later chapters. It is unfortunately difficult to prevent a bald political summary from becoming a dreary catalogue of such words as "constitution," "representation," "democracy," "oligarchy," "liberty," "tyranny," and suchlike respectable but inelegant terms. We are tied down to the use of these deceptive abstracts, and much of the political argument of the day was concerned with their interpretation. Indeed, it is one of the special features of early Meiji controversy that it was a battle about words, and about words that had only just entered the native vocabulary, to represent ideas new to most Japanese. One interesting example may be quoted in order to show how strange, even to men of education, were many of the ideas that presently were to be the subject of bitter strife.

There was nothing in the Japanese language that stood for "popular rights," and a term had to be invented. This was the word *minken,* which within a few years became the war cry of the liberals. Its origin is interesting, for it was adopted in an almost accidental fashion. In 1870 a small group of scholars was engaged on a translation of the French Civil Code. When they came to the words *droit civil* the translation *minken* was suggested, because *min* means "people" and *ken* means "authority" or "privilege." But a discussion arose as to whether "people" had "rights." What did it mean? Objections were raised, and it was only after the chairman of the translation committee had intervened that the unfamiliar idea was accepted. *Minken* thus became the Japanese word first for *droit civil* and then for "the rights of the people." The chairman was Eto Shimpei, one of the Restoration leaders, who later was executed for leading an insurrection against a government that was loath to concede popular liberties.

But Eto himself was not imbued with liberal sentiment. He wanted a change of government because he disliked the ruling coalition, and there were many others of his kind, though not all were prepared to take the same risks. His case throws some light on the nature of the political issues that split the governing class after the Restoration. From a plain record of its principal events the political history of the first twenty years or so appears as a great struggle to reach a national decision for or against democratic principles of government. This may stand as a description of its superficial aspects, though it was complicated by personal antagonisms and long-standing loyalties, which were often more important than principles in deciding the order of battle. But what was at stake was something of deeper import than a choice between two systems of administering national affairs. It was a conflict between traditional sentiment and that idea of progress which was then the guiding principle of the Occidental world.

This concept, this view of life, not very long established in the West, was new to Oriental peoples, though it must be admitted that the Japanese were more ready to receive it than others. In India and China it was unfamiliar and even unpleasing, since it ran counter to religious beliefs or social systems of great antiquity. In India and in the Buddhist countries of Farther India it was only by exception that men nourished hopes of increasing the sum of earthly felicity by human endeavour. In China, less pervaded by a sense of spiritual values, men's minds tended to a matter-of-fact acceptance of the existing order and were generally sceptical of innovation. But the Japanese are a restless people, who seem always to have been more interested in action than in contemplation, for even their version of Zen quietism had its energetic side. They were therefore disposed to accept the theory that a good life can be attained by assiduous devotion to practical matters. To the Japanese after the Restoration the idea of progress was not only welcome, but extremely stimulating. It was interpreted by them not in terms of spiritual enlightenment but of material accumulations — more facts, more wealth, more strength, more manufactures, more men, ships, and guns. Most of the leading men in the country were on the side of progress so defined, and if there was a division of opinion among them it was not as to the kind of progress to be desired but as to the method of attaining it. Though on the surface the political turmoil of these crucial decades looks like a fight for individual freedom, in fact it was little more than a hot dispute, confused by allegiances that had little to do with the real issue, as to the best way of achieving material successes. The most striking feature of the period is not its political clashes, but the alacrity with which the country as a whole seized upon the dogma of perfectibility and threw itself without misgivings into the task of self-improvement.

It is not necessary to pursue this topic here, though it is hoped that the reader will bear it in mind when studying the following narrative. He might also do well to remember that, in Japan as elsewhere, the political alignments of individuals are frequently based upon grievances rather than principles. Thus — to take a simple instance — many of the important figures in political life in Japan in the decisive years of early Meiji were former Bakufu officials who led opposition movements because they were influenced by an inherited dislike of the clans that had brought about the downfall of the Bakufu. This was particularly true of the principal journalists, who with few exceptions supported the liberal opposition for motives that were not entirely idealistic but included an antagonism to the ruling coalition arising from their former loyalty to the Tokugawa régime.

Another point that should not be overlooked in studying the administrative history of the early years of Meiji is the part played by former servants of the Tokugawa. The Bakufu had sent its brightest young men abroad for study for some years before the Restoration, and its officials had been obliged by the pressure of events to attempt constructive reforms while its opponents were still engaged in destructive criticism. It therefore had at its disposal a number of experienced men who knew how to tackle administrative problems and some capable persons who knew about Western life from direct observation. It thus had a wider choice than any single clan, and probably it could draw upon better brains than could either Satsuma or Chōshū. Though political power was seized by individuals from those clans, who were remarkably capable leaders, they could not have exercised that power promptly and successfully without the support of trained administrators who had learned their business under the Bakufu. Thus, paradoxically, a good deal of the talent that destroyed the Bakufu system was furnished by the Bakufu itself. In the early years of Meiji it was said of the minority of former Bakufu servants who refused posts under the new government that they were displaying *yase-gaman,* which means spiting their stomachs to save their faces. Among Tokugawa retainers who threw in their lot with the new régime were Enomoto, who had been sent abroad for study in 1863 and, after fighting for the Tokugawa in 1867, became an admiral and then an ambassador in the service of the Meiji government. With Katsu Awa, another Bakufu man who was sent abroad, he was the founder of the Japanese navy. Katsu himself was one of the chief figures in the Restoration and displayed great talent as a negotiator.

It may not be out of place here to speculate in very general terms why Japanese culture offered less resistance to new ideas than Chinese or Indian culture. The problem is not easy to understand, though many explanations have been offered. Perhaps a clue may be found in the fact that Japanese culture, especially in its political features, contained a number of anachronistic and even irrational elements. In so far as it was based upon the assumptions of early Shinto, a primitive theocratic creed, modified by Buddhism and overlaid by feudal thought, it was riddled with contradictions and had not the strength and coherence of such great systems as Confucianism and Hinduism. In fact it might be argued that the Japanese never worked out a satisfactory and stable system of political life, but were always experimenting. This is a view that their disturbed and changeful domestic history tends to confirm; and it is significant that when, under the Tokugawa, they arrived at some degree of stability, it was achieved by disregarding indigenous precedents and calling in the aid of Confucian teaching. It is not surprising that when they were faced with a realization of their country's weakness the leaders of the Restoration movement and their immediate successors should have been ready to sacrifice much of a system that had already proved obsolete. Equally it was to be expected that they would arouse opposition from both conservative and progressive quarters and would be charged with going too fast or too slow as seemed expedient to their critics.

But this did not mean a complete break with tradition. Certainly the presentation of new ideas to the Japanese people was a most important feature of early Meiji history, and new ideas must often fly in tradition's face. A first glance at the course of events gives the impression that one belief after another, one institution after another, fell before the attack of Western influence. Yet a closer examination shows that many of the important changes that took place in political and social life came about not by direct imitation of Western models but by a natural process of evolution which produced results similar to those which had arisen in the West out of similar circumstances.

This is one of the themes to be discussed in ensuing chapters and need not be enlarged upon in this prefatory note. But it may be useful to cite one example by way of illustration: it is generally held that the Constitution framed by Ito and promulgated in 1889 was a result of direct German influence, and even of the personal influence of Bismarck himself. This is only true in a most general way, for as a strict historical statement it cannot stand, because it neglects the fact that the relevant circumstances of Germany resembled those of Japan at the same time. Ito found useful material in German history and German political literature because German sentiment about monarchy and armies was like Japanese sentiment on those matters; and it will scarcely be contended that Japanese sentiment (which had a strong tradition behind it) was created or even influenced by German example. The most one can say is that Ito felt at home in a German atmosphere.

2. The Remnants of Feudalism

THE FIRST task of the leaders of Japan when the Shogun had formally returned his powers to the Emperor was to replace the complex and heterogeneous rule of the Tokugawa by a single and uniform control over the whole country. This could be done only by stages, and the first central government to be formed was only provisional. Its purpose was little more than to symbolize the assumption of power and to hold the position until more suitable forms could be worked out. What was important at this juncture was not the detail of its organization but the character and antecedents of its members, for it was their decisions that would shape policy in the crucial years to follow and thereby fix a pattern for the future development of Japan which it would be difficult to vary. This may not have been apparent at the time, but subsequent history shows that the small oligarchy that guided the first steps of Japan after the Restoration did in fact lay down lines of national policy from which even violent opposition could not force them or their successors to depart.

The early stages in the development of a central authority though brief and experimental are therefore of peculiar interest. They belong to a time when public opinion was fluid and even bewildered, when political views had not crystallized in intellectual circles. Such conditions were favourable to rapid and arbitrary decisions by those in authority. The first government was a simple structure, consisting of a Supreme Controller and senior and junior Councils of State. The Controller was an Imperial Prince and under him as deputies were two court nobles of the highest rank, Iwakura and Sanjo. These appointments were necessary in order to emphasize the power of the throne and the civil aristocracy, which the military aristocracy had for so long usurped.

KIDO JUNICHIRO (KŌIN) (1834–77)

A Chōshū samurai, one of the leaders of the
Restoration movement and a member
of the first Meiji government

But in the Controller's department there served men who, though they had played an important part in the overflow of feudalism, had been military retainers of feudal lords. They were youngish samurai of modest origin from those powerful clans of Satsuma, Chōshū, Tosa, and Hizen which, by throwing their strength on the side of the Emperor, had made the defeat of the Tokugawa possible. Among them were Okubo, Kido, Komatsu, and Goto, men of strong character and firm opinion who, it should be noted, were not mere theoretical revolutionaries but former feudal officials experienced in clan politics, conversant with administrative tasks, and imbued with a strong authoritarian sense. They were true members of a military caste. Goto, for instance, when Sir Harry Parkes was attacked by rōnin in 1868, dismounted and cut off the head of one of the assailants with great skill and dis-

GOTŌ SHŌJIRŌ (1837–97)

*A leading Restoration figure and member of
early Meiji governments*

patch. Nakai, a Foreign Office official, also leaped from his horse and sliced off another head. This is not a feat that can be performed without practice and a martial disposition; and most members and officials of the new government were capable of similar exploits.

These were the men who exercised real power, though they acted warily at first and worked behind a screen of high personages. The Senior Council was composed of court nobles and feudal nobles in equal numbers, the Junior Council of courtiers and feudal officers of lower rank. Neither of these bodies had any real authority. This arrangement lasted only a short time. It was modified in February and completely revised in June of 1868, when the aims of the new government were laid down in an Imperial Proclamation. This is an important document, which needs close study,

317

for it is — although not so named — the first Constitution of modern Japan. It opens by citing in full the Charter Oath which had been taken by the Emperor on April 6, 1868 and which may be looked upon as the source and foundation of Meiji policy. For an important charter of this character the oath is remarkably vague, and attempts to translate it faithfully into English reveal that it can be interpreted in several ways. Two authoritative translations, usually cited by foreign writers on Japanese history, read as follows:

A. Hodzumi's Version, as quoted in *Encyclopædia Britannica* (1911)	B. Ukita's Version in *Fifty Years of New Japan*
1. Deliberative assemblies shall be established on an extensive scale and all measures of government shall be decided by public opinon.	Public councils shall be organized and all governmental affairs shall be decided by general discussion.
2. All classes, high and low, shall unite in vigorously carrying out the plan of government.	All classes, both rulers and ruled, shall with one heart devote themselves to the advancement of the national interests.
3. All classes of the people shall be allowed to fulfil their just aspirations so that there may be no discontent	All the civil and military officials and all the common people shall be allowed to realize their own aspirations and to evince their active characteristics.
or All classes of the people shall be allowed to fulfil their just desires as far as possible so that there may not be any discontent among them.	
4. Uncivilized customs of former times shall be broken through and everything shall be based upon just and equitable principles of nature.	All base customs of former times shall be abolished, and justice and equity as they are universally recognized shall be followed.
5. Knowledge shall be sought throughout the world, so that the welfare of the Empire may be promoted.	Knowledge shall be sought for throughout the world and thus the foundations of the Empire shall be extended.

So expressed, the first three articles might well be taken as a statement of intention to set up a national parliament and local assemblies, to introduce democratic principles of government, and to adopt freedom and equality and the pursuit of happiness as the foundation of the national life. The fourth article might be read as a promise to abolish all institutions which are not consistent with the doctrine of natural rights; and the fifth as a decision to adopt Western philosophical beliefs and social practices. But many other interpretations are possible, and domestic political strife in Japan during the ensuing twenty years consisted largely in an argument over the practical intention of these various clauses.

It is not likely that the whole truth can be ascertained, nor is it of great importance, but there is some use in trying to discover what was in the minds of the effective rulers of Japan at the time when the document was made public. If they intended it as a truly democratic charter it can be inferred that they were strongly influenced by Western political thought. But if a less liberal and less precise interpretation is correct, then they had not made up their minds to introduce drastic political reforms but deemed it wise to proclaim liberal intentions in broad terms that committed them to no specific measures.

The first draft of the oath was made by Yuri Kimimasa and Fukuoka Kōtei, and this was amended and expanded by Kido. It was on Kido's advice that the oath was made public, his reason being that the opinion of the clans — he did not refer to the people — was running in various directions and there was danger from them. It was therefore important to give them "a general line" to follow. His Majesty should give a lead to the feudal lords and "the hundred officials," and show the public what his intentions were. A study of some of the preliminary drafts shows that the first article, at least in its early forms, contemplated not a national assembly but a council of feudal lords. Yuri's first draft has no text under the heading Article 1, but simply a note saying "General idea of a deliberative form." The next version, that of Fukuoka, says: "A council of feudal lords shall be established," and this is accepted by Kido without change.

We need not stop for further textual criticism. It is enough to say that the proclamation which ushered in the government of June 1868 cannot be regarded as definitely promising an elective legislature and equal political and social rights for all subjects. All the drafts distinguish between civil and military officers on the one hand and the common people on the other. The first article, in the usually accepted English translations, says "All classes of people" or "High and low." These versions are somewhat misleading, since the Japanese text shows a definite consciousness of division into classes and not of political or social equality. It is true that they represent the meaning ascribed to the Charter Oath by the liberal opposition in the following two decades, and this was also the interpretation later spread abroad by Japanese propagandists anxious to make a good impression in England and the United States. But seeing that when the proclamation was issued feudalism had not yet been abolished, the clansmen had still to be reassured and the general public was neither experienced nor interested in political forms, it is most improbable that the government then in power should have intended to set up popular representative institutions, to allow the ignorant masses to decide the national polity, and to break down all existing class divisions by fiat. They may have thought it wise to hold out such prospects as a distant goal, for there was certainly apparent at that time a widespread if vague desire for reform, which it was important not to disappoint. But in 1868 not many Japanese, even in well-educated circles, had more than rudimentary notions about democratic forms of government. Indeed, the very idea of liberty at that date was startling, if attractive.

It is important to note that the Proclamation of June 1868 did not state in terms anything that had not already been proposed by the Shogunate when it was trying to come to terms with the throne and suggesting means of consulting opinion throughout the country. It was not until some years later that the general public became familiar, through books and speeches and newspapers, with Western political theory and practice. It is therefore reasonable to assume that Kido and his colleagues were temporizing when they devised the Charter Oath, and that their main purpose was to keep public opinion quiet, or to forestall dissatisfaction, while they devoted themselves to immediate problems. If further evidence is needed, it can be found in the extremely bureaucratic system that was in fact adopted after the proclamation had been issued.

The supreme organ was the Dajōkwan or Council of State, in which was concentrated all authority, whether executive, legislative, or judicial. Its several powers were exercised by three bodies which, though distinct from one another, were integral parts of the Council. These were a deliberative chamber comprising an upper and a lower house; an office of the President of the Council; and five departments of state, those of the Shinto Religion, War, Foreign Affairs, Finance, and Justice. The highest offices fell to princes of the blood and to the court and territorial nobility, "because due affection should be shown to relatives of the Sovereign and due respect to persons of rank"; but real power remained in the hands of the advisory officials, who were as before samurai from the western clans — Okubo, Kido, Goto, Itagaki, Soyejima, Saigo, Ito, and Okuma. The deliberative assembly was at first composed only of samurai representing the clans, but a departure was made by extending membership to representatives of the three great cities and of Imperial — that is to say, of former Tokugawa — territory. The assembly proved incapable of any useful discussion or advice and

OKUBO TOSHIMICHI (1832–78)

A Satsuma samurai. He was the most influential member
of the first Meiji government.

lapsed into disuse after a few sessions, not unexpectedly since the matters referred to it were either trivial or were foregone conclusions. The questions on its agenda had already been decided by Okubo, Kido, and their colleagues in consultation with the heads of the government.

It is clear that the first system of government established under the terms of the Charter Oath did not embody any Western forms and was not inspired by any specific Western influence. It was, in fact, as was freely stated at the time, a reversion to pre-feudal institutions. It was modelled on the administration set up in A.D. 701 in imitation of the Chinese system, and established almost exactly the same offices with the same titles. It embodied in particular one very ancient feature: namely, the precedence of the Department of Religion over all other departments of state.

It is true, however, that the new system included some innovations. A deliberative assembly was not part of Japanese tradition, though in ancient and mediæval Japan such communities as great monasteries were governed by councils drawn from their members, and under the successive feudal régimes much business was left by the Shogun to councils or committees. It is therefore not certain that the idea of a deliberative assembly was of foreign origin, though some points in this early Constitution can perhaps be traced to foreign influence of a very general kind, as for example the threefold division of powers, which had already come to the notice of Japanese missions to the United States and to Europe in 1860 and 1861.

The structure of June 1868 needs no further description, for it was modified at intervals until in 1871 a commission was set up to make plans for reorganizing the central government. Still further changes were subsequently made and it was not until 1889 that a permanent form of organization was reached. These numerous revisions reflect the unsettled conditions of the time and may be said to have been the result of a necessary process of trial and error. Though we need not follow this process in detail, it is best for a proper understanding of the institutional growth of the first twenty years or so of Meiji to know something of the problems faced by the small ruling oligarchy that came into power in 1868.

It cannot be too emphatically stated that the steps taken on the way to the form of government reached in 1889 were dictated not by theoretical considerations but by the demands of the domestic political situation. Okubo, Kido, and the other leaders had to consider not how to adapt Western practices to Japanese needs, but how to meet the exigencies of the very precarious situation in which the established government found itself for some years after 1868. Indeed, it is only just within the bounds of truth to call it an established government, since the first care of its members was to preserve its life rather than to consider its anatomy.

In 1868, though such central authority as the late Tokugawa government used to exercise had been destroyed, vestiges of feudalism as an institution and much of the feudal spirit still survived. The nominally centralized government that came into power in 1868 owed its very existence to the support of the great clans that had espoused the Imperial cause, and it was their military strength that had restored the sovereign power. The government had little military or financial strength of its own, and no moral authority except that which it derived from the Emperor, at that time a youth of fifteen. This last was admittedly a powerful advantage, but one that might easily be lost if the government offended the great feudal lords who, though they had combined to displace the Shogun, were still masters in their own domains. They were capable of resisting by force any policy they might hold to be against their own or the nation's interests.

The Restoration would, however, have been in vain if the feudatories were not deprived of their autonomy; and the problem that the new government had to solve was not one of administrative forms but of gradually strengthening itself until it could with safety destroy the still considerable remnants of feudal power. For this purpose it needed not only sound policies which would command substantial approval throughout the country, but also sufficient force to discourage, and if necessary to suppress, any serious opposition that might threaten from either of two sources. One of these was a possible combination of dissatisfied feudal lords; the other was an active discontent among those numerous samurai and rōnin who might, as individuals, stand to lose by changes that were imperative if the government was really to exercise universal authority and to demolish every form of separatism. To meet such emergencies the first need was to equip and train a national army. This was commenced by the introduction of a conscription law in 1870. But time was required for preparation, and the law could not come into effective operation for two or three years. Meanwhile it was essential for the government to attract to itself all the support it could gain from the most powerful groups in the country. These were the great western clans of Satsuma, Chōshū, Hizen, and Tosa. Fortunately they, or a majority of their members, were convinced of the need for a strong central government, and they took action which, though no doubt inspired by regard for their own interests, was none the less enlightened and magnanimous. In March 1869 they voluntarily offered their fiefs to the throne, thus declaring themselves on the side of the government and ready to share in the destruction of feudalism. They made this offer in a document that stated: "There must be one central governing body and one universal authority, which must be preserved intact."

By this time the last resistance of the Tokugawa had been broken and the new administration felt able to treat the defeated vassals with some liberality. This proved unpleasing to certain elements in the clans, in particular that of Satsuma, which was traditionally the bitterest enemy of the Tokugawa house. There was a difficult moment here, for while the Satsuma clan contained a progressive group inspired by Okubo, who held an important place in the new government, the remainder — and this included Shimadzu, the leader of the clan, as well as Saigo Takamori, one of its most influential members and a popular hero — felt jealous of their younger colleagues and were disappointed by the small part that Satsuma as a whole was playing in the new administration. There is no doubt that most of the clans which combined to overthrow the Tokugawa were moved by a desire to destroy a régime that they hated rather than any intention to construct a new central authority; and bodies that have cohered for purposes of destruction frequently fly apart when their task is finished. It would be wrong to suppose that there was uniform opinion in any one clan, but it is certain that in many clans there was a strong element looking forward not to the displacement of feudal rule by centralized power but to a new form of feudalism in which local autonomy would be preserved under some kind of federal council upon which all would be represented. The most powerful clans doubtless entertained hopes that they, or some combination among them, would dominate the national scene, and Satsuma, it is certain, at one time nourished ambitions of replacing the Shogunate under the Imperial ægis.

It was because of dangerous possibilities such as these that the new government had to move cautiously, and the emphasis upon deliberative assemblies which is embodied in the Charter Oath was not a concession to rising democratic sentiment but a safeguard against the ascendancy of a single feudal group. It will naturally be asked why then did the four great clans, which were the most likely pretenders, consent to surrender their fiefs at a time when the newly established government was lacking in force. No full account of their motives is possible, but it is safe to guess that an attempt by one of them to seize power would have raised a coalition against it and brought about a really disastrous civil war. Other and worthier considerations were also in the minds of many clansmen, especially the active-minded younger samurai who were imbued with patriotic feeling and influenced by a spirit of reform that filled the contemporary air. Many of these, moreover, were chafing under the restraints of narrow clan politics, confined by petty local duties and burning to exercise their talents in a wider sphere. For these reasons the young reformers at the centre of government were not in fact so powerless as they appeared. They could, if they were cautious and tactful, mobilize on their side very strong forces, of which not the least valuable was a sense of loyalty to the throne and to the country at large which the stirring events of the Restoration had fostered.

It was in reliance upon this spirit that Okubo, Kido, and their colleagues persuaded the four clans of western Japan to surrender their fiefs. The idea of the surrender of the fiefs was not new. It had been suggested before the Restoration by the Owari branch of the Tokugawa family, though at that time it was expected that the surrendered fiefs would be redistributed by the Emperor. The reformers all thought that it was a logical and necessary sequel of the surrender of the Shogun's powers that the daimyos should make a similar gesture. They were agreed in thinking that the establishment of provincial governments under the crown was necessary in order to unify the nation and also, in Iwakura's own words, "essential if we are to be on a par with foreign countries." It is significant that this care for national prestige recurs frequently in these early documents and there can be no doubt that it was an important factor in persuading reluctant feudal lords to agree to a measure that was contrary to their personal interests. That some were reluctant is clear from the fact that Kido first thought of only a partial surrender of territory, but was persuaded by Ito that it would be a mistake to take half measures.

Thus the reformers passed safely through the most crucial phase in the abolition of feudalism. But there were still obstacles to surmount. The remaining clans, with few exceptions, followed the example of the leaders before the end of the year, but there were still discontented factions in Satsuma and elsewhere, so that the government felt constrained to make a conciliatory gesture. In 1871, therefore, an imposing mission was sent to Satsuma headed by Prince Iwakura as the Emperor's deputy and including Okubo, himself a Satsuma samurai of great influence in the clan. They carried a message from the Emperor to Shimadzu, urging him to throw his weight behind the Imperial government and they proposed changes in the composition of the government which would give him a strong voice in national affairs. Similar visits were paid to Chōshū and other clans that it was important to sweeten, and thus a sorely needed composite support was obtained by the central authority. One valuable result was the formation of a force of some eight thousand men, to which the clans contributed, thus establishing the principle of a national army.

The surrender of the fiefs, though accepted in principle in a decree of August 1869, could not be carried out at once, since the government had at its disposal neither the funds nor the personnel required for the administration of the new territories. Further, and even more important, the actual transfer of the fiefs to civil governors would involve the complete abolition of feudalism, because the resources of the fiefs would belong to the state, and the samurai could no longer continue as the constituents of private armies. How fully these consequences of their gesture were foreseen by the feudal nobles is difficult to tell. The government was not yet ready to put them to the test and made only a modest preliminary move. It assimilated the administration of the surrendered domains to that of the areas already under the jurisdiction of the crown, but left their former feudal rulers in charge as Imperial delegates with the title of governor.

It was not until two years later that the final step in the abolition of feudal institutions was taken by the issue, in August 1871, of a brief decree which announced that feudal domains were henceforth to become units of local administration (prefectures) under the central government. This edict, surely one of the most laconic announcements of a revolution ever made, was reinforced by an Imperial message addressed to the new governors, explaining that the administration meant what it said, that this was not one of those orders which need not be obeyed. Shortly afterwards all the former daimyos were ordered to leave their estates and settle with their families in the capital. This was bold action and bore a strong resemblance to the Tokugawa policy of keeping feudal lords away from their fiefs and in attendance at the Yedo court so that they should not plot mischief at home. It succeeded because, in the interval between April 1868 (the date of the Charter Oath) and August 1871, the government had strengthened its hand by the conciliatory measures already described and by a judicious reshuffling of offices of state which, for the near future at least, assured the support of the great clans.

The general public at this time counted little in the balance of political forces, for the real danger to the administration was not popular objection to change but actual armed resistance by members of the military class. Nevertheless there was some growth of interest in national affairs in the cities, and the government took the precaution of inspiring newspaper articles against feudalism, thus for the first time in Japanese history condescending to take into account the opinions of the general public. The newspaper was a weekly, founded in 1871 at the instance of Kido, largely for this particular purpose.

This was an important departure and resulted in a rapid increase in the influence of the press, which was within a few years to cause great trouble to the government in power. But the most effective single measure that the government was able to take in its campaign to consolidate central authority was the formation of a conscript army. This, as we have noted, was provided for in the Conscription Law of 1870, though there was no army in being until 1873; but it was a key measure in the reform program and meanwhile the government could rely upon the composite force contributed by the clans, which, in case of need, would certainly have been reinforced by much voluntary enlistment from all reformist quarters.

The part played by the gradual building up of a national military force in shaping the character of Japanese political life cannot be underestimated. It is true enough that foreign influence prescribed some of the political forms that were ultimately adopted, but the necessities of the situation in the early years of Meiji, combined with the military antecedents of most of the protagonists, gave to the army a preponderating place in the national life. It brought into the political foreground men like Yamagata Aritomo (later Marshal Prince Yamagata), who may be regarded as the founder of the modern Japanese army. The shaky government in its young days was much strengthened by the force that was formed largely by the western clans, and could scarcely have survived had that group been hostile. Consequently the composition of ministries from 1871 onwards was largely determined by the fact that it was those clans that had made possible the transition from feudal rule to centralized monarchy. For many years men from Satsuma and Chōshū in particular continued to dominate the political stage and to hold key positions in the army and navy. It is obvious that governments so constituted were bound to acquire a special character, which was as important in shaping the national polity of Japan as the foreign influences to which she was submitted. Or, to put it in another way, those influences could operate only within limits set by the history of the Restoration movement and the antecedents of the men who brought it about and carried it through. To look upon the Restoration as a process by which feudal institutions and feudal thought were replaced by unqualified Western forms and ideas would be to misunderstand both its nature and its sequels.

The experiences of the government after the surrender of the fiefs show that its leaders had no grand design for reconstruction. It was not possible for them to look far ahead, and they had to proceed step by step, as was natural and indeed inevitable in times of commotion and uncertainty. Their general aim was to establish a stable central government and to develop the military and economic strength of their country so that it could face the international future with confidence. On long-range polity all parties and factions were agreed; but the immediate problem was to ensure domestic peace and to prevent the coalition of supporting clans from dissolving.

The next step therefore was to provide for the dispossessed rulers compensation for their loss of revenue and prestige, and to treat the now unemployed samurai with a degree of liberality that would keep them at least satisfied enough not to revolt against the new order. This need had already been foreseen when the government in 1869 had granted to the daimyos one half of their revenues upon the surrender of their fiefs. But such generous treat-

ment could not continue indefinitely, since the daimyos were relieved of far more than half of their expenditure, at the charge of
the state. The samurai had been giving varying proportions of
their customary allowances, and this also was a heavy burden upon
the national finances, since they formed an unproductive class,
numbering with their dependants perhaps as many as two million.
The government sought a way out of its financial embarrassments
by sending a mission abroad in 1871, under the leadership of
Iwakura and including Okubo, Kido, and Ito, to ask for a revision
of the treaties that would permit of raising import and export
duties. This attempt failed and, an increase of direct taxation being out of the question, the only means of balancing accounts was
to reduce expenditure on pensions.

Accordingly at the end of 1873 the government announced a
voluntary commutation scheme for the samurai, which was so un-
attractive that few of them accepted its terms. The feudal lords,
meanwhile, were left in receipt of their subsidies and were able,
moreover, to retain such capital sums as they had accumulated under the previous régime. By 1876, however, the government was
obliged under financial stress to introduce compulsory commutation for both daimyo and samurai.

Into details of this new plan we need not enter. It proved favourable to all but the least important daimyos, since the government as well as providing them with good pensions took over some
of their debts. But the small feudal chieftains and a majority of
the samurai suffered a severe cut in their emoluments. A samurai
of good standing whose annual rice allowance was nominally one
thousand bushels in pre-Restoration days, found himself reduced
to about four hundred after 1868, and now in 1876 he was obliged
to accept a payment in bonds and cash which would give him an
annual income equal to the value of one hundred and fifty bushels.
Samurai with low allowances were cut down to a pittance on which
a single man could scarcely subsist. This measure, though it might
be justified by financial necessity, was a gross breach of faith of a
kind common to revolutionary governments, and raised a great
outcry among the samurai. But the plan was carried through with
some modification and reduced the national expenditure by about
one third. It was a bold step to take and it produced some disagreeable results. It may not have been the true cause of a series of
samurai revolts that followed closely upon the announcement of
commutation, but it certainly made already smouldering discontent blaze up in several parts of Japan. There were uprisings
among samurai from 1874 onwards, that being the year in which
the voluntary scheme was announced. The pronunciamentos of
the disaffected groups usually took the form of attacks upon the

government for its policy of abolishing Japanese customs and encouraging Western ideas. Thus the Shimpūren or Divine Wind League, a society formed by Kumamoto men, was an extremely violent and xenophobe body, basing itself upon Shinto tenets. It bitterly criticized the government order of 1876 forbidding the wearing of swords and proclaimed that the toleration of Christianity would lead to selling the sacred soil of Japan to foreigners. In this revolt a number of Shinto priests took part. Other risings, in Hagi, Akidzuki, and Yamaguchi, were of a similar character, but the leader of the Yamaguchi samurai, one Maebara Issei, particularly attacked the pension scheme as an injustice to four hundred thousand innocent samurai.

These local disturbances were put down with little difficulty, but they were followed in 1877 by a rebellion on a large scale, led by Saigo Takamori, a prominent Satsuma samurai, which was suppressed only after several months of bloodshed. Something more must be said about this last struggle of feudal irreconcilables, but we should first examine a little more closely the conditions that produced it.

The great feudal lords did not suffer any serious loss when they were deprived of their fiefs. Few of them had been more than nominal rulers of their own domains, so that they were not conscious of any loss of power. Altogether their position as private individuals after the complete abolition of feudalism was in most cases socially more agreeable and financially more comfortable than it had been when they were only nominally powerful and rich. Many of them were in fact to form a new and influential class of *rentier*, investing in banking, commerce or industry, or serving in legislative bodies, or engaged in other careers where they could display more enterprise and enjoy more freedom than before.

The position and prospects of the samurai were by contrast wretched. They had already in the late Tokugawa period suffered heavy losses, and now, but for a fortunate few, they were ill-fitted for the kind of life offered to them. Their pensions were so small that even the higher grades of samurai were left in straitened circumstances, while the lower grades were reduced to penury or to real destitution. It is remarkable that they should as a class have resigned themselves to such treatment with so little protest. Their traditional contempt of money and their ignorance of its management, upon which they prided themselves, no doubt forbade them to make a public grievance of their poverty.[1]

But they had other reasons for complaint, for almost every

---

[1] J. R. Black, the author of *Young Japan*, who had a wide acquaintance among members of this class, records that he remembers only one instance when a samurai in conversation showed an interest in money (Vol. II, p. 459).

measure announced by the new government deprived them of some cherished privilege or spelled the dissolution of the society in which they had been brought up. From before the Restoration foreign ideas had begun to spread. The very introduction of the musket and the rifle had diminished the martial monopoly of the swordsman, and Western military uniforms had blemished the customary heraldic scene. In 1871 the government had given permission to samurai to wear swords or not, as they pleased. This was in effect to rule that the sword was no longer an indispensable badge of gentility; and in 1872 the people were directed to discontinue the old fashion of hairdressing — the topknot — and to wear their hair short, after the foreign style. This again was regarded as interfering with good old customs to no purpose. The edict announcing conscription for military service was perhaps the most objectionable of all innovations to the samurai, since it meant that, their occupation gone, they would lose their privileged social position. They thought little of farmers as soldiers and felt humiliated by being lumped together with common citizens. In subsequent clashes between samurai and government troops the samurai were often defeated because they despised their adversaries, thinking themselves a match for any number of peasants in uniform.

The tendency of Meiji legislation, though it was not equalitarian in principle, was to break down class distinctions once feudalism was abolished, because the traditional division of the people into four classes was no longer appropriate. Once the soldier had lost his pre-eminence, there was no good reason to continue the division between farmer, artisan, and trader, which was already blurred. Some concession to pride of ancestry was made by dividing the population into three main classes, *kwazoku,* or nobles; *shizoku,* or former samurai; and *heimin,* or commoners, which included all others. The designation of *shizoku* carried with it no rights or exemptions. It meant that as a class the samurai retained nothing but a name. Their profession, their revenues, and their prestige had vanished or sunk to a low level, while new rights were being conferred upon the other classes, who could now choose their own occupations and even obtain title to land. This last change struck at the very heart of feudal pride and privilege, for feudal society rested upon the tenancy of land by the peasant and its ownership by the lord. It was for that reason that Maebara Issei, whose revolt has just been mentioned, attacked the issue of titles in land to private owners as an infringement of the rights of the crown. Private ownership meant an end to the land-revenue economy that had for so long sustained the samurai and their ancestors.

In circumstances like these it is not surprising that the series of samurai uprisings which began in 1874 should have culminated in a large-scale revolt. This was the so-called Satsuma Rebellion of 1877. Its leader, Saigo Takamori, was a popular samurai of the Satsuma clan who had played a great part in the Restoration. Personal ambition and grievances were important among the factors that brought about this rising, but essentially it was the expiring struggle of conservative or reactionary opinion against a govern-

SAIGO TAKAMORI (1827–77)

ment determined to crush all subversive, not to say separatist trends.

The rebellion could not have been planned if there had not existed a great number of discontented samurai in most parts of Japan, but particularly in the west. There the men of Satsuma and Chōshū were divided in opinion. There was a reform party whose members were behind their clansmen in the government; but there was a conservative party, or rather a number of conservative factions, which frankly detested foreign influences upon Japanese culture and at the same time desired a greater share in the power exercised by the central authority.

The final struggle was brought about by a clash of opinion upon a matter of foreign policy. The government, aware of Japan's economic and military weakness, thought it wise to keep free from complications abroad and to concentrate upon internal reform. The conservatives argued that internal reform, which, as they saw it, was nothing but the adoption of foreign ways, was going too fast, and that what the country needed was action which, by raising the national prestige, would stimulate the national energies now flagging under the strain of too much foreign teaching.

Since the Restoration a nationalist school had called for the annexation of the Luchu Islands and the Bonins; the punishment of Korea for an alleged insult to Japan; an expedition to Formosa to chastise the savages who had ill-treated Japanese subjects and whom the Chinese could not control; and finally a stern attitude towards Russia in the matter of territorial rights in Sakhalin. Such adventures would certainly have raised the spirits of the samurai, by providing ample exercise for their swords and thus demonstrating their importance to the state. But when in 1873 Iwakura and his colleagues returned from their mission abroad they were disturbed to find that agitation for an expedition against Korea had grown to such a point that a split in the government had developed. Even Okubo, the mainstay of the party committed to domestic reform, was disposed, in the hope of appeasing the national-prestige party, to agree to an expedition to Formosa as a lesser evil. But his colleague Kido took a firm stand and argued that internal reform must take the first place. An interesting passage in his memorial to the Chancellor reads as follows: "There are now in this country thirty million people who do not yet enjoy the full protection of the government, poor and ignorant persons who have no rights and do not yet know that the nation exists. Though it is the business of the government to see to the protection of the people, the implements are still lacking and little can be done. In my own departments, of Home Affairs and Education, the services that can at present be rendered to the Emperor's subjects are even less than those of former feudal days." The government, however, gave way to pressure, and Kido resigned.

No immediate harm resulted from the Formosan affair, since the Peking government had been "squared," and there were no clashes between Japanese and Chinese troops. The departure of a force of three thousand samurai that went to Formosa in May 1874 removed from the political scene at least for six months a number of turbulent characters. But the government had surrendered on a point of principle without even slaking the thirst of the nationalists for overseas adventure. In justice to the latter it must be said that their view was not one they had hastily adopted for purposes of political manœuvre. It had a somewhat more respectable origin, since for some years before the Restoration the loyalist, anti-Bakufu movement had been inspired by the teachings of such men as Yoshida Shoin, who had argued for the centralization of power under the Emperor as a necessary prelude to Japanese expansion in Asia. Indeed, it is clear enough that ultimate expansionist designs were harboured by most of the leaders of the Restoration, and it need not be supposed (according to the current fashion of ascribing Oriental misdeeds to Occidental corruption) that the foreign wars that Japan waged later in the nineteenth century were inspired solely by the example of contemporary Europe. An urge to expand is visible, though for long periods latent, throughout Japanese history.

It was strongest among the western clans, whose territory fronted on the sea, but all coastal provinces developed at least an interest in foreign trade. It is true that this urge was suppressed by Tokugawa policy after Ieyasu's death, but the seclusion policy inevitably produced a sense of confinement which by the end of the eighteenth century was expressed with increasing emphasis.

The discord between the pacific and bellicose schools in 1873 arose not on a point of international justice but from a difference of opinion as to what was feasible and politic in prevailing circumstances at home. Even among members of the government there were some who favoured what was called a strong, that is to say an offensive, policy towards China and Korea. During the absence abroad of Iwakura, Okubo, and Kido the Council of State and the various ministries were dominated by Saigo, Itagaki, Eto, Soyejima, and Okuma, all men from clans that contained a number of discontented and aggressive samurai. Consequently, after the mission returned to Japan in order to resist the plans of the expansionists, the governing coalition broke up, and in October 1873 a number of the representatives of the western clans withdrew.

The reconstructed government, from which Saigo, Itagaki, Goto, and Eto (from Satsuma, Tosa, Tosa, and Saga respectively) were missing, now included Sanjo and Iwakura in the highest offices, with Okubo, Kido, Ito, and Okuma in important positions as before. It was this government that began to introduce measures, such as the commutation of pensions, that were to strike the final blow at feudalism. The dissident movement began with an attempt on Iwakura's life in January 1874, and was followed by a rebellion in Hizen, led by Eto, who had just resigned from the Council of State, and then by those other risings which have already been mentioned. Saigo, who upon retirement from the Council had withdrawn to his province, meanwhile occupied himself in the military training of young men in Satsuma. He accepted office in the government from time to time, as did his feudal lord Shimadzu, but it was clear that neither had any intention of supporting the domestic policy of the administration. They were aiming at the restoration of feudal powers in one shape or another, Saigo largely on grounds of personal ambition and Shimadzu out of sheer reactionary sentiment. Shimadzu, while professing at times to co-operate in the work of reform, had never been in sympathy with it, and although some of the most progressive members of the government and the civil service were of Satsuma origin, the general run of Satsuma samurai clung stubbornly to their old prejudices. Hatred of the government, inflamed by its successive measures of change, burst out in open warfare after the prohibition of swords went into effect in January 1877. Shimadzu, who was in Tokyo at that time, left in disgust. He with his followers retired along the old Tokaido, the Eastern Sea Road, which had in feudal days seen many brilliant processions of feudal lords with their armed retinues as they proceeded to or from their terms of attendance on the Shogun in Yedo. But on this occasion, symbolic of the last stage in the decline of feudalism, the Satsuma men carried their swords wrapped in cotton bags, and no heralds went before their chieftain to warn bystanders to prostrate themselves as he passed. Arriving in Kagoshima, Shimadzu took no further part in political life and remained in seclusion.

Rebellion broke out under Saigo's leadership early in 1877. Hostilities lasted for six months, not spreading beyond Satsuma, for neighbouring clans remained alert but neutral. They ended in the defeat of Saigo, who was wounded and died on the battlefield, decapitated at his own request by a friend, to preserve his military honour. The government forces numbered 65,000 against 40,000 rebels, and their losses were approximately equal — about 6,000 killed and 10,000 wounded on each side.

This was the real end of six hundred years of feudalism in Japan, the triumph of the new order over the old. Perhaps one of its most striking results was to demonstrate that the new conscript army could fight as well as the flower of the military caste. At the same time the central government drew great strength and confidence from the victory of its soldiers. It could now count upon strong national support and need no longer fear an armed rebellion or depend for its existence upon the fickle western clans.

Before leaving this subject to pass on to a recital of subsequent political events, it is pertinent to consider some singular aspects of the struggle between the forces usually described as "progressive" and "reactionary," seeing that it left traces in later political history. The effort to overthrow the Bakufu had been shared by many parties from different motives, which ranged from a simple desire to seize the Shogun's power to an unmixed intention to establish throughout the country a uniform government in which

MINSTREL PERFORMANCE ON COMMODORE PERRY'S FLAGSHIP
1854

*Drawing by a member of the Japanese delegation
to negotiate the treaty*

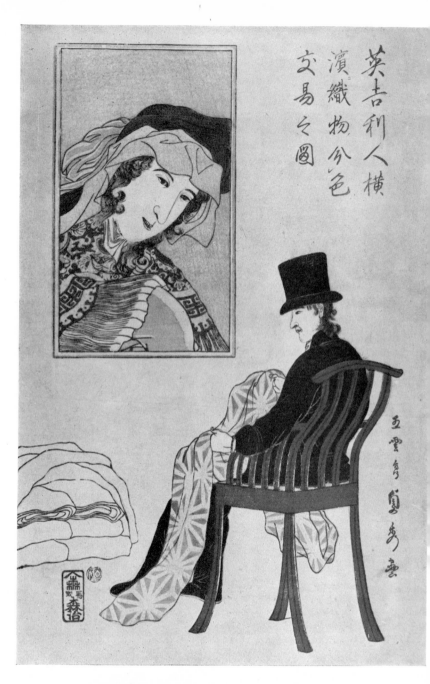

AN ENGLISH MERCHANT IN A YOKOHAMA STORE

Color print by Sadahide, circa 1860. Typical of the Western subjects chosen by print artists after the arrival of foreigners in Japan. (From British Museum collection)

no single faction should preponderate. The only principle which these different parties held in common was that of loyalty to the Emperor, and it was this principle that, by unifying the most diverse opinions, brought the Meiji revolution to a successful and relatively bloodless issue. It resulted that an appeal to the sense of loyalty, which was sincere enough in most cases, became a habitual political device in time of conflict between parties. The watchword of *Kinnō,* or "Revere the Emperor," once a genuine war cry which aroused a fresh patriotic ardour, became in course of time a mere debased currency in political exchanges. It was by a charge of infringing the Imperial prerogative that the revolting samurai justified their attacks upon the government in 1874. Similarly, it was Shimadzu's contention that the men in Tokyo, who had introduced one detestable reform after another, were abusing the power that they exercised in the sovereign's name. In taking this stand he was only repeating a practice as old as feudalism itself, for each military dictator from Yoritomo to Nobunaga had accused his rivals of usurping power and represented himself as a protector of the throne. Conversely, when the government learned of Saigo's revolt, their first care was to proclaim him publicly as a rebel against the Emperor and to appoint an Imperial prince as commander of the expedition against him.

These accusations of treason or disrespect to the throne became a fixed political habit, which was carried over into the controversies of the twentieth century. In his valuable *Political History of Japan* Dr. W. W. McLaren stated that, as a result of the Satsuma Rebellion, "in political theory it was to be no longer possible to separate the throne and the imperial government, or to claim loyalty to the former as a pretext for armed attack upon the latter." This is perhaps true in so far as it concerns large-scale rebellion, but it overlooks the importance of the appeal to loyalty as a device that has remained characteristic of Japanese political strategy throughout modern times. It is true that it has usually been resorted to by bureaucratic governments in order to stifle opposition. They have repeatedly identified themselves with the throne and charged their opponents with disloyalty when government measures have been criticized. But the same argument was certainly used by politicians out of office. Thus, to cite a familiar instance, the Minister of Education in a short-lived party administration of 1898 said in a public speech: "Suppose that you dreamed that Japan had adopted a republican form of government. . . ." He and his colleagues were at once obliged to resign on the ground that they nourished disloyal sentiments.

Similar stratagems were used to upset ministries in later times, and it is well known that in trials for mutiny and political murder, which were frequent for some years from 1932 onwards, the assassins would usually plead in defence that their victims had usurped or abused power that belonged to the Emperor. They were exponents of the traditional appeal to loyalty, by which Saigo had justified his act of treason in 1877, and although none of them became a national hero like Saigo, they did gain considerable public sympathy and approval.

Saigo's career illustrates another characteristic feature of public life in Japan. He was a man of fine physique, great courage, and abundant charm, so that he was almost universally admired. Despite his ambitious follies he is still a venerated figure in the national legend and his statue is one of the ornaments of the capital. Perhaps for lack of political experience the Japanese people as a whole appear to be less interested in principles than in persons, and subsequent political history shows that in Japan as in other Oriental countries personal popularity is often more important than capacity, or even integrity, in a public man.

One further and important political consequence flowed from the Satsuma Rebellion. The government leaders after their victory did not show any resentment towards the mutinous province. They took a sensible and liberal line, which allowed the Satsuma men, many of whom were capable and progressive, a large share in the administration. Indeed, before long the coalition of the four leading clans broke up, owing to the secession of representatives of Tosa and Hizen, and from 1877 onwards the most important offices, both civil and military, were held by men from Satsuma and Chōshū. The strong position thus gained by these two clans gave them a kind of vested interest in affairs of state and led to what was called "clan government," a peculiar phenomenon of Japanese politics, which persisted for two generations or more and had not entirely disappeared before the Pacific war of 1941. The term "clan government" is somewhat misleading, since the clans as such exercised no power, nor can it be said that the clansmen worked in favour of their own provinces. But for a long time it was difficult for outsiders to secure or to hold any post of high importance; and those who succeeded in penetrating the circle often found themselves faced by the resistance of clan solidarity. This feature of Japanese political life is of course not without parallel in other countries, since a governing class is usually composed of men of like social origin. But a complete analogy would demand, for instance, that in England all Whigs in high position should come from Lancashire or Yorkshire.

The predominance of men from Satsuma and Chōshū is of course due to the superior strength of those two feudal principalities and to the decisive role they played in the Restoration.

The samurai who rose to power were not the successors of a feudal aristocracy, since the feudal princes had long before the Restoration let their power slip into the hands of intelligent subordinates of very modest standing. Consequently the sequence of events in Japan after the destruction of feudalism does not offer a close analogy to the development in England of a rich and politically powerful landowning class. The feudal lords, though some of them retained or purchased considerable tracts of arable or forest land, did not hold enough to dominate the agricultural economy and so to secure a predominant political influence. They invested in banking, industry, and trade and to that extent might be politically important, but as a ruling class they were permanently displaced by the young samurai who established themselves at the Restoration as a self-perpetuating oligarchy of bureaucrats and leaders of the armed services. The great careers in Japanese history for several decades thereafter are those of new men who were socially perhaps the near equivalents of small gentry and yeomen farmers in England, though this analogy must not be pressed. Okubo, Kido, Ito, Yamagata, Katsura, Okuma, Inouye, Itagaki, and later men like Inukai, Komura, and Kato, were all of very modest though respectable origin, and the only members of the old nobility to figure prominently in political life were Iwakura, Sanjo, Saionji, and Konoe, not former feudal lords, but members of the court nobility who owed their positions to their connection with the Imperial family rather than to exceptional talent.

Thus, it will be seen, to think of Japanese history since 1868 in terms of European history can easily lead to error. The basic social conditions of Japan at the close of the feudal period were unlike those which obtained in western Europe in one most important aspect. The privileged feudal classes, apart from two or three hundred feudal nobles and a not very numerous body of highly placed officials, consisted of some 400,000 poor and landless samurai, who were for the most part little more than the noncommissioned officers and private soldiers of a modern army.[2] They might be described as the educated class in Japan, but (except for a minority) only in contrast with illiterate peasants and workmen. Thus in Japan the privileged class was economically weak, deriving its strength from a monopoly of weapons and from a tradition of behaviour that gave it a certain solidarity.

Even so, the samurai, though they had a common outlook upon life, can scarcely be regarded as a homogeneous class for political

---

[2] It should be remembered that there were grades among the samurai. The lowest grade, called *sotsu*, were little more than menials. When the division of the population into *shizoku* and *heimin* was made in 1872, the *sotsu* were grouped with the commoners and not with the ex-samurai.

purposes, since clan rivalry prevented close intercourse between fiefs and did not promote a feeling of common interest. It was because samurai opinion was divided that the reformers were able to break up the feudal order without meeting concerted opposition throughout the country, and because for most samurai life had become a conflict between pride and indigence. They found themselves in that situation where an active element in the nation feels that its fortunes may be bettered and can hardly be worsened by change. Such a frame of mind smooths the path of reformers; and the result shows that, while the loss of their income and status brought hardship in many individual cases, as a class the samurai adjusted themselves to new conditions and found employment suited to their capacities. Naturally they carried over into the new life the prejudices of the old, and it is here that one must seek an explanation of certain political trends that developed and hardened during the Meiji era.

In the Restoration movement and the reforms which followed, the mass of the people played no part. It was members of the samurai class who devised it, carried it through, and built up a new political structure. They were men who had been brought up to believe in discipline and firm government, to cultivate martial virtues, and to set duties above rights. It would have been a miracle if they had not applied these ideas in the performance of their political task and fashioned an authoritarian régime. Their aim was to reproduce on a national scale the conditions that had obtained in feudal lordships, where the daimyo was nominally supreme but real power was exercised by his samurai counsellors.

Foreign and even some Japanese writers, discussing today the political development of Japan since 1868, are apt to judge it by standards of twentieth-century democracy or some other fictitious absolute; and they are inclined to scold and condemn the Japanese people for not evolving out of their native materials the forms that Anglo-Saxon institutions have taken after a very long and very different history. It is one of the purposes of this study to show that, even assuming the perfection of Western models, the evolution of modern Japanese political life has been conditioned by a past that made the adoption of purely Western practices unnatural and indeed impossible. This may be deplorable, but the facts of political life are, alas, hard and stubborn things, not to be changed by ideological yearnings.

In the foregoing pages the word "revolution" has been used to describe the process by which the remnants of feudalism were destroyed. But in its origins it was not a revolution comparable to the English Revolution of 1688 or the French Revolution of 1789. It was a civil war fought with both political and military weapons by one section of a dominant military class against another. Its purpose was to replace an administration already obsolete and declining by a more efficient system of government giving scope to new men. The leaders of the victorious party stood for no new political theory, as is clear from the splits that soon divided them; but having achieved their purpose of securing power, they found that in order to keep it they must discard certain institutions. In other and simpler words, "the abolition of feudalism was mainly an afterthought."

3. Western Theory and Eastern Practice

THE SUPPRESSION of the Satsuma Rebellion marked the end of attempts to overthrow the government by force of arms, but attack now came from a new quarter and in a new guise. The clansmen from Tosa and Hizen who had resigned in protest against the government's refusal to adopt a nationalist foreign policy transferred the ground of opposition to domestic affairs. The issue was no longer the abolition of feudalism, but the conflict between conservative and progressive schools of political thought. But though principles were at stake the struggle was complicated, if not dominated, by personal rivalries. As early as 1873, Saigo, Itagaki, Goto, Soyeshima, and Eto had withdrawn when Okubo and Kido had refused to sanction minatory action against Korea. Saigo and Eto, as we have seen, resorted to arms and paid with their lives. Itagaki, Goto, and Soyeshima were not prepared to make a stand on the Korean issue, which was for them secondary. They felt that Okubo, Kido, and Ito were establishing an oligarchy from which they were to be excluded, and they no doubt genuinely believed that the country was being denied the representative government it needed and desired. Accordingly they delivered their attack on the constitutional issue, and thus the political history of the next few years is concerned almost entirely with agitation for popular rights and a struggle for parliamentary government.

Since we are attempting to assess the degree of Western influence upon political development at this time, it may be useful to explain here that proposals to establish a national assembly had been made some years before the Restoration. Even during the seclusion period a vague and elementary knowledge of European institutions had reached Japan through Dutch and Chinese books, and this was of course enlarged after Perry's visit, when Japanese missions began to visit foreign countries. The idea of parliamentary government thus became familiar, though its working was only imperfectly understood. Even Fukuzawa Yukichi, a convinced modernist and advocate of reform, confessed after seeing the English Parliament at work that he found representative institutions "very perplexing." Very soon after 1860, Tokugawa officers, looking for ways of arresting the obvious decline of the Shogunate, began to suggest among other reforms the setting up of an assembly for the discussion of national affairs. Similar proposals, but with somewhat different intentions, were made by officers of various clans whose aim was a compromise by which, while powers would nominally be returned to the Emperor, they would be exercised by feudal authorities through a kind of federal parliament. The Shogun (Keiki) himself was much interested in these plans, and there is good reason to believe that when he surrendered his powers he hoped for the establishment of a bicameral assembly, with an upper house over which he would preside and a lower house of samurai. The upper house would be composed of court and feudal nobles. None of these plans was adopted before the Restoration, but they were not forgotten.

Something of a parliamentary nature was tried under the first Meiji government, when an assembly of samurai representing the clans met in Tokyo in 1868 and 1869, but it proved quite ineffectual. At that time there was no thought of a truly popular assembly, since the people other than the samurai counted for nothing. However, the idea of a deliberative assembly, already approved in the Charter Oath, was now fixed in the public mind, so that when the clans were abolished and the samurai lost their status some decision had to be taken as to the membership and functions of the future national deliberative body. In the view of the progressives it must represent not one privileged caste but the people as a whole. In January 1874 a group of samurai including Itagaki, Goto, and Eto had addressed a memorial to the government in which they demanded the early establishment of a representative assembly. At the same time they launched a public campaign for the same purpose. Some attempt at compromise was made by Okubo and Ito, and Itagaki was persuaded to rejoin the government; but the reconciliation was only temporary and he soon resigned, to carry further the agitation he had commenced.

Before describing this movement it is convenient to notice briefly the changes in government organization that were made by Okubo and his colleagues as soon as the abolition of the feudal system enabled them to replace the temporary fabric that had been erected and from time to time patched up since 1868. A most significant change was the gradual disappearance from effective political life of the former members of the feudal and court nobility who had been nominal heads of the government. They had served their purpose as symbols of co-operation between the civil and military estates and as an impressive screen behind which the real motive forces of the reform could operate discreetly. Now the small group of leaders who had carried through the reform program step by step assumed the key posts in the administration, and the influence of aristocratic statesmen like Iwakura and Sanjo gradually diminished. It was the former samurai who now made decisions, and it is clear that they were reluctant to admit to any position of authority a legislative or even an advisory body that could interfere with their plans. They felt obliged, however, to make a formal gesture in compliance with the Emperor's undertaking that matters of high policy should be decided by public debate, and accordingly in 1871 they set up an advisory council of which the announced function was to examine measures proposed by the administration. In practice this body exercised no authority, since its members were appointed by the Emperor on the motion of the government.

The organization of the central government had been frequently modified since 1868, without much essential change. In 1875, in an attempt to meet the wishes of Itagaki and his supporters, there was a further reorganization. The Council of State (Dajōkwan) was retained and a Senate (Genrōin) and a Supreme Court (Daishin-in) were established. But these arrangements, though giving the appearance of a separation of powers, with a legislature and a judiciary independent of the executive, were in fact illusory. The members of the Senate were nobles and high officials or other persons who had rendered service to the state, and their appointments were made by the Emperor. Their powers were circumscribed and ultimate authority resided in the Council of State, which, though nominally the sovereign's privy council, was in fact a small autocratic body determined to exercise absolute rule in the Emperor's name and to concede as little as possible to the advocates of popular government. The demand for a representative assembly could not be entirely neglected, and a somewhat disingenuous effort to meet it was made by creating an assembly of provincial officials, who were to meet regularly in the capital. The intention of the ruling group was set forth in a rescript in which the Emperor announced that "by assembling representatives from the various provinces of the Empire the public mind will be known and the public interest best consulted." This rescript continues with an admonitory passage that clearly reveals the official attitude: "We hope by these means to secure the happiness of Our subjects and Ourself. And while they must necessarily abandon many of their former customs they must not on the other hand yield to a rash desire for reform."

The assembly of provincial officials could certainly not be regarded as a rash experiment, since it was composed almost entirely of governors of prefectures who owed their position to the central government and were under close supervision and control by the Minister of Home Affairs. It was quite clear that the ruling group had no intention of allowing the people to share in forming the policy of the central government so long as they could prevent it; and far from encouraging local autonomy they saw to it that local government should remain in the hands of a bureaucracy taking its orders from the capital and lacking discretionary powers. The formation of the Provincial Assembly is an interesting example of a characteristic feature of early Meiji politics, in that it was an attempt to dress up traditional Japanese practices in Western garments. There was indeed little to distinguish a powerless assembly from a feudal council that must take orders from the central authority.

Itagaki, after a brief spell of office, seeing that neither the Senate nor the Assembly of Provincial Officials was intended to have any truly representative or elective character, made up his mind that there was no prospect of agreement between his party, which stood for radical change, and the ministry, which was averse to popular government. He accordingly resigned in the autumn of 1876 and set about consolidating an opposition party, which was to agitate for popular rights for the next ten years or more. He had already in 1873 formed a political association — the first of its kind in Japan — with headquarters in Tokyo. It was called the Aikoku-kōtō, or Public Society of Patriots, the word "public" being introduced to show that it was not a secret or illicit society but an open combination against the government. This was a new feature in political life, since hitherto any form of opposition had been treated by the feudal authority as treasonable, and public criticism was regarded as peculiarly subversive in that it encouraged the people to doubt the competence of the ruler. The Aikoku-Kōtō was not a political party in the strict sense, since there was yet no parliament; but it may be regarded as the progenitor of organized political parties in Japan. Owing to the circumstances of its birth, its purpose was to displace the nominally provisional government of the day, which was in bureaucratic hands and did not depend upon party support. Consequently the idea of political parties in Japan was from the early days of Meiji associated with opposition to the bureaucracy rather than with the promotion of a specific political philosophy; and this formative period strongly influenced subsequent political activity.

At the same time as the Aikoku-Kōtō there was founded by Itagaki in his native province of Tosa a political academy or training school, called the Risshisha,[3] designed to spread ideas of self-government and self-reliance while preparing young men for political work. Similar institutions sprang up in other parts of the country, so that before long there developed a strong body of opinion antagonistic to the government and in favour of the speedy establishment of a parliament. The fact that the Satsuma Rebellion had been begun by students of Saigo's academy in Kagoshima somewhat weakened the position of the Risshisha in and after 1877, and all but the extreme wing of liberal reformers were anxious not to be associated in the public mind with Saigo's opposition, since it was based upon reactionary sentiment. Itagaki and most of his followers therefore somewhat moderated their attacks and took the government side during hostilities. Even so they were not averse to embarrassing the administration. The Risshisha sent to the Emperor in June 1877, in the midst of the Satsuma campaign, a memorial praying for an elective assembly and charging the government with usurping the Emperor's authority and obstructing his announced design of granting political rights to the people. The memorial was rejected and certain members of the Risshisha were arrested on suspicion of complicity in a plot to overthrow the government by force.

From this time onward, although the position of the government was greatly strengthened by the defeat of Saigo, the struggle for *Minken*, or People's Rights, became intense. Itagaki and his associates carried on an energetic campaign by means of speeches, newspaper articles, pamphlets, and books. Almost all the national energy seemed to be devoted to political questions, and the country was divided into two main camps — progressives who stood for freedom and the rights of the subject, against conservatives who believed either that absolute rule was best or that the time was not ripe for democratic institutions. In a later chapter some account will be given of the polemical battle that occupied the public mind from 1874 to about 1882; but it may be mentioned here that the progressives drew freely upon Western political literature for their arguments, and quoted Rousseau, Bentham, Mill, and Spencer as the occasion demanded. Pains were taken to instruct the general public by publishing popular works on representative government and related matters. Among these were Fukuzawa's *Tsūzoku Minken Ron*, or *Simple Account of People's Rights*, and Ueki's

[3] The name Risshisha is variously translated as the Society of Independent Men or the Society of Freethinkers, and these are near enough. But as a sidelight on the influence of foreign literature it may be noted that *Risshi* was the word used by the translator of Samuel Smiles to render "Self-Help," and that is what it means in *Risshisha*. It was a society of men who were going to rely upon their own judgment and efforts. It is interesting to note that membership was confined to samurai.

Minken Jiyū Ron, or *Essay on People's Rights and Freedom;* the latter is addressed to "Mr. Farmer, Mr. Merchant, Mr. Fisherman, Mr. Samurai, Mr. Doctor, and Mr. New Commoner," the New Commoner being a former member of the pariah class. The press took part vigorously in the controversy, being for the most part with the progressives and against the government. The government in its turn took very strong measures. The Press Law of 1875 was ruthlessly enforced and many editors were thrown into jail. Political gatherings were made subject to severe restrictions, and agitation against the government thus became extremely difficult.

Some adherents of the progressive party were so angered that they saw no alternative but a resort to violence. An attempt on Prince Iwakura's life had been made in 1874. In 1877, during the hostilities in Satsuma, a number of prominent persons, including Mutsu, then a member of the Senate and later to become Foreign Minister, were found to be plotting an armed revolt. In 1878 Okubo, the most resolute and powerful member of the government, was assassinated. It was evident to his colleagues that the demand for representative institutions had some determined supporters, and probably in an effort to placate them they took what they presented as a step towards the formation of a national parliament by enacting a law setting up elective assemblies in rural and urban prefectures and other measures granting some degree of local autonomy. Though these bills were drafted before Okubo's murder, there can be little doubt that the government was moved by the strength of popular sentiment, as manifested in outbreaks of violence, to hasten somewhat its own program of slow and gradual reform. The concessions they made to democratic feelings were, however, unsubstantial. Any decision of the local assemblies was subject to official veto, while the Home Minister had power to dissolve an assembly of which he disapproved and to call for a new election. The progressive party continued and increased their efforts to force the government's pace. They undertook a political campaign throughout the country, holding national conventions of the Society of Patriots in Osaka in 1878 and again in 1879 and 1880. These were attended by thousands of delegates representing nearly one hundred local societies, and monster petitions were prepared, calling for the immediate opening of an elective national assembly.

The government, on learning of the convention of 1880, took rapid and drastic action. It ordered the dissolution of the convention and speedily enacted laws restricting public meetings and forbidding the amalgamation of local political societies, thus preventing the formation of political organizations on a national scale. These repressive measures did not succeed in checking political agitation. Itagaki and his associates, though unable to take useful action in the capital, toured the provinces and addressed local associations and other public gatherings. This was a new form of political activity in Japan, for in the early years of Meiji speechmaking was an unknown art, and it was even found necessary to invent a word for it.[4]

The government seems not to have been unduly disturbed by the orations of the progressives, and it might have weathered the wordy storm but for one of those scandals which, though unimportant in themselves and irrelevant to the issue at stake, often have greater effect than powerful argument. The sale of certain government properties at a very low price to friends of the administration became known to the public and caused great indignation, though in feudal days the misuse of public funds would have excited little comment. A violent campaign against the government was conducted by the newspapers, and mass meetings of protest were held.

At this time, since Itagaki and others had resigned from office, the government was controlled by former samurai of Satsuma and Chōshū, while the clansmen of Tosa and Hizen, who had shared in the task of abolishing the feudal régime, now found themselves in opposition to their former allies. The direction of affairs had fallen into the hands of a closed group, so that ambitious candidates from other clans could scarcely hope to obtain good posts, much less to reach the highest offices. Among those who did not belong to the inner ring was Okuma Shigenobu, a talented statesman from Saga. He had remained in the government when the other representatives of Tosa and Hizen withdrew and had held important posts dealing mainly with finance. But he was never fully at ease with his colleagues and in 1881 he joined the opposition with a startling gesture. He called a public meeting against the aforesaid scandal, details of which he disclosed, and he indited a memorial to the throne in which he prayed for the establishment of a national assembly in 1883.

The response of the government was immediate. Within a day from the receipt of the memorial the Emperor issued a rescript which declared that a parliament would be established in 1890.

This remarkable result was due in a great measure to Okuma's action. He had timed his coup skilfully at a juncture when the government, weakened no doubt by the loss of Okubo, was already unpopular because of its harsh treatment of political opponents

---

[4] It was the word *enzetsu*, which had been used in a different sense before, referring to formal oral statements. It was Fukuzawa who gave it currency, and he also invented terms for "proposing" and "seconding" and other points in the procedure of meetings.

and its ruthless handling of the press. It is unlikely that he would have succeeded had not Itagaki's campaign already aroused feeling throughout the country, but there is no doubt that Okuma's personal qualities were important in forcing the government to pay attention to a popular demand. Whether in the long run he hastened the constitutional development of Japan is open to question. His action and its sequels belong to the commonplace of political manœuvre and as such are of little interest; but they are worth examining for such light as they throw upon certain characteristic features of Japanese political development. Okuma no doubt held more advanced views than his ministerial colleagues as to the adoption of a parliamentary form of government. They for the most part thought that it was premature to entrust decisions of great import to an inexperienced electorate. He, on the other hand, seems genuinely to have believed in parliamentary rule, but a dominant motive of his secession seems to have been personal ambition coupled with a lack of co-operative spirit. He was not alone in the administration in resenting the virtual monopoly of power by Satsuma and Chōshū clansmen and he seems sincerely to have believed that the only way of breaking down the system of clan government was to establish a national assembly that would make votes and not partisan connections the road to high offices of state. If this view is correct the struggle for a parliament was in essence not a clear issue between traditionalists and the advocates of Western principles of government, but rather the perpetuation of old rivalries in a modern setting.

Okuma's sudden bolt did not succeed in destroying the close alliance of Satsuma and Chōshū. On the contrary it strengthened the coalition, which now included no representatives of Tosa, Hizen, or other clans and was composed of Ito, Inouye, Yamagata, Matsukata, Kuroda, and the younger Saigo. These drew closer together now that they had to face an enlarged opposition containing Okuma, a redoubtable enemy who knew a great deal about the inner workings of government. They forestalled his resignation by relieving him of office on the day of the Imperial Rescript, and all those who were known to be his followers were deprived of their posts at the same time. They also girded up their loins for the battle they expected before the opening of the promised national assembly in 1890.

In describing the political struggle between the government on the one hand and the opposition led by Itagaki and Okuma on the other, it is easy to fall into the error of representing the government as a group of wicked tyrants wantonly depriving virtuous liberals of their elementary rights. This is not a true picture. The oppressive measures of the government were deplorable, though by the standards of a decade or so before they would have been regarded as wretchedly weak. But their general line of policy was logical and defensible in the light of the responsibilities that they bore and the circumstances in which their country was placed. The reforms they had already accomplished were remarkable. They had succeeded in carrying through a political and social program of a revolutionary nature with surprisingly little violence and, when one takes into account the native habit of slow and cautious compromise, with surprisingly little delay. They knew only too well the military and economic weakness of their country and the political inexperience of the majority of their compatriots — features that the reader will have deduced from the description of town and country life already given. It was natural that they should hesitate to confer upon an untrained and uninstructed electorate political freedoms likely to be used to the detriment of their main task and duty, which as they conceived it was the rapid organization of national strength. Brought up in an authoritarian tradition and imbued with the belief that firm government is good government, they were not disposed to apply in practice Western theories of natural rights and popular rule unless they could be shown to contribute to the purposes of the national state.

Here their ingrained Confucian sentiment clashed with the new Western doctrines, which were attractive to the people at large and especially to a numerous group of impressionable young men. Confucian philosophy holds that it is the business of the ruler to govern and of the people to obey, whereas the current nineteenth-century English and American teaching, then widespread in Japan, was or seemed to the Confucianists to be based upon the shocking theory that the people know best. Prince Ito, who was an influential member of the government during the struggle for popular rights and may be regarded as expressing moderate conservative opinion, describes the situation in the following illuminating passage from his reminiscences:

We were just then [about 1880] in an age of transition. The opinions prevailing in the country were extremely heterogeneous and often diametrically opposed to one another. We had survivors from former generations who were still full of theocratic ideas and who believed that any attempt to restrict an imperial prerogative amounted to something like high treason. On the other hand there was a large and powerful body of the younger generation educated at a time when the Manchester theory was in vogue, and who in consequence were ultra-radical in their ideas of freedom. Members of the bureaucracy were prone to lend willing ears to the German doctrinaires of the reactionary period, while on the other hand educated politicians among the people, having not yet tasted the bitter significance of administrative responsibility, were liable to be more influenced by the dazzling words and lucid theories of Montesquieu, Rousseau, and similar French writers. A work entitled *History of Civilization* by Buckle, which denounced every form of government as an unnecessary evil, became the great favorite of students of all the higher schools, including the Imperial university. But those same students would not have dared to expound the theories of Buckle before their own conservative fathers. At that time we had not arrived at the stage of distinguishing clearly between political opposition on the one hand and treason to the established order on the other.

If the conservatives were strengthened in their dislike of representative government by a selfish fear that it would break up the coalition of Satsuma and Chōshū clansmen, the motives of the advocates of political freedom were not invariably pure; and this explains though it may not justify the repressive measures to which the government resorted. It is interesting to examine the forces that assailed the government under the banner of liberalism. Itagaki, their leader, left the government in 1873 because he professed to be disappointed by the failure of his colleagues to take strong action against Korea, of a kind that might easily lead to war. In fact Itagaki himself recommended the dispatch of a force to "chastise" the Koreans. This, to say the least of it, was a strange and inauspicious motive for breaking with the government in order to lead a liberal movement. Itagaki was a fighting man by origin and vigorous by character, and this may account for his bellicose attitude; but his liberal principles were also open to some doubt, for it is clear that he and a number of his fellow clansmen from Tosa bitterly, and not without reason, resented the virtual monopoly of power held by men of Satsuma and Chōshū. It is known that he did not, at the beginning of his campaign, envisage a wide suffrage or a parliament of representatives from all classes. In his own writings he stated more than once that what he proposed was nothing like a universal franchise, and he contemplated an assembly composed of officials, of samurai from all the clans, and some representatives of rich merchants and farmers. As the campaign developed, his views no doubt moved in the direction of a more genuine democracy, but certainly when he first left the government he would have been satisfied with much less than was demanded by a popular sentiment that he himself aroused.

In the study of Japanese liberalism in its early phases the position of Itagaki is important, for it seems to have determined the course of later political development in Japan. It is difficult to reconcile his democratic professions with his conviction that the unassailable position of the Emperor was the key to the political stability of Japan and with the aggressive nationalism expressed in his support of a punitive expedition against Korea. We must return to this question later, and meanwhile it may be sufficient to say that Itagaki's liberalism was apparently not much more than a moderate approval of parliamentary forms.

Among his followers there were no doubt a large number who had been convinced by the arguments of Western writers and sincerely believed in representative government, while there were many ardent young men whose generous impulses led them to a hatred of oppression, a desire for change, and an optimistic belief in the wisdom of majorities. But at the same time a great proportion of Itagaki's following consisted of disappointed politicians and office-seekers, of discontented and turbulent samurai ready to join any movement against authority, and of all the flotsam and jetsam left by the waves of change that had swept away most of the old life of Japan. Among these was a considerable element inclined to disorder and violence, the *sōshi* or strong-arm men, a class of political hangers-on that, under the disguise of patriotism, sullied political life in Japan in subsequent years.

The goverment from which Itagaki and later Okuma seceded found itself constantly embarrassed by threats of violence. The Satsuma Rebellion was inspired by reactionary ideas that Itagaki and his associates did not share, but while the government was fighting sedition, advocates of constitutional practices did not hesitate to press their claims, not only by legitimate political action but also by violence. They recruited, or at least accepted in their ranks, a number of adherents who had nothing in common with their political views except a wish to overthrow the government. They could depend upon the support of many discontented factions whose grievances were sometimes genuine, sometimes not. The peasants subscribed to their program because they wanted taxes reduced, and some landlords, but not all, took part in the movement for reasons of their own. Certainly the movement was not inspired by an urban bourgeoisie and backed by mercantile interests, as was that of the United Kingdom, which it in some respects followed. It was rural and agrarian rather than urban and mercantile, but in essence, except perhaps in the extreme left wing of the liberal party, it was a struggle for political power. That this is substantially true is shown by the gradual degradation and sacrifice of principle that was later displayed by the new parties as they turned into organs for securing place and profit.

Itagaki and other leaders did not approve of violence, but they were unable to stop it. The attempt upon Iwakura's life, the murder of Okubo, Mutsu's plot, and local riots and disturbances fomented by agitators who mostly had no desire for reform but thrived upon mischief, all these and similar modes of opposition naturally disposed the government to take extreme measures of repression. It cannot of course be proved, but there is some reason to think that Japanese political development would have followed a smoother and more liberal course if the apostles of freedom had not pressed to extremes the conflict between gradual progress, which was the professed aim of the government, and sudden perfection, which was what the advanced party required. The point, while only one of conjecture, is of some interest because, although the campaign for people's rights was supported by citing Western theories and practice, it is doubtful whether direct Western influence was an important factor in the political developments that fixed the pattern of Japanese institutions from about 1881.

The intellectual background of the constitutional movement was certainly provided by Western political philosophy, and its polemical writers drew freely for their arguments upon Western literature, ranging from French or Russian revolutionary writings to the solid treatises of English empiricists. The various foreign teachings undoubtedly influenced Japanese minds and created a passing fashion in the intellectual world, especially among the younger generation. Even the fiction of the period treats almost exclusively of political themes, and its lovers sit in shady bowers talking of Spencer and Mill or comparing the merits of Gladstone, Salisbury, and Bismarck in those interminable conversations that are so pleasing to the unwearied youthful mind.

But in the practice of politics, one must recognize, the course of events was governed not by theory but by the exigencies of a unique domestic situation and by ideas which, though they might at times be given European labels, were native in origin. In studying the conflict between absolutism and freedom one cannot help feeling that the debate was conducted in terms of Western thought which had little relation to the issues really at stake. This was to be expected, since the political philosophies of nineteenth-century Europe were a response to conditions resembling only in a most general way those which obtained in Japan. It is true that once the last feudal survivals were done away with, it was necessary to find a new form of government; and since the Japanese had no experience of any other forms but the obviously unsuitable systems of antiquity, they were bound to light upon something that corresponded in part to Western models. In that limited sense they came under Western influence, but once the study of political history is pursued beyond the point that we have now reached, it becomes clear that what was finally adopted was, if Western in shape, thoroughly Japanese in colour and substance.

There is one very marked contrast between the political history of Japan and that of England and America. In those countries it was parliament that produced organized political parties, but in Japan it was political parties that produced parliament. In neither case was it political theory that divided parties, but rather a conflict of interests and a struggle for power that led to the study of political theory. Though the history of Japan in the first twenty years after the Restoration is full of references to Western authorities on political science, it may well be that their careful arguments had less effect upon Japanese social and political thought than the unorganized sentiment of Rousseau; for whereas on paper one form of government looks very much like another, the idea of natural rights was very welcome to a people long accustomed to despotic rule. At the same time it was new and startling, and when it came to applying it in practice it was found that the Japanese vocabulary had no suitable words to express such notions as civil liberty. Even public speaking was so unfamiliar that it was at first felt to be slightly improper for a man to presume to disclose his views aloud and without decent restraint.

So far we have considered the democratic movement only in its purely political aspects. The abolition of the rigid, hereditary class distinctions of the feudal era might give the impression that, parallel to the people's rights movement, there was a demand for all-round social equality. It is true that a formal or legal division into classes no longer existed, but hierarchical sentiment remained strong, and the old arrangement of classes was succeeded by an accepted order of society in which birth still counted, but talent and to a less extent wealth gave entry into higher social ranks. As is natural in a bureaucratic state, social position tended to correspond to official position, and a new aristocracy developed as titles and honours were conferred upon public servants. Class barriers were lowered and could be crossed, but no strong equalitarian trend is visible in the early Meiji period. Yet while class distinctions persisted, relations between members of different classes were generally easy and amicable, no doubt because they were conducted in accordance with a convention that prescribed suitable forms of speech and deportment for all occasions. The strong social sense of the Japanese included a liking for ritual in everyday life.

4. Political Parties

WITH the announcement that a national parliament would be created in 1890 the political societies formed in 1877 had served their purpose, and from 1881 onwards there came into being a number of new associations that were now described as political parties in anticipation of campaigns for election to the Diet. The first of these was the Jiyūtō, or Liberal Party, established in 1881 by Itagaki and Goto. It was followed in 1882 by the Rikken Kaishintō, or Constitutional Progressive Party, under the leadership of Okuma, and the Rikken Teiseitō, or Constitutional Imperialist Party, which was conservative and supported the government.

Now confronted by two powerful opposition parties under capable and popular leaders, the government felt obliged to take strong measures to counter their influence, which so long as they joined forces was formidable. It was from this time that the repressive action of the bureaucrats in power was carried to extremes. A law restricting the right of public meeting and speech, first enacted in 1880, was amended in 1882 in such a way that nearly all the normal activities of a political association became, if not illegal, extremely difficult. Police powers of interference with public meetings were almost unlimited and local political bodies were forbidden to amalgamate or even to correspond with similar bodies elsewhere. The Press Law was so rigorously enforced that often several editors were in jail at the same time and it became the practice of newspapers to employ an editor whose chief duty it was to serve prison sentences. It is difficult to understand how, in an age when the words "freedom" and "enlightenment" were on everybody's lips, the government, composed as it was of men not without reforming spirit, should have gone to such lengths of despotism. But it seems that the members of the government were but little influenced by the new concepts of liberty and popular rights, their minds being still imbued with the harsh principles of feudal discipline, which regarded criticism of the existing order as a form of treason. It must be remembered too that the use of vindictive police measures had been characteristic of the Tokugawa régime, which bore many resemblances to a modern *Polizeistaat*.

The liberal opposition itself was not innocent of a tendency to use force instead of persuasion. Its leaders were probably not directly responsible for uprisings and seditious plots, but many of its members were implicated in insurrectionary movements depending upon violence. On more than one occasion there were serious manifestations of force in the provinces, which necessitated the calling out of troops. It is doubtful whether there was at any time an organized attempt sponsored by the opposition to overthrow the government of the day, but riots took place frequently from 1882 to 1884, resulting in loss of life and destruction of property. Their origins were by no means exclusively political, though they usually assumed a political complexion. They were mostly led by genuine reformers, but often joined if not fomented by numbers of former samurai of the class already mentioned, headstrong men without fixed occupation ready to join in any attack upon authority. Their grievances, like those of the peasants and workmen with whom they combined, were partly economic, since trade was languishing from about 1880 and prices were rising owing to a mistaken currency policy. Some of the rioting was the work of peasants and others oppressed by high taxes and rents, who formed Shakkin-tō, or Debtors' Parties, which were linked with radical elements in the opposition political parties. Genuine as were many of these complaints, the leaders of Itagaki's liberal party (the Jiyū-tō) and Okuma's progressive party (the Kaishin-tō) could not afford to be identified with subversive plots, and late in 1884 the Jiyu-tō broke up in order to clear itself of suspicion. The Kaishin-tō, while not at once dissolving, lost Okuma and other important leaders for similar reasons. It should be added that certain industrialists and landowners who had supported the opposition in their own interest were ready enough to resign when they found that the local party leaders were taking a very radical line and asking for too much in the way of reduction of taxes and rent in rural areas.[5]

These internal weaknesses of the liberal opposition somewhat eased the position of the government, though its members could still find in acts of violence an excuse for continued rigour in their treatment of political adversaries. They also skilfully exploited the personal failings of their chief opponents and thus contributed to a split between the two "progressive" parties, whose union had never been more than temporary. Okuma's party, the Kaishin-tō, was mainly bureaucratic in composition and stood for a very moderate program of reform, which most members of the government might well have advocated had they been out of office. It had little in common with the Jiyū-tō, which contained a number of advanced reformers, equalitarians in favour of a single chamber, and a left wing of revolutionary tendency. By contrast the Kaishin-tō was conservative.

While the opposition thus fell into confusion and disunity, their respective leaders were unable to agree, for both were self-willed and ambitious. This state of affairs suited the government very well and it was not long before they succeeded, by playing off one against the other, in reducing both to relative impotence. Having thus rendered the democratic movement for the time ineffective, they took the precaution of strengthening rather than relaxing their measures of repression.

[5] These were of course exceptional cases. The landlords and the peasants mostly supported the Jiyū-tō in its demands for tax reduction, because they felt that they were being called upon to support the government's industrial program and generally to bear a disproportionate tax burden. But landlords did not like low rents.

In 1882 certain scandals, which had to do with the alleged receipt of money from official sources, had blemished the name of Itagaki and involved Okuma in charges of improper dealings with industrial concerns. Whatever the truth of these charges, they aroused great public anger, widened the breach between Jiyū-tō and Kaishin-tō, and ended by discrediting all political parties in the popular mind, to the great satisfaction of the government. Thus the coalition of Satsuma and Chōshū samurai found itself by about the end of 1885 in virtual command of the political arena and free to develop at leisure its plans for meeting party opposition when the new parliament should hold its first session.

The foregoing bare description of the first phase of the modern political development of Japan does not pretend to be complete. It leaves out much that is important, such as the economic bases of the liberal movement and the conflict between agrarian and urban interests. It may have given the impression that the energies of the government were mainly devoted to suppressing the opposition, and this would be mistaken, since they got through a great deal of constructive work in many fields. It therefore no doubt unduly simplifies the complex issues that were at stake. Its main intention, however, is not to record political history in detail but to trace and assess the effects of Western influence upon Japanese political thought and action; and perhaps it will be sufficient for that purpose. A careful examination of the evidence bearing on this question leads to the conclusion that the liberal movement, started with high hopes and seemingly with almost universal acclaim, was in fact much weaker than it appeared. Many reasons can be offered for its failure. The Japanese public is given to enthusiasms that evaporate quickly unless they are concerned with matters close to its daily life, and it is not easily induced to struggle for unfamiliar principles though it is extremely tenacious of old habits. The liberal parties were on the whole earnest, but divided among themselves, and they had behind them no solid tradition but only a medley of ill-assorted theories of foreign origin, as is clear from their readings in Western literature, which they so freely cited and so often misunderstood. They were trying to lead on the road to independence a people schooled by centuries of obedience to authority, and they lacked the unity, perhaps even the honesty of purpose, essential for such a task. They could oppose no coherent resistance to the uniform and skilful pressure of a government that knew its own mind. A sympathetic observer of the Japanese liberals might have said in 1885:

> . . . The bad
> Have fairly earned a victory o'er the weak,
> The vacillating, inconsistent good.

All these and other plausible reasons for the liberal failure can be summarized by saying that Japan was not ready for democracy. Her past history was against it, and there was force in the argument, with which those in power repeatedly countered pleas for an immediate grant of popular rights, that it was too soon to pass the conduct of affairs into inexperienced hands. The liberal reply was: "Yes, it is true that democratic institutions were the result of centuries of evolution in Europe. But that is also true of modern science and art and machinery, as well as of political forms. Would you have us abstain from the use of steam or electricity until we have gone through all the stages that ended in their discovery?" This was an ingenious retort, but it raises without answering the whole question of cultural relationships between East and West, for history so far has shown that machines will enter where ideas cannot penetrate.

One further aspect of the influence of European political thought upon Japan deserves some notice. Students of Japanese history, thinking in terms of twentieth-century political canons, are apt to forget that Victorian England — to say nothing of America and the rest of Europe — did not teach only one gospel. It would, for instance, be a mistake to suppose that faith in parliamentary democracy was universal in England. Indeed, most of those eminent Victorians who believed in parliaments regarded them not as a means of extending the people's share in government, but rather as bulwarks against democracy, and they stood for a very limited franchise. Many Victorian radicals were anti-parliamentary, and what today in England might be regarded as orthodox democratic views were held mainly by Chartists and other extremist minorities. Similarly in the field of politico-economic theory it cannot be said that Adam Smith and laissez-faire were unchallenged. Neither Mill nor Spencer accepted them, and they were not alone in their disbelief. Even the idea of progress, which in retrospect seems to have dominated Victorian life, was challenged and ridiculed by many eminent Englishmen, as can be seen from a comparison between the gloom of Matthew Arnold and the cheerful march of Tennyson's mind along the ringing grooves of change.

Such examples as these may perhaps make the apparent inconsistencies in Itagaki's conduct more intelligible. It has been suggested by some Japanese historians that Itagaki, with Eto, Soeshima, and others, was at the same time a radical, a strong nationalist, and a strong supporter of the Imperial prerogative, and that the only way to reconcile his views on popular government with his absolutist principles is to conclude that he was afraid of republicanism and regarded a parliament as a safeguard against abuse of the Emperor's trust by arbitrary or incompetent ministers. In that sense Itagaki and his colleagues who left the government on the Korean issue are to be regarded as the true fighters in the anti-feudal struggle, whereas the government itself was substituting one kind of feudal dictatorship for another. This is not an easy view to follow, but it is of interest in the light of what has been just said about Victorian attitudes towards parliamentary democracy. At least it goes some way towards explaining why the Japanese in the eighties should have been baffled by European thought and should not have seen the light that to most twentieth-century minds seems so pure and clear.

5. Conservative Triumphs

THE POLITICAL history of the period between the announcement of 1881 and the opening in 1890 of the parliament that it promised shows a reaction against the reforming enthusiasm of the seventies, setting in slowly at first and gradually gathering momentum until, by the first session of the Diet, conservative sentiment had grown in strength and was coloured by some antagonism to Western cultural influences.

When the political parties after a few years of energetic strife went into eclipse owing mainly to the withdrawal of their leaders, the public lost interest in the cause of popular rights, and the unruly acts of its extremist members cost the liberal movement much of the sympathy it had so far enjoyed. The government was thus free to proceed with its plans without fear of serious opposition. The general line of its leaders was a very gradual development of parliamentary rule, always subject to the ultimate authority of the crown and its advisers.

The key to the system that they had in mind was the position of the Emperor as the supreme head of the state, by whom all rights were granted and to whom all duties were owed. This concept of an absolute monarch, venerated and remote, was carefully fostered throughout the Meiji period by a process of indoctrination for which it is hard to find a close parallel in modern times, though the mass propaganda methods of authoritarian states in recent years resemble it in some respects. It promoted the Emperor to a position that he certainly had not previously held in Japanese history, for despite his legendary attributes he had not in the past been the sole focus of national loyalty, but rather a shadowy figure that one feudal leader after another had captured and used for his own aggrandizement. There is little to distinguish this political device from that which was adopted by the principals in the Restoration movement, who gained power precisely as their predecessors had done by claiming to exercise authority on behalf of the crown. The difference was that they gave a modern dress to the figure on the throne and adjusted the theory of his supremacy to suit contemporary circumstances. To say this is not to suggest that their action was dishonest or conceived merely out of lust for personal power. They had at hand, in a long and well-based tradition, the materials for forming a sentiment of national unity, and these they sensibly and indeed almost inevitably used. Monarchy in the nineteenth century was a valuable and imposing institution for which they would have been hard put to it to find a substitute.

Consequently the government and its supporters were careful when introducing any new measure to represent it as conforming to the wishes of His Majesty, and they tended to treat opposition as a form of disrespect to the throne. Conversely, the opposition parties were as a rule careful to avoid words or acts that might be twisted into expressions of disloyalty, and it is noticeable that most political manifestoes of whatever colour contained a reference to the dignity of the throne. The invocation of the Imperial name thus became an important advantage, which the administration constantly used in its efforts to check the advocates of speedy reform. When the Parliamentary Rescript of 1881 was issued, the Emperor was made to rebuke the people for their impatience, saying: "We perceive that the tendency of Our people is to advance too rapidly . . . and we warn Our subjects, high and low, to be mindful of Our will. Those who may advocate sudden and violent changes will fall under Our displeasure."

Thus sheltered by the Imperial utterance, the members of the ruling group were able to disregard most forms of opposition. On the one hand they were firm in repressive measures, on the other they continued with a program of administrative change which, though presented as a gradual devolution of powers to representative bodies, both central and local, served in reality to strengthen the hold of the bureaucracy upon all branches of government. The Prefectural Assemblies, which in 1878 followed the discredited Assembly of Provincial Officials, were, it is true, elective bodies, and in 1880 similar elective assemblies were formed in cities, towns, and villages. Nominally representative institutions, their powers were so restricted by rights of revision and veto held by official members that they cannot be looked upon as an extension of popular rule, though they doubtless had the merit of acquainting local authorities with public opinion and of giving their unofficial members some insight into problems of administration. This was as far as the ruling oligarchy were prepared to go, and the same policy of gradual and largely illusory concessions to democratic principle was followed by them in other measures, which they took in order to strengthen the executive branch of the government and to limit the powers of the legislature that was to be created in 1890.

Soon after the Parliamentary Rescript of 1881, Ito (at that time Home Minister and the most powerful member of the government) was ordered to prepare the draft of a constitution, a necessary preliminary to the creation of a parliament. He went abroad in April 1882 with a numerous staff and (to use his own words) began "an extended journey in different constitutional countries to make a thorough study of the actual workings of different systems of constitutional government, of the various provisions, as well as of theories and opinions actually entertained by influential persons on the stage of constitutional life." Here was a very definite instance of an endeavour to profit by Western experience, though (as we shall see) the model which Ito finally selected was that of Germany and bore little resemblance to the forms that had been so warmly advocated in Japan by admirers of French, English, or American methods. It was surprisingly like the constitution that would have emerged in Japan if, without reference to foreign example, the government had logically pursued the line of development that it had already taken during its conflict with opposition parties.

Upon Ito's return early in 1884, a bureau was formed for the special purpose of drawing up a constitution. It was made part of the Ministry of the Imperial Household and not of the Home Ministry, in order to emphasize the fact that the constitution was to be a gift of the Emperor and at the same time to prevent public discussion while the work was conducted in privacy.

Meanwhile a full reorganization of the administrative system was planned, and carried out in 1885. This also was in part influenced by the German system of the period. The Dajōkwan or Council of State was now abolished and its place was taken by a Cabinet, composed of ministers of the several departments of state and presided over by a Prime Minister. Under this arrangement the Emperor remained as an absolute monarch, nominally exercising personal rule with the advice of the Prime Minister. In fact, the position of the ruling oligarchy was unchanged. It may even be regarded as strengthened, since during the Emperor's minority it had been a kind of council of regency, but now the Prime Minister and his colleagues could always counter opposition by claiming that they were carrying out the Imperial commands. So strong was the veneration for the throne, which they had sedulously fostered, that the liberal parties were almost silenced and public interest in domestic politics declined. There was nothing to do but await the announcement of the Constitution and to see what powers would

be given to the Diet. As for the leaders of liberal or radical opinion, they also were quiescent. They could not openly attack the
government on the constitutional issue, since the government was
careful not to disclose the nature of the instrument that was being
drafted, and even suppressed speculation as to its contents. It remained therefore to find some other count on which they could
rouse public opinion. This was offered to them in the field of
foreign and not domestic politics.

In the foregoing outline of political history no attention has
been paid to the foreign relations of Japan, though it may well be
said that the government which came into power had them constantly in mind. Indeed, its attitude towards domestic problems
was conditioned by anxiety lest Japan should fail to develop such
national unity and strength as would ensure first her safety, and
then her eminence, in international life. This concern for security,
which in the government's view could be obtained only by the
most scrupulous husbanding of its country's moral and material
resources, was (apart from a natural authoritarian bias) what determined its resistance to the agitation for popular rights. The government thought, perhaps rightly, that the independence of Japan
was in danger, and it considered that there was no time for an experiment in democracy. Japan had come late upon the international stage; she was far behind the great powers in military and
economic strength as well as in the technical capacity that a modern state requires. It must therefore use its autocratic powers to
prevent the national energies from being dissipated in domestic
political struggles likely to cause delay in fulfilling its duty to make
the country strong.

It can of course be argued that they could safely have slackened
the speed of modernization and paid more attention to developing
a public experienced and responsible in political matters. This
may be so, but there are indications that the Japanese people were
more enthusiastic for national prestige than for a share in domestic
policy. Certainly the political events of 1887 tend to show this, for
although the clamour for popular rights had by then died down,
the government's handling of treaty revision aroused the greatest
public indignation and caused it perhaps more embarrassment
than the attacks of the liberal reformers.

The public had from time to time been agitated by the problem of treaty revision, and national pride had been more and more
offended as years passed without bringing the fiscal and judicial
autonomy that they so ardently desired. The hated treaties limited
Japan's power of levying customs duties and stipulated that consular courts and not Japanese courts should try all cases, criminal or
civil, in which foreign nationals were concerned. The general at-

titude of foreign residents did little to diminish this grievance, which was no doubt intensified by a humiliating feeling that in some respects Japan was still a backward country obliged by unkind circumstance to adopt foreign customs. These sentiments before long produced a strong conservative reaction and a nationalistic temper of which one expression was a growing hostility to foreigners, strongest among the educated classes but not confined to them. This was at a time when for reasons of policy the government was encouraging social intercourse with foreigners and doing its best to persuade them that the Japanese were such apt pupils in foreign ways that they should be treated on equal terms by foreign nations.

But it became known in 1887 that the Foreign Minister was negotiating with foreign representatives in Tokyo, lavishly entertaining them and preparing to sign an agreement abolishing extraterritorial rights in principle but providing for the trial of suits involving foreign nationals in mixed courts on which foreign judges were to sit with Japanese. Public anger was aroused by this proposal. A storm of protest obliged the government to repudiate the negotiators and accept the resignation of the Foreign Minister. Even in the bitterest days of the struggle for popular rights the government had not yielded so promptly to public pressure, and that it did so on this occasion testifies to the strength of popular feeling. No doubt it hoped that this demonstration would persuade the foreign powers that their demands were not acceptable, for it is a common diplomatic device to plead the strength of public opinion even in countries where it counts for very little. But the national temper was aroused and the government knew that the opposition would surely seize upon any false step that it might make. The stoppage of the negotiations did not, however, appease public discontent. Formal denunciation of the treaties was called for, and the movement, which had acquired an unfortunate antiforeign complexion, became so embarrassing that it was suppressed by most drastic measures introduced *ad hoc* on December 25, 1887.

The public agitation for the abolition of the treaties had favoured a revival of political activity by the opposition parties. They were in substantial agreement upon this one issue, and also upon other questions of foreign as distinct from domestic policy. They joined in attacking the government for its weakness in agreeing with China to recognize the independence of Korea and in other ways insisted upon what they called Thoroughness in Japan's attitude towards foreign states. Thus, it will be seen, the radicals who once had fought for popular rights were now turning into upholders of national prestige and advocating aggressive measures that might have been expected from a military oligarchy but not from disciples of Mill and Spencer. Barred from open political association by the existing law, they resorted to the formation of secret societies and the use of the political rowdies known as *sōshi,* some of whom were merely hired ruffians, others of a better sort but given to violence under pretentious names. They would attack the persons or property of members of the official class and generally terrorize the citizens. It was their disorderly conduct that impelled the government to issue and enforce the Peace Preservation Ordinance (Hoan Jōrei) of December 25, 1887. This declared a sort of martial law or state of siege in Tokyo, for it empowered the authorities to banish any person suspected of disturbing the public peace from within seven miles of the Imperial Palace. The Tokyo garrison was reinforced, official buildings and residences were guarded, and more than five hundred persons were arrested and conveyed out of Tokyo. Among them, besides a number of gang leaders, were some of the most prominent liberal politicians and journalists, redoubtable fighters for popular rights and parliamentary government who were to play an important part on the political stage a few years later.

It was in such an atmosphere that the government faced the nation in the year before the Constitution was to be announced. The most burning issue was treaty revision, and in an attempt to compromise with popular feeling Okuma was taken into the Cabinet as Foreign Minister. But no progress was made. On the contrary there was a set-back since a solution suggested by Okuma was violently rejected, and he himself was attacked and severely injured by a bomb. The negotiations were called off.

The politicians who had been sent out of Tokyo and their less dangerous colleagues who had remained began to renew their pressure, by forming a loose confederation under the cry of *Daidō Shōi,* which means "Agreement in great things, Difference in small," thus proclaiming that its members, though at odds about some matters, were unanimous in disliking the government. This group provides another interesting example of the Japanese habit of following persons rather than principles. This has been noticed in respect of Saigo, whose rebellion was joined by many admirers of his character though they did not like his policy. Similarly the Daidō Shōi association owed many of its adherents to the engaging character of its founder, Goto Shōjiro, a Tosa samurai who had taken an active part in all the main events since before the Restoration.

6. The Constitution and Parliament

The foregoing summary of political events will have shown that the opposition parties pressed upon the government the adoption of political forms that most nearly resembled those of English origin, and they freely invoked the support of English and American theory. The government, for its part, in resisting these demands did not as a rule call in the aid of theory, but dealt with its problems on empirical lines. It did not commit itself to any particular doctrine but took steps to examine the practical working of the systems of government in use in the leading countries of the West, in order to ascertain which was most appropriate to the needs of Japan. Ito, as we have noticed, went abroad in order to study "the actual workings of different systems" and "opinions actually entertained" by practical statesmen. The use of the word "actual" is significant here. He was not going to be guided by theory, but by personal observation and discussion with men of experience. In the light of this determination the stormy public debates of the preceding decades appear to have little importance in so far as they consisted of arguments between schools of political thought, basing themselves upon written authorities. What counted most was direct acquaintance with systems and men; and this is a point to be borne in mind when discussing the nature and extent of Western influence upon Japanese life. A study of what we may call literary influences, though tempting to the historian, may be misleading, for often they do not penetrate beyond intellectual circles and find little response in practical life. It is probable that, despite the great number of Western books circulated in Japan during the first twenty years of Meiji, their effect was not so great as the aggregate influence of individuals consulted by Japanese on their journeys abroad and of foreign advisers employed in Japan, who were in close touch with officials and students destined later to hold important posts.

It was to be expected that when Ito reached Europe he would not go out of his way to find a form of government like those liberal, parliamentary systems which Itagaki and his associates had recommended. These, after all, were precisely what Ito and his colleagues in office had been resisting. He was on the contrary much attracted by the strong monarchical, anti-parliamentary principles of Bismarck and he spent most of his time abroad in Germany.

This is not the place for an analysis of the Constitution which was promulgated in 1889, but it may be said in general terms that it included a great deal that was of German or Austrian origin and very little of the English or French political philosophies which had been publicly recommended in Japan for the previous twenty years. Ito and his colleagues perceived similarities between the position of Germany and that of Japan, since both countries were in process of consolidation and both were somewhat behind the leading Occidental states in international prestige and particularly in industrial organization. The governing class in both countries was determined to keep liberalism in check, and indeed when Ito visited Germany, Bismarck had not long before passed repressive legislation against Social Democrats and the liberal government had resigned, to be succeeded by a conservative cabinet. It is not surprising, therefore, that Ito, encouraged by Bismarck's successes, should have concluded that the German Constitution offered a suitable pattern for adaptation to Japanese needs. He had conversations with Bismarck (upon whom he is said to have modelled his own views and deportment in later years) and with Lorenz von Stein, whom he subsequently told that while the Japanese parliament embodied some features of the English system, the Constitution, which controlled its functions, was derived mainly from German example. In drafting the Japanese document Ito acted on the advice of Stein in making the text simple and broad, in keeping it free from statements of theory, and in referring as little as possible to the Emperor. By following this advice he allowed some latitude in interpretation and consequently left room for development in its working.

Though it was in some respects a reactionary document, it was not so illiberal as is often alleged. Like most legislation of the kind, much depended upon the spirit in which it was applied. Sir William Anson, when asked his opinion, said of it that it was not inconsistent with the development of a strong parliament capable of challenging an arbitrary government. But just as Bismarck was able to flout the Prussian parliament owing to the Austrian and French wars, so Ito was able to override opposition in Japan because of the war with China in 1894 and, it must be admitted, because of the internal weaknesses of the opposition and the irresolute conduct of its leaders.

It would thus appear that German influence was very strong in Japan in the third decade of Meiji, though it must be remembered that, conditions in both countries being similar in many respects, the Japanese government would, even without German experience to draw upon, have produced a system very close to that which was adopted. Both had an autocratic and warlike tradition, a strong monarchy, a powerful conservative ruling class (samurai and junker) and a determination to make up for lost time by building up national strength at the expense of civil liberties. The adoption by Japan of German methods of administration, of military organization, and of economic control cannot therefore be looked upon as an example of strong cultural influence. It did not result in any important deviation from traditional Japanese principles, whereas if the Japanese had adopted any substantial part of the English, French, or American practice in those departments a radical change in Japanese life would have ensued. What is remarkable is not the influence exerted by German example, but the almost complete failure of liberalism after twenty years of the most diligent study and ardent advocacy of responsible parliamentary government and individual freedom.

Yet is it so remarkable after all? Japan before 1868 was a loose federation of autonomous units, particularist in outlook, suspicious of their neighbours, and jealous of central authority. It was the task of the Meiji leaders to weld them into one nation. But a nation cannot be made without nationalism, and the cultivation of a nationalistic spirit is rarely compatible with the encouragement of liberal thought.

The growth of such a spirit is usually accompanied by positive traditionalist reactions against foreign influence, and some of these we should now examine. But before passing on to the more deliberate kinds of conservatism it may be useful to notice some examples of a natural adherence to custom that is not a positive or intentional rejection of the lessons of foreign experience.

One of the most striking examples of the persistence of old forms during a period of seeming political renovation is to be found in the history of a feature peculiar to public life in Japan for many years after the Restoration — namely, the prominence of a small class of men known as the Genro, or Elder Statesmen. The word *Genro* (which is reminiscent of the Toshiyori or Old Men who formed the Council of State of the shoguns) means literally the Original Seniors, the wise old men of the tribe — or one might say the Founding Fathers — who saw it through its time of troubles. The beginning of the Elder Statesmen of the Meiji era can be seen in the formation in 1875 of the Genro-in or Senate, a body composed of eminent persons who had rendered conspicuous service to the state in the years just before and after the Restoration. The special deference paid in the Far East to age and official distinction brought into prominence a small group of men who at all times, whether in or out of office, exercised great influence in national affairs. The Senate was in due course abolished, but its members or other men of the same kind continued to command respect and to wield personal authority because of their prestige. Later in the Meiji period, as they grew older, a small and diminishing élite consisting of Yamagata, Matsukata, Oyama, and a few others became recognized advisers to the throne and to ministries. It cannot be said that they played a part behind the scenes, since it was well known that on all crucial occasions in public affairs their guidance was sought by the government of the day, and indeed the public would have been dissatisfied had they not been

THE STRUGGLE BETWEEN THE OIL LAMPS AND THE LANTERNS

consulted. The last of the Elder Statesmen was Prince Saionji, some years before whose death at a great age in 1940 this extra-legal institution lapsed, to the regret of many good citizens.

The political tradition of Japan seems to call for an advisory organ, neither legislative nor executive nor judicial, which shall oversee the government of the country and stand above partisan feeling. It is doubtless for this reason that, as the most weighty Elder Statesmen left the scene, the Privy Council in some measure replaced them. This also was a body that, though legally constituted, was inconsistent with true parliamentary government. It was created in 1888 for the purpose of advising the Emperor on matters of high policy, its first task being to approve the Constitution before promulgation. Unlike the group of Elder Statesmen, it was and remained an integral part of the organization of the state. Nominally advisory, its powers of review and veto were such that in practice it could exercise a decisive influence upon policy in both domestic and foreign affairs. It could not initiate legislation, but it could suggest and within limits determine the character of laws and treaties. It may therefore be regarded as a perpetuation in Western dress of the traditional advisory councils that under the Shogunate had often been the effective instruments of policy-making; and it was generally regarded by the executive officials as interfering and obstructive.

When it was formed, the Privy Council was officially defined as a body composed of "personages who had rendered signal service to the state" whom the Emperor desired to consult. These were the words that had been used to describe the Senate of 1875, and so the institution of 1888 was not so modern as its name.

7. Traditionalist Reactions

Having traced the main lines of Western influence upon Japanese political thought in the period of its greatest effect, which covers approximately the first twenty years of Meiji (say from 1868 to 1887), we may now look back and examine separately the more important manifestations of conservative sentiment expressed during that period in reactions against foreign culture.

It should at once be said that the flood of reform at first flowed so strong and deep that it submerged most of the defenders of the past, and the extreme traditionalist movements that took place had very little effect. It is easy to give a false impression of their importance by selecting a number of exceptional or picturesque instances of protest against the invasion of new ideas, but the account which follows should not be read as an argument that the great changes which took place in Japanese life were brought about in the face of strong reluctance or opposition. The interest of these reactions is not in their contemporary effect but in their foreshadowing of a more widespread and more effective conservative sentiment that began to develop in the last years of the nineteenth century.

We have already noticed the Shinto revival of the first years of Meiji and seen that this was not specifically an anti-foreign movement. At that time there was no longer any room for effective anti-foreign demonstrations, since the majority of the Japanese people were so enthusiastic for new things and ideas that opposition would have been unpopular and might even have been regarded as unpatriotic. The Japanese, moreover, are partial to strangers, whom they are accustomed to treat with kindness and hospitality. Even during the height of the agitation against "barbarians," when Westerners stood in danger of attacks from enraged or drunken samurai, the ordinary citizen treated them with friendly interest. But intellectual or religious revival movements by their very nature were forms of resistance to foreign cultural influence and therefore deserve some study.

The failure of Shinto to gain an advantage over Buddhism by securing a monopoly of state patronage brought a certain benefit to Buddhism after 1872. There was a revival of sectarian activity among Buddhists and they were able to recover from the harsh economic treatment of earlier years. There was a Buddhist newspaper and this played some part in political discussion from 1874, though only for a short time. Buddhists if not Buddhism were prominent in such anti-foreign agitations as took place at this time. The best known of them was an eccentric of extreme views named Sada Kaiseki, who wrote diatribes against modern things as well as modern ideas. It was he who published an essay entitled *Rampu Bōkoku Ron*, or "On Lamps as a National Disaster." Oil lamps were regarded as representative of Western culture and therefore insidious in their effect. A cartoon of the day shows a duel between a mineral-oil lamp and an old-fashioned *andon*, a lantern in which candles or vegetable oil were used, and this conflict was supposed to represent the struggle between native and foreign thought. Sada, who attacked both oil lamps and Copernican astronomy, also expressed his scorn of foreign things in a *Baka-Bandzuke* or List of Fools, modelled upon the programs of wrestling matches which name the contestants in order of precedence. The Champion Fool was the man who ate bread instead of rice, the next the man who used a foreign umbrella, and so on down to the child who preferred foreign to Japanese toys.

Neither the Shinto nor the Buddhist traditionalists could make much headway against the stream of modern ideas, but the position of Confucianism was somewhat different. In the early years of Meiji the reaction against Confucian philosophy was severe because of its association with feudal institutions, or perhaps it would be better to say that it suffered from neglect rather than positive antagonism. But it was not to be expected that a system which had played so great a part in the formation of Japanese ideals of conduct could be swept away. It went into hiding, so to speak, to emerge later when conditions were favourable. Its fundamental principles of loyalty and piety, which had become part of the stock of Japanese ethical ideas, continued to influence men's lives in some degree, if only because Western thought had not yet offered a positive substitute or successor. Foreign ethical doctrines were studied, but largely as interesting theories and not as guides to conduct. Christianity, while it was to play an important part, was rivalled by materialistic doctrines that came in with English utilitarian philosophy and the theory of evolution.

Although there was no very active school or movement of Confucian revival, certain individuals exercised some influence on behalf of Confucianism. Among these was Motoda, the Confucian tutor of the Emperor from 1875. It is known that his views were embodied in the draft of the Imperial Rescript on Education of 1890, and that he consulted other Confucianists, including Inouye Kowashi, who later became Minister of Education. In 1881 Motoda wrote a preface to a book on the Essentials of Learning for the Young, which was published by the Imperial Household Department and is said to have been issued at the request of the Emperor because he thought that Western ethical teaching was not suitable for Japan. This work may be regarded as the first textbook on moral training in modern Japan and is therefore an important landmark, since in later years the inclusion of moral lessons in the curriculum of elementary schools gave to the authorities a powerful means of controlling national thought. It was at this time that the Minister of Education (Fukuoka) laid it down that the teaching of morals should be based upon "the native doctrine of the Empire and the principles of Confucianism."

Another influential Confucianist was Nishimura Shigeki, who was at the same time a student of Western teachings and a translator of Western books. He was a pupil of Sakuma Shōzan and of Yasui Sokken, men who had been in the forefront of the struggle to open Japan. In 1873 he had joined a group of intellectuals in forming the Meirokusha (that is, the Meiji Six Society, as one might say the Seventy-three Club), a literary society for the encouragement of Western studies, which issued a journal, the *Meiroku Zasshi,* containing articles by men like Fukuzawa, Nakamura Keiu (the translator of *Self-Help*), Kato Hiroyuki, and other leading men of letters. But when he saw that from about 1872 the educational policy of the government dwelt upon material success in life and had little to say about such classical virtues as loyalty, piety, and righteousness, he began to feel grave misgivings and presently ranged himself with the Confucianists. In 1875 he wrote a work called *Shūshin Chikoku Hinito Ron,* or *Moral Training the Only Way of Governing the Country.*

A body called the Tokyo Shūshin Gakusha, a society for the

encouragement of moral training, was founded in 1876. It was expanded in 1883 and called the Nihon Kōdō Kwai, its purpose being to promote lectures on Japanese ethical principles. This new society was formed under the auspices of two Imperial Princes and had several hundred members. But neither undertaking had much success. Their general line was that Christianity and other Western ethical teachings were not suited to the national character of Japan or consistent with its social and political structure. An ethical, not a religious foundation was needed, and that must be Confucian in essence, since it was Confucian principles that had governed the conduct of the dominant classes in Japan for three hundred years past. Some Confucianists went so far as to admit that Confucian principles alone would not suffice in modern conditions, and they toyed with the idea of a compromise between Eastern and Western ethics, which should be the warp and weft of present-day morality.

Deliberate attacks upon Christianity were unusual at this time, though an occasional extremist would use violent language, like that of Megata Sakae, who in 1883 wrote a work entitled *The Irrationality of Western Religion,* in which he denounced Christian doctrine as evil and the Bible as the work of demons. In 1875 the veteran Confucianist Yasui Sokken had written his *Benmō* or *Exposure of Falsehood,* which was a violent attack upon Christianity from the point of view of traditional Japanese sentiment. His criticism of the Bible was trenchant and not without effect. His book had a preface by Shimadzu Hisamitsu, the very conservative lord of Satsuma. In general, however, anti-Christian sentiment was not positive, but only implicit in such revival movements as those fostered by the Confucianists. Thus the propaganda of the Shūshin Gakusha and the Kōdōkwai was only partly and indirectly anti-Christian, and the same is true of the teaching of such Confucian scholars as Naka Tsūko and Nishimura Shigeki. Perhaps the most interesting of the anti-Christian trends was the attitude of the government during its struggle against the people's rights movement when it suggested that the advocates of freedom were "not true Japanese." This, however, misfired and threw a number of Japanese Christians into the Minken movement.

Nishimura in 1886, at a time when in order to facilitate treaty revision the government was deliberately encouraging the adoption of foreign habits, lectured for three days at the University of Tokyo on Japanese principles of virtue. He argued that while in science, politics, and law Western countries were ahead of Japan, they must not be blindly copied out of admiration for their wealth and strength and their superiority in some branches of knowledge. There must be discrimination between good and bad, and Western ideas could not be adopted without modification in moral and physical surroundings differing from those in which they had evolved. This kind of sentiment began to spread and conservative reactions, which had been sporadic and insignificant during the period of Western fever, developed into an influential movement from about 1887, when the negotiations for treaty revision broke down because of popular dissatisfaction. It seems that the pride of a great number of patriotic Japanese was injured by the proposal that foreign judges should sit in Japanese courts, and they felt that the nation's efforts to assimilate foreign culture had been wasted. This sentiment caused some revulsion of feeling against the West. It also led to criticism of the government, which had by example as well as by precept encouraged the adoption of Western habits to an excessive degree.

No doubt there were other and more rational grounds for the impending conservative reaction, but that it was connected with the failure of treaty revision is scarcely to be doubted. This view is borne out in an entertaining way by an incident in which members of the government figured during the life of the abortive conference. In May 1886 the representatives of seventeen powers gathered in Tokyo for discussions. Now was the time for a display of all the most modern European social habits which had been naturalized or given the status of alien residents in Japan. The highest in the land set the example of social intercourse with foreigners upon a grand scale. In 1883 an international club had been opened in a new building, called the Rokumeikwan (which means the Mansion of the Baying Stag). Here Japanese and foreigners together played cards and billiards, conversed, danced, and listened to music. Many fashionable bazaars were held, and attended by the nobility and gentry. This was the age of grand entertainments which were part of a hospitable movement, not without political motive but none the less kindly, intended to make pleasure-loving foreigners feel at home.

The zenith of cosmopolitan gaiety was reached at two splendid parties given respectively by Ito, the Prime Minister, and Inouye, the Minister for Foreign Affairs, in the spring of 1887, only a few weeks before the treaty discussions were abruptly ended. The Prime Minister gave a costume ball in his own residence. Over four hundred guests took part. The Prime Minister appeared as a Venetian nobleman, Prince Arisugawa as a mediæval European warrior, Inouye as a strolling musician, the Director of the Legislative Bureau as a mendicant Buddhist monk, the Chancellor of the University as a pilgrim to Buddhist shrines, the chief of the Metropolitan Police as Bingo Saburo, a loyal knight of early feudal history. The wives and daughters of these high officials appeared as romantic or poetic characters in Japanese legend and were much sought after as partners by the young foreign gentlemen, many of whom appeared in Japanese dress. It must have been a charming occasion and the costumes were no doubt striking, for nobody is better at that sort of thing than the Japanese. But the angry conservatives — who were not in office — were shocked by the spectacle of the great men of the land dressed up like actors and dancing with foreign women. Even the modern chronicler (1922) from whom these details are borrowed writes as if it were a very deplorable affair. All such gaieties were condemned in sober circles, and political opponents of Ito and Inouye, whether in such circles or not, found useful material for their tirades in the lavish entertainments that were frequent at this time. One wrote a tract entitled *Twenty-one Current Evils,* in which he said darkly that extravagant balls and banquets would be thought by the public "to lead to unusual behavior." Another severe moralist observed that this country had learned the decadence of the Roman Empire without first reaching its pinnacle of glory.

Though it was unreasonable thus to attack the innocent pleasures of the great and the rich, it must be admitted that the craze for Western things had gone to absurd lengths. Associations to promote the use of Roman letters for writing the Japanese language, to reform the classical theatre and classical painting, to abolish ideographs, the native costume, and the native diet might singly be tolerable and even useful, and there was no great harm in trying to show that the Japanese were of Caucasian origin.[6] But the cumulative effect of all these attempts to improve old Japanese habits out of existence was naturally to create a feeling of resistance in conservative quarters.

Perhaps the best illustration of the growth of conservative feeling is to be seen in the foundation in 1888 of the magazine *Nippon Jin* by a group under the leadership of Miyake Yūjiro (Setsurei). Its declared purpose was the conservation of the essence of the national culture and it was the organ of a society formed by Miyake and his collaborators for the same purpose, the Seikyō-sha or Society for Political Education. Miyake was by no means prejudiced or reactionary, for he was a scholar of considerable attainments, familiar with both Eastern and Western philosophy, who had

---

[6] An extreme case of intoxication with Western ideas was that of a writer named Takahashi Yoshio, who in 1884 published a book entitled *The Improvement of the Japanese Race,* in which he argued that the Japanese were physically and mentally inferior to Occidental peoples, with whom they could never compete. He recommended that Japanese men, bearing in mind the laws of natural selection and the survival of the fittest, should divorce their wives and marry Western females of superior physique and intellect. He did not suggest a similar policy for Japanese women.

reached the conclusion that Confucian and Buddhist thinkers were "able to master recesses of philosophy more profound than even German philosophy." He thought that if Japan succeeded in assimilating scientific knowledge, there was nothing to prevent her from becoming "foremost in philosophy among the countries of the earth."

Miyake's school of thought was opposed by a rival magazine, *Kokumin no Tomo* or the *People's Companion,* founded in 1887 by Tokutomi Iichiro (Soho). It was written in a simple style and was popular among advanced young men who were in favour of modern ways. It argued against conservatism that it easily became a narrow nationalism. One of Tokutomi's most effective essays included the following retort to conservative arguments: "If you hate dancing and therefore free social intercourse between men and women, if you hate luxuries and therefore free trade, if you hate relations with foreign people and therefore mixed residence,[7] then feeling for Japan grows strong and feeling for the world at large grows weak, the ideal of the state flourishes and the ideal of the people withers. The spirit of conservatism grows, the spirit of progress dies — and then our country loses its vital power."

It is characteristic of the confusion of ideas that prevailed in Japan at this time that the Kokusui Hozon movement, which being committed to preserving the national essence was antagonistic to foreign influence, found its conservatism no obstacle to joining forces with the liberals in attacking the government; so that the magazine which disliked liberal notions supported the purveyors of foreign doctrine, although the government that it attacked preferred national prestige to popular rights as a political goal. Nevertheless the conservatism for which Miyake stood, though open to the criticism that it did not define the national essence which it praised, served a useful purpose in that it brought an end to indiscriminate admiration of Western civilization and moved the Japanese to re-examine their own culture and Western culture in a critical spirit. It also contributed to a revival of interest in the national literature and to the foundation in the Imperial University of a department of Japanese literature, with courses of classical study. At the same time there developed a general movement favouring a study of the native literature. The Kokugaku-In or Academy of National Letters was founded in 1890 and the production of new editions and collections of classical works received a great impetus. Education was also reformed by placing a greater emphasis upon the national language, literature, and history. This

---

[7] "Mixed residence" (*Zakkyo*) referred to that part of treaty revision which was to permit foreign nationals to live outside the areas originally designed as foreign "settlements."

was an important departure from the standpoint of the days when it was proposed that all teaching should be in English, and even that the Japanese language should be abolished. In the educational as in the political world foreign influence had produced a reaction and had strengthened traditions that had been under attack.

Notes on CHAPTER 13

BIBLIOGRAPHICAL. For those aspects of early Meiji history which are discussed in this and the following chapters I cannot do better than refer the student to an excellent selected bibliography of works in English and Japanese printed by Herbert Norman at the end of his *Japan's Emergence as a Modern State* (published in 1940 in the Inquiry Series of the Institute of Pacific Relations). It would be hard to improve upon this.

Most of the books that he lists have been consulted for the purpose of this study. In addition, since the writer of cultural history must know the lineaments and postures of the actors as well as the text of the play, I have paid attention to biographical works and collections of correspondence, as well as reading — not with undiluted enjoyment — a number of novels, newspaper extracts, and other fugitive pieces of the first three decades of Meiji. To quote copiously from them would have encumbered these pages, but some knowledge of materials of this kind is indispensable for an understanding of the "atmosphere" of the period, though I am by no means certain that I have drawn the right conclusions on all points.

THE CHARTER OATH. In order to simplify the narrative I have omitted details of the *Seitaisho* or Statement of the Forms of Government, which in June 1868 followed the Charter Oath and amplified it. This document expands the abstract principles of the oath and sets forth the functions of the various departments of state. It was drafted by Fukuoka and Soyeshima, and its text throws some light on the intentions of the government at that time. It refers specifically to the separation of powers, and in one clause it provides for the election of officials for a period of four years, both of these being ideas suggested by the American system. Fukuoka is known to have read an account of the government of the United States in 1862.

For interesting details of the background of the Charter Oath the student is referred to *Meiji Boshin* (edited by Ichijima Kenkichi, Tokyo, 1928), which is a collection of essays on the events of 1868. It contains useful evidence as to the state of mind of the members of the government at that time. The most valuable paper is one by Dr. Osatake, which gives the texts of early drafts in a convenient form. There can be little doubt that the immediate purpose of the oath and the statement was to encourage unity of opinion among the clans, who were hesitating as to the next move after Keiki's defeat and might have split again had they not been given a line to follow. What was needed was confidence in the new government among nobles and samurai; and Yuri Kimimasa in particular urged this as an essential prelude to the success of the new note issue for which he was responsible. It is interesting to note that, of the several drafts of the oath, the "Tosa" draft (Fukuoka's) shows more consciousness of class division than the "Echizen" draft, which was by Yuri, who had been under the influence of Yokoi Shonan and the vague republican ideas that he entertained. But the general impression given by these data confirms, I think, what has been said in chapter xiii — that there was no plan to introduce parliamentary government, and that ideas of political or social democracy, if held at all, were rudimentary.

The more one studies the background of early Meiji history, the more is one convinced that a perusal of its public documents alone may give a wrong impression. Western writers on Japan have so far not gone into these questions very thoroughly, and there is a tendency to rely upon the texts of laws and proclamations without knowledge of the circumstances in which they were drawn up and the minds of their authors. Mr. Norman, in his *Japan's Emergence as a Modern State,* has gone far to remedy this defect, but there remains a good deal to be done in fields that he has not covered.

THE FORMOSAN EXPEDITION. Among the curiosa of early Meiji literature is a report submitted by Okuma to the Emperor in 1875. In his capacity as president of the Formosa Commission he described the whole sorry business, including the negotiations in Peking, as if it had been a magnificent and heroic enterprise. He then said that, had no steps been taken by Japan to chastise the savages, a land of cannibals would have been established forever, and Japan would have been disgraced in the eyes of the world. But happily the expedition was successful and its glory would not pale before great deeds done in ancient times. He went on to exhort the Emperor not to stop with the chastisement of savages, but to exalt his works of wisdom to the very highest pinnacle of glory.

Other countries have boasted of their exploits in subduing defenceless savages; but this piece of hyperbole from the leader of a movement styled progressive is a rarity even in the annals of political nonsense.

A very interesting account of the negotiations in Peking is to be found in a study, based on Chinese documents, by T. F. Tsiang: "Sino-Japanese Diplomatic Relations, 1870–1894," in the *Chinese Social and Political Science Review,* Vol. XVII, of April 1933. This paper is also valuable for the origins of the war against China of 1894–5.

A study of the Formosan affair brings out some interesting points of domestic history. It shows that the leaders who, united by a common purpose, were able to carry through the Restoration movement, began to drift apart by the end of 1871, if not sooner. There was ill feeling between Okubo and Kido, which developed while they were on the mission abroad in 1872, and there were serious clashes of temperament and differences of opinion among Okubo, Saigo, Ito, and Okuma, to say nothing of other leaders. Personal jealousies and rivalries had a great deal to do with shaping political events thereafter, and it would be a mistake to think of the Meiji leaders as a happy band of unselfish patriots. During the absence of Okubo and Kido the caretakers (Okuma, Saigo, and others) broke their promise to take no decisive steps and only to hold the position at home. The Tosa men and the Hizen men tried to consolidate their respective groups and thus collided with Inouye, while there were continuous quarrels between members of each group. They agreed only in their antagonism to Satsuma and Chōshū statesmen. Okubo comes best out of the story.

Motoda Eifu. Readers not familiar with Japanese will find an account of the life of Motoda, together with specimens of his lectures to the Emperor in English translation, in Volume XL of the *Transactions of the Asiatic Society of Japan* (Tokyo, 1912). This includes his lecture on a hexagram in the *Book of Changes,* which is said to symbolize the connection between the divine and the secular elements of kingship.

The Constitution of 1889. This document has been much criticized as illiberal and undemocratic, and it certainly included some objectionable features from the point of view of a believer in responsible parliamentary government. But like most political arrangements its form is less important than the spirit in which it was worked. Ito was no democrat, but it is fair to say that he framed it in such a way as to allow for further development in the direction of democratic government, since it contains provisions for its own amendment. It is true that it made the Cabinet responsible to the throne and not to the Diet or the people, that the budgetary powers of the lower house were inadequate, and that the upper house had powers of veto that were difficult to circumvent. But these defects could have been remedied had there been in the Diet or in the country at large any general determination to bring about by entirely legal processes, if not at once, at least by steps, a genuinely democratic form of government. It was probably because they were well aware of this possibility that the autocratic elements in the governing class buttressed the absolutist structure by certain extra-constitutional devices that were far more serious obstacles to progress than the terms of the Constitution itself.

Chief among these was a rule, initiated by the Privy Council in 1898, by which the posts of War Minister and Navy Minister could be held only by a general or an admiral on the active list. This meant that no cabinet could be formed without the approval of the service departments, and any cabinet could be destroyed or held to ransom if the military and naval leaders threatened to withdraw their nominees.

It will thus be seen that discussions as to the nature of the Constitution of 1889, or as to its resemblance to a German model, have little relevance to the actual political system that was developed in Japan after the war with China. It has been argued in this chapter that this system cannot properly be ascribed to German "influence." Dr. McLaren, in his *Political History of Japan,* when treating of the text of the Constitution quite correctly speaks of "Prussian influence" (p. 182) and "Prussian innovations" (p. 205); but later in his book, when he comes to the working of the system, he refers to "the immediate failure in Japan of the system adopted from Germany" (p. 229) and points out that the minds of those who framed the Constitution were "imbued with theories of the native policy" and "fortified by a study of . . . Tudor England and Hohenzollern Prussia" (p. 365). The word "fortified" here is important. It does not mean "inspired."

He is of course right in saying that in 1889 practically every institution and principle that had been used by Bismarck made its appearance in Japan. But he could have gone on to say with equal truth that the imitation turned out to be very unlike the genuine article, and wear and tear revealed it to be of domestic manufacture after all. If I may be permitted a spirituous simile, it was not unlike those liquors that used to be sold in Japan in bottles labelled "Scotch Whisky." They were made of the right kind of ingredients and were potable enough, but they would not have passed muster in the Highlands.

THE REMNANTS OF FEUDALISM. It is difficult to write about Japanese history without using the word "feudalism," though it stands for different things at different times and leads to confusion unless it is clearly defined. I am afraid that I have erred myself, but the loose way in which writers and speakers on contemporary Japan explain present-day phenomena by dismissing them as "feudal" is truly alarming. It tends to become a synonym for "undemocratic"; and the height of absurdity is reached when it is applied not only to economic or political forms but to novels, plays, food, dress, behaviour, and speech — and I dare say to archery, hawking, fencing, and wrestling.

Japanese feudalism in the Middle Ages has been clearly described by the late Dr. Asakawa in his *Documents of Iriki* and other works. But Tokugawa Japan was in many respects the antithesis of a feudal country. Granted that the object of the shoguns was to preserve the appearance of feudal relationships between themselves and their vassals, the reality was far otherwise. The supremacy of the Tokugawa was maintained not because they stood at the apex of a pyramid of feudal loyalties, but because they kept a precarious balance among the Fudai and Tozama fiefs by a policy of bullying, cajoling, intriguing, and spying, combined with a financial and military strategy designed to keep the feudatories weak and unable to combine against their nominal suzerain. Nobody can say that Satsuma and other great Tozama fiefs were, a hundred years after Sekigahara, anything but autonomous states in practice — or let us say tributary states, but certainly not tenants by virtue of an obligation of service sustained by loyalty and rewarded by land. As for the late eighteenth and early nineteenth centuries I can see very little that was feudal except certain social traditions and the vestiges of overlordship over Fudai daimyo and hatamoto — this being political rather than economic. Indeed, as the eighteenth century progressed the economic concomitants of a feudal system, where they persisted, became negligible and almost nominal. The Shogun could not keep his contract with his own direct retainers, and the hatamoto and samurai in Tokugawa domains were little more than "soldiers" in the original sense of that word — the officers and men of an army paid a wage for their services. Conditions in the several clans were somewhat different, but even here the system was only quasi-feudal and might be better described as paternal. There is perhaps no harm in saying that in certain quarters a feudal spirit survived after the Restoration and that its vestiges are still to be perceived in Japan. But that does not justify writers on present-day Japan in saying of any political or social circumstances which they dislike that they are "feudal" when what they mean is that they are conservative or traditional.

CHAPTER
14

EARLY MEIJI: WESTERN INFLUENCES

1. Popular Sentiment

WHEN the rallying cry of "Expel the Barbarians" died down because it was no longer useful as a political device to embarrass the Shogunate, and when six of the leading feudal lords said in a memorial to the authorities: "Let the foolish argument be abandoned which has hitherto described foreigners as dogs, goats, and barbarians," the new government began to encourage the adoption of Western ways. This was part of their plan to destroy what were called *kyūhei*, or bad old habits, and to build up national strength by assimilating those material and practical features of Occidental life which were supposed to be the true foundation of a powerful modern state. The townspeople, always lively and much given to new fashions, responded with almost feverish enthusiasm; and they were followed, though slowly and with misgivings, by the peasants, who thought that change might better their condition but were puzzled and even frightened by innovations that seemed to run counter to cherished customs and beliefs.

The subsequent craze for Western things and Western ideas lasted for a space of about two decades, described by some Japanese historians as the period of intoxication. This almost fanatical phase is of peculiar interest in the history of European influences upon Asiatic peoples and deserves therefore some detailed description.

Naturally it was the visible and tangible features of Occidental civilization that first attracted the attention of the Japanese people at large, since its unfamiliar modes of thought were not easy to fathom. The æsthetic bent of the Japanese makes them peculiarly sensitive to fleeting movements on the surface of life; and because their visual perception is acute their artists are often quicker than their writers to seize upon changes in popular taste or shifts of public interest. Throughout Japanese history the student often finds the mood or sentiment of a time expressed more vividly in the plastic arts than in literature, and it happens that this is especially true of the period of transition in the middle of the nineteenth century. Long before the Restoration, Japanese colourprint artists had begun to turn their attention to themes that would satisfy or even anticipate a popular interest in Western things.

In 1848 Hokusai, the Old Man Mad with Painting, was eightynine, Hokkei was sixty-eight, Kunisada sixty-three, Kuniyoshi fiftytwo, Hiroshige fifty-two, and Eisen had lately died. Hokusai's *Mangwa* was yet to be completed, and so was Hiroshige's *Tōkaidō Meisho Dzuye;* but popular art had passed its zenith and was in full decline. This was the year in which the Russian "black ships" came to the coast of Matsumae. This was the year in which the feudal lord of Saga had started to build a reverberatory furnace and Sakuma Shōzan had constructed a field gun upon a recent European model. New movements were afoot and were soon to be reflected in painting. The following year shows already the beginning of a change. No longer the lovely ladies and the pleasant landscapes untouched by time and dusty business, but now less romantic and less familiar themes bespeak the print artist's brush if he is to satisfy the capricious taste of the citizens of Yedo and Osaka. In 1848 the leading print artists begin to concern themselves with political matters, thus mirroring the confused pattern of contemporary life, the uncertainties that prevail. Kuniyoshi and a number of his colleagues are questioned by the authorities concerning prints that are in effect political satires. In 1853, when Perry's ships have arrived, Kuniyoshi and his publisher are fined for issuing a series of prints professing to be a selection of genre paintings reminiscent of the masterpieces of Matahei, but really poking fun at dissolute goings-on in the inner apartments of the Shogun's palace. The citizens are beginning to deny respect to their feudal masters. Certain artists now devote themselves to a type of black-and-white picture, struck off from clay blocks, and called Perry Tile-Prints *(Perry Kawara-ban)* to show how up-to-date they are. These are broadsheets depicting chiefly contemporary events, and the production of prints tends to become less an artistic undertaking than a kind of rudimentary journalism. The number of copies sold increases month by month. The prints develop as a medium of information about foreign customs and about changing domestic conditions. Their titles reveal this trend, for the Perry prints are followed by the Red Hair prints, which depict the persons and habits of northern Europeans as distinct from Portuguese and Spaniards, people whose appearance has already been freely portrayed since the sixteenth century. There is also a series known as *Kaikwa-ban* or Civilization-Prints, showing some of the external aspects of that Western culture which Japan is on the brink of adopting with fervour. Their subjects are intensely modern. They represent steamships, foreign architecture in brick and stone, exhibitions (still pretty new in Europe), trousers and hats, bustles and bonnets. The colour, the composition, the sentiment of the traditional *ukiyoe* begin to vanish. Here is visible one of the first evil effects in the æsthetic field of the impact of Western civilization upon Japan, and in this lapse from former standards the use of cheap imported pigments played a wicked part.[1]

A gradual degradation becomes clear as one studies colour prints and book illustrations from about 1850, yet the decline is not universal. Hokusai just before that had done a landscape showing surveyors at work, which may be said to have a slightly modern touch; but it preserves all his great qualities. Kuniyoshi does Yokohama street scenes with a slightly foreign flavour, and Hiroshige rather later a scene at the railway station. Sadahide, *circa* 1860, is still able to display brilliant design and harmonious colour in a triptych representing foreign vessels loading cargo. This last is indeed a minor masterpiece, which has some of the quality of work of the best Ukiyoe period, though instead of Yedo beauties poised upon airy bridges it portrays the massive hulls of ships, dock workers plodding up a gangway, and elegant foreign females in crinolines, waving their hands from little rowboats. Even a print by Kiyochika (1847–1915) of an iron foundry manufacturing pots and kettles contrives to make good play with the glow from the furnace and the straining figures of the workmen. This is of 1879, and now and again one comes across pictures of an even later date showing traces of that happy gift of the great print artists which enabled them to perceive and record the pictorial essence of unpromising scenes.

It was hard for the print artists of Meiji to preserve the old qualities of their school as they inevitably turned to depicting such phenomena of the new age as shawls, capes, and umbrellas, locomotives and factory chimneys, street lamps and telegraph poles. Yet even here some ingenious painters contrived to find decorative elements, just as their early predecessors had portrayed with gusto such striking subjects as the large noses and the baggy breeches of Portuguese captains or the tall cadaverous figures of Jesuit fathers. But it must be said that European dress and deportment of the nineteenth century were lacking in picturesque qualities, and the merchants and seamen who came ashore in Yoko-

---

[1] Japan took part in the International Exposition in Vienna in 1872. A description of the process of making colour prints was prepared, but when it was published later in Japan the illustrations were done in imported aniline colours, which were in vogue at the time. The pure Japanese colours were available.

hama offered less attractive models to Japanese artists than did those who landed in Nagasaki from caravels some three hundred years before. Nevertheless some interesting traces of foreign influence can be found in the popular arts of the day, though it is social rather than æsthetic. The print men and the illustrators, perhaps responding to some subconscious wish, are apt when representing Japanese ladies and gentlemen in foreign dress to idealize their subjects and to give them an extremely Western air. The ladies are tall and slender — as indeed were the seductive females imagined by Utamaro. They wear their foreign dress with charming ease. The gentlemen, especially the high officials in tight breeches, have extremely long legs and well-turned calves, which would have pleased Sir Willoughby Patterne but are certainly not the sturdy members that usually support the Japanese male. Both sexes have beautiful fair complexions. In imposing salons the gentlemen lean over the seated ladies in intensely deferential poses, which certainly do not accord with the traditional habit of Japanese society.

While popular art was thus being transformed by foreign influence the classical schools of painting, of their nature unable to adjust themselves to new conditions, suffered from neglect and even from contempt as the movement in favour of "modern" — that is, of Occidental — taste developed and brought with it a positive reaction against the ancient and traditional. Two masters of classical Japanese painting, Kano Hogai and Hashimoto Gaho, were almost starving ten years after the Restoration, and their works were sold at street corners, where they could be bought for a few pence. The treasures of Buddhist monasteries were thrown away or sold for a song. Precious wooden sculptures were used as fuel. Sacred buildings were destroyed, partly because political trends had fostered an anti-Buddhist movement, but largely because the mood of the day was iconoclastic and what was old was thought to be bad because what was bad was sometimes old. In 1879 an American connoisseur, Alfred Fenellosa, who had studied and appreciated Japanese painting and sculpture, lectured at Tokyo University on the value of early Japanese art and implored the authorities to take protective action. But the tide of foreign influence was too strong and it was not until some years later that a reaction set in with sufficient strength to afford protection to national art treasures and support to living artists. It is perhaps significant that a Japanese word (*bigaku*) for "æsthetics" was coined about 1880, when foreign theories were in high favour and Japanese art was at a low ebb.

This description of the condition of Japanese art in the early years of Meiji will give some measure of the violence of the foreign fever that then raged in Japan, for it attacked the very essence of

Japanese culture, its deeply rooted æsthetic tradition. That it should have affected more superficial aspects of daily life is not remarkable, though even here there are some curious features that show not so much the strength of foreign influence as the weakness of a society in a period of drastic political change, when old habits are challenged and new standards have not been fixed.

While foreign political ideas began, as we shall presently see, to make a strong impression upon Japanese minds in the early years of Meiji, the first and most apparent changes brought about by contact with the West were naturally those which showed themselves in the field of material culture. Thus military uniforms of Western type were adopted for obvious reasons of utility before the Restoration of 1868, and thence it was but a short step to the issue in 1872 of an ordinance prescribing foreign dress for court and other official ceremonies. This was an important departure, for it so to speak legalized trousers and abolished flowing robes, thus symbolizing the current change from a leisurely, processional life to a busy, practical striding about the market place. To wear foreign-style clothes and leather shoes was now correct and up-to-date, not ludicrous as it had been as late as 1859, when an Englishman named Tilley reported that the Japanese in Yedo were extremely amused by European costume. They had greeted with loud laughter his "tail coat and a curly-brimmed London hat which would have been fashionable in the Botanic Garden on Wednesday." Less than twenty years later the Tokyo newspapers were reporting that the most prosperous tradesmen in Tokyo were the tailors of foreign garments and that shoemakers were doing a thriving business. Of course few Japanese in 1875 or thereabouts could afford a complete foreign wardrobe, but it was usual to wear one or two articles of foreign clothing. Some interesting combinations were thus devised, such as a kimono over trousers, or a broadcloth frock coat and a silk divided skirt with two swords in the belt; and these naturally drew the fire of Japanese satirists. Traditional Japanese costume permits of few ornaments, but diamond rings and gold watches became very popular as marks of advanced views and good social standing — a sorry departure from the frugal standards of an earlier day. Foreign umbrellas (called by the Japanese "bat shades," from their resemblance to the wings of that creature) unhappily displaced the decorative bamboo-and-paper implements that had formerly brightened rainy streets. Cheap glass began to displace pottery and lacquer, and tin cans were more prized than utensils made by craftsmen. Here and in many other ways traditional articles of great beauty gave way to drab things with no merit except perhaps durability.

Such changes had a measure of august approval, since the Imperial ordinance just cited was followed by a message stating that old-style costume was not appropriate to the times. The people must not be soft, but must strive to build up a martial state. These are interesting words, for they suggest that the purpose of abolishing what the authorities called "old evils" was not to adopt a kind of civilization recognized as superior but to mobilize and stiffen the hitherto inert masses for national purposes that had little to do with cultural reform or the pursuit of happiness. There were other changes encouraged by the government in order to promote such ends. It became fashionable to eat beef, and notices were issued by local authorities recommending this unorthodox diet on the ground that it would create energy for the performance of patriotic duties and strengthen the national physique. The public was assured that eating meat would not as hitherto be regarded as defiling worshippers at shrines. One of the most widely read books of this early period was *Aguranabe* (1871), a series of sketches by a popular comic writer and prolific journalist, Kanagaki Robun, in which he describes the customers in an eating-house of which beef stew was the specialty. It gives their occupations, samples of their talk, their views on modern life, and their taste in Western things. It suggests that you could not be civilized unless you ate beef stew (*gyunabé kuwaneba hirakenu*); and among its numerous illustrations is a drawing of a young man who has placed his umbrella on the floor behind him, is gazing at an enormous gilt watch, and is about to consume a dish of beef. To these insignia of modernity he adds a coiffure which, though in the old style, has been sprinkled with eau-de-Cologne.

Ranking with beef, umbrellas, and watches as signs of advanced thought were oil lamps, knitted underwear, blankets, telegrams, and horse-carriages. The list might be enlarged to include almost any simple mechanical contrivance or handy utensil that could be adapted to use in Japanese daily life; but perhaps the state of affairs is best illustrated by a song composed for children in 1878. It was called the "Civilization Ball Song" and was designed to impress on young minds the advantages of Western culture. They were to count the bounces of the ball by reciting the names of ten objects deemed to be the most worthy of adoption — namely, gas lamps, steam engines, horse-carriages, cameras, telegrams, lightning-conductors, newspapers, schools, letter post, and steamboats.

Rather less material aspects of Western life that were urged upon the confused but obedient public were the use of the English language and the observance of decency. The former calls for no comment, but the latter needs a rather roundabout explanation. It has to be remembered that when the so-called treaty ports were opened to foreign trade and residence in 1868, the Emperor issued an edict announcing that the treaties concluded by the Bakufu with foreign countries had his approval, but that they contained some harmful clauses that must be amended in accordance with international justice. This is the first official statement on the subject of treaty revision, a question that was to claim the attention of successive Japanese governments for nearly thirty years. It is not too much to say that the problem of securing new treaties on a footing of equality with other powers overshadowed all other problems and influenced not only foreign but also domestic policy throughout that period. The attitude of the authorities towards the adoption of Western institutions and customs was to a great extent shaped by their anxiety to show to Western nations that the Japanese people had assimilated enough of Western culture to justify their claims to be treated as members of a civilized modern state. They wanted Western nations to agree that the constitution and laws of Japan were enlightened and that her standards of public and private behaviour were high enough to make their country a respectable and worthy member of international society. No doubt they privately thought that their own civilization was in many ways superior to the materialistic culture of the industrialized Occident, but they did not say so; and they were consistent in urging upon the Japanese public the reform of practices that to the foreign eye might look unpolished or even barbarous.

The steps they took to modernize their political and economic structure need not be considered at this point, but it is proper in the present context to pay some attention to the effect upon daily life of the concern of the rulers of Japan lest their people should be regarded by foreigners as inferior in behaviour or capacity to those of the dominant nations in the nineteenth-century world. The frantic zeal with which foreign ideas and habits were adopted in the first two decades after the Restoration seems at first sight to testify to the overwhelming effect of Western culture and gives the impression that its most obvious features were borrowed by the Japanese as gladly as were the main elements of Chinese culture in the seventh century. But this view leaves out of account the necessities of the situation as the Japanese saw it after the threatening visits of Russian and American warships round about 1850. In many respects they felt that they had no choice. It was true that the Western nations did not explicitly impose upon Japan the task of reshaping her social and political life along Western lines, but the Japanese saw clearly that if they were to enter the dangerous circle of international comity they must in self-defence forge for themselves the kind of weapons which, it appeared, gave to the great modern states their supreme position in world affairs. This meant that they must equip themselves as rapidly as possible not only with a military machine but also with a modern apparatus of administration, law, industry, and commerce. These ends, they were convinced, could not be fully achieved unless they secured full political independence, and this was not possible so long as the first treaties remained in force and denied them such conditions of full sovereignty as judicial and fiscal autonomy.

They made up their minds to take over foreign ways of life not so much because they recognized the absolute merits of Western culture — a point on which in truth they were at that time not able to form a rational judgment — as because the sooner they could display to the world a colourable imitation of Western society, the sooner would the unequal treaties be revised. This was their goal, and much that is obscure in early Meiji history becomes clear when it is looked at in the light of these circumstances. That treaty revision was a controlling factor in the political life of Japan until it was accomplished in 1894 is clear enough from the most cursory study of political documents; but day-to-day social life also reveals, in curious and unexpected ways, how important it was thought by Japanese leaders that their countrymen should make a good impression on the outside world by showing themselves as earnest followers of Western example. Their anxiety sometimes took an extreme form. So thirsty were they for approval that they developed a nervous dread of ridicule. A study of the vernacular newspapers for a few years after 1870 reveals some interesting evidence of this fear of foreign criticism. Such is an announcement in the *Nichi-nichi* newspaper at the end of 1871 of an order issued by the Tokyo municipal authorities against nakedness. The writer explains that rikisha men and day-labourers must give up their old comfortable practice of stripping to the loincloth during their exertions. They must cover themselves with something, for the headline says: "You must not be laughed at by foreigners." So the new rule goes into force, and from time to time a simple countryman is arrested for indecent exposure because he has tucked up his kimono and bared his sunburned thighs. Next the public bathhouses engage the attention of the functionaries. The proprietors are told to put screens before the entrance and to separate the sexes, and this is done though the barriers are often only symbolic. Again, under the headline: "Do not be laughed at by foreigners," the newspaper explains that this and similar reforms need not be construed as condemning good old customs outright but simply as measures to prevent ridicule by prudish aliens. Shortly after this the diligent municipal officers summon a theatre manager and two writers of farces to warn them that henceforward they must produce only edifying and not naughty plays. Obscene performances are offensive to high-class Japanese as well as to foreigners and will not be permitted. Nor may the actors make jokes and puns about famous historical figures, since that might confuse school-children. They must at all costs be instructive. Another official order forbids the display or sale of Spring Pictures — a polite way of describing pornographic art, as Spring Tales is the general name for erotic writings.

The solicitude of the authorities extended even to the conduct of Japanese travelling abroad. A leading newspaper in 1870 prints an article under the title: "Bad Behavior of Japanese Tourists." It relates the dreadful conduct of a Native of our Empire who, while at sea on a Pacific Mail steamship, smoked in bed and chanted Chinese poems in a loud voice, to the distress of other passengers. A miscreant more dangerous to the reputation of Japan had, while staying at a hotel in the United States, attempted to seduce the chambermaid and sullied the white wall of his room with an improper sketch. The writer of this piece reminded the public that the doings of one business man could cast shame upon the Japanese people in the eyes of the whole world, since in modern days the press could spread small items of news over thousands of miles to hundreds of thousands of readers.

Of somewhat more significance than the trivia just recorded was the attitude of the Japanese newspapers towards an attempt made by the authorities in 1871 to abolish the sale of girls as prostitutes or geisha. The *Nichi-nichi* newspaper announced the impending reform in a column headed: "Traffic in Human Beings Forbidden. The Caged Birds return to the Sky. Geisha and Harlots released by Order." But to relieve the distress of those who might be pained by such drastic interference with ancient custom, the writer added: "But this is only on account of foreign opinion." A few days later the Department of Justice, in defence of its policy, stated that these unfortunate women, having been sold to their owners, were deprived of human rights and had become like horses and oxen. Upon this the newspaper observed that horses and oxen could not pay their debts, so that the owners would get no indemnity or refund. Another protector of vested interests wrote the consoling sentence: "Anyhow these girls are not enjoying their freedom"; and for lack of public support the new order was not enforced.

This incident, occurring at the height of the craze for foreign things, shows that old and deeply rooted habits did not easily succumb to foreign influence, and that change was slow to penetrate beneath the surface of Japanese life. The truth is that, for the most part, it was only foreign things and not foreign ideas that had an immediate appeal to the mass of the Japanese people, who could not be expected to grasp the principles which guided Western behaviour, since they were of an intellectual origin far remote from the ancient springs of conduct in Far Eastern countries. Thus it was puzzling for a thoughtful Japanese to discover that, while Europeans thought it shocking to expose the naked human form, they displayed in their homes and in public places paintings and statues of the nude body which had no place in the repertory of Japanese artists, who would have deemed them merely an exaggerated form of Spring Pictures. Similarly in a country that had developed no doctrine of human rights it seemed absurd to prevent indigent parents from selling their daughters into a profession that served a recognized social purpose; and they were not likely to change that opinion so long as they observed that the brothels in the treaty ports were thronged with foreign visitors.

Indeed, as was to be expected, it was not very long before the first flush of enthusiasm for Western ways and manners began to produce a critical and conservative reaction in some quarters. A more detailed study of the effect of Western thought must be reserved for a later chapter, but it is convenient here to examine some of the earliest expressions of scepticism by individuals who asked themselves whether Western culture, represented to them as morally and materially more advanced than their own, was in reality so flawless as it pretended to be. Perhaps the first sign in literature is a work entitled *Seiyō Anasagashi,* which means Picking Holes in the West. This essay in fault-finding, published in instalments in 1879 by the recently founded Keio University, quoted foreign evidence of foreign delinquency, for it was composed mainly of extracts from *Palace and Hovel or Phases of London Life* and *The Light and Shadow of New York Life.* It is true that this is a solitary instance among a crowd of translations of European classics; but it may be taken as showing that the pretensions of the West were no longer being accepted without question in educated circles; and it is the more significant in that Keio University was founded for the very purpose of spreading knowledge of the English language and Anglo-Saxon institutions.

In less sophisticated or more stubbornly conservative circles it is easy to trace a strong anti-foreign sentiment, freely expressed by factions in apostolic succession to those which had raised the cry of "Expel the Barbarians" as soon as they saw that their own cherished beliefs were endangered by the arrival of foreigners spreading new doctrine. An interesting example of such early conservatism is to be found in the treatment of Japanese Christians in the first years of Meiji.

The government installed immediately after the Restoration was organized on lines similar to those of the administration set up in A.D. 702 after the Taikwa Reform. The movement that brought this about was described as the Return to Antiquity, and one of its main features was an attempt to restore the indigenous (Shinto) religion to its primacy in the state. Above the six ministries was placed a Department of Religion, whose President ranked next to the Chancellor of the Realm; and when the Emperor took his Charter Oath in 1868 he swore not to his subjects but to the national deities, following an ancient ritual that had been used by his ancestor when he announced to the gods the conversion of Japan to Buddhism.

Underlying this procedure was a very early concept of the unity of government and worship, in which the sovereign was seen as an intermediary between the gods and the people. In that sense the new structure was a return to antiquity, though it is true that its main purpose was to make a clean break with the tradition of feudal rule and to reassert the absolute power of the throne. It could not long withstand the rough winds of political controversy, but for a brief period it survived uneasily and meanwhile gave a certain authority to the Shinto enthusiasts who presided over the Department of Religion, and to the officials of its dependent institution the Daikyō-in or Board of Religious Instruction. These took advantage of their position to harass and humiliate their Buddhist colleagues, of whom a few were admitted to the board on sufferance and only for form's sake, since in fact only Shinto doctrines were taught.

This revival movement, as an attempt to restore Shinto as the state religion, was abortive and had little effect upon the religious or social life of the day. Though it would scarcely deserve mention on its own account, it is of some historical significance as the forerunner of similar movements in later times — movements that differed from it, however, in having a strong political complexion. It is interesting chiefly as an expression of traditional feeling running against the intellectual tide of the day. The Shinto doctors, successors of Mabuchi, Motoori, and Hirata, the great Kokugakusha or National Scholars, who by their studies of the native literature had contributed to the downfall of the Shogunate, felt that their services should be rewarded and that the government should support them in their assault upon foreign creeds, by which they meant Buddhism and Confucianism and — though it was not usually a direct object of their attack — Christianity. They were especially hostile to Buddhism and resented in particular the combination of Buddhism and the indigenous faith that was called Dual Shinto. Thus curious syncretic system permitted Buddhist images and paintings in Shinto shrines and Shinto emblems in Buddhist chapels. It was a compromise that had the sanction of long usage, and when the Shinto shrines were urged to throw out

Buddhist articles and the monasteries to surrender Shinto emblems a great deal of unseemly and riotous conduct ensued, which led in some provinces to the destruction of sacred buildings and their contents, with subsequent reprisals. It was this quarrel that was chiefly responsible for the loss of many art treasures, already described.

These stupid and intolerant excesses were thought in some quarters to have the approval of the government, and did in fact result from a policy for which the Chancellor, Prince Iwakura, was responsible, though he cannot have foreseen its results. In certain provinces, notably in Satsuma and Chōshū, where there was a strong anti-Buddhist feeling among followers of Hirata and Yoshida Shōin, Buddhism was for a time almost eradicated, and elsewhere a great deal of Buddhist property was destroyed under the impression that it was the government's aim to abolish Buddhism.

These episodes, typical of a period when a hundred conflicting doctrines in religion, social ethics, and politics were striving for adoption, had sequels that must have sadly disappointed the Shinto doctors. The great popular Buddhist sects, in particular the Amidists of the Hongwanji, were moved from lethargy to action by the hostility of Shinto and were before long able to regain great influence, particularly in such regions as Satsuma, which had been swept and garnished for them by the recent excesses, since no rivals were left to compete with them.[2] Moreover, as a result of its excessive zeal the Board of Religious Instruction, the chief organ of Shinto propaganda, was abolished in 1876, and the parent Department of State soon followed it into oblivion. The field of religious and ethical controversy was left clear for Buddhists, Confucianists, and freethinkers alike.

The times were not propitious, however, for Confucian philosophers. Their teaching, which encouraged virtuous behaviour and self-discipline, might perhaps have been adapted to the require-

[2] An interesting footnote to the history of this period is furnished by the relationships of this great Buddhist sect with certain Restoration leaders. The Eastern Hongwanji had been favoured by the Tokugawa at the expense of the Western Hongwanji, with the result that the Western branch nourished a certain animosity against the Bakufu. When Chōshū and Satsuma rebels were in Kyoto setting the court against the Bakufu, they were offered sanctuary in the Western Hongwanji, where they were free from the attentions of the Shogun's police. Chōshū and Satsuma samurai remembered this after the Restoration, and men like Ito, Inouye, Koduma, and Terauchi did the abbots favours, thus aiding the revival of Buddhism in their provinces. Later, when the people of the western provinces, in particular Chōshū, resisted new taxes imposed by the Meiji government, the Chōshū men in the administration asked the Hongwanji to persuade members of the sect that the taxes ought to be paid.

It is difficult to understand early Meiji history without some knowledge of the private relationships of its chief actors. Often obscure features only become clear when one learns the personal friendships and quarrels or the family connections behind them.

ments of the modern life upon which Japan was now entering; but (as the Japanese phrase goes) it smelt of China. It was also tainted with feudal associations, since the Tokugawa administration had been, at least in theory, based upon the Confucian ideal of government by superior men — a system not at all consistent with the prevailing desire for freedom and popular rights. Consequently, though there were some early attempts at a Confucian revival, promoted by Yasui Sokken and other scholars, they had little success and it was not until after 1880 that Confucianism began to regain some small measure of influence. The truth is that in the era of "enlightenment," which lasted approximately from 1868 to 1888, the only doctrine that could be successfully preached in Japan was a utilitarian philosophy, suitable to a country which was aiming at the material development of the nation and the individual.

It is perhaps surprising, but nevertheless appropriate, to deal with Christianity under this rubric. Reactions against Buddhism, Confucianism, and even Shinto as old-fashioned and therefore unsuitable to the times did not extend to Christianity. Indeed, they even worked in its favour, since there was current a feeling, not very precisely formulated, that Christian teaching was closely connected with and perhaps even accounted for the success of Western countries in managing their own affairs. This feeling was of gradual growth, because it had to contend with a long tradition of hatred and suspicion dating back to the persecutions of 1597. In 1868 the ban on Christianity, imposed and renewed time after time since the massacre of Shimabara in 1638, had not yet been withdrawn. On the very day of the Emperor's Charter Oath, which bade his subjects "seek knowledge throughout the world," the authorities had (in place of those of the Bakufu) put up new notice boards that still proclaimed: "The evil sect of Christians is forbidden as heretofore." The reason for this action is not clear. It is known that in this year the government sent to Nagasaki as advisers to the newly appointed Governor of Kyushu two officials, Okuma and Inouye Kaoru, who were later to hold great offices of state. They, or their subordinates, learning that there were some practising Japanese Christians in the near-by village of Urakami, had them arrested. The foreign consular representatives in Nagasaki moved their ministers in Tokyo to make strong complaints to the authorities of the central government, who were extremely dilatory. They were no doubt stiffened in their resistance to pressure by the strength of the Shinto revival that has just been described; and being technically on firm ground because the old anti-Christian laws had not been repealed, they procrastinated for fear of being accused of submitting to foreign interference in domestic affairs. The government then installed at Kyoto sent to Nagasaki one of its most important members, Kido Junichiro. He, in conversation with the British Consul, said that he considered it desirable for the welfare of the country to put Christianity down, since ill feeling against it existed among the people and he feared disorder. He blamed Roman Catholic priests for much of the trouble and described missionaries as men sent to Japan to teach the Japanese to break the laws of their country. He was friendly but quite firm, and a few days after this talk a number of the arrested Christians were put aboard ships and dispersed in various fiefs. This was regarded as an act of clemency, giving the converts an opportunity to reform. It was not until 1873 that the problem was solved by Ito and Okubo, who had gone with Iwakura's mission to America and Europe, "seeking knowledge throughout the world." One piece of useful knowledge acquired on this journey (which was made for the very purpose of securing some relaxation in the conditions imposed upon Japan by the agreements of 1858) was the fact that there was no prospect whatever of treaty revision so long as Christianity was forbidden by Japanese law. In every country that they visited they were asked why Japan was persecuting Christians. The government at last gave way, though even then it did not openly repeal the edicts but merely caused the notice boards to be withdrawn, having released the imprisoned Christians and paid them an indemnity.

Thus ended the long and tragic tale of Christian martyrdom in Japan. Small Catholic communities that had continued to practise their faith in secret since the first great persecution had managed to survive for over two centuries. Little groups in Urakami (where later stood a cathedral, destroyed by an atomic bomb in 1945) and on lonely near-by islands had been smoked out by the authorities during the Tokugawa period. There had been searches in the years round 1806, 1827, 1840, and 1856; and the last of these revealed a number of suspects, who were imprisoned, some of them dying in jail after torture. Yet this harsh action did not eradicate the faith. Hidden Christians cautiously made themselves known to French missionaries who arrived in Nagasaki after 1862, and upon further inquiry the fathers estimated their total number to be as high as twenty or even fifty thousand. These figures are doubtful, but it is certain that there were thousands rather than hundreds. They grew bolder under the protection of the missionaries, but in 1867 the local authorities rounded up about one hundred suspects and continued to make arrests until more than four thousand had been placed in custody or sent to forced labour in other provinces. It was these acts that gave rise to the protests of foreign consuls in 1868.

Further discussion of the influence of Christianity in Japan must be left for a later chapter, since here we are considering it only as one of the many Western influences to which the Japanese were subjected after 1868. For the moment we are more concerned with the conservative reactions to foreign culture in general which can be discerned in the early years of Meiji. Among these is the attitude of the peasant population, which, as might be expected, was more cautious and less fickle than that of the lively townspeople.

It is difficult, in examining the behaviour of the peasants or even of more sophisticated members of rural society, to find any uniformity of sentiment in regard to the social and political changes that were imposed upon them in rapid succession from the beginning of Meiji. In one province they would placidly accept what in another had caused loud complaint or even violent resistance, while at times they would be moved to rioting by baseless rumours which aroused their superstitious fears. In general they were ignorant if shrewd, and inclined to suspect that any new measure would be harmful to their interests, for though they had little to lose they clung to their exiguous property and cherished their old comfortable habits. Thus when, the Emperor having accepted the surrender of the fiefs, the government, instead of allowing the feudatories to remain as prefectural governors, ordered them to reside in the capital, the peasantry, so inured were they to feudal rule, in some districts rose to prevent their one-time overlords from deserting them. In Niigata in 1872 the rioters carried banners inscribed: "Restore the Tokugawa. Down with the enemies of the state." Such demonstrations had little political significance, and many of them were fomented by agitators and vagrants for their own selfish purposes; but they were none the less expressions of a general uneasiness.

At times the new government in its zeal for reform was clumsy and hasty, as when it was officially announced that compulsory military service was to be introduced. This was in 1873, when the new measure was described as a blood tax (*ketsuzei*), it being explained that in foreign countries it was so named because "the people contribute their lifeblood for the sake of the country." Nothing could have been more alarming to the simple countrymen who for centuries had been denied the right to bear arms and had been told that fighting was the business of a superior military caste. By a curious twist of circumstance, it happened that of all the foreign articles familiar in Japan at that time almost the only one of use to peasants was the cheap woollen blanket, which they could throw over their shoulders or drape over a wooden bench. It was usually dyed red, and so favoured was it by countryfolk that the word *akagetto* or "red-blanket" was a common name for a rustic among city-dwellers. So when the peasants heard of the blood tax, wild rumour flew around that the government intended to draw their blood and sell it to foreigners, who would use it for dyeing blankets or drink it as medicine. Some even said that it would be smeared upon telegraph wires so as to speed the messages along. It is not surprising to learn that, following upon this carelessly drafted announcement of the blood tax, there were numerous risings against conscription in 1874.

Another grievance of the farmers reveals in an interesting way how deeply rooted in Japanese life was the sense of class distinction, the feeling for social hierarchy. It was natural that the samurai should object to conscription, because it deprived them of their standing as members of a privileged order. But the peasants had their class feeling also, and when in 1872 the classifications of *eta* and *hinin* (the pariahs) were abolished, there were revolts with violence in many parts of the country. In Arima, to take one example, some five thousand villagers banded together in protest, burning and smashing property until they were suppressed by police using firearms. The peasant's loathing for the outcast was greater than the contempt of the samurai for the trader, and the fact that there was no longer any official distinction between the pariah and the farmer, who had always ranked higher than the merchant and the artisan, aroused bitter anger in country districts.

Further instances could be related of the suspicion with which new measures were regarded by many of the peasants, but it will be enough to mention a few more of their real or fancied grievances, so as to show their general nature.

In 1872 a Tokyo newspaper reports that in rural areas in western Japan it is believed that the transmission of messages by wire is a trick of the Christians; that the wires have to be smeared with the blood of virgins; and that the recent preparations for a census are in reality a device for finding out how many young girls are available for sale to foreign countries, while the numbering of houses is to show the order in which they will be taken.

For a year or more after 1872 there were agrarian risings in several parts of the country. It is clear that some of these were due to false rumours spread by persons who wished to shake the people's confidence in the government of the day and thus to hamper the proposed reforms; but there was also genuine and not unjustified misgiving among the peasants, whose real grievances were not always those against which they revolted. For example, though they complained about the Gregorian calendar, which was introduced in 1873, and were disturbed by new regulations about dress and deportment, or alarmed by the policy of favouring Shinto at the expense of Buddhism, these were in the nature of a general dislike of change. But a study of documents in which their specific complaints are recorded shows that what caused them most anxiety was fear of material losses. A typical case is that of a rising in Tottori prefecture in the summer of 1873, when one or two thousand men armed with bamboo spears and a few guns marched about the countryside destroying official buildings and schools. On examination of the ringleaders it was found that what they really wanted was a lower price of rice, improved conditions of land tenure, and the abolition of primary schools. These were specific economic demands rather than objections to reform in general, for a high price of rice meant a heavy payment of rent and elementary schools meant a new burden of taxation.

Such in broad outline was the reaction of the average Japanese citizen to the changes that were being imposed upon him by officials or recommended to him by leaders of the new movement for Westernization. It cannot be said that there was any powerful or concerted resistance and indeed it is doubtful whether the mass of the people realized how great a task their country had undertaken or how far-reaching would be the results of the plans of their rulers. Old habits of obedience and of respect for established authority, though a little shaken, were not destroyed, so that while the government had to cope with opposition from diverse quarters it was usually able to appeal with success to a strong sense of national unity and a characteristic desire for improvement. The opposition came from several factions, each concerned to protect its own interests. The samurai were disappointed because they had lost their social status and their assured incomes, and those who could not find suitable employment tended to drift into subversive movements. Scholars of the old style resented the prestige that new kinds of learning had acquired, and felt betrayed when they saw that ignorant upstarts with a smattering of English could set up as men of wisdom and earn an easy livelihood. The peasants, as we have seen, feared for their scanty earnings. Buddhists, Shintoists, and Confucianists saw dangers ahead for their respective creeds; and honest conservatives, whether they did not believe in progress at all or whether they had grave doubts of the superiority of Western culture, felt that traditional Japanese institutions were being destroyed to no good purpose.

But the government itself had no great difficulty in appeasing or breaking down a resistance so diversified in its motives and its aims. It was easy enough for those in power to play off one faction against another. Their most dangerous opponents were in their own camp, the advocates of reform who were themselves striving for political power or the intellectual leaders who wanted even more sweeping changes than the men in office thought wise in the national interest. Here the struggle was not exclusively between old and new but between different schools of modern political thought, so that the history of the first two decades of Meiji politics is in essence the record of an administration working on the one hand to counter conservative movements among the people at large and on the other hand to check progressive movements among its political rivals and their intellectual vanguard.

In order to understand the somewhat confused political events of this period it is necessary to have some knowledge of the intellectual currents of the time, and it is to these matters that we must now turn.

2. Literary Trends

JUST as it was principally by means of pictures and imported goods that ordinary Japanese citizens gained their first notions of everyday life in Western countries, so it was through translations or summaries of Western literature that the more educated classes were able to reach some understanding of the intellectual background of European culture.

It happened that in the closing years of the Tokugawa period the native literature was at a very low ebb. Little was produced but a mass of indifferent novels and salacious comic pieces. It may be that this decline was a symptom of the disorder that had attacked the national life at the turn of the century, when Japanese culture seemed to come to a standstill. It is a tempting hypothesis to suppose that in the long period of seclusion Japan had used up her native cultural resources as she had seemingly exhausted the possibilities of her economic development, and therefore stood in need of refreshment from alien springs. Certainly her civilization had turned in upon itself from about 1700 and tended thereafter to produce little but variations upon well-worn themes; but it would be mere speculation to suggest that without the intervention of foreign ideas there was no possibility of further growth. All we can say is that the native arts and literature, together with the traditional philosophies, were almost lifeless by the middle of the nineteenth century. The æsthetic spark was not entirely extinguished, but literature had reached its lowest point at the time of the Restoration and there it remained for twenty years. A foreign critic should perhaps not commit himself to so severe a judgment, but it has the support of the important Meiji man of letters Tsubouchi Yūzo (1859–1934), who in his essay *Shōsetsu Shinzui* or *The Essence of the Novel,* written in 1885, called for literary reform and said of early Meiji novels that if they were not the dregs of Bakin they were tawdry copies of Ikku and Shunsui, two masters of fiction who flourished about 1830. His argument was that literature should be independent of morality in a narrow sense. It should deal with truth and not conventions. He was here giving expression to literary views then held in Europe and at the same time deriding the professed aims of Tokugawa novelists, which were summarized in the phrase *Kwanzen Chōaku*, "to encourage good and rebuke evil." Most of the popular literature that Tsubouchi condemned was either bawdy or bloodthirsty, though garnished for the sake of propriety with spurious moral sentiments. The public of the day would read anything quite indiscriminately, whether original or not, decent or not, or well or badly written. This is perhaps not to be wondered at, since the times were disturbed and most readers sought escape from their own troubles. Those who were prepared to take a plunge into the new life preferred books on practical matters such as geography, arithmetic, foreign languages, history, and even political philosophy; and consequently their demand for original Japanese works fell and enthusiasm grew for translations from European literature.

Here the problem of choice presented itself, and since very few Japanese at that time had knowledge or discrimination enough to judge of the merit of foreign works, their selection was erratic and guided often by chance. Thus, to take an extreme case, Shakespeare's *Hamlet* was first brought to the attention of the general reading public in Japan by a traveller who, on his return from a visit to the United States, wrote in 1880 a book called *The Splendours of New York,* which contained in a chapter devoted to the theatre an account of the play and a description of its performance. Before this date, when few Japanese had travelled abroad, to select works for translation was a matter of almost purblind choice.

A study of the titles and dates of the earliest translations reveals some interesting aspects of contemporary Japanese taste. In general what was sought after was the kind of book that would give information about life in foreign countries and might, it was hoped, by explaining the character of Western peoples, reveal the secret of their success. It is true that *Robinson Crusoe* had been translated as early as 1859, and *Æsop's Fables* had been known since the Jesuits printed a Japanese version in 1593. These were popular works, appreciated less for their didactic qualities than for their interest as tales. But in general readers seem to have sought instruction rather than entertainment; and that no doubt explains why, as early as 1870, Smiles's *Self-Help* was enthusiastically welcomed by a public that was anxious to get on in the world. If the enterprising Westerners needed the kind of advice that was offered by

Smiles, it was natural that the bewildered Japanese should look for similar guidance. Indeed, in studying Japanese reactions to the changing world of the nineteenth century, it is as well to remember that European as well as Asiatic peoples were finding it difficult to adjust themselves to modern life. Western Europe was then in the vanguard of reform, but in other parts of that continent there were people who lagged behind and were touchingly anxious to catch up. When in their endless discussions on political and social reform the characters in Russian novels of about 1860 praise English or French methods; when in *Fathers and Sons* Bazarov says that an English wash-basin stands for progress; when Pavel Petrovich lards his conversation with English and French phrases and is upset by a slighting reference to Sir Robert Peel, then those characters are behaving very much as the Japanese will behave perhaps a decade later.

Following in rapid succession upon *Robinson Crusoe* and *Self-Help* there appeared in Japan complete or abridged translations of biographies of great men, such as Homer, Bacon, Shakespeare, Voltaire, and Napoleon; children's stories from Æsop and the Bible; *Self-Help* again; *Pilgrim's Progress*, translated from a Chinese version of 1853 and published serially in a Kobe newspaper from 1876 to 1879; part of the New Testament (1876); *Robinson Crusoe* again (1877) and Rousseau's *Contrat social* in the same year.

These works, all belonging to the first ten years of the Meiji era, need no special comment, though it should perhaps be mentioned that the quality of the translations was generally poor. The translators themselves were none too competent and the Japanese written language was ill-adapted to the clear expression of unfamiliar Western ideas. It was not until the following decade that a suitable method was evolved, when the work of translation was taken up by men with appropriate training. One of the best-known of these was an interesting character named Oda Junichiro. He had studied law at Edinburgh University and had been the tutor of a young Japanese nobleman during his travels in Europe. Returning to Japan in 1878, he devoted himself to the translation of English novels. In 1879 he completed a Japanese version of Bulwer Lytton's *Ernest Maltravers,* which was published in instalments of about fifty pages at a very high price. His work was enthusiastically received and his publishers made a handsome profit.[3] Oda used for his translation a style known as *kambun chokuyaku,* which is Chinese prose read in accordance with Japanese syntax. He gave it the title *Kwaryū Shunwa,* which means "A Spring Tale of Flowers and Willows." This seemingly inappropriate description of Lytton's

[3] He died in poverty in 1919. One of his later translations was of *East Lynne.*

novel was chosen because to Japanese ears flowers and willows speak of beauty and elegance, while the word "spring," according to context, may evoke either tender or erotic sentiment. So freely were these words used in the titles of books in order to tempt readers that rising young authors like Tsubouchi were obliged to resort to the same vernal, blossomy descriptions. His serious translation of part of *The Bride of Lammermoor* (1880) was entitled "A Spring Breeze Love Story" and his *Romeo and Juliet* was offered as a "Flower and Moon Romance," because, as he told an inquirer long afterwards, he and his friends "had to use words like 'spring' and 'moon' because of the influence of Oda's titles." Evidently this usage, as well as perpetuating an old literary fashion, represented the mood of the times. Current feeling had its romantic element, due probably to a reaction against the rather solemn canons that had dominated taste in the upper levels of Tokugawa society.

But if romance was in the air, so was a deep interest in politics; and the success of *Ernest Maltravers* in Japan is to be accounted for not by its seductive title but by its contents, which related in a flamboyant style suited to current Japanese taste and against an interesting political background the efforts of a talented youth to rise to high position, his love affairs, separations, disappointments, and then, all obstacles overcome, a happy ending. This was the kind of life that ambitious young men in Japan now saw themselves destined to lead, so that the translator had struck a lucky vein. He followed his first success with *The Last Days of Pompeii* and *Paul Clifford*. Further works of Lytton that were translated at about this time were *Rienzi* (1879?), *A Strange Story* (1880), *Kenelm Chillingly* (1885), and *Night and Morning* (1889). All these were very popular. The vogue for political novels continued and several writers tried their hands at translations of Lytton and also of Disraeli. *Kenelm Chillingly* was much approved because it seemed to have some bearing on political issues of the moment. Its title in Japanese was "A Statesman's Life," while *Coningsby* was named "Spring Warblings" (1883), though the title page bore also the legend, " A Tale of Political Parties."

The demand for novels with a didactic purpose is illustrated in an interesting way by the preface to a new translation of *Robinson Crusoe*. It presents this classic not as a tale of adventure but as a work which, though cast in the form of a novel, was intended to teach English youth how to endure hardship. "It should not be regarded as trivial," says the translator, "for if men will read it carefully they will see that it shows how by stubborn determination an island can be developed." In other words it should be

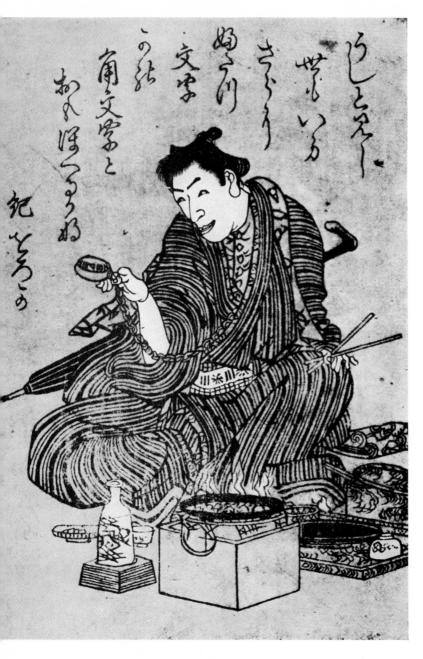

SYMBOLS OF WESTERNIZATION

*A young man-about-town displays his Western taste. He has an umbrella,
an imported watch and chain, and is eating beef. (Illustration
to Kanagaki Robun's* Aguranabe, *1871)*

KAWAKAMI OTOJIRO AS PELOPIDAS IN *Keikoku Bidan*

studied as a handbook on the training of Japanese political reformers who wish to make their insular kingdom rich and strong.

Related to the demand for works with a political moral was a
taste for tales of adventure and discovery, which was amply satisfied by the scientific romances of Jules Verne. This was an age in
which the belief in progress was at its most optimistic, and books
like *Round the World in Eighty Days* or *A Journey to the Moon*
were the very thing to please the Japanese as after long seclusion
they gazed upon new horizons, for they encouraged a belief that,
given an adventurous spirit and the proper scientific knowledge,
nothing was impossible. Prophetic works of this kind seem to have
suited Japanese taste from an early date, since among the first
translations of the Meiji period was *A Dream of the Future* (1874),
based apparently on a Dutch original that describes the experiences of Professor Dioscurides in company with Roger Bacon and
a lady named Miss Phantasy, in A.D. 2065 while on a visit to London, then called Londinia. There is no record of the reception of
this surprising work in Japan, but there is no doubt as to the
popularity of Jules Verne's romances or of another French prophetic novel, *Le Vingtième Siècle,* by Albert Robida, which was
translated in 1887. Japanese readers must have been puzzled, if
entertained, by this somewhat flippant book, which describes
Paris in 1952, with aerial omnibuses, the telephonoscope, a mechanical President of the Republic, and regular decennial revolu-
tions lasting for three months, thus giving time to clean the machinery and allowing a long national holiday.

A Japanese man of letters, Kurimoto Jōun, who was prominent
in the early years of Meiji and had been a Tokugawa retainer of
some standing, made a penetrating observation on the popularity
of Jules Verne's novels. He said that readers were tired of the
Chinese and Japanese novels of the old school, which get their
characters into great difficulties and surround them with perils
from which only divine or demoniac forces can save them. This
was an unsuitable solution of human problems in an age of Self-
Help; and Japanese of modern inclinations preferred the current
Occidental pattern, well exhibited by Jules Verne, whose heroes
extricate themselves from difficult situations by means of money.
What Kurimoto said was not literary criticism, but a sage observation on social changes that were then taking place in Japan. The
Japanese gentleman of a generation before, whether soldier or
scholar, had despised money, but his sons were born into a world
where money talked; so that in the popularity of Jules Verne's
novels we have not an influence upon Japanese literary taste but
rather a pointed testimony to the effect of the new mercantile spirit

upon traditional moral standards. It was because he had money in his pocket that Mr. Phileas Fogg of the Reform Club could scurry round the world and, even though he was appropriately delayed in Yokohama in 1872, win his wager in the end.

It would be wearisome to prolong this list of early translations, but it is worth while to mention certain works that, though today they may be regarded as curiosities of literature, evidently responded to some contemporary need when they were published, and therefore help in the understanding of the cultural scene. The first is *Heneromu Monogatari* (1879), in which the ingenious student may recognize Fénelon's *Aventures de Télémaque;* the second is a group of extracts from *Chambers's Encyclopædia,* including articles on Scandinavian mythology, on rhetoric, and on belles-lettres; the third, and most astonishing, is a life of Epaminondas of Thebes.

It may well be asked what were the motives for selecting such seemingly unsuitable subjects, but the explanation is simple enough. *Télémaque,* described as a European novel of adventure, goes rather well into a florid, classical Japanese style; and since it describes how Telemachus spurned the soft pleasures offered by Calypso in her grotto and listened instead to the call of duty, it seemed to teach a timely lesson in morals and in politics. The articles from *Chambers's Encyclopædia* were published by the Ministry of Education, and the subjects chosen were clearly such as, in the view of that department, would aid in the understanding of European culture. If the Japanese reader learned what magic spells, what gods, ghosts, and demons, sprang from the imagination of Western people, then he might be seized of the essence of their spiritual life and perhaps discover the sources of their mystifying behaviour. The life of Epaminondas, which was a historical romance based upon Plutarch and not a direct translation, needs more explanation.

It was published in 1883, under the title of *Keikoku Bidan* or *A Noble Tale of Statesmanship,* and the cover bore in English the words "Young Politicians of Thebes." It is strange that in a country so dedicated to modernity such ancient historical episodes should have been found edifying, yet the book was most popular. Epaminondas became a model for aspiring youth in Japan, and the hero of a stage play produced a few years later. It was one of several successful works describing heroic struggles for independence and the deeds of patriots who strove against oppressors, and it shows very clearly that the rising generation of Japan was already filled with hopes for national greatness and a certain hostility towards the great powers of the West. It was written by Yano Fumio, a rising young author full of political ardour, and in that sense it is in the same category as the translations of Lytton and Disraeli — and even of Shakespeare, for *Julius Cæsar* was translated under the name of *The Last Blow of the Sword of Freedom* (1884) by Tsubouchi, who though essentially a man of letters was at that date active in party politics on the side of popular rights.

It will have been noticed that most of the translations published were from English originals. This was due in part to the close political connection of the United States and Great Britain with Japan and to their leading position in Far Eastern trade, which made English the foreign language most useful to the Japanese in diplomacy and commerce. But it was also due to the prestige of Great Britain, which rested upon her stable political institutions, her sea power, and her economic strength — features that the Japanese were anxious to develop in their own country. Consequently in the first ten years or so of Meiji the European cultural influences that affected literary movements in Japan were almost exclusively English, and even French works were usually introduced by translation from English versions. From 1884 onwards, for reasons that will be discussed in a later chapter, there was a disposition to correct what was thought by the authorities to be an excessive dependence upon English models, but before that date very little literary influence from other than English sources had made itself widely felt in Japan.

A not very important exception was a fleeting interest in Russian literature just before 1883. This was a time when political feeling ran high and almost every kind of political doctrine was studied by the youth of the country. Russian works describing Nihilism, such as Stepniak's *Underground Russia,* or accounts of the activities of terrorists, political assassinations, treason trials, and so forth had a temporary vogue. Young members or supporters of the Japanese Liberal Party, which was fighting the government bitterly at that time, were moved by tales of revolutionary courage and suffering. They seem, however, to have favoured the spread of such works not in order to promote Nihilism but rather to warn or threaten the government. Theirs was perhaps a mild form of terrorism, and in fact some acts of violence were commited by advocates of the democratic movement. They were sporadic, however, and not representative, and if they had any effect it was to cause some popular reaction against the Liberal Party. At this time the interest in Russian literature was not sustained. It was only some years later that the writings of Pushkin, Turgenyev, Dostoyevsky, and Tolstoy became well known in Japan and exerted a considerable influence in the literary but not the political world.

Enough has been said to give some general idea of the kind of

European literature that became known to the Japanese in the first twenty years after the Restoration. It is perhaps going too far to say that it had an important effect upon Japanese thought, for it usually met a requirement that had already been formed, though no doubt it often gave precision to vague trends of opinion. The desire for knowledge of Western habits, the taste for politics, the interest in science, the belief in progress had already been present before the Meiji revolution was accomplished, and these literary importations did little more than furnish raw materials required by the Japanese in the cultural amalgam they were compounding. By 1868 they had already begun to picture themselves as a modern people. They saw developing — it would not take long if they were assiduous and scientific — a busy industrialized state, where machines whirred, great enterprises were afoot, and great fortunes were made. There was nothing Oriental about their aspirations and their methods. They did not belong to the Oriental society of which Kinglake wrote in that well-known passage describing how he bade farewell to the East on the Pass of the Lebanon:

Behind me I left an old decrepid world — Religions dead and dying — calm tyrannies expiring in silence — women hushed and swathed and turned into waxen dolls — Love flown and in its stead mere Royal and Paradise pleasures. Before me there waited great bustle and strife — Love itself an amorous game — Religion a Cause and a Controversy, well smitten and well defended — men governed by reasons and suasion of speech — wheels going — steam buzzing — a mortal race and a slashing pace and the Devil taking the hindmost — taking me, by Jove, if I lingered long on the difficult Pass that leads from Thought to Action.

In some such words a spokesman of Young Japan of the 1880's might well have adressed the easy-going feudal past as he looked forward to the mortal race and the slashing pace of an industrial future.

The active leaders of Japanese life had already crossed that difficult Pass. No lingering for them. They must hurry, hurry on the road to success, which understandably enough in those days meant becoming a rich country with a strong army. All must be sacrificed to those ends. Japan must not passively submit to foreign influence, but must weigh and test, adopt and reject, according to her own practical requirements. It is interesting to note, in this connection, that from about 1887, after a decade or so of indiscriminate borrowing, more judgment was used in the choice of books for study and translation. Japanese novelists began under Western influence to write original works, and this in turn created a more exacting taste among readers of translations. Now the works most popular among educated readers were for the most part those which had been well received in their country of origin, and the translations were written in a more palatable style.

Indeed, of all the foreign influences brought to bear upon Japan at this time that which had the most visible and lasting effect was perhaps the influence of translations upon the literary language. The early translators had been faced with a difficult problem, for it was only by a rare accident that classical Japanese or Sinico-Japanese suited the language of Western originals. Strange and awkward devices were resorted to in an attempt to render the sense and the movement of English prose. Thus the translator of *Télémaque* (from an English version) used the kind of language that was familiar to readers of Japanese romances, a metrical prose with a Chinese flavour, which was not unsuitable for florid passages. It was quite easy to put into the Japanese of metrical romances or the dramatic recitative called *"jōruri"* such a syrupy sentence as: "The rivulets that with soothing murmurs wandered through meadows of intermingled violets and amaranth formed innumerable baths that were pure and transparent as crystal." This is from Hawkesworth's translation, published in Edinburgh in 1799, which the Japanese translator used. He rendered it as follows:

> *Amaki idzumi wa sensen to*
> *Nagarete otsuru suishō-ike ni*
> *Kakewatashitaru hashi-ishi wa*
> *Sanagara menō to miru bakari.*

This gives the same sort of impression as the English, though it leaves out violets and amaranth. But when he came to simple phrases like "adorned with a thousand flowers" he recited a long list of the plants that usually adorn a formal Japanese garden.

This dressing-up of English in conventional Oriental garments was an unsatisfactory device, and little by little the translators developed for their own purposes a new kind of literary Japanese, which made increasing use of colloquial forms. This style of writing (known as *gembun-itchi,* which means a compound of the colloquial and the literary) was brought to perfection by Japanese novelists under the leadership of Futabatei Shimei, whose translation of *Rendezvous* (1889), one of Turgenyev's *Sportsman's Sketches,* was a turning-point in Meiji literary history. It fixed the quasi-colloquial as an accepted literary medium and served as a model for younger writers who founded the naturalistic school of novelists a few years later. In this sense it may be said that English, through translations rather than directly, had a revolutionary effect upon the Japanese language in that it broke down the old distinction between speech and writing and made colloquial forms respectable in prose. Such a reform was necessary if Japan was to lead a modern life, where popular education and journalism play an important part, since the conventional literary style delighted in learned phrases and obscure classical allusions. It was rather a means of communication between scholars than a medium for the wide spread of knowledge.

It can also be argued, though perhaps with less force, that European influence brought about a permanent change in the very nature of Japanese literature as well as in the language in which it was written. This is the opinion of a good Japanese authority, Professor T. Tanikawa, who says: "Whether the starting-point of Meiji literature be the political novel, or Tsubouchi's *Shōsetsu Shinzui* or Futabatei's *Ukigumo,* all these men started out under the influence of European literature. And that has now become the literary tradition, for new movements almost always start with the importation of movements from Europe. The contemporary literature of Japan [he was speaking in 1935] has now a tradition of fifty years or more and some present-day writers have been brought up in that tradition. It is none the less true that the influence of the West is always the guiding spirit of our literature. . . . That is the chief reason why contemporary literature is separated from society in general. In painting the spirit of the Orient is still alive and the tradition still vital."

If this view is correct it affords a striking example of a deep and lasting cultural influence, and it will be noticed that whereas the literary tradition of the Tokugawa age was not strong enough to stand up against new forces, the æsthetic heritage of Japan was able in the fine arts to defend itself against intrusion.

It would be presumptuous for a foreign student to question a native authority in matters of literary criticism, but not all Japanese scholars would agree that Japanese literature has failed to escape from Western influence. In the period with which we are now specifically dealing — let us say the first twenty years of Meiji — it is true that both the language and the content of the Japanese novel were transformed by the example of European writing, and the old Tokugawa standards became obsolete. But it is by no means certain that modern Japanese literature has not progressed far beyond that stage and, throwing off its comfortable Occidental fetters, evolved upon essentially Eastern lines. It is a moot point and one of great interest, but it cannot be settled until much more is known about the whole corpus of Meiji literature and the effect upon the minds of Meiji authors of the foreign works with which they were familiar. Of all cultural influences it is literary influences that are easiest to allege and hardest to measure.

A further somewhat revolutionary movement in Japanese literature was the introduction of new verse forms. These also originated in translations, since English poetry could not be suitably rendered in conventional Japanese poetical modes. A book entitled *Shintaishi-shō* (*A Selection of Verse in New Forms*), published in 1882, contained translations from Shakespeare, Gray, Campbell, Longfellow, and Tennyson, together with some original poems in the new manner.

This New Verse had a passing vogue and continued to appear for some time, but it was never truly naturalized, no doubt because native forms were the truest expression of native feeling. It seems that poetry and religion are the aspects of a people's culture that most stubbornly resist alien influence. When the Tokyo wits in the early days of Meiji satirized the frenzied adoption of foreign habits, one of the incongruities they ridiculed was "men in Western garments reciting Eastern poems." A study of some of the earliest New Verse suggests that they were right in seeing here a mating of incompatibles. The new poets seem to have been earnest scholarly men — one of them was a celebrated philosopher, Inouye Tetsujiro [4] — whose purpose was not to appeal to the emotions. They did not pretend to be inspired but only to instruct and to elevate. They explained that Meiji poems must be poems of Meiji, not old classical stuff; and they furnished rather free metrical or rhythmic versions of pieces like *The Charge of the Light Brigade, The Mariners of England* and Gray's *Elegy*, which happily appealed to the martial and melancholy moods — for both are characteristic — of their countrymen. Such poems as these were for a time very popular and were even sung to Western tunes. The Ministry of Education went so far as to publish a volume of verses in the new style, some being translations from English, others old Japanese chants and legends refashioned for use by children as school songs. The new form was not very startling after all, for it made use of the traditional alternation of five and seven syllables. But it differed from the old form in that the pieces consisted of several long stanzas, whereas the normal Japanese poem is a brief impressionistic statement of thirty-one syllables or less. It is impossible without quoting from Japanese originals to give a fair account of this attempt to reach a poetical compromise between East and West. One can say that Hamlet's soliloquy opens not unskilfully:

Shinuru ga mashi ka	Is it better to die?
Ikiru ga mashi ka	Is it better to live?
Shian wo suru wa	The thing to consider
Koko zo kashi.	Is here indeed.

But it gets into difficulties as it proceeds. Yatabe's translation of Gray's *Elegy* on the other hand is faithful and not without charm.

---

[4] And two others were professors at the university — Yatabe and Toyama.

The poem seems to suit the Japanese temperament, which is sensitive to the fleeting moods of nature and, under the influence of Buddhist thought, deeply conscious of the evanescence of glory. The translation runs like this:

> *Yama yama kasumi*   *iriai no*
> *Kane wa naritsutsu*   *no no naka wa*
> *Shidzuka ni ayumi*   *kaeriyuku*
> *Tagayasu hito mo*   *uchitsukare*
> *Yōyō sarite*   *ware hitori*
> *Tasogare dokini*   *nokorikeri.*

It reproduces well enough the feeling of the first stanza. But since Japan is not a pastoral country, the translator moves in some mountains and omits the lowing herd that winds slowly o'er the lea. This treatment well illustrates the formidable difficulty of transposing the imaginative literature of one people into the idiom of another. It is a hopeless task to seek in Oriental life and legend the exact emotional equivalent of the ivy-mantled tower, the storied urn, the animated bust, the long-drawn aisle, the fretted vault, or the pealing anthem, which all speak of a landscape and a history peculiar to the West.

Several volumes of New Verse by other writers followed this first collection. It must be said that they are for the most part painfully flat and didactic. They are of interest only as revelations of the matter-of-fact thought of the day, and its preoccupation with current national problems. A good example is a poem *On Liberty* by an ardent patriot named Komuro, in which he addresses his subject like a lover with the words

> *Jiyū yo Jiyū ya yo Jiyū*

which might be rendered "O Liberty! Ah! Liberty, Liberty O!" and seem like an echo of the "O Huncamunca, Huncamunca O" of Fielding's parody. It continues:

> Liberty, we two are plighted until the world ends.
> And who shall part us? Yet in this world there are
> clouds that hide the moon and winds that destroy the
> blossoms. Man is not master of his fate.
> > It is a long tale to tell
> > But once upon a time
> > There were men who wished
> > To give the people Liberty
> > And set up a republican government.
> > To that end . . .

This poet, who was known also as the writer of important political manifestoes, wrote a *Song of Diplomacy,* of which the first lines run as follows:

In the West there is England,
In the North, Russia.
My countrymen, be careful!
Outwardly they make treaties,
But you cannot tell
What is at the bottom of their hearts.
There is a Law of Nations, it is true,
But when the moment comes, remember,
The Strong eat up the Weak.

These curious outpourings need not be taken as evidence of a sad decline of poetical spirit. They are cited here rather as pointing to the zeal with which political questions were being discussed in the period under survey, and of the anxiety with which the Japanese regarded their weak international position. It was no doubt in order to encourage a more confident mood that a number of songs and poems at this time dealt with martial themes, such as *Japanese Spirit in Battle* (by Yamada Bimyōsai, a popular literary figure) and *The Song of the Drawn Sword*. Yamada's poem can be judged from the first line and the last, which run respectively:

Though our enemy may be numbered by myriads

and

What is there to fear? What is there to fear?

Such verses were often put to pseudo-European music and sung by students. They were bad poetry, but so are most national anthems and patriotic songs.[5]

Another interesting category of popular poetry is that of the kind sung by strolling entertainers. Of these there were many sorts. They were mostly variations upon familiar themes, sometimes comic, often vulgar, and they included a number of political ditties. Few of these have been preserved, for they were ephemeral, but the following specimens will give some idea of their nature. One was a very topical, up-to-date little piece entitled *Dynamite*, evidently addressed to the government at a time when there was a certain interest in Russian Nihilism. It ran:

Increase the national wealth!
Increase the people's happiness!
Nourish the people's strength!
If this is not done, then
Dynamite, BANG!

[5] It should be explained that Western influence was not strong enough to persuade Japanese poets to regard romantic love as a respectable theme. There are no odes to a geisha's eyebrow, no pleas to a cruel mistress, but only invocations to Minerva or Bellona, or their Oriental counterparts.

There was a longer poem, addressed to those conservative members
of the upper class who resisted political and social reform. It ran
somewhat as follows, though the translation does not do it justice:

> People who don't believe in the franchise and public welfare
> Must be given a dose of Liberty Medicine.
> They look very smart
> In their mantles and bonnets,
> Their trousers and coats.
> Outwardly this lady and gentleman
> Are very fine,
> But inwardly they are lacking
> In political ideas.
> Nor do they understand
> The principles of natural philosophy.

Here is all the popular jargon of the day, words used with little
exact knowledge of their meaning, but seeming to offer an agreeable prospect of wealth and happiness to multitudes. Liberty,
Votes, Science, Enlightenment, Reform, Progress, Gas, Steam, Machines, Telegraphs — everything that mortal but modern man
could desire, the answer to all life's problems, for which ancient
philosophy had found no solution.

Contemporary drama, like fiction and poetry, contained a
strong political element. The traditional Japanese theatre continued to stage classical pieces, but the new theatre, which began
in Osaka about 1888, was devoted to modern plays and realistic
acting, thus departing from the strict Kabuki convention, in which
dancing, posturing, and an orchestral recitative were important
features. The modern drama developed after the period with
which we are now dealing, but it is convenient to discuss it here
because it is closely connected in its origins with the literary movements already described in this chapter. It was not a direct imitation of Western drama, but resembled it in so far as it dealt with
modern life and used modern, everyday language.

Some idea of its character can be gained from the career of its
chief (though not strictly speaking its first) exponent. This was a
curious character named Kawakami Otojiro, a samurai of humble
rank who at the age of twenty became a policeman but soon resigned to lead a bohemian life. He became one of the peripatetic
speakers who were numerous at the time. His attacks on the government and his other misdemeanours got him into trouble, and
he is said to have been arrested over a hundred times. It is an interesting sign of the degree to which political issues entered into
almost every department of Japanese life that although he frequented the society of gamblers and other ne'er-do-wells in Kyoto
and Osaka, and was forbidden to make political speeches by the

police, when he turned to the profession of humorous reciter and mimic he still found a ready audience for comic songs and scandalous tales on political topics. Tiring of this field of endeavour, he joined some strolling players of his acquaintance, rented a theatre in Sakai in 1891, and there staged what was described in the posters as "A Greek Historical Play. *Keikoku Bidan,* a Noble Tale of Statesmanship." This was a dramatized version of Yano Fumio's life of Epaminondas of Thebes. It was a failure, and so was a piece called *The True Story of the Peril of Mr. Itagaki,* which dealt with attempted political assassination. The company moved to Yokohama, but their performances were forbidden by the police. They then went on to Tokyo, where Kawakami somehow raised funds and, in a large theatre in August 1892, performed *Keikoku Bidan.* It had a resounding success and there are still extant colour prints or theatrical posters showing Kawakami in the role of Pelopidas the Spartan. The scene is purely Japanese — but for a modern oil lamp — and the characters wear Japanese costume of the late Tokugawa period.

The new theatre was not refined. It catered to the taste of the townspeople of Yedo and Osaka, who (like the townspeople of the previous era) had a taste for lewd or bloodthirsty plays and novels. Consequently the most popular plays of early Meiji took for their theme crimes of passion, which were freely reported in the contemporary press. The prototype of such melodramas was a play representing the career of a celebrated murderess. No history of popular taste in the first half of Meiji should neglect to mention this lady. Her name was Takahashi O Den, and though her sordid story is of no particular interest we may pause to relate it briefly in order to show that not all the citizens were content with political tales. O Den was a pretty young woman, cursed with a temperament both amorous and acquisitive. Of her numerous lovers she killed at least two. Her first husband, who suffered from a mortal disease, she poisoned or strangled. This and other crimes were not discovered until, in order to furnish money to her latest paramour, she had enticed a man into a tea-house and stabbed him to death, imprudently leaving clues behind her. Her trial and her execution (at which she behaved with cool courage) caused a tremendous sensation, and her adventures were recorded in gruesome detail in newspapers and novels, while they served as the plot of several dramas, one of which was written by a leading playwright (Kawatake Mokuami) and played by a cast that included Danjuro and Sadanji, two celebrated actors of the classial school of Kabuki. Other plays, books, and pictures dealt with episodes in the careers of O Kuni and O Matsu, two contemporary murderesses of a similar sort. They and O Den were the heroines of a type of novel that Japanese writers distinguish as a special class, called *Dokufu-mono* or Works on Poisonous Women.

It may be inferred from the foregoing description that the new drama in its early phases was not a credit to the Japanese theatre, and it is true that it made slow progress, while the classical stage never lost its popularity. Attempts to reform and modernize it were subsequently made, principally by literary men like Tsubouchi, who encouraged the performance of translations of European plays and himself translated most of Shakespeare and established a private school for the study of the drama among students of Waseda University. But these belong to a later date and need not be discussed here.

3. Men and Books

THE FOREGOING outline of literary trends may be usefully filled in by some biographical details of certain individuals seen as typical products of the new age. The figures here described are selected not for their prominence in political or intellectual life but rather for the interest of their careers as authors or translators who played a part in interpreting Western culture to their country-men. The origins and characters of the transmitters are important aspects of the transmission of cultural influence. Most of these men, it will be seen, were of samurai origin, as might be expected, since they belonged to a class that had for centuries held a virtual monopoly of learning. In character they varied, and not all can be regarded as representative of their class; but the eccentric and the unorthodox often reveal more than the usual and the common-place.

It would be pleasant to be able to record more intimate details of the lives of these interesting individuals, but unfortunately Japanese literature is poor in biographical works and collections of familiar correspondence. Indeed, biography, and especially autobiography, is a literary form which, even at the height of the period of borrowing, attracted hardly any attention among Japan-ese writers, possibly because discretion and reserve are cardinal features of Japanese social life and to enlarge upon one's own affairs is thought presumptuous.

KAWASHIMA CHŪNOSUKE may be taken as an example of the kind of young man of an inquiring mind but no great talent who, from a simple rural life in feudal Japan, emerged into the great world, travelled in Europe, and returned home to become one of the leading interpreters of Western civilization. Brought up in the remote and mountainous province of Hida, he moved to Tokyo on his father's death, intending to study medicine. This proved impossible and he found employment as a draftsman at the Yokosuka Ironworks in 1869. He studied English and French in his spare time and then found employment with a French dentist. In 1870 he became a pupil in a naval engineering school and two years later was appointed to a minor post in the Navy Department at a salary of twelve yen a month, afterwards being transferred to a silk filature in the provinces as a revenue officer. He soon left official employment, became a clerk in a Dutch business house in Yokohama, and, having acquired some commercial knowledge, went to Italy on a mission to sell silkworm egg-cards. Returning to Japan in 1877, he completed a translation of Jules Verne's *Round the World in Eighty Days,* which was published at his own expense. He thus became the pioneer of Western novels in Japan. In 1881 he wrote a book about the suppression of Nihilist plots, and in the following year he went to France as manager of the Lyons branch of the Yokohama Specie Bank, a post for which his qualification seems to have been a knowledge of sericulture. His banking duties were not onerous, for in his leisure he studied law at the university and devoted himself to reading European classical literature, in particular Plutarch's *Lives.* He happened in 1883 to meet Yano Fumio, who was on the editorial staff of the newspaper *Hōchi,* and it was doubtless then that the idea of *Young Politicians of Thebes* was born. Yano was immersed in politics, but Kawashima remained in the service of his bank, becoming a director and later manager of the head office. He died at the age of seventy-nine, a respected man of affairs who had sown his literary wild oats by publishing his translation of Jules Verne a few months before the appearance of *Ernest Maltravers,* thereby gaining the distinction of being the first to translate a modern European novel into Japanese.

A literary career in strong contrast to his was that of SHIBA SHIRO, better known perhaps by his nom de plume of Tōkai Sanshi, the Wanderer of the Eastern Sea. He was born in 1852, the son of an Aidzu samurai; and his younger brother, Shiba Goro, true to the warlike tradition of his clan, was a soldier who was to make a name for himself at the siege of Peking during the Boxer rising of 1900. As a youth he studied Chinese and subsequently French and English. He was sent to study in America and after a course at a commercial school in San Francisco was graduated from the University of Pennsylvania. Returning to Japan in 1884, he became private secretary to the Minister of Agriculture and Commerce, and shortly after this published his celebrated *Kajin no*

Kigu. He was elected a member of the Diet in 1891, and in 1892 became the first director of the Osaka *Mainichi Shimbun,* one of the leading newspapers.

Kajin no Kigu — the title means *Strange Encounters of Elegant Females* — was so popular that it was said in a frequent but pleasant hyperbole to have "raised the price of paper in the metropolis." Some account of its contents ought to be given, because as well as being an influential novel it was a description, not of the author's life (since nobody could have lived on such a lofty plane for so long as his hero), but of his own professed ideals and consequently of the ideals of the numerous young men who drank in his gospel.

It is as well to premise that it is a deplorably bad novel, today unreadable except by a conscientious historian of manners blessed with great powers of endurance. In the first chapter it discloses the Wanderer of the Eastern Seas at Philadelphia in Independence Hall, musing upon the Liberty Bell. The Wanderer is Tōkai Sanshi, the hero and the author. While he is communing with himself on the successful struggle of the colonies against the brutal tyranny of the King of England, there enter two ravishing European beauties, one of whom gives her companion an account of the War of Independence, with suitable reflections on Bunker Hill, Valley Forge, and other historic sites. The Wanderer stands by the window eavesdropping in a refined way; and here, as throughout the book, his thoughts are recorded at length, frequently in Chinese verse or with difficult allusions to Chinese history. The ladies leave after a coy glance at him. A day or two later he takes a boat and rows up the Delaware River, where he encounters them both again. He is addressed by one, who explains that she and her companion have been impressed by his romantic character, for they first saw him brooding upon a historic scene and now find him enjoying the beauties of nature in a secluded spot where, it so happens, they are living in retreat. He is invited to join them, and with but little encouragement they tell him the stories of their lives.

One is named Yūran, or Mysterious Orchid, and the other is Kōren, or Crimson Lotus. It transpires that Yūran is the daughter of a noble Spaniard who in his struggle to make Spain a constitutional monarchy has incurred the hatred of the republican party and is in danger of his life from assassins. He has brought his daughter to America for safety and returned to the fray in Europe. Kōren is a golden-haired beauty, the daughter of an Irish patriot who died in jail, the victim of tyrants. Their several experiences are related at great length in high-flown discourse, which includes mention of a great number of characters in history and legend, from Socrates to Macaulay's New Zealander. When Kōren has told her story, the Chinese butler who has been filling their wineglasses discloses himself as a once distinguished rebel against the Manchus, but now an indigent exile. He also tells a long tale of oppression and tyranny, by which the Wanderer is moved to anger and grief at the wickedness of men.

He is consoled by Yūran, who holds out bright prospects for Japan and encourages him to believe that he can render great service to the cause of freedom in his own country. At this he weeps copiously and his tears fall upon the dress of Yūran. He begs her to forgive him and wishes to wipe the moisture from her skirt with his handkerchief, but Yūran stops him, saying that she is grateful to receive his tears, which are more precious than gold, more lovely than falling petals. At this point the hero, explaining that he too has suffered in freedom's cause, recounts in abundant detail the history of the Restoration in Japan and the fate that overtook him and his family, who were members of the Aidzu clan and fought against the Imperial army. The young samurai of Aidzu were cruelly treated by the new government, and this may account for the author's hatred of oppressors.

By this time it has grown late, the moon has risen. Yūran throws open the window and says: " Let us not spend this delicious night in melancholy. Let us be brave and cheerful. Let us dance and sing." Thereupon, to an accompaniment played on harps by the two ladies, they all sing the *Marseillaise*, in a Chinese version obligingly furnished by the butler. There is more music, drinking, and dancing. The ladies become slightly tipsy and the party breaks up not long before dawn. Tōkai Sanshi, who is asked to stay until morning, dreams that he has been wounded in a revolutionary struggle and rescued by Yūran, who passes through a storm of missiles to pick him up on the battlefield. It is clear from the conversation at breakfast that a harmony of political views has developed into a more tender sentiment between the Wanderer and the two beautiful Europeans. It is not disclosed which is his choice, but Yūran has taken steps to declare her feelings, for Kōren inquires mischievously who has taught the white parrot to say "Oh, do not desert me" when he appears. He leaves that morning, promising to come back in a few days, but he is prevented by illness, and when he is able to visit the retreat again, the ladies have vanished. He discovers that Yūran's father is in prison and they have flown to his rescue, which (he learns subsequently) Kōren accomplishes by amorous play with the governor of the fortress where he is confined.

After such a prelude it might be supposed that a thrilling love story would follow. But nothing comes of it. The rest of the book is little more than a guide to modern revolutionary movements.

The scene moves to Ireland, Egypt, the Sudan, Burma, China, Korea — all round the world to countries where minorities are struggling. Mysterious Orchid and Crimson Lotus appear from time to time, and it is clear that both of them are in love with the Wanderer. But his bosom is so filled with patriotic fervour, with hatred of tyrants and contempt of human folly, that it cannot give permanent lodging to more romantic emotions. The book ends by disappointing the reader of his hopes for a passionate climax, but leaves him crammed with information about four and twenty nations in revolt.

Its literary merit is negligible, but it is of value as evidence of the way in which patriotic Japanese minds were working after some twenty years of international intercourse. It is said that there was not a remote mountain village in Japan in which some young man had not a copy in his pocket, and the Chinese verses that so freely stud its pages were recited everywhere with great relish. Even its congested prose seems to have been imitated by younger writers, but no doubt its political complexion was what gave it the most of its success. One passage may be cited as summarizing the strong nationalistic views that were spreading among the official class when *Kajin no Kigu* was written in 1885.

When Tōkai Sanshi falls into deep gloom after hearing so many tales of the oppression of the weak by the strong, Yūran encourages him in the following words: "Now that your country has reformed its government and, by taking from America what is useful and rejecting what is only superficial, is increasing month by month in wealth and strength, the eyes and ears of the world are astonished by your success. As the sun climbs in the eastern skies, so is your country rising in the Orient. Your August Sovereign has granted political liberty to the people, the people have sworn to follow the Imperial leadership. So the time has come when, domestic strife having ceased, all classes will be happy in their occupations. Korea will send envoys and the Luchu Islands will submit to your governance. Then will the occasion arise for doing great things in the Far East. Your country will take the lead and preside over a confederation of Asia. The peoples of the East will no longer be in danger. In the West you will restrain the rampancy of England and France. In the South you will check the corruption of China. In the North you will thwart the designs of Russia. You will resist the policy of European states, which is to treat Far Eastern peoples with contempt and to interfere in their domestic affairs, so leading them into servitude. Thus it is your country and no other that can bring the taste of self-government and independence into the life of millions for the first time, and so spread the light of civilization."

It was this moving language that caused the flow of the Wanderer's tears. It evidently set forth the author's view of the international scene and of the destiny of his own country. It reveals a growing antagonism to the West and it may be taken as one of the first clear signs in Meiji literature of a reaction against the foreign influences that, it was felt, threatened to destroy what was best in the native culture. The thinking is confused, and one detects beneath the sympathy for oppressed peoples a conviction that it is Japan's birthright to succeed to the empire of Asia. This is not surprising, for it is in the nature of a vigorous organism to expand, and in an age when the Japanese were building up a strong national consciousness it would have been remarkable if her leaders had not nourished high ambitions. Without the encouragement of such purposes they might well have flagged at their task. But it is none the less interesting to find in a popular novel so clear and early a presage of future political sentiment. Historians who base their judgments upon economic analysis may argue that, as she developed from an agrarian into a capitalistic state, Japan was obliged to follow the Western example of mercantile and colonial expansion, and this can hardly be denied. But when Tōkai Sanshi wrote, Japan had barely reached the stage of industrial capitalism, and yet attacks upon Formosa and Korea had already been proposed a decade before.

A photograph of the author shows him as a good-looking young man of a sensitive and melancholy cast of countenance. A Byron *manqué*, he wears a fez and a braided tunic, the uniform of a cosmopolitan littérateur. But returning from foreign parts he was taken up by politics and journalism, "to go no more a-roving by the light of the moon."

Another prominent literary figure was SUYEHIRO TETCHŌ, the author of *Setchūbai,* or *Plum Blossoms in the Snow* (1885), a political novel that made a great impression in the years of political strife before the opening of the Diet in 1890. It went through several editions and some three hundred thousand copies are said to have been sold. Suyehiro was the son of a samurai of Uwajima and attended the clan school, where, after a further study of the Chinese classics in Kyoto, he was later employed as a teacher. He then became a minor official, serving first in a prefectural office and then in the treasury in Tokyo. But he was not suited to official work and turned to journalism. He became a newspaper editor and was imprisoned for offences against the Press Law, which he attacked in his journal. He was active in party politics and his novel was, to use his own words, "nothing but a political tract sprinkled with novel-powder." Like most of the political novels of the day it has no literary value, but drawing as it does upon his

own experiences, it throws an interesting light on the party manœuvres of the day and the life of the rank and file of the opposition.
As a Japanese literary historian has observed, it belongs to a group
of novels that might be described as the Voice of Young Japan,
as Disraeli's works were said to be the Voice of Young England.
Suyehiro was in the thick of party politics from 1875, when he was
in his twenty-fifth year, and was able from his own knowledge to
describe the life of young students and other political enthusiasts,
their meetings and speeches, and the underground movement with
its plots of violence and the harsh police measures they evoked.

Setchūbai, written in 1886, opens with a prologue describing
a scene in Tokyo on October 3 in the year 2040, the one hundred
and fiftieth anniversary of the first opening of Parliament in Japan.
Two gentlemen exchange congratulations on the great prosperity
their country is now enjoying as a result of constitutional government. "Yes," says one of them, "we have the good fortune to have
been born in this happy era and to spend our declining years in
peace and comfort. Look out over the city of Tokyo, stretching
more than ten miles in every direction. It is covered with tall
brick buildings and a great spider's web of telegraph lines. Railway trains come and go from all points of the compass. The streets
by night are lit by electricity as bright as the day. In the great port
of Tokyo the merchant ships of all nations are moored and commerce is more flourishing than in London or Paris. On land we
have a powerful army of a hundred thousand men, on the sea ride
hundreds of strong warships. There is no place where the Rising
Sun flag does not fly. Education is universal and no country where
literature and learning flourish can rival us."

At this point in the text there is an illustration giving a bird's-
eye view of Tokyo, A.D. 2040. It consists largely of tall chimneys
flying great pennants of smoke. The Western reader who has
dwelt in an industrial town is tempted to ask: "And was Jerusalem
builded here among these dark Satanic mills?" But no such misgivings trouble the speaker, who proceeds to attribute all these
blessings to the Virtues of the Emperor and the Wisdom of the
elected Parliament, in which progressives and conservatives debate
with courtesy and cabinet changes are smoothly effected. There is
no need to relate more of this prophetic dream, for it has not so
far come true, except for the smoke. But we may single out one
further passage to show what loyal patriotic visions filled the minds
of Japanese liberals in the days of their agitation for freedom and
justice. Having further descanted on the perfection of Japanese national life in the twenty-first century, the elder speaker says: "Until
a hundred years ago our country was said to be the weakest and
poorest in Asia and we were despised by Europe and America.

The great increase in our national strength that has taken place in so short a time is due to the virtue of our wise sovereign, who at an early date decreed a constitutional form of government and opened our Parliament this day one hundred and fifty years ago. Truly it behooves us and our descendants to serve the Imperial house with fullest loyalty."

The scene then shifts back to the nineteenth century, and the actors are young men fighting for popular rights against an autocratic government cruelly using police powers and killing that very movement which, if successful, would lead to the glorious era imagined in the prologue.

A career not unlike Suyehiro's was that of SUDO NANSUI, born in 1858, son of a leading official of the Uwajima clan. He went through the usual training of a young samurai in Confucian studies and military exercises and then became a teacher in an elementary school. His interest turning to politics, he took to journalism first as a reporter and then as a member of the editorial staff. He became popular as a specialist in crime stories — especially the Tales of Poisonous Women already mentioned. Later he turned his attention to political novels, of which the best-known is *Ryokusa Dan*. The author's preface explains that he wrote it first when a youth, after reading English books on self-government. Later, as the taste for political novels grew, he revised and enlarged it and gave it a topical flavour. In the preface he said: "Its true subject is the conflict between centralization and local autonomy, but if the reader wishes to savour it only superficially he will find a love interest in every chapter. If however he wants to get to the marrow of it he will find it replete with political argument throughout."

Neither as a love story nor as a political tract can this work be recommended, but its illustrations are entertaining and instructive. There is a view of a racecourse attended by fashionably dressed people; a tender tête-à-tête interrupted by a jockey; a young student interrogated by the police on suspicion of having purchased dynamite though he really wanted a diamond; and many other pictures showing, if not the real social life of the day, the life that modern-minded Japanese lived in their moments of fantasy, an elegant, busy mixture of politics and romance.

A somewhat different character is BABA TATSUI. Born in 1850, the son of a Tosa samurai, he was sent at the expense of his clan to study in Yedo and entered Fukuzawa's school. Later (1870) he was sent to study in England, where he attended Warminster Grammar School and University College, London, and studied law in the Temple. Returning to Japan in 1878, he engaged in political activities as a supporter of the movement for an elective assembly.

He wrote on political matters and was regarded as the most eloquent orator of the day. He was versatile but superficial, turning from history to law, from law to economics, translating the *Kojiki* into English, and engaging in propaganda abroad which took the form of praising his country but damning its government. He was arrested in 1885 on suspicion of purchasing explosives, but acquitted upon trial, after suffering for several months in jail. He died in Philadelphia in 1888.

His best-known work was an essay on Natural Rights (1882), which is an attack upon Kato Hiroyuki, then president of the university. He may be regarded as typical of those Japanese educated in the West who were strong liberals abroad and strong nationalists at home, though it must be said in his favour that he remained antagonistic to the government and did not, like many of them, change his views in order to obtain official employment. He was one of the brilliant but unstable failures of liberalism in early Meiji; and many of his successors in later years went through a like experience of theoretical conversion and practical apostasy. An interesting chapter of modern Japanese history could be written by tracing the careers of clever young men educated in liberal surroundings in England or America who returned to Japan flushed with democratic enthusiasms and in course of time lapsed into a bitter nationalism accompanied by a strong dislike of the West, which had nourished their youthful ardours. Not long ago an able and experienced member of this class observed to me that most of his contemporaries, products of Western education, had turned against the Western democracies feeling that their liberalism was a sham.

Two other literary figures may be described, not on account of their works, but in order to show what variegated careers were followed by the youths who grew up as the nation was subjected to violent change. NARISHIMA RYŪHOKU, born in 1837 in a samurai family, was trained as a tutor in the Shogun's palace, and in 1856 he was instructing the Shogun Iemochi in reading. He did some historical research and wrote sketches of Yedo life and some satirical poetry, which brought him punishment in 1863. After three years under house arrest he was pardoned and made a captain in the reorganized army of the Bakufu. He left this career as the Bakufu collapsed and opened a school in the Hongwanji temple at Asakusa. After a voyage to Europe he wrote for newspapers and magazines, published what was probably the first detective story in Japan, was imprisoned for breaches of the Press Law, and followed the fighting during the Satsuma Rebellion as a war correspondent.

HATTORI SEIICHI, born in 1842, was the son of a Confucian scholar. In 1874 he wrote a work entitled *The New Prosperity of Yedo,* a humorous description of life in the new capital written in Chinese style. This was a survival from the Yedo period which today, says a critic, "seems like the fossil of a long-extinct organism." He then turned to political journalism, which in those days included some scandalous writing. His magazine was suppressed for libelling the Foreign Minister's daughter, who seems to have been indiscreet; but he repeated the story in serial form in another journal. He ended as a teacher of composition in a secondary school.

It will be seen that journalism and translation and novel-writing were the favourite occupations of the bright young men of the period, and this was natural in a society that was not yet stabilized and where official employment, trade, and industry did not yet offer plentiful opportunity to young men without money or influence. It resulted that the press in Japan developed rapidly and played an important part not only in purveying news and scandal but also in spreading knowledge of the Western world. This feature of political and social life deserves some separate notice as one of the main channels through which Western influence reached the general public.

A bridge between belles-lettres and journalism is furnished by the literary career of KANAGAKI ROBUN, who may be described as a product of transition. He was the son of a Yedo fishmonger and devoted his early youth to study. Born in 1829, he had before the Restoration become the most prolific comic writer in Japan. He poured out a stream of novels, sketches, and humorous verse which endeared him to the townspeople, especially to the denizens of the theatres, the tea-houses, and such centres of gossip as the public baths. In 1873 he moved to Yokohama, where he was employed by the Prefect in the astonishing post of Inspector of Public Sentiment, employment for which he was well fitted, since popular sentiment was exactly what his writings tickled. He soon returned to Tokyo, where he engaged in journalism for the least literate class of reader, promoting the *Kana Shimbun* and the *Iroha Shimbun,* both of which made free use of the simple syllabary. He also published the *Tokyo E-iri Shimbun,* an illustrated sheet. His pseudonym "Kanagaki" comes from his employment of the syllabic *kana* script in preference to the ideograph. Though not an important figure, he is an entertaining specimen of his class, representing the irreverent, scandal-loving citizen of Yedo as it turned into Tokyo. He even ventured to make fun of the serious Mr. Fukuzawa, whose popular work on natural science he parodied under the title of *Kyūri Dzukai,* which by a change of characters in his version stood not for Illustrations of Physics but for How to Use Cucumbers.

4. The Press

THE DEVELOPMENT of the press in Japan is a definite example of direct Western influence, since newspapers published by foreign residents in Japan provided an example that the Japanese could

KANAGAKI ROBUN 1829–93

Popular comic writer and journalist of early Meiji.

study at first hand. The Shogun's government in the latter part of the seclusion period had paid some attention to news from foreign countries, which they obtained usually through Dutch traders, but also from Chinese sources. From 1862 the *Batavia News* was regularly translated, not for public information but for use of the officers of the Bansho Torishirabe-dokoro, the office for the study of barbarian writings. The first Japanese journals after the official news-sheets were poor productions, struck off from wood blocks on unsuitable paper, and could hardly be described as newspapers, but rather as a kind of magazine appearing at irregular intervals. They count for little in the history of journalism, but are interesting for the fact that they were mostly published by former servants of the Bakufu who resented the authority of the Western clans and violently attacked them. The most important was the *Kōko Shimbun,* controlled by Fukuchi Genichiro, who complained that the new government was worse than that of the Shogun. All these were suppressed and Fukuchi was tried and condemned to imprisonment.[6] The only surviving paper was the *Dajōkwan Nisshi,* a kind of official gazette first published in 1868. It was followed by the *Shimbun Zasshi* (1871), a periodical used by Kido for presenting the official view.

The lack of printing presses and an inadequate technical experience of newspaper organization delayed the growth of good daily newspapers in Japanese, but soon after the opening of the treaty ports the foreign residents in Japan began to publish their own journals. The first of these was the *Nagasaki Shipping List and Advertiser* (1861), which soon became the weekly *Japan Herald* under English management. This was followed by the *Japan Express,* an American-owned paper, in 1862. Within the next few years there appeared several other newspapers, English, French, and German, of which perhaps the most prominent was the *Japan Gazette.* There was even a *Japan Punch.* These proved useful sources of information to Japanese who could read English and were carefully perused by the government, who from time to time made use of them for the dissemination of official news and opinions.

A Scottish journalist named J. R. Black (author of an interesting book called *Young Japan,* which contains useful information on Japanese history between 1858 and 1877) was editor of the *Herald* and later the *Gazette.* He also produced one of the first regular newspapers in the Japanese language, the *Nisshin Shinjishi* or *Reliable Daily News,* and he exerted some influence through articles written by himself or by Japanese political writers. He attacked the government at the time of the agitation for a national assembly and was offered an official post in the hope of silencing his adverse comment. His influence on Japanese journalism was considerable though it is not always fully recognized in Japan.

The first regular daily Japanese newspaper was the *Mainichi,* published in Yokohama in 1872, which used an imported printing press; and from that date the number of dailies increased rapidly. According to Black their quality was poor at first, for they did not dare to comment seriously on the events of the day and "their columns were defaced by such filthy paragraphs as to render them worse than contemptible." This charge may be true, since newspapers of a much later date were not always scrupulous in their choice of material; but certainly the press made good progress from

---

[6] Fukuchi ten years later was editing the government paper, the *Nichi-nichi.*

about 1873 and by 1875 there were more than one hundred periodicals in Japan. It had gained great influence, which the government found embarrassing, and efforts were made to suppress criticism. But journalists were not long in finding ways of circumventing official orders and, profiting by public sympathy, they soon grew bolder and more powerful.

FUKUCHI GENICHIRO

*A leading journalist of early Meiji, at first hostile
to the government, but later editor of* Nichi Nichi,
which became the official organ.

Born during a period of political strife, the leading newspapers of the early years of Meiji, say until about 1887, were not organs of public entertainment intended to give news and to earn profits by wide circulation. They were as a rule the personal undertakings of individuals or groups, designed for the purpose of political discussion and public education. Their editors and chief contributors were not as a rule professional journalists, but leading figures in political or literary life, and each journal was associated with a particular coterie or a particular school of thought. Thus the *Yūbin Hōchi* was controlled by liberals of the type of Yano Fumio (the author of the *Young Politicians of Thebes*), Ozaki Yukio, and Inukai Ki; the *Mainichi* by Shimada Saburo; the *Tōyō Jiyū Shimbun,* which had a socialistic tinge, by Prince Saionji and Baba Tatsui; and the Tokyo *Nichi-nichi* by Fukuchi Genichiro, who at that time hated the government.

All these were men who played important roles in current politics, though rarely in office, and it is significant that with very few exceptions the newspapers of the period were on the side of the opposition. The fact that the government was obliged to gain control of one organ (the *Nichi-nichi*) for expression of the official view, and also resorted to bribery, testifies to the growing power of the press. As the controversy over popular rights grew hot the government, as we have seen, enacted a Press Law, much more stringent than the first regulations of 1873 and 1875, and enforced it ruthlessly. Even this did not discourage the newspapers though they were fined and their editors imprisoned with alarming frequency; but when after the dissolution of the so-called Government Party (the Imperial Constitutional Party) in 1883 the need for a government organ vanished, the opposition papers took to belabouring one another and to a kind of mutual blackmail, which brought about a fall in quality and a loss of public interest.

These circumstances, combined with government pressure, diminished the role of the newspapers as organs of instruction and platforms for discussion. Within a year or so they had lost influence and become only purveyors of news and not leaders of opinion. This rise and fall of the power of the press is an interesting testimony to the waxing and waning of public enthusiasm for politics in the years between 1868 and 1883. In the early part of that period they had served a most useful purpose as an educational medium, often publishing translations or summaries of Western books or instructive articles on Western life. Many translations of European classical works first appeared in their columns, one of these being *Pilgrim's Progress,* which ran for three years in instalments in a Kobe newspaper. So much did the early newspapers depend upon translations that great numbers of students and other young men of the samurai class eked out a scanty livelihood by occasional journalism of this type, and in novels of the day the hero is often a poor youth who cannot pay his rent because the translation fees have not come in.

It was probably the writing, printing, and publishing of newspapers and books that, next to employment as functionaries, offered the most suitable opening to the more literate of the samurai who were obliged to find work to supplement their pensions. The Scottish journalist Black, in his description of the growth of the press in Japan, says that it gave employment to thousands of samurai of all ranks. His account of his own experience is worth quoting for the interesting picture it gives of the staff of a Japanese newspaper about 1873:

It is remarkable that the compositors of all the Japanese newspapers in Tokyo, and I fancy elsewhere, are samurai. Their steady industry, regularity and general good behavior are their marked features. I speak from experience. On the *Nisshin Shinjishi* for four years I had over sixty of them employed. . . . There was not one who hadn't the manners of a gentleman. . . . The editor was of an old hatamoto family under the Shogunate and had been vice-governor of Hakodate. He had one failing, an unconquerable objection to modifying his style of writing — from the most scholastic to which he and all of his standing had been accustomed — and bringing it down to the comprehension of the multitude. Everyone said how beautiful was his language, but it often took some of his professed admirers a long time to understand it. It had the effect however of placing the paper very high in the estimation of the most cultivated classes.

All the subordinates were men of equally good family. The manager of the paper was formerly treasurer of one of the most powerful southern clans and the clerks under him were well-born men of a northern clan. The chief reporter was paid a high salary and employed his own men. They were all his former retainers under the old régime. And even the office messenger was a samurai.

He goes on to praise their courage in writing what they thought at a time when the Press Law was ruthlessly enforced and journalists were always being hauled off to jail. Medicine and engineering, he thought, attracted the next largest number of samurai after journalism and related occupations. Black's account incidentally calls attention to an interesting point in the distribution of political talent after the Restoration. We have already noticed that the driving force was furnished almost entirely by men of samurai origin. Moreover many of the most capable of them were not, as might have been expected, from the clans that had opposed the Shogunate, but were former administrators, officials, and scholars who had been in the employment of the Bakufu. A list of prominent figures serving under the early Meiji government includes many names of direct Tokugawa retainers and of clansmen who had before the Restoration transferred their services from their own fiefs to the administration in Yedo, as civil servants or technical advisers. Thus it came about that the bureaucrats who worked under the leadership of the Satsuma-Chōshū coalition were officials of a conservative type, content to place their talents at the disposal of the government in power and rarely playing any political role. On the other hand it was samurai of a nonconforming type who were unwilling to serve the clan coalition and gravitated towards journalism as a means of protest, with the result that almost every newspaper was hostile to, or at least critical of, the government. These circumstances gave a special character to the Japanese press, which it retained for a long time.

5. Intellectual Currents

So far we have considered only the effects of Western influence upon sentiment as it was expressed in changing habits or reflected in popular literature. It remains to discuss — if the distinction can be properly made — the development not of material but of intellectual life in an atmosphere of contact or conflict between traditional and modern trends of thought. This is a difficult matter, for it has to be borne in mind that many of the Western doctrines that came to the notice of the Japanese in the second half of the nineteenth century were by no means fully established throughout Europe, nor were they in every case unanimously accepted in their country of origin. Here we have not a simple example of one ancient culture confronting another, but rather the spectacle of an old Asiatic culture, itself in a state of flux, being subjected to the same kind of doubts and questionings as had not long before exercised men's minds in Europe when their habits began to undergo rapid change to meet the demands of a growing industrial society. It is true that this change had been slowly brewing in Europe since the Renaissance, and that Japanese society had not been transformed, as had Western European society, by the growth of scientific knowledge and the spread of commerce. Nevertheless, Japan of the eighteenth century was not inferior to most European states in culture and enlightenment; and after the turn of that century she had in a general way been apprised of the main events of modern European life. She was therefore not entirely unprepared for the new ideas that were presented to her just before and after the collapse of feudal rule. This is not to say, of course, that the impact of Western ideas at that time was neither violent nor disturbing, but merely to suggest a partial explanation for the relative ease with which Japan made the transition from ancient to modern life.

Much of the transformation achieved was creditable indeed, but not miraculous. Those who have long resided in Far Eastern countries will agree that the adoption and use of Western mechanical devices never presented any serious difficulty to peoples skilled in handicrafts that require nimble fingers and quick minds. It betokens "a certain condescension in foreigners" to suppose that only they themselves have the secret of manipulating levers and

valves. Western things were easy enough to borrow, and the remotest spots in Asia soon became familiar with the use of repeating
rifles, steam engines, and, in due course, other products of the machine age. When Commodore Perry presented to the Emperor of
Japan, as gifts symbolic of Western civilization, a telegraphic apparatus, a miniature locomotive, rifles, carbines, pistols, several
baskets of champagne, and a barrel of whisky, Japanese at once
came forward who understood the uses of these Occidental products, and the workmen who helped to set up the various machines
proved as handy as the artificers from the American ships.

There was no great difficulty about Western things. The
trouble was with Western ideas, which could not be handled like
physical objects but needed careful study before they were used,
for they might be dangerous. Consequently a great deal of the
intellectual activity of early Meiji was taken up with the examination of foreign teachings in philosophy and in political and economic science. A brief survey of the works on such subjects that
were first studied in Japan is the most convenient way of examining the effect of Western thought upon Japanese intellectual life
in this early period, when their relatively small number makes it
easy to trace which were the most widely read and presumably the
most influential.

Without question the subject that most interested the Japanese
of the years just before the Restoration and the two following
decades was the theory and practice of political science. This was
to be expected since they, like the Chinese, who had guided their
first steps in philosophy, have always been interested less in metaphysical speculation than in inquiry into the principles and methods of government. This question of government was moreover of
peculiar urgency after the fall of the Shogunate, since it was necessary without delay to erect a new structure in place of that which
had been destroyed, and the whole future of Japan seemed to hang
upon the choice that was to be made. At first it was thought possible to revert to methods of administration which had the sanction of antiquity, but little else, in their favour. These, it was soon
found, did not meet the practical needs of the day; and though
there were many Japanese who thought it possible to borrow certain convenient Western forms while retaining the spirit of native
institutions, this could not always be done because the new social
and economic life upon which Japan was entering exacted methods
of regulating national activities for which Japanese history offered
no precedent. There was, however, a fairly wide range of choice
between different Occidental systems, and it was the study and
discussion of these various alternatives and their underlying principles that absorbed most of the intellectual energies of the Japan-

ese people as soon as the confusion following the Restoration was cleared up and it became possible to look ahead and chart a new political course.

What formed the views of the small group of leaders who retained power for some years after the Restoration is best discussed in the context of a record of their political activities, for although they were influenced by Western political theories they were also moved by considerations of expediency. What for the moment concerns us here is the growth, the ups and downs, of political opinion among the Japanese people and the influences by which it was formed.

In the spread of public knowledge about Western political systems a leading part was played by three men, whose influence was so far-reaching that the history of political thought between 1860 and 1880 might well be written in the form of their biographies. They were Fukuzawa Yukichi, Kato Hiroyuki, and Itagaki Taisuke. Of these Fukuzawa deserves special attention as a pioneer of Western learning in many fields. This remarkable man may be taken as an epitome in his own person of those qualities of mind and heart which characterized the active leaders of reform in the crucial period just before and after the Restoration. He owed a great deal of his success to the early training that he received in the modest samurai family from which he came. Though unorthodox and antitraditional, he was none the less a typical exponent of those virtues which were the most admirable features of the feudal code of behaviour — a high sense of duty coupled with self-control and a certain contempt for worldly goods. His father was a trusted retainer of the head of the Okudaira clan of Nakatsu in Kyūshū. As overseer of the clan treasury he had to spend most of his time in Osaka (where the young Fukuzawa was born in 1835), transacting the affairs of his feudal lord and therefore dealing with rich rice-brokers and moneylenders. It is a striking illustration of the standards of the best sort of samurai that the father, by nature a scholarly man of rigid principles who despised the contamination of money, was obliged by the loyalty he owed to his chieftain to devote himself to distasteful financial business. So deep-seated was his contempt for the counting-house that when he heard that his small sons were being taught the multiplication table he took them away from school in a rage, crying: "It is abominable that innocent children should be taught the use of numbers — the tools of shopkeepers. What will the teachers do next?"

It was in such an atmosphere that many young samurai grew up, and it is therefore not surprising that the growth of commerce and industry in Japan should have brought about a clash between old and new standards of morality. This conflict, as might be expected, was the thread of most discourse in Japan, and there were few novels that did not treat of it in one form or another, but it is interesting to note that as late as 1899 the most popular novel of the day dealt with this very theme of the struggle of the old, stern traditions of family life and duty against the new spirit of progress, the feverish desire to rise in the world, to make money, and to break down social distinctions that in feudal days had barred a man from leaving the station in life to which he was born.

The novel in question is *Konjiki Yasha* (which might be rendered as *The Demon Gold*), a work by Ozaki Kōyō, the leading writer of the realistic school of fiction. Every educated Japanese man and woman of the generation that became adult at the end of the nineteenth century was familiar with this book, and it may be regarded as a landmark in social as well as in literary history. It tells the story of Kwanichi, a promising young student about to enter the university, and Miya, his betrothed, who for reasons of money is promised by her parents to a flashy young business man, the son of a rich banker. Few readers were unmoved by the farewell scene in which Kwanichi, accusing Miya of falsity and greed, knocks her down and kicks her as she lies weeping on the moonlit shore of Atami.

Although Fukuzawa was brought up in the belief that man should strive to acquire virtue rather than wealth, and was himself free from avarice, he was a convinced modernist, and consequently his teaching ran counter to the moral precepts of the feudal élite, since he did all in his power to encourage a matter-of-fact, utilitarian outlook upon life among his fellow countrymen. As a youth he resented the stiffness of feudal society, which kept ambitious young men in their place; and here he was representative of most of his contemporaries, for the force that contributed most powerfully to the downfall of feudalism was without doubt the desire of able young samurai of low rank to get out of the groove to which their pedigree condemned them and to obtain power commensurate with their talents.

In his twentieth year, just before Perry's return to Japan in 1854, he determined to strike out for himself and went to Nagasaki to learn Dutch and gunnery, subjects that offered some hope of a career. He had a good grounding in classical Chinese studies, a good memory, and an active mind. He made rapid progress and, rather than return to the dull life of a small castle town, he went on to Osaka, where he continued his studies under Ogata Kōan, a physician who practised Western medicine. He and his fellow students, a group of turbulent young men from different parts of Japan, studied not only Dutch but any other subject that seemed likely to be useful in the new society that was already forming. In their enthusiasm they would dissect stray dogs and decapitated criminals, do experiments in chemistry and electricity, or laboriously make copies of Dutch books on scientific matters. In 1858 he was sent to Yedo to give lessons in Dutch to the young men of the clan on duty there. One day, on a visit to Yokohama, he spoke to some foreign merchants in Dutch and found that they did not understand him. It was thus that he discovered that English, not Dutch, was the language of the future, and set about learning it at once. He shortly afterwards contrived to be taken on a voyage to America in a Japanese vessel, the *Kanrin Maru,* which in 1860 escorted the ship carrying the Shogun's envoys to the United States for the purpose of ratifying the treaty of 1858. He returned to Japan in 1860, at the height of the anti-foreign agitation, which was so violent that the captain of the *Kanrin Maru* was advised not to carry ashore an umbrella he had bought in San Francisco, lest he be cut down by a fanatical samurai. Fukuzawa's own life was in some danger, for at that time all students of Western languages were regarded as traitors by the patriotic extremists.

Some information on Western systems of government had reached Japan before the Restoration, and the mission of 1860 made useful additions to this knowledge. The envoys gained some understanding of elected legislative bodies by attending sessions of the Congress in Washington. It is true that one of them, disturbed by noisy exchanges across the floor of the House, observed that the scene reminded him of the fish market at Nihombashi, the Yedo equivalent of Billingsgate; but this blemish did not turn their minds against parliaments.

In 1861 a mission was sent to visit England, France, Prussia, and other European countries. It was on his return to Japan after this journey that Fukuzawa began to devote himself to the spread of information concerning foreign, and especially English, social and political ideas and practices. His first essays were based mainly upon such sources as encyclopædias and college textbooks, which were not always the most reliable or recent authorities. He appears not to have known of standard works like those of Hallam or Bagehot, but he was successful in disseminating some general knowledge of the English parliamentary system and of democratic principles as they were then expounded by English political thinkers. He also drew upon his observations in the United States, though he had found American political methods difficult to understand.

The work that made Fukuzawa's reputation was *Seiyō Jijō,* or *Conditions in Western Lands.* It was a simple account of Atlantic civilization, describing the political and military systems of the principal states, national debts, taxation, joint-stock companies, railways, steamships, post offices, banks, libraries, museums, schools, the highly developed sense of the rights of the citizen, and similar features of the national life of modern Western countries. The Japanese people were not entirely ignorant of these things, but Fukuzawa's book responded to, and even created, a demand for fuller information. It was an influential, indeed an epoch-making work. Of the first edition 150,000 copies were sold at once, and pirated editions quickly multiplied that number. Fukuzawa, because of his whole-hearted belief in Western culture, became the champion of English-language study in Japan. He devoted himself to educational reform, arguing that schools and colleges must prepare youth for practical life, and he founded in 1863 a school that later developed into Keio University, where the curriculum was devoted mainly to modern subjects and stressed the study of English.

He was a most prolific author, and so familiar did his name become as an authority on Western matters that in the early years of Meiji all foreign works were popularly known as *Fukuzawa-bon* or "Fukuzawa books." Some idea of the range of his writing may be gained from a list of the chief subjects he dealt with after the issue of his *Conditions in Western Lands*. It will also show in what kind of knowledge the general public were at that time deficient.

1867	A Guide to Foreign Travel	
	Western Ways of Living	On food, clothing, houses, etc.
1868	An Illustrated Account of Natural Science (*Kyūri Zukai*)	Elementary physics, chemistry, etc.
1869	The English Parliament	
1872	Lessons for Children	Illustrated by moral tales from the West
1872–6	Encouragement of Learning (*Gakumon no Susume*)	Seventeen pamphlets on education
1873	Book-keeping Procedure at Meetings	Rules for conducting conferences, etc.
1875	Outline of Civilization (*Bummei Gairyaku*)	An essay (6 vols.) on the nature and purposes of modern civilization and its meaning for Japan
1876	The Division of Powers (*Bunken Ron*)	On decentralization
1877	Popular Economics (*Minkan Keizai Roku*)	

ILLUSTRATION FOR THE NOVEL *Konjiki Yasha*

Kwanichi kicks Miya on the shore at Atami.

THE EMPEROR'S CONFUCIAN TUTOR

Motoda Eifu, author of Essentials of Learning for the Young
(*1881*)

1878	Popular Discourse on People's Rights (*Tsuzoku Minken Ron*) Popular Discourse on National Rights	
1879	Reform of National Sentiment	A discussion of the effect of modern civilization on the minds of the people. It foreshadows the establishment of Parliament.

The reader will have gathered from the foregoing descriptions that the chief intellectual activity of the first two decades of Meiji was directed to politics, and indeed it may well be said that the dominant interest was political throughout the whole period. This was to be expected since, the overthrow of feudalism having been brought about by compromise rather than by the triumph of a single revolutionary doctrine, the achievements that opened the new era, remarkable as they were, still left unsettled many fundamental political questions. To these all other aspects of the national life were perforce subsidiary.

This feature of the cultural history of the early part of Meiji is brought out very clearly by a study of the controversies that occupied the minds of scholars as well as statesmen and politicians when the last revolt had been quelled and the country had to consider what institutions it should adopt in place of those which had been destroyed. It was natural, indeed inevitable, that they should turn to Western models and try to profit by Western experience. They found in Europe and America no uniform pattern of political theory or practice, and their instinct led them to seek some composite form of government that, while it suited what they conceived to be their own requirements, could be justified by the doctrines of one or another school of philosophy among those then dominant in the West. Accordingly the teachings of Montesquieu and Rousseau, of Mill and Spencer, of Bluntschli and Biedermann, and of the Founding Fathers were all carefully and somewhat indiscriminately studied, not as academic subjects but in the hope of finding practical guidance for policy and, perhaps even more important, ammunition for debate. Since the Japanese people (with the exception of an ineffectual minority who believed in the Return to Antiquity) were striving not to evolve a new political structure from their own past but to build one anew from such materials as they could find at home or abroad, it is not surprising that, especially between 1875 and 1885, the intellectual scene presented a picture of confusion, which reflected the prevailing uncertainty in politics.

As early as 1868 one Nakamura Keiu (the first translator of *Self-Help*), returning from study in England, had published translations of the Constitution of the United States, of Washington's Farewell Address and some of Emerson's essays. He also formed a society for spreading English ideas on the moral education of youth, and thus followed closely in Fukuzawa's footsteps. English influence at this early date was considerable and remained important if not dominant for fifteen or twenty years.

Here was an interesting change from the Japanese attitude towards England in the first half of the century. The visit of H.M.S. *Phaeton* to Nagasaki in 1808 — when her crew were said to be as fierce as tigers — had caused both anger and fear; and the Opium War with its sequels had, as we have seen, caused Japanese patriots to regard the English as a dangerous people with sinister intentions upon their country. But after the bombardment of Kagoshima by a British squadron in 1862 the Satsuma men developed a respect, soon to turn into friendship, for a people who (in harmony with good Satsuma practice) were resolute and knew how to look after their own interests in a decisive fashion. There was evidently something to be said for the gunboat policy in those days, as Commodore Perry would doubtless have agreed, on condition that the gunboats were not British.

But what strengthened this growing admiration for England was, no doubt, the favourable report brought back by the mission to Europe of 1861. Its members, including the young Fukuzawa, gave glowing accounts of English strength and wealth, they were impressed by English political institutions, and they felt that one island kingdom might well take hints from another, which had raised itself to the pinnacle on which Great Britain stood in that illustrious Victorian phase of her history. These various factors go far to explain why among the earliest works on political philosophy to be widely studied in Japan where John Stuart Mill's *Considerations on Representative Government* (translated in 1871); part of Herbert Spencer's *Social Statics* (translated in 1877 by Ozaki Yukio, later to become the leading liberal in Japanese politics and to be known as the God of the Constitution); Sir William Anson's writings on Parliament and the Crown; and Sheldon Amos on *Political Science*.[7]

Spencer's influence was particularly strong, for he was the prophet and philosopher of the scientific movement that was overwhelming European thought in the second half of the nineteenth century. His *Development Hypothesis* encouraged optimistic be-

---

[7] Notice that Ozaki translated in 1877 an early work of Spencer's (1850). The choice of works for translation was rather peculiar, and the translators were often behind the times.

liefs among those Japanese who had abruptly turned their backs upon the past, while their sanguine temper was stimulated by *Progress, Its Law and Cause,* though it might have been better for them if he had written a volume on Progress, its Cause and Cure. It was perhaps unfortunate for Japan that she entered international society at a moment when European self-confidence had reached its loftiest peak. A few decades sooner, or a few decades later, and she might have been spared much disillusion. But in the 1870's Spencer was the man for their taste, because he reduced the universe to a simple system and made a synthesis of all knowledge which could not but be attractive to a people just emerged from seclusion and faced with an extremely complicated existence. After all, they were not alone in taking him at his own valuation, for his philosophy was widely accepted in Victorian England and even more in America, so that the enthusiasm of the Japanese for his gospel was in the circumstances to be expected.

It is scarcely necessary to add that Huxley and Darwin also had an important effect upon Japanese thought, since the theory of evolution, as applied to politics and sociology, opened attractive vistas to their forward gaze, and perhaps made them feel that they were helping in the universal process as they strove to develop their country. The survival of the fittest was a cry that struck a most responsive chord, and its rendering into Japanese, *Yūsho Reppai* (Superior Wins, Inferior Loses), was freely used in political debate as an argument for abolishing what you did not like or building up your strength against possible enemies.

French influence upon political thought in Japan began at an early date with the foundation in Tokyo in 1868 of a small school for the study of the French language. This led to the translation of French works on political philosophy, of which the first was Montesquieu's *De l'esprit des lois* in 1876.[8] His eulogy of the English Constitution and his argument for the division of powers made a great impression, and perhaps his influence should be reckoned as English rather than French in view of his Anglophile sentiments. A year later, in 1877, Rousseau's *Contrat social* was translated, under the title of *Ro-shi Minyaku Ron,* by Hattori.[9] His theory of natural rights was enthusiastically adopted as the intellectual basis for attacks on the government of the day, which was determined not to concede political power to the people at large. It was the warmth and vigour of Rousseau's feelings rather than the logic of his argument that appealed to the generous in-

[8] It is said that Montesquieu was translated as the result of a suggestion made to Kido, by some prominent Washington lawyers, during his visit to America in 1872.

[9] There were several translations of the *Contrat social.* That of Nakae Chōmin was in pure Chinese.

stincts of the young Japanese of the period, many of whom felt that the Restoration would have been in vain if the social distinctions and the political privilege of the feudal régime were not utterly destroyed.

But at the same time a contrary tide was beginning to flow in educated circles, and this can be conveniently illustrated by some account of the career of Kato Hiroyuki, a leading scholar of the day. Born in 1836, the son of a samurai of good standing who was frequently employed in Yedo on the business of his clan, young Kato studied the Dutch language, gunnery, and military science under Sakuma Shōzan and other teachers, showing such aptitude that he was made an assistant professor in the Bansho Torishirabe-dokoro, an institution set up by the Bakufu for the study of foreign documents. In 1862 (?) he wrote an essay called *Tonarigusa* or *Sketches of Our Neighbour*,[10] which gave an explanation of constitutional government. It was not thought suitable for publication in the prevailing atmosphere and was circulated only in manuscript. At this time he began to study German, being the first Japanese to learn that language. He made rapid progress in official employment, holding in succession several important posts, which mostly had to do with education; and when the new government was formed in 1868 he continued as a public servant, being appointed president of the Kaisei Gakkō, a government college that succeeded the Bansho Torishirabe-dokoro and later became the Imperial University of Tokyo under his direction. In 1875 he was nominated a member of the Genrō-in or Senate, but soon resigned. He served in several ministries and by 1890 he had been made a member of the House of Peers. He died full of honours in 1916.

Between 1868 and 1882 he published a number of works on political matters connected with the burning question of the day, the form of government to be adopted by Japan. The liberal, equalitarian views that he held as a younger man gradually gave place to more conservative opinions as he became more involved in problems of administration and more imbued with bureaucratic sentiment. In 1870 he had published his *Shinsei Taii*, or *Outline of True Government*, which was the precursor of a number of works by younger authors pressing for democratic reforms and included probably the earliest references to socialism and communism in Japanese literature. In 1875 he wrote his *Kokutai Shinron* or *New Thesis on National Polity*, which was a critique of traditional concepts of the function of the state in Japan. In this work he made favourable mention of republican government and used language that was deemed injurious to the Imperial

---

10 The Neighbour was China, and he was criticizing his own government under the disguise of an account of conditions there.

dignity. The book was withdrawn. By 1882 he had changed his mind and issued his *Jinken Shinsetsu* or *New Views on Human Rights,* in which he revised opinions he had previously expressed in support of Rousseau's doctrine of natural rights. He had already gone over to the official view that it was premature to set up an elected legislature, and thenceforward he fought against the Liberal Party, which was demanding a parliament and a wide suffrage. This change of attitude is to be ascribed to two causes. The first is Kato's enthusiastic acceptance of the theory of the survival of the fittest, which he never ceased to expound in his later writings; and the second is his conversion to the German doctrine of the supremacy of the state, which he owed to his study of German literature. It is a strong testimony to the influence of German thought that Kato, who was the first to advocate freedom and popular rights, should have later turned to Bluntschli and Biedermann and looked on Bismarck with the highest admiration. He had published the gist of Bluntschli's *Allgemeines Staatsrecht* under the title of *Kokuhō Hanron* in 1870. His late works bear such titles as *Competition and the Rights of the Strong* and *Contradictions between Nature and Progress.* He had lost his early belief in perfectibility and now regarded man as a helpless puppet. Whatever may be thought of his political philosophy, he was a man of great ability and considerable learning. He must be esteemed as a leading figure in the intellectual history of Meiji, and in its literary history too, for he expressed himself in a lucid and scholarly language, which, together with Fukuzawa's easy style, made an important contribution to the development of good, fluent, popular prose in modern Japan. In this latter respect he was on the side of reform. Some measure of the simplifications of language brought about by these two men is given by the fact that selections from *Shinsei Taii* and *Seiyō Jijō* were used as readers in elementary schools.

The main schools of political thought which divided opinion after the Restoration were both under the influence of strong nationalistic feeling, and there was little place for socialistic views that emphasized the brotherhood of man, while the idea of equality seemed strange to a people with a strong hierarchical sense. In the early years, when the appetite for Western knowledge was both voracious and undiscriminating, some traces of an interest in socialism can be perceived, but it was transitory and thin.

The first mention of modern socialism and communism in Japanese literature appears to be a passing reference, for explanatory purposes only, which we have already noticed in Katō Hiroyuki's *Shinsei Tai-i* (1870). No doubt some attention was paid to these schools of thought by students soon after that, but until about 1879 there is no definite evidence of anything more than desultory discussions of the need for social reform, the evils of poverty, and the defects of capitalism. In that year the Tokyo *Nichi-nichi* newspaper published an account of the theory and purposes of socialism, which was probably the first popular explanation to be printed. For the next year or two liberal politicians were inclined to include in their programs some items of social reform or to dwell in their speeches upon the distress of the poor, which they ascribed to the mistaken policies of the government then in power. Thus Hara Kei (many years later to become Prime Minister of the first party cabinet in Japan) wrote in 1880 an essay on the relief of distress, urging that it was the duty of government to see to the welfare of the poor. In the same year Ozaki Yukio wrote in the magazine *Rikugo Zasshi* an article on the misery of the poor and the general discontent arising from the sickness of contemporary society, for which he urged Christianity as a remedy.

In 1882 a popular journal uttered warnings against subversive doctrines such as Nihilism and socialism and inquired why rebellious ideas of this kind were springing up in the minds of Japanese. In this year also several books appeared which dealt with socialism, but their treatment was descriptive and gave no support to socialist theory, except for a work by Harada called *Zaisan Heikin Ron* or *An Essay on the Equalization of Wealth*.

While these writings no doubt responded to some current desire for information about socialism in practical politics, it made little or no progress. A "Far Eastern Socialist Party" was formed in 1882 in the remote district of Shimabara in Kyushu, where in 1638 thousands of peasants had been slaughtered when they took arms to protect themselves against the final persecution of Christians. But it was promptly dissolved by the police and its leaders severely questioned. In 1883 and 1884 some small movements, socialistic in character, were set on foot by workmen in Tokyo and the provinces, but these also were promptly suppressed. They were of no immediate significance and are interesting only as the first attempts to give corporate expression to labour's grievances, which were beginning to grow as industry expanded. It cannot be said that at this time a definite labour movement had developed or that socialism was in any way organized either among workmen or intellectuals. What was taking place was not more than a gradual realization of the existence of a social problem, which was discussed but not tackled. In particular a magazine called *Kokumin no Tomo* or the *People's Companion,* published from about 1887 a number of articles which called attention to the condition of the labouring class, deplored the gap between the rich and poor, proposed May Day celebrations, and generally pleaded the cause of the working people. It contained a good deal of Christian socialism. But all this was still rather superficial, ill-digested, and without foundation in public sentiment. It was not until after the war with China that a more solidly based movement and a more coherent theory began to take shape.

6. Economic Thought

Economic thought in Japan was subjected to the same kind of foreign influence as was political thought after the Restoration, but there is a difference between the two processes that arises from the previous history of economic inquiry in Japan. The discussion of Western political theory became an important, indeed a pre-eminent feature in Japanese intellectual life only when the urgent question of finding a durable substitute for feudalism arose. But economic problems had demanded the attention of Japanese thinkers long before the fall of the Shogunate and throughout most of the Tokugawa age. A considerable body of economic doctrine, heterogeneous and unsystematic, had been worked out by them during the Tokugawa age. It is true that this grew out of the consideration of problems peculiar to an agrarian economy, but the expanding use of money and the growth of industry in its later days obliged the feudal leaders to seek a solution of economic difficulties that crowded upon them; and consequently the ground was somewhat better prepared for the critical study of Western ideas in the field of economics than it was in the field of politics. Here also we have to remember that European economic thought was by no means uniform, nor could it be said that practice had shown the permanent truth of any particular theory. European doctrines could claim attention because they were the fruit of a wider experience and a more extended study than those of Japanese scholars; and perhaps the true difference between the native economists and their Western brethren lies not in their respective attainments but rather in their method of approach. While Western thinkers in time came to distinguish economics as a separate discipline, the Japanese, imbued with classical Chinese philosophy, tended to treat their subject as a branch of social ethics and attempted to discover how man should, rather than how he does in fact, behave in his environment. It was not until some years after the Restoration that Japan had any scholars who could be regarded as specialists in economic theory.

The general public made its first acquaintance with Western economic ideas through the writings of the versatile and prolific

Fukuzawa. His *Western Conditions*, first published in 1867–9, gave some elementary facts on commerce and banking, and his *Minkan Keizai Ron* (1877) was a popular statement of economic principles. The early work of Kato Hiroyuki, *Shinsei Taii*, though largely political, touches economic questions in its discussion of the functions of government and, drawing upon foreign sources, argues in favour of a minimum interference with the lawful activities of the subject, from which naturally flows an advocacy of free trade.

Following closely upon Fukuzawa and Kato came a writer who holds an important place in the history of economic studies in Japan, though it cannot be said that his views were in the long run influential. This was Taguchi Ukichi, who was the chief exponent in Japan of English laissez-faire doctrines, was deeply read in Adam Smith and was familiar with English commercial history.[11] In 1878 he published his *Jiyū Kōeki Nihon Keizai Ron,* or *A Free Trade Policy for Japan.* This work, of which new editions came out at intervals during the next twenty years, treats of the division of labour and argues strongly against state protection of industry. In his argument Taguchi makes an interesting point by asserting that to protect infant industries would in effect give favourable treatment to members of the samurai class and so encourage them in their traditional lazy habits. He himself was a hard-working man of humble origin and prejudiced against gentlemen of leisure, but there is also in this statement a hint of at least one of the reasons why free-trade doctrines could not make headway in Japan. The government, especially in the first ten years or so after the Restoration, had always to bear in mind when framing its policies, whether social or economic, the danger of creating a numerous body of malcontents of samurai origin. These men, with all their faults, were still the flower of the nation and no administration, until it was most solidly entrenched and backed by a loyal majority among the most active elements of the people, could afford to disregard them. However powerful might be the theoretical arguments in favour of a given Western doctrine, the political realities of the moment had to be taken into account, and these were in large measure still shaped by conditions that had no close parallel in Europe but had been carried over from Japan's very recent feudal past.

11 Taguchi also founded the magazine *Keizai Zasshi*, an economic journal. He was also a moving spirit in the promotion of historical research, and it is due to him that the important collection of historical material known as *Kokushi Taikei* was compiled and published and the historical magazine *Shikai* was founded. He was a man of high character, perhaps the best representative of a small body of true and ardent liberals of an "Anglo-Saxon" type of political philosophy. Like Fukuzawa he remained independent and refused all offers of official posts.

There is consequently a somewhat unreal quality about the presentation of Western economic theses to the Japanese people by those scholars or spokesmen who from their private forum were adressing a public still without power or knowledge enough to determine national policy. Taguchi continued to advocate free trade through the eighties and nineties, Fukuzawa wrote and spoke copiously and with vigour in favour of the individualist utilitarian principles that the study of English and American examples had nourished in their minds. Malthus, Adam Smith, Jevons, Cobden, Mill, and later Alfred Marshall — all the exponents of those principles in their several variations — were translated, studied, and discussed. The attitude of English economic thinkers, the characteristic English empiric philosophy, appears to dominate the intellectual scene, and it might be supposed that some at least of their teaching would have been translated also into political action. But that was not the outcome of the economic controversies of the day, for despite the great efforts of the English school the economic policy of Japan developed upon German rather than English lines.

Taguchi published in 1882 his *Keizai Saku,* or *Economic Policy,* an attack upon the protectionist line that the government had begun to take as early as 1869. He was followed a little later by Amano, also a trained economist, who published two important and widely read books on *The Principles of Economics* and *Standards of Commercial Policy.* These were based upon J. S. Mill and other advocates of free enterprise, but they show already a dilution of the pure milk of doctrine. Amano denies that Adam Smith and Mill are out-and-out upholders of laissez-faire and he agrees to state intervention in certain undertakings of national importance if it is found in practice that private monopoly is not conducting them in the public interest. He would therefore permit state ownership or control of railways, gas, electricity, and shipping if (as seemed likely at that time) private owners should abuse their power. He also opposes protective tariffs in principle, but allows them in special circumstances, such as infant industries, dumping, or retaliation against duties imposed by foreign countries.

This was an entering wedge, and the theories of free-traders soon began to encounter polemical opposition from avowed protectionists, while even the stalwart utilitarian Fukuzawa, nourished upon English individualism and strong upholder of free trade in his early days as a champion of liberty, within half a dozen years after the beginning of Meiji was arguing in favour of protective duties. He was followed in this apostasy by such men as Kanda Kōhei, also an individualist at one time, and by Kato Hiroyuki, whose lapse we have already noted. Even Oshima Sadamasu, the

translator of List and among Japanese economic writers the strongest advocate of economic nationalism, had been inclined to economic liberalism until about 1880, when he changed his mind and
followed List — who, it will be remembered, had himself once
held free-trade views, but fell from grace as he grew older. The
protectionist movement, which had begun thus early, grew in
strength as young Japanese industries struggled to expand and
vested industrial interests were created. Attacks upon free trade
which drew upon protectionist arguments used in Europe and
America became increasingly frequent and did not scorn to use
the dialectical trick of insulting your opponent. They would describe those who stood for freedom as obsolete old scholars or as
raw students smelling of mother's milk, who had only just learned
the alphabet and were bemused by foolish Utopian dreams. An
English work, *Sophisms of Free Trade,* by J. B. Boyles, was translated in 1877, but the chief support of the official protectionist
view came from German sources, notably the works of List, which
were freely drawn upon from about 1888.

This battle of the books was only a kind of academic skirmish,
which had little to do with the main struggle; in that encounter
other and more powerful forces were engaged. Scholars and a few
interested members of the general public might argue for this imported theory or for that; Western precept and example might
thereby become better known and understood in Japan; and to
that extent the Japanese were subjected to strong Western influence. But the history of English economic thought in Japan shows
very clearly that a well-established culture does not easily absorb
even the most persuasive of foreign intellectual influences unless
they are welcome to the *sette de' tempi,* the prevailing climate of
opinion, in the country upon which they are exerted.

To the men who were ruling Japan the question to be settled
was one that overrode all debate upon points of political or economic theory. It was the simple question: What are to be the
national aims of Japan? The decision upon that issue would dic-
tate the appropriate policy in economic as in other spheres of
national effort. It was an issue that could not be considered in the
light of Western theory or practice, since in part it was predetermined by Japanese history and for the rest, like most great issues, it must depend upon national sentiment rather than upon
systematic thought. Foreign influence might play some part, in so
far as foreign experience or foreign reasoning offered guidance in
a choice between alternative courses. To this extent it is true that
Western economic science made a contribution to the development
of Japan. But it is important to distinguish between direct and
specific influences and those resemblances which occur through

the sharing of a like experience with others and do not necessarily result from imitation. It is interesting to conjecture what institutions Japan would have developed if she had had no advice from Western authorities. One may hazard a guess that, by trial and error, she would have arrived at a position not very different from that which she reached by a road provided with a confusing number of signposts.

What in reality controlled or shaped the development of economic policy in the years under review was the decision taken by the Japanese people when they adopted as their national watchword the phrase *Fukoku Kyōhei,* "A Rich Country and a Strong Army" — in other words, when the Japanese ruling class were confident that they had the whole Japanese people behind them in their determination to secure first the independence and then the fullest possible economic and military development of their country. The methods pursued to that end might be the subject of domestic political argument, but in the long run, so strong was the tradition of respect for government, a policy presented as contributing to national strength or national prestige could count on enough popular approval to nullify factional opposition. It is for reasons such as these that no Western doctrine had any prospect of adoption on a national scale so long as it was claimed by the government in power to be inimical to their general plan of rapidly increasing national wealth and strength. Consequently although the early years of Meiji present at first sight a picture of the enthusiastic adoption of Western habits, on closer examination one discovers beneath the surface a strong resistance to many of the essential features of Western culture. The general public had, from even before the Restoration, responded to the desire of the authorities that they should modernize their way of life. They were willing enough to raise their material standards and they were prepared to make use of every Western appliance, to profit by every Western discovery, that would demonstrably serve the nation's purpose. But this did not mean that they were ready to abandon all their own ideas about life and society, which had deep roots in their history.

Notes on CHAPTER 14

THE ANTI-CHRISTIAN LAWS. The full story of the withdrawal of the notice boards is a curious one. When the government realized how strong the pressure was in all Western countries, they saw that they must give way, and on February 24, 1873 the order of the Dajōkwan was issued, which said:

"Henceforward when orders and regulations are issued their text shall be posted up in convenient places for 30 days, so that they may become familiar to the public. The notice boards that have hitherto been used shall, in view of the fact that the public will be fully informed, be withdrawn."

This order did not specifically cancel the edict against Christianity, but its issue was a convenient and face-saving, if somewhat disingenuous, way of permitting Christian missionary work.

At about this time Mori Arinori (Japanese Minister to the United States) wrote in English a memorial addressed to the Prince Sanjo in which he set forth the case for religious freedom. It was published shortly after Iwakura's return from his mission. Iwakura when in Washington had replied to a question put to him by the Secretary of State that the notice boards barring Christianity were in fact "dead" and that in practice there was freedom of religion in Japan. He was sharply taken up by DeLong (the United States Minister to Japan) who was present at the interview and quoted the case of Ichikawa.

THE JAPANESE PRESS. There is an interesting illustrated article by F. M. Jonas on "Foreign Influence on the Early Press of Japan" in the *Transactions of the Japan Society of London,* Vol. XXXII (1924–5). From this it appears that the *Batavia Shimbun* appeared only once (1862) and was followed by the *Kaigai Shimbun,* which also contained translations from Batavia newspapers.

CHAPTER
15

EARLY MEIJI: WESTERN INFLUENCES
(continued)

1. Prefatory

So far we have looked at cultural influences only in such spacious fields as politics and literature, where it is difficult to say of any one feature that it is characteristic, and still less that it results from the impact of foreign ideas.

But there are certain narrower fields in which foreign influence can be clearly discerned and even measured, though not with much precision. These are the aspects of national life that find expression in well-defined institutional forms, such as law, education, and religion. Here we have documentary evidence which within certain limits is detailed and convincing. This is particularly true of law, which sets forth in carefully chosen language the principles or rules by which society is governed and therefore furnishes trustworthy data for comparative study. It is somewhat less true of education, because a written code lays down a system but does not tell us in what spirit it is followed; and it is still less true of religion, where institutional features do not necessarily reveal the essential nature of belief or its intensity.

None the less, each of these three forms of corporate life, though they do not allow for the unusual, can be studied profitably in the light of written materials that are more exact than descriptions of political thought or surveys of what are called, often out of politeness, intellectual trends. While the truest impression of political history can at times be gained from the individual, the eccentric, and even the scandalous, law, education, and religion are embodied in systems of a definite character. They are therefore treated separately, though by no means exhaustively, in this chapter.

2. Law

ONE of the most interesting examples of the difficulties attending a fusion of cultures is provided by the history of the legal reforms that followed the Restoration. Quite apart from the natural desire of the leaders of the country to introduce new laws that should define and embody the changes then in progress in political and social life, there was an extremely strong motive for revising and so far as possible codifying existing laws. This was the desire of the government, enthusiastically shared by the people, to rid themselves of the extraterritorial jurisdiction which had been conceded to the treaty powers in 1858. The Western powers had reserved to themselves the right of jurisdiction over their own nationals, on the ground that the customs and laws of Japan did not ensure the safety and well-being of foreign residents. The Japanese, for their part, regarded the position as anomalous and disgraceful and very soon after the Restoration began to press for a revision of the treaties and in particular for the withdrawal of the clauses dealing with jurisdiction. Each time the appeal was made, the reply of the foreign governments was that the laws of Japan were incomplete, and it was only after many years of difficult diplomatic negotiations (which, as we have seen, were reflected in domestic political strife) that at last agreement was reached. The treaties would be revised on condition that the Japanese government framed new codes, it being understood that the new treaties would not come into force until the new laws had been adopted and put into effect.

It will be seen that the motives for legislative reform were twofold. Both internal needs and foreign pressure, besides giving a certain urgency to the task of compilation, naturally tended to influence the character of the new laws, for it was necessary, while adjusting them to Japanese traditions, to pay respect to Occidental principles of jurisprudence.

As early as 1870 a bureau of investigation was set up, which completed a translation of the French codes, and this gave to Japanese students their first comprehensive notions of the nature of Western legal thought. In 1875 an official committee was appointed to compile a new civil code, and a draft was submitted to the government in 1878. It followed too closely the French civil code and was not acceptable to the authorities. Subsequently a French jurist, Professor Boissonade de Fontarabie, then a legal adviser to the Japanese government, was asked to prepare a new draft, which he submitted in 1881. After protracted study and argument a new draft was completed and adopted by the government in 1888. It was in part the work of Boissonade and in part of

Japanese jurists, and it was actually embodied in a law of the year 1890, which was to go into operation from the beginning of 1893.[1]

Thus after fifteen years of preparation Japan now possessed a code of private law for the first time in her history, for the early codes such as those of Taihō (702), though remarkable documents, were not comprehensive, and the codes of later periods were concerned almost exclusively with feudal society. But the new law aroused most violent controversies among lawyers and statesmen, as well as among members of the general public. One party favoured its enforcement, another called for postponement and a full revision; and there was thus afforded the interesting spectacle of a hot public dispute between Japanese as to the merits of different schools of European jurisprudence.

The Japanese jurists who had studied English law either in England or the United States or in the University of Tokyo objected to the new code, while lawyers of the French school were in favour of its enforcement. English law had been taught at the university since 1874, and already by 1888 a majority of important judicial and legal appointments were held by graduates of that school. But students of French law, though in a minority, also held some influential posts, and French legal theory was not without strong support in both academic and official circles. The dispute between the two schools of legal thought continued for some time, in somewhat anomalous circumstances, since the Civil Code, a charter of fundamental importance, had been adopted by the government — though it was not in operation — before the new Constitution was promulgated and before the first meeting of the Diet. To resolve this difficulty a bill was introduced in the Diet providing that the Civil Code as already adopted should not be enforced, but that its operation should be postponed pending revision. A codification commission was then set up and as a result of its labours a new code, promulgated in instalments, was adopted and enforced in 1898.

The composition of this commission deserves some notice. It was presided over by the Prime Minister (Ito) and included representatives of parliament, the law, commerce, and industry. Academic jurists representing each of the foreign schools of jurisprudence were appointed, the government being anxious that the new code should not take any one school as an authority or any one national code as a model. The commission was to hammer

---

[1] A curious story is told of Boissonade's experiences while working in the Ministry of Justice, which shows how old evils existed alongside of new ideals in the confusion of early Meiji. Boissonade, seated at his desk before a draft dealing with civil rights, heard a commotion downstairs. He investigated and found in a cellar an unfortunate suspect being tortured by officers of the law. He threatened to resign, and after some delay torture was made illegal in 1876.

out an amalgam of different elements which would take into account the conditions of Japanese life, and it is significant that the drafting committee was composed of three professors of law who had studied in different European countries: Hozumi, a barrister of the Middle Temple who had spent some time at the University of Berlin, Tomii, who had studied French law in France, and Ume, who had studied in both Germany and France.

We need not enter into details of the work of the commission, but it is interesting to note that it studied more than thirty foreign codes or drafts of codes. In the words of Dr. Hozumi, it "gathered materials from all parts of the civilized world and freely adopted rules or principles from the laws of any country, whenever it saw advantage in doing so."

The result of their work was a composite law, of which it is often said that it followed the civil code recently adopted in Germany. This is denied by Dr. Hozumi, though he admits that the drafting committee found valuable material in the Saxon code and in the early drafts of the German code. But perhaps the most interesting feature of the new Japanese code is not the similarity of some of its provisions to those of one foreign code or another, but rather its adoption of one characteristic principle of modern European law which introduces an entirely new concept into Japanese legislation. This is the concept of rights as contrasted to obligations. Here we have a distinct and undoubted case of the exertion of direct Western influence upon Japanese culture, for the notion of rights is foreign to the jurisprudence that Japan borrowed from China in the seventh century and on which all her subsequent legislation was based. Indeed, not only in its laws but in its customs the social system of Japan was penetrated by the idea of duties to the exclusion of the idea of rights. So unfamiliar was the concept of the rights of the individual subject that in purely Japanese legal writings there is no term that closely corresponds to the word "rights" as expressing something that is due to a person and that he can claim; nor indeed did familiar speech include such a word in its vocabulary. It was necessary to coin a new term, and this was done by a Japanese scholar who had been sent to the University of Leiden to study law, and on his return in 1868 published a *Treatise on Western Law,* in which he explained the new idea and invented the compound word *kenri,* made up of *ken,* meaning "power" or "influence," and *ri,* meaning "interest." [2] Accordingly the first code to be drawn up in Japan after the Restoration contained chapters on rights *in rem* and *in personam,* which marked the abandonment of traditional legal assumptions.

[2] For the translation of *droit civil,* see p. 312 *supra.*

There was another important respect in which the new code departed from, or rather reversed, traditional notions, and this was the very fact of its publication. The earliest Japanese codes were not made public, but were compiled only for the information and guidance of officials; and throughout the Tokugawa period the laws were in principle (though not always in practice) kept secret, it being held sufficient that from time to time certain simple orders and injunctions should be proclaimed on public notice boards, while rules as to trial and punishment were communicated only to administrative and judicial officers. In fact it may be said that during the Tokugawa period there was no general body of law that must be known to and followed by the citizen. It was his business to obey the orders of officials, whose actions were arbitrary except in so far as they were governed by administrative orders. This is a feature of feudal society that should not be overlooked by students of Japanese history, since the feudal ruler was not bound by statutes. He could make or change the law at will by fiat, and consequently discussions as to what was the law at a given time are apt to be fruitless when the actions of a feudal dictator are in question.

This attitude towards the subject persisted during the first years of Meiji, and it was not until 1873 that the Chinese [3] legal principle of keeping the people in ignorance of the law was done away with by an announcement in the preamble to the revised Criminal Code that henceforth every law should be posted up in convenient places "for the information of the people."

It will be seen that with the introduction of these new concepts Japanese civil law, in the words of Dr. Hozumi, "passed from the Chinese to the European family of law," and there can be no doubt that since then European principles of jurisprudence have continued to exercise an important influence upon legal theory and practice in Japan. But it is important to notice that the legislation of the early Meiji period, though it contained many imported elements, recognized and perpetuated certain traditional features of Japanese social life. This is particularly apparent in those portions of the Civil Code which deal with the family as an institution. Care was taken by the legislature not to tamper too rashly with the old and deeply rooted customary sentiment that was embodied in the family system, which was looked upon as an important element in preserving the stability of the social structure. The task was delicate and difficult, for the accept-

[3] "The people must not know the law, they must obey it." It is perhaps unjust to describe this as a Chinese principle. It is based upon a passage in the Analects (VIII, 9), which runs: "The people can be made to obey, but they cannot be made to understand." The Japanese took this as applying to law, and also to education, though this is perhaps not what the Master intended.

ance of the Western principle of individual rights was in some ways inconsistent with indigenous beliefs and practices.

Traditionally the unit in Japanese society was the family and not the individual. The problems raised by this difference are too specialized and intricate for treatment here, but some idea of their nature may be gained from selected examples. Perhaps the most instructive instance is that of the difficulties presented by the incorporation in a modern legal instrument of rules touching the ancient practice of ancestor-worship, since this involved certain contradictions between the concept of the "family" and the concept of the "house."

The distinguishing feature of the Japanese family system is the importance of the house as contrasted with an indeterminate group of blood relations loosely described as a family. The House has been described by Japanese legal historians as "a legal entity originally founded upon ancestor-worship." To be more precise, the House is composed of the head of the House and of members who are subject to his authority. Those members may include not only his kindred by relationship of blood, but also persons, male and female, who are not his blood relations and who enter the House with his consent. The House is in fact a name group and not a blood group, and its purpose is the continuation of ancestor-worship. So important and customary was this arrangement that when national registration was introduced in 1871, the unit of registration adopted was the House, and not the family or the individual. It will be seen, therefore, that in so far as the Civil Code of 1896 laid more weight upon the House than upon the group of kindred, modern Japanese legislation approved and encouraged the practice of ancestor-worship. At the same time the state, having adopted the principle of individual rights, was obliged, when the code was in draft, to recognize that in certain aspects of his life a person could not be treated solely as a member of a House. He had also the capacities of a member of a family and (if adult) of an individual subject with prerogatives and obligations that the head of the House could not limit. Consequently in the new code it was necessary to introduce certain modifications of customary practice. The simplest of these was the provision of some means of registering individual status,[4] as distinct from House or family membership, and this was dealt with in the Law of National Registration, which was enacted as a pendant to the Civil Code.

But a more difficult question arose in regard to the succession of House members to property. Originally not only authority over

___

[4] In Japanese, *mibun tōki*. This law still bears the name of Koseki-hō, or Law of *House* Registration.

the House but also over the property of the House was vested in the House head, because (it was argued) the sole object of inheritance was the perpetuation of ancestor-worship by the House. But the Civil Code, without departing from the principle that the House head succeeds to his position in order to secure the continuity of worship, was obliged to distinguish between succession to headship and succession to property. At the same time the law took every precaution against the extinction of a House and the consequent lapse of worship, by such measures as the legal recognition of adoption and restrictions upon the freedom of the legal heir to renounce succession or inheritance.

The provision of the new Civil Code by which a House member could own, succeed to, or bequeath property as an individual was a complete reversal of tradition, since before 1868 no House member could exercise separate, personal-property rights. Whatever he possessed, he possessed not as owner but by permission of the head of the House. All the relevant legislation of early Meiji tended to break down this rule, because it was incompatible with the new economic life upon which Japan was entering; and it is perhaps the most notable feature of the Civil Code that while in matters of function it made no significant changes in the prevailing family system, in regard to property it was obliged to approach very closely to Western practices.

There was a special reason for this departure from tradition. As will be readily perceived, it had to do with changes in the economic structure of the country, which began as soon as, or even before, the Meiji government was formed. It will be recalled that one of the motive forces of the Restoration was the ambition of samurai, mostly of low rank and without pecuniary resources, to use their talents and their energies in public service and to build up independent careers as statesmen, officials, or soldiers. In those early years many such men found themselves in possession of fair sums of money that they had received by way of grants, pensions, or annuities, in recompense for their labours. This was a new form of property, which, together with official salaries, it would have been unjust to treat as the income of the House to which they belonged. Most of them had divested themselves of private responsibility for the sake of their public duties, and were not heads of Houses; and it was for this reason that there developed a new category of independent ownership of property by House members as individuals. Similar results followed the rapid growth in the early years of Meiji of property in the form of bonds, stocks, debentures, bank deposits, and title deeds, which were registered in the names of individuals and therefore could not be disposed of by the House head. Conversely, the House head could not be held responsible for debts contracted in respect of such transactions by individual members of his House. From this it was only a short step to modifying the practice by which property left by a House member on his decease went to his House. The new code provided that such property should go to his descendants in equal shares, irrespective of the House to which they might at that time belong.

In such ways the introduction of Western commercial and financial methods inevitably brought about changes even in the most cherished customs, modifying an old and well-established segment of the Japanese social system. Many other examples of this process can be adduced to justify the conclusion that, among all forms of Western influence, direct or indirect, it was the economic changes following the Restoration that brought about the most notable and the most enduring modifications of Japanese life.

The foregoing summary has paid no attention to other important features of the Civil Code, such as the position of women, nor has it touched upon questions of criminal law or commercial law, or various codes of procedure, since these are matters that require expert treatment. But it can be safely said that a careful and detailed study of all branches of the legislation of early Meiji would repay much labour by revealing numerous instances of the conflict between Western and Eastern cultures and the compromises that resulted therefrom as Japanese life in many of its external features was subjected to the demands of an industrial society.

Those compromises have not all been on one side, as may be seen from the following quotation of the closing words of *The Making of Modern Japan,* written by J. H. Gubbins in 1922, after many years' residence in Japan and a close study of Japanese legislation. He said: "It would be in no way surprising to those who have studied Japanese progress during the last fifty years if . . . the present Civil Code, based on that of Saxony, were to be revised with the object of bringing it more into harmony with Japanese tradition and sentiment."

3. Education

EDUCATION under the Tokugawa was not regarded as a function of the state except in so far as it was necessary for the training of a governing class. Even had the idea of universal education taken hold in the Yedo period, the social order was such that instruction would have had to follow the lines of class, separate schools being provided for nobles, samurai, peasants, and traders. In fact, such education as was provided during the period fell into those categories. The Bakufu provided colleges for its retainers in Yedo and the territories under its direct administration, the principal establishments being the Shōhei-kō or Confucian College in Yedo and smaller colleges in places like Nagasaki. The several fiefs provided education for their samurai in clan schools. For the populace the feudal rulers provided no education, it being an accepted principle that the people must be made to obey and not to learn. Their instruction was therefore left mainly to the Buddhist clergy, who maintained what were called *terakoya* or "temple schools" in town and country. These the Bakufu neither helped nor hindered, though as its power declined and class distinctions became less rigid, the children of samurai began to attend the *terakoya* and some commoners' children were admitted to clan schools.

There were in addition to these a number of private schools throughout the country, at most of which the chief subject of study was the Chinese language and classical Chinese literature. With few exceptions instruction in all these colleges and schools was based upon Confucian philosophy, principally of the official Chi Hsi school; but towards the end of the Tokugawa régime more attention began to be paid to study of the native literature and to "Western" subjects, in which were included foreign languages, geography, and elementary natural science. The Bakufu, recognizing the importance of Western subjects, had created the Bansho Shirabe-dokoro, or Office for the Study of Western Writings, in 1855. At that time this meant the study of Dutch books, but the curriculum was enlarged in 1860 to include English, French, German, and Russian, and a little chemistry was taught. After 1862 it sent students abroad for study, one of the consequences of this policy being that, when a new government was set up after the Restoration, it had to depend upon former servants of the Bakufu for much of its knowledge of Western institutions.

One of the remarkable features of Western studies in the pre-Restoration period was the great attention paid to surgery and medicine. A scholar named Ogata Kōan is said to have taught more than three thousand students in his school at Yedo in the twenty years before 1862, and there were many other private schools, all teaching Western medical and surgical methods and related subjects. From medical science it was only a short step to pharmacology, chemistry, and related subjects. Thus it will be seen that by 1868 the country was by no means unprepared for a further development of education on Western lines.

The history of education in the early years of Meiji is of great interest because it shows a certain conflict between Japanese traditions and the requirements of modern education of a Western type. The Japanese had no experience of organizing elementary or secondary education on a national scale, nor were they very well acquainted with the subjects that must be prominent in a curriculum of foreign studies. They were thus ill-fitted to devise or operate a modern educational system and were obliged at first to follow Western example somewhat uncritically and to rely largely upon foreign advisers and teachers. At the same time they were reluctant to abandon certain principles that they cherished. Consequently the educational policy of the first few years of Meiji presents a somewhat confused picture in which custom is at odds with necessity. It is much to the credit of the new government that, immediately upon coming into power, it turned its mind to the question of education. Its first steps were not entirely successful, for policy fell into the hands of the Shinto or National Scholars, who headed the movement for the Return to Antiquity. They were anti-Buddhist and anti-Confucian, and they took advantage of their position by insisting that the basis of education should be the national language, history, and religion, while Chinese and Western studies were to be attached "like two wings" to the main body. This attempt was bound to fail, since it left out of account the claim of advanced studies in Western science, law, and languages upon which Japan's future depended. It also provoked the Confucianists, who did not like being regarded as the Chinese wing of a Japanese bird. It was almost as if in England the study of early Anglo-Saxon history and literature should have been promoted over the classical humanities.

However, the government at this time revived the old Bansho Torishirabe-dokoro, and this under the name of Kaiseisho became the centre of Western studies, ultimately forming the nucleus of the University of Tokyo. In 1869 a number of foreign teachers were engaged. The former medical school of the Bakufu was revived, instruction in medicine and surgery now being given by German teachers, it having been decided that Germany was the most advanced country in those sciences. Also in 1869 the government, having revived the Shōhei-kō (the former Confucian college) which had been the highest institute of learning under the Bakufu, turned it into a University and attached to it the Kaiseisho and the Medical School. By a most curious arrangement it was now declared that the parent body, the former Confucian college, should be responsible for teaching both Chinese and Japanese classics. This naturally resulted in great quarrels between the professors of the two disciplines, which the government endeavoured in vain to compose. They introduced some new rules, which seemed to satisfy the classicists but enraged the professors of Western subjects, who now found both the Japanese and the Chinese schools combined against them. The problem was insoluble, and the university was closed.

It should be explained that the Daigaku, or university, had been intended to administer educational policy as well as to be the venter of higher learning.[5] In this latter capacity the university was re-established in 1871, the separate schools of Western studies and medicine continuing as government colleges, but the schools of Japanese and Chinese classics disappearing. It was now necessary to create a new organ for the control of education, and a Ministry of Education was formed in the same year.

These curiosa of academic history are related here to show that, in spite of the prestige of classical learning in Japan, in matters of national education it was obliged to give way to the requirements of the modern world. Confucian sentiment and the traditional Far Eastern attitude towards learning were not consistent with an organized, regulated instruction designed to meet practical needs. There was a conflict of principle here, and it is worth while to give some consideration to the nature of the dispute, since feelings about education are an important part of national culture.

The Japanese, like the Chinese, have a great respect for learning, and a teacher in their countries is looked upon as a most important kind of person, to whom deference must be paid throughout his life by his pupils, and thank-offerings brought from time to time. This rare and agreeable attitude towards educators springs from a concept of learning that differs radically from that which prevailed in England during most of the Victorian era. In Japan of the feudal age it was held that the purpose of education was not to fill a young man's mind with useful facts but to make him virtuous by teaching him the wisdom of gods or sages and so forming his character to meet the needs of the society — and particularly the class — of which he was a member. Not less indispensable to a teacher than learning was a high character, which should influence the moral development of his pupils; and the reverence in which great teachers were held was called forth not by their skill in expounding nor by their store of knowledge, but by exemplary conduct and lofty principles.

To those who continued to hold such views, and there were many, it came as a surprise to learn in the early years of foreign intercourse that teaching was a science and must be organized in one system. If this were true, then a master might discuss virtue with his pupils, but could not show it to them in his own person. In

[5] This also was part of the Return to Antiquity, since under the administrative code of A.D. 710 the university (Daigaku) had been a department of government responsible for education.

other words, the aim of the new education was to impart facts, whereas in the old education this had been merely a by-product of moral training. Education in the West, it seemed, was needed only to turn out men who would be useful, to fit them for the practical business of life. That was the English utilitarian view, or what was thought to be such, and certainly it was the view of Fukuzawa, who was the pioneer of modern education in Japan. He was not by any means blind to the importance of good behaviour, but he was impatient of the traditional standards of Japanese culture, which in his view paid far too much deference to useless knowledge. He expressed his opinions so forcefully that it is best to explain them by direct quotation from his writings. They are set forth in his *Gakumon no Susume,* or *Encouragement of Learning,* a book published in instalments between 1872 and 1876, of which all together over three million separate parts were sold. His attack upon Chinese studies, the equivalent of the classical humanities in Europe, is interesting not only as displaying his controversial method but also as showing the tendency of the party of root-and-branch reform to regard any old-established custom as useless baggage to be thrown overboard without to-do. In a typical passage he wrote:

The only purpose of education is to show that Man was created by Heaven to gain the knowledge required for the satisfaction of his needs for food, shelter, and clothing, and for living harmoniously with his fellows. To be able to read difficult old books or to compose poetry is all very nice and pleasant but it is not really worth the praise given to great scholars of Chinese and Japanese in the past.

How many Chinese scholars have been good at managing their domestic affairs? How many clever men have been good at poetry? No wonder that a wise parent, a shopkeeper, or a farmer is alarmed when his son displays a taste for study! . . . What is really wanted is learning that is close to the needs of a man's daily life.

A man who can recite the Chronicles but does not know the price of food, a man who has penetrated deeply into the classics and history but cannot carry out a simple business transaction — such people as these are nothing but rice-consuming dictionaries, of no use to their country but only a hindrance to its economy. Managing your household is learning, understanding the trend of the times is learning, but why should reading old books be called learning?

Such views presaged an important change in national thought, because while antagonistic to pre-Meiji ideals they created a wider interest in education, which was now presented as a necessary preparation for the life of all citizens and not as a private road to dignified accomplishment. This was supposed to be the prevailing view in European countries, though it left out of account the importance of liberal studies, which were still pursued in practical, commercial England. But Japan had no time for arts and graces, or at least so thought Fukuzawa and his school. To encourage classical learning would be to delay the acquisition of the modern languages, the scientific and technical knowledge, which were needed if the country was to be transformed into a modern industrial state. Nor could the young Japanese devoting himself to Western studies hope to master the dead languages, the ancient history and philosophy that constituted the humanities in Europe; so that inevitably higher education in Japan tended to neglect the spiritual, or let us say merely the ornamental aspects of learning and to apply itself to the immediately useful. Already by 1872 it was reported that a very few students were taking courses in Japanese language and literature, and that twice as many were entered for "Western" subjects as for the Chinese studies which had so far been regarded as essential for a man of breeding and culture.

Fukuzawa's own school, which he founded in 1858 for the study of Dutch, became in time the leading centre of instruction in the English language, economics, law, and other subjects that would prepare young men for practical careers in commerce or industry. The iconoclastic Fukuzawa, true to his samurai tradition, attached importance to moral training, and though he had violently shaken himself loose from feudal ethics he endeavoured to instil into his disciples a moral code that he hoped contained the best of both Eastern and Western principles. He placed the greatest emphasis upon independence and self-respect and regarded education as the proper means of inculcating those principles and showing men how to apply them in their own individual lives. This traditional concern for the moral aspects of learning fell into the background for some time as the government proceeded to organize education in a highly systematic manner, but it constantly reappears throughout the history of educational policy. Ministers become alarmed by utilitarian, even antimoralistic, tendencies among students and issue exhortations to both teachers and pupils, and after a decade or so of eclipse Confucian insistence upon the ethical purposes of learning emerges again. The Confucian revival, which has already been mentioned as part of a general conservative reaction, though no doubt not unconnected with professional jealousy, was stimulated in part by anxiety as to the effects of "modern" education upon the character of youth.

When the Ministry of Education was formed in 1871, it proceeded to encourage Western learning and decided that a complete national system of education must be devised and enforced. One of its high officials, Tanaka Fujimaro, was sent as a commissioner to examine the systems of Europe and America. He returned in 1872, and in that year a most detailed and voluminous Education Act was issued, which laid the foundations of state-controlled compulsory education. The plan was ambitious, providing for universities, middle schools, elementary schools, normal schools, and technical schools on a large scale, and the statement of policy that accompanied it made it clear that, in future, education was to be organized on Western lines. The classical curriculum had been defeated and here the attitude towards education expressed by the act was, to judge from internal evidence, inspired by Fukuzawa, who regarded old-fashioned scholars as rice-consuming dictionaries. The persons concerned in devising educational policy at this time were almost exclusively men distinguished for their knowledge of conditions in the Occident, and included (as well as Fukuzawa, who had no official position) Kato Hiroyuki and the leading professors of the modern schools which were all that remained of the university.

Two quotations from the proclamation that announced the issue of the Act of 1872 will suffice to reveal the ideas by which it was inspired. The first is a sentence that runs: "Learning is the key to success in life, and no man can afford to neglect it," which shows that the authorities took a utilitarian view of the purposes of education. The second says: "Every man shall of his own accord subordinate all other matters to the education of his children." It shows a determination to enlist the support of the whole nation, and it must be said that, after some initial grumbling, the whole nation nobly responded.

The system adopted was modelled upon French practice, and besides centralizing control over education it aimed at a high degree of standardization. This was in harmony with the general attitude of the new government towards all questions of administration. The new leaders had not been able to free themselves from that passion for regulating the life of the citizen which distinguished their feudal predecessors. The new system, however, proved unworkable. It was too big and costly and it was introduced at a time when the new government was not yet quite firmly settled and had not succeeded in overcoming local prejudices. In the provinces there was a growing sentiment against complete centralization or at least a mistrust of the government's intentions. An American adviser, Dr. David Murray, who was himself against standardization, warned the authorities that they were going too fast and risking definite opposition to their program. The public did not understand what the government was driving at and feared that heavy taxation would be levied to support the new scheme. Tanaka Fujimaro, the new Minister of Education, who while in America had been impressed by the autonomy in educational matters enjoyed by the several states of the Union, was inclined to

isten to Murray's advice. At the same time there had since the first
year of Meiji been a considerable and important development of
private schools, which had rendered useful services, and their promoters were influential men who were disturbed by the official
attitude.

Accordingly in 1879 a new ordinance was issued that laid down
new principles in broad terms and left it to local governments to
apply them by prefectural regulations subject to the approval of
the ministry in Tokyo. This reversal of policy had the unexpected
effect of causing a decline in public interest in education, which
was probably due to some extent to fear of increases in local taxation. The revolt against standardization did not last long. In 1880
the ordinance was revised and the government resumed control,
the new Minister proclaiming that elementary education was an
inescapable duty of the state. The program of compulsory education in primary schools (with a minimum of three years' attendance) was vigorously carried out, but the position as to other
schools and universities was little changed for the time being.

The financial resources of the government did not allow of a
rapid increase in the number of secondary schools and colleges, but
in the early years of Meiji the gap was filled by private schools of
all descriptions and these played an important part in supplementing state-controlled establishments. Since many of the private
schools were founded by Christian bodies or by Japanese who were
opposed to the official policy of standardization, a conflict developed that presently became acute as a conservative trend, beginning in the eighties, gathered strength. But there was little sign of
this in the years when the educational system had not yet crystallized, and the services rendered by the so-called "foreign" private
schools deserve some mention at this point. It was they that did
most for the spread of foreign learning in Japan. The first and
most influential was Fukuzawa's Keiōgijuku, but there were plenty
of other schools founded by Japanese educators in which the emphasis was laid chiefly upon English studies, and also some German and French schools. All these were valuable at a time when
standards were low in the state schools owing to lack of money and
suitable instructors. Among them may be mentioned the Dō-
jinsha, founded in 1873 by Nakamura Keiu, an accomplished Confucian scholar who while a Bakufu official had spent some time in
England before the Restoration of 1868. He was impressed by the
influence of Christianity on English life and in 1872 he wrote in
Kido's organ, the *Shimbun Zasshi,* an article advocating not only
the toleration but the positive encouragement of Christianity in
Japan, pointing out that if important elements of Western culture
were to be borrowed the religious system of which they were an

outgrowth must not be neglected. He believed that Confucian ethics could be taught in terms of Christian morality, and his private school was intended to educate youth on that eclectic basis. Respected as a man of high character and known to every student in Japan as the translator of *Self-Help,* he attracted a great number of young men to his academy and with the Keiōgijuku it became one of the most important organs for the interpretation of Western ideals.

Another important institution was the Dōshisha, a Christian college founded in 1875 by Niishima Jō (often called Joseph Neesima), who had braved the edicts in 1864 and worked his passage to America, where he stayed until 1874, coming under strong religious influence during his studies in New England. The Dōshisha subsequently played a very significant part in education in Japan, its character being distinct from that of Fukuzawa's school in that it stressed spiritual training while the Keiōgijuku, reflecting the free-thinking, utilitarian propensities of its founder, was secular and practical. Other Christian schools, supported and sometimes controlled by foreign missions, played a prominent part in secular as well as religious instruction at this time.

The decade in which these schools were founded and flourished was notable for the strong influence of English and American thought in intellectual circles. It showed itself not only in schools but in public educational activities undertaken by private individuals who had themselves lived abroad and who made efforts to diffuse English social and political ideas by means of lectures and periodical literature. An interesting expression of this trend was an association of Japanese studying in London who formed a club there in 1873 and on their return to Japan held regular meetings, with lectures and speeches, which continued until 1880, when the law restricting public gatherings brought them to an end. It was this fraternity that founded the magazine *Meiroku Zasshi,* already referred to, and secured contributions from leading public men who stood for national enlightenment as to the nature of Western civilization.

It might be supposed from the foregoing description that official education policy was strongly influenced by the views of these prominent men, and it is true that they did establish a certain tradition of independent thought. But they were for the most part without political power and were not strong enough to resist the bureaucratic tendency, which had been only temporarily checked. Their efforts did not prevent the educational system from developing on lines of rigid standardization. The attitude of the government was well described by Mori Arinori, who became Minister of Education at the end of 1885 and brought in his new act in 1886.

He said that the object of education was to serve the purpose of the state. "In the administration of all schools, it must be kept in mind, what is done is not for the sake of the pupils but for the sake of the country." The regulations creating the new university open with an article stating that the purpose of a university is to teach

MORI ARINORI 1847–89

Minister of Education from 1885. Assassinated
for an alleged insult to the Isé Shrines in 1889.

the arts and sciences essential to the state, and the educational system is conceived throughout not in a spirit of free inquiry but in conformity with strong nationalistic principles of a predominantly utilitarian trend.

It is convenient to mention here the college, now Waseda University, founded by Okuma upon his retirement from the government in 1881 in circumstances already described.[6] As he was in opposition, a thorn in the side of Ito, it was to be expected that this private university should stand for a freedom of thought and ex-

[6] See p. 345.

pression that was none too palatable to the government; and it is highly probable that an official character was deliberately stamped upon the Imperial University so that it should counteract the influence of Waseda, Keiō, and other private institutions.

As an administrative feat the building of a vast structure of universities, colleges, and schools from almost rudimentary beginnings was a most creditable performance. It testifies not only to great and single-minded energy on the part of the government but also to a remarkable response by the people. The idea of compulsory education was unfamiliar to them and it imposed a heavy burden of tax, but it was not long before the whole nation was convinced of the importance of education, and the sense of obligation among parents grew so rapidly, with very little pressure from government, that the percentage of children receiving elementary education rose from 46 in 1886 to 61 in 1896 and 95 in 1906. Secondary and higher education made an equivalent progress.

These were commendable results, but what concerns us here is the kind rather than the amount of education. The revision of the system undertaken by Mori was in one sense the logical sequel of following the Western practice of compulsory primary education, and it was Western in so far as foreign rather than native subjects dominated the curriculum, especially in middle and higher schools. But the underlying theory that learning must subserve the purposes of the state and train only the kind of individuals that the state required, though it had some kinship with French and German views, was not essentially Western but a reversion to the outlook that had inspired feudal rulers to treat one doctrine as orthodox and all others as heretical. When the Shinto doctors in the early years of Meiji had contended that the "national learning" was to be the basis of education, they were insisting that Shinto tenets as to the nature of the Japanese state should be articles of universal belief. This, as we have seen, was inconsistent with the government's educational aims and caused the closing of the university, which the Shintoists attempted to dominate. It cannot be said that Mori's new policy was in any sense a concession to their views. On the contrary Mori was a very modern-minded man, described by Ito as more like a foreigner than a Japanese in his outlook. He took no stock of most Japanese traditions and he laid stress on the teaching of English; but his emphasis on the supremacy of the state in the scheme of education brought him nearer to the stand of the conservative "National Scholars" and to Confucianists like Motoda than he would have cared to admit. His reforms, while in matters of organization following an Occidental pattern, were reactionary in spirit, and certainly they ran counter to all those liberal ideas of American, English, or French origin which had been current in the intellectual, if not the official world for the previous twenty years.

It must be admitted that there was much to be said for a revival of the neglected national studies. The university was for a time without a department of Japanese and Chinese literature, while in some schools English but not Japanese literature and history were taught and even the readers used for moral instruction were translations of foreign textbooks. Such deficiencies were made good by the establishment in the university of departments of classical Chinese and Japanese, and by introducing courses in Japanese legal history and Oriental philosophy, while approved school textbooks were compiled by the authorities. These were proper measures, not of themselves reactionary; but the general trend was towards the dissemination of a fixed official doctrine by a prescribed official method, and from this it was only a short step to the limitation of academic freedom and then the pursuit of heresy. The prefixing of the word "Imperial" to the title of universities after 1886 symbolized the imprint upon higher learning of the absolutist concept that was beginning to dominate the form of all national institutions. There is good ground for believing that Mori owed his appointment to Ito, with whom he was in close touch while they were both in Europe, and it is highly probable that the educational policy introduced in 1886 was designed by them in consultation so as to harmonize with the constitutional principles, particularly the doctrine of the supremacy of the state, which Ito planned to embody in his draft.

As for the pursuit of heresy, there is a convincing illustration in what may be called the *locus classicus* in the history of academic freedom in Japan. This was the case of Professor Kume, a historian who contributed to the historical journal *Shikai* in 1891 an article arguing that Shinto was a survival of a primitive form of worship. This not very startling view caused the greatest resentment among nationalists, and Kume was expelled from the university.

It will be seen that, whereas Western influence was strong in the organization of education and the choice of pedagogic methods, educational policy in general was in its essence neither enlightened nor progressive by contemporary Occidental standards. Something can be said in defence of the official attitude. Standardization and state control were calculated to raise the level of instruction more rapidly than voluntary effort, and they contributed to the formation of a homogeneous national sentiment, something that was needed if the particularism surviving from feudal times was to be reduced. Both of these were legitimate ends, granted that Japan was obliged to lose no time in the development of her national strength.

Moreover, education in Europe and America was not at the time we are now considering as uniformly widespread and progressive as the most thoughtful educators could have wished. Foreign descriptions of Japanese policies, in education as in other matters, in the early part of Meiji tend to judge them by standards that were proclaimed but not always reached in Western countries.[7] It is therefore important to remember that in England, for instance, it was not until 1870 that a comprehensive Elementary Education Act was passed, and this more than thirty years after the state had begun to concern itself with elementary education. It was only in 1880 that the system of universal compulsion was completed, and there still remained to be settled many problems in secondary education. The highly centralized French state system, though it started from the principle of compulsory primary education laid down in 1791, was revised and reformed in many ways after the war of 1870 and was not stabilized when the Japanese took it as a model in 1872. As for German education, so much in advance that the wars of 1866 and 1870 were said to have been won by the Prussian schoolmaster, it might have been suitable for adaptation by Japan, but the situation in Germany, though superficially similar, was unlike that of Japan in one fundamental particular. The German problem was complicated by the need to reconcile diverse political and religious interests and consequently had to allow for a good deal of decentralization and for local variations in type of school and curriculum.

The truth is that for Japan the problem of education was much simpler than that which faced most European countries in the middle of the nineteenth century. Political and social conditions were not unfavourable to uniformity, because there had been a clean sweep in 1868. The Japanese people were culturally homogeneous and there were no deep-seated differences of religion or custom to prevent a simple schematic treatment. Indeed, one of the most impressive contrasts between Japanese history on the one hand and European history on the other emerges when one considers the part played by religion in almost every aspect of European life. European history is rich in political and intellectual movement that springs from a diversity of religious belief, for which China and Japan offer no close parallel. In this respect Far Eastern history is wanting in variety and presents a somewhat monotonous spectacle of the minor vicissitudes of great, uniform systems that are essentially stable. European history since the beginning of our era could be written in terms of religious events with-

[7] This is not true of the *History of Japanese Education* of H. L. Keenleyside and A. F. Thomas (Tokyo, 1937), which pays attention to educational policies in Western countries.

out omitting any vitally important facts, but this is hardly true of Far Eastern history, for if it is in one aspect a history of religious tolerance, in another it is a history of indifference. In the particular case of Japan no religious creed, no ecclesiastical authority, was ever allowed for more than a brief space to dominate the political stage, and the conciliation of religious interests was never a cardinal feature of feudal administration. Consequently at the Restoration there were no deep religious gulfs dividing the nation, and the governing class was neither in educational nor in other matters obliged to take religious feelings into account.

The contrast with European experience is most striking, as a glance at the history of educational measures in England, France, and Germany shows. In each of those countries the early influences that determined the character of education were almost entirely religious. It is true that in Japan, and to a less extent in China, the Buddhist church was for a long time the chief repository of learning, but in both countries such public institutions as existed were mostly secular in character. There was nothing to correspond to the great mediæval universities of Europe, which were independent schools of higher study, not necessarily theological, but obtained their charters from the Church. Nor was there anything to correspond to the great struggle in the field of learning that took place in Europe as the revival of classical, humanistic studies led to conflict or compromise with scholastic, theological disciplines. The progress of learning in the Far East was vivified by no such controversies. Far Eastern societies were not split from top to bottom by protestant movements or enlivened by widespread sectarian disputes.

The foregoing reflections upon the religious element in European history may appear to be only remotely connected with the question of education in modern Japan, but they may serve to throw some light upon it by showing that the foundations were laid in conditions of deceptive simplicity. In England it was necessary to reconcile secular and denominational principles as well as to find a way of including in one national system both voluntary and public schools. In France it was felt necessary to carry the principle of secularism so far that it produced an acute conflict between Church and State. In Germany the *Kulturkampf* was waged largely in the field of education, while political divisions made it impossible to avoid separate treatment for different states and localities.

No such difficulties confronted those who framed the education laws of Japan in 1886 or drafted the Imperial Rescript of 1890. Uniformity and centralized direction were so easily imposed that the system which was finally developed could scarcely fail to be rigid and lifeless. It would not be difficult to make a case against the modern educational system of Japan, showing that her history would have taken a different turn if her rulers, even at the expense of what was deemed efficiency, had encouraged rather than repressed originality or at least diversity in academic life. In this respect it cannot be said that they submitted to a characteristically Western influence.

The Imperial Rescript, though it may be said to lay down broad principles of educational policy, is by no means specific; and it is in reality a document of much wider import than appears from its contents. It must be considered in the light of the conservative reaction against Western culture, which, as we have noted, began to gather force in the 1880's. Its full text is as follows:[8]

Know ye, Our Subjects:

Our Imperial Ancestors have founded our Empire on a basis broad and everlasting, and have deeply and firmly implanted virtue; Our subjects ever united in loyalty and filial piety have from generation to generation illustrated the beauty thereof. This is the glory of the fundamental character of Our Empire, and herein also lies the source of Our Education. Ye, Our Subjects, be filial to your parents, affectionate to your brothers and sisters; as husbands and wives be harmonious, as friends true; bear yourselves in modesty and moderation; extend your benevolence to all; pursue learning and cultivate arts, and thereby develop intellectual faculties and perfect moral powers; furthermore, advance public good and promote common interests; always respect the Constitution and observe the laws; should emergency arise, offer yourselves courageously to the State; and thus guard and maintain the prosperity of Our Imperial Throne coeval with heaven and earth. So shall ye not only be Our good and faithful subjects, but render illustrious the best traditions of your forefathers.

The Way here set forth is indeed the teaching bequeathed by Our Imperial Ancestors, to be observed alike by Their Descendants and the subjects, infallible for all ages and true in all places. It is Our wish to lay it to heart in all reverence, in common with you, Our subjects, that we may all attain to the same virtue.

The 30th day of the 10th month of the 23rd year of Meiji.

It will be observed that the language is studiously elevated, that the reference to education is brief, and that the document as a whole is not a charter of learning but an announcement of ethical principles that are henceforward to govern the thoughts and actions not only of teachers and pupils but of the whole nation. In that respect it is in keeping with the most ancient Japanese practice, for the first document of its kind in Japanese history, the so-

[8] This is the accepted translation, and the reader must bear with its atrocious style.

called Constitution of Prince Shōtoku (A.D. 604) was also a statement of moral maxims designed to support a national policy; and
subsequent rulers of Japan were given to the issue of moral exhortations to the people with a like political intention. The Rescript of 1890 proclaims a return to native tradition and implicitly
gives notice to the people that they are not to be led astray by

INOUYE KOWASHI (KI) 1843–95

*A Kumamoto samurai who held important posts in the
Meiji government. He became Minister of Education
in 1889, after working on the draft of the Rescript
on Education, which was issued in 1890.*

Western ideas in moral and political philosophy. It reasserts the
doctrines of ancestor-worship, of filial piety, of loyalty to superiors,
and of duty to the state, and it concludes by affirming that these
doctrines go back to an ancient past and are valid for all times and
in all places.

These are considerable claims, but it is not unusual for governments to say that their principles are universally and eternally true.
The interest of this Rescript lies not so much in its dogmatic tenor
or its lofty style as in the circumstances that brought about its
issue. It can be regarded as the culmination of a movement in favour of native traditions and away from that pragmatic, utilitarian

view of life which (as the governing classes saw it) was destroying the ancient morality of Japan — what they called the National Essence — and putting in its place nothing but a dangerous utilitarianism and a subversive materialism.

It would be difficult to find in the Far East a more pragmatic, and utilitarian group than the ruling élite of that time in Japan, but in so far as their fears were genuine they cannot be blamed, for the student of Meiji history is bound to admit that there was some reason for the alarm betrayed by the conservatives. It was true that the rapid growth of trade and industry, combined with the collapse of former political and social institutions, had almost inevitably led to a relaxation of old standards of conduct. No doubt the phase of intoxication, the "Western fever," had gone too far, and it was time for the Japanese to examine their condition and chart their future course. That was the feeling in advanced intellectual circles where there was no special animosity to Western culture but only an anxiety as to how much Japan could absorb without doing violence to her own national character.

As for the country at large, it should be remembered that from the time of the preliminary conference in Tokyo in 1882 the minds of both government and people had been exercised by the problem of treaty revision. Indeed, the influence of this vexed question can be seen in almost every department of Japanese life between the Restoration and 1894, when it was settled to the satisfaction of Japan. While it was still under discussion, national pride called for the denunciation of all special privileges accorded to foreigners, but when from about 1887 it seemed that a solution was in sight the public suddenly became aware that the conclusion of "equal" treaties meant throwing the country open to unrestricted foreign trade and residence. Enthusiasm vanished and doubts arose. The most unexpected fears were voiced. The influence of foreigners would spread all over the Empire, their beliefs and customs would corrupt the national spirit, and Christian missions would be used to cover Western designs of aggression. Hostile opinion was stirred up by agitators for ends of their own, and the government of the day was not innocent of using it as a lever in negotiation with the treaty powers. But if much of the alarm was baseless and foolish — at times it amounted almost to panic — there was a residue of genuine fear that Japan would be overwhelmed and lose her cultural identity. This real concern to preserve the national character from alien influence must be recognized as an important factor in the conservative movement, which reached its peak about 1889, when the government was forced to suspend the pourparlers by the violence of public sentiment.

But the Imperial Rescript of 1890 was not a mere expression of concern. It was a most categorical assertion of future policy in regard not only to education but to every aspect of the relationship between the people and the state. It was the crowning item in a sequence of public acts which had led to the promulgation of the Constitution. The purpose of the Rescript was to stamp with Imperial approval, and so to reinforce, principles already announced in legal form by a series of measures designed to strengthen the system of government that the bureaucratic leaders had carefully and patiently built up. The key to the system was the absolute power of the Emperor, which must ultimately depend not upon documentary provisions but upon the creation of a sentiment of respect amounting to veneration for the throne. It is for such reasons that the Rescript appeals to ancestral tradition and, with conspicuous success, endeavours in one coherent scheme to relate the customary morality of the Japanese people to a concept of the nature and function of the sovereign for which there was only an imperfect historical warrant.

We have dealt elsewhere with this aspect of statecraft, and here we need consider the effect of the Rescript only in the field of education. It meant that from the moment of its issue education in Japan was closely bound up with the indoctrination of youth on lines conformable to the authoritarian principles of the government. Consequently the curricula and the pedagogic theories of subsequent years show a reaction against American and English influence and a search for some method that would combine in due proportions utilitarian instruction and moral training. Regulations issued in 1891 for the guidance of teachers in primary schools laid down the following rule: "In education the greatest attention should be paid to moral culture. Hence, whatever is found in any course of study relating to moral or national education should be taught with care and assiduity. All teaching should be based upon matters essential to life, lessons should be so taught that they may all be turned to practical uses."

Questions as to the ultimate value of such principles are outside the scope of this study; but there can be no doubt that the ethical teaching given in Japanese schools had a large measure of success in the fulfilment of an official policy designed to create a strong and uniform sentiment of loyalty and discipline. It is difficult to judge how far this result should be ascribed to deliberate indoctrination; but it is certain that it could not have been achieved without the aid of old established ideas and habits. In that sense the history of Japanese education in the nineteenth century provides a useful example of a reaction against foreign influence and a return to tradition in the midst of a strenuous process of "modernization."

4. Religion

A<small>PART</small> from an early attempt to elevate Shinto by oppressing
Buddhism, the history of religion in Japan in the period under re
view, which is roughly the first twenty years of Meiji (or more ac
curately from the year 1868 to the promulgation of the Rescript
on Education in 1890), is mostly concerned with the progress of
Christian evangelization and its effect upon Japanese religious
thought.

We have already seen that until the very early years of Meiji
the official attitude towards Christianity remained hostile, and the
people in general, schooled by two centuries of ruthlessness on the
part of the authorities, continued to look upon the foreign religion
with fear and suspicion. The common dread of punishment for
even the most tenuous connection with the "evil sect" is well illustrated by an incident related by an officer of Perry's flagship.
He had asked a Japanese visitor aboard to write his autograph on
the fly-leaf of a book. It was a prayer-book, and when the guest,
with his brush poised, saw a cross on the title page he hastily threw
it down and would not touch it again.

It was to be expected that in such an atmosphere the renewal
of Christian evangelism in Japan would meet with great resistance,
and so in fact it did until the Japanese government, in circumstances already described, withdrew the anti-Christian edicts in
1873. Before that date Christian teaching had been tacitly permitted in some places and a few missionaries who arrived in Japan
soon after the 1858 treaties came into force were able to work
within the very narrow limits of residence and travel then allowed
to foreigners. But for several years they were handicapped not
only by restrictions on their movements but by popular prejudice
and fear. One of the first missionaries, Guido Verbeck, of the
Dutch Reformed Church in America (who arrived in Japan in
1859), said at this time that when a religious question was mooted
in the presence of a Japanese, "his hand would almost involun-
tarily be applied to his throat to indicate the extreme peril of such
a topic." Japanese servants in missionary households were in constant fear of spies, and it was very difficult to obtain the services of
a Japanese language teacher.

As late as 1871 a Japanese named Ichikawa Einosuke, who had
given language lessons to an American missionary in Nagasaki, was
arrested and imprisoned. The evidence against him was that he
possessed a Japanese translation of part of the New Testament. He
died in jail some eighteen months later; for such were the rigours
of confinement in those days that the record of many political

offenders ends with the grim words "died in prison while awaiting trial." The case of Ichikawa is of especial interest because it brought out into the open the official attitude toward Christianity and contributed to the withdrawal of the edicts. Missionaries who called upon the authorities to plead for him were told that if he had received baptism he could not escape the death penalty. The American Minister in Yedo appealed to Iwakura, the head of the government, and was told that Japan was not answerable to foreigners for the treatment of Japanese subjects. The minister warned him that ill treatment of Christians would affect the friendly relations of the United States with Japan, and when Iwakura shortly afterwards went on his mission to America and Europe he found that the story of Ichikawa was well known in official circles. It was not long after this that the ban upon Christian teaching was removed.

The circumstances of this withdrawal throw some light upon the general attitude of the new government towards religion. It has already been pointed out that shortly after the Restoration a determined attempt was made by a conservative group to establish Shinto as a state religion and to repress Buddhism. The inner history of this movement is somewhat obscure. It seems, however, that the court party in the government were its chief supporters, because they felt that while their samurai colleagues enjoyed the backing of the military caste, their own position needed strengthening. The elevation of Shinto to the position of an official doctrine would fortify the throne and the court aristocracy, providing as it did a coherent theory of direct Imperial rule. This fitted well enough into the plans of the new government, in so far as it promoted Shinto at the expense of Buddhism, which had some traditional patronage from the Shogunate and was therefore out of favour. Accordingly Okubo and Kido were not opposed to religious projects favoured by Iwakura and Sanjo, though they cannot have had very much faith in them. For a few years Buddhism was under attack. It lost government grants, and in February 1871 an official order placed Shinto priests in charge of certain important Buddhist foundations, including the great mausoleum of Ieyasu at Nikko. These attempts to rehabilitate Shinto failed because the mass of the people were not much interested in its doctrinal aspects and held to their Buddhist faith, which, though it may not have been profound, was part of their customary life. By the end of 1872 the government gave up its attempts to regulate religious belief and began to take a neutral position, no doubt because Okubo, Kido, and their colleagues felt that they had more important matters in hand.

The Department of Religion (*Jingi-kwan*), which was concerned only with the national cult, was replaced by an office of lower rank, called the Board of Religious Instruction (*Kyōbu-shō*), under which was a college of lecturers whose function was to impart and supervise ethical teaching. The college was called the Daikyō-in, or College of the Great Doctrine, and the Great Doctrine was based upon three colourless principles that were supposed to be acceptable to Shinto and Buddhism alike. They were, in fact, scarcely religious principles at all, but ethical rules, which, it was hoped, would facilitate government by encouraging loyalty and obedience to officials.[9] But the Shinto leaders did their best to give this institution a strong Shinto flavour. When the college was opened in June 1873 with great ceremonies, these took place in the ancient Buddhist monastery called Zōjōji, which belonged to the Pure Land sect of Amidism and contained the mausolea of several Tokugawa shoguns. Many of its Buddhist parishioners were present, and they were horrified to find that the ritual took the form of worship of the divine Imperial ancestors, in which Buddhist lecturers of the college were obliged to take part, serving at the altar in Shinto robes — a spectacle that is said to have reduced many devout Buddhists to tears.

Such arbitrary action naturally stimulated antagonism among the Buddhist clergy, and though the college continued for some time it soon lost any influence it may have had, and by 1877 the parent Board of Religious Instruction was abolished. This abortive attempt to regulate religious thought showed the authorities that they were on dangerous ground. They knew that they would presently have to face the problem of Christian teaching in Japan, and early in 1873 the edict against Christianity as an "evil sect" was removed from the public notice boards. This did not in theory change the law, but it meant that the government did not intend to enforce it. Consequently from 1873 onwards the work of Christian missionaries in Japan entered upon a new phase. From 1859 to 1872 inclusive their task had been only preparatory. They had made few converts,[10] but they had begun educational and medical work and had organized small religious communities in Yokohama and in other places where circumstances were not unfavourable, and they had made some progress in the translation of the Scriptures. The first translation into Japanese under Protestant auspices of a portion of the Bible was printed in 1871, though before that there were available in Japan copies of Chinese translations of

---

[9] The principles were: (1) reverence for the national deities and love of country; (2) the Law of Heaven and the Way of Man; (3) loyalty to the throne and obedience to the authorities.

[10] At the beginning of 1872 there were only ten baptized Protestant converts. The first Japanese Protestant convert to be baptized in Japan was a physician named Yano in 1864. He was baptized *in extremis*.

the New Testament and of religious tracts, which educated Japanese could understand.

More than the letter of the law it was the return in 1873 of Iwakura's embassy from America and Europe that improved the prospects of Christian missions in Japan. Its members were impressed by the importance of Christianity in Western life and saw clearly that they could not hope for good relations with Western states so long as Japanese subjects were denied religious freedom. Some leading men went further than that and asked whether it was possible to take over the civilization of Western countries without adopting their religion, and within a year or two of the abortive Shinto revival we find more than one eminent thinker recommending the adoption of Christianity. Even in government circles the idea seems to have been seriously entertained, for it is on record that in 1873 members of the Japanese Legation in Berlin inquired of Professor Gneist whether he thought that Japan should introduce Christianity as the state religion.

No doubt such speculations and inquiries were prompted by a feeling that Japan as a Christian nation would be treated as an equal of other Christian countries; but they also tend to show that in the early years of Meiji there was among the educated Japanese no profound and unanimous conviction of the truth of their own traditional religious beliefs. Those were times of intellectual confusion, and it might be supposed that such circumstances were favourable to Christianity. In a limited sense that is true, since Buddhism did not offer any serious positive resistance to Christianity, nor at the early stage was Shinto, as an organized cult under official auspices, a major obstacle to Christian propaganda. The difficulties that Christianity had to surmount lay not in active opposition by systematic religions but rather in the strength of traditional ways of thought of the Japanese people and in their social customs, which stood as a strong barrier against change. The mass of the people were indifferent, not hostile to Christianity. The uneducated were tenacious of old ways and the rural population in particular continued its simple Buddhist observances often out of habit rather than conviction. The educated classes had for the most part followed the moral principles of Confucianism and were by training and inclination sceptical. They might, as a social duty, think it well to belong to a Buddhist sect and would see nothing incongruous in performing Shinto ritual, but they were not fundamentally religious, and it is significant of their general outlook that agnostic and rationalistic schools of Western thought found a ready response among Japanese intellectuals who followed Confucius in thinking that human life was hard enough to understand and nothing useful could be known about the hereafter.

In addition to these difficulties, Christian missionaries were confronted with a political situation, or rather with a series of political convulsions, which for some years after 1873 produced strong currents of feeling against foreign influences. The opposition to Western culture was by no means clear-cut, since there were many dissident factions whose aim was to embarrass the government, not to resist all Western influences. But in effect they worked against Western religion, and they made it difficult for the government to grant any benefits to Christian missions.

The subversive movements that culminated in the Satsuma Rebellion of 1877 were of political origin, but they mobilized conservative feeling in many parts of the country, and it was easy for agitators to lay the commotions of the day at the door of a government which was introducing all kinds of Western ideas. Of these Christianity was perhaps the easiest to attack, and many malcontents from various motives joined in the campaign. Such anti-Christian activities were as a rule incidental features of a secular movement, and seeing how unruly that movement was, it is remarkable that they were not more frequent and more violent. That they were not all mere by-products of political strife is clear from the nature of some contemporary anti-Christian literature. A work called *Bemmō*, or *An Exposition of Falsehood,* has already been mentioned, and some further account of it may suitably be given here. It was written in 1875 by a leading Confucian scholar, formerly in Bakufu service, and it was furnished with a preface by Shimadzu Saburo, an irreconcilable conservative who was the leader of the reactionary wing of the Satsuma clan. This preface dwells on the central theme of the book, which is the contention that the teaching of Christ is in conflict with those Confucian doctrines of filial piety and loyalty to superiors which are the very foundation of the state. It also objects that Christianity is incompatible with ancestor-worship. The tone of this book is trenchant and bitter rather than abusive. It gives closely reasoned arguments that present at their clearest the principles of Far Eastern social ethics and it includes some shrewd thrusts at Christian practice as distinct from Christian doctrine.

The importance of such works as these should not be overrated, but they had a fairly wide circulation. *Bemmō* in particular was reprinted in 1881 and was still read by young men a generation after it was written. Christian missionaries thought that they could trace its influence in the arguments used by many of their adversaries in debate.

It is not surprising that in the decade between 1873 and 1883 the Protestant church in Japan made little progress as measured by the number of converts. Statistics for the beginning of 1883 show 93 Protestant churches with 145 foreign workers, while the number of missionary societies in Japan had risen to 18, with a proportionate increase in the number of foreign evangelists. The multiplication of Christian sects gave Japanese critics cause to complain that Western controversies were being transferred to Japan, and even among Japanese Christians there was a feeling in favour of unity, while Japanese officials argued that, though the Roman Catholic Church was one body, it was difficult for the government to negotiate with the Protestant church because it had so many denominations. It was true that the number of converts did not seem to justify the increased number of separate missionary bodies, for by the beginning of 1883 there were only some 4,000 adult Japanese church members in the whole country.

But the success of Christian teaching cannot be judged only by statistics of conversions, since Christian influence was making itself felt in many indirect ways. Much depended at this time on the secular educational work in which many missionaries were engaged, and upon the efforts of a small body of Japanese evangelists and pastors who braved not only abuse and hatred but also bodily dangers in their endeavour to spread Christian beliefs in parts of Japan where sentiment was peculiarly hostile. A notable example was the so-called Kumamoto Band, composed of thirty youths who made a covenant to stand up for Christianity in Kumamoto in Higo at a time of insurrection when feeling against foreigners ran dangerously high. Not all of them kept to their resolution, but a small nucleus in 1876 entered the Christian college known as the Dōshisha, then newly founded by Neesima (Niishima Jō). The personal influence of men like Neesima, coupled with the zeal and, most of all, the evident integrity of certain leading foreign missionaries, was powerful in spreading a respect for Christians if not a belief in Christianity among Japanese of all classes. This in turn favoured the undertakings of the missionaries and in particular increased confidence in the schools and hospitals they founded. That such support was still needed may be judged from the fact that as late as 1880 some provincial officials endeavoured to check the spread of Christian ideas, and even the central government was at times loath to approve of missionary undertakings such as teaching and the publication of Christian literature.

Something should be said here about the translation of the Scriptures into Japanese. A translation of the New Testament was completed in 1880, of the Old Testament in 1888. The work was one of extreme difficulty, not only because it was a corporate undertaking of all the missionary societies in Japan, but because of the many problems that arose from the differences in structure and vocabulary between the two languages. To acquire a real mastery of Japanese is at the best of times a severe task, while the early Protestant missionaries were especially handicapped by a scarcity of apparatus in the form of dictionaries and grammatical works. A great deal of preparatory labour had to be faced, as for instance in the compilation of a Japanese-English and English-Japanese dictionary in the Roman alphabet. This was achieved by Dr. Hepburn, of the American Presbyterian mission, a pioneer task Sisyphean rather than Herculean, since (as a later scholar observed) "nowhere is finality more unattainable than in the field of Japanese lexicography."

Most baffling among the linguistic obstacles were the problems of selecting suitable equivalents for such words as God, Spirit, Soul, Atonement, Grace, Conscience, and, notably, Logos; for literal renderings often produced ludicrous results. As the Jesuits had found long before them, the translators were faced with an almost insuperable difficulty in their search for means of expressing ideas that were unfamiliar, if not unintelligible, to Japanese minds. Even the Japanese Christians who were brought in to help the translation committee were not able to give much help, since they were not familiar enough with the English language, far less with Greek and Hebrew. A further difficulty was the choice of style, since the Japanese literary language had several modes of expression, ranging from a relatively pure native prose to a stiff and learned compound in which Chinese elements predominated. Somehow solutions were found for all these problems and the publication of the complete Bible in Japanese in 1888 was an important landmark in the history of Protestant missions in Japan. It was used not only by converts, but by non-Christian Japanese as an adjunct to their language studies and an aid to the understanding of Western ideas; and of course it much facilitated the work of the missions since it could be placed in the hands of their Japanese helpers.[11]

11 The first translation of a portion of the Bible in Japan is said to have been made by Xavier's helper Yajiro in a tract that included quotations from the Gospel of St. Matthew. This has not been preserved, but in 1592 the Jesuit press in Amakusa issued a work called *Doctrina Christiana* in Japanese (in Roman letters), which included the Lord's Prayer, the Ten Commandments, and extracts from St. Matthew (v, 3–10).

In 1880 Professor Chamberlain (an Englishman who held a chair of Japanese at Tokyo University) essayed a rendering of some of the Psalms and read a paper on the subject to the Asiatic Society of Japan. He used a poetical language akin to that of the longer poems in the great anthology called *Manyōshū* — a considerable tour de force for a foreigner.

Other translations by foreigners were not so successful. Thus one of the early missionaries gave a rendering of the hymn "Jesus loves me" in the following words, which will be appreciated by students of the Japanese language as a near approach to "pidgin":

Although, as we have seen, a general conservative reaction against Western influence set in from about 1882, the fortunes of Christianity in Japan do not seem to have followed this pattern closely, for it made more progress in the ensuing decade than ever before. This would indicate that its influence was gaining rapidly, though it has to be borne in mind that, having overcome certain initial obstacles, it would naturally spread at an increasing rate so long as there was no positive official antagonism to overcome. A favourable event was what has been called the "disestablishment" of religions in 1884. This is a somewhat deceptive term, since it refers to an announcement by which the government disassociated itself from control over the appointment of Buddhist and Shinto priests to positions they had formerly held as instructors or as incumbents of certain temples and shrines.

Strictly speaking, neither Shinto nor Buddhism was at this time an established religion, but the action of the government was in practice a recognition, however tacit and incomplete, of religious freedom; and as it followed closely upon Ito's return from abroad it is probable that the step was taken in preparation for the grant of a constitution in which a general recognition of civil liberties was to figure. There was in fact among leaders of public opinion, especially in official circles, some disposition at this time to give a qualified approval to Christianity on what may be called prudential rather than moral grounds. The conspicuous success of missionary schools and colleges in secular education, particularly in the education of the daughters of well-to-do families that were not Christian, contributed to this new esteem.

But undoubtedly an important factor was a more general sentiment that it would be advantageous to Japan if it were regarded abroad as a Christian country, at least to the extent that Christianity was among the religions approved and commonly professed. Newspaper articles of the day, especially in the *Jiji Shimpo* under Fukuzawa's direction, endorsed Christianity as a useful contribution to civilization and politically beneficial. One such article contained the following passage, most revealing in its frank simplicity: "We cannot persuade Shintoists to change their views, but we can tell them that they should look at the ascendancy of Christianity in our country as an event in the natural course of things, and that for the sake of the country they should refrain from dis-

Jesus loves me, this I know	*Yaso ware wo aisu*
For the Bible tells me so	*Sayo seisho mosu*
. . . . . .	. . . . .
. . . . . .	. . . .
Yes, Jesus loves me	*Hai! Yaso aisu*
Yes, Jesus loves me.	*Hai! Yaso aisu.*

turbances. We do not propose that a majority of our people should become Christians, a small proportion would be enough. All that is necessary is to accept the name of a Christian country." This was in 1885, at a time when in the provinces there were still occasional outbursts against Christians; but by now the central government was on the watch and took measures to prevent such incidents.

In general it may be said that the more violent forms of opposition to Christianity had now come to an end, and that although there was still a strong movement of resistance in some intellectual circles, Christianity had passed beyond the stage of toleration and had some positive support in influential quarters. By 1889 its legal position also was unassailable, for article 28 of the Constitution promulgated on November 11 assured freedom of religion to all Japanese subjects.

But of course legal freedom was not enough, for ultimately the fortunes of Christianity depended not only upon the efforts of the missionaries but upon the disposition of the Japanese people. Judging by figures alone, the progress made between 1883 and 1889 was satisfactory if not remarkable, for the total Japanese adult membership of Protestant churches rose from 5,591 to 29,000, and the number of self-supporting churches had increased. Out of a population of some 40,000,000 this was an almost negligible proportion, and even allowing that Christian influence was spread far beyond the direct membership of churches it cannot be said that it had conspicuously affected the foundations of Japanese culture. Neither had the Roman Catholic and Greek Orthodox (Russian) churches grown very rapidly. The former reported for 1881 a total of under 25,000 adult Japanese converts, which had risen to about 40,000 by 1889, in which year the latter claimed some 18,000 baptized members, of whom it was currently said that they were often lukewarm in their faith and not easily distinguishable from the non-Christians around them.

A leading Protestant missionary well acquainted with conditions in Japan, reviewing the situation after 1890, made some interesting observations which may be cited here as a carefully considered estimate of the prospects of Christianity at that date. He said:

So far as the laws of the land are concerned the Christians have little to seek. The acquisition of this liberty however has not lessened the severity of the ordeal to which they are subjected. The very recognition of the rights of Christians may be said to betoken a kind of indifferentism in matters of religion, which is widespread and which has affected more or less unfavourably those who are supposed to reap its greatest benefits, in that it has (as is always the case in similar circumstances) weakened their power of resistance to the more subtle temptations attendant upon prosperity. For they breathe the same air as their countrymen, and cannot fail to be affected by every general movement which affects the nation.

The writer here lays a finger upon a very definite characteristic of Japanese life then, and perhaps at all times — a strong feeling for social duty, but a lack of deep religious sentiment as it is understood by Western peoples. This is a crude statement that needs much qualification, but in general it is borne out by the history of Japanese religious institutions.

Certainly at the time when the authority just quoted was forming his opinions the country was absorbed in practical affairs and little interested in spiritual matters. Growing prosperity, the new element of competition which had been brought into daily life by industry and commerce, and an intense preoccupation with secular learning left little room for an interest in the claims of religion. It might even be said that, if there was any notable growth of religious fervour, it was easily diverted from the Church to the state and expressed itself in an ardent patriotic sentiment, which was not without morbid elements. However that may be, leading missionaries judged that the forces making themselves felt in Japanese society from about 1890 were for the most part "unfriendly to the progress of organized Christianity," a condition that they ascribed chiefly to the growth of a strong nationalistic feeling. The same writer continues:

Among the more intellectual classes visions of the great part Japan is to play in the world's life have led to a depreciation of what she has already received and what other nations have to give. Among others the new opportunities of amassing wealth or improving social position have led to an epicurean view of life and an impatience under the restraints which religion imposes. The churches have suffered sadly from this cause.

As a contemporary observer's view of the process of reaction at work this is of great interest. It is confirmed by many other manifestations of a growing conflict in Japanese life, in its effort to accommodate new ideas with old convictions. Thus Japanese Buddhism found its hold relaxing in part through the diversion of some of its believers to Christianity, but much more through the growth of indifferentism or of a positive antireligious "rationalist" trend of thought among educated Japanese. Certain Buddhist sects, in particular the Shinshū (or "True Sect" of Amidism), went so far as to present their doctrines as not inconsistent with but superior to Christianity, and by "modernizing" their teaching made it appear monotheistic and gave to the merciful Amida in

Buddhism the position of the Saviour in Christianity. At the same time the teachers of this and other sects pointed out that Buddhist cosmology was consistent with the principles of modern science, since it did not, like Christianity, assume that the Deity could be persuaded by prayer to change the decreed course of nature. Such attempts can scarcely be regarded as important, except in so far as they show that not only Christianity but also the traditional religions of Japan suffered from a prevailing scepticism.

That this sceptical mood was strong is clear from the literature of the eighties and nineties, for the gospel of most intellectuals in Japan was the gospel of Herbert Spencer, and it is clear that a widespread belief in the "real" and the "practical" made the agnosticism of the mid-Victorian era very palatable to educated Japanese.

But, lest it should be assumed that the impact of nineteenth-century ideas had killed all that religious fervour which had been displayed by the humble converts of the Jesuits in the sixteenth century, it would be wrong to overlook the appeal of certain forms of Christianity to the emotions of a great number of converts. The history of revival meetings in modern Japanese Christian churches affords some striking parallels to the scenes of tearful bliss recorded in the early Christian communities during the sixteenth century and, as we have noted, in the congregations of the Pure Land sect of Amidism. Descriptions of revival meetings, frequent and well attended, are to be found in missionary reports from all parts of Japan, especially from 1883 and for some years later. Perhaps a sufficient general impression of their nature can be gained from one account, describing a succession of joint prayer meetings (of several denominations) at Sendai in 1886:

At the commencement of these meetings a brother came to the realization of his sins and seeking for peace he found it with joy. The first meeting was very impressive, and the Spirit was present with power, many being convicted of their sins. The meetings on the next evenings were still more wonderful. The audiences were very large, and many were so deeply impressed that they went into the fields and the mountains to pray. Others remained in the churches until the morning, unable to sleep from deep emotion caused by the conviction of sin . . . and many confessed their sins publicly in the meetings. . . . During an address the whole audience was in tears and one of the hearers rushed out of the church with the cry "God help me! God forgive my sins!"

Such manifestations of religious excitement caused alarm to some of the pastors, but they continued and spread from churches to schools, where children are said to have spent hours together "in tears and prayer," in classrooms and dormitories. All these meetings are characterized by confession, loud cries, tears, and a general frenzy that it is difficult to distinguish from a mass hysteria. We cannot attempt to explain this phenomenon though it is of great psychological interest, but it may be noted that several cases of something like mass hysteria are reported among the urban populations in the early years of Meiji, when crowds would assemble, nobody knew why, and march the streets shouting monotonously some meaningless phrase in unison.

Distantly related to this overflow of religious feeling is the almost apocalyptic attitude of some of the early converts among young samurai. The Kumamoto Band has been mentioned as an example of burning enthusiasm, and it is interesting to note that one of the most judicially minded foreign missionaries felt that their dominating, even headstrong spirit was a deterrent to more sober but equally earnest converts. However that may be, it seems clear that many young samurai converts were inflamed by an abnormal apostolic conviction. Dr. Anezaki, in his *History of Japanese Religion,* says that they were filled with aspirations to work out the spiritual resurrection of the nation in conjunction with a new political life. He remarks that their faith was more ethical than religious, and quotes first-hand evidence that they were inspired by the Acts of the Apostles rather than by doctrines of sin and redemption in other parts of the New Testament. Their samurai spirit, it seems, was invigorated by Christian enthusiasm, and the single-minded perseverance of the apostles was in harmony with their inherited Confucian ideals of fortitude. They were sincere and high-minded, but one cannot help feeling that some of them may have been at times unbalanced in their ardours. In any case, it is a striking fact that the political thought of young men of their type was in those early days infused with fervent religious sentiment.

It is of course not suggested that the Christian church in Japan made converts principally among emotionally disturbed persons. That would be very far from the truth, for many distinguished and important figures in Japanese life have been of the Christian faith. But all missionaries would agree that it was among a sceptical and self-controlled educated class that they found their most effective adversaries. It was the author of *Bemmō* who represented that class at the time when he wrote and he was followed and preceded by other formidable opponents of Christianity, some of whose works have already been mentioned (in the sections of the preceding chapter dealing with literary and intellectual trends).

In this context we may single out one category of anti-Christian movement that is closely related to the attitude of the educated class, since it arose out of a conflict between national educational policy and the principles of education as understood by the missionary bodies who supplied both funds and guidance to a large number of colleges and schools. It will be recollected that the failure of the negotiations for treaty revision resulted in or strengthened a wave of anti-foreign feeling that in its more reputable aspects was expressed by the formation of such societies as the Nihon Kōdō-Kwai and the publication of organs like the magazine *Nihon-Jin,* which announced in 1880 that it stood for "the adoption of systems of religion, education, art, government, and production conformable to the ideas of the Japanese people and the environment provided by all the natural features of their country."

Such movements, led by scholars of distinction, could not be dismissed as exhibitions of ignorant prejudice. They usually kept within the bounds of propriety, though there were not wanting some instances of extremist behaviour which might be ascribed to their influence. Thus the assassination of Mori Arinori, the Minister of Education, as he left his house to attend the ceremony of the promulgation of the Constitution on November 11, 1889, was a violent expression of hatred because he was regarded as entirely subject to Western and therefore to Christian influence. He was in fact, though modern-minded in respect of the material benefits of Western civilization, essentially a conservative man, and his educational policy was fundamentally nationalistic and militaristic, for he planned to give rifles to elementary school-children for their drill and to make the dormitories of normal schools resemble military barracks. This did not protect him from the assassins, however, who alleged that he had profaned the great shrine at Ise; and the cause of his murder was summarized in the liberal magazine the *People's Companion* by saying that he fell a victim to the reactionary thought that he himself had aroused.

The conflict over educational policy became exceedingly bitter, as may be seen from the titles of articles that appeared in the leading magazines from about 1889, when a teacher in a state middle school was accused of refusing to pay reverence to the Imperial Rescript on education at an opening ceremony. He was attacked by Buddhists, and the leading philosopher of the day, Professor Inouye Tetsujiro, apparently at their instance, wrote articles on "The Conflict between the State and Christianity," to which Christian Japanese writers responded. The polemical battle continued for some time, and Christianity found some warm supporters, among whom was Takahashi Goro, who struck his blow at Inouye with an article entitled "False Arguments of a Mock Philosopher." But the outcome was on the whole unfavourable to Christianity, for the majority of educators were on Inouye's side. The opposition of the Buddhists, though not of itself redoubtable, had some effect in combination with other anti-Christian influences, and even within the Japanese Christian churches there were signs of a conservative, ultra-nationalistic reaction. It should be added that, in the opinion of some missionary writers, there were other signs of internal weakness in the Japanese Christian church. They point on the one hand to the excesses of the revival movement, and on the other to the disruptive influence of a multiplication of sects and denominations. Perhaps more significant is another feature they mention: namely, the growth of an interest in critical theology which tended to "endanger the foundations of faith."

The important Christian college, the Dōshisha, soon after 1887 was affected by the new criticism. The development of scientific studies in secular institutions had encouraged a sceptical if not hostile attitude towards Christianity. It was based largely upon the theory of evolution, but relied also upon Hegelian philosophy, which was seized upon as supporting Buddhist rather than Christian views. The University of Tokyo became the intellectual stronghold of disbelief, the more so as it was opposed to the relatively free teaching of the private universities, Waseda and Keiō, founded respectively by Okuma and Fukuzawa; and it is clear that Ito and other members of the government looked to the University of Tokyo to defend official doctrines against subversive influences, of which Christianity was felt to be the most dangerous.

But we should not lose sight of internal dissensions as a cause of weakness in the Christian church in Japan. Disputes that had arisen among Christians in the West were imported into Japan. A group of young theologians came near to wrecking the Dōshisha by their heretical views on cardinal points of belief. Nor can there be any doubt that fragmentation had an adverse effect upon the spread of Christianity. By 1896 there were some thirty separate Protestant denominations represented by missions, including such small bodies as the Universalists, the Hephzibah Faith Association, the American Evangelical Lutheran Mission, and a few others. The Japanese also noted that Protestant sects often had national titles prefixed to their names, such as the American Methodist, the Anglican, the Canadian Methodist, the Scandinavian Alliance, the Dutch Reformed, and the German and Swiss Evangelical. Suspicious minds thought that these bodies enjoyed political support in their several countries, while it was noted that the Catholic Church claimed to be universal and not national.

It was secular rather than religious opposition that the Christians had most to fear. Feeling throughout the country was moving in a direction generally unfavourable to Christianity and incidentally discouraging to the foreign missionaries, who were as a rule orthodox and conservative and naturally out of sympathy with nationalistic reactions against Western culture. The new education policy of 1886 worked against them, since it was based upon Confucian principles of morality and was designed to exclude religious influence from schools. This antireligious trend was hardened by the Rescript on Education of 1890, which made it incumbent on teachers to oppose Christianity by supporting the ethical principles laid down by the state. Its results were soon apparent, for the records of the Protestant missions show a fall in the number of baptisms in the five years after 1890, and only a very small increase in the total church membership.

Strong opposition to Christianity came from that body of thought which is loosely described as Shintoism, and this at first sight may appear to be a form of religious conflict. But Shintoism as an aspect of the anti-Christian, conservative movement is not exclusively or even primarily a religion, but rather a complex of social and political ideas grouped around the concept of the supreme power of the Emperor and his position as the focus of all the loyalties of the Japanese people. It is (or was) a religion only in the sense that among its most devoted and sincere adherents are some who display a patriotic fervour that at times seems to partake of the character of a religious mysticism. It has very little to do with the old theocratic myth, or if it has, this is refashioned to meet modern political requirements. In the early part of Meiji it was not, what it later became, a systematic official propaganda designed to strengthen and sustain nationalistic sentiment. It was, despite its artificial elements, an attempt to express in one coherent doctrine traditional Japanese feelings about the state, the community, and the family; and these could scarcely have been drawn together and turned to political purposes if they had not been deep-seated and sincere.

Thus while Christians in Japan might fear the propagation of an artificial Shinto because it taught a limited ethical system, they were forced to recognize that the basis of the distinctive Japanese morality was within its limits firm and genuine. A review by the leading missionary from whom I have already quoted of what he describes as "the ethical situation" after the promulgation of the Constitution and the Rescript on Education, includes some interesting observations on this point. They provide a useful contemporary estimate of forces which were deemed unfavourable to Christian mission work:

During the early part of the period under review [he writes], under the influence of an over-wrought patriotism there was much both said and written about Japanese morality, it being assumed that morality is a national matter. A sufficient foundation for this morality was found, so its advocates claimed, in the virtues of filial piety and loyalty. Even more strenuous efforts were made than before to show that Christians by the very fact of their faith were both unfilial and disloyal. Teachers in Government schools were forced to resign their positions because of their unwillingness to bow before the portrait of the Emperor. In itself considered there is no more objection to bowing before the Emperor's portrait than in kneeling before the portrait of George II, as Thackeray tells us his Hanoverian subjects were accustomed to do. There was, however, practically this difference, that the common people considered the salutation demanded as divine worship, and few if any were found willing to say publicly that it was not.

There are here revealed the elements of a disagreement not unlike that which produced the Rites Controversy in China, and the Japanese authorities came forward with a solution not unlike that of K'ang Hsi by pronouncing that such acts of reverence were not acts of religious worship. But the fundamental difference of opinion was not removed, because it was not confined to procedure but extended to principles. The attitude of strict Japanese Christians was described by a pastor (the Reverend J. T. Yokoi, a son of that Yokoi Shōnan who was one of the leaders of the Restoration movement) in the following terms, in an article dealing with the statement of Japanese moral principles set forth in the Rescript on Education:

The illustrations and examples of moral principles must be drawn from Japanese sources. Japanese history has been ransacked for anecdotes illustrative of the virtues of loyalty and filial piety. Numbers of textbooks appeared, filled with stories of men and women who at times of great emergencies sacrificed their lives in devotion to the service of their sovereigns or parents. So much insistence was laid on the unusual and heroic sides of these virtues that it must have appeared to young minds that only on such unusual and critical occasions could these virtues be practised, while the quiet peaceful performance of daily duties small and unheroic seemed to fall into comparative neglect.

Referring to the current movement to revive Shintoism, or to produce a New Shintoism that was to "codify the old Japanese spirituality," the same writer said:

It seems to me to be the sacred task of the leaders of thought today to supply some adequate philosophy which shall not only furnish a basis for the old distinctive "spirituality" but be comprehensive enough to include and present in due proportions the new ideas which are needed to make up the defects in the old system. In this philosophy, I am convinced, individualism will have to occupy the central position.

Much has been spoken and written since that time on the conflict between Western individualist thought and the Japanese view,
partly customary and partly created by indoctrination, that the
Imperial house is supreme and sacred and that the life of the individual must serve the purposes of the state. But these early examples are of special value as descriptions of the situation of the
Christian church in Japan, while throwing light upon the development of Japanese thought in reaction against Western influence.

This was the main religious problem of the early Meiji period.
No important developments took place in the position or nature
of Buddhism beyond the clash with Shinto in the course of the
abortive Back to Antiquity movement already recorded. The great
Buddhist sects, in particular the two Hongwanji branches of
Amidism, made some recovery, but it cannot be said that they
prospered. Some Buddhists joined in movements against Christianity, but among Buddhist leaders in general there seems to have
been an uneasy feeling that Buddhism itself was ill-adapted to
modern life and stood in need of reform. Certain Buddhist sects
even took hints from Christian example and began to encourage
the singing of hymns by congregations, to found hospitals and or-
phanages, to form Sunday schools, Young Men's Associations and
generally to imitate modern Christian institutional practices. Between 1872 and 1875 a commission of priests of the Shin sect
travelled abroad to study Western religious organizations, and
from that time onwards increasing attention was paid to the study
of Buddhist texts. But this proceeded from a scholarly rather than
a pious enthusiasm, and even a temporary vogue later enjoyed by
the works of Nichiren was a literary fashion and not a true revival
of the Lotus sect. Neither these measures nor the attempts to reinterpret Buddhist doctrine in the light of modern thought succeeded in restoring the fortunes of Buddhism in Japan, and though
there was some growth of private interest in Buddhist doctrine
from about 1880, the strong secular trend in the national life that
became manifest soon thereafter was almost as hostile to Buddhism
as to Christianity. From 1890 there was even a tendency for the
two religions to combine in resistance to it.

It is a curious fact that, although the National Scholars like
Mabuchi, Motoori, and Hirata, as proponents of Pure Shinto,
continued to attack Buddhism throughout the greater part of the
Tokugawa period, there is little sign of any effort by Japanese
Buddhist leaders to defend their faith. Thus Buddhism in Japan
was already weak before the Meiji Restoration, and it never recovered its prestige. The Buddhist clergy appear to have been
apathetic, and with few exceptions were content to enjoy their
emoluments and to carry out their duties in a perfunctory man-

er. As obliged by law, they kept registers of all parishioners, and
hey performed some religious services, of which funeral rites were
he most important. But there is no evidence that they exercised
any marked social or political influence. Even after the Restora-
ion, when they had regained some of their losses, their activities
betray a lack of confidence. Buddhist literature of the early Meiji
period consists largely of apologetics, in which a common line of
argument is that certain doctrines have the support of the conclusions of Western philosophy and Western science. Buddhism as expounded in European languages by Japanese writers at this time
is scarcely recognizable, so much do they strive to describe it in
Western terms. Although subsequently Buddhism profited by a
reaction against Western thought and regained some of its former
influence, it is difficult to believe that it became a real power in
the national life.

It would be rash, however, to reach a firm view on this last
point without close examination of the work of Buddhist scholars
and the effects of education in the Buddhist colleges that were
founded about 1890 and whose graduates often became teachers
and directors in state schools. This is more than can be undertaken
here, but it is as well to mention the activities of Inouye Enryo,
a learned scholar, monk of the Otani branch of the Hongwanji,
and the leader of literary attacks upon Christianity, since he was
one of the early promoters of Buddhist education of a modern
type. His hostility towards Christianity grew out of a desire (not
free from political colour) to reinvigorate Buddhism, and it is
thus an interesting expression of a contemporary intellectual trend.
His *Shinri Kinshin* (*Essence of Truth*) and *Bukkyō Kwatsuron*
(*On the Vitality of Buddhism*) appeared in parts between 1885
and 1890 and are said to have exerted much influence upon the
rising generation of students.

These works are an attempt to counter the influence of rationalistic thought in Japan by arguing that an educated Japanese
could, consistently with a belief in the findings of modern science
and the latest philosophical systems of the West, hold to Buddhist
doctrine and thus remain in conformity with a national intellectual tradition. The reasoning is not always scrupulous, but it
is true that both Hinduism and Buddhism contain within their
spacious metaphysic ideas corresponding to nineteenth-century
theories as to the nature of the universe and the evolution of man.
To Inouye the Hegelian dialectic was analogous to the analytic
logic of the Tendai sect, and the doctrine of Karma (which had
attracted Huxley's attention) was an anticipation of the development hypothesis then finding favour in Occidental countries. With
regard to Christianity his line of argument is that any form of

theism must be unacceptable to Western philosophy and science
Therefore Christianity is false, but Buddhism is true. The interes
of his writings lies perhaps less in his reasoning than in the pur
pose for which he wrote. He reflected the political sentiment o
the day and expressed the greatest concern for Japan's cultura
independence. He said: "If we are to abolish our Oriental culture
and lose our independence, there is nothing more to be said. Bu
if we want to preserve our culture and promote our independence
then we must strive for the invigoration of Buddhism." He took
part in the conservative movement led by Miyake, and joined the
staff of the magazine *Nihon Jin,* which was its organ.

As a pendant to the foregoing summary of religious trends
some mention should be made of certain popular sects that are
usually described as outgrowths of Shinto but seem rather to have
been manifestations of religious feeling which could only find full
expression when the Tokugawa régime was weakening and no
longer kept strict watch on religious movements for fear of political conspiracies. The best-known of these sects are those which
go by the names of Tenri-kyo and Konko-kyo. Both were founded
by peasants before the Restoration and both teach simple theistic
creeds that the founders claimed to be based upon revelation.
Except in so far as they show some slight Christian influence in
their later development, they are outside the scope of this study,
and all that need be said of them here is that they must have
arisen to satisfy some need that Buddhism and orthodox Shinto
did not fill. They bear a resemblance to Christian Science in that
they teach that faith is essential to the cure of bodily as well as
spiritual illness.

For purposes of comparison it is convenient to add here some
account of the attitude of the Chinese authorities towards Christianity after the Treaty of Nanking had placed the relationships
of China and Western states upon a new footing. It will be noticed that religious toleration was granted by the Chinese government sooner and more freely than by the Japanese, though perhaps
more out of weakness than benign intention.

The first diplomatic agreement to include specific undertakings as to the treatment of Christians in China was negotiated by
the French in 1844. Their trade interests were not great and they
attached less importance to their commercial treaty than to arrangements for restoring the influence of the Catholic Church.
The French negotiator succeeded in obtaining the issue of a decree
that in effect placed Chinese converts under the protection of
French diplomatic representatives in China; and in 1846 the Em-

peror was persuaded to order that church property confiscated in previous reigns should be restored to the appropriate Christian bodies. When new treaties were made by other powers a clause was incorporated guaranteeing that the Chinese government would not discriminate against Chinese Christians. This applied to Protestants, of course, as well as Catholics, since Protestant missions dated from the arrival of Robert Morrison in China in 1807, and had thereafter increased in numbers and influence. The French, unlike the English, Americans, and Russians, were not satisfied with a simple promise of toleration. They aimed at securing positive rights of intervention in favour of Chinese Christians and they insisted upon stipulations in their 1858 treaty which virtually removed converts from Chinese jurisdiction in some respects; and they obliged the Chinese government to rescind all previous official orders and pronouncements inimical to Christianity.

The Chinese authorities were naturally not active in enforcing provisions that, besides encroaching upon sovereign rights, caused great trouble and annoyance to the official class and engendered ill feeling against converts among non-Christian Chinese who resented their claims to special privilege. The converts insisted that they should not be called upon to contribute to the cost of official ceremonies of a religious nature and they were often supported by their priests in resisting the exactions of local authorities. The natural antagonism of the literati to a faith that openly expressed contempt of indigenous beliefs was matched by a superstitious dread of Christianity on the part of ignorant peasants. Before long, anti-Christian movements appeared in many places. The native Christians were the special object of attack, though occasionally a foreign missionary was killed or injured. The converts were accused of neglecting ancestor-worship or of destroying ancestral tablets — charges that were often true; but more fantastic accusations were also made, as when it was alleged that they used magic arts on young children and took out their eyes for the ingredients of medicines. It was even said that the foundling hospitals of the missionaries were only a disguise for kidnapping. These and similar rumours gained such credence that in 1870 there were riots in Tientsin, which ended in the destruction of mission property and the massacre of a number of French mission workers and other foreigners.

This incident caused great trouble between France and China. It was not settled until an indemnity had been paid and an official apology made by a Chinese envoy sent to France for that purpose. At this time France was in the throes of her war with Germany, and her diplomatic position was weak; but she could count upon the support of the other Western powers, not excluding her German enemy, in a matter that touched the safety of foreign nationals in China.

It will be noticed that, at a time when the Chinese government was too weak to resist pressure exerted on behalf of Christian missions, the Japanese government was still adhering to its traditional anti-Christian attitude. Despite its own comparative weakness, it submitted to foreign pressure only to the extent of tacitly permitting missionaries to work in Japan without any special privilege as to residence or travel. This firmness is in part to be explained by the earlier history of Japan's treaty negotiations, for it is clear that the United States government was anxious lest Perry's mission should be wrecked by disputes about religious freedom. Perry's instructions from President Fillmore referred to the known hatred of the Japanese for Christianity, and he was told to say that the United States was not like other Christian countries, since it did not interfere in religion at home, much less abroad. The President's letter to the Shogun refers to the Constitution and laws of the United States as forbidding intervention in the political or religious affairs of other countries — a somewhat disingenuous argument in the circumstances of Perry's visit — and goes on to say that Perry has been ordered to avoid any action likely to disturb the peace in Japan. There is no reference to religion in any of the treaties concluded in 1854.

It is a perhaps more striking fact that the treaties of 1858 contain no toleration clauses like those in the Chinese treaties of the same year. They allow foreigners in Japan to practise their own religion and they state that neither Japanese nor foreigners shall do anything to excite religious animosity. But there is no undertaking to protect native Christians and there was no change in the law against Christianity. In the Dutch agreement of 1857 it is laid down that the Japanese government has abolished the practice of trampling upon a sacred image (the *fumi-e*), but that this does not mean that Christianity may be propagated in Japan or that Christian literature or pictures may be imported.

Coming to a later period, it must be remembered that by 1868 the new Meiji government was for reasons of domestic policy committed to the doctrine that the Emperor was of divine origin. It could therefore not afford to be so tolerant as to incur charges of weakness from the extreme loyalists, who were fiery upholders of the Shinto view of the Japanese state.

Notes on CHAPTER 15

LAW. For this section of chapter xv I have consulted a number of works in Japanese on the history of Japanese legislation, which will be familiar to students who can read the language. I have also drawn upon my recollection of conversations and correspondence with the late Dr. Hozumi, who was one of the committee of three that drafted the Civil Code and wrote in English and Japanese a number of works on legal questions.

RELIGION. For the history of the Protestant missions in Japan in the first part of Meiji there are two useful works in English: *A History of Christianity in Japan,* by Otis Cary; *A History of Protestant Missions in Japan,* by H. Ritter (translated from German original).

The Missionary Research Library at Union Theological Seminary, Columbia University, New York, has an extensive collection of works dealing with missions in Asia, including reports and correspondence from Japan. Anezaki's *History of Japanese Religion* contains interesting details and opinions.

In Japanese there are several works by Y. Hiyane, including *Nihon Kirisuto-kyō Shi,* a history of Christianity in Japan in five small volumes.

CHAPTER
16

THE NINETIES

1. The Failure of Parliamentary Rule

To continue the story of political developments after the Constitution of 1889 came into operation brings us to the first meeting of the Diet in the following year. This took place in November 1890, nearly two years after the Constitution was promulgated, and as may be imagined the interval was long enough to permit of a great deal of manœuvre and diatribe on both sides. There were definitely two sides. But these were not two great political parties; they were respectively the government and the parliament itself. From the beginning the two assumed a mutually hostile attitude, a state of affairs due in the first place to the authoritarian principles of the government leaders, but exacerbated by the unruly and sometimes unprincipled conduct of the opposition parties during the two years in question. Agitation against the official policy on treaty revision had taken an anti-foreign turn. In 1889 on the day when the Constitution was promulgated the Minister of Education had been assassinated for his alleged unpatriotic views; and in 1890 the Minister of Foreign Affairs (Okuma) was badly injured by a bomb. Both incidents were characteristic of the violence attending political controversy in Japan, for assassination had been a habit since the murder of Yokoi Shonan in 1869 and was to claim many victims in years to come.

The elections of 1890 therefore took place in a heated atmosphere, but with far less disturbance than might have been expected. The result of the voting, which was remarkable for both the number of candidates and the number of voters, was to confront the government with the prospect of a lower house comprising 60 members of Goto's [1] Daidō or "general agreement" group, 50 members each of the Liberal Party (Jiyūtō) and the Progressive

---

[1] Goto himself had joined the government in 1888, together with Okuma. Both served under Kuroda, the minister whom Okuma had attacked for corruption in 1881. Thus the party of General Agreement, kept together by Goto's personality, lost its leader and its unanimity at the same time.

Party (Kaishintō), and the remainder of the 300 made up of 140 members who were independents and had nothing else in common.

Practically the whole house, with the exception of a few independents, was hostile to the government, and for once the various opposition parties were united in a common cause. The government itself was weak, because the leading statesmen were careful to leave office or to refuse it before the first Diet session, knowing that it would be stormy and preferring to wait for better political weather. Before the session there was a good deal of shifting between parties — not to be surprised at in the absence of fixed principles — but there was agreement on tactics, and from the opening of debate the government was under attack from all sides.

The main target was the budget, though there was also violent criticism of the administration for its oppressive police measures, its handling of treaty revision, and its program of taxation. Although there was a powerful majority against the government, which could find but little help from the independents, the new Constitution did not confer the power of the purse that characterizes the kind of parliamentary democracy for which the Liberals had been struggling. Certain categories of expenditure could not be challenged and even if the Lower House refused to adopt the budget as a whole, the government need not resign but could proceed on an interim working budget within the limits of the expenditures of the previous fiscal year. Consequently there was no constitutional means of forcing the resignation of a cabinet, and the opposition was therefore reduced to causing all possible embarrassment to the administration by unremitting obstruction and abuse.

The first session of the Diet ended with its dissolution in December 1891, and the administration remained in power, the situation being that the party men were determined to continue their obstructive tactics and the government was determined to make no concessions on major political issues. This unfortunate precedent fixed the pattern of political life for a generation or more.

The dissolution of 1891 was followed by an election in February 1892 during which the government (under a new Prime Minister) resorted to both open and concealed pressure of an illegitimate kind on behalf of official candidates, but obtained less than 100 seats. When the session opened, the Lower House attacked the government on the budget and other issues. The Liberal opposition moved an address to the throne in which it was urged that the Cabinet, having a parliamentary majority against it, should resign and thus give effect to the principle of representative government. But the Cabinet had no intention of admitting responsibility to parliament, nor in fact was it legally obliged to do so, for the Constitution was specific on the point that ministers were responsible to the Emperor and not to the Diet.

During this short and very stormy session the government resorted to a device that, as we have seen, had in one form or another been used by oligarchies in Japan for centuries past. It invoked the Imperial name and thus made opposition to government policy appear disloyal if not even treasonable. The opposition was helpless, for if the constitutional point were pressed, the Cabinet could — and on subsequent occasions did — secure from the throne a rebuke addressed to parliament. Such a step did not prove necessary in the 1892 session, since the motion for an address to the throne failed for the very reason that a majority of members opposed it, not because they lacked faith in their own cause, but because it was a delicate and even dangerous matter to involve the Imperial name in party conflicts. Thus the position of the Cabinet was theoretically unassailable. But in practice it was untenable because the obstructive methods of the opposition hampered administration and the government was unpopular throughout the country. Even the most obstinate of cabinets could not continue to govern in such a hostile atmosphere. Accordingly the Diet was prorogued and the Cabinet resigned in August 1892. Responsibility fell upon Ito, who must now find out whether the system he had devised could be made to work. He was sensible and experienced enough to endeavour to create a more favourable public sentiment, but it was quite impossible for him to placate the Diet, which was not to be satisfied by a change of ministers. What the opposition wanted was a change of system.

During the session that opened in November 1892 and continued through February 1893 the battle between oligarchy and responsible government was resumed. This was to decide whether the struggle for *"Minken,"* or People's Rights, which had filled the public mind for the first twenty years of Meiji, was to reach a successful issue.

The Lower House voted a reduction of the budget estimates, the Cabinet rejected their amendments. The House then moved, and this time adopted, an address to the throne, in which it brought accusations of misgovernment against the Cabinet. The Cabinet retorted promptly by securing from the throne an Imperial message which instructed both sides to the dispute to co-operate harmoniously, but was in effect a rebuke to the Diet. The opposition knew well enough that they had been tricked by the Cabinet, but again they were obliged to submit, out of respect for the throne. A compromise was reached on the estimates, and the session closed in comparative calm.

One incident, not without its comic aspect, seems like a survival from the days of the shoguns. Since the Diet would not approve the full amount of a budget estimate for naval construction, the Emperor's message contained a passage directing all military and civil officials (and therefore all members of the Diet) to contribute one tenth of their salaries during the six years of the building program. This was almost exactly the method of financing national defence that had been used by the Bakufu when it cut down the rice allowances of its samurai. Indeed, these appeals for harmonious co-operation and loyal conduct and patriotic sacrifice sound like an echo of admonitions from a remote past. But though their sentiment of reverence for the throne was no doubt genuine, the opposition members of the Diet resented Ito's ingenious coup and willingly joined in a manœuvre that was to take revenge upon him. Okuma hated the Satsuma and Chōshū bureaucrats who were monopolizing power. Ito had somehow managed to win over the Liberal Party (Jiyū-tō) under Itagaki (the onetime stalwart defender of the people's rights), and Okuma therefore made a tactical agreement with the leader of a reactionary party and brought accusations of misfeasance against a Jiyū-tō member who had before Itagaki's shift been appointed President of the Lower House. This man (Hoshi Tōru) was expelled from the Diet. The opposition, led by Okuma and supported by some genuine liberals, then drove hard at the Cabinet, not on questions of policy or principle, but by bringing accusations of corrupt financial dealings against individual members of the government. We need not enter into the sordid details of this campaign. It is enough to observe that the procedure of an address to the throne was again used, and that again the government secured an Imperial reply which closed the question by specifically asserting that no interference by the Diet could be tolerated in the appointment or dismissal of ministers, this being the sovereign's prerogative. The Diet was dissolved at the end of December 1893, while the opposition was discussing a further address to the throne on the subject of treaty revision.

A general election took place in March 1894, and when the new Diet assembled in May it began an impeachment of the government but was dissolved out of hand by an Imperial order after sitting for less than three weeks. This brings to an end the history of the first struggle for parliamentary reform, since before a new Diet could be elected Japan (on August 1, 1894) went to war against China, and the opposition could no longer complain that the government's foreign policy was weak. Nor could they object to the handling of treaty revision, for by 1894 (July 16) a new treaty had been concluded with Great Britain, which provided for the surrender of extraterritorial rights in Japan.

It will be seen from an examination of this very summary account of early parliamentary history that (as has been already suggested) whereas in all the public discussion — the speeches, books, and pamphlets — of preceding years there seemed to be an overwhelming opinion in favour of democratic institutions of an Occidental type, what eventually emerged was something that had a very strong Japanese flavour and bore little resemblance to its reputed models. It is possible to argue that the influence of Prussian example is very patent, and this is no doubt true of forms. But the manner in which both government and parliament behaved during the short period that has just been sketched shows the clearest imprint of Japanese tradition. The oligarchy in its struggle to keep parliament down may resemble an Occidental counterpart, but its pedigree is Japanese. The manœuvres of Ito and his colleagues are dictated by considerations of clan solidarity as much as by reasons of state, and the splits and fusions in the opposition are unseemly and erratic because they have less to do with principles than with clan connections or personal antagonisms in which old clan rivalries are reflected. There can be little doubt that the dominating feature of Japanese political life at this time was the tension between Satsuma and Chōshū on the one hand and the outside clans on the other. This division, carried over from pre-Restoration times, determined the autocratic nature of Japanese government, the rule by a self-renewing oligarchy, for at least two generations; and (it may be added) the failure of the opposition, so powerful in numbers, to combine on matters of principle can be ascribed to similar causes. The Constitution itself, while as a document it naturally resembles other documents supporting a monarchy in theory unlimited, perpetuated pre-Meiji concepts as to the divinity of the sovereign and as to the general nature of the state.

It would seem therefore mistaken to stress the similarity between German and Japanese political institutions, while overlooking the fact that similar conditions are likely to produce similar results. In other words, it was Japanese tradition rather than Occidental influence that determined the course of political events. On the whole, if one may judge by the views of the opposition parties and the support they gained in the early elections, it was the idea of responsible party government that had gained most popular support in Japan. So that, if it comes to a judgment as to the origin of the political thought that most influenced Japanese public opinion, one is bound to conclude that English, French, and

American ideas had the greatest effect. Nevertheless what guided the government was not public opinion but the convictions of its leaders, which were those of all autocratic statesmen East and West.

2. The War against China

Of Japanese legislators it may be said *inter arma silent,* and accordingly the wordy duel between Cabinet and parliament was suspended upon the outbreak of war in 1894. The opposition spoke only to vote military expenditure and to declare its patriotic ardours. No voices were raised against war, and the only note of dissent, if it may be so called, was a suspicion that the government would make peace too soon.

This warlike attitude of liberals as well as militarists deserves some study, since its origin can be traced far back, and it thus furnishes an interesting example of the effect of old tradition in a modern state. It will be remembered that in 1873 Okubo hurried back from his travels abroad when it appeared that, during his absence, the ministers whom he had left in charge had brought Japan to the brink of war with China. A warlike group in the ministry, led by Saigo, Itagaki, Goto, and others, had desired to "rebuke" Korea for insulting behaviour. It is true that Saigo's motives were not the same as those of his colleagues. His desire — so it is said by his admirers — was to cleanse the country in the fires of war, because he thought that a true revolution had not been accomplished and a purge of national sentiment was necessary. Theirs was a more commonplace intention, for they wanted to embarrass their Satsuma and Chōshū colleagues in the government and thought that they could mobilize public opinion on their side by an appeal to national pride.

However that may be, there was no opposition in principle to an aggressive foreign policy, but only hesitation upon practical grounds. It is clear from Okubo's correspondence that he had no objection in principle to taking a threatening line with China, but he did not think that the time was ripe. He suspected the motives of the warlike party, and he was firmly of opinion that Japan must settle her domestic problems before taking risks. This was a view that had been fully confirmed by his observations while in Europe, where he had been much impressed by Bismarck's discourses on the importance of developing internal strength. He set forth his views in a list of "Reasons why it is too soon to start hostilities against Korea." Here he says that the foundations of the new government are not yet firmly established; its foreign and domestic debt is a matter of concern; it will take years to complete its in-

dustrial program; the balance of foreign trade is adverse; if Japan
were to become involved in Korea, Russia would fish in dirty
waters, and England would take advantage of the situation to
intervene in Japan's internal affairs, and finally the prospects of
treaty revision would recede. He threatened to resign and at last
got his own way, though at the cost of a breach with Saigo and
much discontent among the samurai. It was partly to soothe injured
feelings that in 1874 Okubo agreed to the Formosan expedition,
to which the government had been committed by precipitate action on the part of the bellicose party; but he did his best to forestall trouble by going to Peking himself and arranging a solution
by which China paid a small indemnity and the Japanese force
was withdrawn from Formosa.

It is clear from these incidents that relations between Japan
and China were on a dangerous footing. There was a war party
in Japan, and all its members were not in the wilderness. There
was another dangerous incident in 1882, when anti-foreign feeling
in Korea ran high and was directed chiefly against the Japanese,
and another in 1884 when the Chinese garrison in Chemulpo
clashed with some troops that Japan maintained there for the protection of her nationals.

The Japanese government came to an agreement with the Chinese, by which the independence of Korea was recognized in 1885,
and the risk of conflict was thus for a time diminished. But the
situation offered temptation to the warlike elements in Japanese
political life, and revived ambitions that had been nourished long
before the Restoration. Satsuma men began to quote leaders of
opinion like Yoshida Shōin, who had laid down for Japan a policy
of almost unlimited expansion on the Asiatic mainland. Similar
views of Japan's destiny had been expressed by other apostles a
century or more before his day and found a response in patriotic
bosoms. A strong military spirit, which had been latent, but not
far beneath the surface, since 1868, now began to make itself felt
throughout the country. It is more than probable that it was stimulated by the slow progress of treaty revision and by the disappointment of the public at the obvious failure of the new parliament to
solve current problems. Life was becoming difficult under the
impact of industrialization, high taxes, and currency troubles, and
the nationalistic feeling that the government had fostered as a
means of unity was easily stirred up in favour of foreign adventure.

The martial sentiment was by no means confined to professional military circles. The leaders of the army and the navy naturally carried on a warlike tradition, and, it must be added, they
had great power in the state, since they inherited the prestige of the

former military caste from which they sprang. It is not easy to stamp out a warlike tradition, especially in times when (as in the decade we are considering) other nations are in a predatory mood. The civilian statesmen were of the same lineage as the military leaders; and pacifism was a notion that, though just entering Occidental minds, was incomprehensible to men who had won their way to power by fighting. It is therefore not surprising that a country like Japan should have seen in war the quickest way of satisfying her far-reaching ambitions. Everything in her past history pointed that way, and the international scene was not so calm as to encourage a belief in peaceful progress.

The war against China ended in a decisive victory for Japan, which brought her a handsome indemnity, the rich island of Formosa, the Pescadores, and a foothold in south Manchuria. Her career of expansion had begun. The signature of the Treaty of Tientsin on April 17, 1895 marks the end of the phase of her cultural history that I have attempted to analyse.

3. Economic Change

A FULL study of the effects of industrialization upon Japanese life would require a voluminous and skilful treatment far beyond my competence, and we must therefore confine ourselves to tracing some of its more obvious features. In a general way it is true to say that the introduction of modern methods of manufacture, trade, and finance brought about changes in Japanese life that can be vaguely ascribed to Western influence. The conversion of an agrarian economy into an industrial economy is naturally accompanied by social changes, which, if carried far enough, may end by giving to a national culture a new character, in which old traditions of behaviour can no longer be observed. But the process is complex and gradual, and its operation is not always easy to detect.

Thus, while it may be said that the introduction of power-driven machinery brought to bear upon Japanese life a strong influence of Western origin, this is true only with qualifications. If we take separate instances we can see that modern inventions may well be used to counter foreign influence in other directions. Printing and binding machinery, for example, increases the number and circulation of books and newspapers, of which the contents may well be such as to spread ideas critical of foreign countries. This is perhaps a somewhat tendentious argument from a special case; but there is no lack of analogies. It might even be regarded as characteristic of Western influence upon Eastern peoples that it carries the germ of its own destruction. Of this the most striking and tremendous example is probably to be found in the modern history of India, where English political teaching created the spirit of revolt against English political authority, and the record of English constitutional growth provided precedents for rebellion. It would not have occurred to any Hindu in the days of Akbar, Aurangzeb, or Shah Jehan to quote the Koran against them; but the Indian Congress, founded by an Englishman,[2] was always ready to confound the Viceroy with citations from the whole corpus of English literature on freedom.

It is true that Western clothing, food, transport, and communications, as well as Western ideas, have enlarged and diversified Japanese life, but they have not necessarily changed its essential character. The cumulative effect of industrialization upon a people whose material culture is simple must destroy much of what is indigenous; but the impact of an advanced Western culture upon an advanced Eastern culture may, despite far-reaching superficial changes, succeed in producing resistance, or even hostile reactions in matters of vital import — in the totality of a people's feelings about life and society. This may not hold true over long periods, since it is possible that industrial life will one day bring about a world-wide uniformity of drabness. But nobody will dare at this date to predict what life will be like in Asiatic countries in the twenty-first century, or in European countries for that matter.

Here, however, we are dealing only with a very limited length of time, and our object is not to prophesy but to describe the impact of the West upon Japan in the first twenty-five years or so of the Meiji era. It used to be supposed that within that short space Japan abolished most of her ancient civilization and adopted as if by a miracle all the material and intellectual apparatus of a modern Western state. Few people believe this now, but it is worth while to give a broad outline of the early steps in the development of an economy similar to that of the leading industrial states of the Occident.

In the first place it should be understood that before Commodore Perry's arrival in 1853, Japan had already gone through the preliminary stages of transition from an agrarian to a mercantile economy, and even manufacturing industry was fairly well developed in certain lines. There were no power-driven machines beyond a few hydraulic flour-mills of ingenious construction,[3] but there were complicated hand-looms for weaving silk and cotton

---

[2] This was Allan O. Hume, a good and upright official who — most ironically — came under the spell of the pseudo-Oriental mysticism of Madame Blavatsky. What a complicated case of cultural influence!

[3] In 1946 I saw one of these, occupying a considerable floor space. It was constructed entirely of wood, without any iron nails, and it had been in use for 150 years. Near by was an airfield, littered with hundreds of wrecked aircraft.

in elaborate patterns, and a few processes in mining and metallurgy were tolerably well understood. Many handicrafts, using small mechanical devices, had long reached a high state of perfection. Shipbuilding and the manufacture of iron and steel had made fair progress under foreign guidance before the Restoration. Japan was therefore already prepared to develop machine industries and to learn the necessary technical lessons from more advanced countries in the West, without being subjected to an unbearable strain, or relying exclusively upon foreign instructors — who, however, played a very important part in early stages.

As to commercial organization, it had already during the Tokugawa period developed independently many of the characteristics of trade in Western countries. Thus the rice-merchants dealt in "futures" and there were numerous transactions in the shares of guilds and other trading associations which were similar to, though not identical with, dealings in the stocks and shares of modern commercial companies. Monetary transactions were intricate and the credit system had special features that were imposed upon it by the peculiar structure of feudal society. But in general it can be truthfully said that already in the eighteenth century economic life in Japan was highly developed within its own categories, urban society was in an advanced phase, transport was organized on a large scale, while mercantile and financial organs of considerable complexity had been evolved. There were present at least in embryo some of the principal elements of a capitalist system of the modern Occidental type. Consequently when Japan was opened to foreign intercourse in the middle of the nineteenth century she experienced no great difficulty in bringing most of her economic institutions and practices into line with contemporary Western standards.

Details of the economic history of the Meiji era are to be found in many books, and for a penetrating analysis of early industrialization, with its political and social concomitants, the reader is referred to the excellent work of Herbert Norman, *Japan's Emergence as a Modern State,* which is full of good historical data and valuable commentary. Here we can deal with these questions only in an impressionistic manner by reciting a few leading events and adding some glosses on their cultural significance.

Although Japan was in 1868 not entirely unprepared for a rapid development of industry and trade on Occidental lines, her economy as a whole could not of course be regarded as modern. It has been well described by a good authority, Dr. John E. Orchard, in his *Japan's Economic Position* (1930), as comparable not to that of eighteenth-century England on the eve of its industrial revolution but rather of England in Tudor times, when the

499

country was predominantly agricultural and its manufactures were produced by domestic handicrafts. Some change, but only by way of expansion rather than development, had taken place since the time when Richard Cocks (writing in 1620) reported to the East India Company that good repair work could be done in Japanese shipyards, saying "for iron work there is no want, and smiths that can make anchors of 20 or 30 hundredweight if need be." Japan derived a certain benefit from being in, if not of, the post-Newtonian world, which was only on the horizon in Elizabethan days, since she had for about a century before 1868 been subject to its influence, though in a diluted form. Both the Bakufu and certain clans had installed machines of various kinds and engaged foreign technical instructors or obtained their advice as early as 1850, if not before, principally for the purpose of making artillery and building warships. These first steps were taken for military reasons and thus gave a special character to the further growth of the national economy, since it continued, as it began, with an emphasis upon heavy industry, thus reversing the usual order of development as it had taken place in the West. In England the industrial revolution began with the manufacture of textiles and continued with other light industries until new mechanical inventions simplified the construction of large and powerful engines; whereas in Japan the full development of textile production was retarded. This contrast, as well as being an interesting item of economic history, is of some importance in the study of cultural influences, because it shows that the past experiences of Japan determined the manner and the degree in which she was to follow Western example in her economic policy, or — since it was not wholly a matter of deliberate choice — in her economic evolution.

The fact that the greater part of her early industrial effort was put into production of goods of direct or indirect strategic importance affected not only the trend of technical progress but also the financial aspects of manufacture and trade. Heavy industries, railway transport, and steam navigation require the investment of large capital sums, and private accumulations of capital in Japan were insufficient for their rapid development.[4]

---

[4] The construction of the first railway in Japan was financed by a foreign loan of about one million pounds sterling at nine per cent, raised in London in 1870. The Japanese government was chary of borrowing abroad because it feared that foreign capital might force the country's economic development into channels differing from those which Japan ought in her own interest to select. A second loan was raised in 1873 in London, to release funds for the commutation of pensions due to the feudal lords and retainers. But apart from these exceptional cases where there was a special urgency, no money was borrowed abroad for twenty-five years, although the government was often in sore financial straits. This deliberate self-denial is a clear example of resistance to foreign economic influence. As Mr. Norman observes in the work cited above, the result of the cautious policy of Japanese

It is true that there was already in Japan a class of wealthy merchants whose fortunes by previous standards had been very great. But for national purposes their accumulations were not adequate, or were not available because their experience was narrow and in the early part of Meiji they were mostly reluctant to invest in new enterprises. They preferred to put their money into land or to finance the domestic trades with which they were familiar. Consequently it was the government that had to bear the burden, by promoting, owning, or subsidizing the most important undertakings. Some of these, which had previously been operated by the Bakufu or by progressive clans — arsenals, shipyards, mines, and foundries — it confiscated and sold at low cost to those few financial supporters who were enterprising enough to come to its aid. Thus from an early date there was fixed a pattern of state ownership, state control, or state assistance from which the government never entirely departed. This phenomenon, again, was one that was in part predetermined by earlier history.

There are, it is true, certain influences which — East or West — cannot be escaped as a modern economy develops. The old domestic hand industries, such as cotton spinning and weaving, are everywhere damaged or destroyed first by the importation of machine-made textiles and then by their manufacture at home. What had happened to weavers in England and India [5] happened in Japan, and the poor country-dweller was forced to seek new ways of supplementing a scanty income. At the same time such changes in the character of production bring about small changes in everyday life, as when in Japan lamps burning mineral oil displaced the old-fashioned lanterns and candles, and aroused sad feelings in conservative circles; or when cheap foreign goods were substituted for beautiful objects made by craftsmen and so attacked the native æsthetic tradition.

But there is not much profit in discussing whether material changes in Japanese life resulting from industrialization should be ascribed to foreign influence or treated as parts of a movement that happened to originate in Europe. It would be of more interest to examine some of those changes separately and to see whether their moral effect can be measured. A few of them have already been touched upon in a previous chapter, where for instance it was pointed out that the revised Civil Code had to take a new view of inheritance because of the growth of new forms of property and income. There was a conflict here between the rights of the in-

statesmen was to accentuate certain characteristic features of Japanese capitalism, such as the growth of state enterprise, the concentration of private capital in a few hands, and the unequal distribution of the burden of taxation, which served industry at the expense of agrarian well-being.

[5] See chapter vii.

dividual and his duties as member of a family. In other ways also the old family system was modified as industrial activity expanded. In the period with which we are dealing the expansion had not gone far enough to make any great inroads upon the customary life of the majority of the people; but by about 1890 factories had already begun to draw workers from the countryside and so to make a small breach in that family solidarity which was the foundation of Japanese society. Yet even this was not a new trend, but rather the extension of an old one, for the drift of rural workers to the towns had begun long before the nineteenth century.

What effect the growth of machine industry and large commercial companies had upon other departments of life it is most difficult to estimate; but for some time the traditional relationship between employer and workman persisted, and even in relatively large undertakings a kind of family or community spirit was maintained, while the old system of apprenticeship survived in many trades. So far as concerns the mass of the population, since at least seventy per cent of all households were engaged in agriculture as late as 1885, new industrial developments had little direct bearing upon their lives. The growth of silk exports tended to increase the cash incomes of farmers in some areas, but new forms of taxation and changes in the system of land tenure, besides disturbing their minds and making them hostile to reforms (which they associated with foreigners), kept the purchasing power of the peasants at a low level and thus denied them the benefits of increased production in other fields of export. They could not afford the new consumption goods that came on the market as manufacturing industry and import trade expanded. Further, despite the increasing use of machines, a large proportion of Japanese manufactures was still produced in both town and country by hand workers using old processes and organized in the old native fashion in guilds or other associations or in the family circle.

Perhaps the most far-reaching sequel of the modernization of Japan was the rapid growth of population concurrently with the development of industry and the application of medical science. It is of course a phenomenon that has accompanied industrialization everywhere, and Japan does not show any peculiar features in this respect. The famines that had at intervals swept over the country in previous periods ceased as food production was intensified, prices kept fairly stable, and distribution improved. The resulting increase of population created a surplus of labour in rural areas, which in the early years of Meiji could not be absorbed by factories in towns, but struggled for employment in the countryside, thus causing congestion in the villages and keeping the standard of living at a low level. These are conditions that must be ascribed less to the adoption of a modern economy than to its slow and one-sided development. They arose from (or were at least accentuated by) the traditional methods of small-scale cultivation in Japan, which made peasants cling desperately to their little plots. They thus contributed to the growth of small household industries, or of farmed-out piece work to supplement small earnings from the soil, which for long remained a characteristic of Japanese manufacture. Here again we see the shape of the new economy dictated in part by the nature of the old.[6]

The biographies of advocates of Western intercourse and the record of events before the Restoration will have made it clear that one of the most compelling reasons adduced for opening the country was the need to use Western science and Western machines for the purpose of national defence. It was this motive, carried over into the Meiji era, that dictated the shape of Japan's industrial economy and imposed on it a certain distortion from which it never fully recovered. The emphasis upon industry, and heavy industry in particular, was accompanied by a comparative neglect of agrarian interests, which caused great trouble in the early years of Meiji and (it might be argued) postponed indefinitely the solution of an agrarian problem which, in different forms at different times, had always harassed Japanese governments. Meanwhile the hesitation of the old class of rice-broker and moneylender to venture capital in modern industry, and the absence of a class of small investor ready to take a speculative risk, gave a special importance to those few wealthy houses of merchant bankers [7] — Mitsui, Iwasaki, Sumitomo, Yasuda, Konoike, and a few others — who did come to the aid of the government and, thanks to favours received in return, developed into those powerful combinations known as the Zaibatsu, the financial oligarchy that went hand in hand with the Hanbatsu, or the oligarchy of the clans. Thus, it will be seen, legacies from a period little touched by foreign influence stamped a deep imprint upon the modern Japanese economy. The habit of state intervention in commerce and industry was formed in Tokugawa days. Trading monopolies and the privileges of sole contractors had in the past been enjoyed by favoured merchants, and

6 This is not to say that the tenant problem in Japan is that of feudal times. It is not, since the landlords after the Restoration were not feudal lords but "modern" capitalists large and small. Nevertheless Japan did not develop large-scale farming by owner cultivators for the simple reason that, in addition to topographical and climatic conditions, the peasant's attachment (in both senses of the word) to the soil and to the family home prevented a transition from intensive to extensive agriculture. Here again ancient habit clashed with modern trends.

7 The development of financial organs in Japan after 1868 presents a most interesting example of the fusion of imported and native elements. This can be studied in the history of banking after the National Bank Law of 1872, and the special relationship of banking to government.

brewers had been powerful in rural Japan no less than in rural England. None of these phenomena was of foreign origin, most of them were rooted in old custom, and their effect was to resist or to moderate the influence of contemporary Western example.

There is not evidence enough to show that because she adapted Western machines and commercial practices to her own uses Japan became Western in the essence of her national character by the close of the nineteenth century. Whether a similar conclusion as to the first half of the twentieth century would emerge from a survey of its cultural history is beyond the scope of the present inquiry. Yet a study of the earlier period raises doubts whether any of the chief civilizations of Asia will, even if they voluntarily follow a Western economic pattern, submit to Western precept or example in political, social, or religious life.

There is one feature, however, absent from all the manifestations of foreign influence we have examined, and that is a deliberate intention on the part of one country to influence the civilization of another. An exception should be made in respect of Christian propaganda, which was an essential part of the policy of the Catholic states of Europe in the sixteenth and seventeenth centuries and of course had the support of the universal church. But in more recent times, though European and American governments have given some political support to Christian missionaries, the propagation of religion has not been part of national policy. It is only since the war of 1914–18 that organized efforts on a national scale have been made by one country or a group of countries to impose a full system of thought and behaviour and a distinctive economy upon another society. The first of these was the attempt of the Allied and Associated Powers to determine the nature of German political development. The second was that of the Soviet Union, through a special organ, to convert other states to its own doctrines. Of a different nature, though in many respects similar in purpose, are the efforts now being made by the Allied Powers to encourage and persuade Germany and Japan to adopt democratic principles of government and appropriate social philosophies.

The processes studied in the foregoing pages are not of this kind, and they therefore throw but little light on the possibility of success where cultural influence is supported by powerful political pressure and a highly organized propaganda.

THE END

Paupertas cartæ finem imponit verbositati.
(Gregory of Tours)

I N D E X

(Long syllables are marked in Japanese words)

i

Index

Index

Index

Index

Index

Index

Index

TYPE NOTE

The text of this book has been set on the Linotype in a type-face called "Baskerville." The face is a facsimile reproduction of types cast from molds made for John Baskerville (1706–1775) from his designs. The punches for the revived Linotype Baskerville were cut under the supervision of the English printer George W. Jones.

John Baskerville's original face was one of the forerunners of the type-style known as "modern face" to printers: a "modern" of the period A.D. *1800.*

The typographic scheme and the binding design are by W. A. Dwiggins. The book was composed, printed, and bound by The Plimpton Press, Norwood, Massachusetts.

WAD